ORIGINAL STORY
HIROYUKI MORIOKA
CONSTRUCTION
AYA YOSHINAGA
COMIC'S AUTHOR
TOSHIHIRO ONO

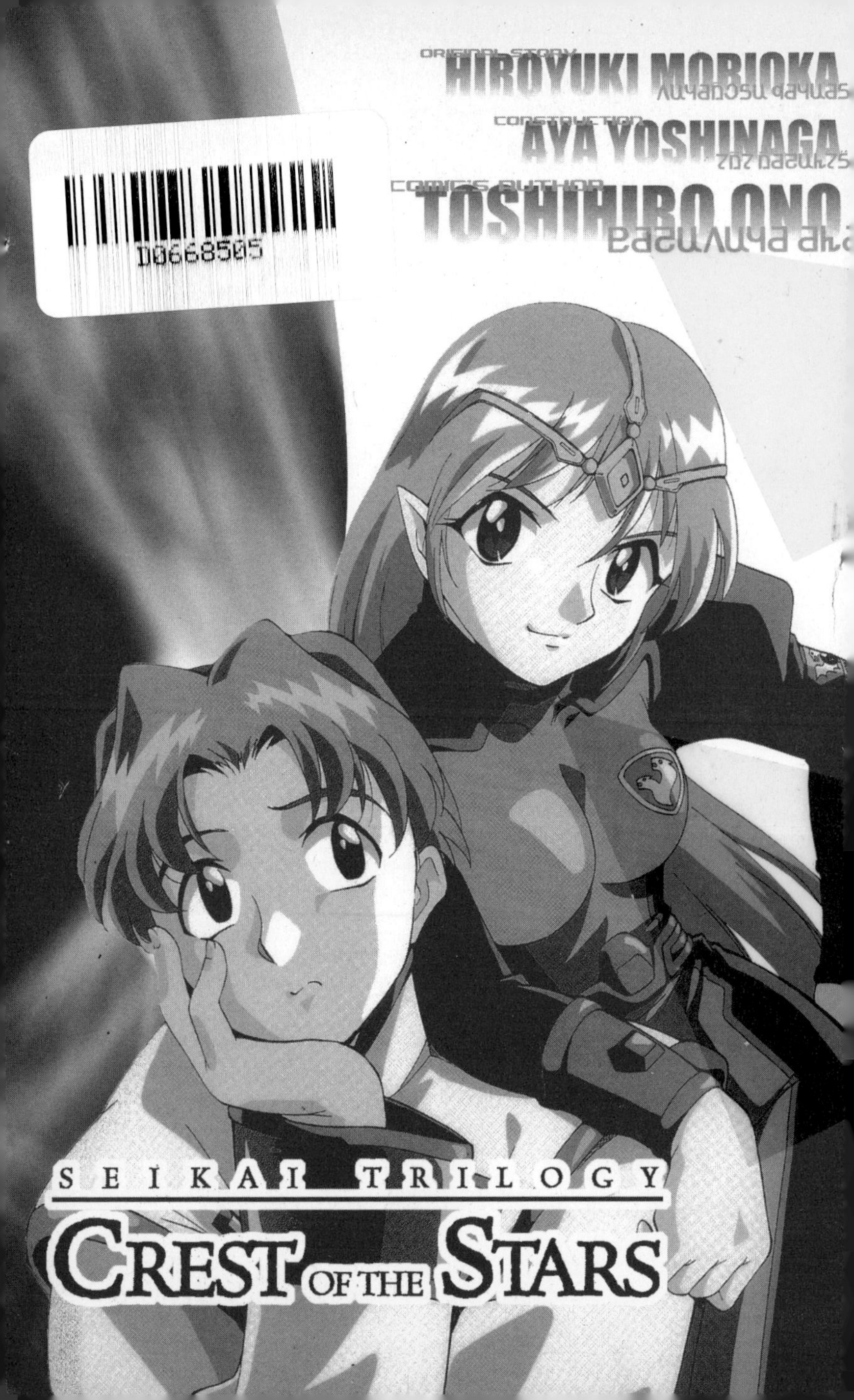

SEIKAI TRILOGY

CREST OF THE STARS

Translator - Bryan Masumoto
English Adaptation - Dan Borses
Retouch and Lettering - Yoohae Yang
Graphic Artist - James Lee
Cover Layout - Patrick Hook

Editor - Luis Reyes
Digital Imaging Manager - Chris Buford
Pre-Press Manager - Antonio DePietro
Production Managers - Jennifer Miller, Mutsumi Miyazaki
Art Director - Matt Alford
Managing Editor - Jill Freshney
VP of Production - Ron Klamert
President & C.O.O. - John Parker
Publisher & C.E.O. - Stuart Levy

E-mail: info@TOKYOPOP.com
Come visit us online at www.TOKYOPOP.com

A  Manga

TOKYOPOP Inc.
5900 Wilshire Blvd. Suite 2000
Los Angeles, CA 90036

Sekai Trilogy Vol. 1 - Crest of the Stars

ISBN: 1-59182-857-0

First TOKYOPOP printing: June 2004

10 9 8 7 6 5 4 3 2 1

Printed in the USA

SEIKAI TRILOGY

CREST OF THE STARS

VOL. 1

Original Story by
HIROYUKI MORIOKA

Composition by
AYA YOSHINAGA

Art by
TOSHIHIRO ONO

TOKYOPOP®

LOS ANGELES • TOKYO • LONDON • HAMBURG

Chapter 1
Kin of the Stars
KARSAL GULULAK

05

Chapter 2
Baron Febdash Territory
RUMUSKOL FEBDASH

49

Chapter 3
Pride of the Abh
PAL REPENEW

83

Chapter 4
Planet Clasbul
NAHENU CLASBUL

113

Chapter 5
Collaboration Request
LADOFOS LOFT

145

Chapter 6
Battleground at Sufugnof Gate
LAISHAKAL WEK SODAL SUFUGUNOM

169

Chapter 7
Trouble Soaring Through Heaven
LOBYUASH SESULA

197

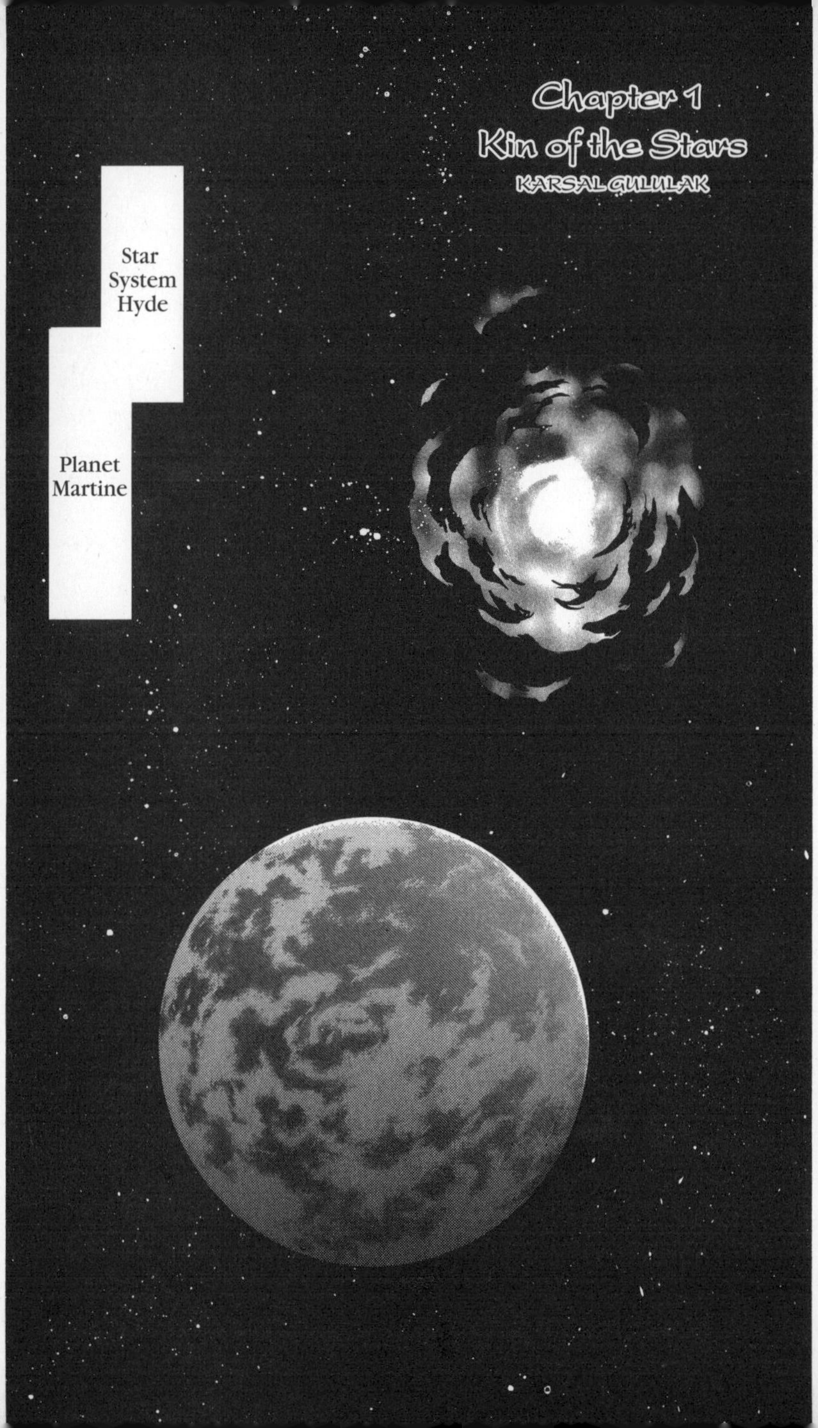
Chapter 1
Kin of the Stars
KARSAL GULULAK
Star System Hyde
Planet Martine

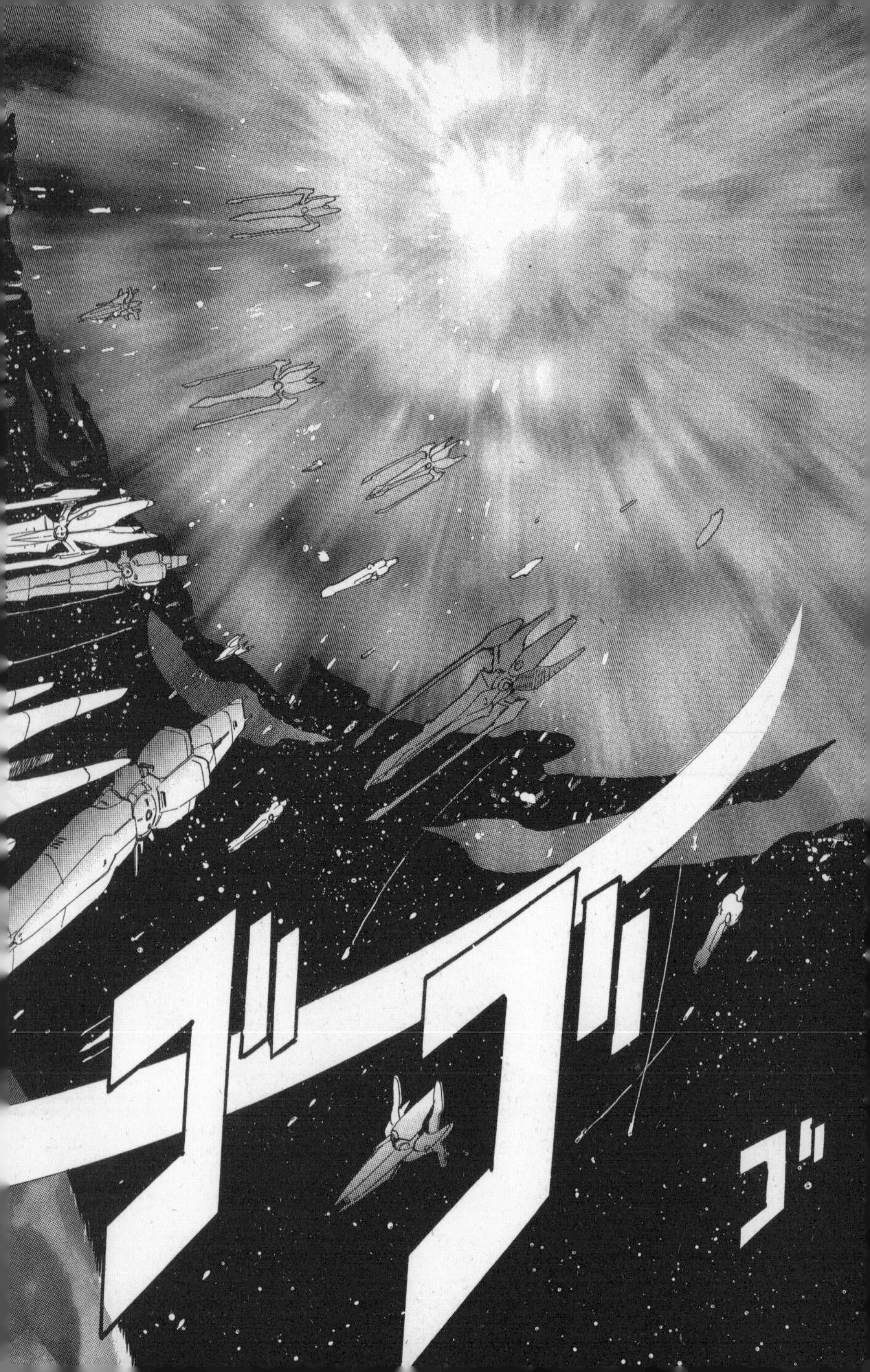
ゴゴ
ゴ

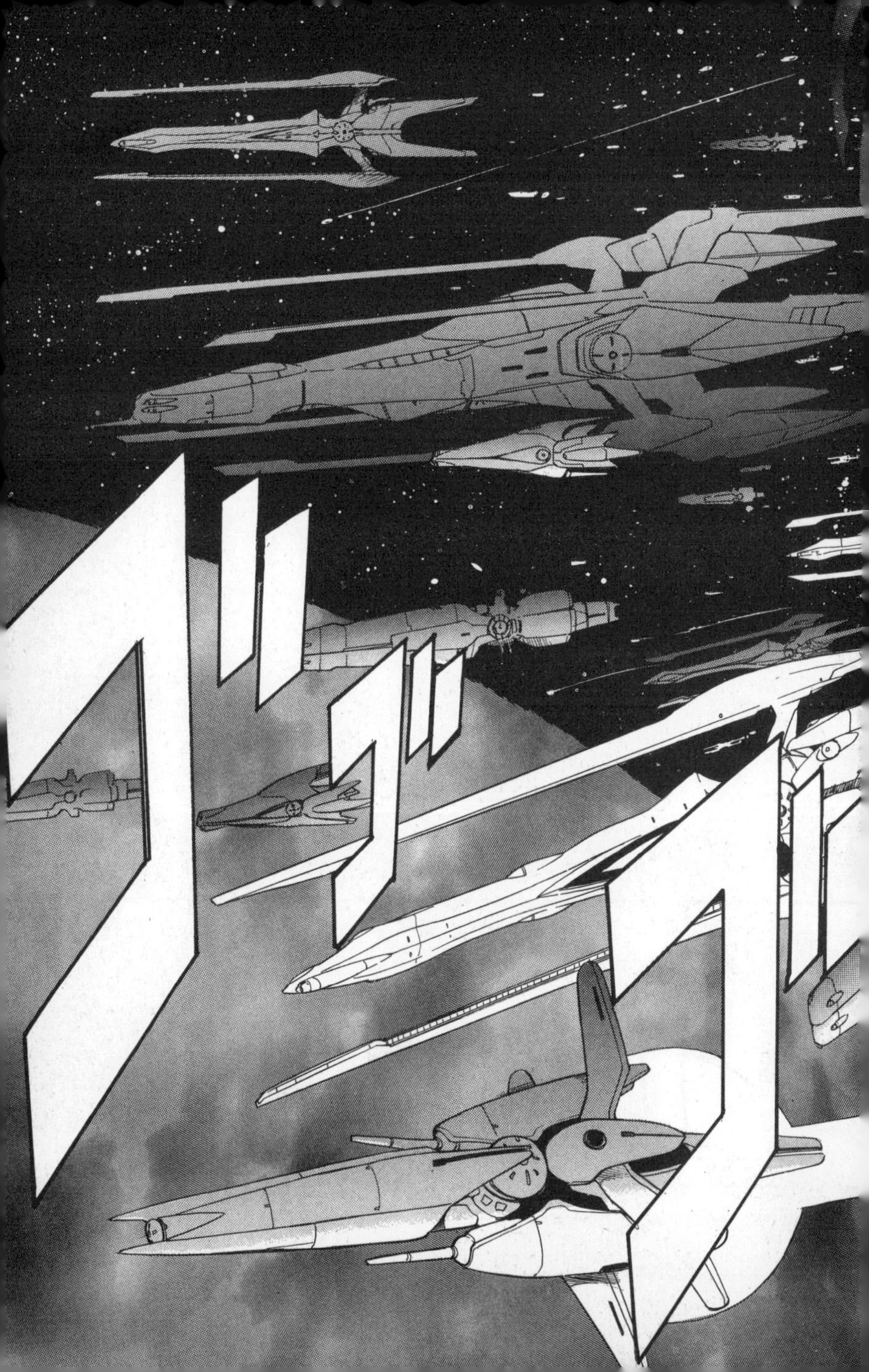
ゴゴゴ

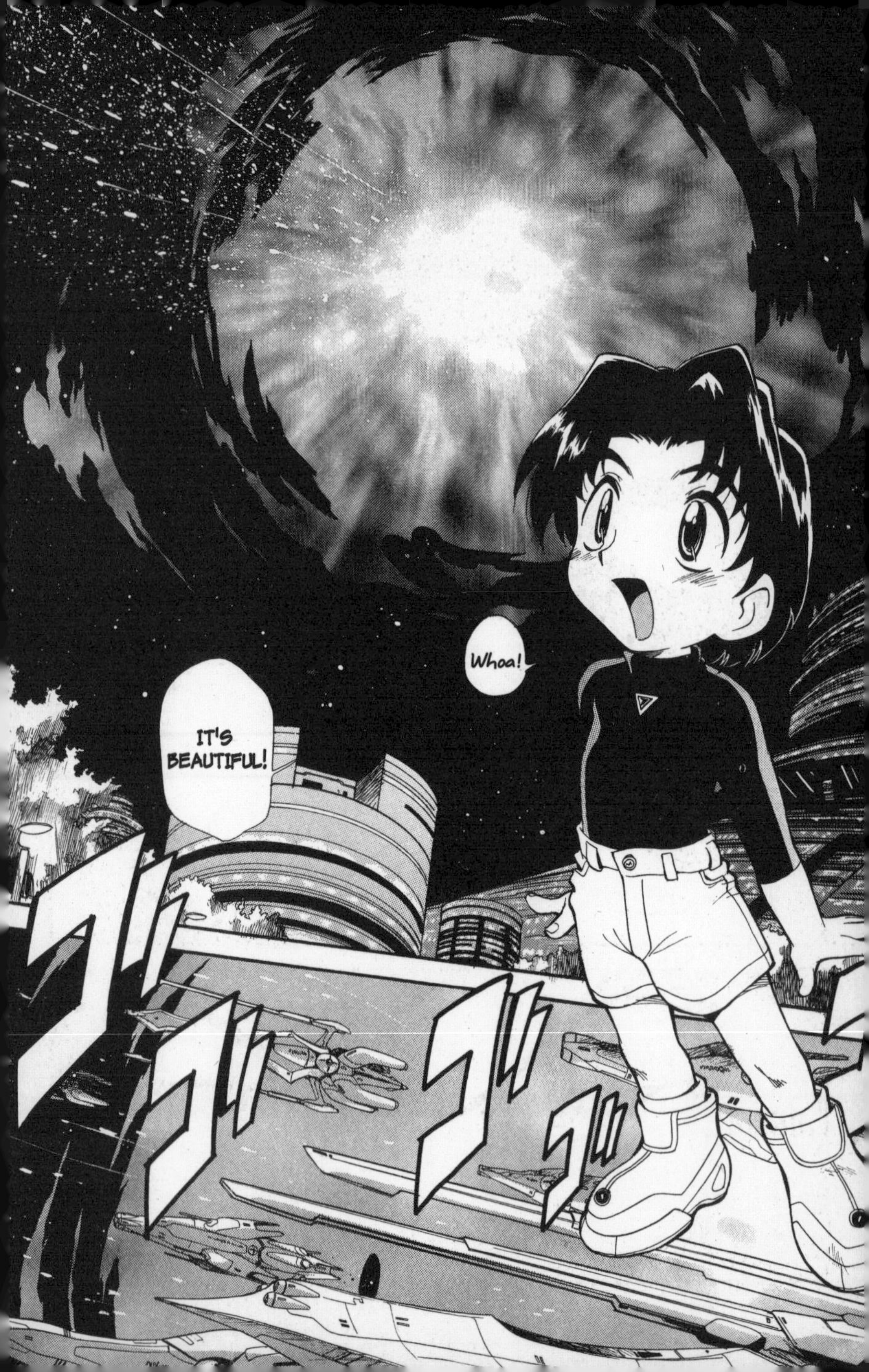
Whoa!
IT'S BEAUTIFUL!

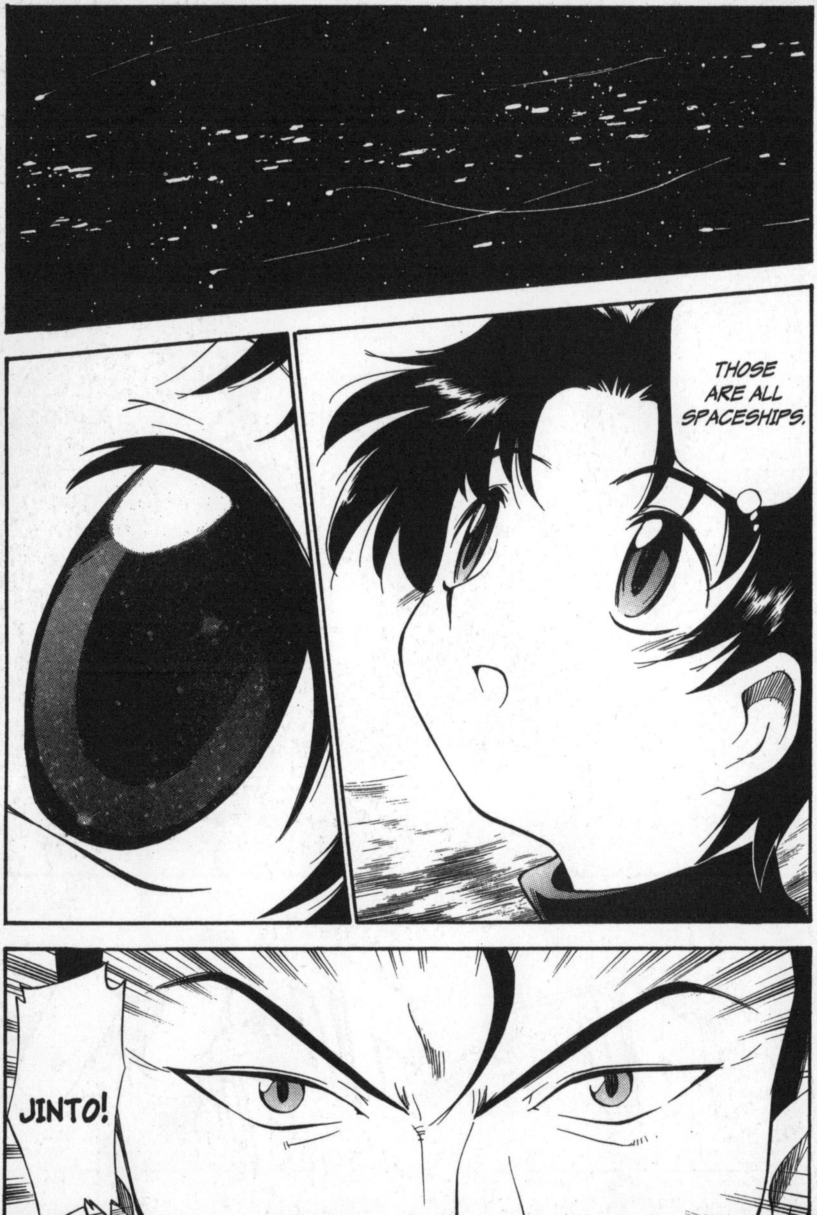
THOSE ARE ALL SPACESHIPS.
JINTO!

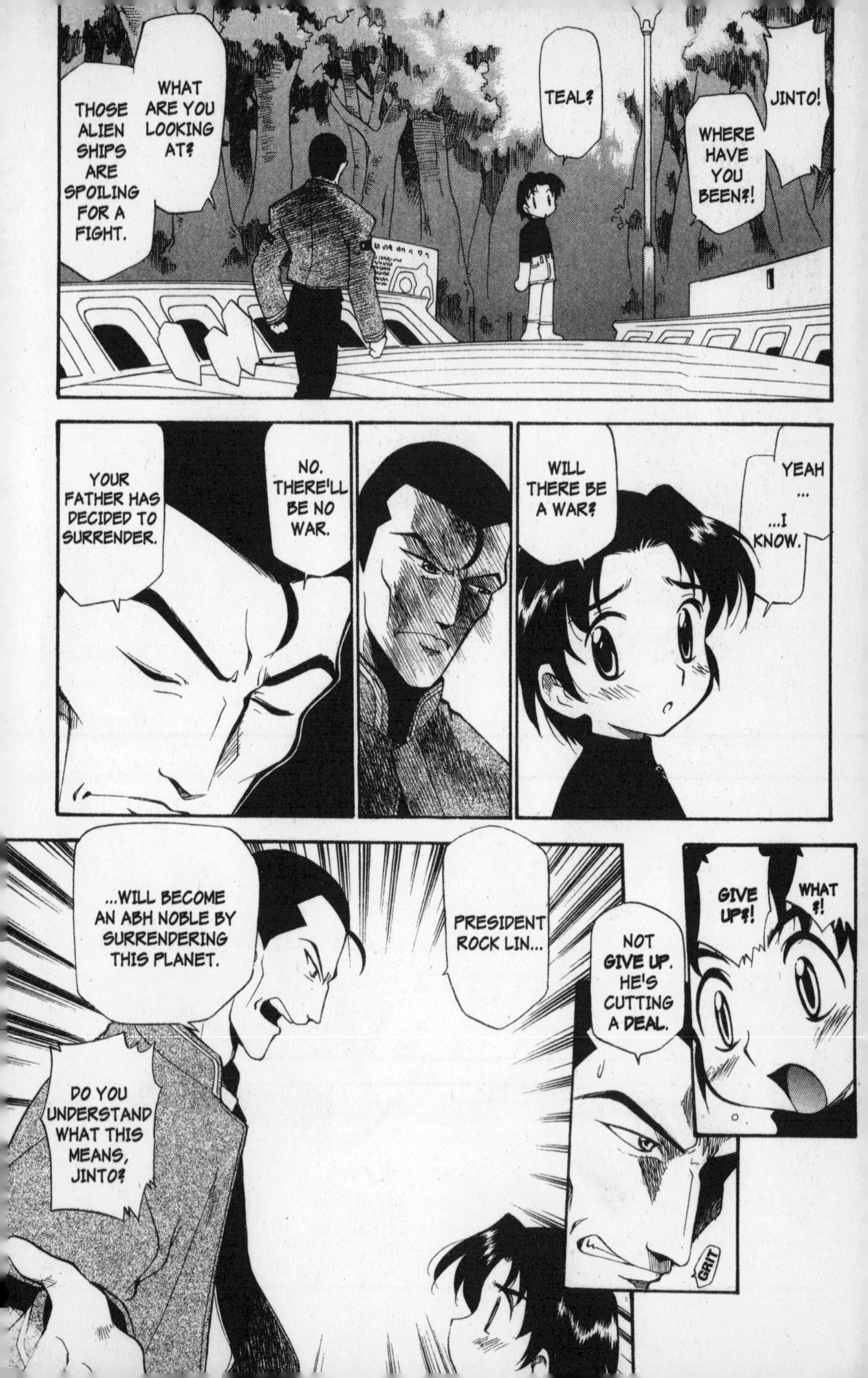
JINTO!
WHERE HAVE YOU BEEN?!
TEAL?
WHAT ARE YOU LOOKING AT?
THOSE ALIEN SHIPS ARE SPOILING FOR A FIGHT.
YEAH... ...I KNOW.
WILL THERE BE A WAR?
NO. THERE'LL BE NO WAR.
YOUR FATHER HAS DECIDED TO SURRENDER.
WHAT?!
GIVE UP?!
NOT GIVE UP. HE'S CUTTING A DEAL.
PRESIDENT ROCK LIN...
...WILL BECOME AN ABH NOBLE BY SURRENDERING THIS PLANET.
GRIT
DO YOU UNDERSTAND WHAT THIS MEANS, JINTO?

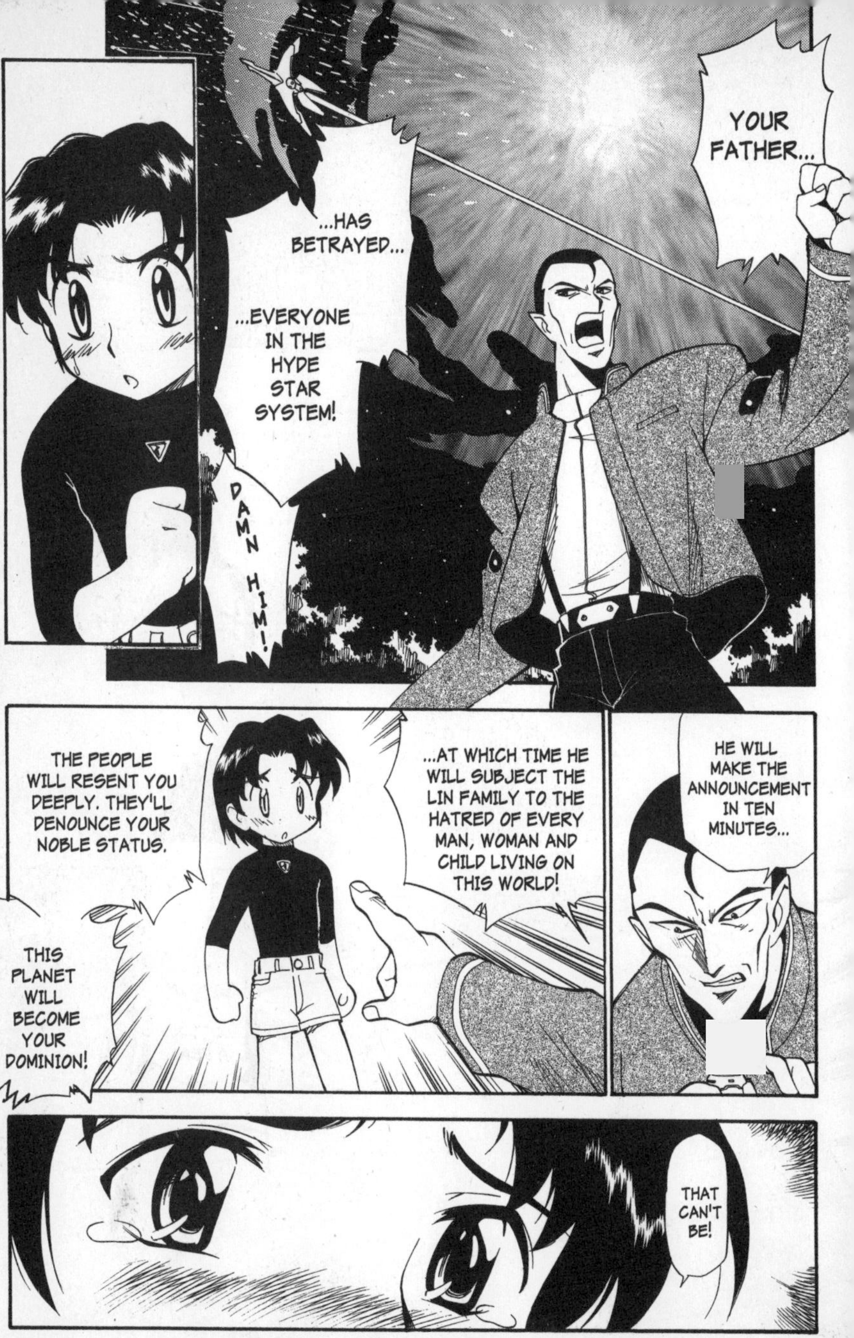
YOUR FATHER...
...HAS BETRAYED...
...EVERYONE IN THE HYDE STAR SYSTEM!
DAMN HIM!
HE WILL MAKE THE ANNOUNCEMENT IN TEN MINUTES...
...AT WHICH TIME HE WILL SUBJECT THE LIN FAMILY TO THE HATRED OF EVERY MAN, WOMAN AND CHILD LIVING ON THIS WORLD!
THE PEOPLE WILL RESENT YOU DEEPLY. THEY'LL DENOUNCE YOUR NOBLE STATUS.
THIS PLANET WILL BECOME YOUR DOMINION!
THAT CAN'T BE!

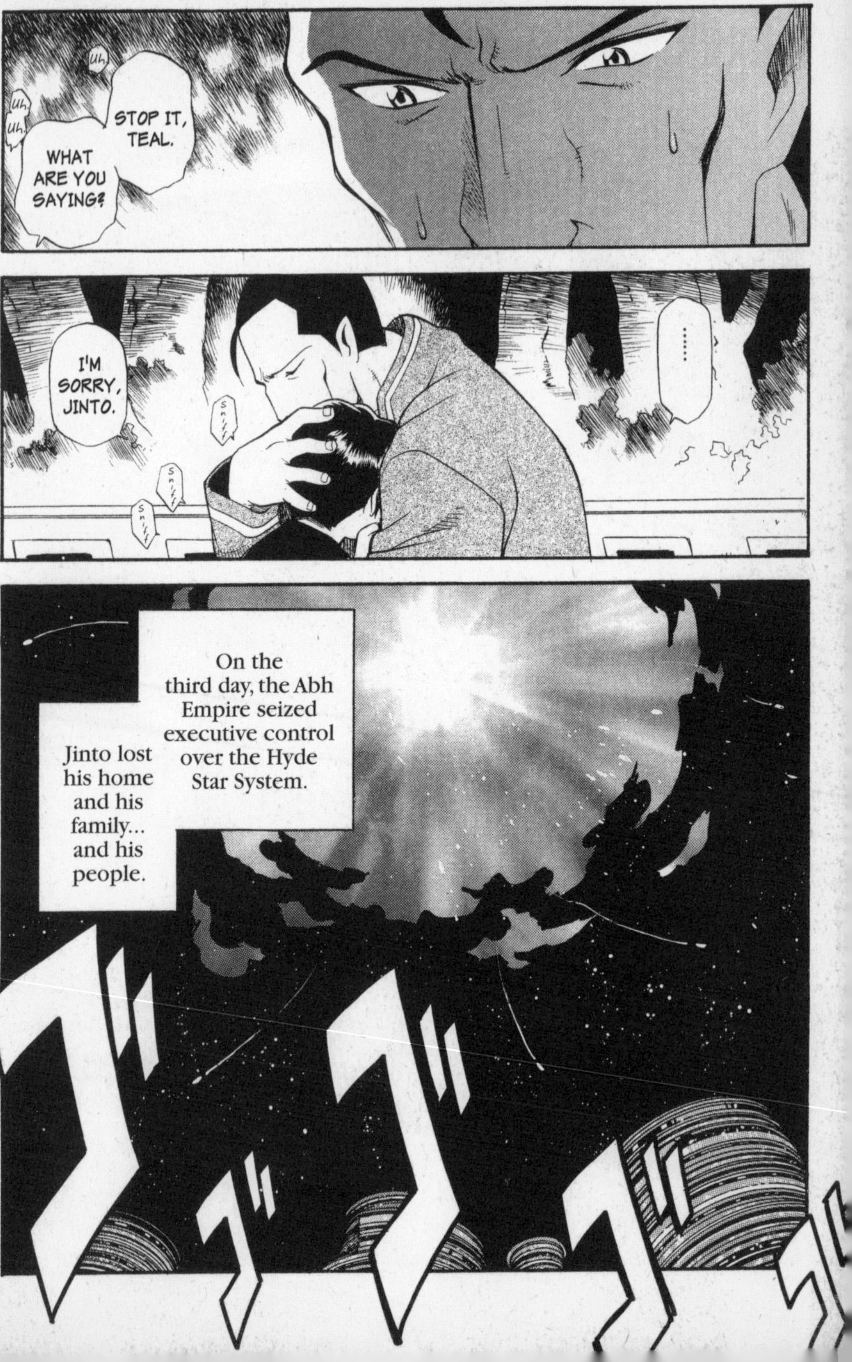
Uh
STOP IT, TEAL.
Uh
Uh
WHAT ARE YOU SAYING?
......
Sniff
I'M SORRY, JINTO.
Sniff
Sniff
On the third day, the Abh Empire seized executive control over the Hyde Star System.
Jinto lost his home and his family... and his people.

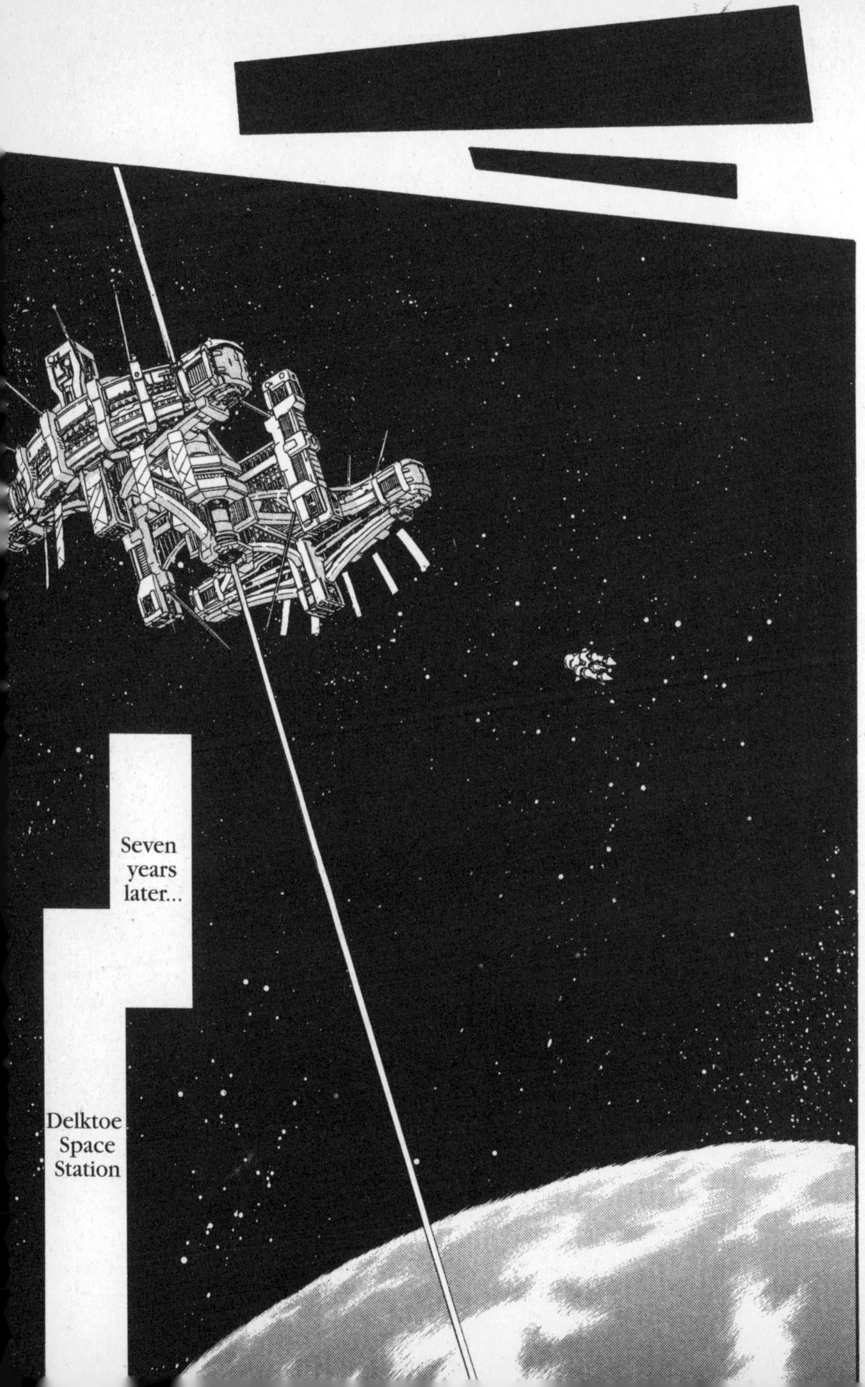
Seven years later...
Delktoe Space Station

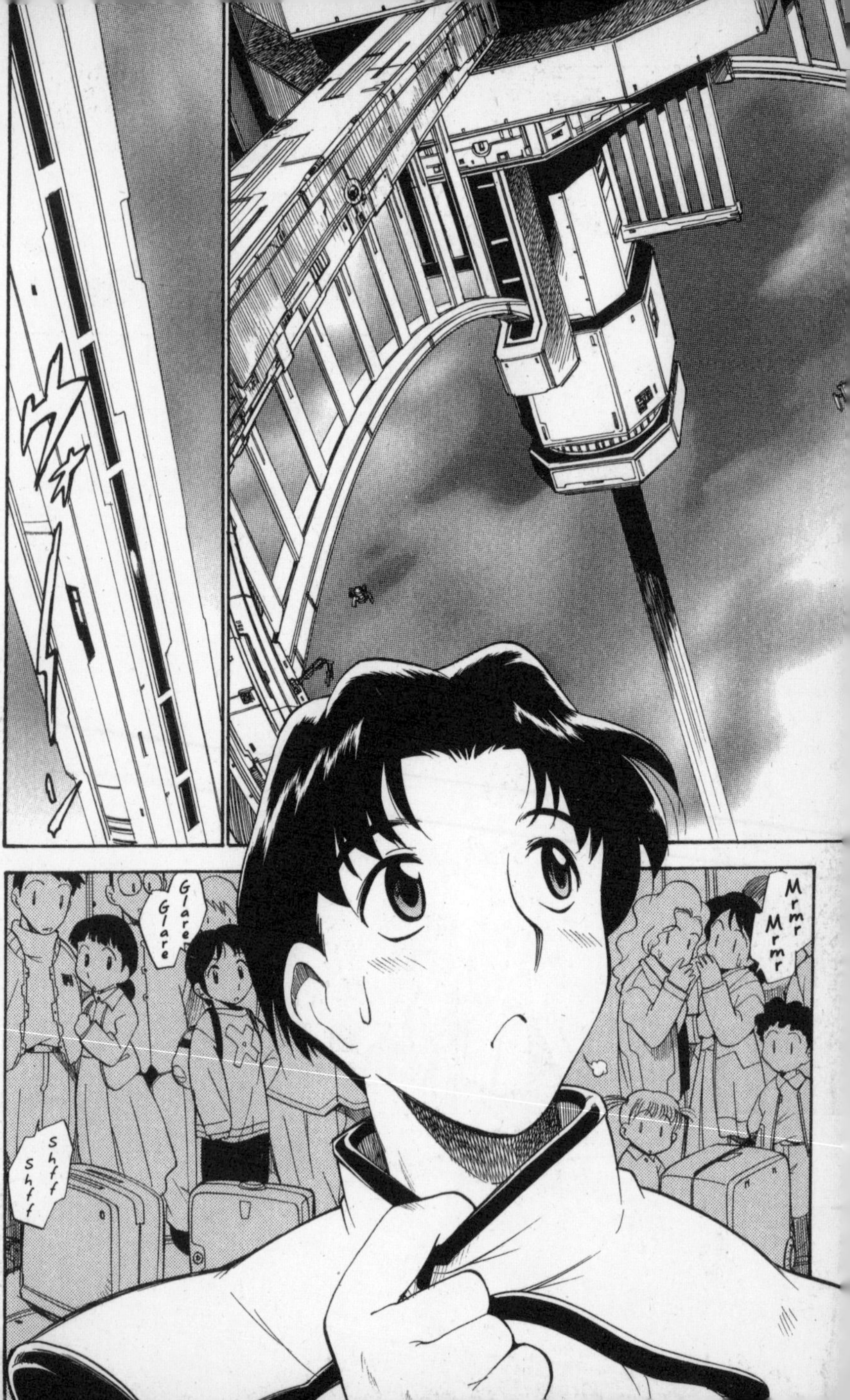
Mrmr
Mrmr
Glare
Glare
Shff
Shff

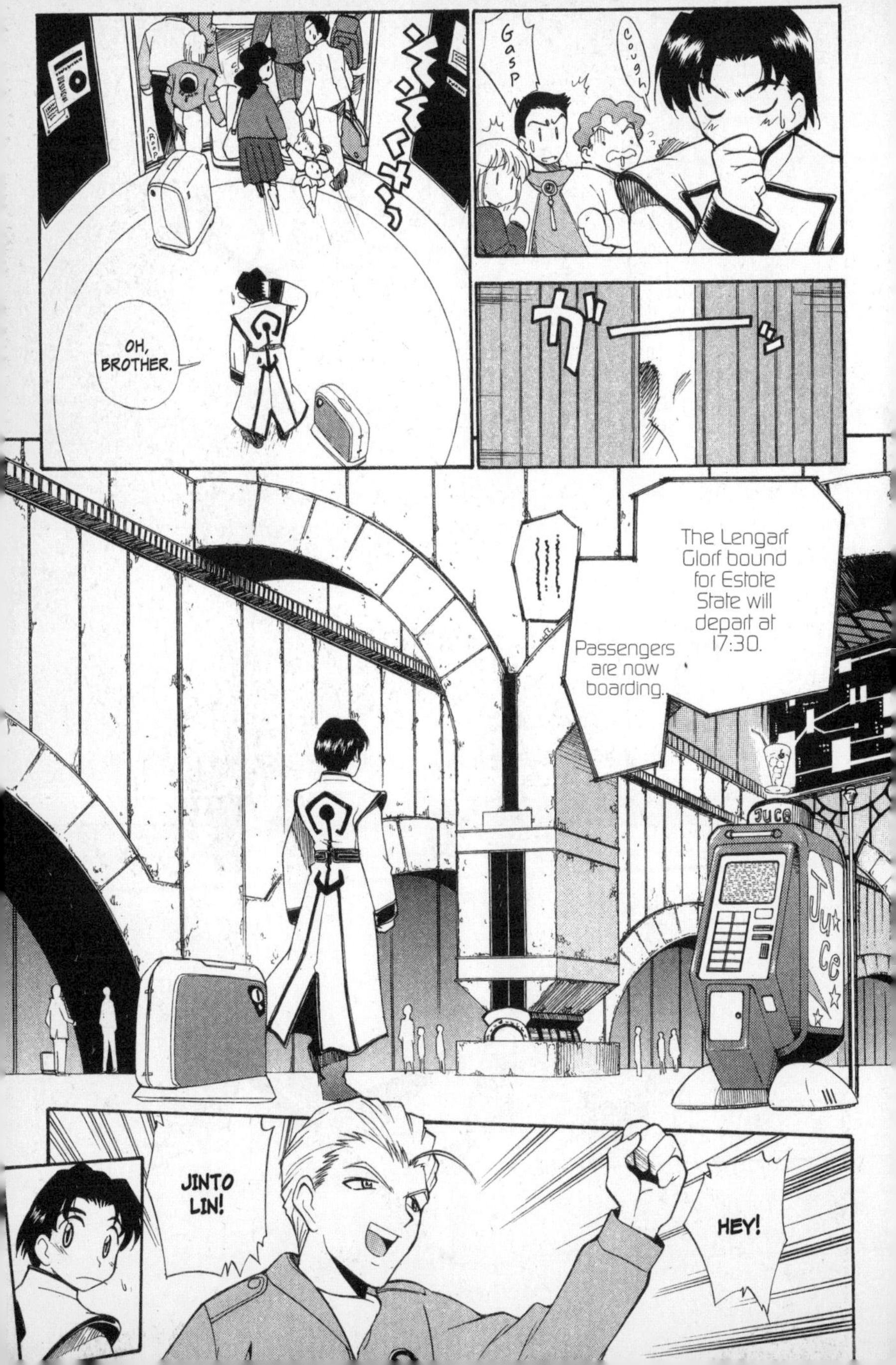
Gasp
Cough
ガーーッ
OH, BROTHER.
The Lengarf Glorf bound for Estote State will depart at 17:30.
Passengers are now boarding.
……
HEY!
JINTO LIN!

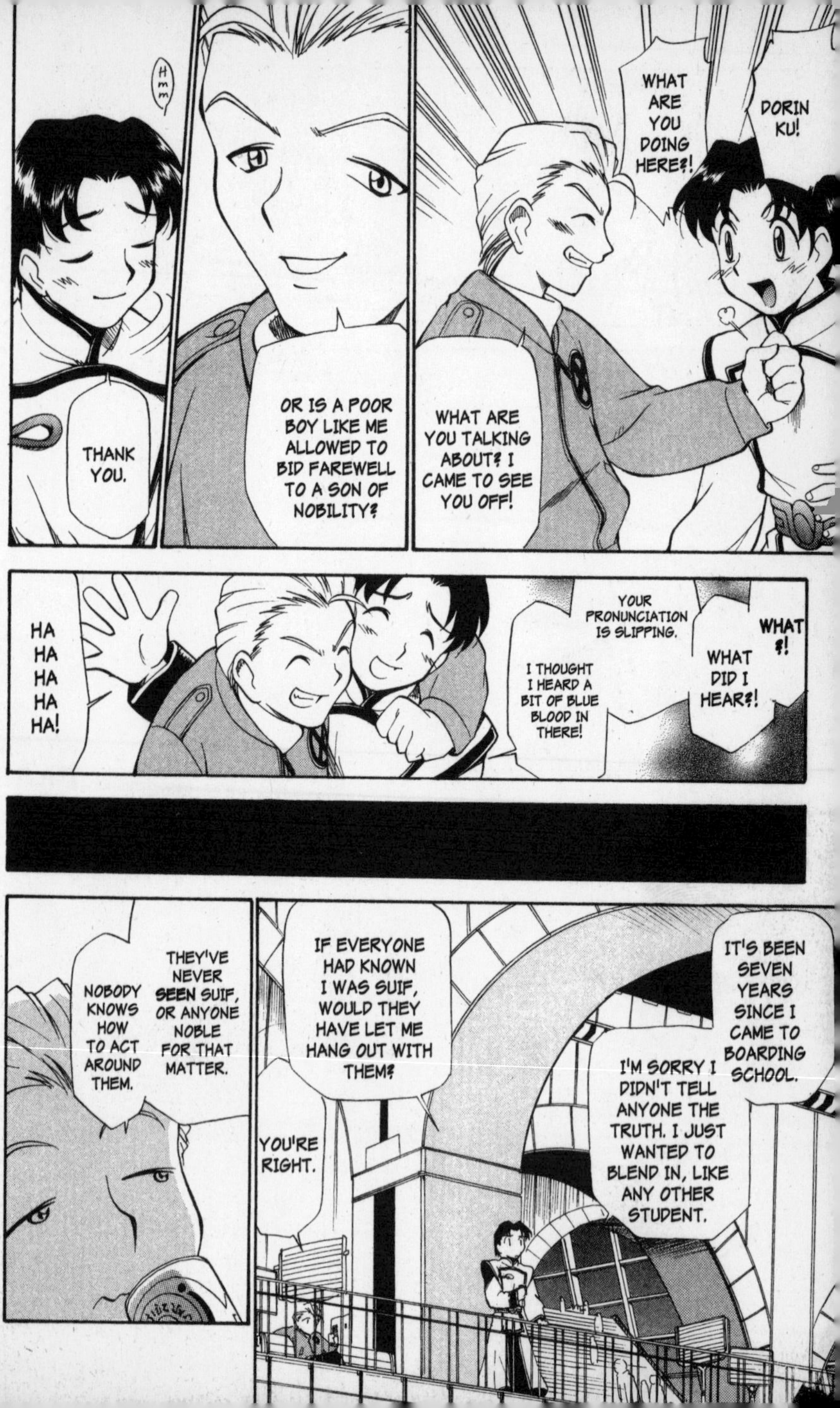

DORIN KU!
WHAT ARE YOU DOING HERE?!
WHAT ARE YOU TALKING ABOUT? I CAME TO SEE YOU OFF!
OR IS A POOR BOY LIKE ME ALLOWED TO BID FAREWELL TO A SON OF NOBILITY?
Hmm
THANK YOU.
WHAT?!
WHAT DID I HEAR?!
YOUR PRONUNCIATION IS SLIPPING.
I THOUGHT I HEARD A BIT OF BLUE BLOOD IN THERE!
HA HA HA HA HA!
IT'S BEEN SEVEN YEARS SINCE I CAME TO BOARDING SCHOOL.
I'M SORRY I DIDN'T TELL ANYONE THE TRUTH. I JUST WANTED TO BLEND IN, LIKE ANY OTHER STUDENT.
IF EVERYONE HAD KNOWN I WAS SUIF, WOULD THEY HAVE LET ME HANG OUT WITH THEM?
YOU'RE RIGHT.
THEY'VE NEVER SEEN SUIF, OR ANYONE NOBLE FOR THAT MATTER.
NOBODY KNOWS HOW TO ACT AROUND THEM.

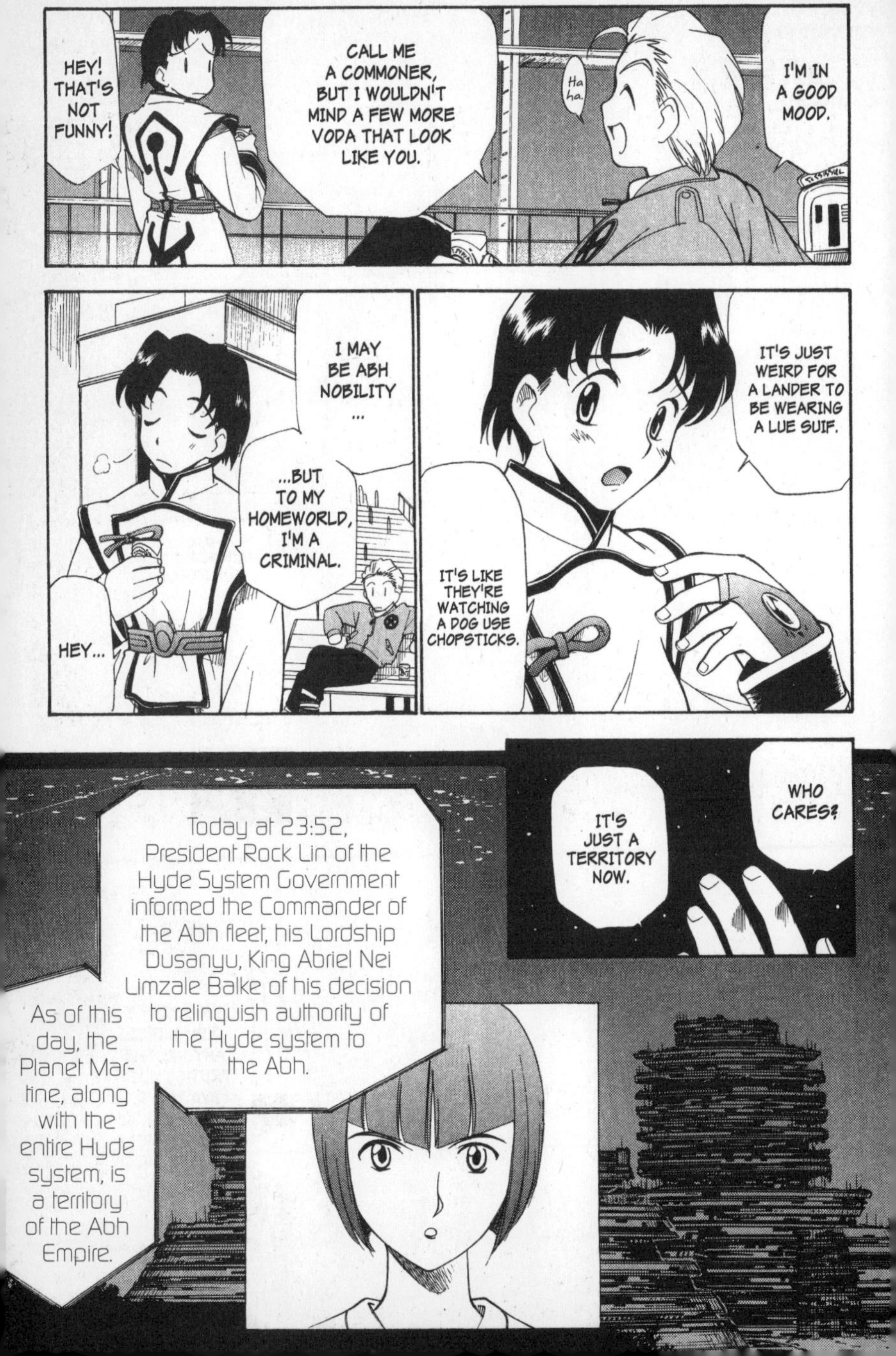
I'M IN A GOOD MOOD.
Ha ha.
CALL ME A COMMONER, BUT I WOULDN'T MIND A FEW MORE VODA THAT LOOK LIKE YOU.
HEY! THAT'S NOT FUNNY!
IT'S JUST WEIRD FOR A LANDER TO BE WEARING A LUE SUIF.
IT'S LIKE THEY'RE WATCHING A DOG USE CHOPSTICKS.
I MAY BE ABH NOBILITY ...
...BUT TO MY HOMEWORLD, I'M A CRIMINAL.
HEY...
WHO CARES?
IT'S JUST A TERRITORY NOW.
Today at 23:52, President Rock Lin of the Hyde System Government informed the Commander of the Abh fleet, his Lordship Dusanyu, King Abriel Nei Limzale Balke of his decision to relinquish authority of the Hyde system to the Abh.
As of this day, the Planet Martine, along with the entire Hyde system, is a territory of the Abh Empire.

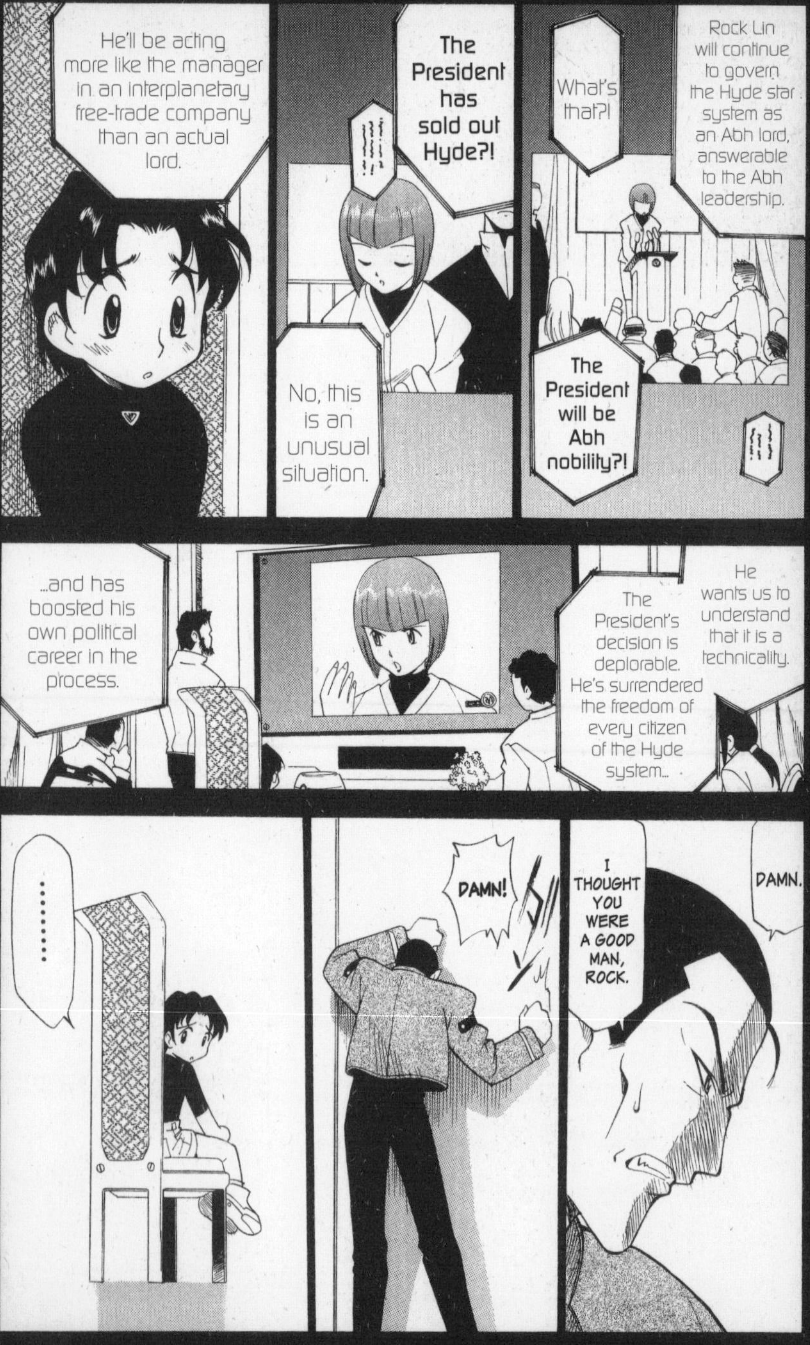

Rock Lin will continue to govern the Hyde star system as an Abh lord, answerable to the Abh leadership.
What's that?!
The President will be Abh nobility?!
The President has sold out Hyde?!
No, this is an unusual situation.
He'll be acting more like the manager in an interplanetary free-trade company than an actual lord.
He wants us to understand that it is a technicality.
The President's decision is deplorable. He's surrendered the freedom of every citizen of the Hyde system...
...and has boosted his own political career in the process.
DAMN.
I THOUGHT YOU WERE A GOOD MAN, ROCK.
DAMN!
......

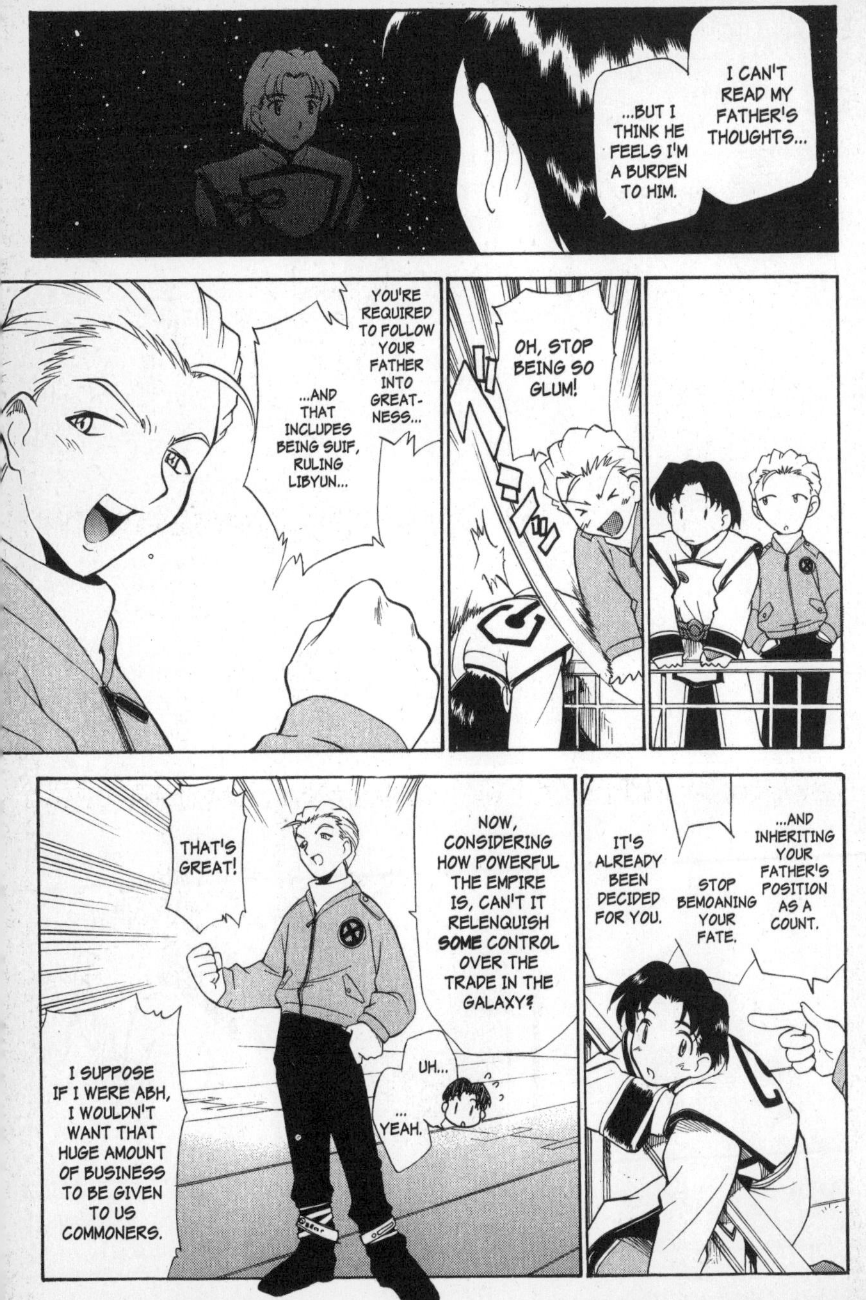
I CAN'T READ MY FATHER'S THOUGHTS...
...BUT I THINK HE FEELS I'M A BURDEN TO HIM.
OH, STOP BEING SO GLUM!
YOU'RE REQUIRED TO FOLLOW YOUR FATHER INTO GREAT-NESS...
...AND THAT INCLUDES BEING SUIF, RULING LIBYUN...
...AND INHERITING YOUR FATHER'S POSITION AS A COUNT.
STOP BEMOANING YOUR FATE.
IT'S ALREADY BEEN DECIDED FOR YOU.
NOW, CONSIDERING HOW POWERFUL THE EMPIRE IS, CAN'T IT RELENQUISH **SOME** CONTROL OVER THE TRADE IN THE GALAXY?
THAT'S GREAT!
UH...
...YEAH.
I SUPPOSE IF I WERE ABH, I WOULDN'T WANT THAT HUGE AMOUNT OF BUSINESS TO BE GIVEN TO US COMMONERS.

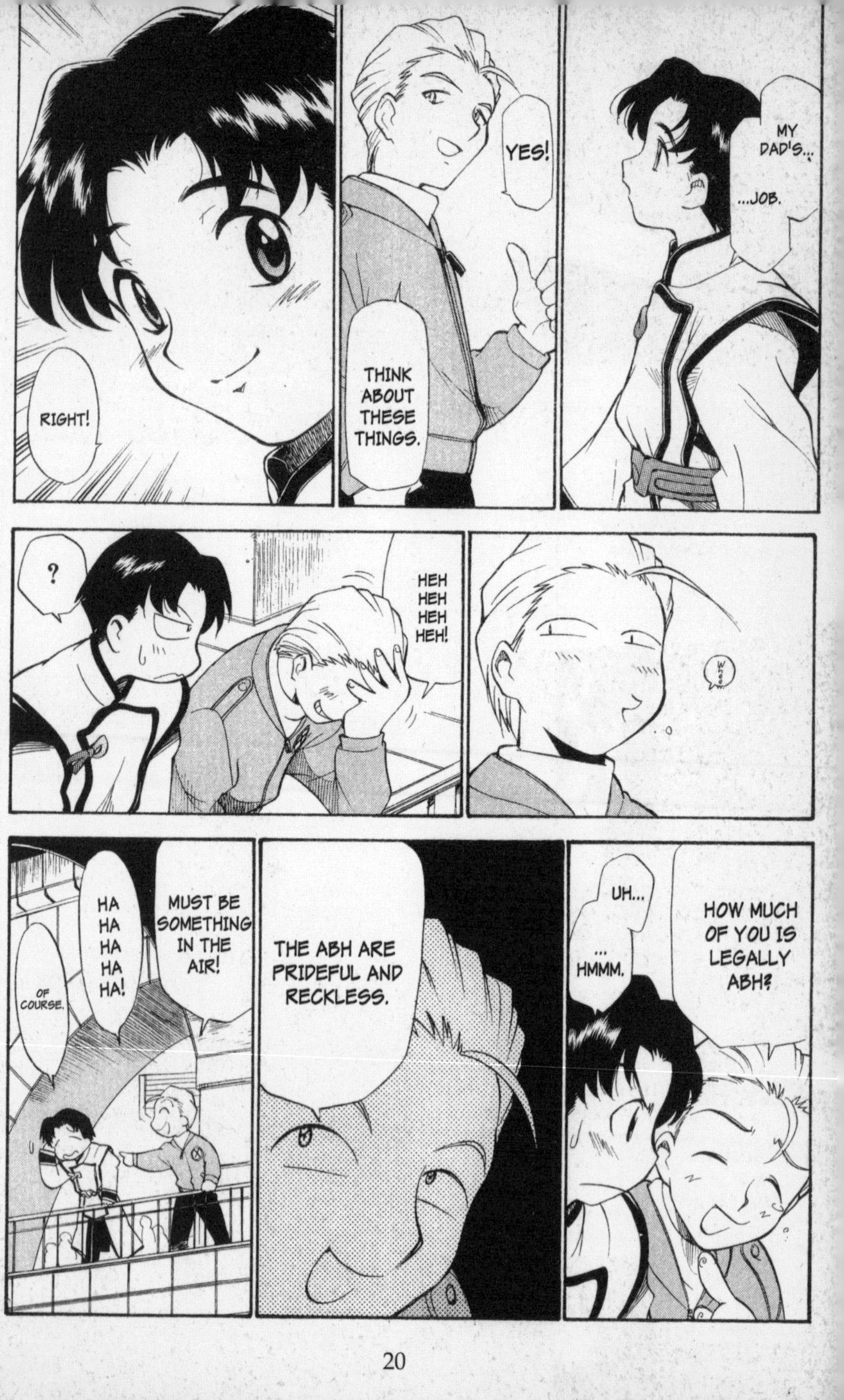
MY DAD'S...
...JOB.
YES!
THINK ABOUT THESE THINGS.
RIGHT!
HEH HEH HEH HEH!
?
HOW MUCH OF YOU IS LEGALLY ABH?
UH...
... HMMM.
THE ABH ARE PRIDEFUL AND RECKLESS.
MUST BE SOMETHING IN THE AIR!
HA HA HA HA HA!
OF COURSE.

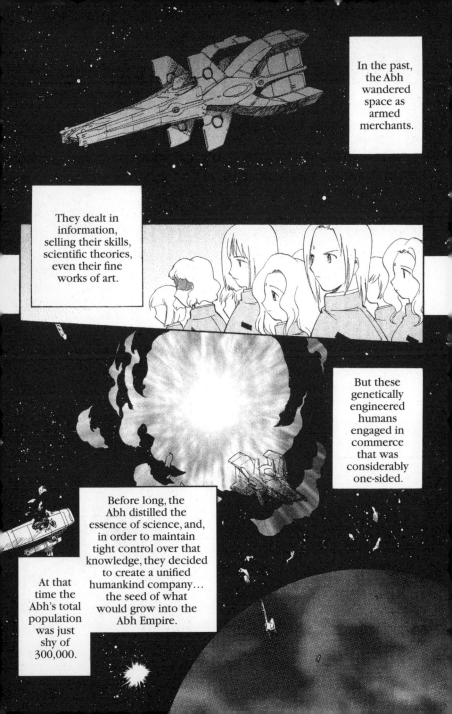

In the past,
the Abh
wandered
space as
armed
merchants.

They dealt in
information,
selling their skills,
scientific theories,
even their fine
works of art.

But these
genetically
engineered
humans
engaged in
commerce
that was
considerably
one-sided.

Before long, the
Abh distilled the
essence of science, and,
in order to maintain
tight control over that
knowledge, they decided
to create a unified
humankind company…
the seed of what
would grow into the
Abh Empire.

At that
time the
Abh's total
population
was just
shy of
300,000.

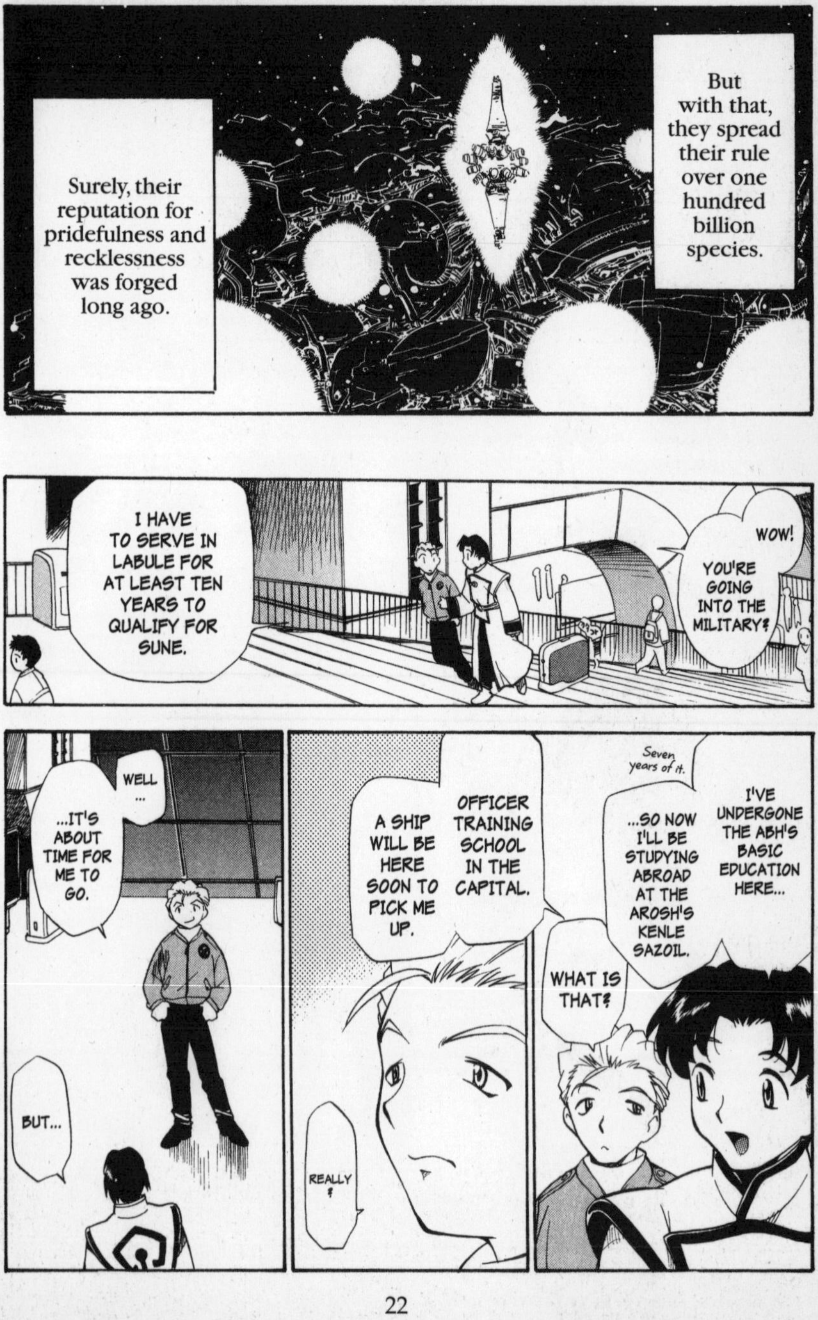
But with that, they spread their rule over one hundred billion species.
Surely, their reputation for pridefulness and recklessness was forged long ago.
WOW!
YOU'RE GOING INTO THE MILITARY?
I HAVE TO SERVE IN LABULE FOR AT LEAST TEN YEARS TO QUALIFY FOR SUNE.
I'VE UNDERGONE THE ABH'S BASIC EDUCATION HERE...
Seven years of it.
...SO NOW I'LL BE STUDYING ABROAD AT THE AROSH'S KENLE SAZOIL.
WHAT IS THAT?
OFFICER TRAINING SCHOOL IN THE CAPITAL.
A SHIP WILL BE HERE SOON TO PICK ME UP.
REALLY?
WELL...
...IT'S ABOUT TIME FOR ME TO GO.
BUT...

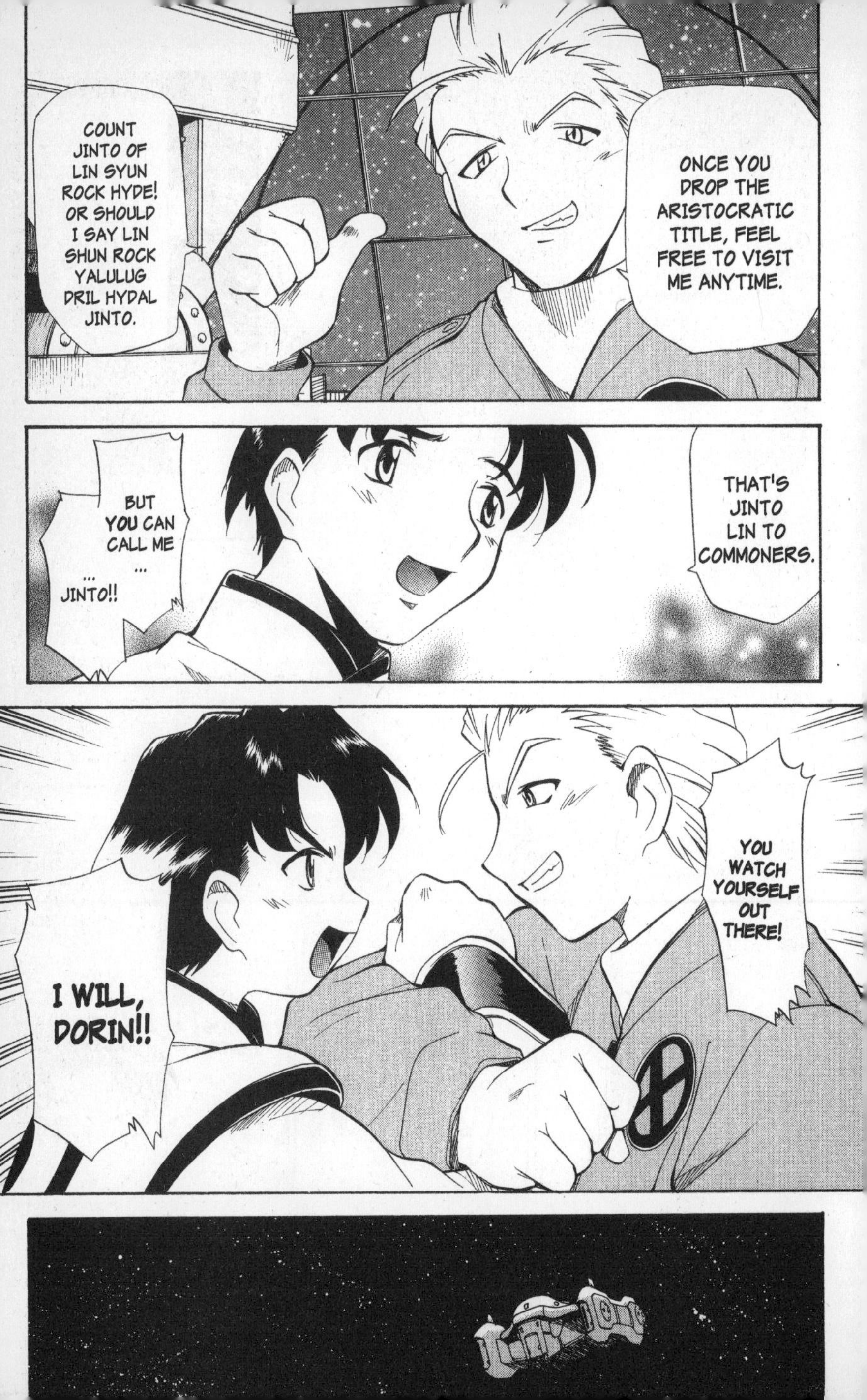
ONCE YOU DROP THE ARISTOCRATIC TITLE, FEEL FREE TO VISIT ME ANYTIME.
COUNT JINTO OF LIN SYUN ROCK HYDE! OR SHOULD I SAY LIN SHUN ROCK YALULUG DRIL HYDAL JINTO.
THAT'S JINTO LIN TO COMMONERS.
BUT YOU CAN CALL ME ... ... JINTO!!
YOU WATCH YOURSELF OUT THERE!
I WILL, DORIN!!

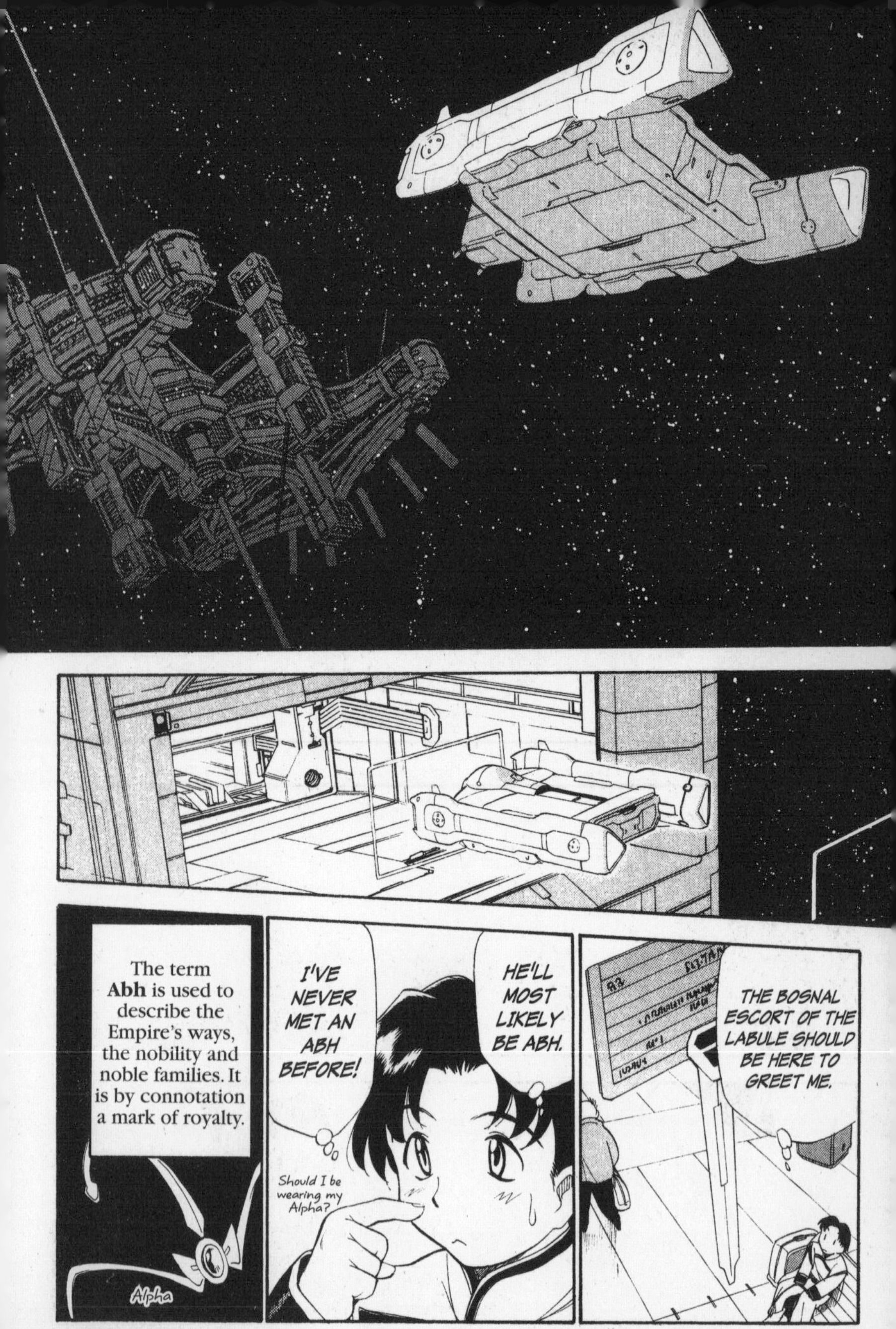
THE BOSNAL ESCORT OF THE LABULE SHOULD BE HERE TO GREET ME.
HE'LL MOST LIKELY BE ABH.
I'VE NEVER MET AN ABH BEFORE!
Should I be wearing my Alpha?
The term Abh is used to describe the Empire's ways, the nobility and noble families. It is by connotation a mark of royalty.
Alpha

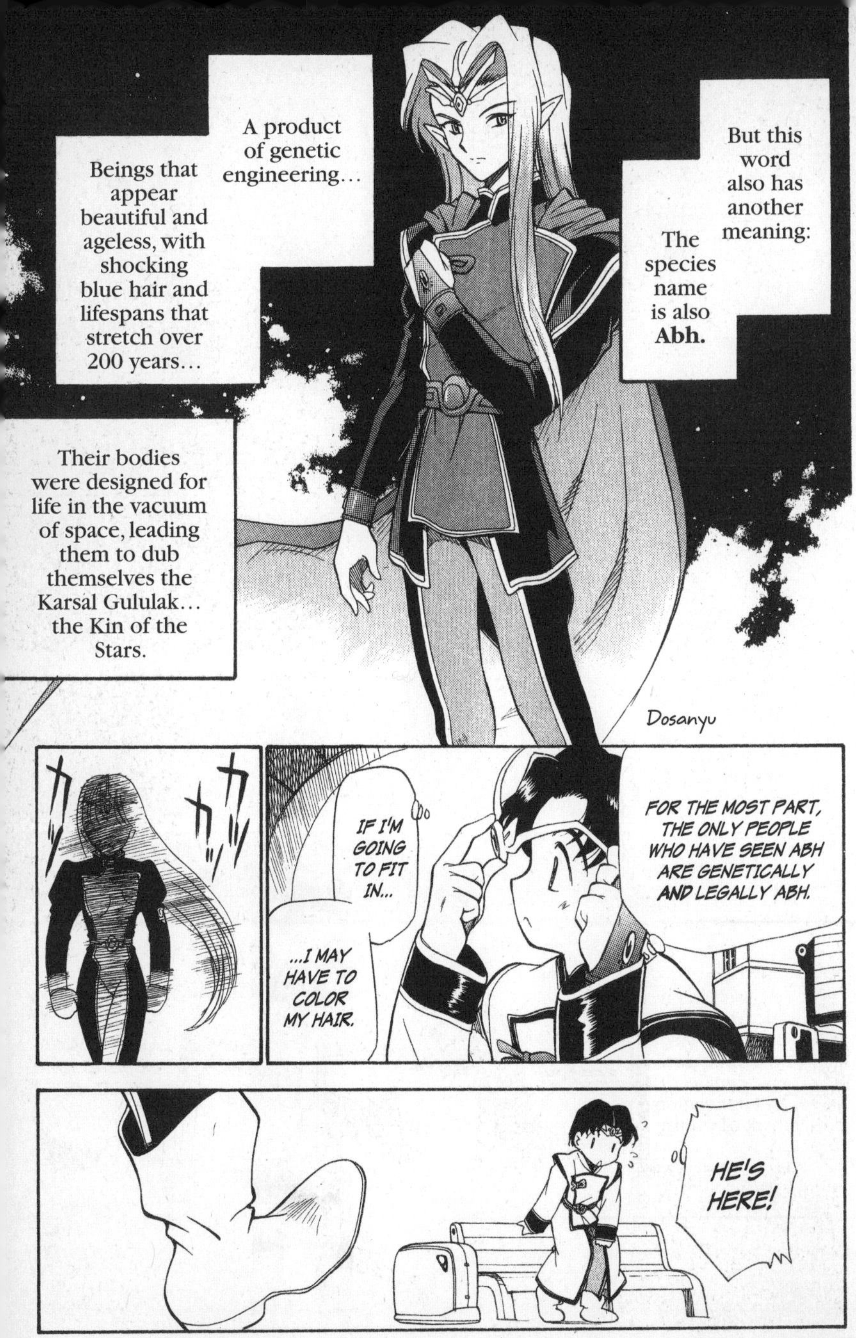

But this word also has another meaning:
The species name is also **Abh.**
A product of genetic engineering…
Beings that appear beautiful and ageless, with shocking blue hair and lifespans that stretch over 200 years…
Their bodies were designed for life in the vacuum of space, leading them to dub themselves the Karsal Gululak… the Kin of the Stars.
Dosanyu
FOR THE MOST PART, THE ONLY PEOPLE WHO HAVE SEEN ABH ARE GENETICALLY AND LEGALLY ABH.
IF I'M GOING TO FIT IN...
...I MAY HAVE TO COLOR MY HAIR.
HE'S HERE!

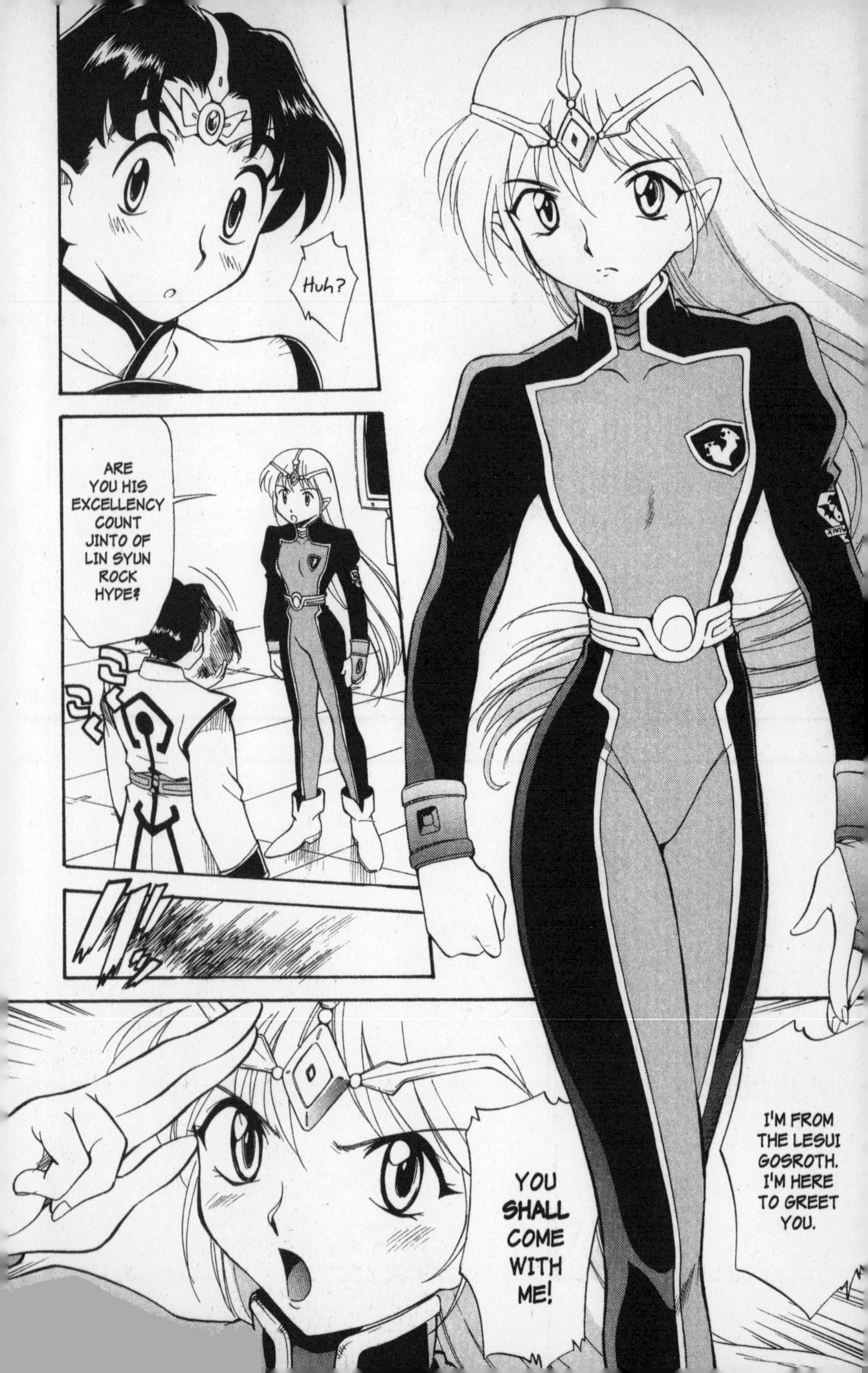
I'M FROM THE LESUI GOSROTH. I'M HERE TO GREET YOU.
Huh?
ARE YOU HIS EXCELLENCY COUNT JINTO OF LIN SYUN ROCK HYDE?
YOU SHALL COME WITH ME!

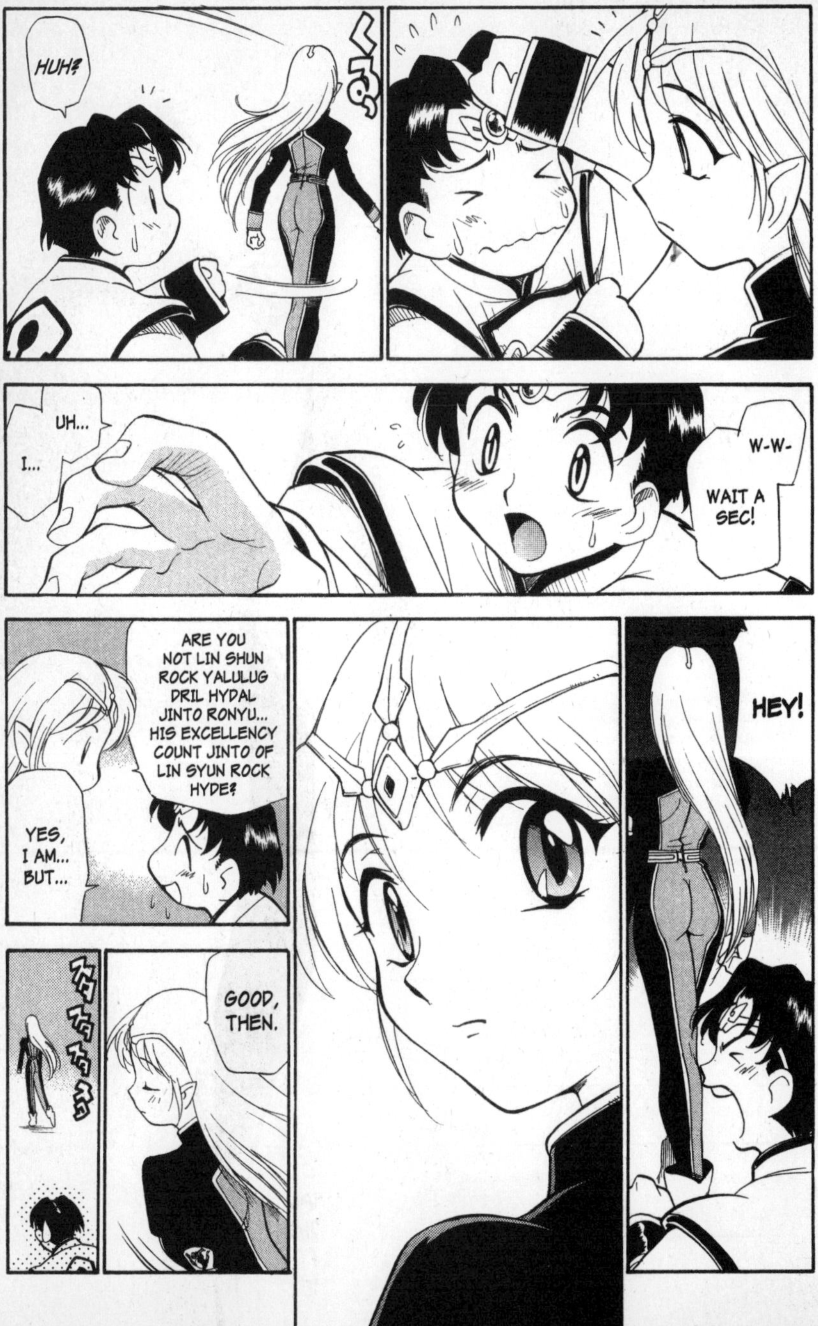
HUH?
W-W-
WAIT A SEC!
UH...
I...
HEY!
ARE YOU NOT LIN SHUN ROCK YALULUG DRIL HYDAL JINTO RONYU... HIS EXCELLENCY COUNT JINTO OF LIN SYUN ROCK HYDE?
YES, I AM... BUT...
GOOD, THEN.

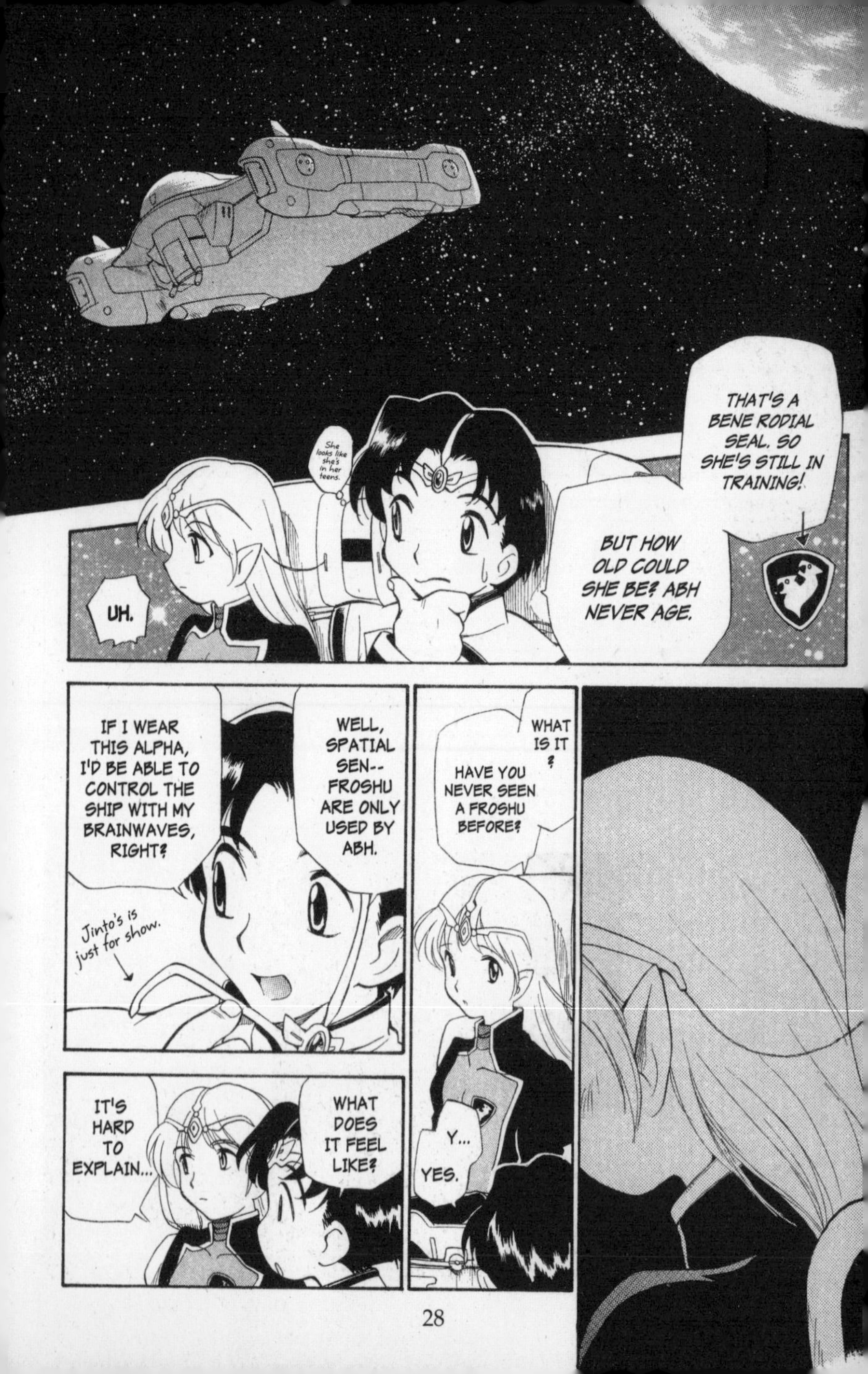
THAT'S A BENE RODIAL SEAL. SO SHE'S STILL IN TRAINING!
BUT HOW OLD COULD SHE BE? ABH NEVER AGE.
She looks like she's in her teens.
UH.
WHAT IS IT?
HAVE YOU NEVER SEEN A FROSHU BEFORE?
Y... YES.
WELL, SPATIAL SEN-- FROSHU ARE ONLY USED BY ABH.
IF I WEAR THIS ALPHA, I'D BE ABLE TO CONTROL THE SHIP WITH MY BRAINWAVES, RIGHT?
Jinto's is just for show.
WHAT DOES IT FEEL LIKE?
IT'S HARD TO EXPLAIN...

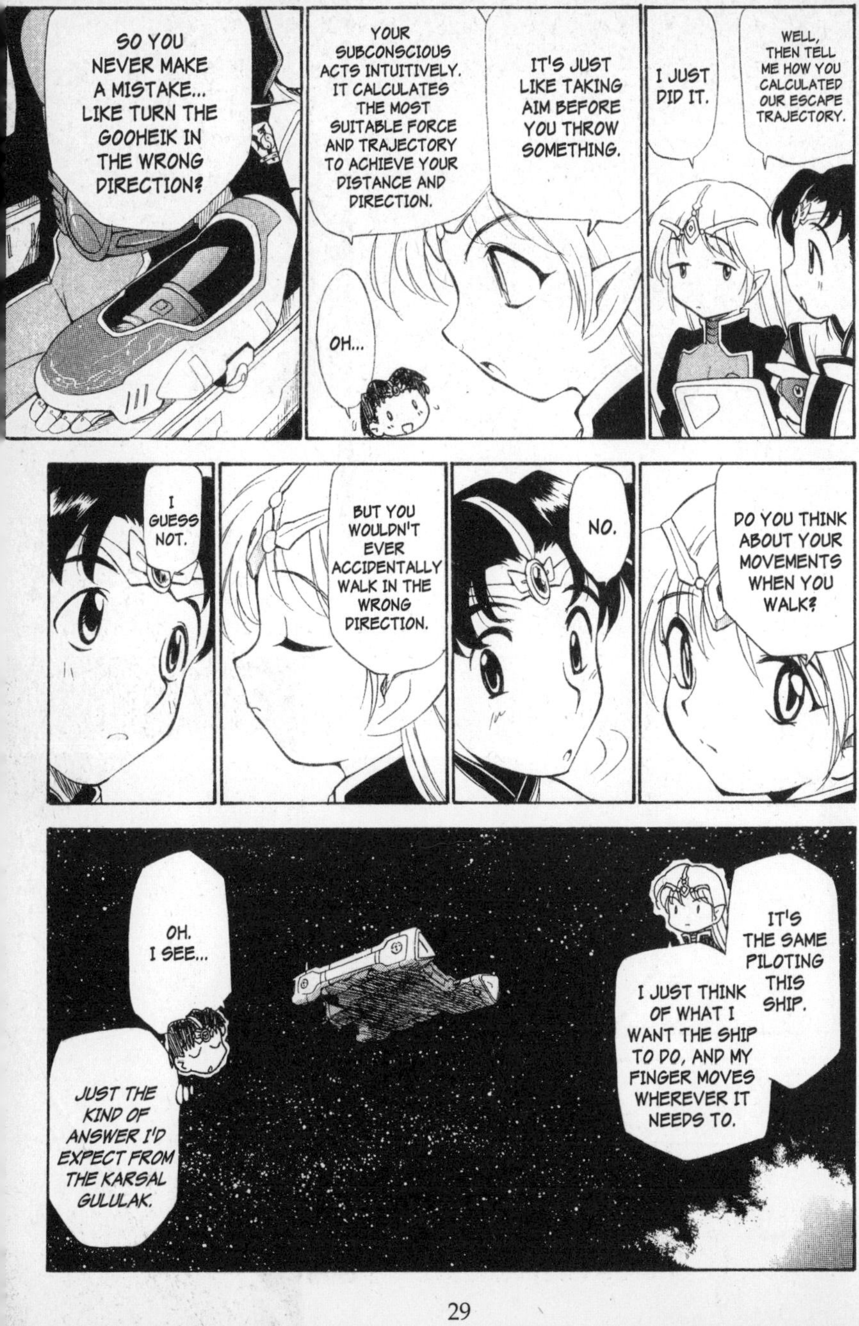
WELL, THEN TELL ME HOW YOU CALCULATED OUR ESCAPE TRAJECTORY.
I JUST DID IT.
IT'S JUST LIKE TAKING AIM BEFORE YOU THROW SOMETHING.
YOUR SUBCONSCIOUS ACTS INTUITIVELY. IT CALCULATES THE MOST SUITABLE FORCE AND TRAJECTORY TO ACHIEVE YOUR DISTANCE AND DIRECTION.
OH...
SO YOU NEVER MAKE A MISTAKE... LIKE TURN THE GOOHEIK IN THE WRONG DIRECTION?
DO YOU THINK ABOUT YOUR MOVEMENTS WHEN YOU WALK?
NO.
BUT YOU WOULDN'T EVER ACCIDENTALLY WALK IN THE WRONG DIRECTION.
I GUESS NOT.
IT'S THE SAME PILOTING THIS SHIP.
I JUST THINK OF WHAT I WANT THE SHIP TO DO, AND MY FINGER MOVES WHEREVER IT NEEDS TO.
OH. I SEE...
JUST THE KIND OF ANSWER I'D EXPECT FROM THE KARSAL GULULAK.

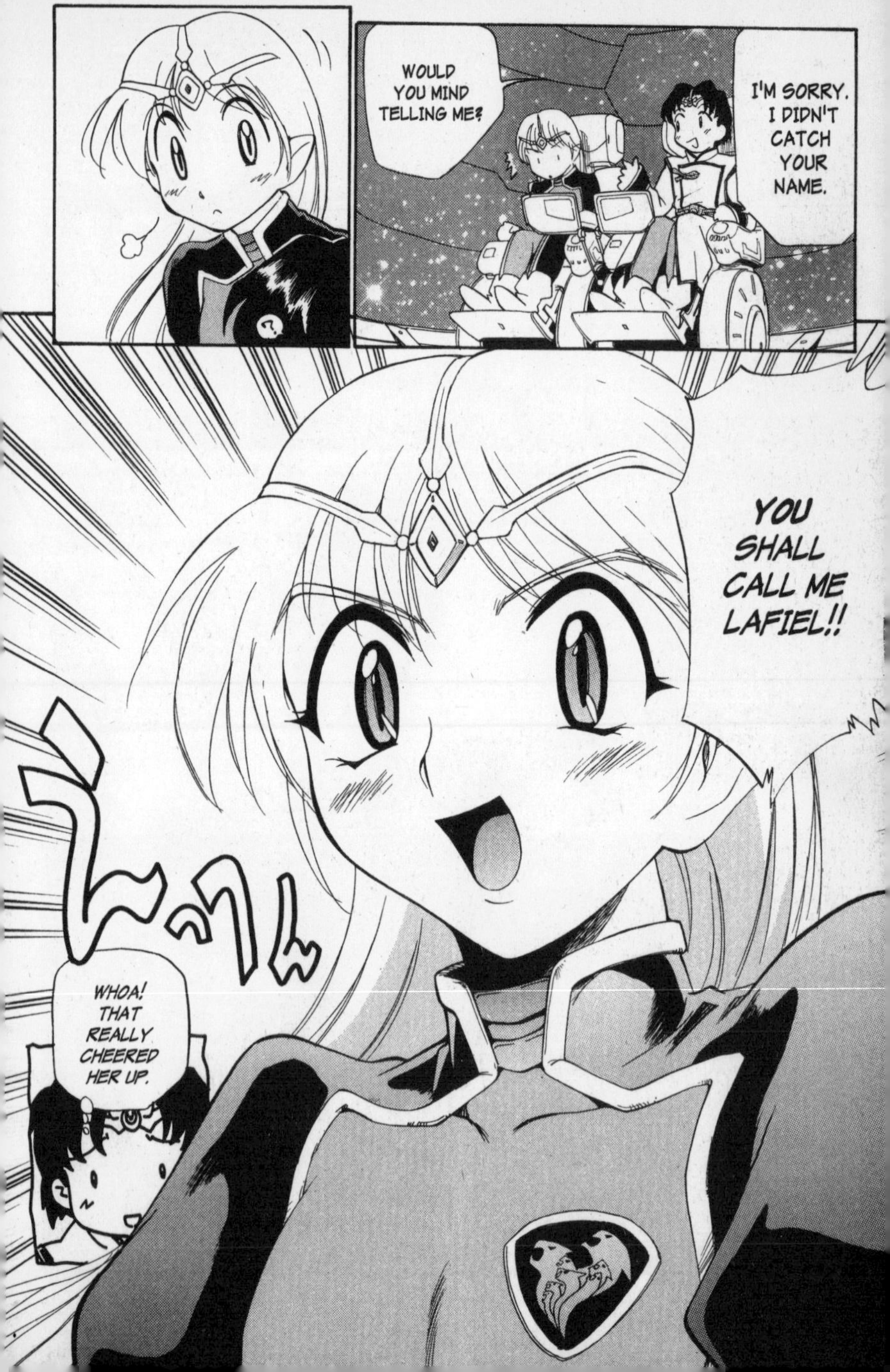

I'M SORRY. I DIDN'T CATCH YOUR NAME.
WOULD YOU MIND TELLING ME?
YOU SHALL CALL ME LAFIEL!!
WHOA! THAT REALLY CHEERED HER UP.

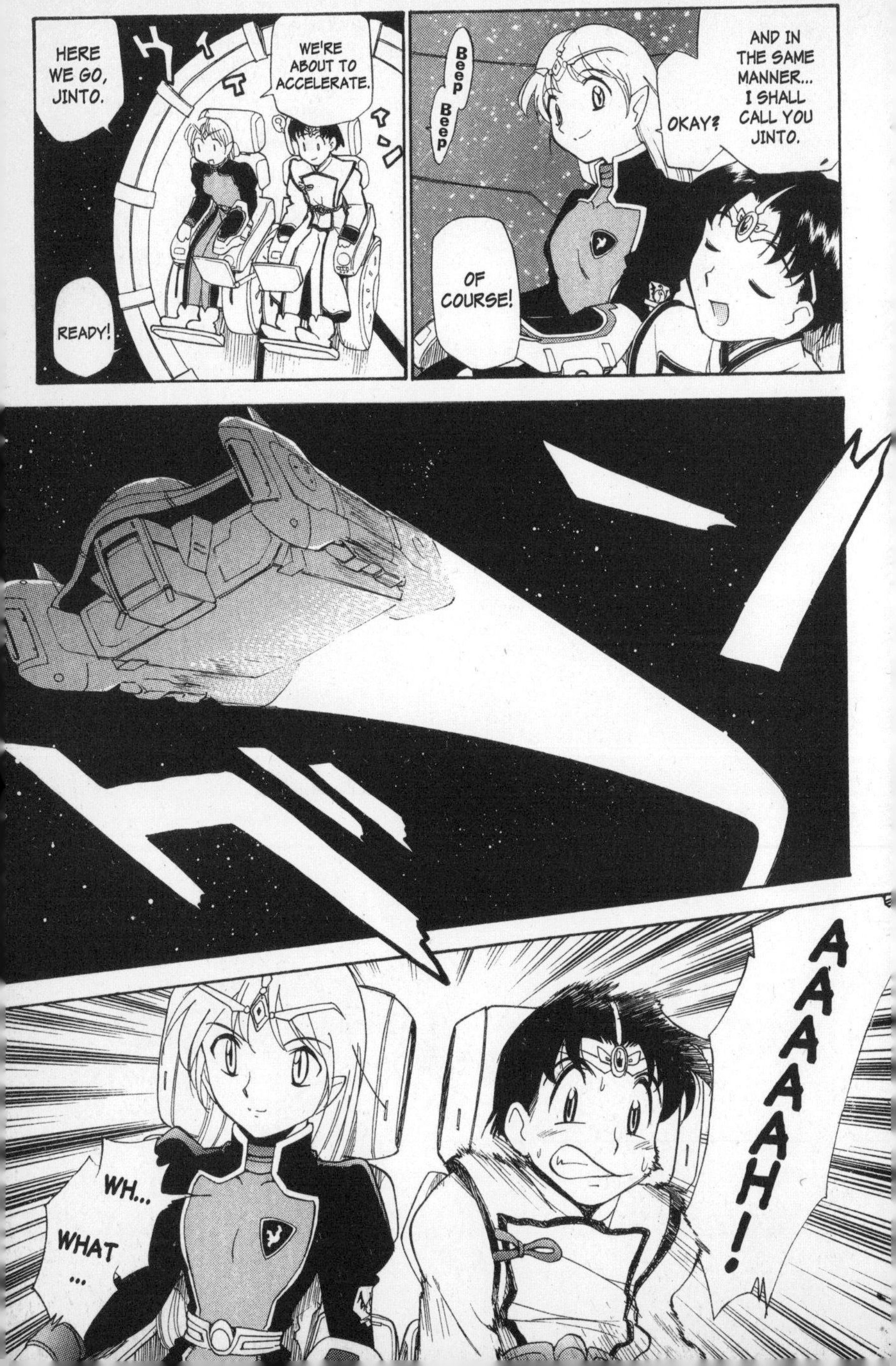
AND IN THE SAME MANNER... I SHALL CALL YOU JINTO.
OKAY?
Beep Beep
OF COURSE!
WE'RE ABOUT TO ACCELERATE.
HERE WE GO, JINTO.
READY!
AAAAAH!
WH...
WHAT ...

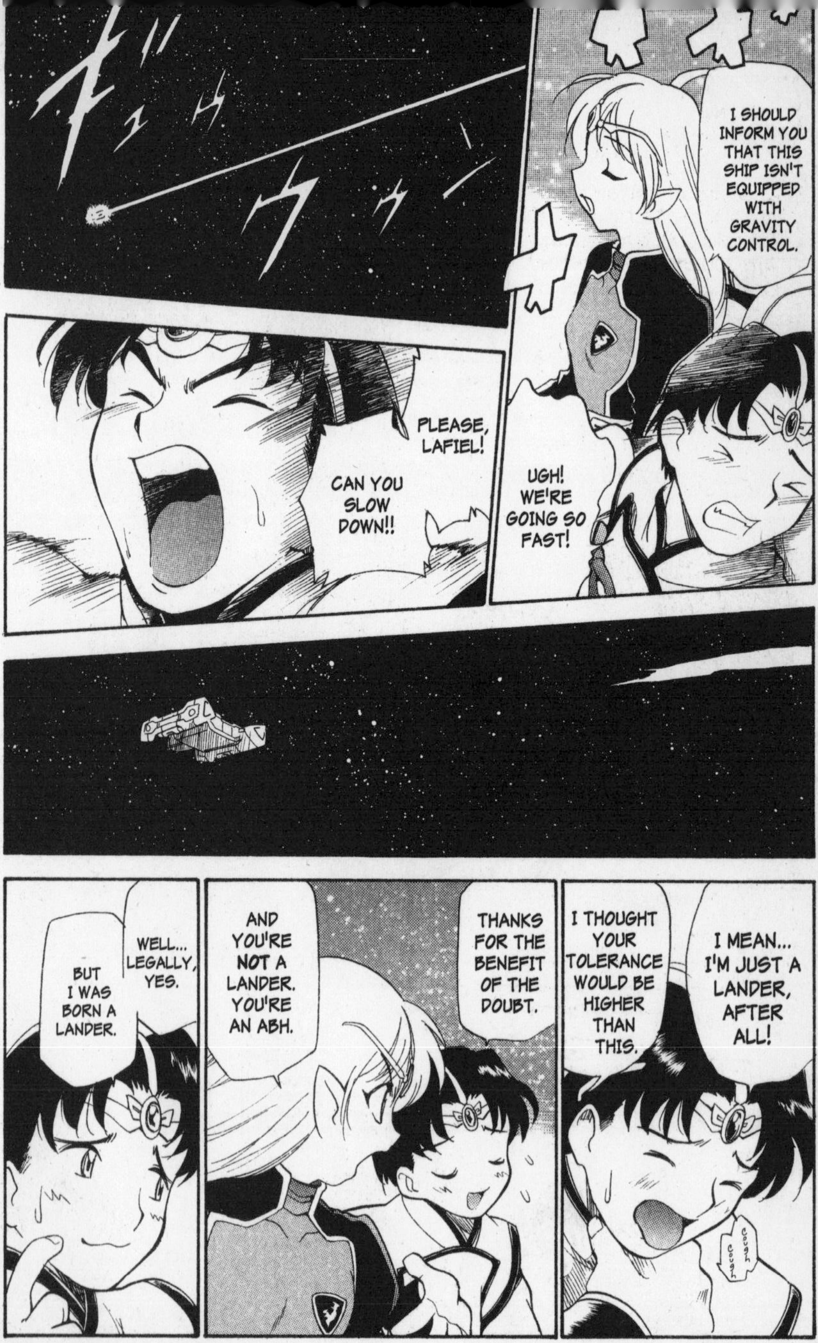
I SHOULD INFORM YOU THAT THIS SHIP ISN'T EQUIPPED WITH GRAVITY CONTROL.
UGH! WE'RE GOING SO FAST!
PLEASE, LAFIEL!
CAN YOU SLOW DOWN!!
I MEAN... I'M JUST A LANDER, AFTER ALL!
I THOUGHT YOUR TOLERANCE WOULD BE HIGHER THAN THIS.
Cough Cough
THANKS FOR THE BENEFIT OF THE DOUBT.
AND YOU'RE **NOT** A LANDER. YOU'RE AN ABH.
WELL... LEGALLY, YES.
BUT I WAS BORN A LANDER.

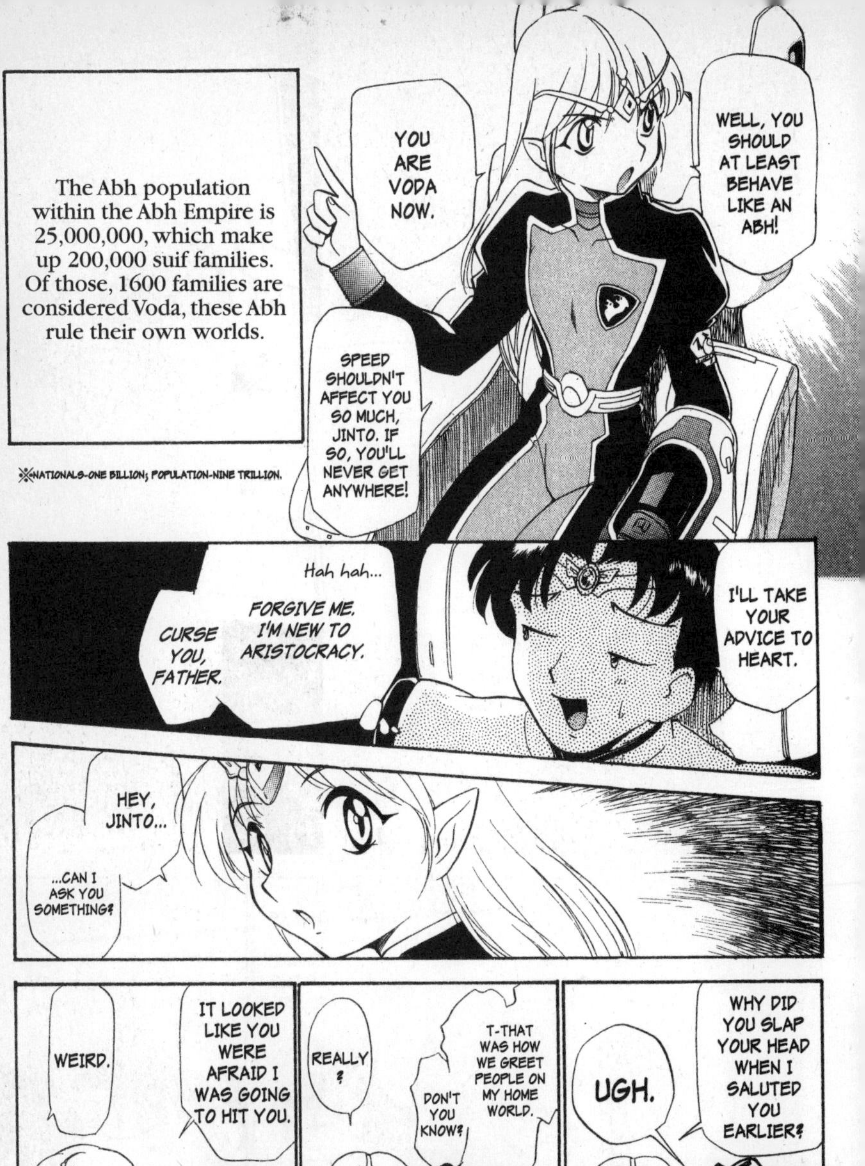
WELL, YOU SHOULD AT LEAST BEHAVE LIKE AN ABH!
YOU ARE VODA NOW.
The Abh population within the Abh Empire is 25,000,000, which make up 200,000 suif families. Of those, 1600 families are considered Voda, these Abh rule their own worlds.
SPEED SHOULDN'T AFFECT YOU SO MUCH, JINTO. IF SO, YOU'LL NEVER GET ANYWHERE!
※NATIONALS-ONE BILLION; POPULATION-NINE TRILLION.
I'LL TAKE YOUR ADVICE TO HEART.
Hah hah...
FORGIVE ME. I'M NEW TO ARISTOCRACY.
CURSE YOU, FATHER.
HEY, JINTO...
...CAN I ASK YOU SOMETHING?
WHY DID YOU SLAP YOUR HEAD WHEN I SALUTED YOU EARLIER?
UGH.
T-THAT WAS HOW WE GREET PEOPLE ON MY HOME WORLD.
DON'T YOU KNOW?
REALLY?
IT LOOKED LIKE YOU WERE AFRAID I WAS GOING TO HIT YOU.
WEIRD.

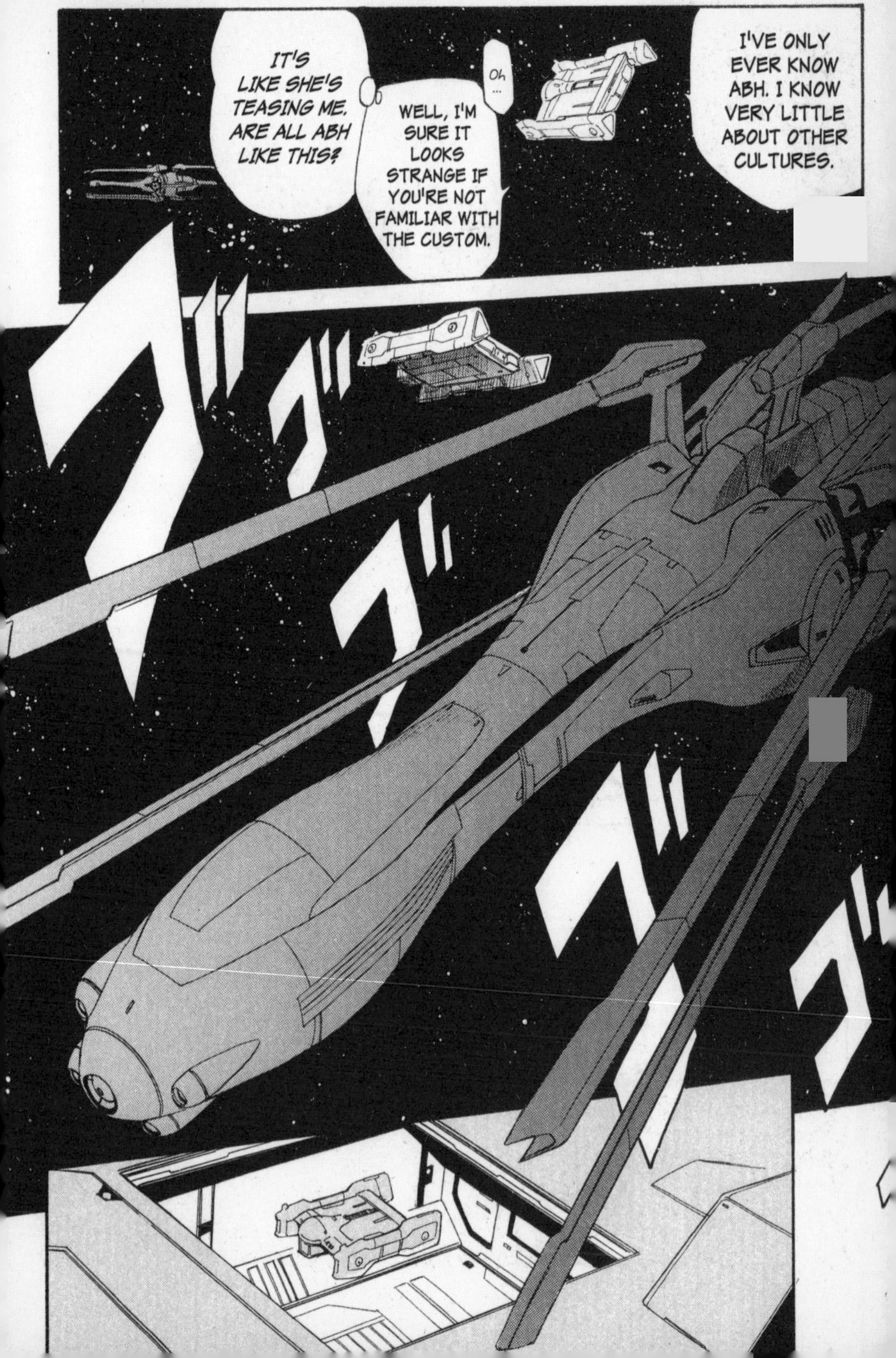
I'VE ONLY EVER KNOW ABH. I KNOW VERY LITTLE ABOUT OTHER CULTURES.
Oh ...
WELL, I'M SURE IT LOOKS STRANGE IF YOU'RE NOT FAMILIAR WITH THE CUSTOM.
IT'S LIKE SHE'S TEASING ME. ARE ALL ABH LIKE THIS?

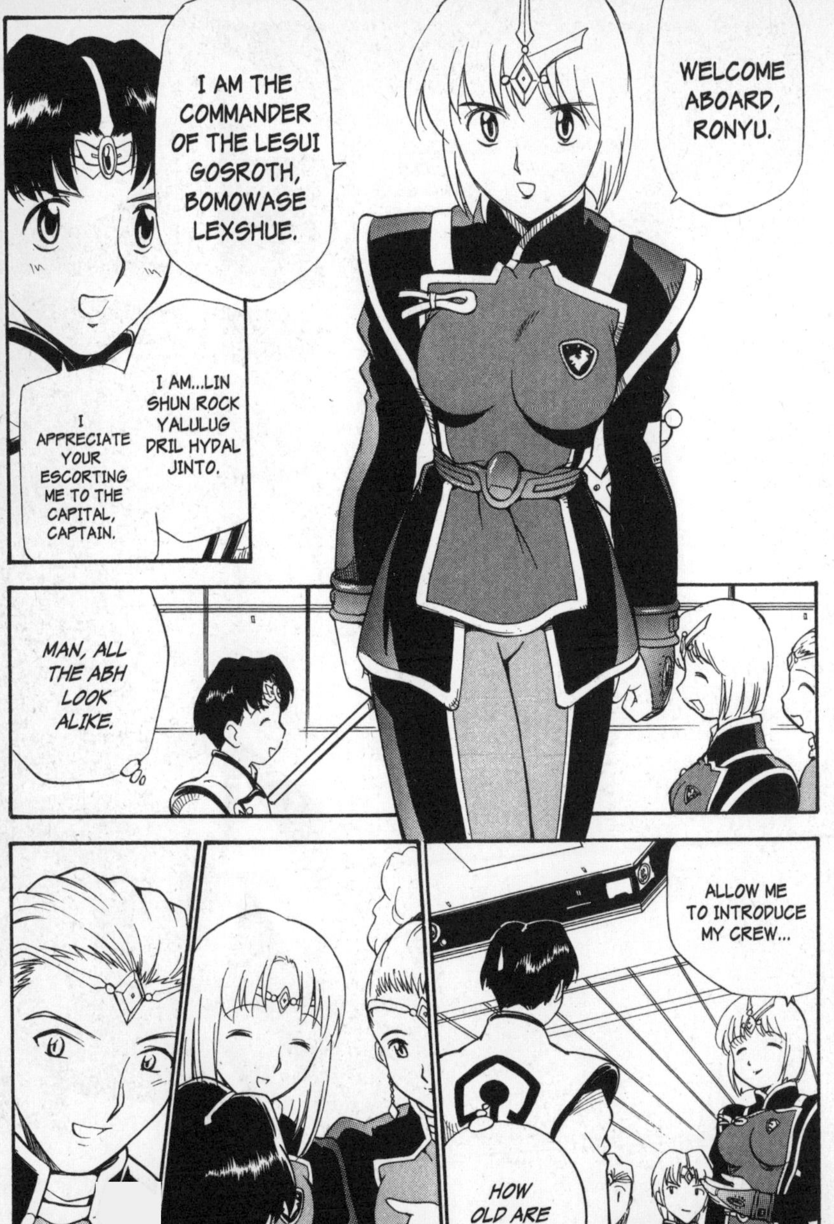
WELCOME ABOARD, RONYU.
I AM THE COMMANDER OF THE LESUI GOSROTH, BOMOWASE LEXSHUE.
I AM...LIN SHUN ROCK YALULUG DRIL HYDAL JINTO.
I APPRECIATE YOUR ESCORTING ME TO THE CAPITAL, CAPTAIN.
MAN, ALL THE ABH LOOK ALIKE.
ALLOW ME TO INTRODUCE MY CREW...
HOW OLD ARE THEY?

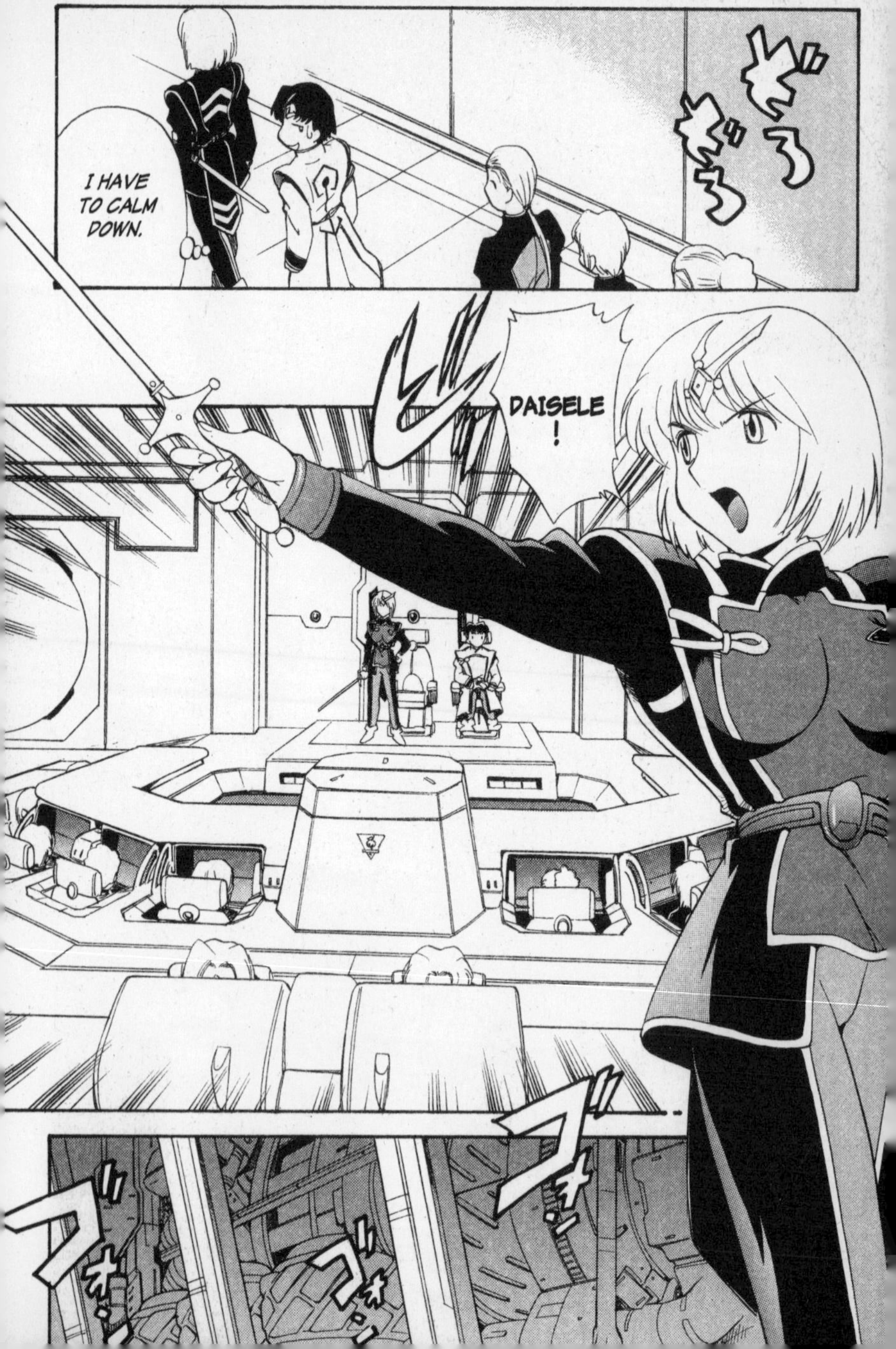
I HAVE TO CALM DOWN.
DAISELE!

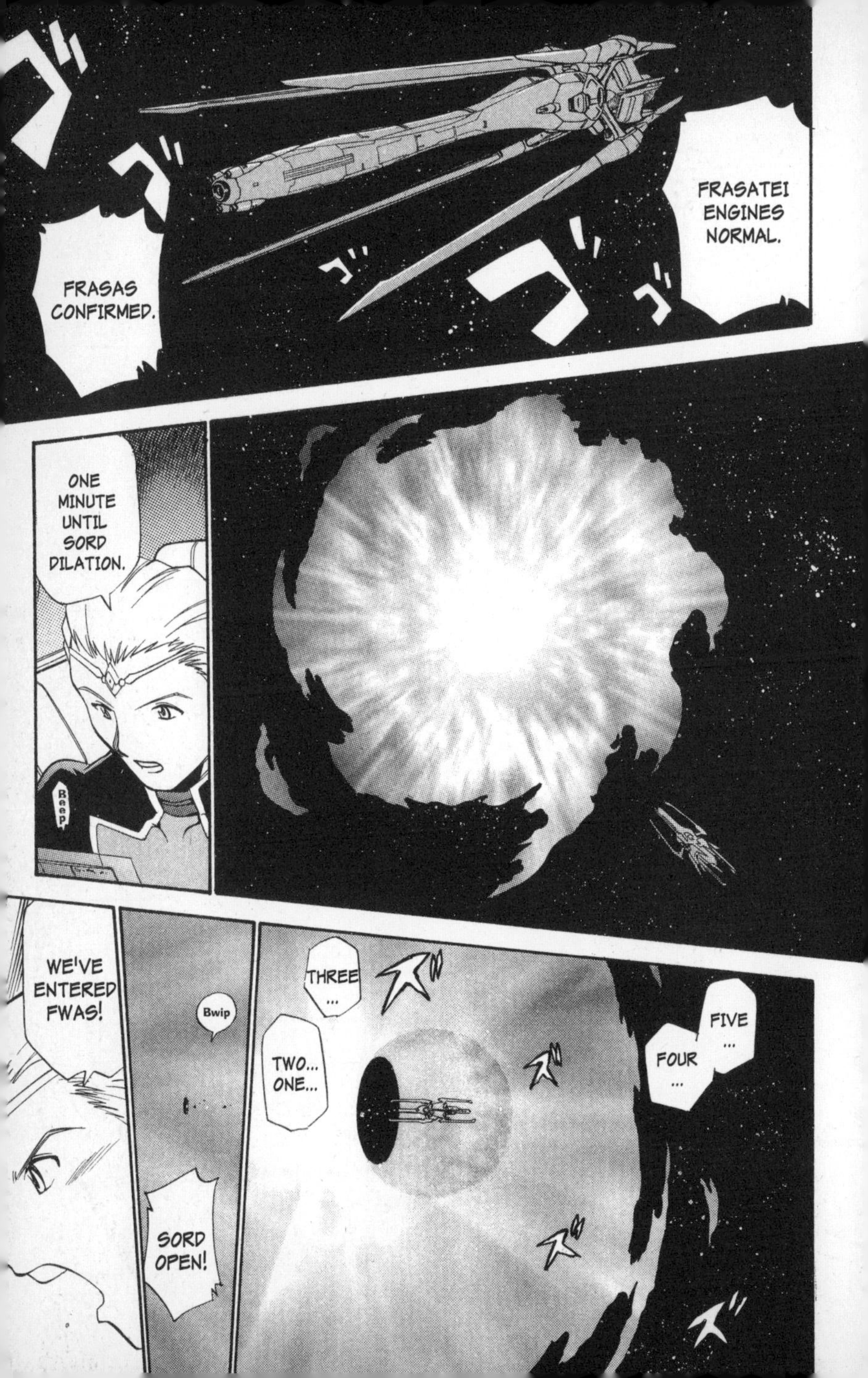
FRASATEI ENGINES NORMAL.
FRASAS CONFIRMED.
ONE MINUTE UNTIL SORD DILATION.
Beep
FIVE ...
FOUR ...
THREE ...
TWO... ONE...
Bwip
SORD OPEN!
WE'VE ENTERED FWAS!

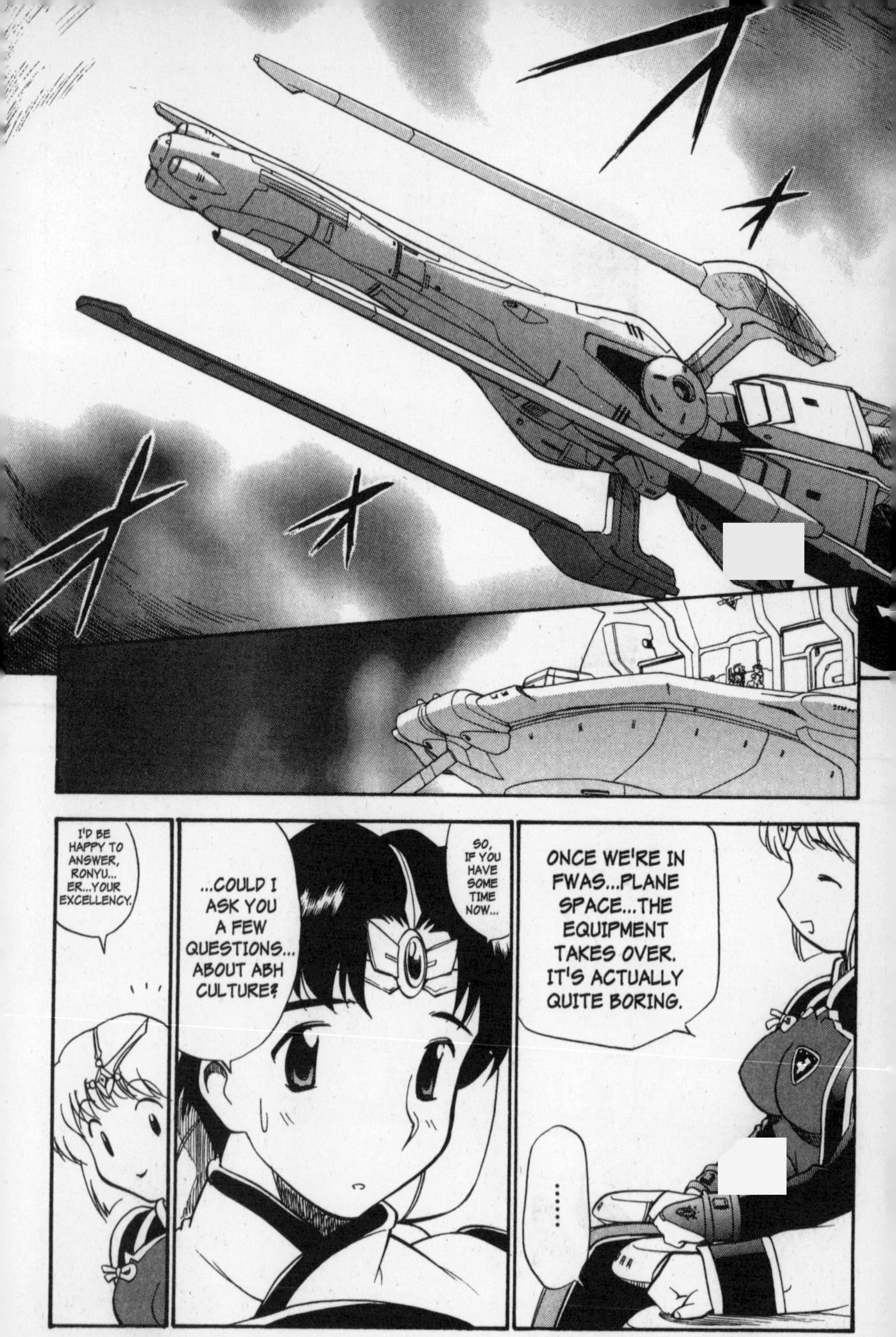
ONCE WE'RE IN FWAS...PLANE SPACE...THE EQUIPMENT TAKES OVER. IT'S ACTUALLY QUITE BORING.
......
SO, IF YOU HAVE SOME TIME NOW...
...COULD I ASK YOU A FEW QUESTIONS... ABOUT ABH CULTURE?
I'D BE HAPPY TO ANSWER, RONYU... ER...YOUR EXCELLENCY.

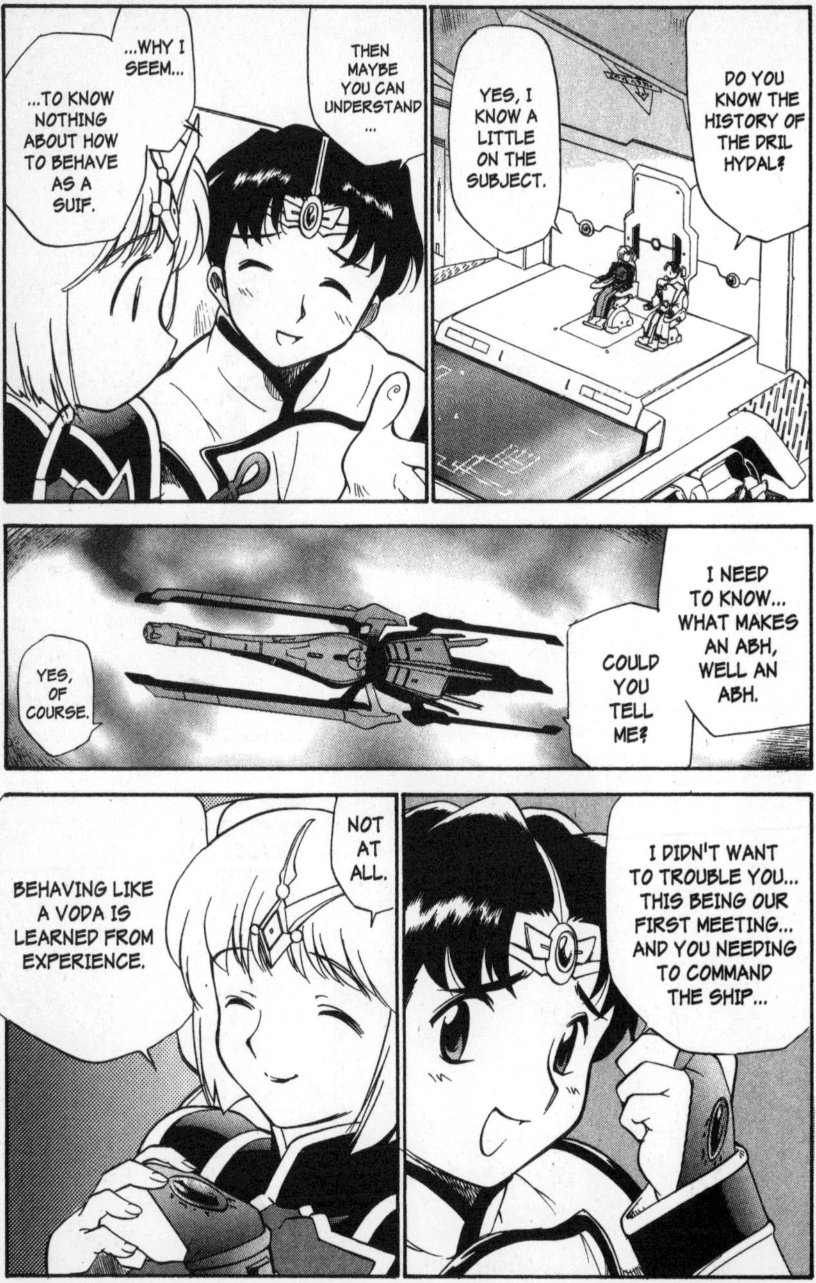
DO YOU KNOW THE HISTORY OF THE DRIL HYDAL?
YES, I KNOW A LITTLE ON THE SUBJECT.
THEN MAYBE YOU CAN UNDERSTAND ...
...WHY I SEEM...
...TO KNOW NOTHING ABOUT HOW TO BEHAVE AS A SUIF.
I NEED TO KNOW... WHAT MAKES AN ABH, WELL AN ABH.
COULD YOU TELL ME?
YES, OF COURSE.
I DIDN'T WANT TO TROUBLE YOU... THIS BEING OUR FIRST MEETING... AND YOU NEEDING TO COMMAND THE SHIP...
NOT AT ALL.
BEHAVING LIKE A VODA IS LEARNED FROM EXPERIENCE.

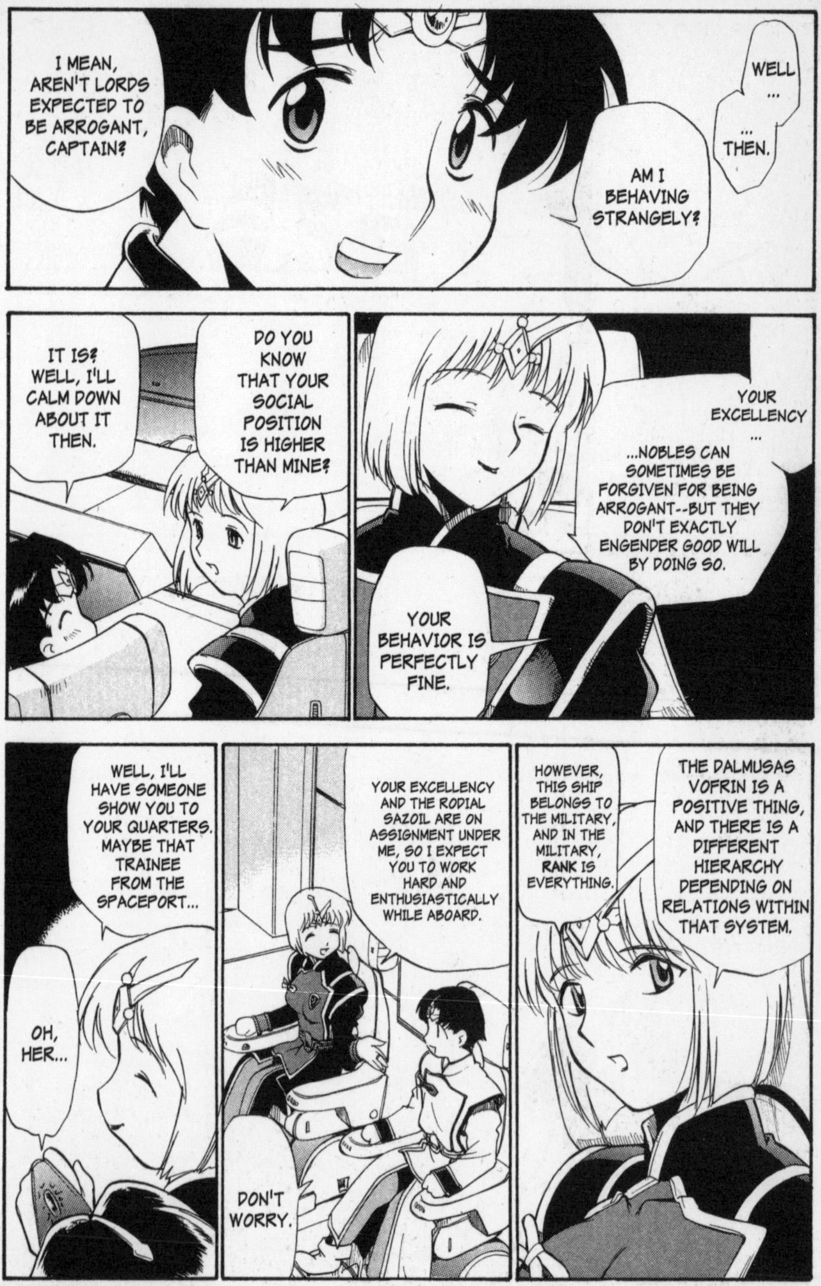
WELL ... ... THEN.
AM I BEHAVING STRANGELY?
I MEAN, AREN'T LORDS EXPECTED TO BE ARROGANT, CAPTAIN?
YOUR EXCELLENCY ...
...NOBLES CAN SOMETIMES BE FORGIVEN FOR BEING ARROGANT--BUT THEY DON'T EXACTLY ENGENDER GOOD WILL BY DOING SO.
YOUR BEHAVIOR IS PERFECTLY FINE.
DO YOU KNOW THAT YOUR SOCIAL POSITION IS HIGHER THAN MINE?
IT IS? WELL, I'LL CALM DOWN ABOUT IT THEN.
THE DALMUSAS VOFRIN IS A POSITIVE THING, AND THERE IS A DIFFERENT HIERARCHY DEPENDING ON RELATIONS WITHIN THAT SYSTEM.
HOWEVER, THIS SHIP BELONGS TO THE MILITARY, AND IN THE MILITARY, RANK IS EVERYTHING.
YOUR EXCELLENCY AND THE RODIAL SAZOIL ARE ON ASSIGNMENT UNDER ME, SO I EXPECT YOU TO WORK HARD AND ENTHUSIASTICALLY WHILE ABOARD.
DON'T WORRY.
WELL, I'LL HAVE SOMEONE SHOW YOU TO YOUR QUARTERS. MAYBE THAT TRAINEE FROM THE SPACEPORT...
OH, HER...

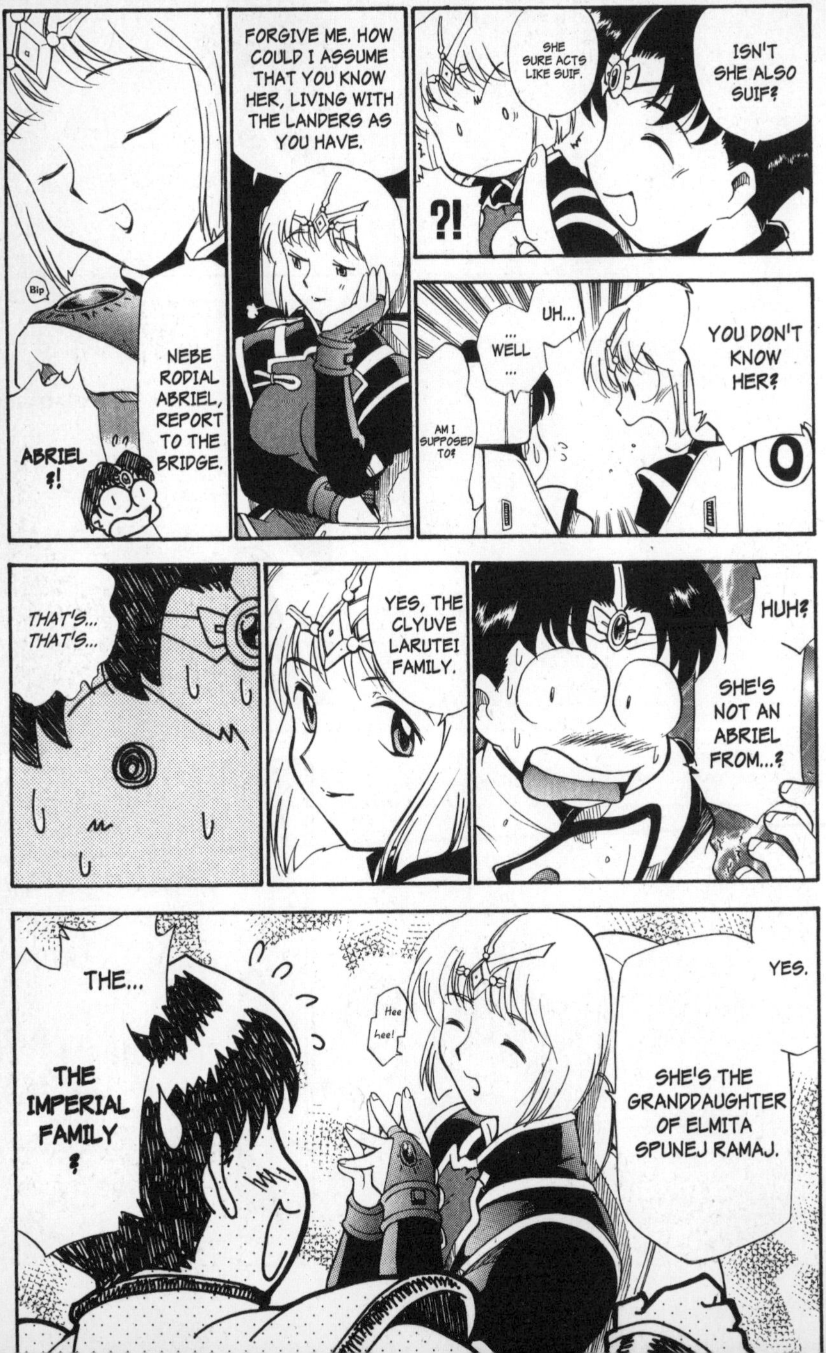
ISN'T SHE ALSO SUIF?
SHE SURE ACTS LIKE SUIF.
?!
YOU DON'T KNOW HER?
UH...
... WELL ...
AM I SUPPOSED TO?
FORGIVE ME. HOW COULD I ASSUME THAT YOU KNOW HER, LIVING WITH THE LANDERS AS YOU HAVE.
NEBE RODIAL ABRIEL, REPORT TO THE BRIDGE.
Bip
ABRIEL ?!
HUH?
SHE'S NOT AN ABRIEL FROM...?
YES, THE CLYUVE LARUTEI FAMILY.
THAT'S... THAT'S...
YES.
SHE'S THE GRANDDAUGHTER OF ELMITA SPUNEJ RAMAJ.
Hee hee!
THE...
THE IMPERIAL FAMILY ?

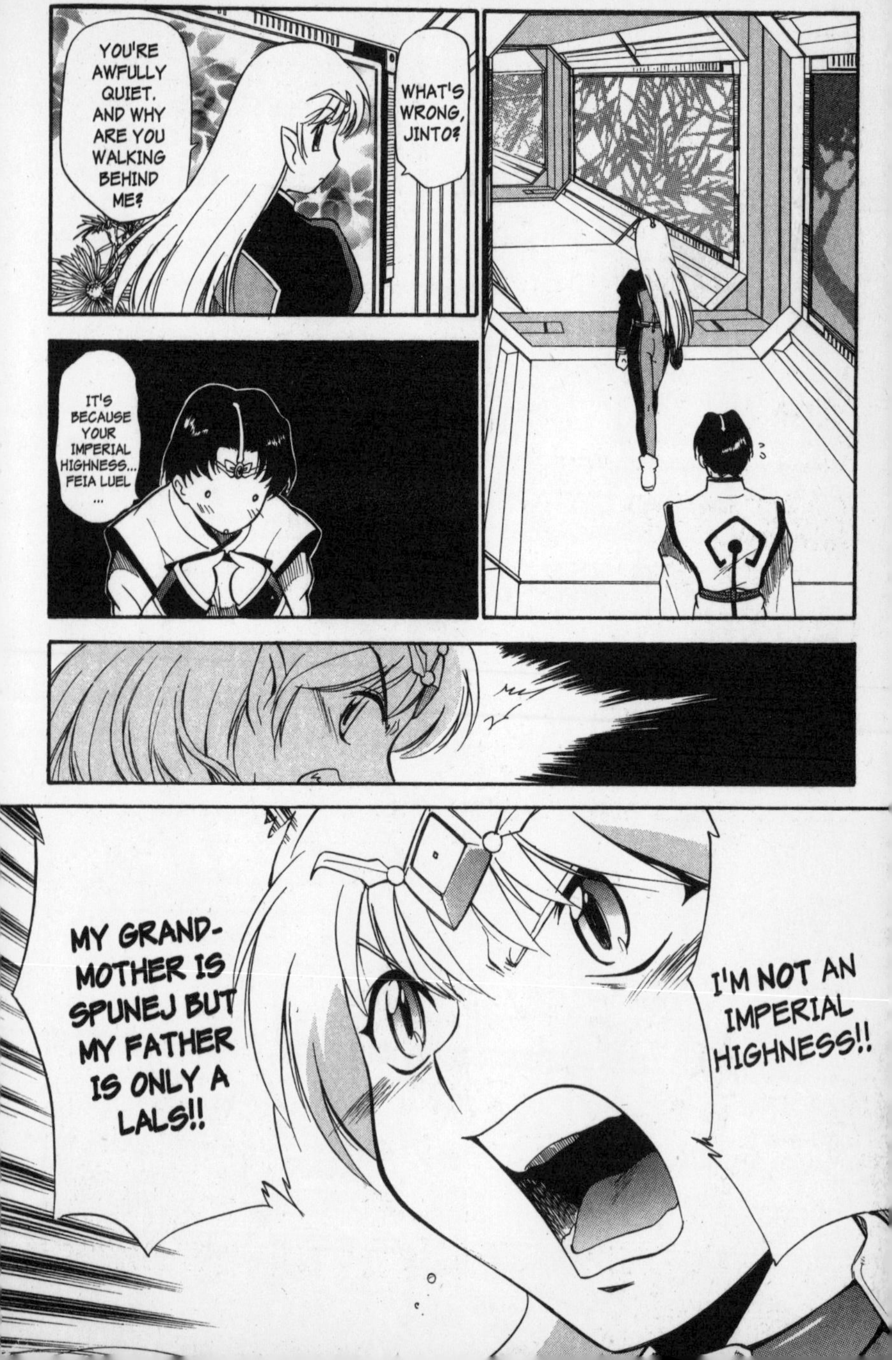

WHAT'S WRONG, JINTO?
YOU'RE AWFULLY QUIET. AND WHY ARE YOU WALKING BEHIND ME?
IT'S BECAUSE YOUR IMPERIAL HIGHNESS... FEIA LUEL ...
I'M NOT AN IMPERIAL HIGHNESS!!
MY GRAND-MOTHER IS SPUNEJ BUT MY FATHER IS ONLY A LALS!!

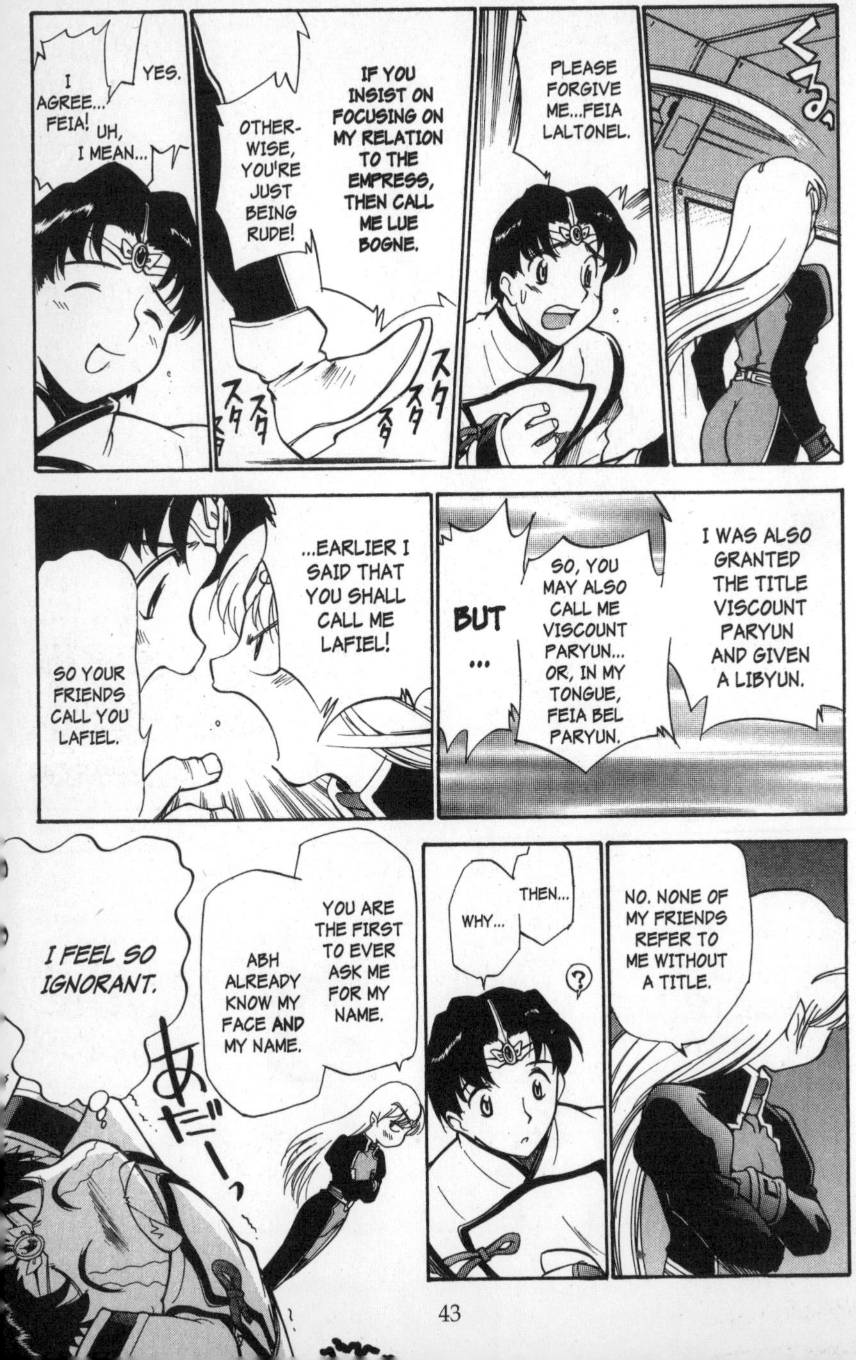
くるっ
PLEASE FORGIVE ME...FEIA LALTONEL.
IF YOU INSIST ON FOCUSING ON MY RELATION TO THE EMPRESS, THEN CALL ME LUE BOGNE.
OTHER-WISE, YOU'RE JUST BEING RUDE!
スタスタ
YES.
I AGREE... FEIA!
UH, I MEAN...
I WAS ALSO GRANTED THE TITLE VISCOUNT PARYUN AND GIVEN A LIBYUN.
SO, YOU MAY ALSO CALL ME VISCOUNT PARYUN... OR, IN MY TONGUE, FEIA BEL PARYUN.
BUT ...
...EARLIER I SAID THAT YOU SHALL CALL ME LAFIEL!
SO YOUR FRIENDS CALL YOU LAFIEL.
NO. NONE OF MY FRIENDS REFER TO ME WITHOUT A TITLE.
THEN...
WHY...
?
YOU ARE THE FIRST TO EVER ASK ME FOR MY NAME.
ABH ALREADY KNOW MY FACE AND MY NAME.
I FEEL SO IGNORANT.
あだーっ

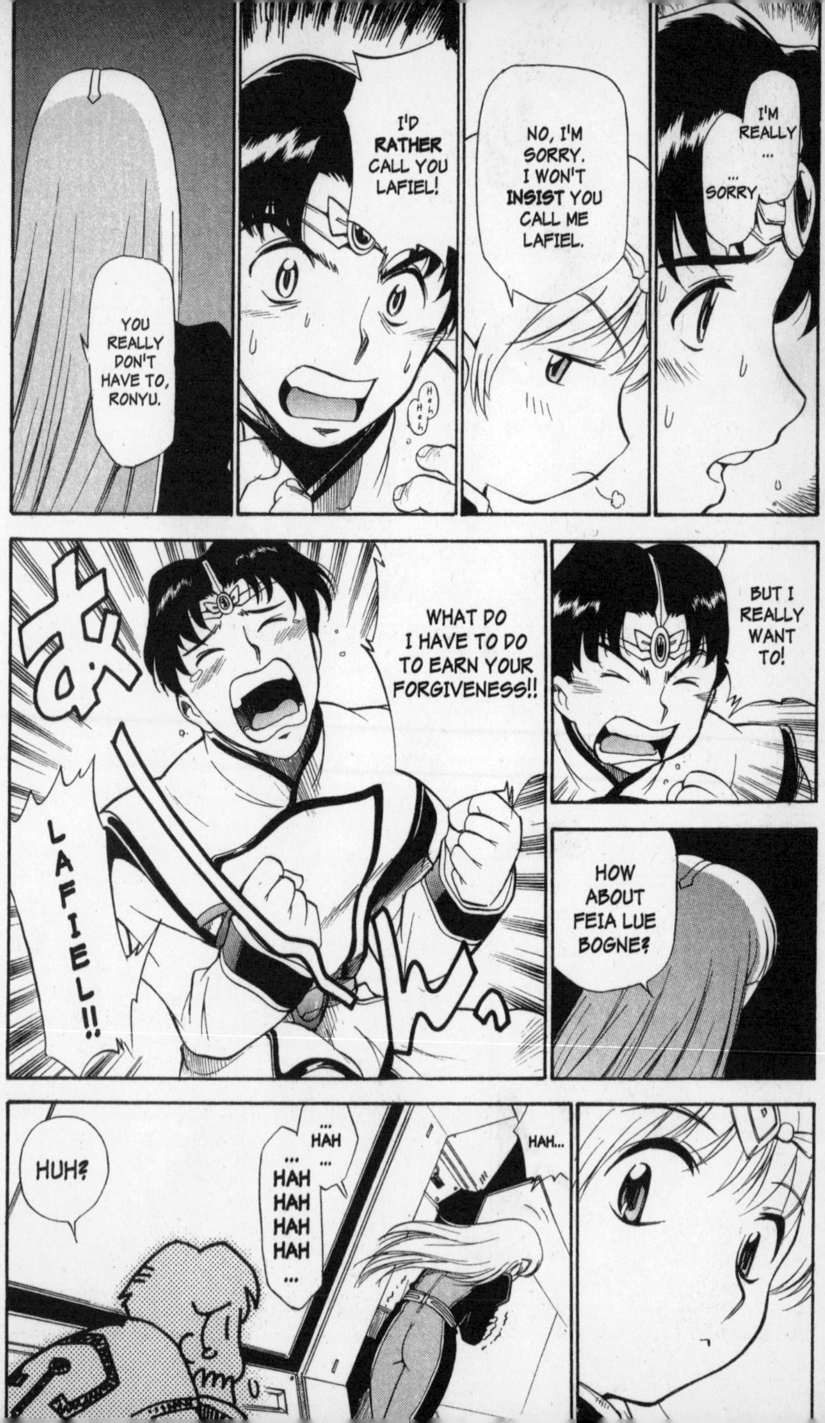
I'M REALLY ... ... SORRY
NO, I'M SORRY. I WON'T INSIST YOU CALL ME LAFIEL.
I'D RATHER CALL YOU LAFIEL!
Heh Heh
YOU REALLY DON'T HAVE TO, RONYU.
BUT I REALLY WANT TO!
HOW ABOUT FEIA LUE BOGNE?
WHAT DO I HAVE TO DO TO EARN YOUR FORGIVENESS!!
LAFIEL!!
HAH...
... HAH ... ... HAH HAH HAH HAH ...
HUH?

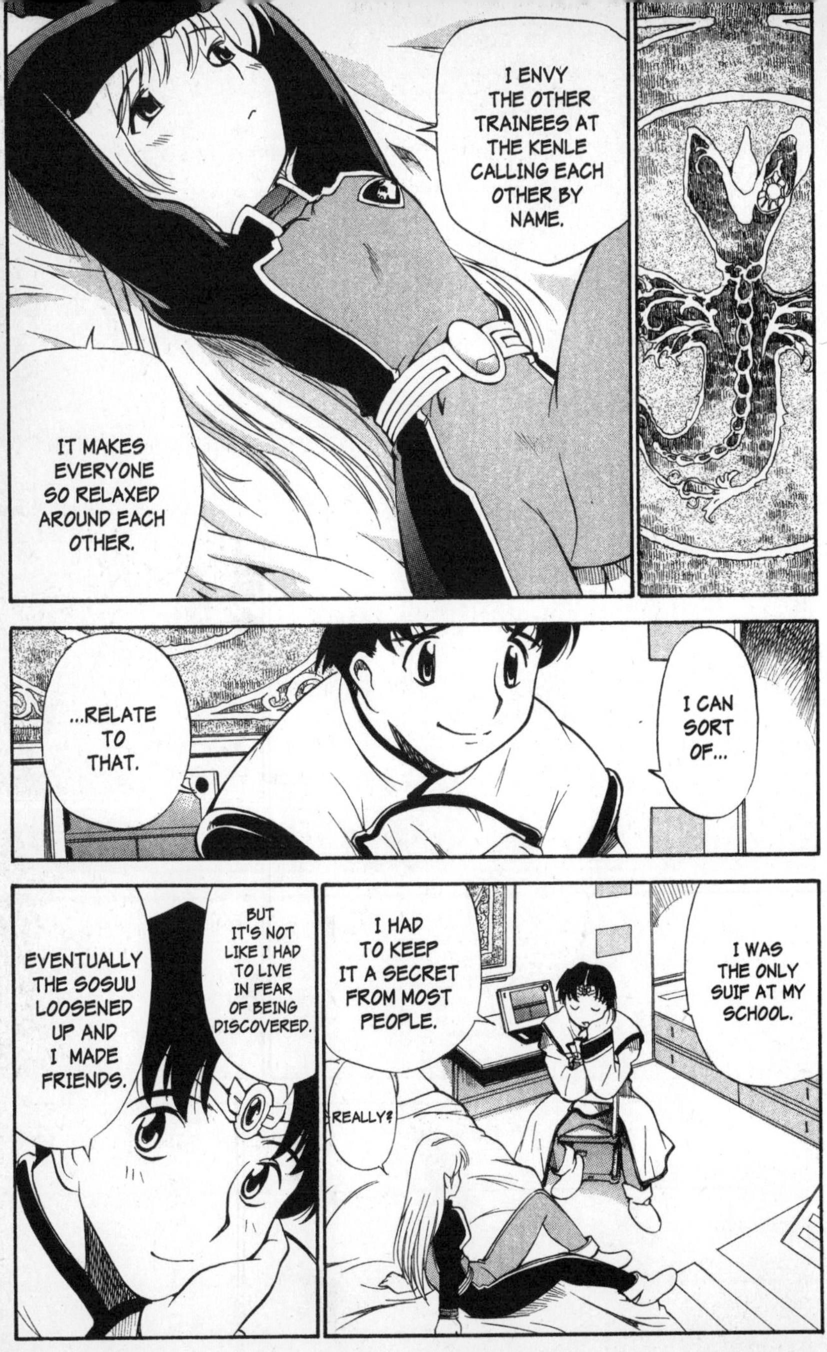
I ENVY THE OTHER TRAINEES AT THE KENLE CALLING EACH OTHER BY NAME.
IT MAKES EVERYONE SO RELAXED AROUND EACH OTHER.
I CAN SORT OF...
...RELATE TO THAT.
I WAS THE ONLY SUIF AT MY SCHOOL.
I HAD TO KEEP IT A SECRET FROM MOST PEOPLE.
REALLY?
BUT IT'S NOT LIKE I HAD TO LIVE IN FEAR OF BEING DISCOVERED.
EVENTUALLY THE SOSUU LOOSENED UP AND I MADE FRIENDS.

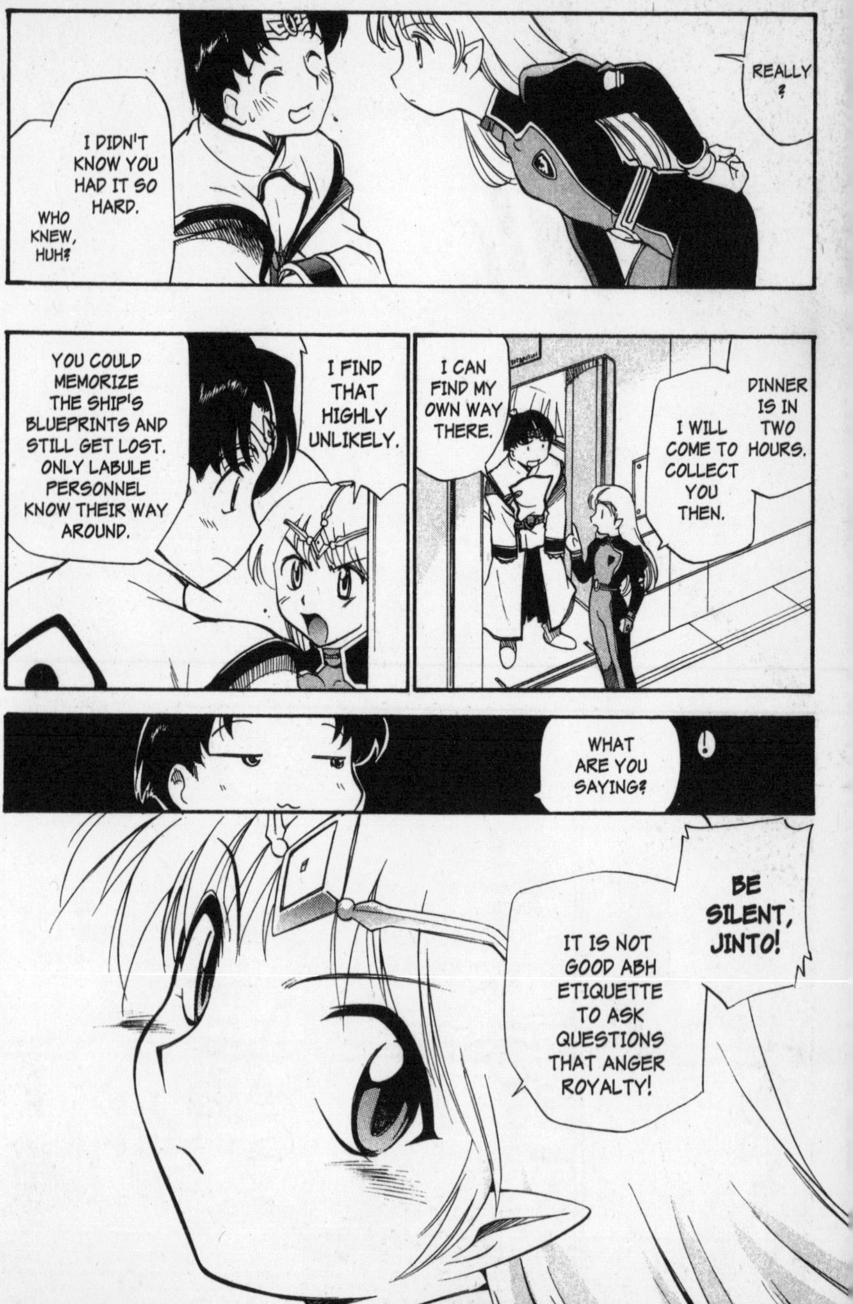
REALLY?
I DIDN'T KNOW YOU HAD IT SO HARD.
WHO KNEW, HUH?
DINNER IS IN TWO HOURS.
I WILL COME TO COLLECT YOU THEN.
I CAN FIND MY OWN WAY THERE.
I FIND THAT HIGHLY UNLIKELY.
YOU COULD MEMORIZE THE SHIP'S BLUEPRINTS AND STILL GET LOST. ONLY LABULE PERSONNEL KNOW THEIR WAY AROUND.
!
WHAT ARE YOU SAYING?
BE SILENT, JINTO!
IT IS NOT GOOD ABH ETIQUETTE TO ASK QUESTIONS THAT ANGER ROYALTY!

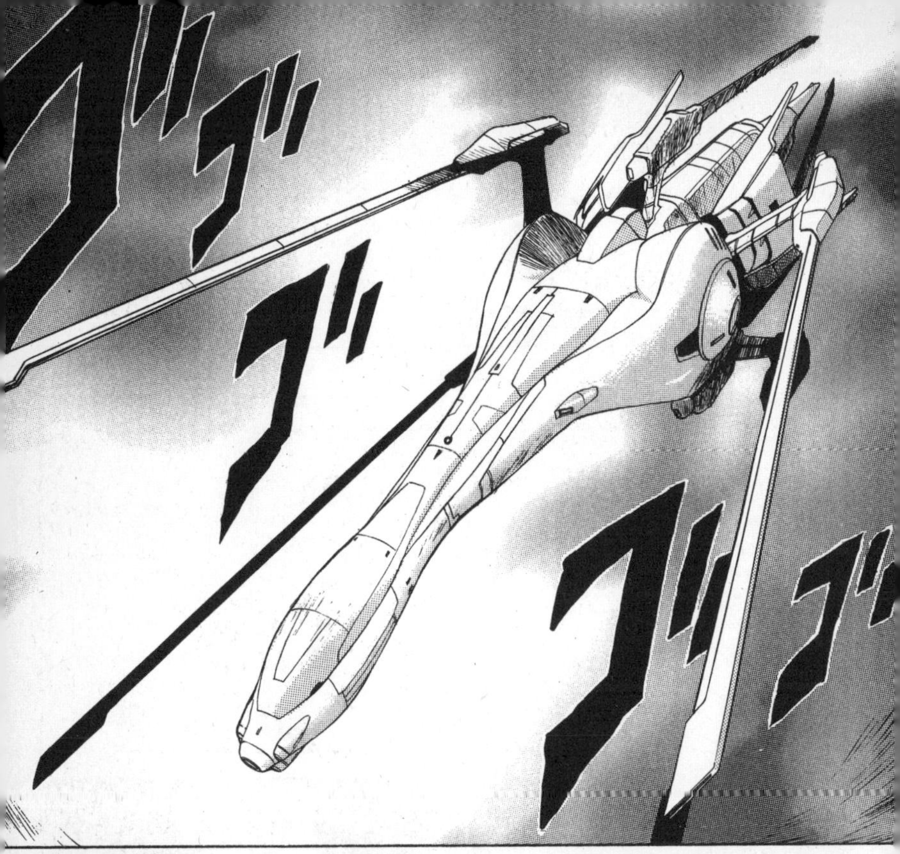

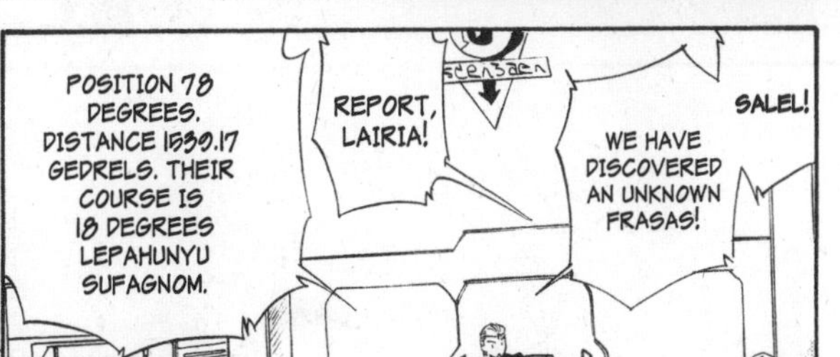
SALEL!
WE HAVE DISCOVERED AN UNKNOWN FRASAS!
REPORT, LAIRIA!
POSITION 78 DEGREES. DISTANCE 1539.17 GEDRELS. THEIR COURSE IS 18 DEGREES LEPAHUNYU SUFAGNOM.

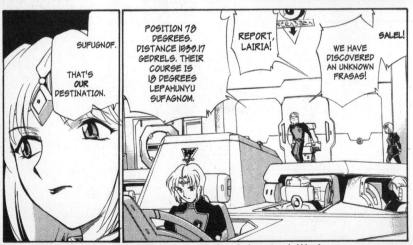

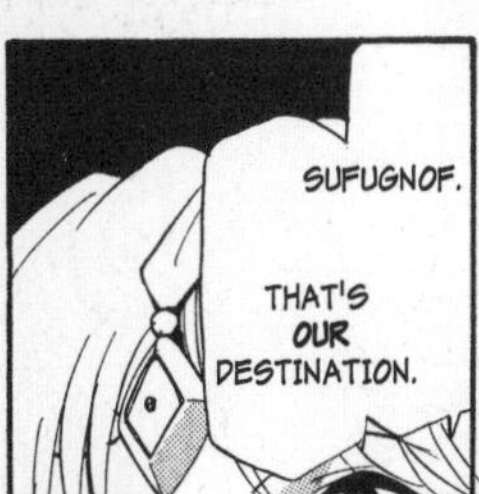
SUFUGNOF.
THAT'S **OUR** DESTINATION.

When a warship travels through Plane Space, its surroundings burst forth creating a bubble of power. In general, the space-time continuum only maintains all four dimensions inside these clusters. From the Hayakawa Library, *Crest of the Stars Handbook*.

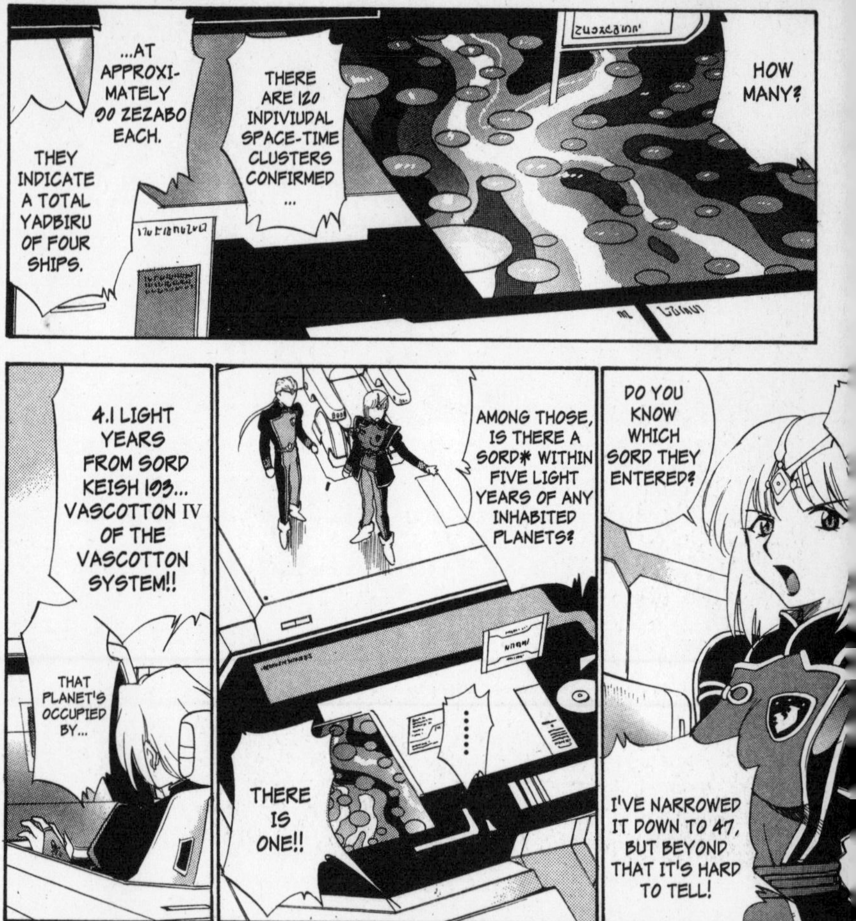
HOW MANY?
THERE ARE 120 INDIVIUDAL SPACE-TIME CLUSTERS CONFIRMED ...
THEY INDICATE A TOTAL YADBIRU OF FOUR SHIPS.
...AT APPROXIMATELY 90 ZEZABO EACH.
DO YOU KNOW WHICH SORD THEY ENTERED?
I'VE NARROWED IT DOWN TO 47, BUT BEYOND THAT IT'S HARD TO TELL!
AMONG THOSE, IS THERE A SORD* WITHIN FIVE LIGHT YEARS OF ANY INHABITED PLANETS?
......
THERE IS ONE!!
4.1 LIGHT YEARS FROM SORD KEISH 193... VASCOTTON IV OF THE VASCOTTON SYSTEM!!
THAT PLANET'S OCCUPIED BY...

*Sord - a passage that connects normal space and plane space.

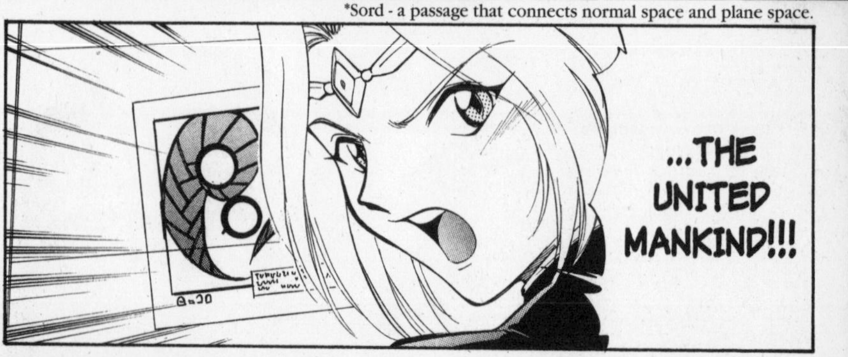
...THE UNITED MANKIND!!!

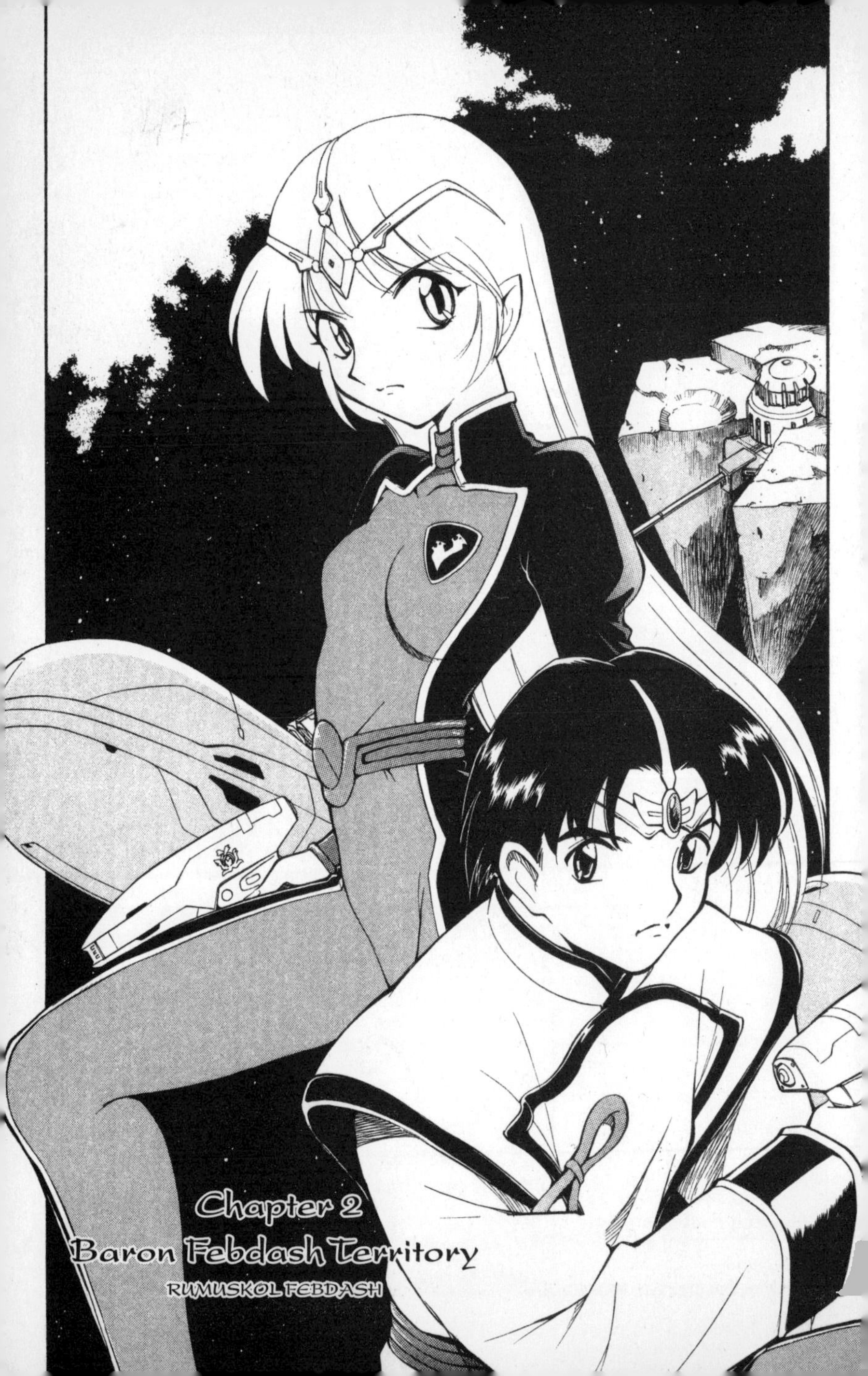
Chapter 2
Baron Febdash Territory
RUMUSKOL FEBDASH

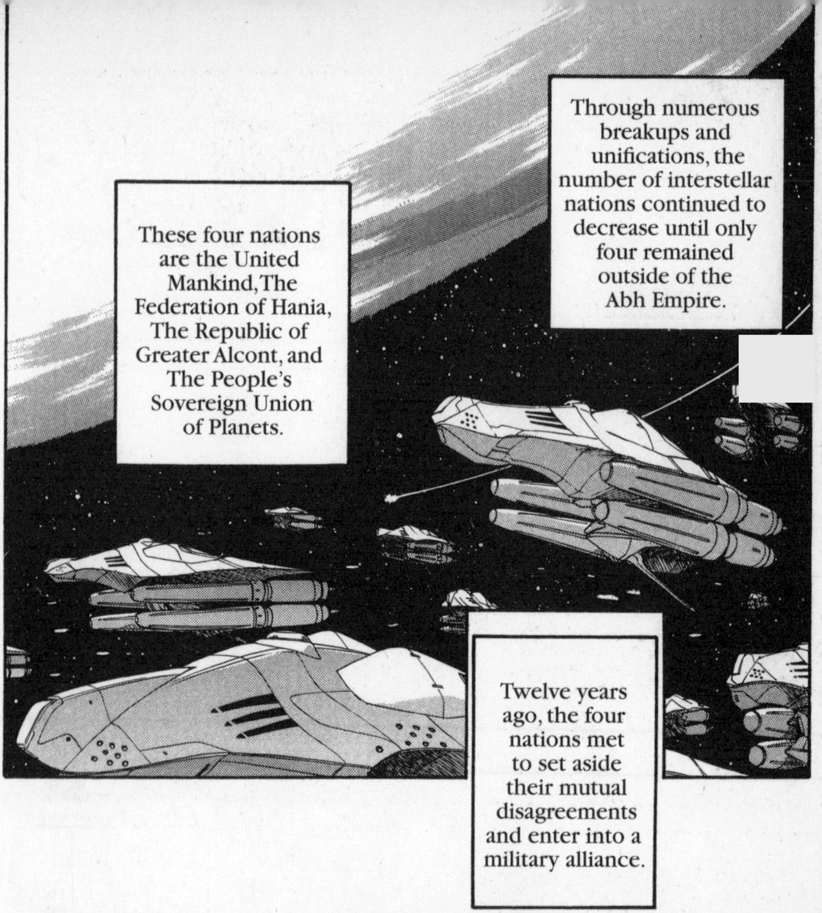
Through numerous breakups and unifications, the number of interstellar nations continued to decrease until only four remained outside of the Abh Empire.
These four nations are the United Mankind, The Federation of Hania, The Republic of Greater Alcont, and The People's Sovereign Union of Planets.
Twelve years ago, the four nations met to set aside their mutual disagreements and enter into a military alliance.

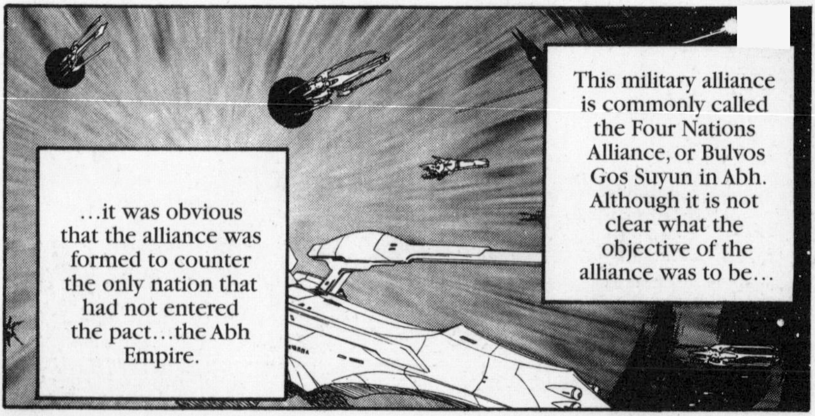
This military alliance is commonly called the Four Nations Alliance, or Bulvos Gos Suyun in Abh. Although it is not clear what the objective of the alliance was to be...
...it was obvious that the alliance was formed to counter the only nation that had not entered the pact...the Abh Empire.

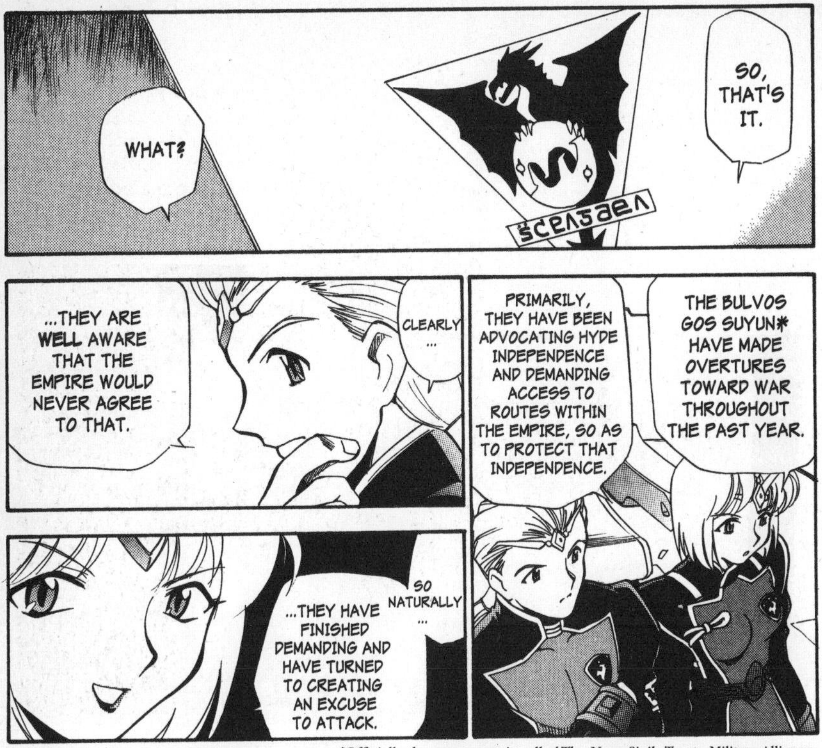
SO, THAT'S IT.
WHAT?
THE BULVOS GOS SUYUN* HAVE MADE OVERTURES TOWARD WAR THROUGHOUT THE PAST YEAR.
PRIMARILY, THEY HAVE BEEN ADVOCATING HYDE INDEPENDENCE AND DEMANDING ACCESS TO ROUTES WITHIN THE EMPIRE, SO AS TO PROTECT THAT INDEPENDENCE.
CLEARLY ...
...THEY ARE WELL AWARE THAT THE EMPIRE WOULD NEVER AGREE TO THAT.
SO NATURALLY ...
...THEY HAVE FINISHED DEMANDING AND HAVE TURNED TO CREATING AN EXCUSE TO ATTACK.

*Officially the agreement is called The Nova Sicily Treaty Military Alliance.

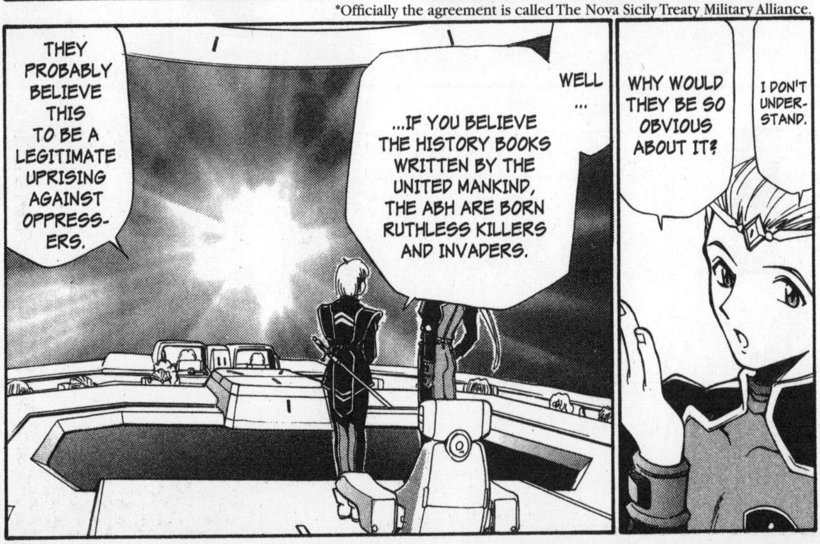
I DON'T UNDER-STAND.
WHY WOULD THEY BE SO OBVIOUS ABOUT IT?
WELL ...
...IF YOU BELIEVE THE HISTORY BOOKS WRITTEN BY THE UNITED MANKIND, THE ABH ARE BORN RUTHLESS KILLERS AND INVADERS.
THEY PROBABLY BELIEVE THIS TO BE A LEGITIMATE UPRISING AGAINST OPPRESS-ERS.

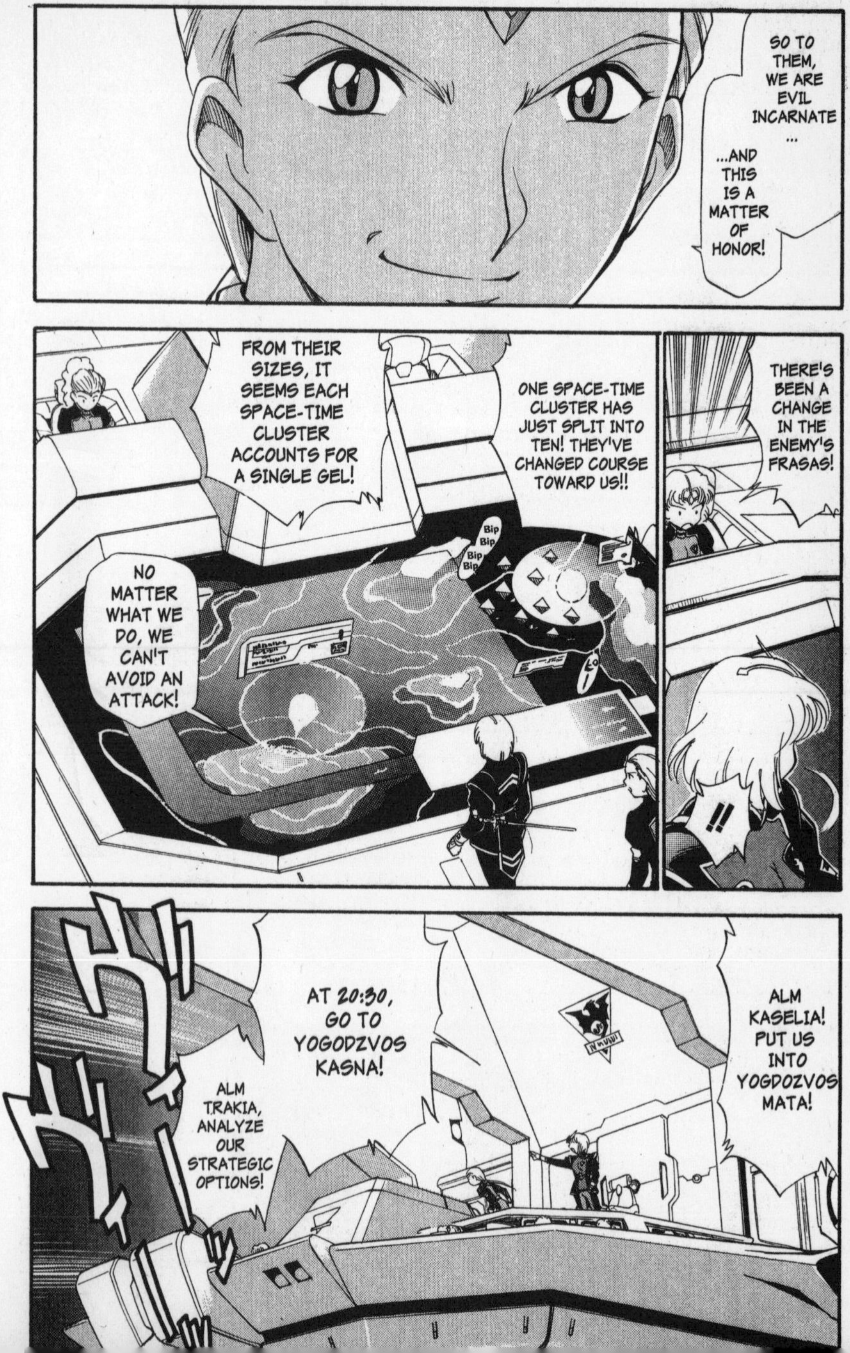
SO TO THEM, WE ARE EVIL INCARNATE ...
...AND THIS IS A MATTER OF HONOR!
THERE'S BEEN A CHANGE IN THE ENEMY'S FRASAS!
!!
ONE SPACE-TIME CLUSTER HAS JUST SPLIT INTO TEN! THEY'VE CHANGED COURSE TOWARD US!!
FROM THEIR SIZES, IT SEEMS EACH SPACE-TIME CLUSTER ACCOUNTS FOR A SINGLE GEL!
Bip Bip Bip Bip
NO MATTER WHAT WE DO, WE CAN'T AVOID AN ATTACK!
ALM KASELIA! PUT US INTO YOGDOZVOS MATA!
AT 20:30, GO TO YOGODZVOS KASNA!
ALM TRAKIA, ANALYZE OUR STRATEGIC OPTIONS!

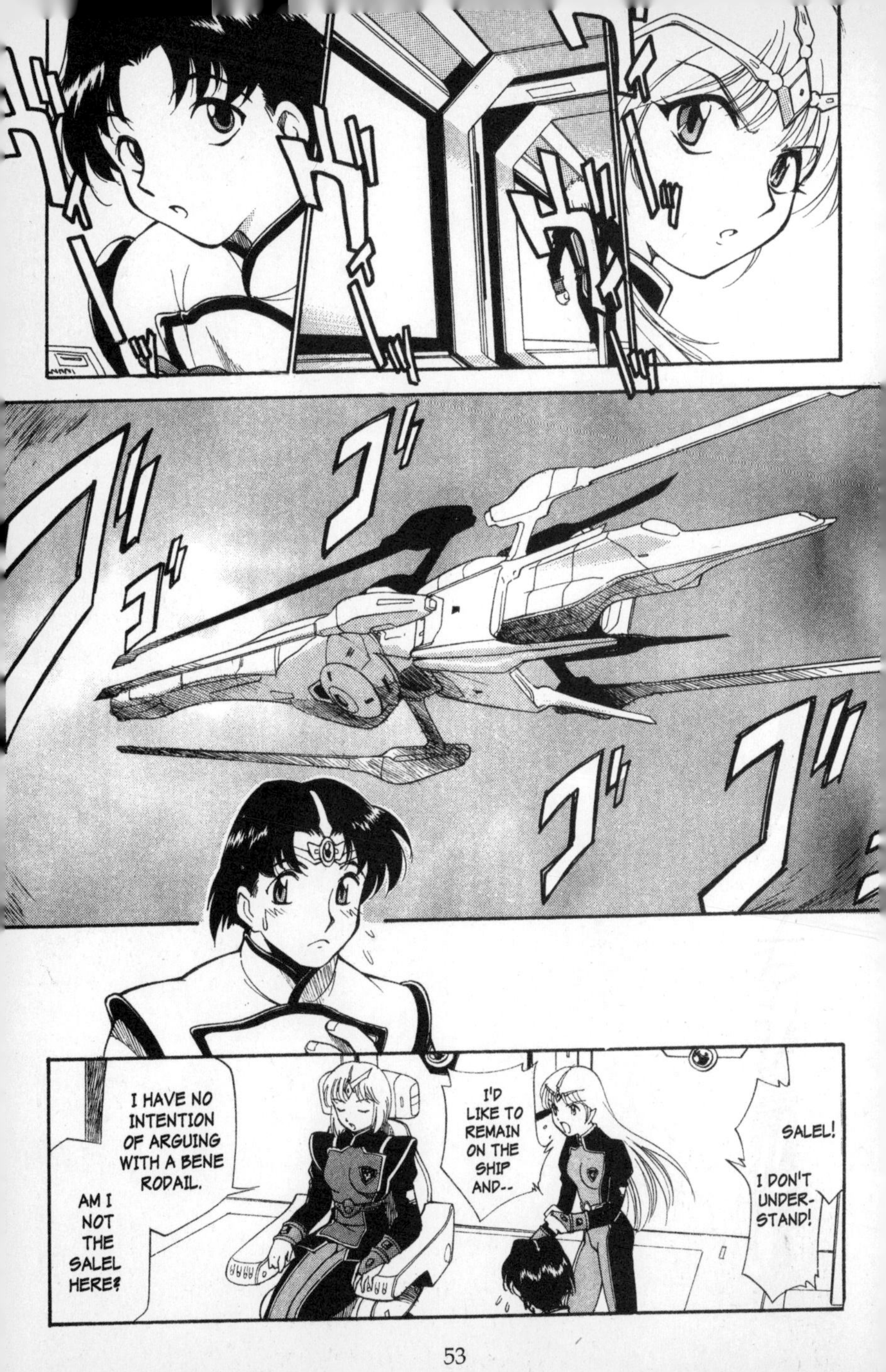
SALEL!
I DON'T UNDER-STAND!
I'D LIKE TO REMAIN ON THE SHIP AND--
I HAVE NO INTENTION OF ARGUING WITH A BENE RODAIL.
AM I NOT THE SALEL HERE?

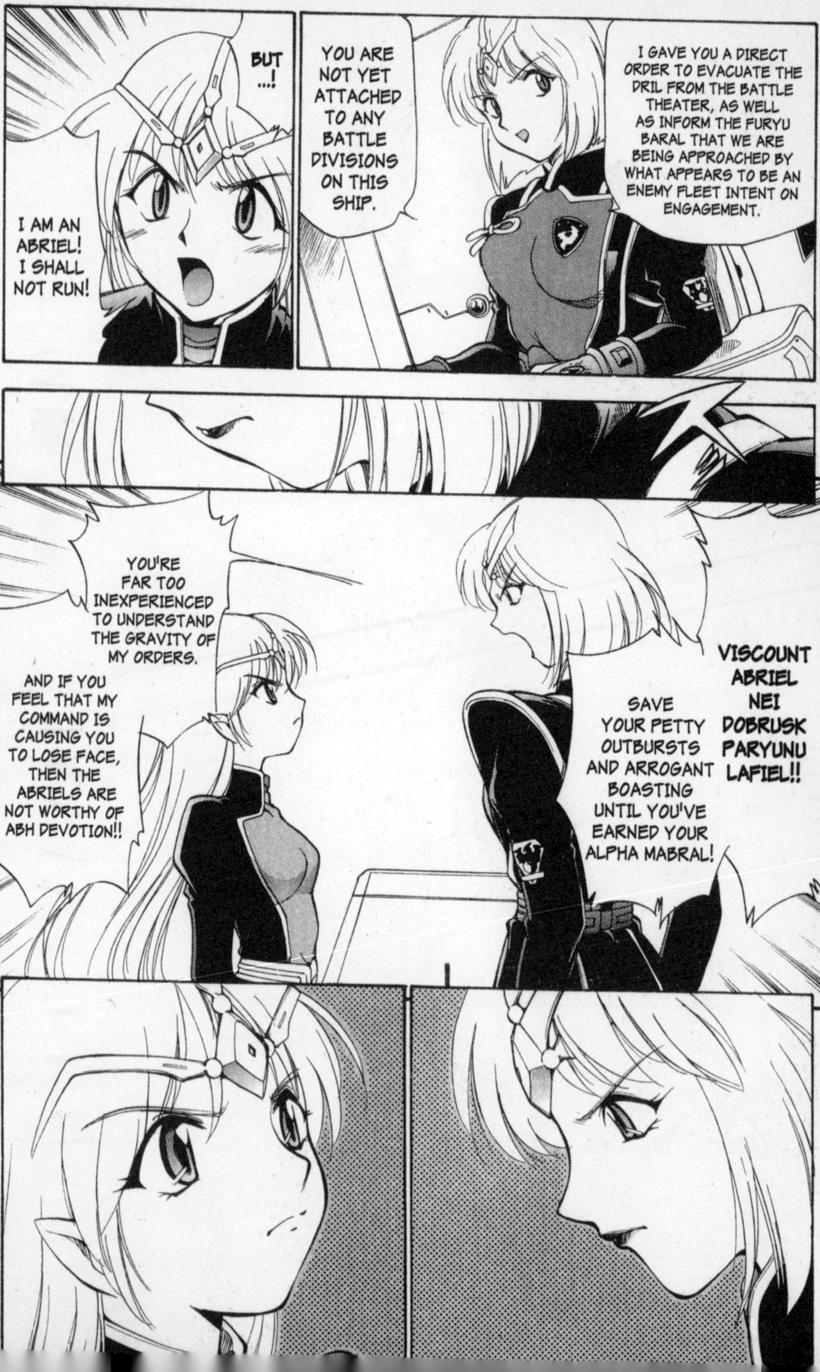
I GAVE YOU A DIRECT ORDER TO EVACUATE THE DRIL FROM THE BATTLE THEATER, AS WELL AS INFORM THE FURYU BARAL THAT WE ARE BEING APPROACHED BY WHAT APPEARS TO BE AN ENEMY FLEET INTENT ON ENGAGEMENT.
YOU ARE NOT YET ATTACHED TO ANY BATTLE DIVISIONS ON THIS SHIP.
BUT ...!
I AM AN ABRIEL! I SHALL NOT RUN!
VISCOUNT ABRIEL NEI DOBRUSK PARYUNU LAFIEL!!
SAVE YOUR PETTY OUTBURSTS AND ARROGANT BOASTING UNTIL YOU'VE EARNED YOUR ALPHA MABRAL!
YOU'RE FAR TOO INEXPERIENCED TO UNDERSTAND THE GRAVITY OF MY ORDERS.
AND IF YOU FEEL THAT MY COMMAND IS CAUSING YOU TO LOSE FACE, THEN THE ABRIELS ARE NOT WORTHY OF ABH DEVOTION!!

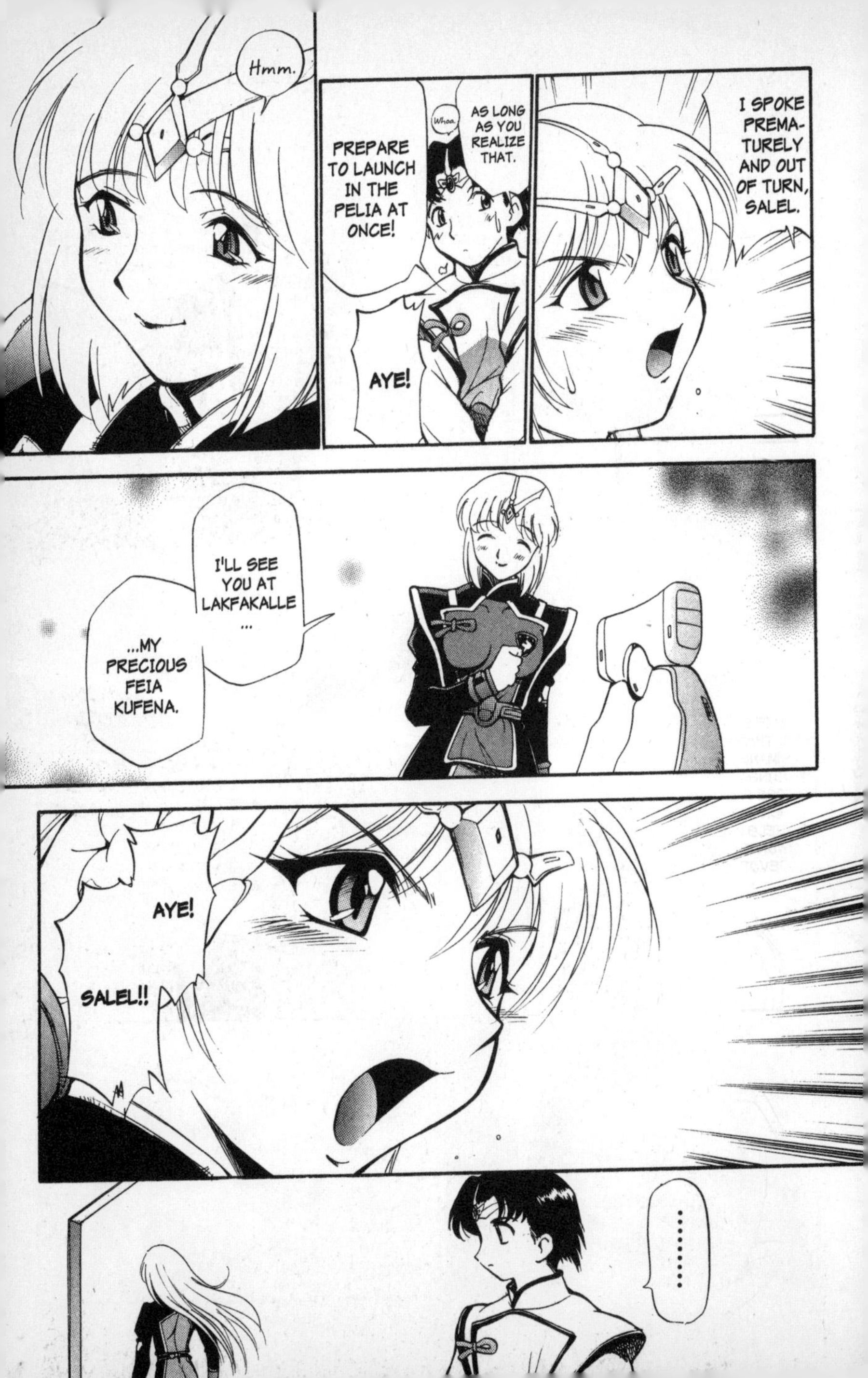
I SPOKE PREMATURELY AND OUT OF TURN, SALEL.
AS LONG AS YOU REALIZE THAT.
Whoa
PREPARE TO LAUNCH IN THE PELIA AT ONCE!
AYE!
Hmm.
I'LL SEE YOU AT LAKFAKALLE ...
...MY PRECIOUS FEIA KUFENA.
AYE!
SALEL!!
......

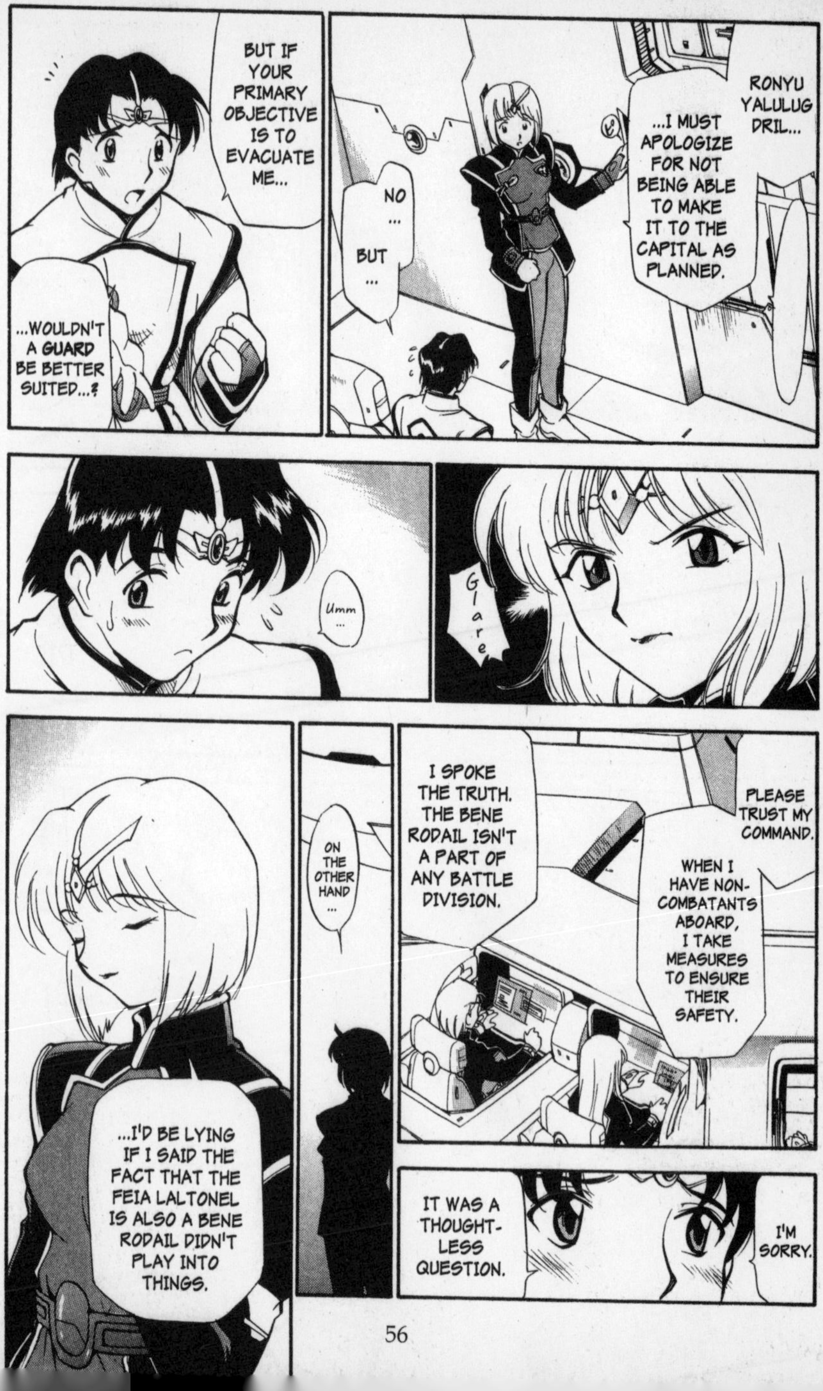
RONYU YALULUG DRIL...
...I MUST APOLOGIZE FOR NOT BEING ABLE TO MAKE IT TO THE CAPITAL AS PLANNED.
NO ... BUT ...
BUT IF YOUR PRIMARY OBJECTIVE IS TO EVACUATE ME...
...WOULDN'T A GUARD BE BETTER SUITED...?
Glare
Umm ...
PLEASE TRUST MY COMMAND.
I SPOKE THE TRUTH. THE BENE RODAIL ISN'T A PART OF ANY BATTLE DIVISION.
WHEN I HAVE NON-COMBATANTS ABOARD, I TAKE MEASURES TO ENSURE THEIR SAFETY.
I'M SORRY.
IT WAS A THOUGHT-LESS QUESTION.
ON THE OTHER HAND ...
...I'D BE LYING IF I SAID THE FACT THAT THE FEIA LALTONEL IS ALSO A BENE RODAIL DIDN'T PLAY INTO THINGS.

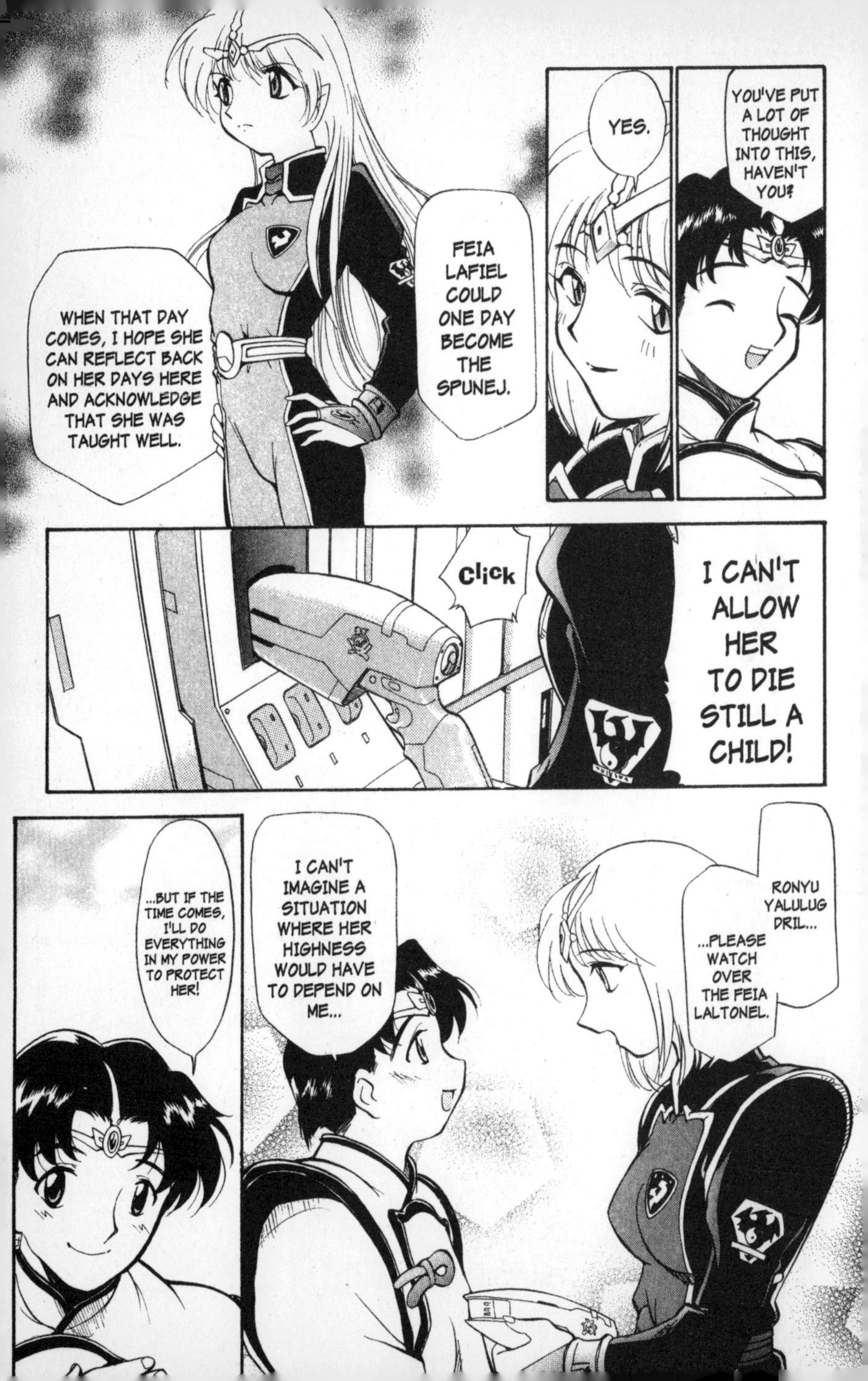
YOU'VE PUT A LOT OF THOUGHT INTO THIS, HAVEN'T YOU?
YES.
FEIA LAFIEL COULD ONE DAY BECOME THE SPUNEJ.
WHEN THAT DAY COMES, I HOPE SHE CAN REFLECT BACK ON HER DAYS HERE AND ACKNOWLEDGE THAT SHE WAS TAUGHT WELL.
I CAN'T ALLOW HER TO DIE STILL A CHILD!
Click
RONYU YALULUG DRIL...
...PLEASE WATCH OVER THE FEIA LALTONEL.
I CAN'T IMAGINE A SITUATION WHERE HER HIGHNESS WOULD HAVE TO DEPEND ON ME...
...BUT IF THE TIME COMES, I'LL DO EVERYTHING IN MY POWER TO PROTECT HER!

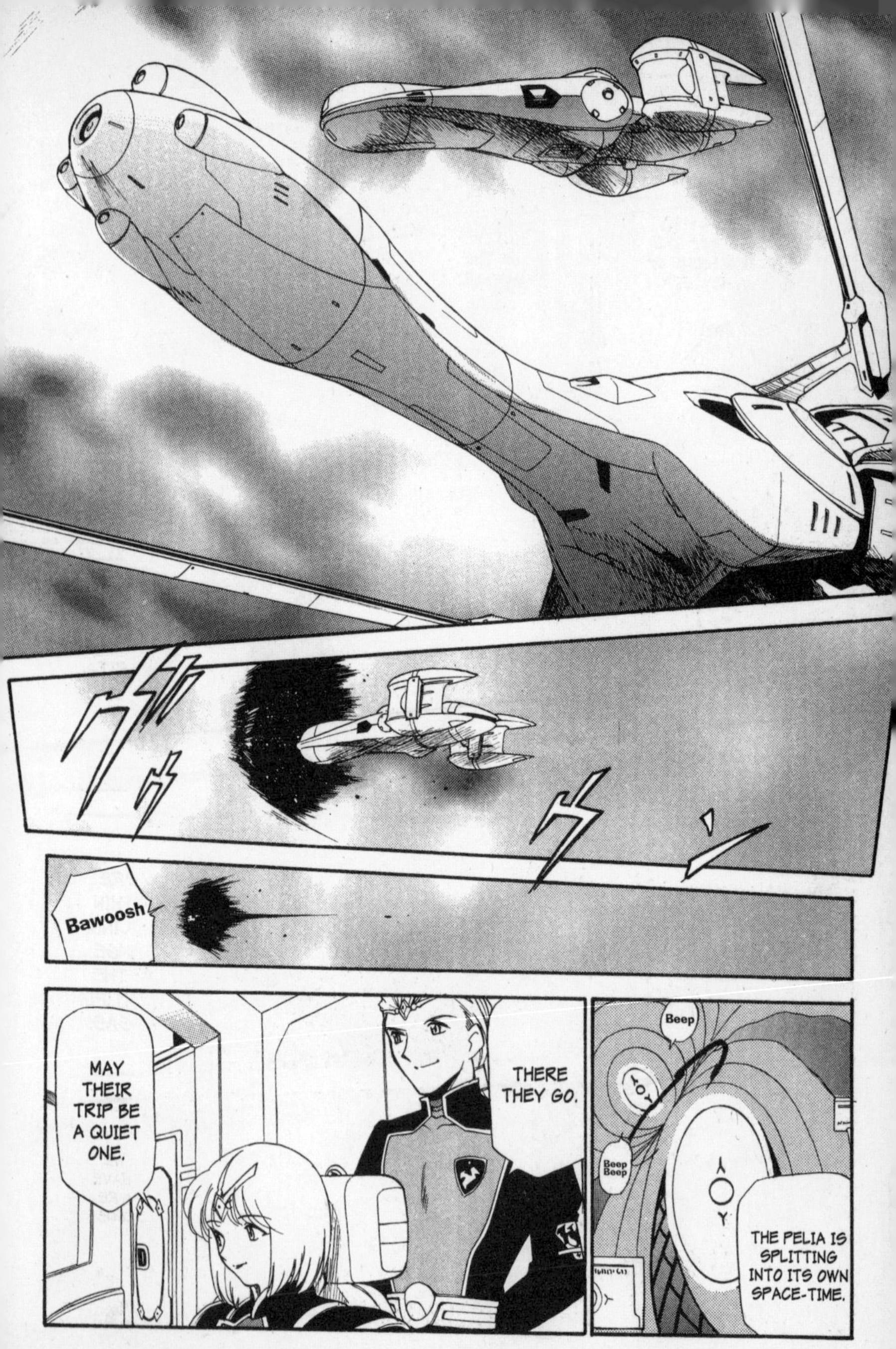
Bawoosh
Beep
Beep Beep
THE PELIA IS SPLITTING INTO ITS OWN SPACE-TIME.
THERE THEY GO.
MAY THEIR TRIP BE A QUIET ONE.

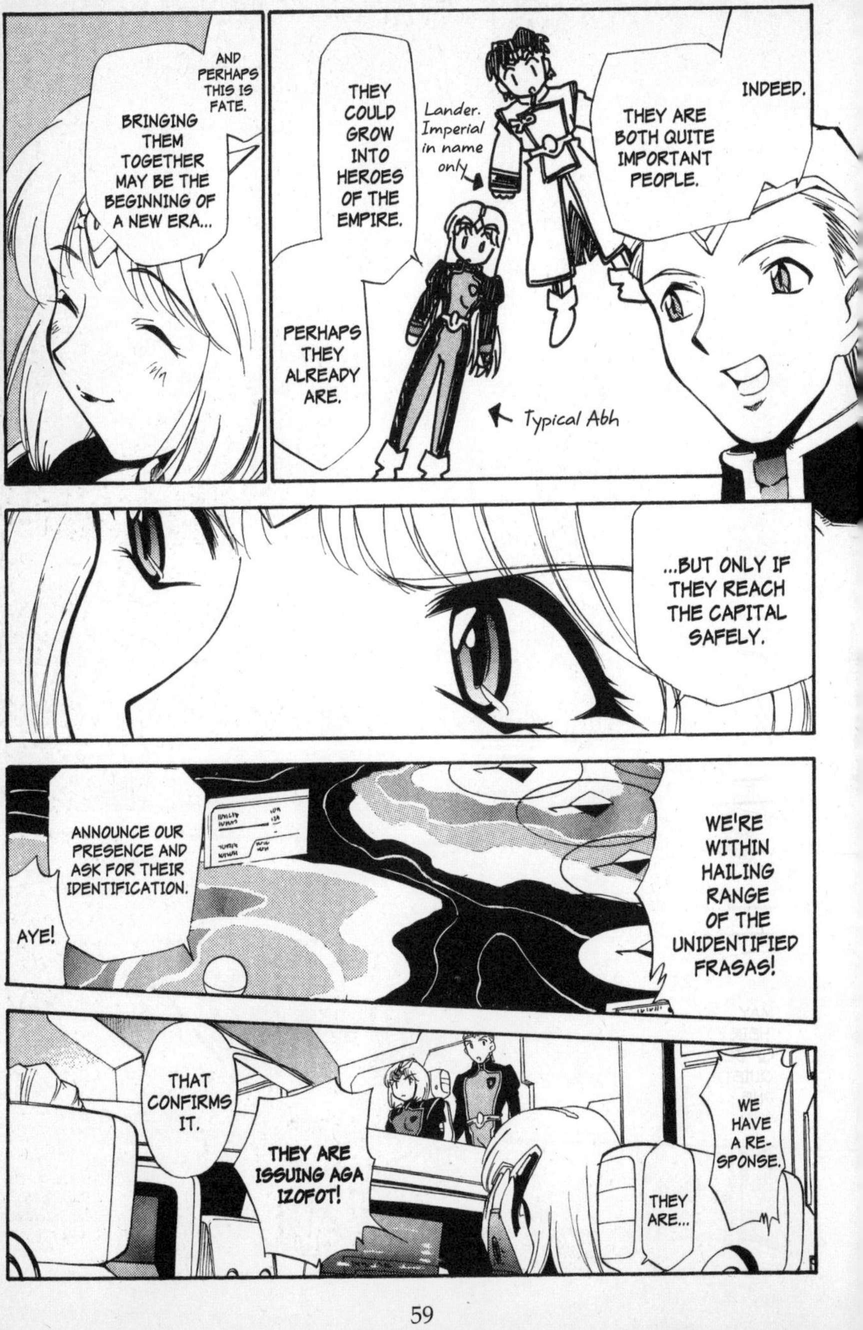
INDEED.
THEY ARE BOTH QUITE IMPORTANT PEOPLE.
Lander. Imperial in name only
THEY COULD GROW INTO HEROES OF THE EMPIRE.
Typical Abh
PERHAPS THEY ALREADY ARE.
AND PERHAPS THIS IS FATE.
BRINGING THEM TOGETHER MAY BE THE BEGINNING OF A NEW ERA...
...BUT ONLY IF THEY REACH THE CAPITAL SAFELY.
WE'RE WITHIN HAILING RANGE OF THE UNIDENTIFIED FRASAS!
ANNOUNCE OUR PRESENCE AND ASK FOR THEIR IDENTIFICATION.
AYE!
WE HAVE A RE-SPONSE.
THEY ARE...
THEY ARE ISSUING AGA IZOFOT!
THAT CONFIRMS IT.

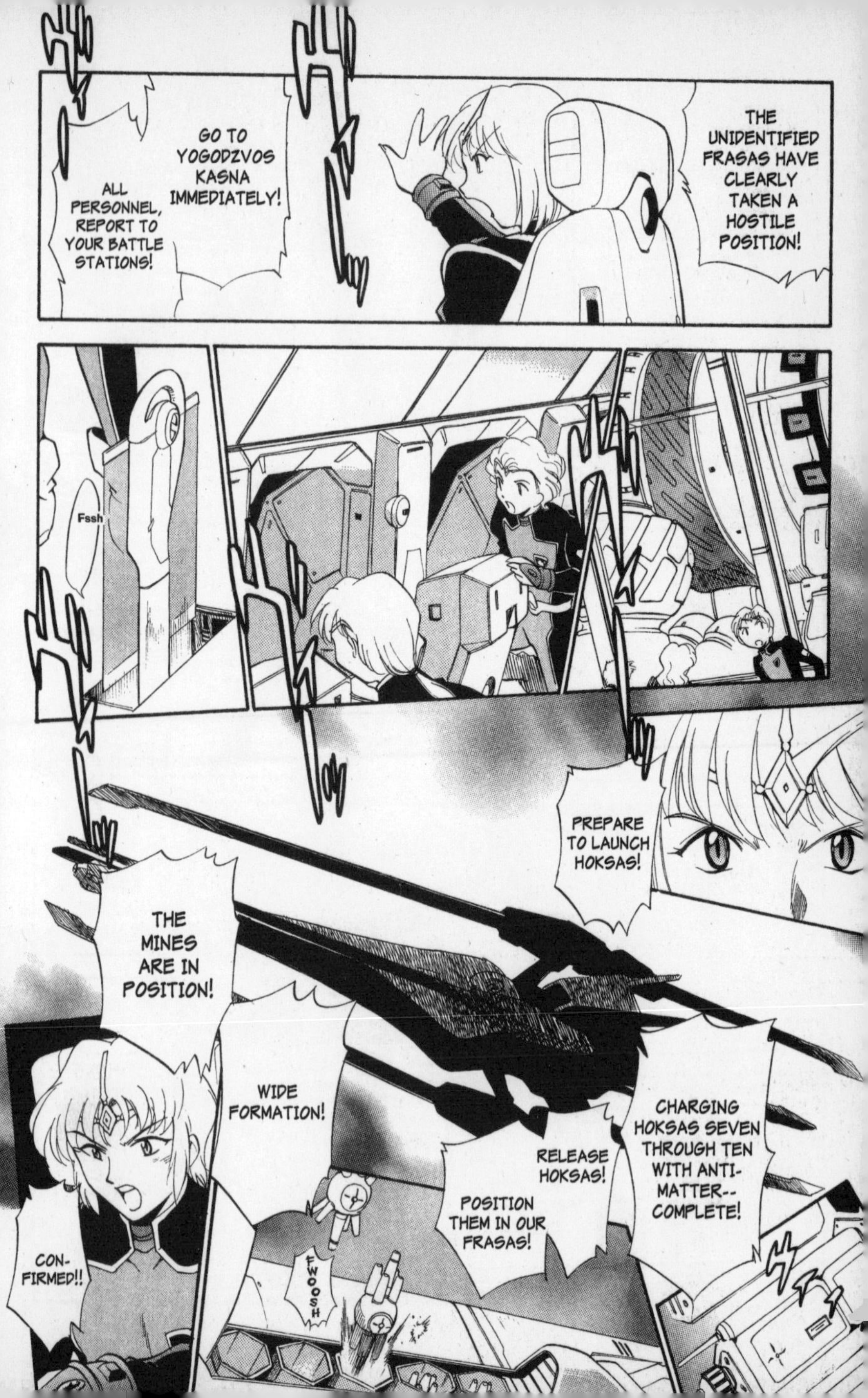
THE UNIDENTIFIED FRASAS HAVE CLEARLY TAKEN A HOSTILE POSITION!
GO TO YOGODZVOS KASNA IMMEDIATELY!
ALL PERSONNEL, REPORT TO YOUR BATTLE STATIONS!
Fssh
PREPARE TO LAUNCH HOKSAS!
THE MINES ARE IN POSITION!
CHARGING HOKSAS SEVEN THROUGH TEN WITH ANTI-MATTER--COMPLETE!
RELEASE HOKSAS!
POSITION THEM IN OUR FRASAS!
WIDE FORMATION!
FWOOSH
CON-FIRMED!!

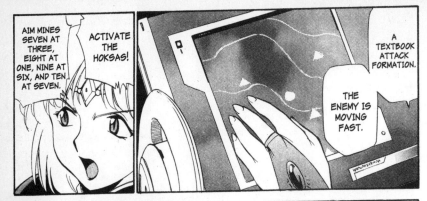

A TEXTBOOK ATTACK FORMATION.
THE ENEMY IS MOVING FAST.
ACTIVATE THE HOKSAS!
AIM MINES SEVEN AT THREE, EIGHT AT ONE, NINE AT SIX, AND TEN AT SEVEN.
MY PRECIOUS CREW!
IT BEGINS!
SABO LUGA!
HOKSAS!
Whoosh
Fssh

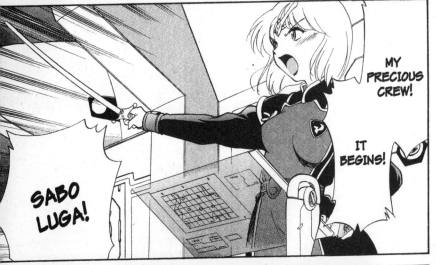

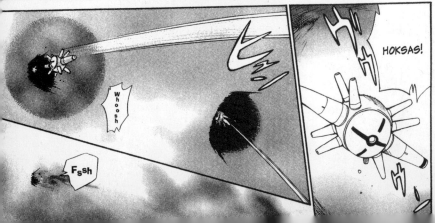

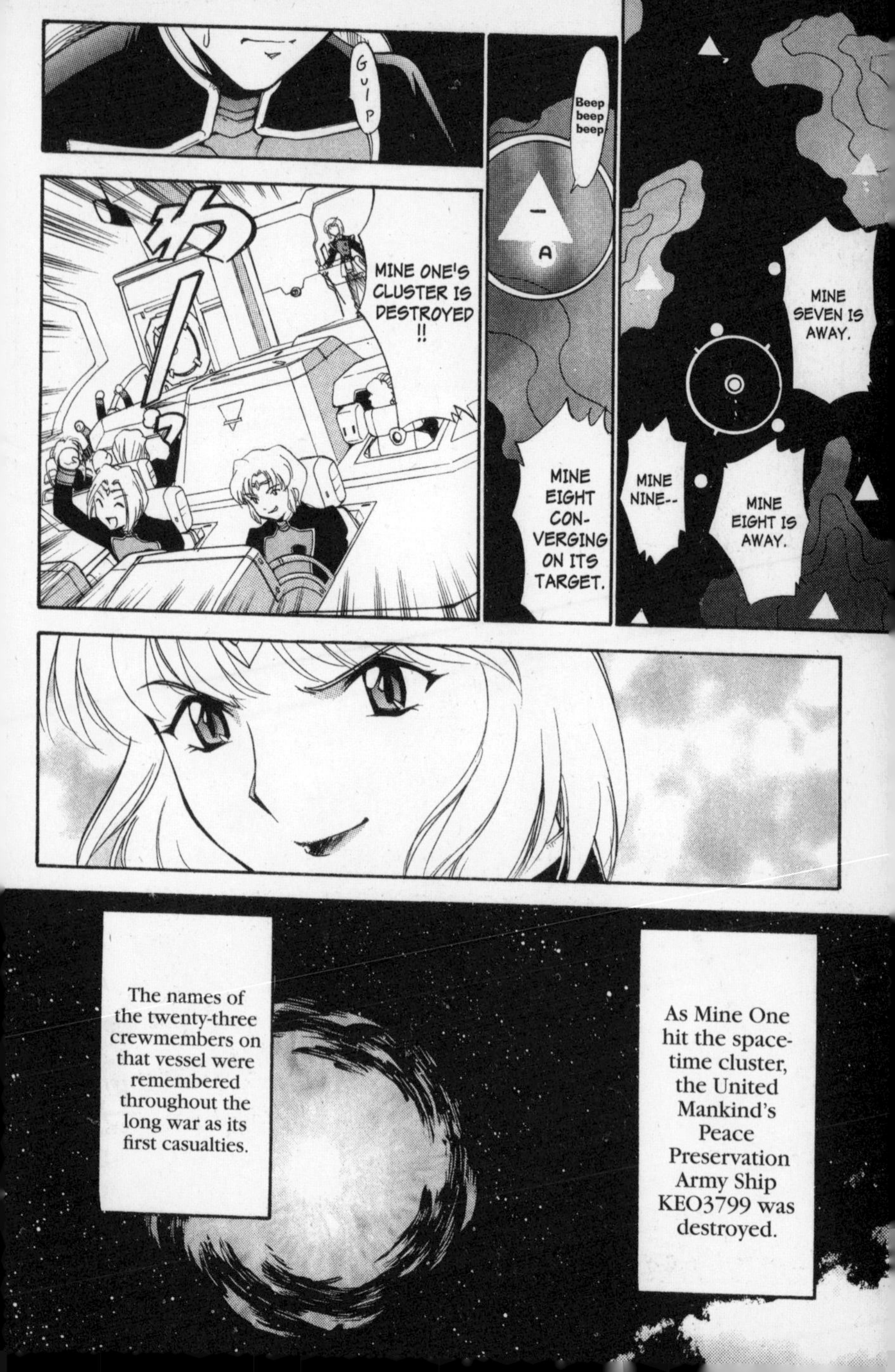
MINE SEVEN IS AWAY.
MINE EIGHT IS AWAY.
MINE NINE--
MINE EIGHT CON-VERGING ON ITS TARGET.
Beep beep beep
GULP
MINE ONE'S CLUSTER IS DESTROYED!!
As Mine One hit the space-time cluster, the United Mankind's Peace Preservation Army Ship KEO3799 was destroyed.
The names of the twenty-three crewmembers on that vessel were remembered throughout the long war as its first casualties.

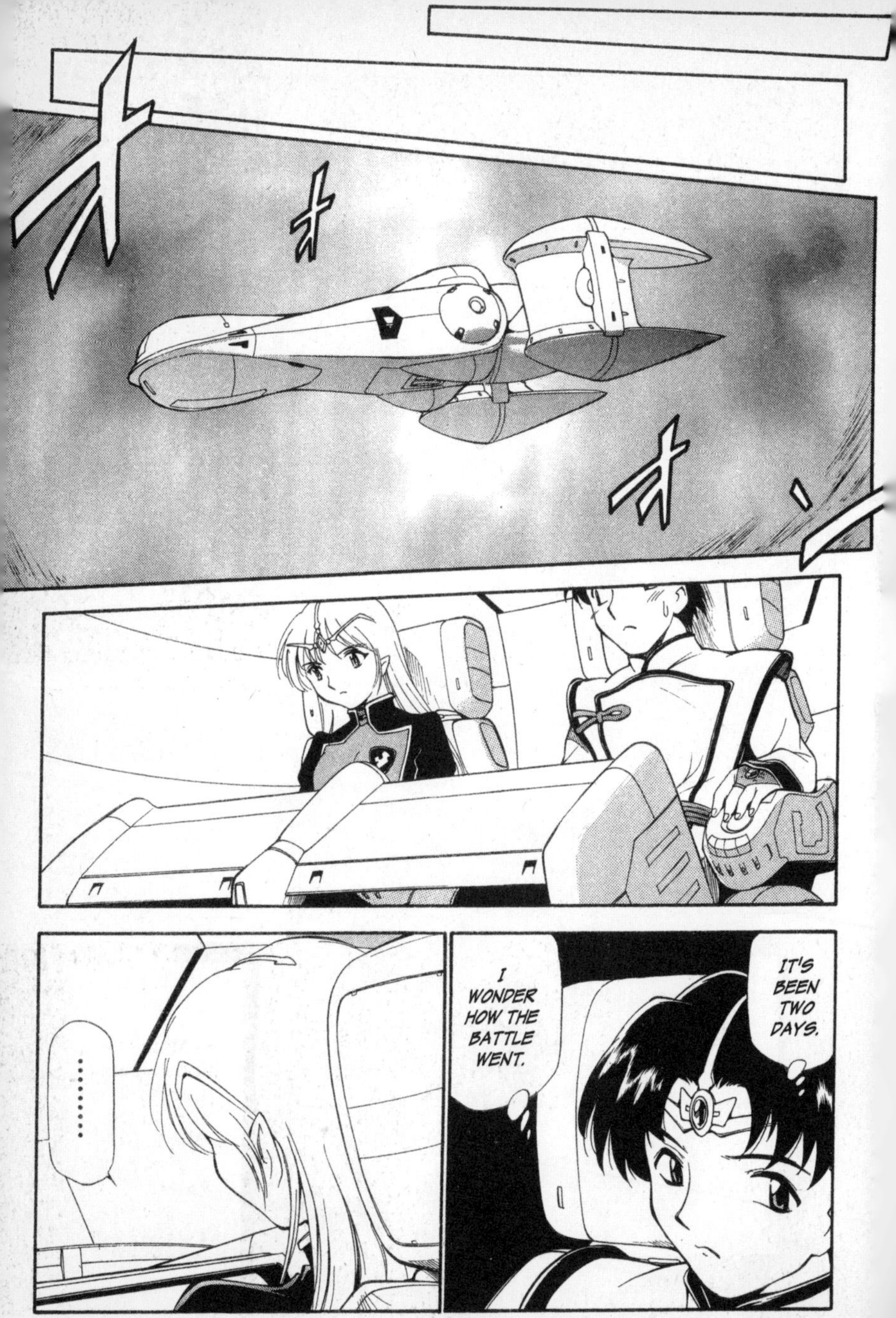
IT'S BEEN TWO DAYS.
I WONDER HOW THE BATTLE WENT.
....

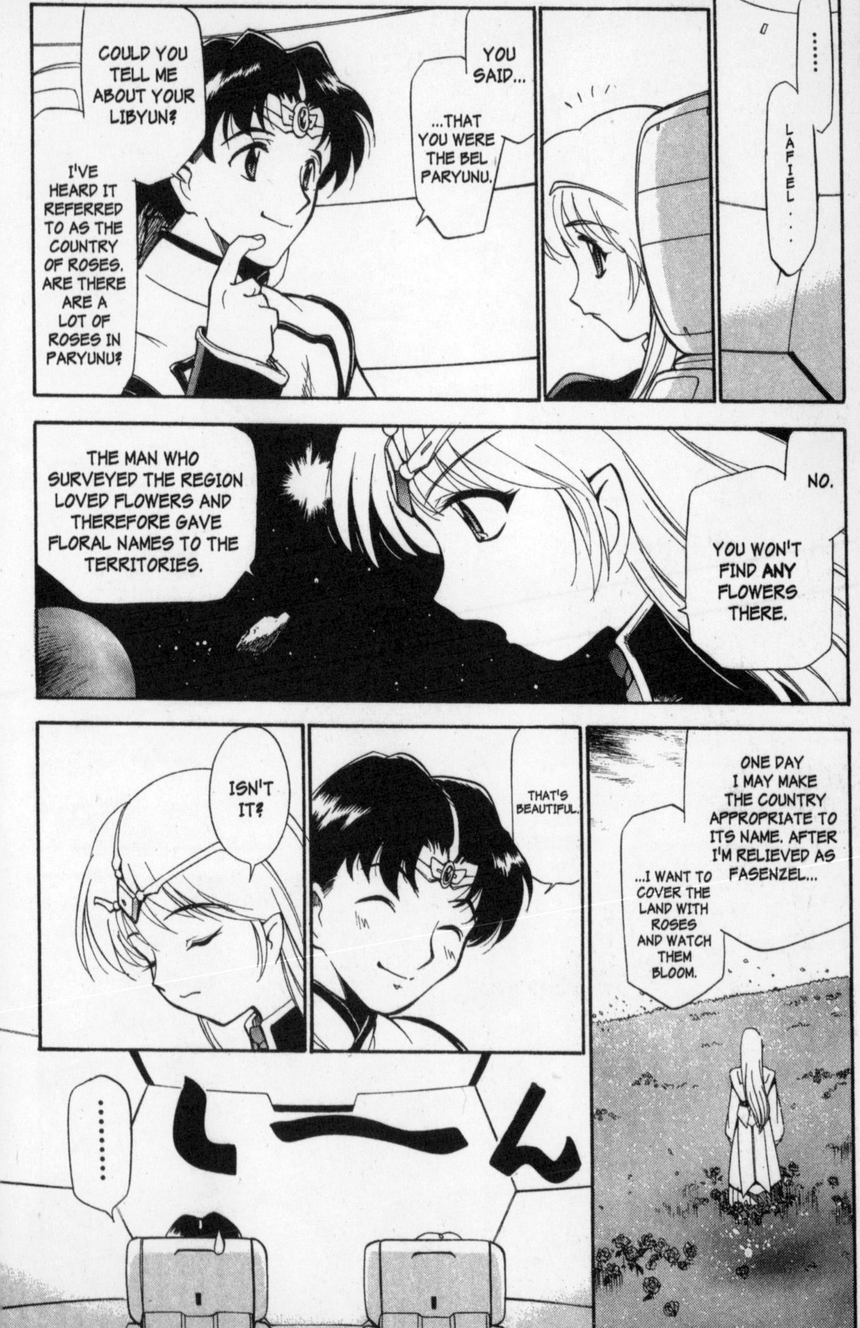
......
LAFIEL...
YOU SAID...
...THAT YOU WERE THE BEL PARYUNU.
COULD YOU TELL ME ABOUT YOUR LIBYUN?
I'VE HEARD IT REFERRED TO AS THE COUNTRY OF ROSES. ARE THERE ARE A LOT OF ROSES IN PARYUNU?
NO.
YOU WON'T FIND ANY FLOWERS THERE.
THE MAN WHO SURVEYED THE REGION LOVED FLOWERS AND THEREFORE GAVE FLORAL NAMES TO THE TERRITORIES.
ONE DAY I MAY MAKE THE COUNTRY APPROPRIATE TO ITS NAME. AFTER I'M RELIEVED AS FASENZEL...
...I WANT TO COVER THE LAND WITH ROSES AND WATCH THEM BLOOM.
THAT'S BEAUTIFUL.
ISN'T IT?
....
しーん

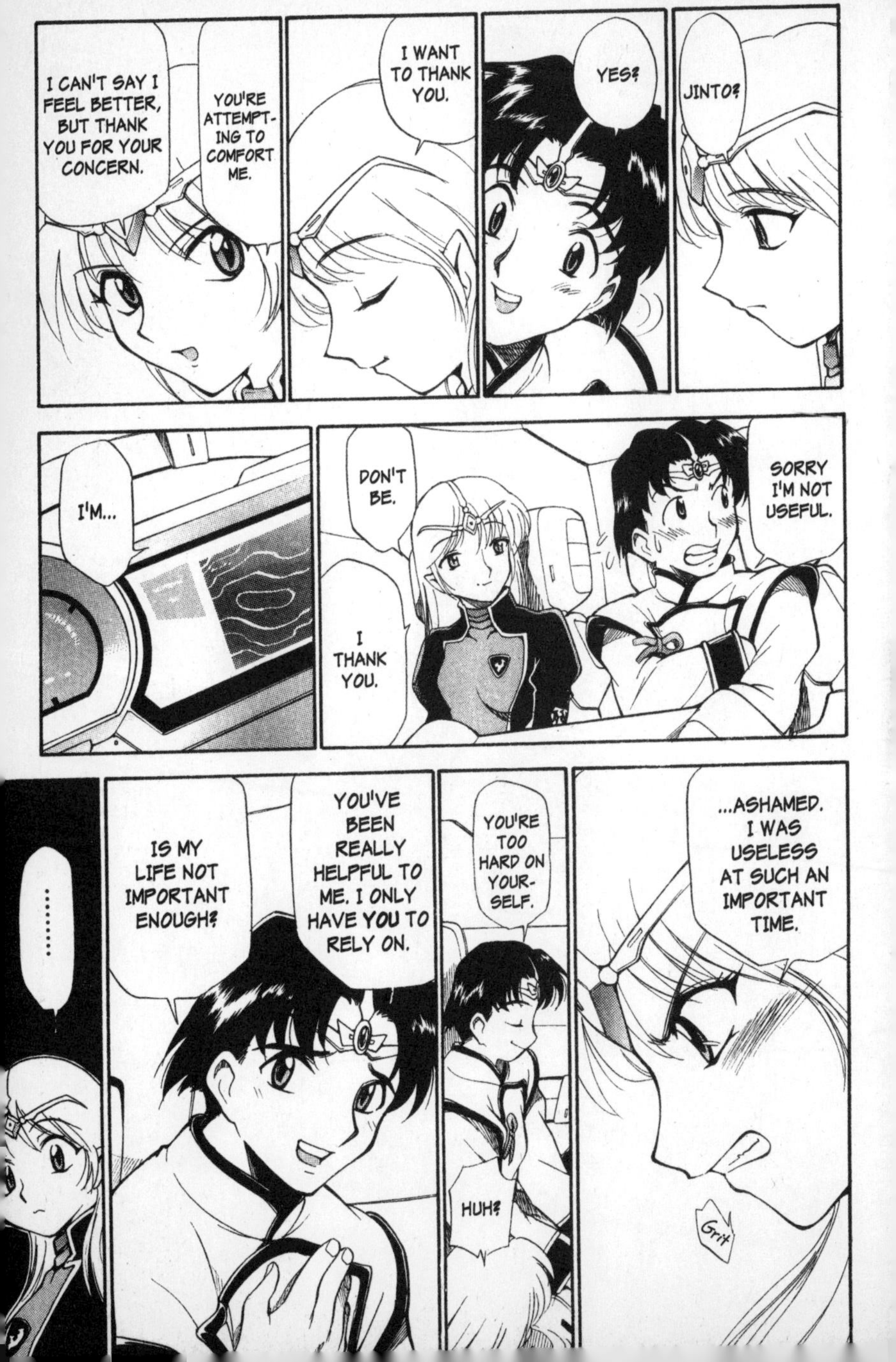
JINTO?
YES?
I WANT TO THANK YOU.
YOU'RE ATTEMPT-ING TO COMFORT ME.
I CAN'T SAY I FEEL BETTER, BUT THANK YOU FOR YOUR CONCERN.
SORRY I'M NOT USEFUL.
DON'T BE.
I THANK YOU.
I'M...
...ASHAMED. I WAS USELESS AT SUCH AN IMPORTANT TIME.
Grit
YOU'RE TOO HARD ON YOUR-SELF.
HUH?
YOU'VE BEEN REALLY HELPFUL TO ME. I ONLY HAVE YOU TO RELY ON.
IS MY LIFE NOT IMPORTANT ENOUGH?
....

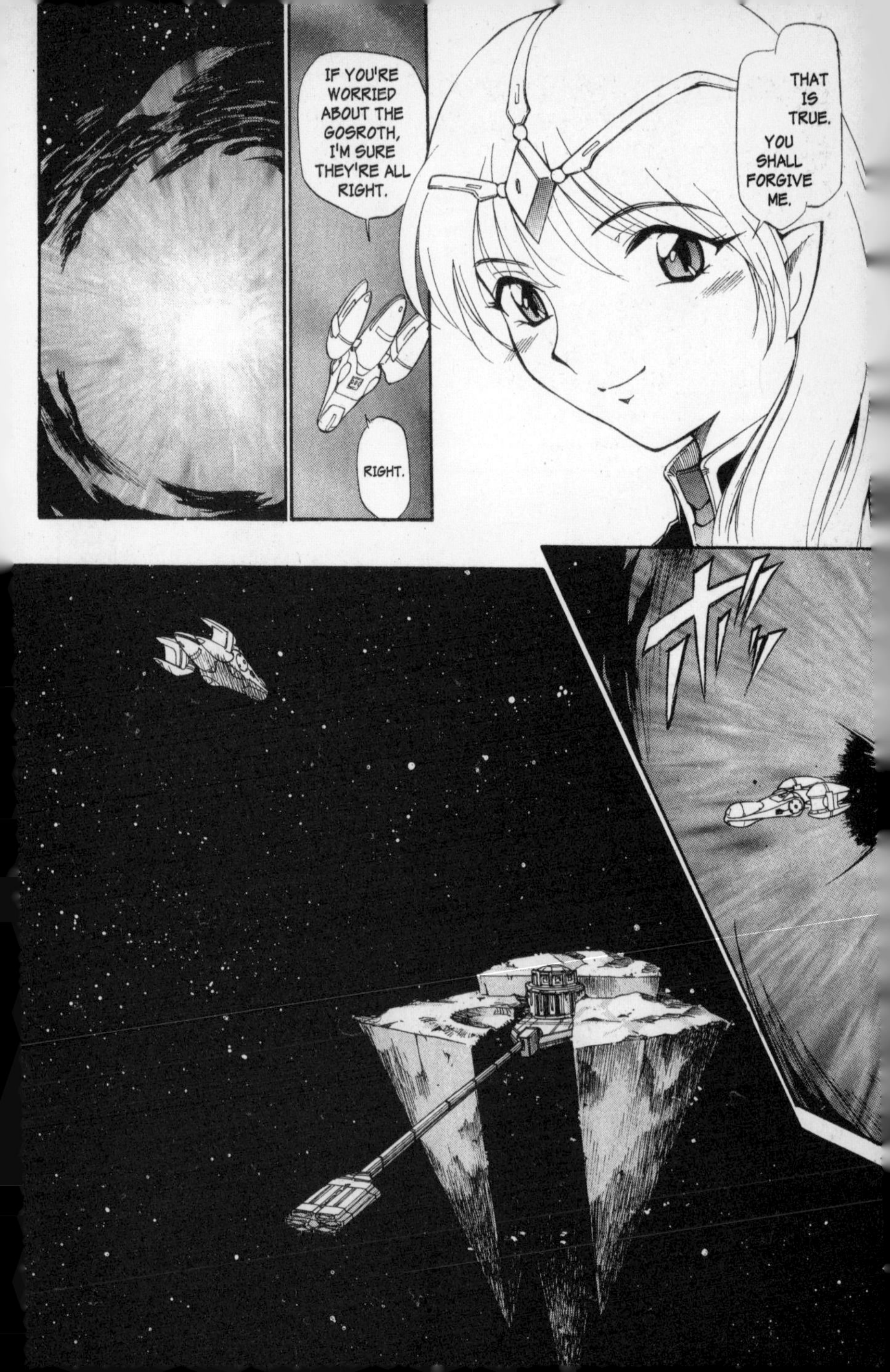
THAT IS TRUE.
YOU SHALL FORGIVE ME.
IF YOU'RE WORRIED ABOUT THE GOSROTH, I'M SURE THEY'RE ALL RIGHT.
RIGHT.

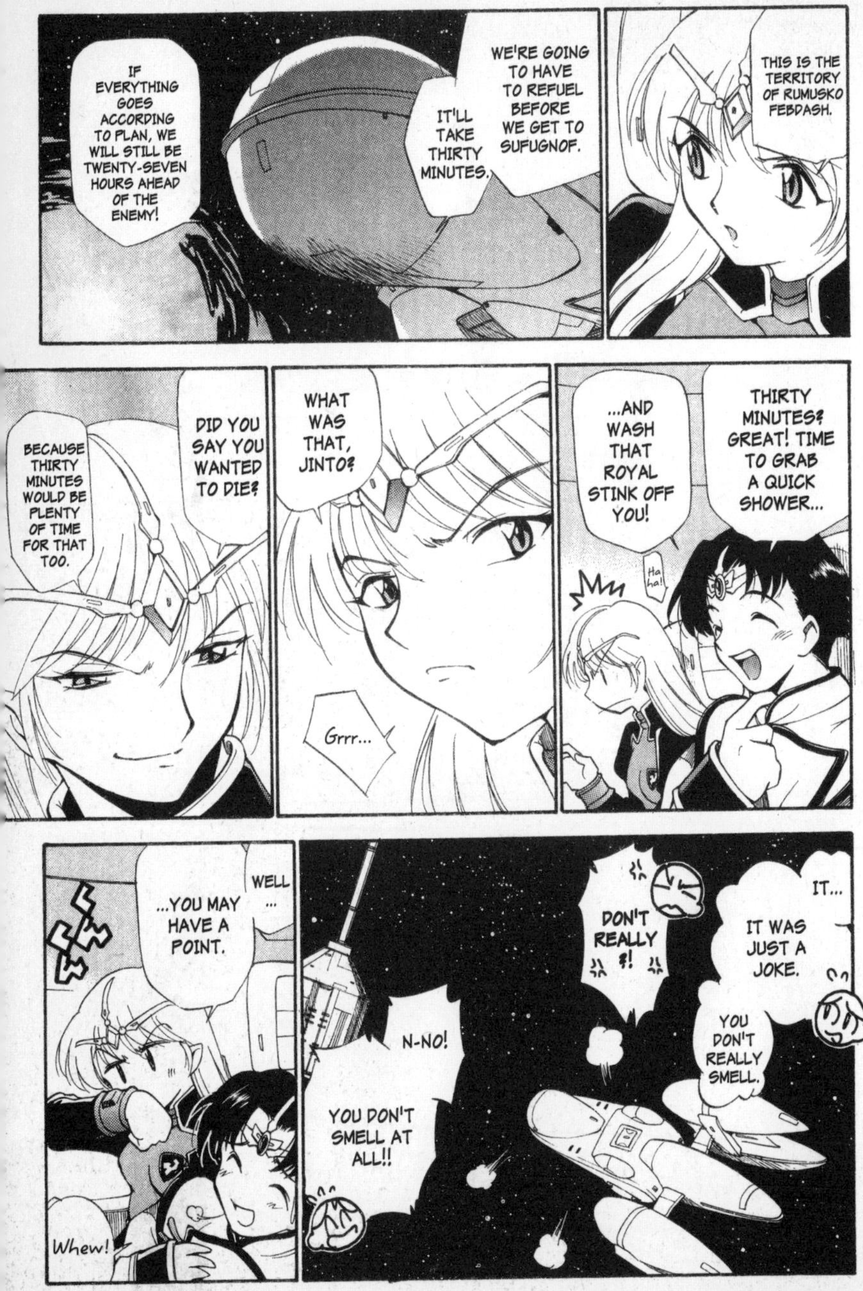
THIS IS THE TERRITORY OF RUMUSKO FEBDASH.
WE'RE GOING TO HAVE TO REFUEL BEFORE WE GET TO SUFUGNOF.
IT'LL TAKE THIRTY MINUTES.
IF EVERYTHING GOES ACCORDING TO PLAN, WE WILL STILL BE TWENTY-SEVEN HOURS AHEAD OF THE ENEMY!
THIRTY MINUTES? GREAT! TIME TO GRAB A QUICK SHOWER...
...AND WASH THAT ROYAL STINK OFF YOU!
Ha ha!
WHAT WAS THAT, JINTO?
Grrr...
DID YOU SAY YOU WANTED TO DIE?
BECAUSE THIRTY MINUTES WOULD BE PLENTY OF TIME FOR THAT TOO.
IT...
IT WAS JUST A JOKE.
DON'T REALLY ?!
YOU DON'T REALLY SMELL.
N-NO!
YOU DON'T SMELL AT ALL!!
WELL ...
...YOU MAY HAVE A POINT.
Whew!

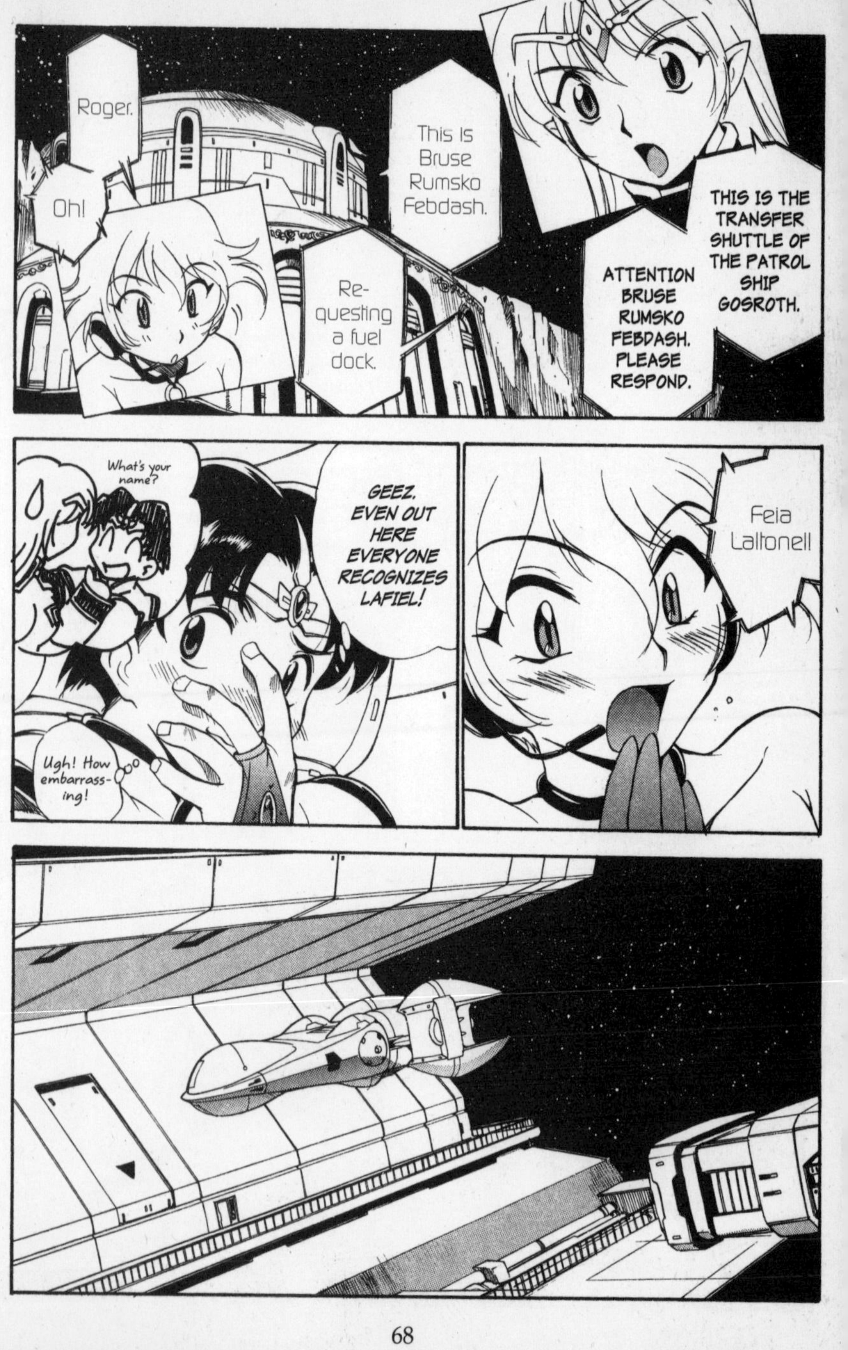
THIS IS THE TRANSFER SHUTTLE OF THE PATROL SHIP GOSROTH.
ATTENTION BRUSE RUMSKO FEBDASH. PLEASE RESPOND.
This is Bruse Rumsko Febdash.
Re-questing a fuel dock.
Roger.
Oh!
Feia Laltonel!
GEEZ. EVEN OUT HERE EVERYONE RECOGNIZES LAFIEL!
What's your name?
Ugh! How embarrass-ing!

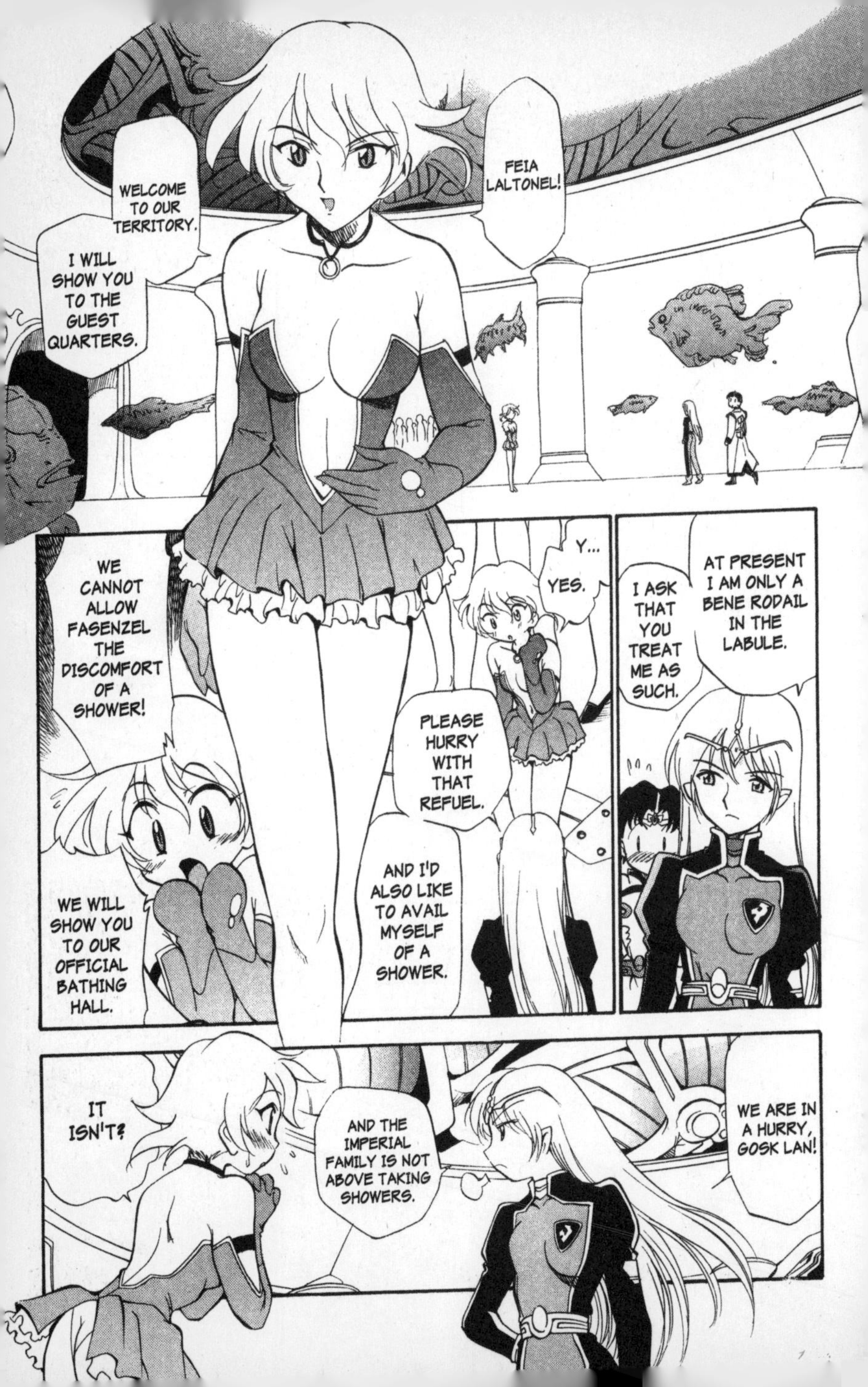
FEIA LALTONEL!
WELCOME TO OUR TERRITORY.
I WILL SHOW YOU TO THE GUEST QUARTERS.
AT PRESENT I AM ONLY A BENE RODAIL IN THE LABULE.
I ASK THAT YOU TREAT ME AS SUCH.
Y...
YES.
PLEASE HURRY WITH THAT REFUEL.
AND I'D ALSO LIKE TO AVAIL MYSELF OF A SHOWER.
WE CANNOT ALLOW FASENZEL THE DISCOMFORT OF A SHOWER!
WE WILL SHOW YOU TO OUR OFFICIAL BATHING HALL.
WE ARE IN A HURRY, GOSK LAN!
AND THE IMPERIAL FAMILY IS NOT ABOVE TAKING SHOWERS.
IT ISN'T?

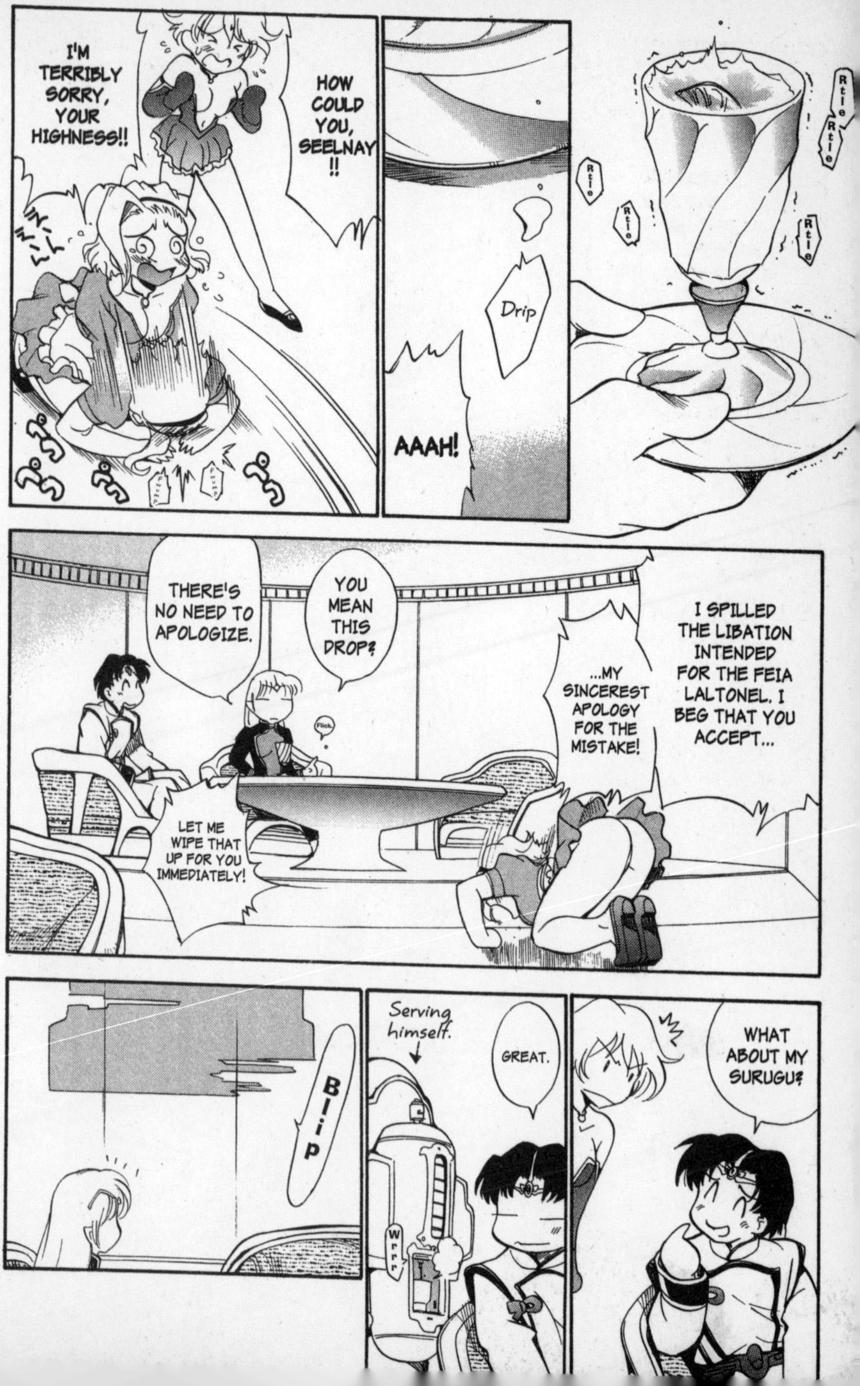
Rtle
Rtle
Rtle
Rtle
Rtle
Rtle
Drip
AAAH!
HOW COULD YOU, SEELNAY!!
I'M TERRIBLY SORRY, YOUR HIGHNESS!!
I SPILLED THE LIBATION INTENDED FOR THE FEIA LALTONEL. I BEG THAT YOU ACCEPT...
...MY SINCEREST APOLOGY FOR THE MISTAKE!
YOU MEAN THIS DROP?
Flick.
THERE'S NO NEED TO APOLOGIZE.
LET ME WIPE THAT UP FOR YOU IMMEDIATELY!
WHAT ABOUT MY SURUGU?
GREAT.
Serving himself.
Wrrr
Blip

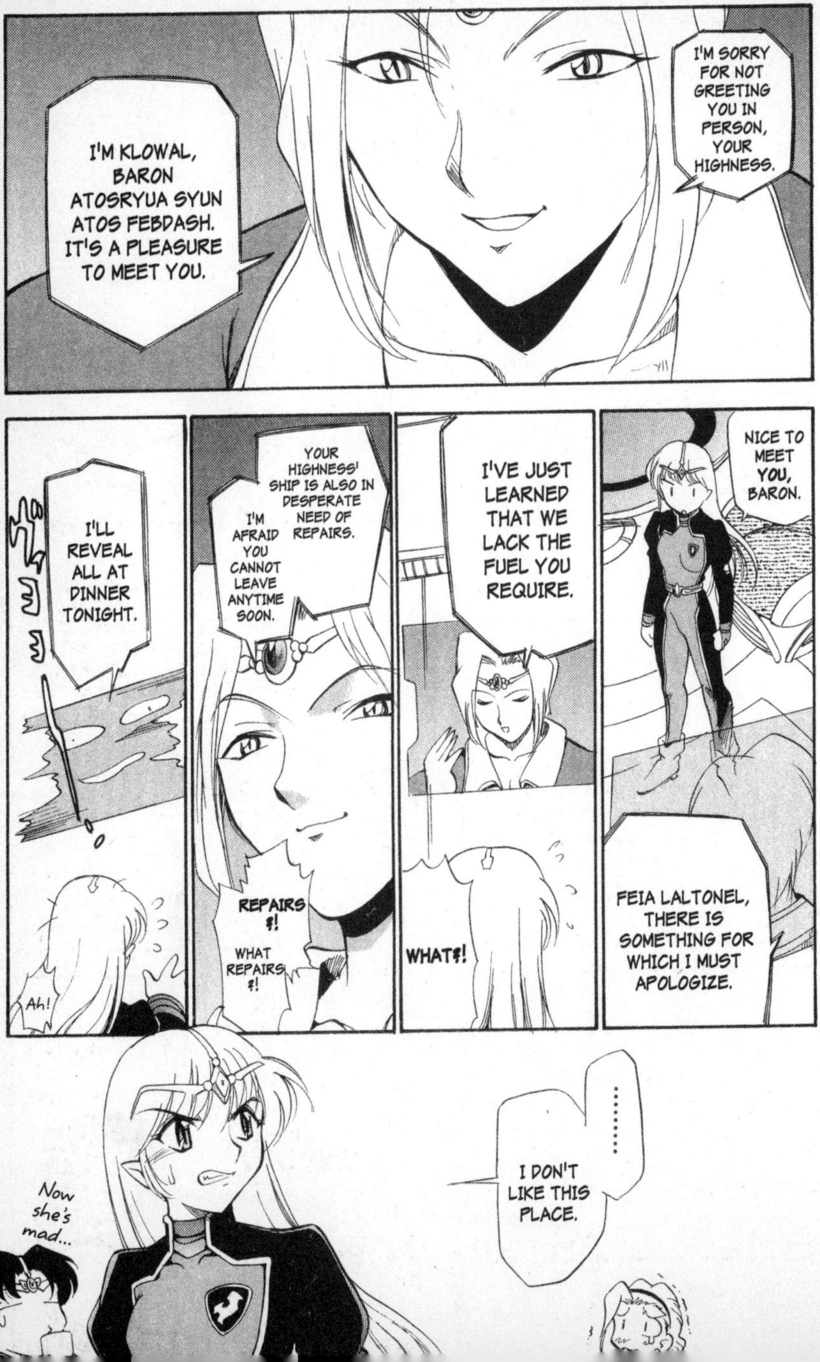
I'M SORRY FOR NOT GREETING YOU IN PERSON, YOUR HIGHNESS.
I'M KLOWAL, BARON ATOSRYUA SYUN ATOS FEBDASH. IT'S A PLEASURE TO MEET YOU.
NICE TO MEET YOU, BARON.
FEIA LALTONEL, THERE IS SOMETHING FOR WHICH I MUST APOLOGIZE.
I'VE JUST LEARNED THAT WE LACK THE FUEL YOU REQUIRE.
WHAT?!
YOUR HIGHNESS' SHIP IS ALSO IN DESPERATE NEED OF REPAIRS.
I'M AFRAID YOU CANNOT LEAVE ANYTIME SOON.
REPAIRS?!
WHAT REPAIRS?!
I'LL REVEAL ALL AT DINNER TONIGHT.
Ah!
....
I DON'T LIKE THIS PLACE.
Now she's mad...

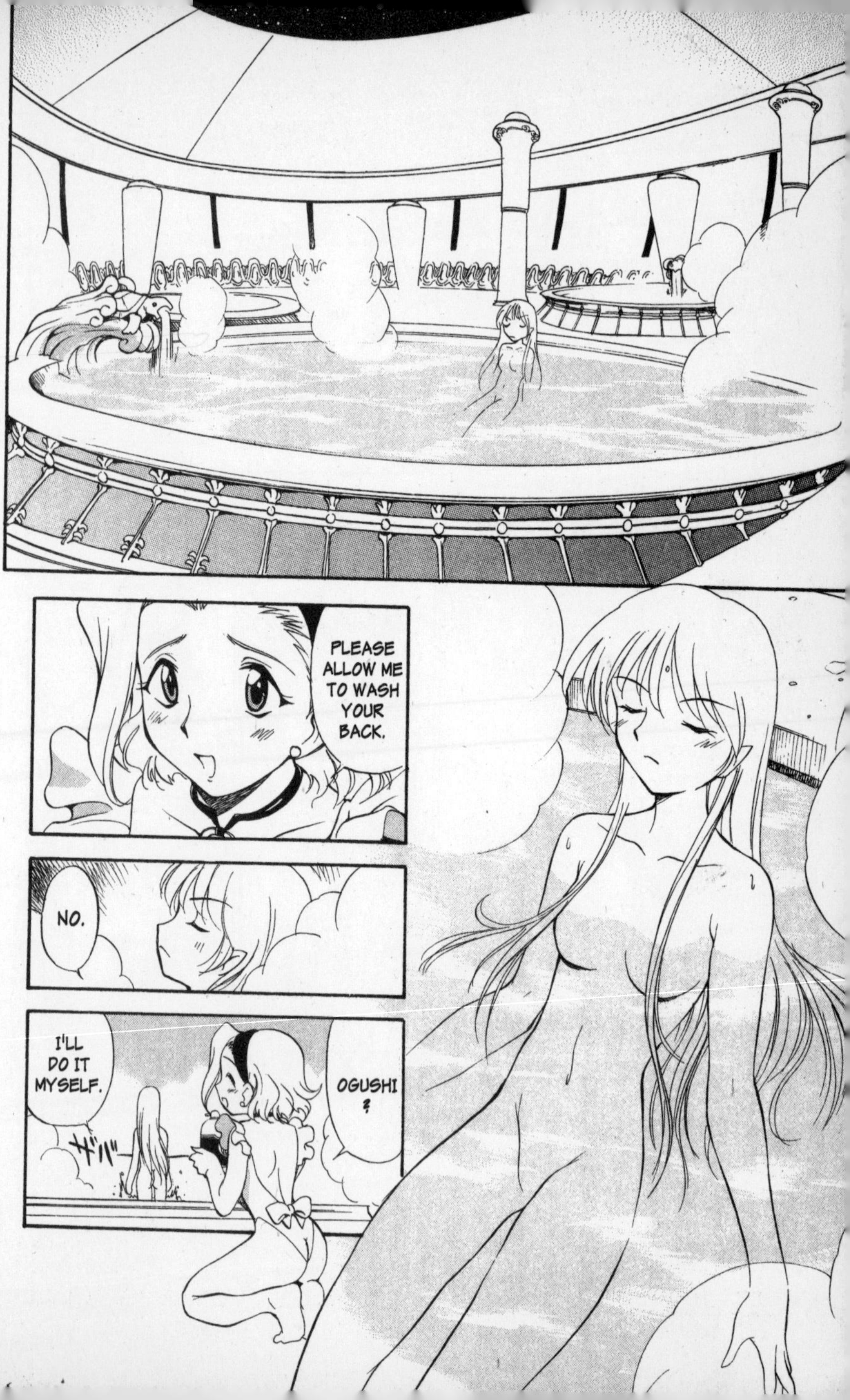
PLEASE ALLOW ME TO WASH YOUR BACK.
NO.
OGUSHI?
I'LL DO IT MYSELF.
ザバ

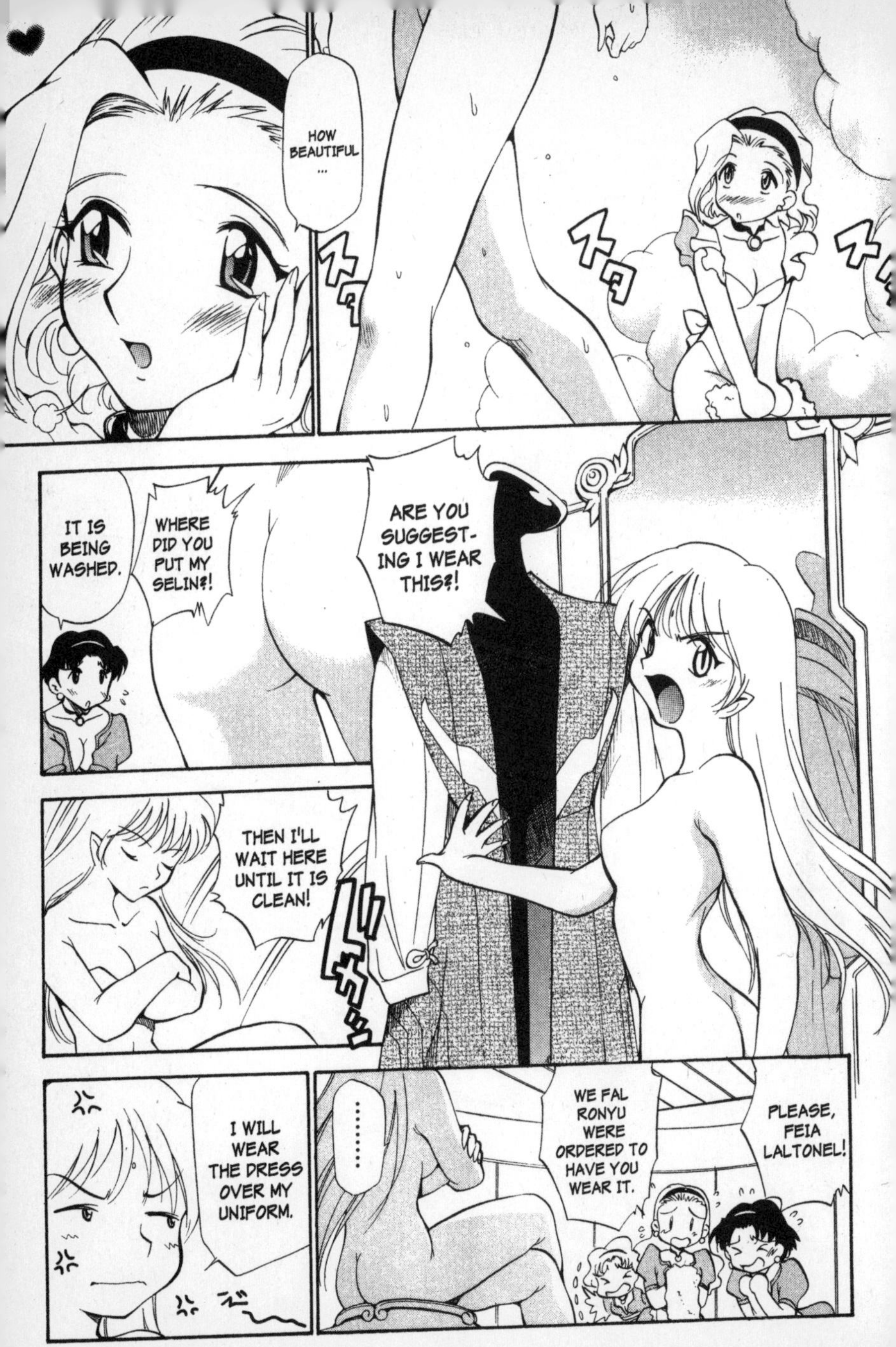
HOW BEAUTIFUL ...
ARE YOU SUGGEST-ING I WEAR THIS?!
WHERE DID YOU PUT MY SELIN?!
IT IS BEING WASHED.
THEN I'LL WAIT HERE UNTIL IT IS CLEAN!
PLEASE, FEIA LALTONEL!
WE FAL RONYU WERE ORDERED TO HAVE YOU WEAR IT.
....
I WILL WEAR THE DRESS OVER MY UNIFORM.

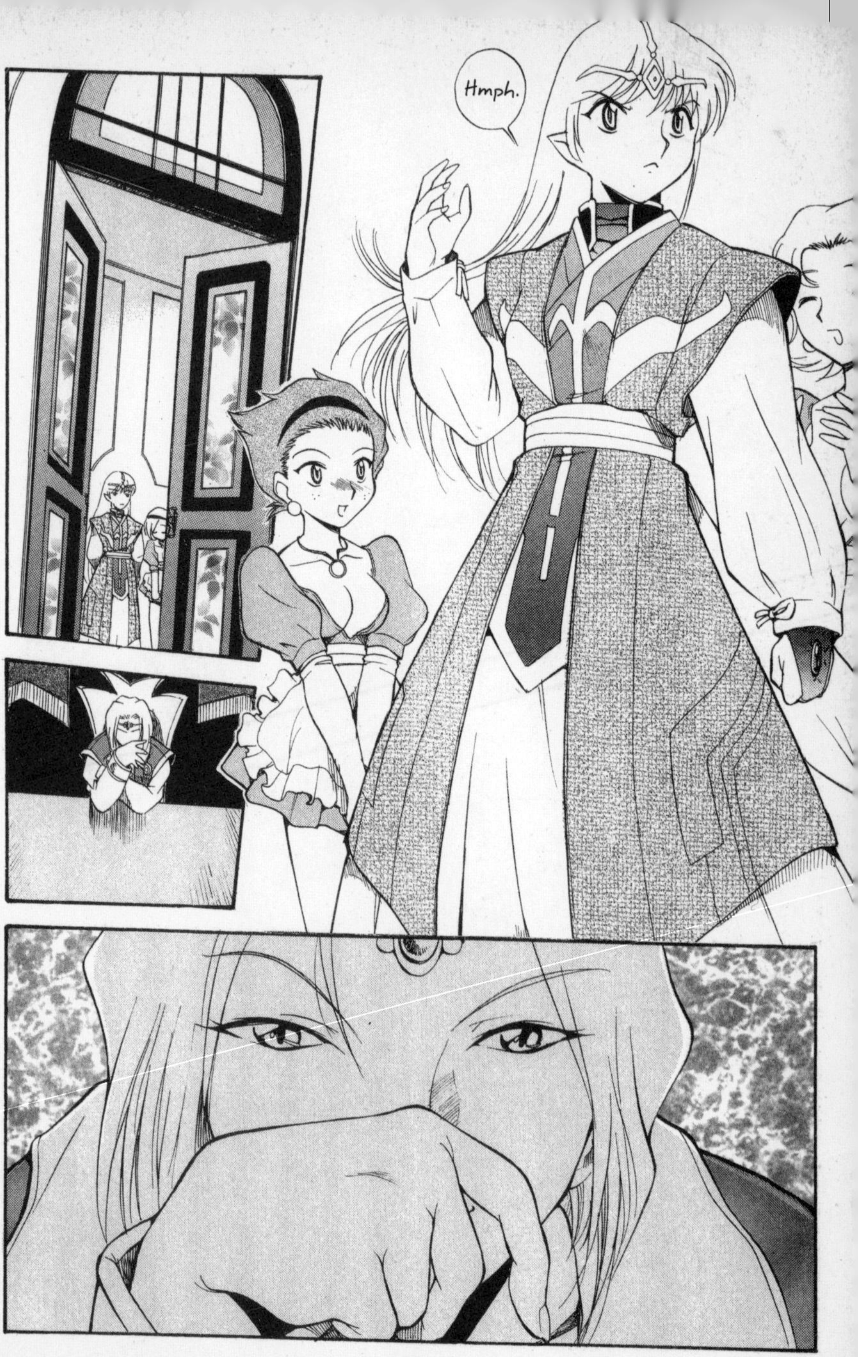
Hmph.

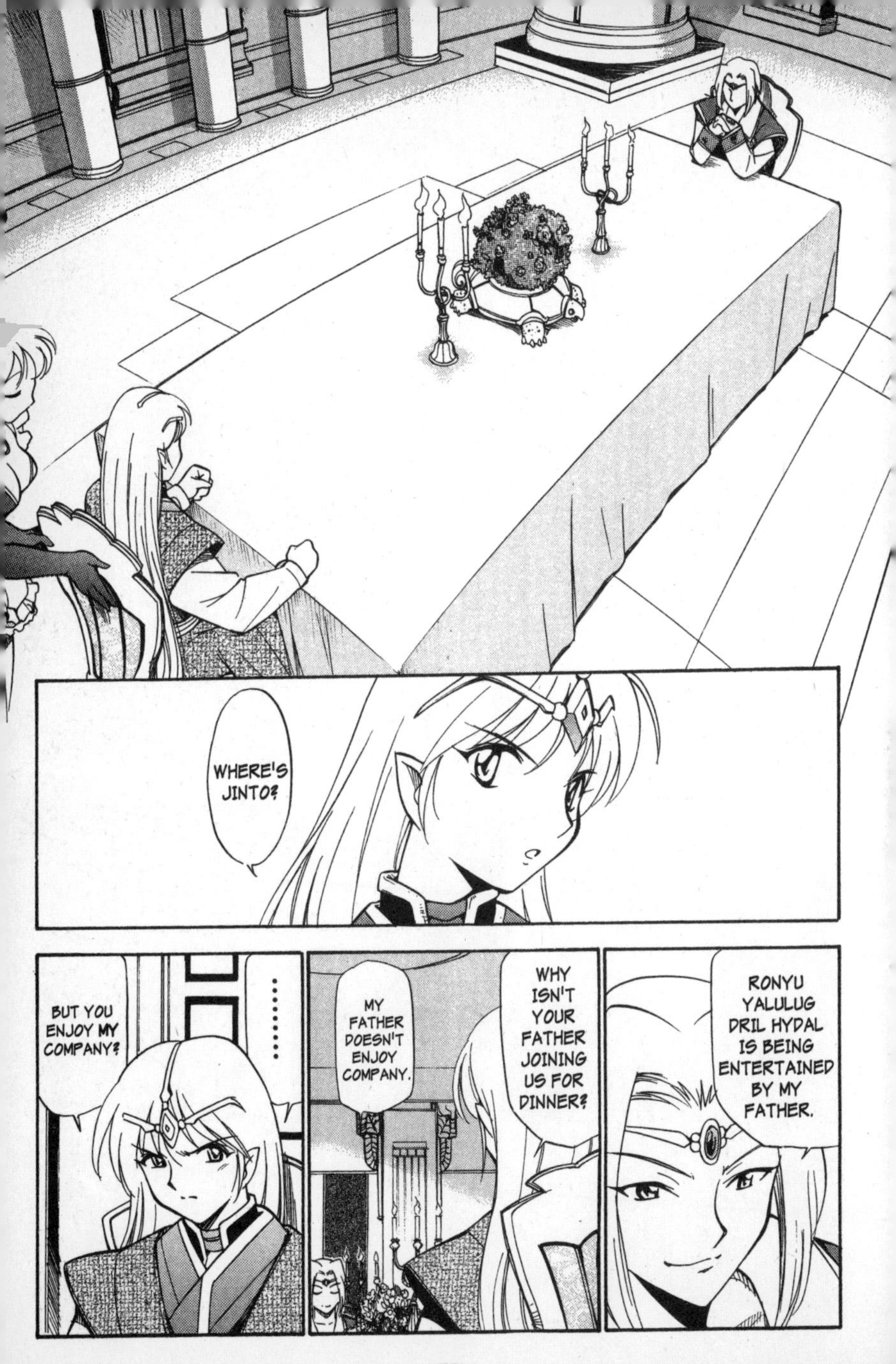
WHERE'S JINTO?
RONYU YALULUG DRIL HYDAL IS BEING ENTERTAINED BY MY FATHER.
WHY ISN'T YOUR FATHER JOINING US FOR DINNER?
MY FATHER DOESN'T ENJOY COMPANY.
....
BUT YOU ENJOY MY COMPANY?

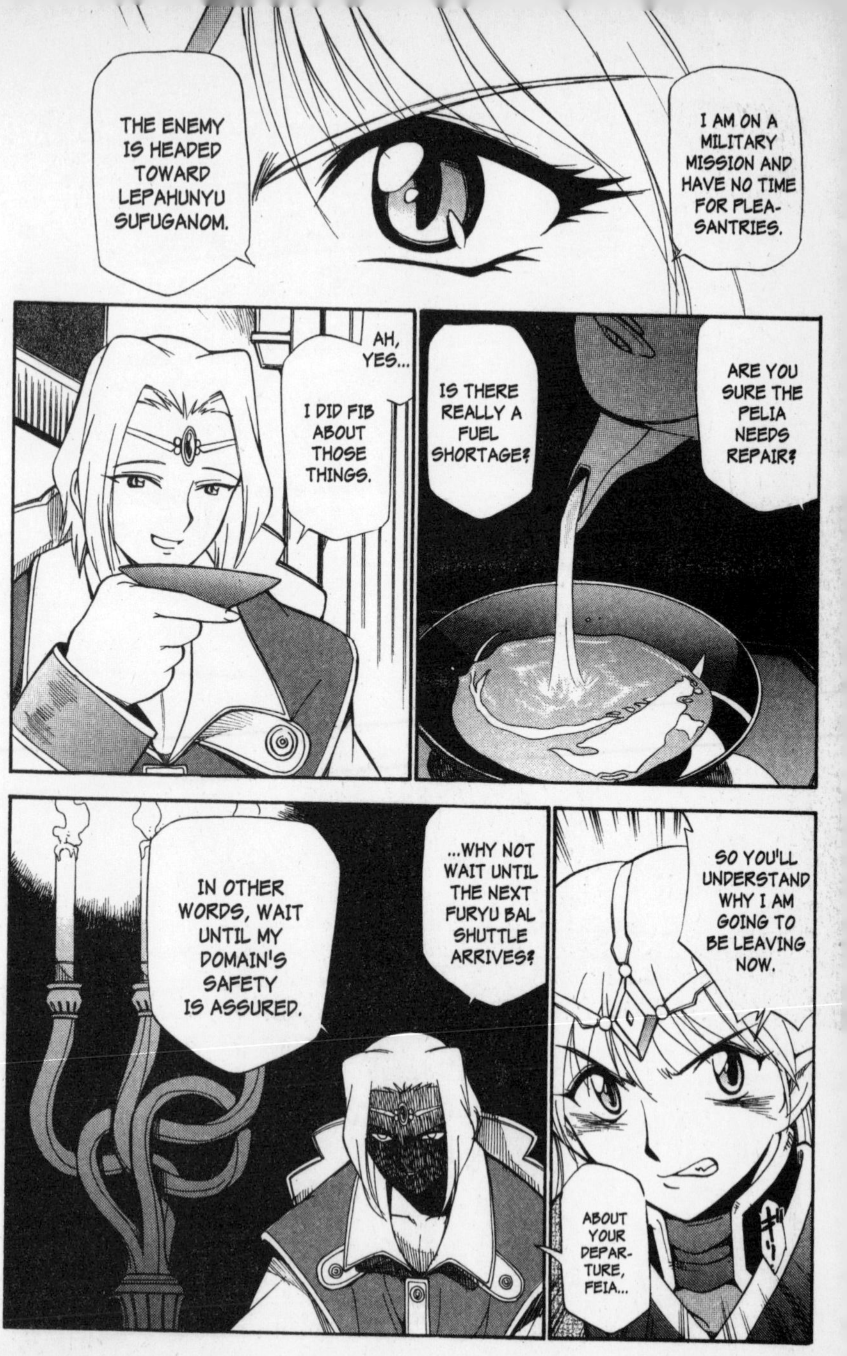
I AM ON A MILITARY MISSION AND HAVE NO TIME FOR PLEA-SANTRIES.
THE ENEMY IS HEADED TOWARD LEPAHUNYU SUFUGANOM.
ARE YOU SURE THE PELIA NEEDS REPAIR?
IS THERE REALLY A FUEL SHORTAGE?
AH, YES...
I DID FIB ABOUT THOSE THINGS.
SO YOU'LL UNDERSTAND WHY I AM GOING TO BE LEAVING NOW.
ギリ
ABOUT YOUR DEPAR-TURE, FEIA...
...WHY NOT WAIT UNTIL THE NEXT FURYU BAL SHUTTLE ARRIVES?
IN OTHER WORDS, WAIT UNTIL MY DOMAIN'S SAFETY IS ASSURED.

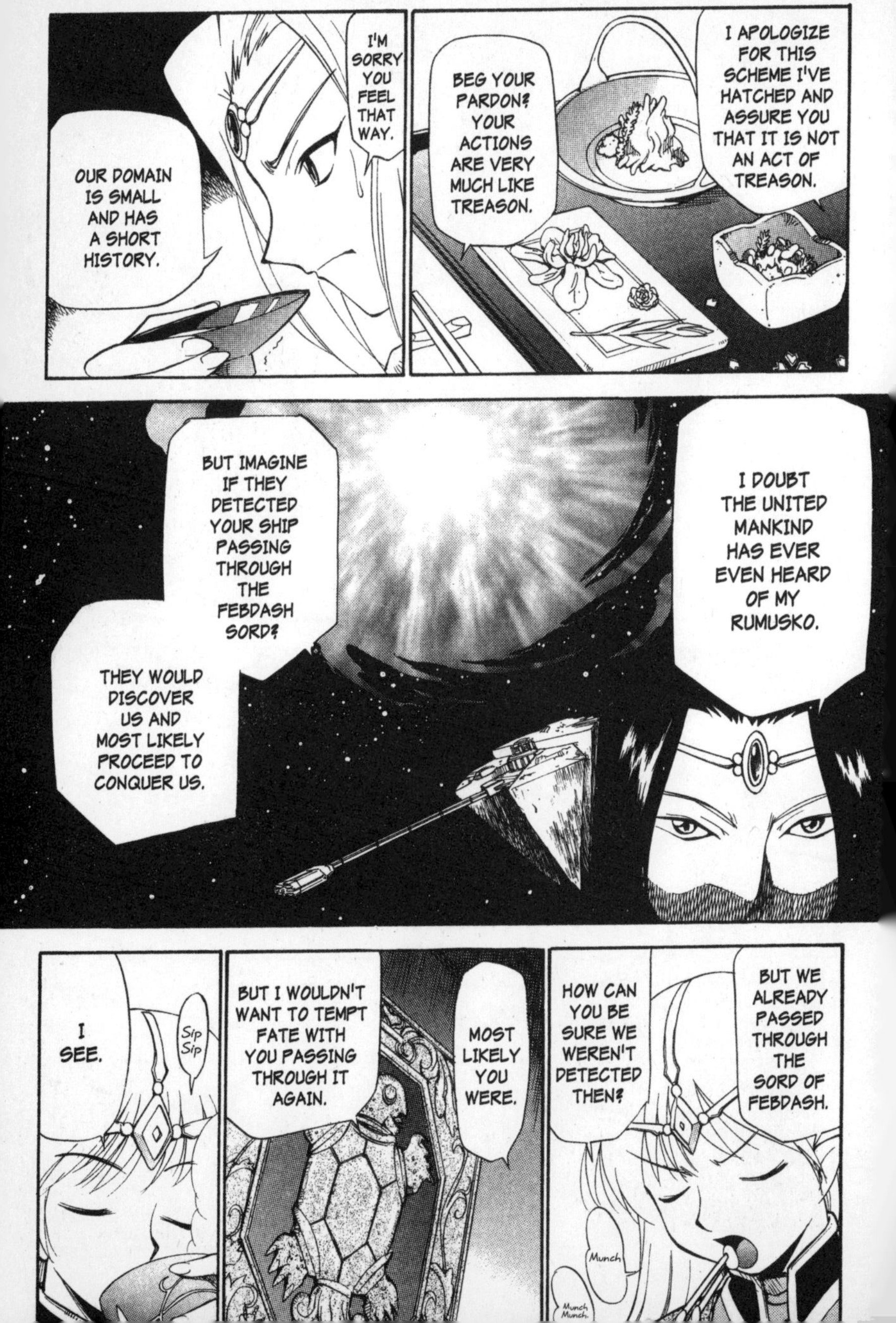
I APOLOGIZE FOR THIS SCHEME I'VE HATCHED AND ASSURE YOU THAT IT IS NOT AN ACT OF TREASON.
BEG YOUR PARDON? YOUR ACTIONS ARE VERY MUCH LIKE TREASON.
I'M SORRY YOU FEEL THAT WAY.
OUR DOMAIN IS SMALL AND HAS A SHORT HISTORY.
I DOUBT THE UNITED MANKIND HAS EVER EVEN HEARD OF MY RUMUSKO.
BUT IMAGINE IF THEY DETECTED YOUR SHIP PASSING THROUGH THE FEBDASH SORD?
THEY WOULD DISCOVER US AND MOST LIKELY PROCEED TO CONQUER US.
BUT WE ALREADY PASSED THROUGH THE SORD OF FEBDASH.
HOW CAN YOU BE SURE WE WEREN'T DETECTED THEN?
Munch
Munch Munch
MOST LIKELY YOU WERE.
BUT I WOULDN'T WANT TO TEMPT FATE WITH YOU PASSING THROUGH IT AGAIN.
Sip Sip
I SEE.

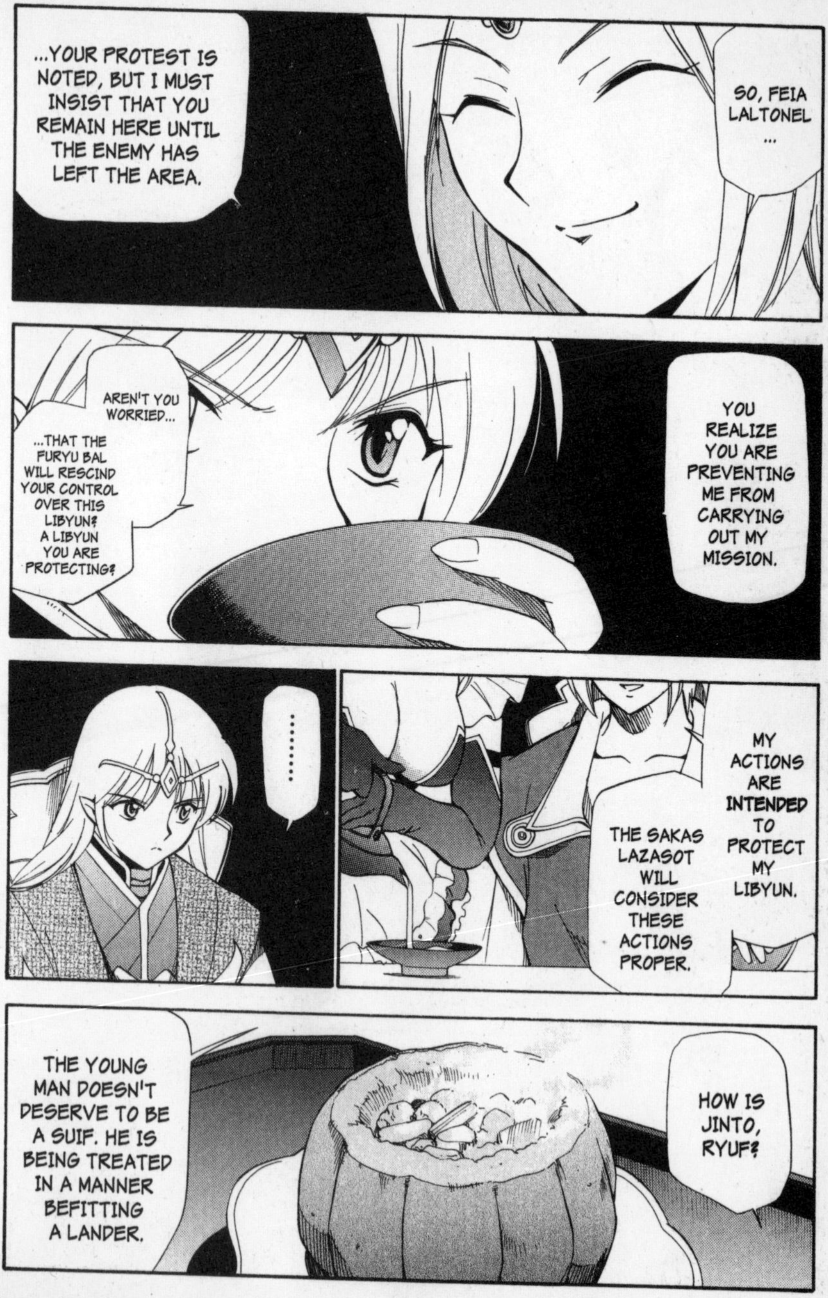
SO, FEIA LALTONEL ...
...YOUR PROTEST IS NOTED, BUT I MUST INSIST THAT YOU REMAIN HERE UNTIL THE ENEMY HAS LEFT THE AREA.
YOU REALIZE YOU ARE PREVENTING ME FROM CARRYING OUT MY MISSION.
AREN'T YOU WORRIED...
...THAT THE FURYU BAL WILL RESCIND YOUR CONTROL OVER THIS LIBYUN? A LIBYUN YOU ARE PROTECTING?
MY ACTIONS ARE **INTENDED** TO PROTECT MY LIBYUN.
THE SAKAS LAZASOT WILL CONSIDER THESE ACTIONS PROPER.
....
HOW IS JINTO, RYUF?
THE YOUNG MAN DOESN'T DESERVE TO BE A SUIF. HE IS BEING TREATED IN A MANNER BEFITTING A LANDER.

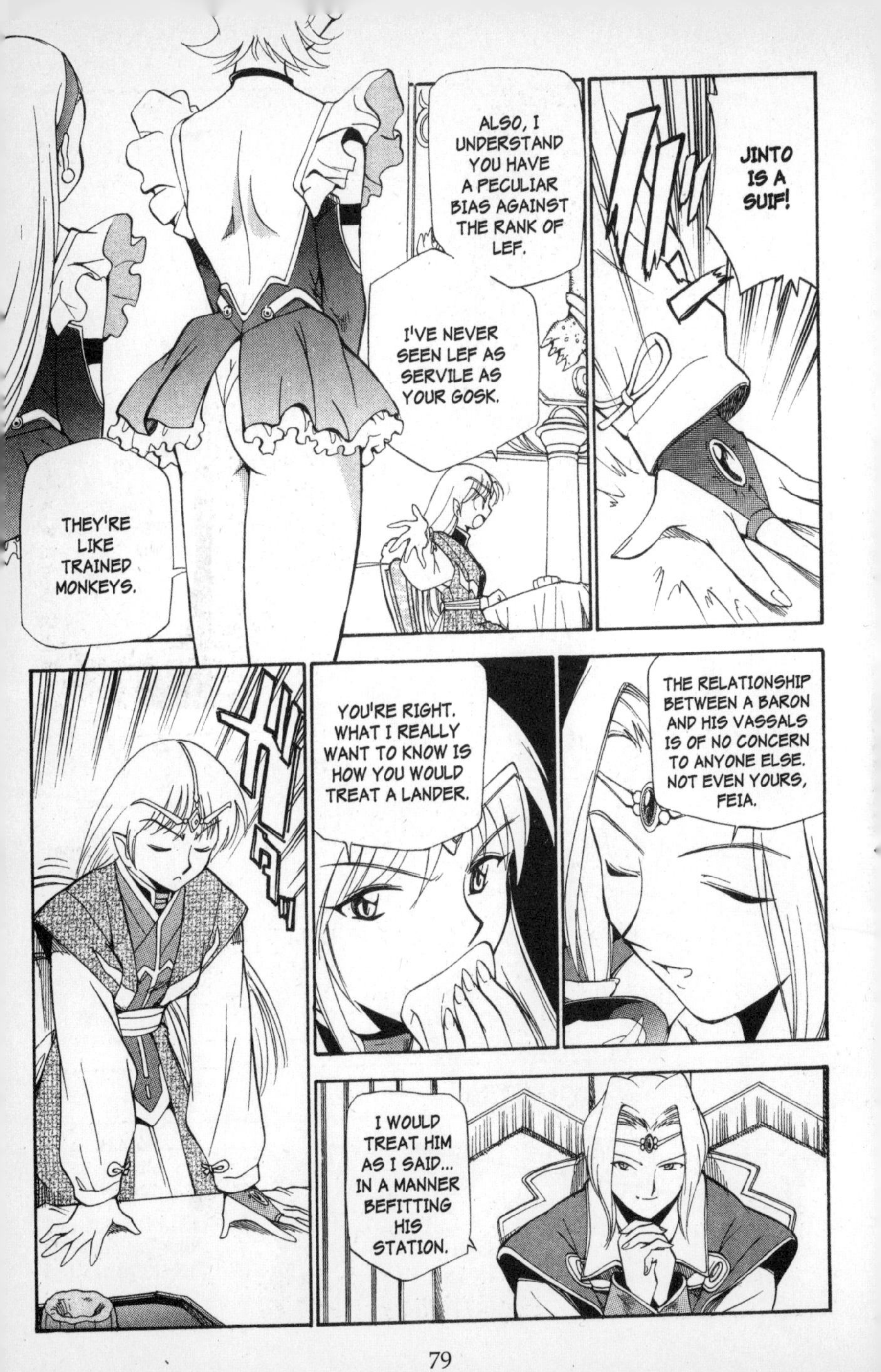
JINTO IS A SUIF!
ALSO, I UNDERSTAND YOU HAVE A PECULIAR BIAS AGAINST THE RANK OF LEF.
I'VE NEVER SEEN LEF AS SERVILE AS YOUR GOSK.
THEY'RE LIKE TRAINED MONKEYS.
THE RELATIONSHIP BETWEEN A BARON AND HIS VASSALS IS OF NO CONCERN TO ANYONE ELSE. NOT EVEN YOURS, FEIA.
YOU'RE RIGHT. WHAT I REALLY WANT TO KNOW IS HOW YOU WOULD TREAT A LANDER.
I WOULD TREAT HIM AS I SAID... IN A MANNER BEFITTING HIS STATION.

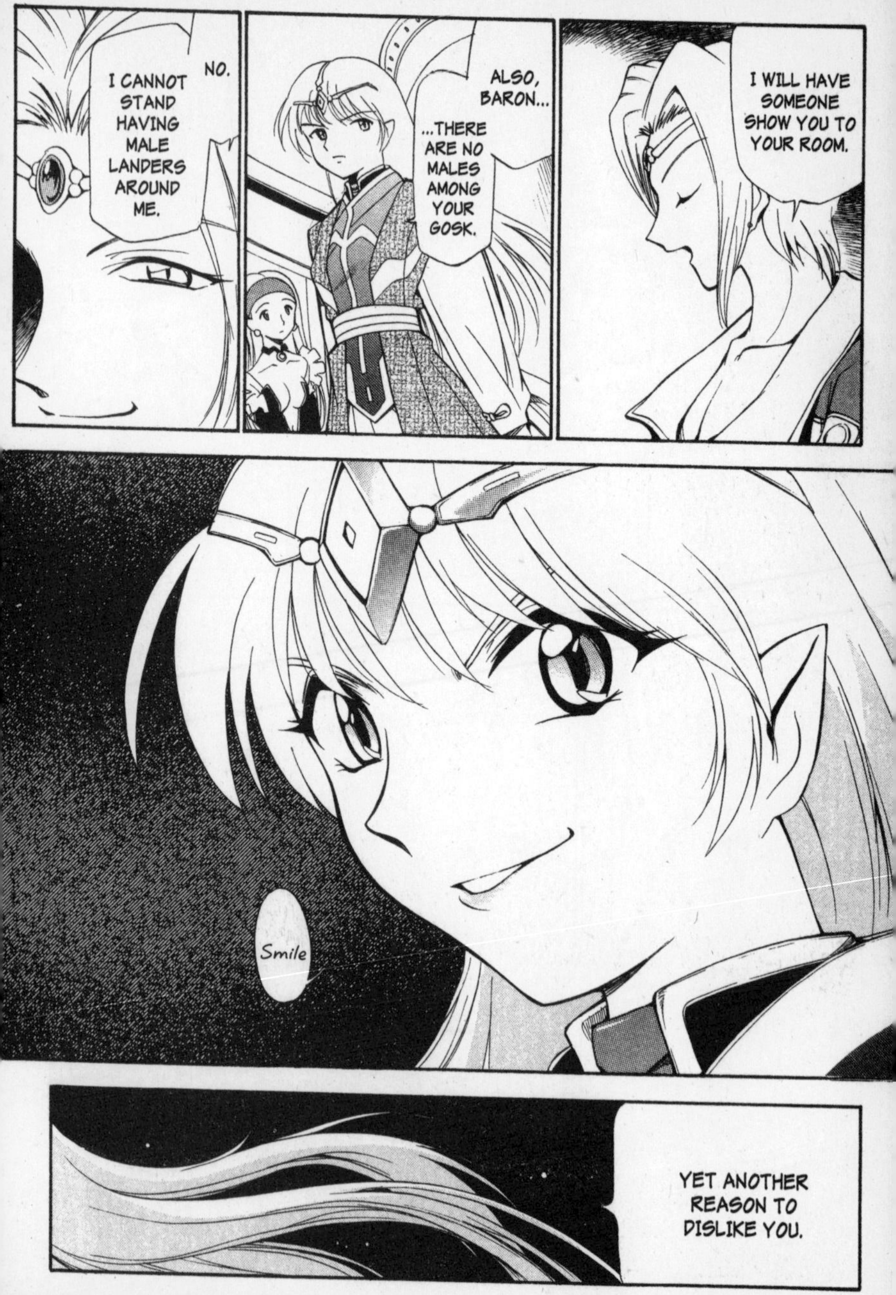
I WILL HAVE SOMEONE SHOW YOU TO YOUR ROOM.
ALSO, BARON...
...THERE ARE NO MALES AMONG YOUR GOSK.
NO.
I CANNOT STAND HAVING MALE LANDERS AROUND ME.
Smile
YET ANOTHER REASON TO DISLIKE YOU.

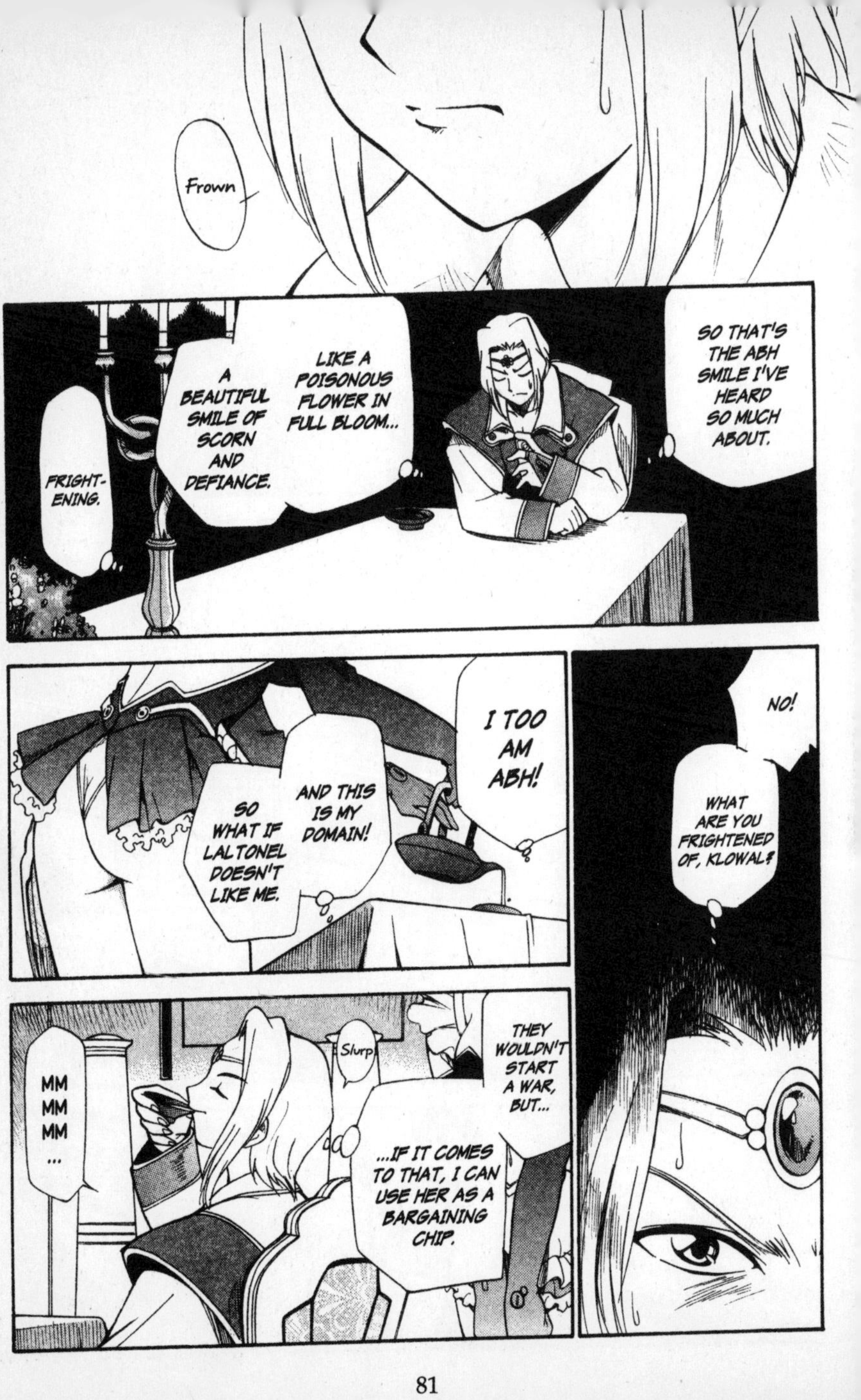
Frown
SO THAT'S THE ABH SMILE I'VE HEARD SO MUCH ABOUT.
LIKE A POISONOUS FLOWER IN FULL BLOOM...
A BEAUTIFUL SMILE OF SCORN AND DEFIANCE.
FRIGHT-ENING.
NO!
WHAT ARE YOU FRIGHTENED OF, KLOWAL?
I TOO AM ABH!
AND THIS IS MY DOMAIN!
SO WHAT IF LALTONEL DOESN'T LIKE ME.
THEY WOULDN'T START A WAR, BUT...
...IF IT COMES TO THAT, I CAN USE HER AS A BARGAINING CHIP.
Slurp
MM MM MM ...

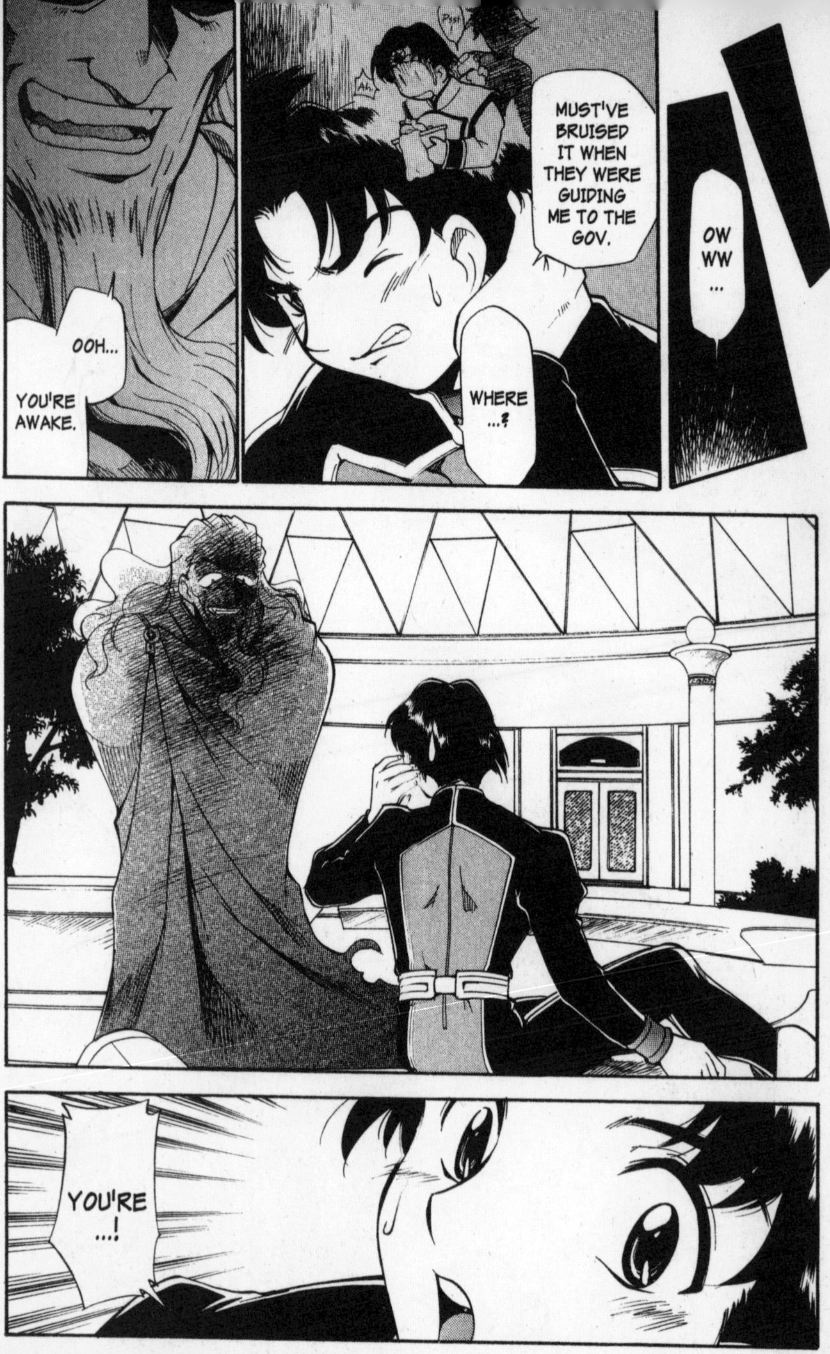

OW WW ...
Psst
Ah
MUST'VE BRUISED IT WHEN THEY WERE GUIDING ME TO THE GOV.
WHERE ...?
OOH...
YOU'RE AWAKE.
YOU'RE ...!

Chapter 3
Pride of the Abh

PAL LEPENEW

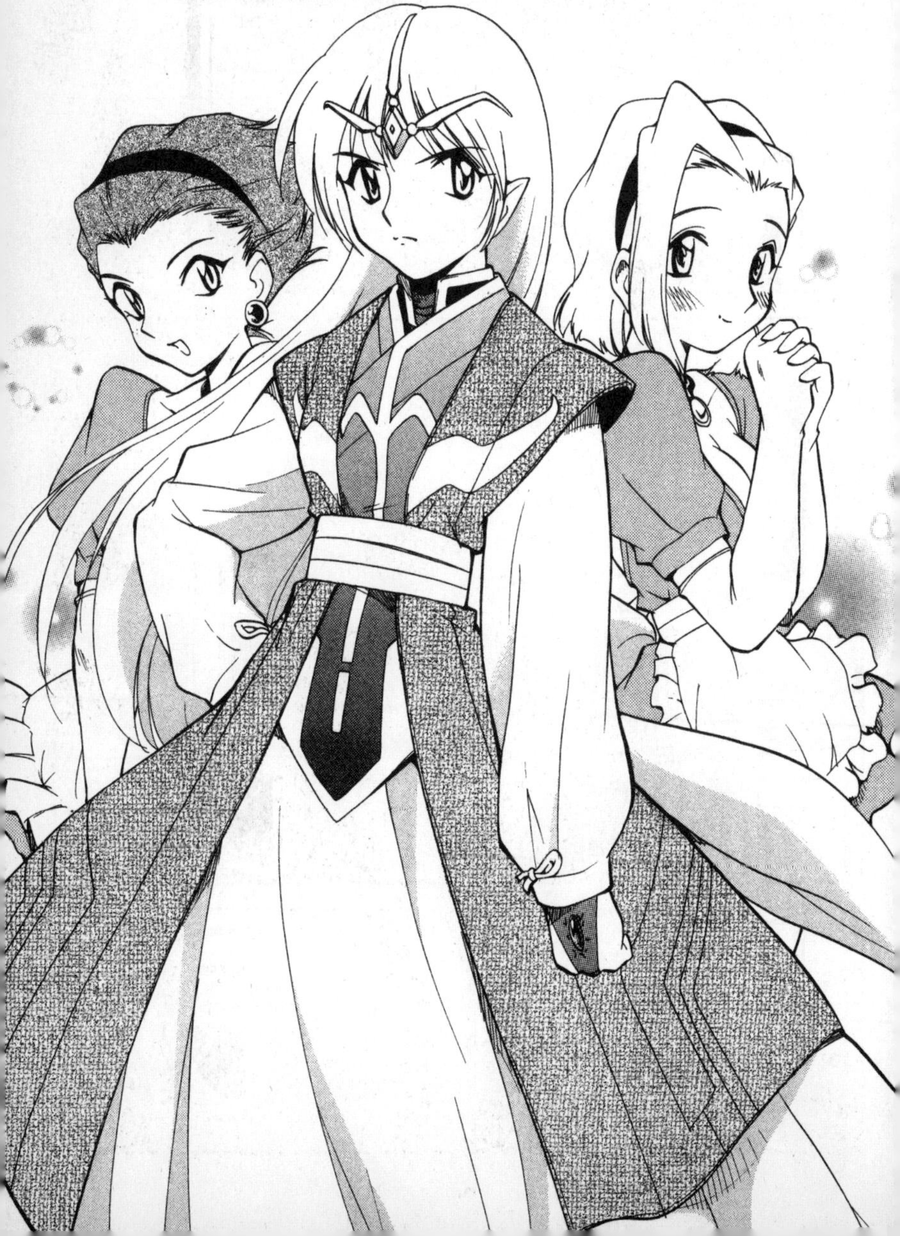

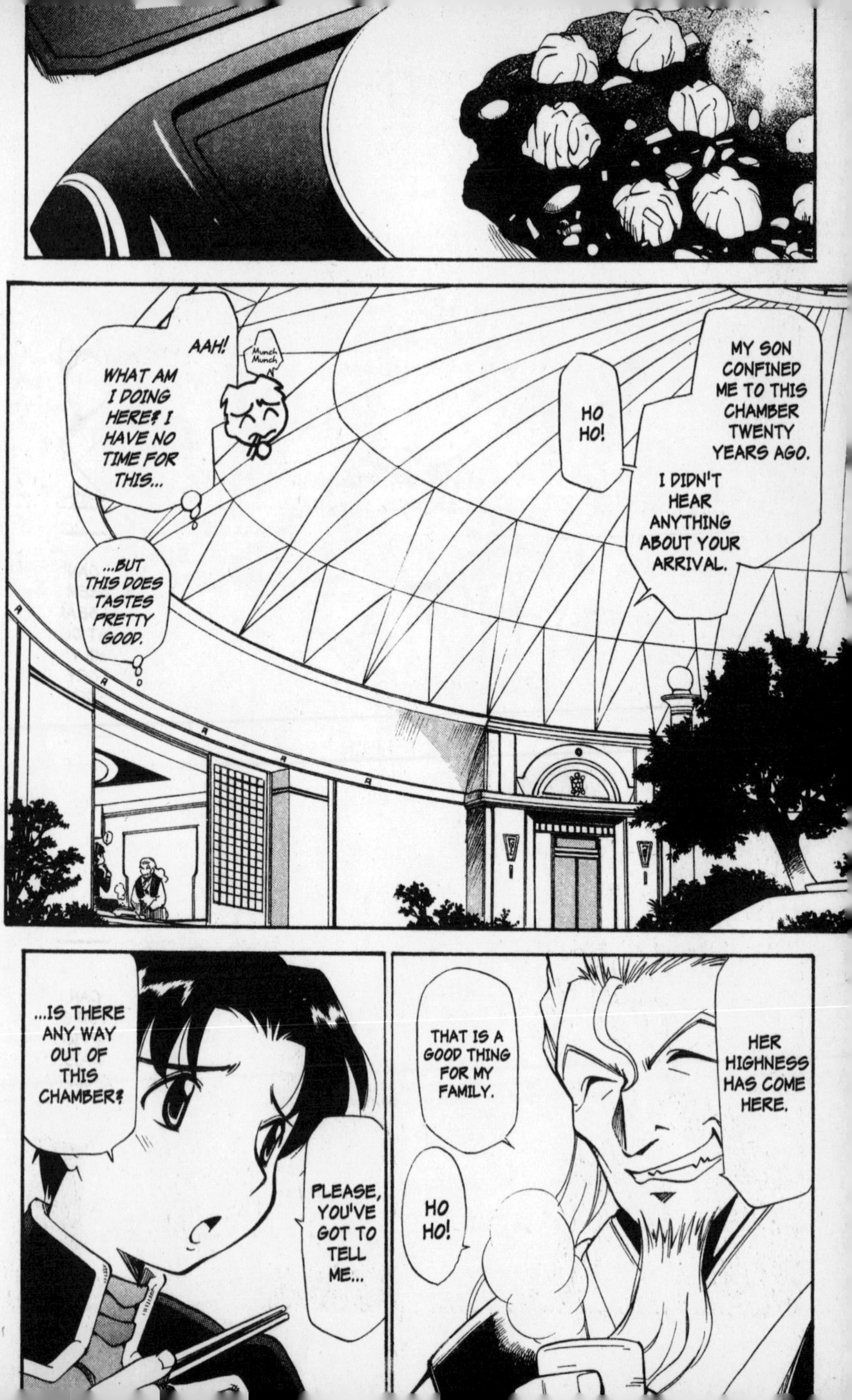
MY SON CONFINED ME TO THIS CHAMBER TWENTY YEARS AGO.
I DIDN'T HEAR ANYTHING ABOUT YOUR ARRIVAL.
HO HO!
AAH! WHAT AM I DOING HERE? I HAVE NO TIME FOR THIS...
Munch Munch
...BUT THIS DOES TASTES PRETTY GOOD.
HER HIGHNESS HAS COME HERE.
THAT IS A GOOD THING FOR MY FAMILY.
HO HO!
...IS THERE ANY WAY OUT OF THIS CHAMBER?
PLEASE, YOU'VE GOT TO TELL ME...

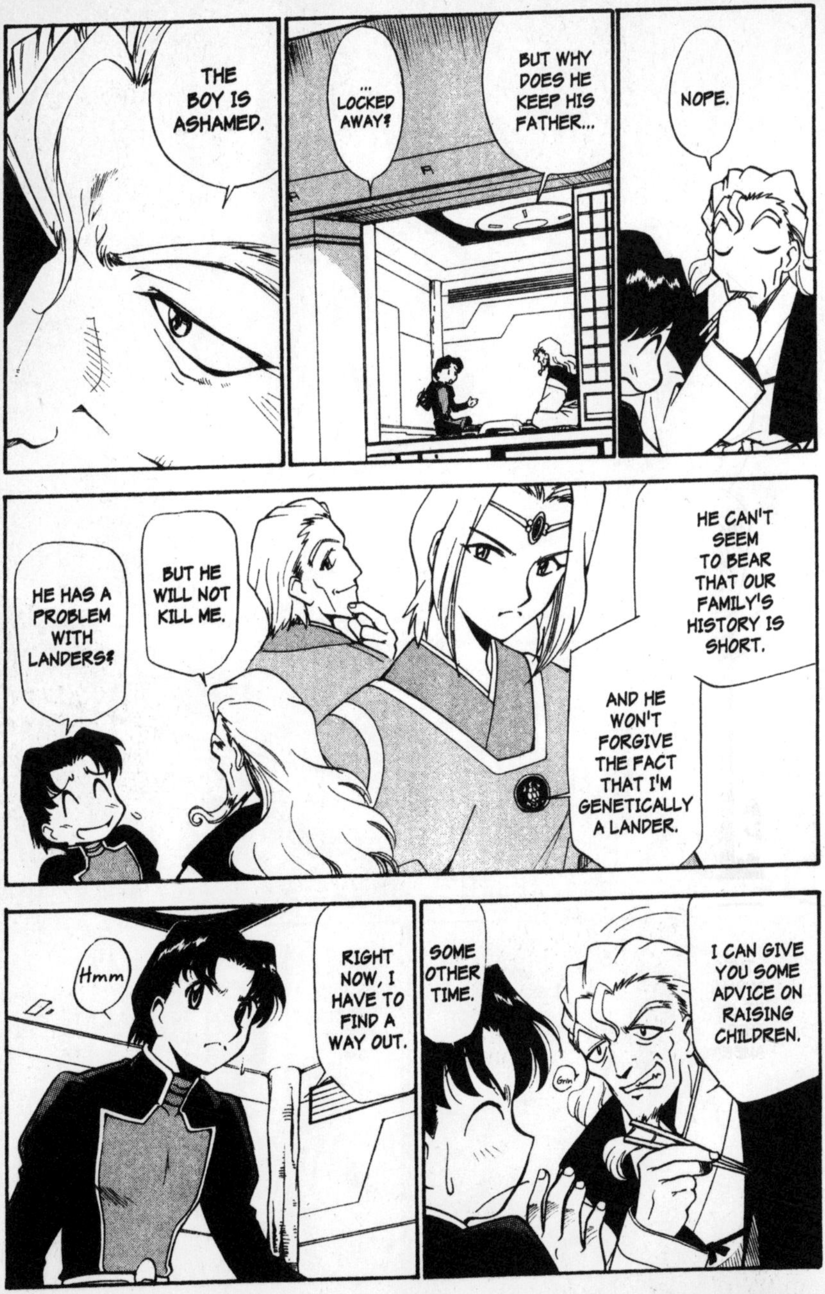
NOPE.
BUT WHY DOES HE KEEP HIS FATHER...
...LOCKED AWAY?
THE BOY IS ASHAMED.
HE CAN'T SEEM TO BEAR THAT OUR FAMILY'S HISTORY IS SHORT.
AND HE WON'T FORGIVE THE FACT THAT I'M GENETICALLY A LANDER.
BUT HE WILL NOT KILL ME.
HE HAS A PROBLEM WITH LANDERS?
I CAN GIVE YOU SOME ADVICE ON RAISING CHILDREN.
Grin
SOME OTHER TIME.
RIGHT NOW, I HAVE TO FIND A WAY OUT.
Hmm

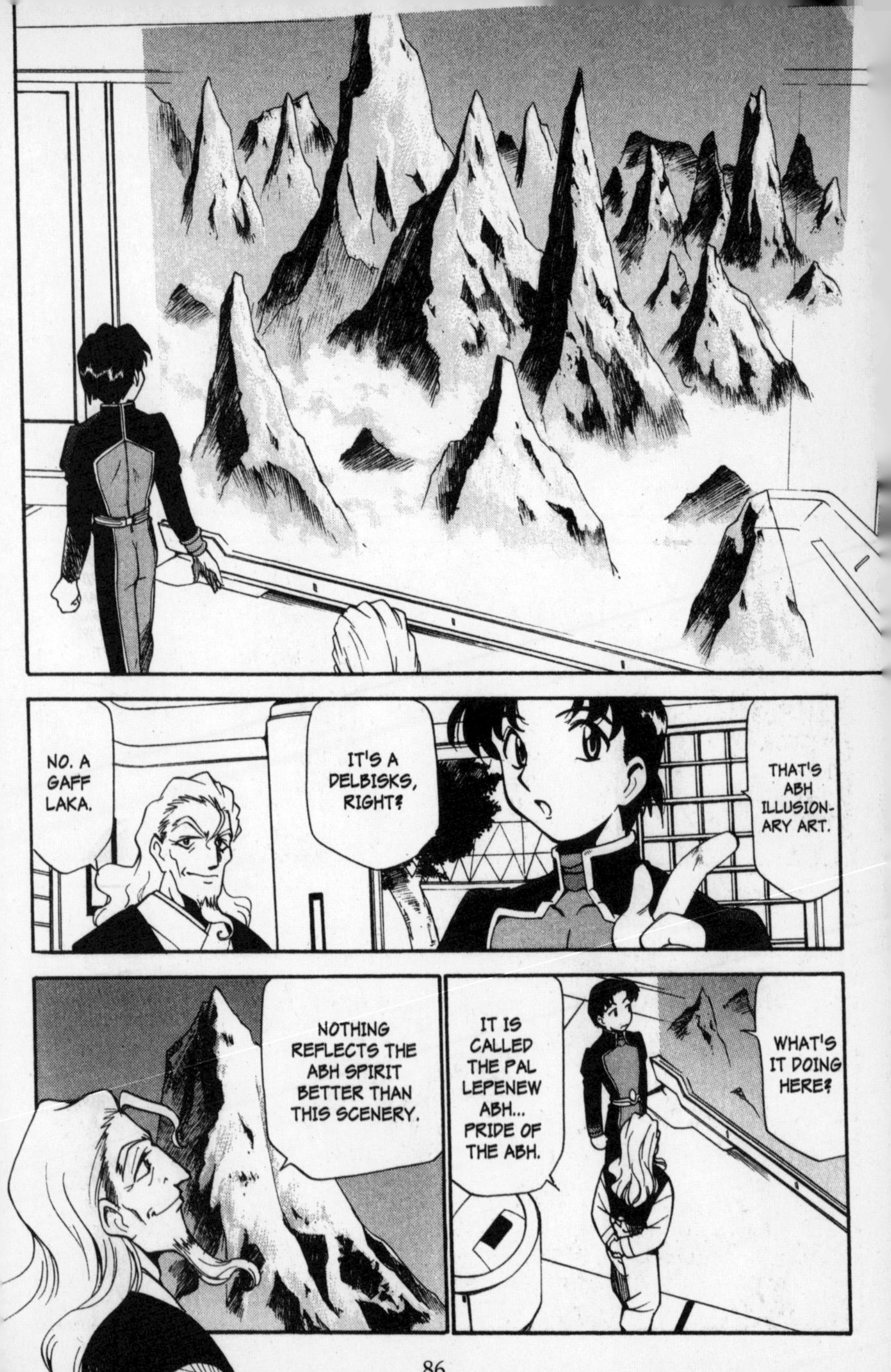
THAT'S ABH ILLUSIONARY ART.
IT'S A DELBISKS, RIGHT?
NO. A GAFF LAKA.
WHAT'S IT DOING HERE?
IT IS CALLED THE PAL LEPENEW ABH... PRIDE OF THE ABH.
NOTHING REFLECTS THE ABH SPIRIT BETTER THAN THIS SCENERY.

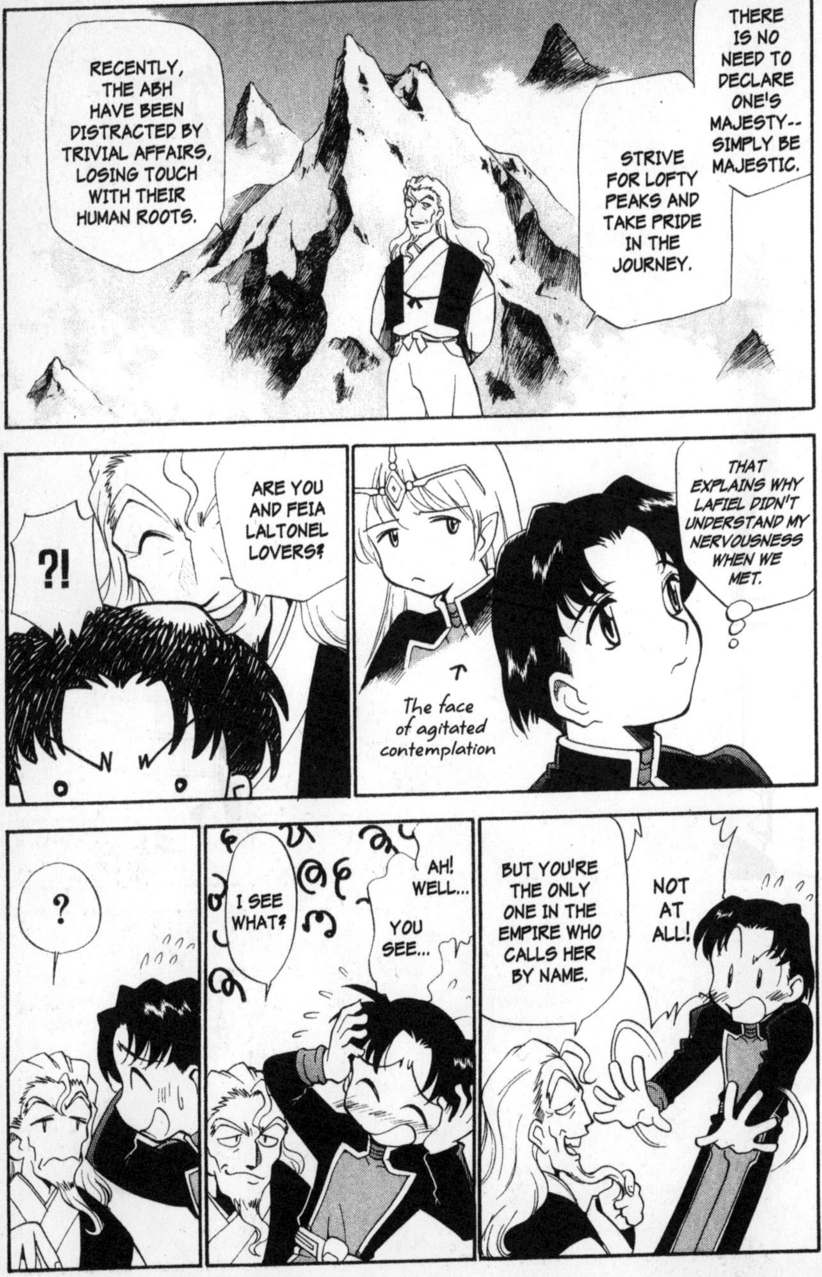
THERE IS NO NEED TO DECLARE ONE'S MAJESTY-- SIMPLY BE MAJESTIC.
STRIVE FOR LOFTY PEAKS AND TAKE PRIDE IN THE JOURNEY.
RECENTLY, THE ABH HAVE BEEN DISTRACTED BY TRIVIAL AFFAIRS, LOSING TOUCH WITH THEIR HUMAN ROOTS.
THAT EXPLAINS WHY LAFIEL DIDN'T UNDERSTAND MY NERVOUSNESS WHEN WE MET.
The face of agitated contemplation
ARE YOU AND FEIA LALTONEL LOVERS?
?!
NOT AT ALL!
BUT YOU'RE THE ONLY ONE IN THE EMPIRE WHO CALLS HER BY NAME.
AH! WELL...
YOU SEE...
I SEE WHAT?
?

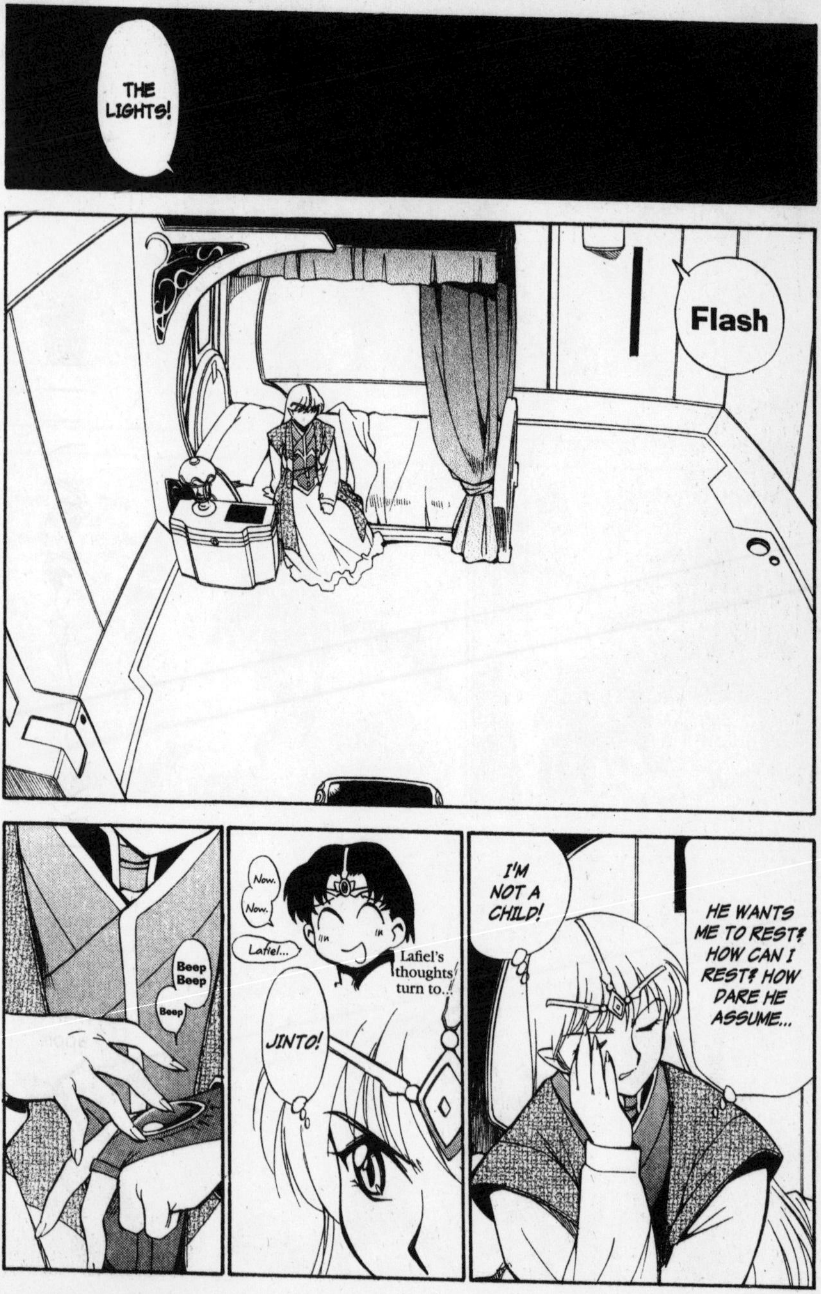

THE LIGHTS!
Flash
HE WANTS ME TO REST? HOW CAN I REST? HOW DARE HE ASSUME...
I'M NOT A CHILD!
Lafiel's thoughts turn to...
JINTO!
Now.
Now.
Lafiel...
Beep Beep
Beep

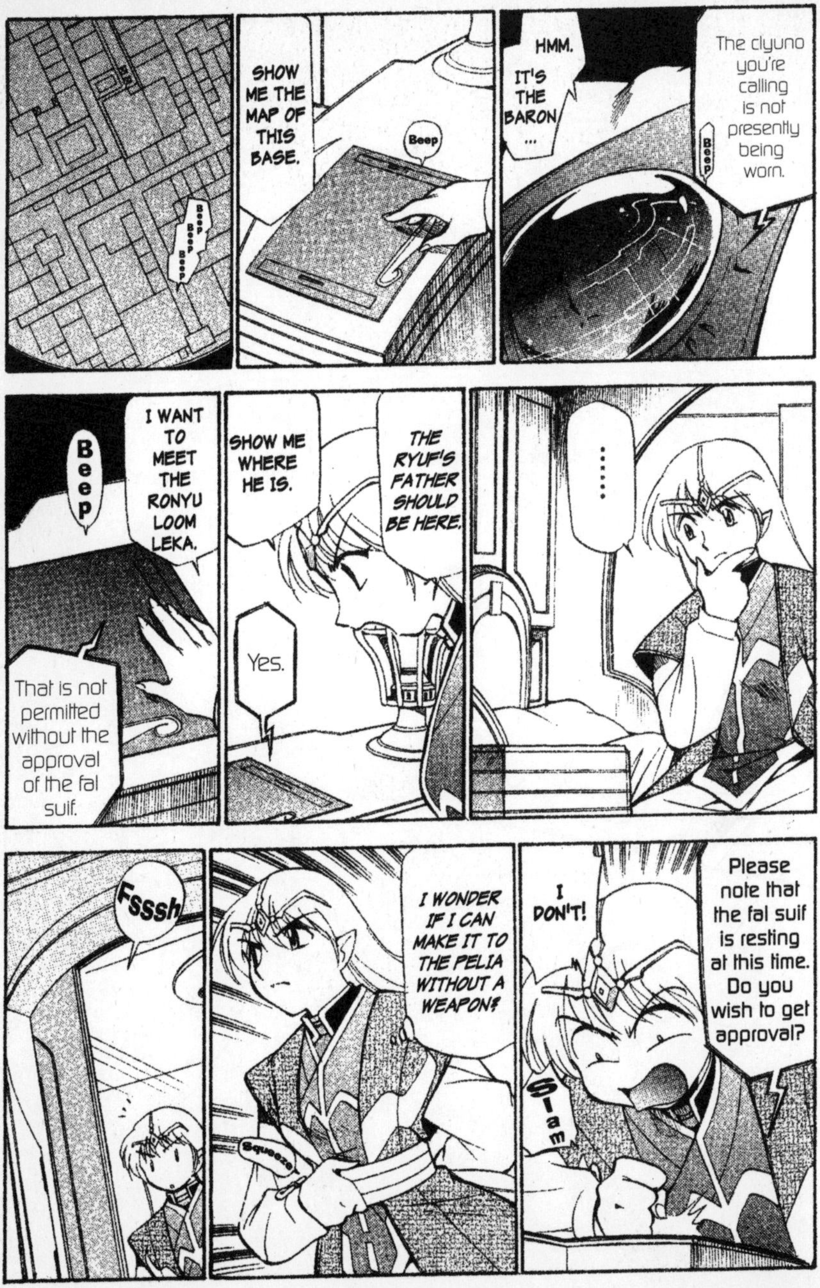
The clyuno you're calling is not presently being worn.
Beep
HMM.
IT'S THE BARON ...
SHOW ME THE MAP OF THIS BASE.
Beep
Beep
Beep
Beep
......
THE RYUF'S FATHER SHOULD BE HERE.
SHOW ME WHERE HE IS.
Yes.
I WANT TO MEET THE RONYU LOOM LEKA.
Beep
That is not permitted without the approval of the fal suif.
Please note that the fal suif is resting at this time. Do you wish to get approval?
I DON'T!
Slam
I WONDER IF I CAN MAKE IT TO THE PELIA WITHOUT A WEAPON?
Squeeze
Fsssh

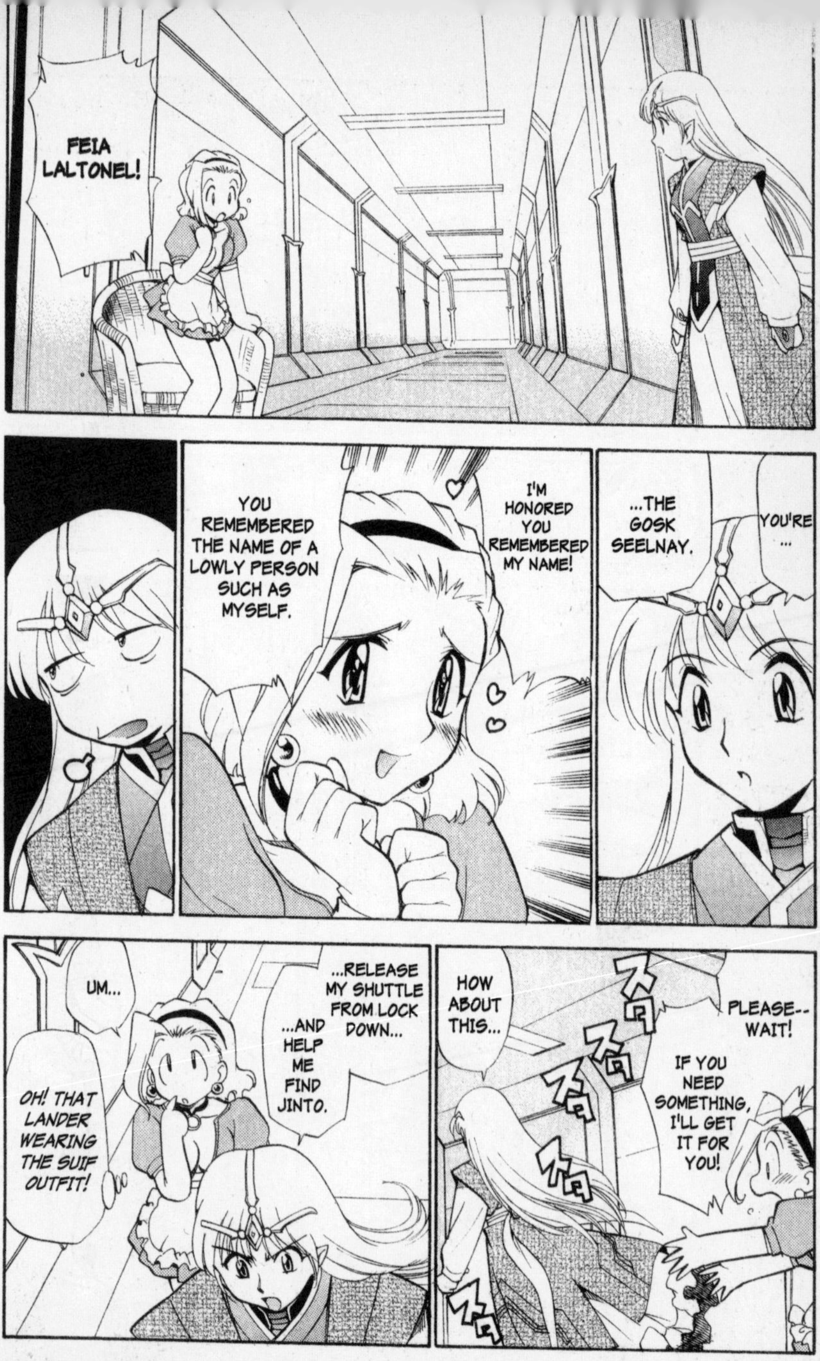
FEIA LALTONEL!
YOU'RE ...
...THE GOSK SEELNAY.
I'M HONORED YOU REMEMBERED MY NAME!
YOU REMEMBERED THE NAME OF A LOWLY PERSON SUCH AS MYSELF.
PLEASE-- WAIT!
IF YOU NEED SOMETHING, I'LL GET IT FOR YOU!
HOW ABOUT THIS...
...RELEASE MY SHUTTLE FROM LOCK DOWN...
...AND HELP ME FIND JINTO.
UM...
OH! THAT LANDER WEARING THE SUIF OUTFIT!

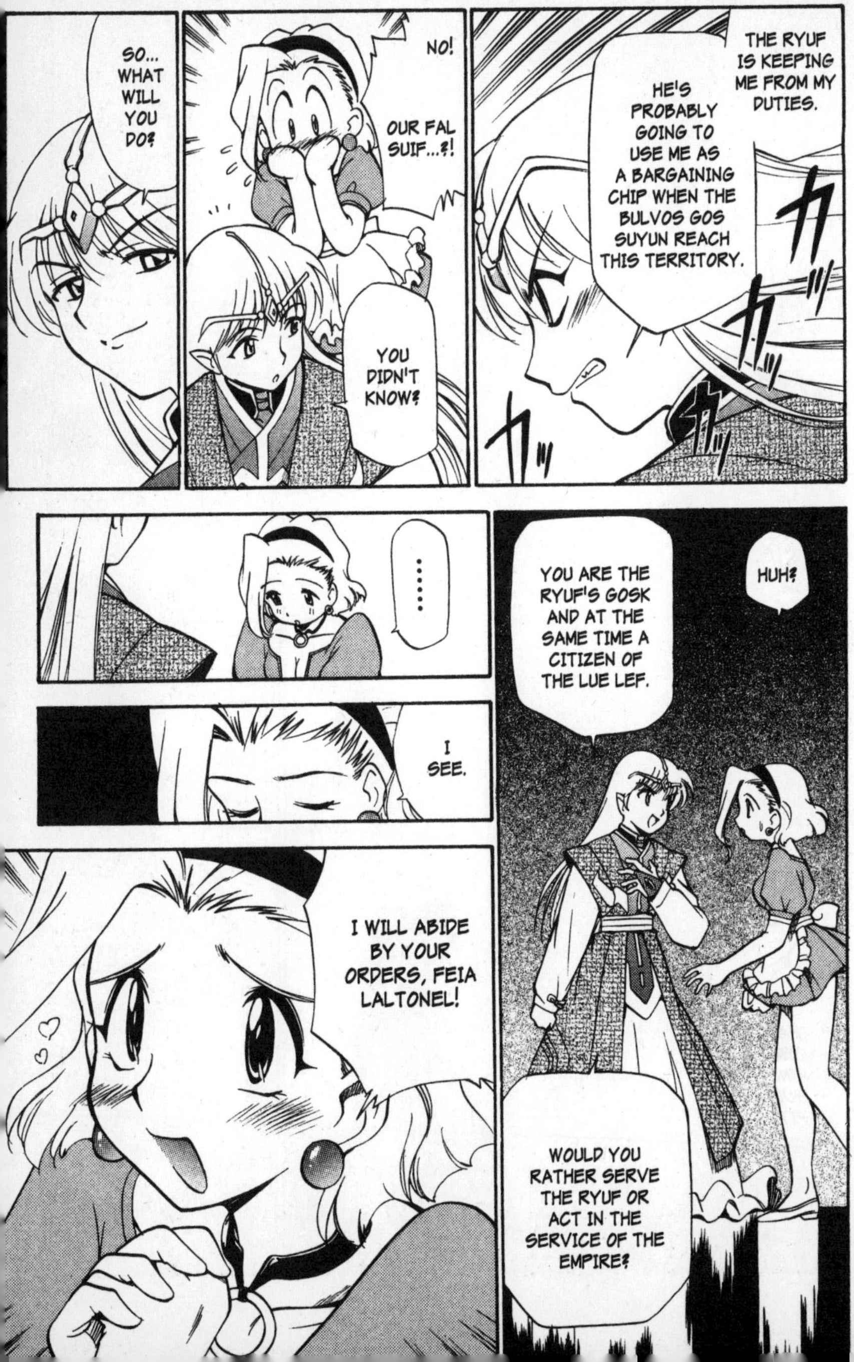
THE RYUF IS KEEPING ME FROM MY DUTIES.
HE'S PROBABLY GOING TO USE ME AS A BARGAINING CHIP WHEN THE BULVOS GOS SUYUN REACH THIS TERRITORY.
NO!
OUR FAL SUIF...?!
YOU DIDN'T KNOW?
SO... WHAT WILL YOU DO?
HUH?
YOU ARE THE RYUF'S GOSK AND AT THE SAME TIME A CITIZEN OF THE LUE LEF.
WOULD YOU RATHER SERVE THE RYUF OR ACT IN THE SERVICE OF THE EMPIRE?
......
I SEE.
I WILL ABIDE BY YOUR ORDERS, FEIA LALTONEL!

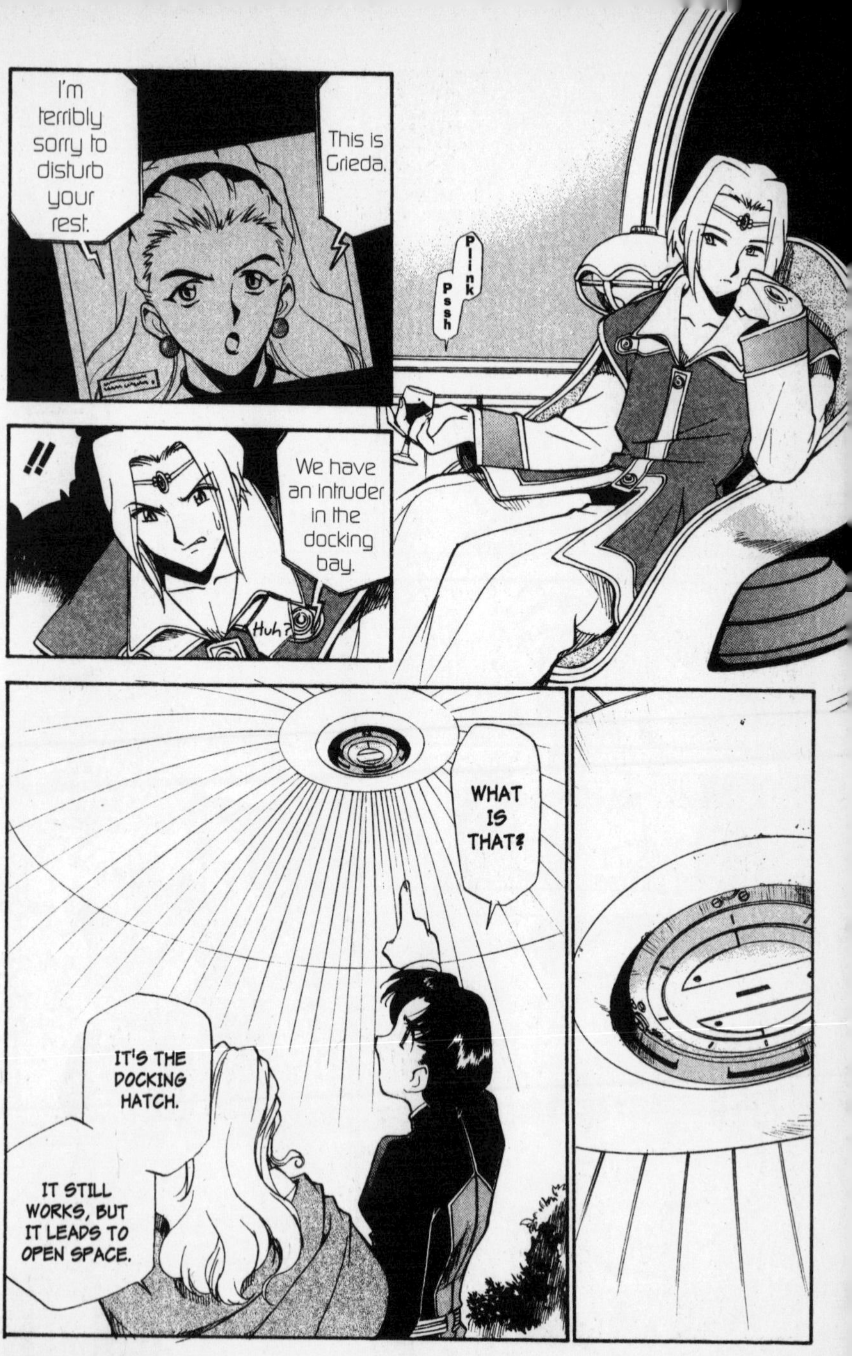
Plink
Pssh
This is Grieda.
I'm terribly sorry to disturb your rest.
We have an intruder in the docking bay.
!!
Huh?
WHAT IS THAT?
IT'S THE DOCKING HATCH.
IT STILL WORKS, BUT IT LEADS TO OPEN SPACE.

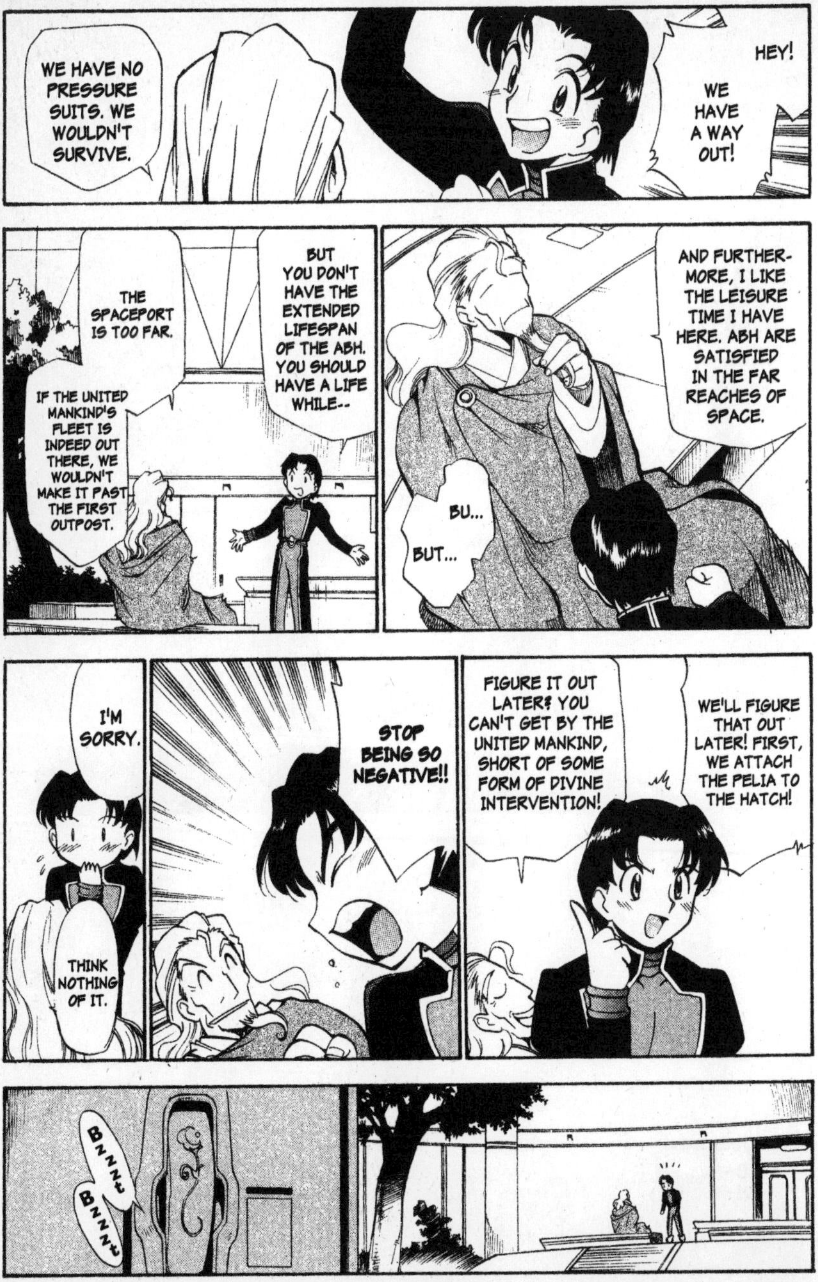
HEY!
WE HAVE A WAY OUT!
WE HAVE NO PRESSURE SUITS. WE WOULDN'T SURVIVE.
AND FURTHER-MORE, I LIKE THE LEISURE TIME I HAVE HERE. ABH ARE SATISFIED IN THE FAR REACHES OF SPACE.
BU...
BUT...
BUT YOU DON'T HAVE THE EXTENDED LIFESPAN OF THE ABH. YOU SHOULD HAVE A LIFE WHILE--
THE SPACEPORT IS TOO FAR.
IF THE UNITED MANKIND'S FLEET IS INDEED OUT THERE, WE WOULDN'T MAKE IT PAST THE FIRST OUTPOST.
WE'LL FIGURE THAT OUT LATER! FIRST, WE ATTACH THE PELIA TO THE HATCH!
FIGURE IT OUT LATER? YOU CAN'T GET BY THE UNITED MANKIND, SHORT OF SOME FORM OF DIVINE INTERVENTION!
STOP BEING SO NEGATIVE!!
I'M SORRY.
THINK NOTHING OF IT.
Bzzzt
Bzzzt

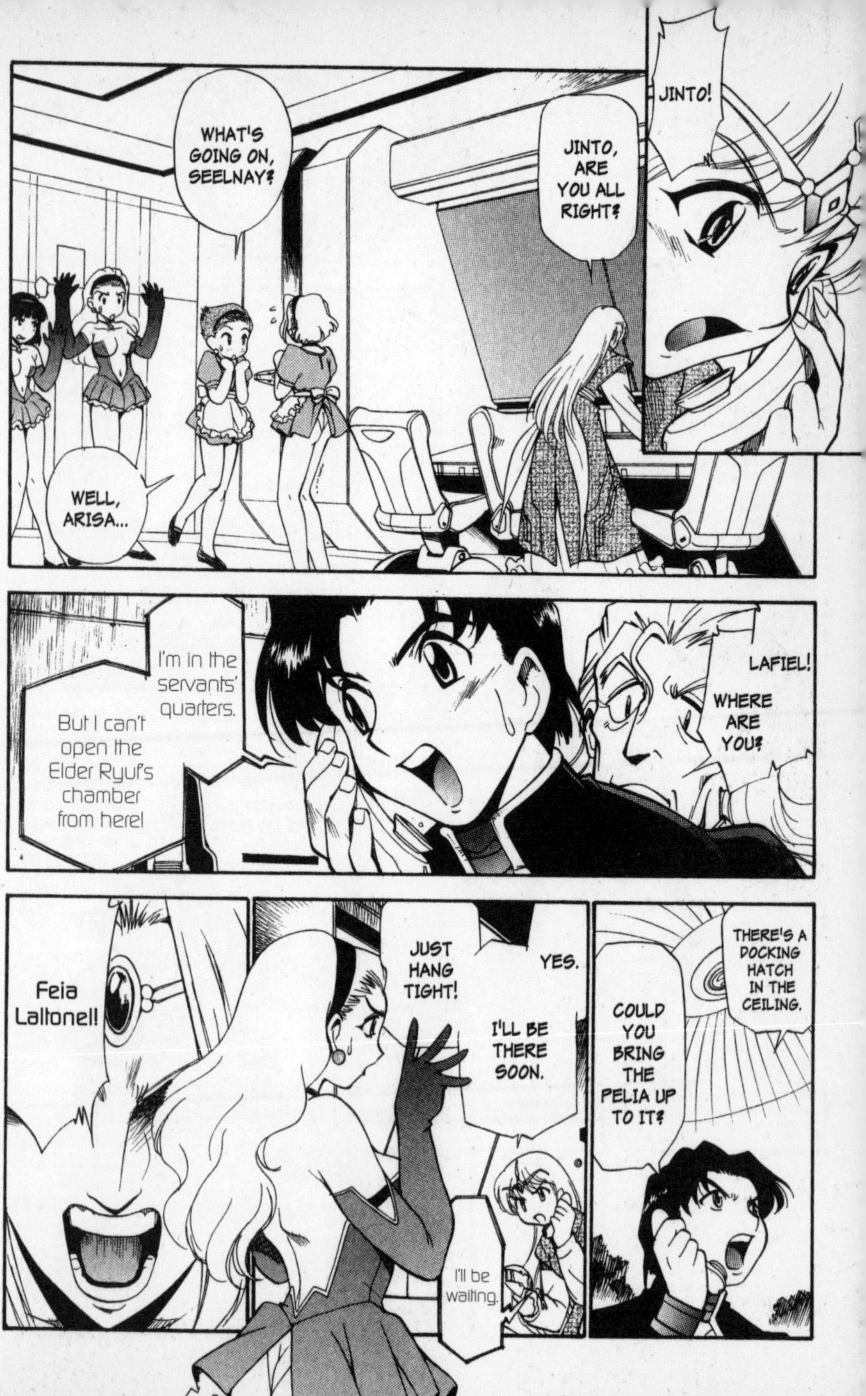
JINTO!
JINTO, ARE YOU ALL RIGHT?
WHAT'S GOING ON, SEELNAY?
WELL, ARISA...
LAFIEL!
WHERE ARE YOU?
I'm in the servants' quarters.
But I can't open the Elder Ryuf's chamber from here!
THERE'S A DOCKING HATCH IN THE CEILING.
COULD YOU BRING THE PELIA UP TO IT?
YES.
I'LL BE THERE SOON.
JUST HANG TIGHT!
I'll be waiting.
Feia Laltonel!

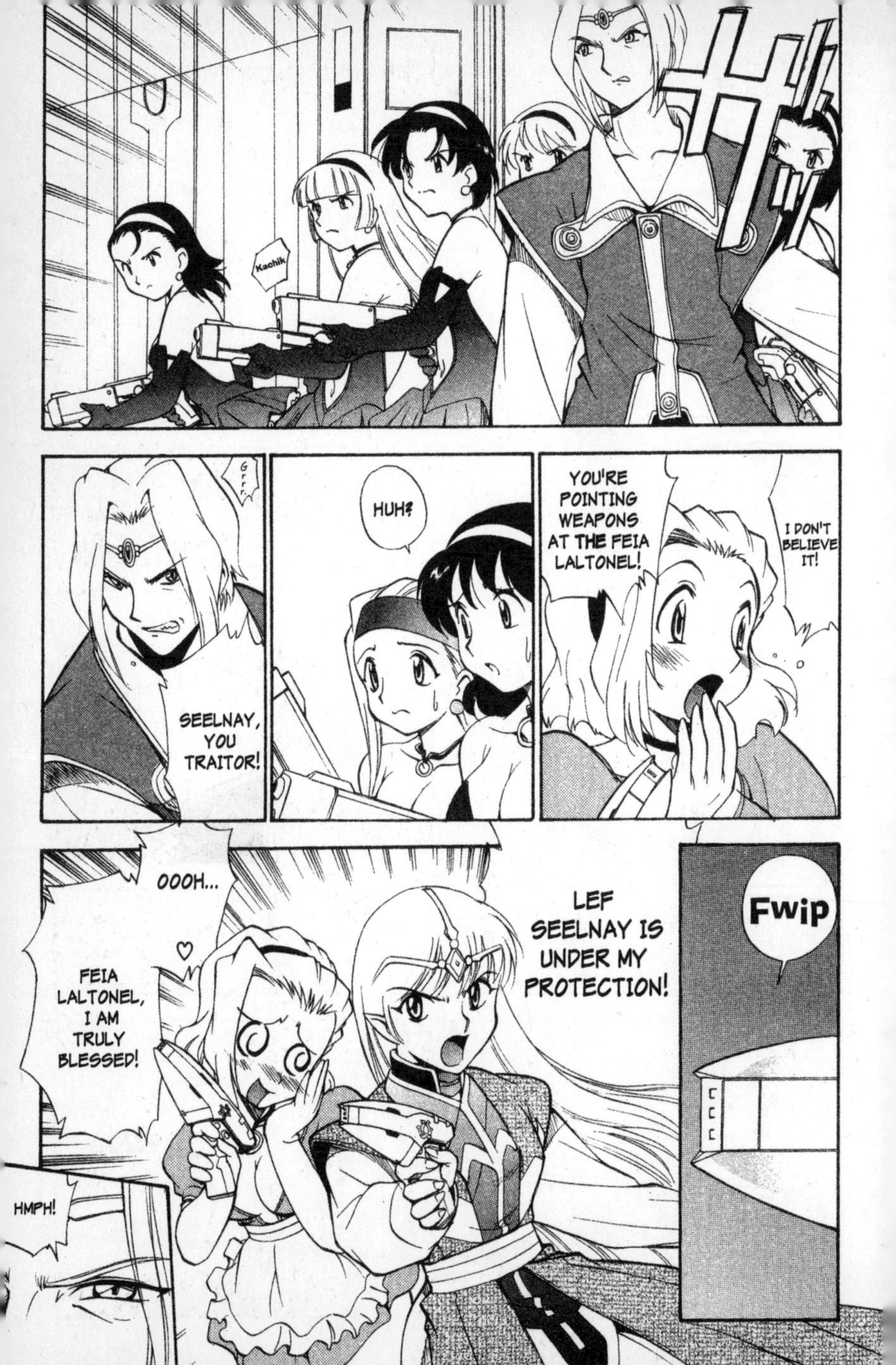
Kachik
I DON'T BELIEVE IT!
YOU'RE POINTING WEAPONS AT THE FEIA LALTONEL!
HUH?
Grrr...
SEELNAY, YOU TRAITOR!
Fwip
LEF SEELNAY IS UNDER MY PROTECTION!
OOOH...
FEIA LALTONEL, I AM TRULY BLESSED!
HMPH!

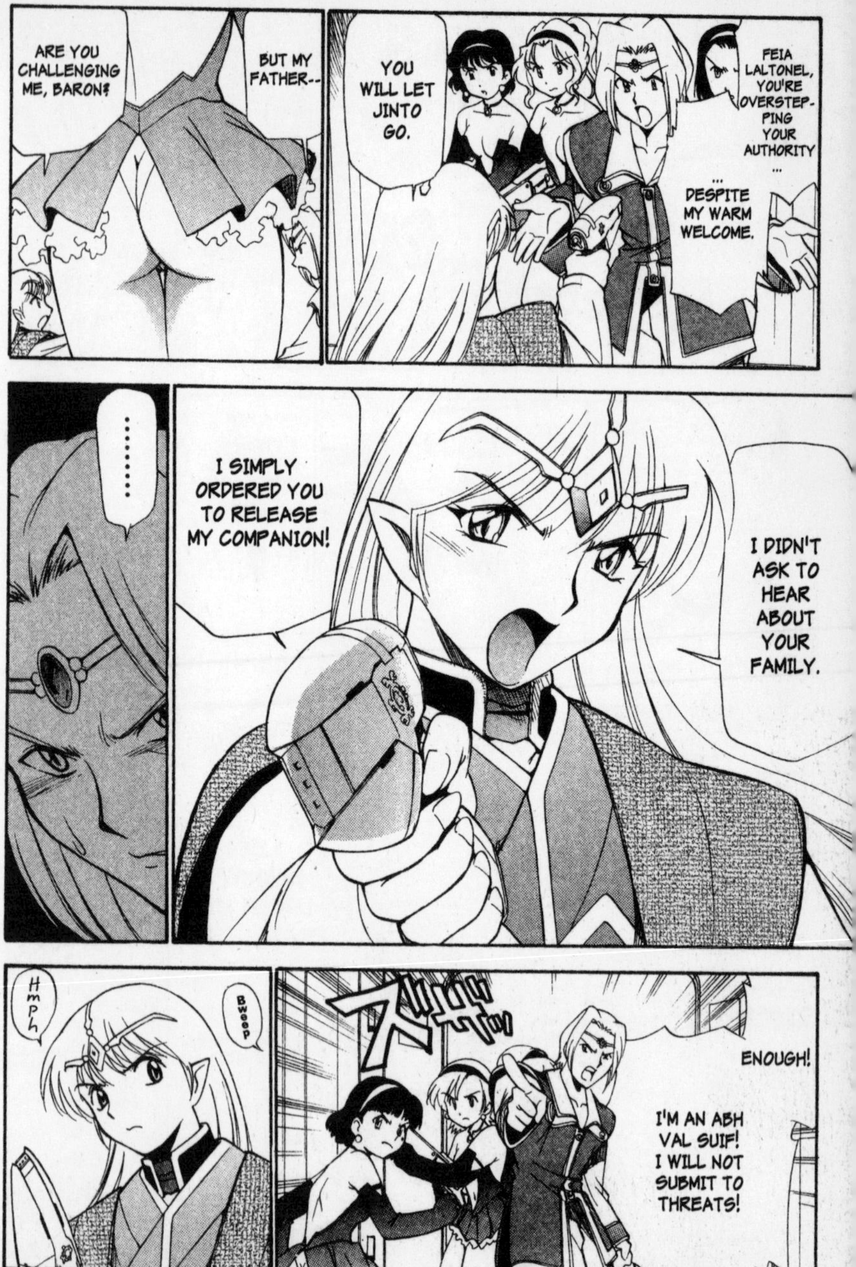
FEIA LALTONEL, YOU'RE OVERSTEPPING YOUR AUTHORITY ...
... DESPITE MY WARM WELCOME.
YOU WILL LET JINTO GO.
BUT MY FATHER--
ARE YOU CHALLENGING ME, BARON?
I DIDN'T ASK TO HEAR ABOUT YOUR FAMILY.
I SIMPLY ORDERED YOU TO RELEASE MY COMPANION!
........!
ENOUGH!
I'M AN ABH VAL SUIF! I WILL NOT SUBMIT TO THREATS!
Bweep
Hmph

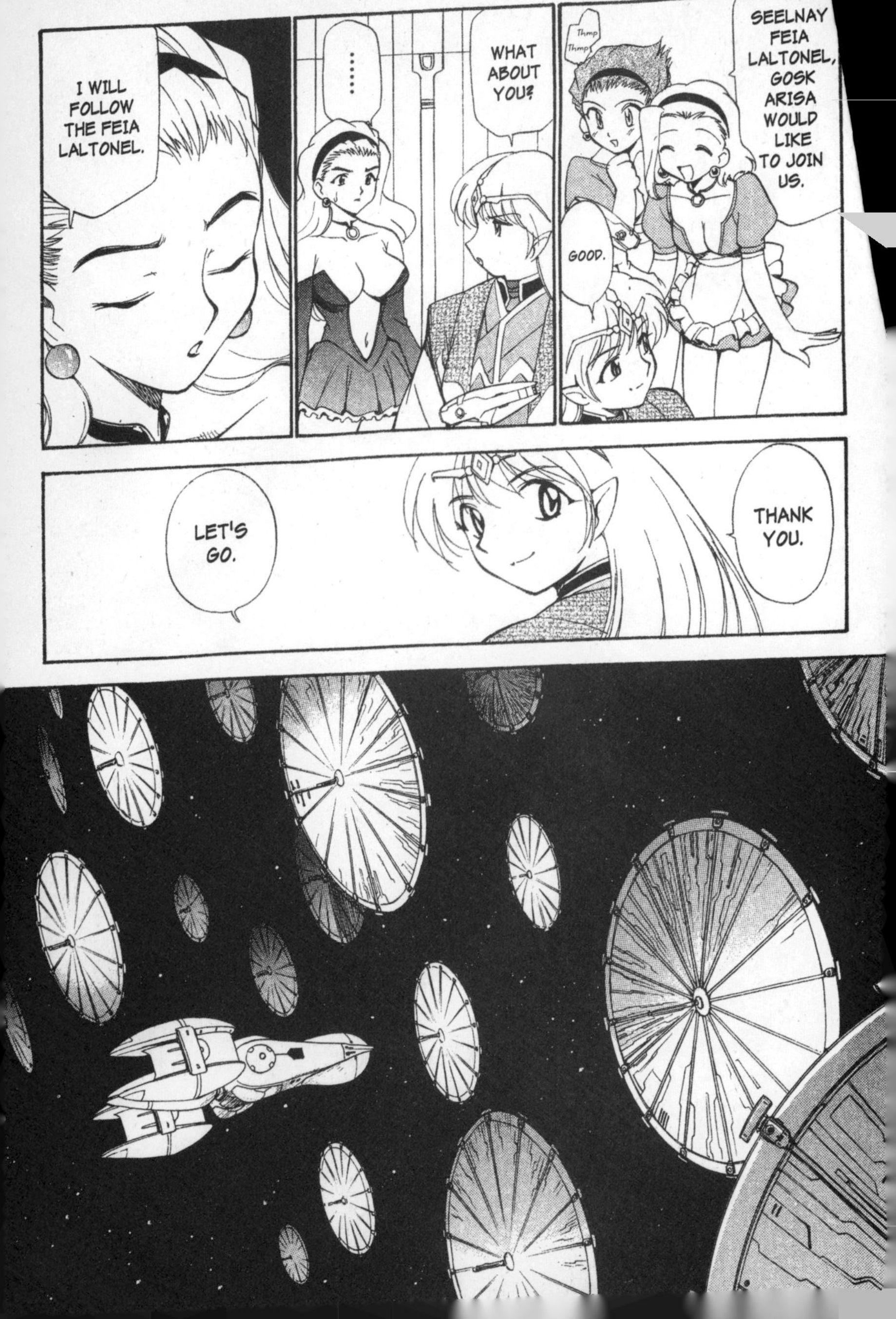
SEELNAY FEIA LALTONEL, GOSK ARISA WOULD LIKE TO JOIN US.
Thmp Thmp
GOOD.
WHAT ABOUT YOU?
......
I WILL FOLLOW THE FEIA LALTONEL.
THANK YOU.
LET'S GO.

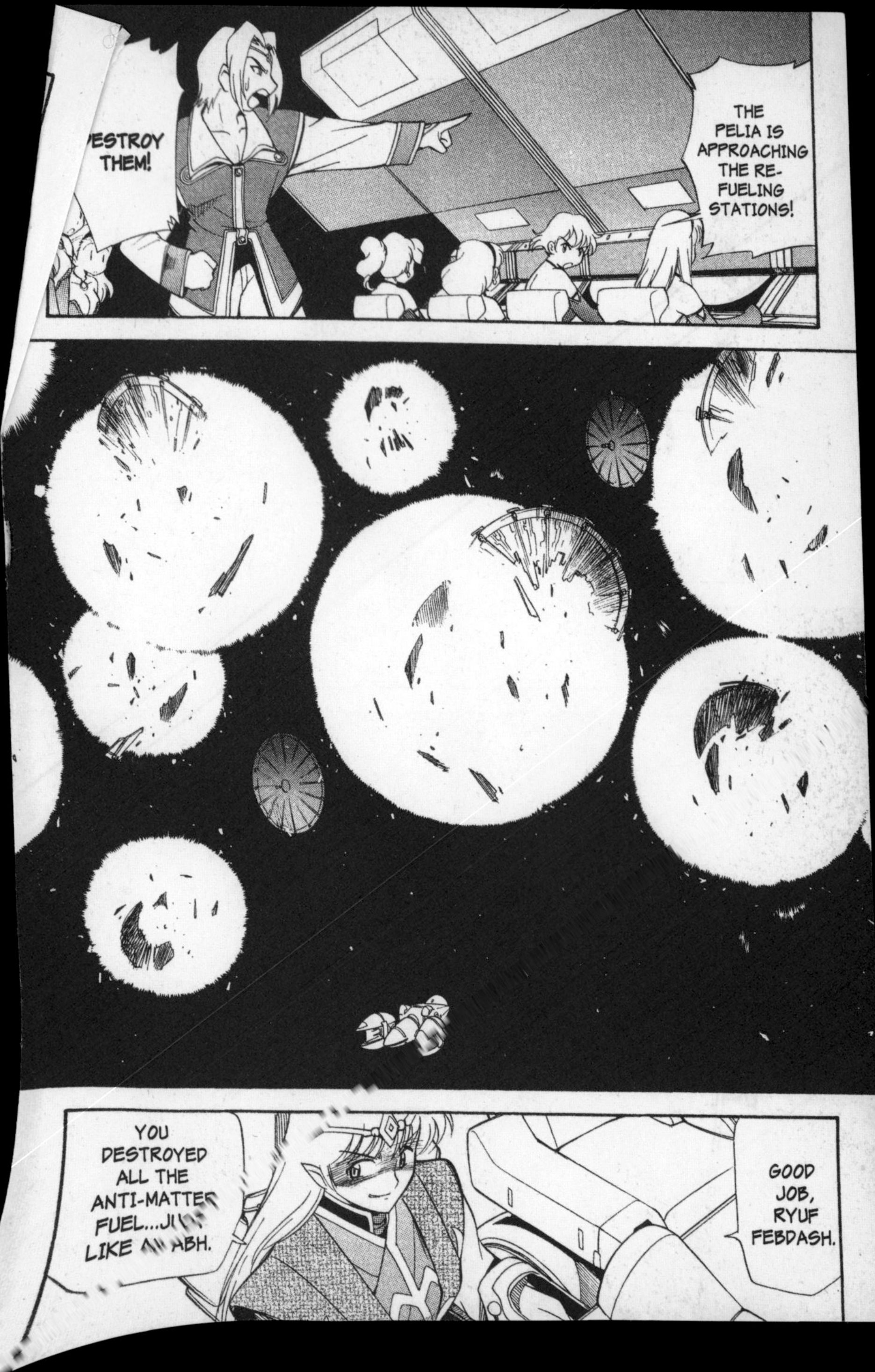
THE PELIA IS APPROACHING THE RE-FUELING STATIONS!
DESTROY THEM!
GOOD JOB, RYUF FEBDASH.
YOU DESTROYED ALL THE ANTI-MATTER FUEL... LIKE

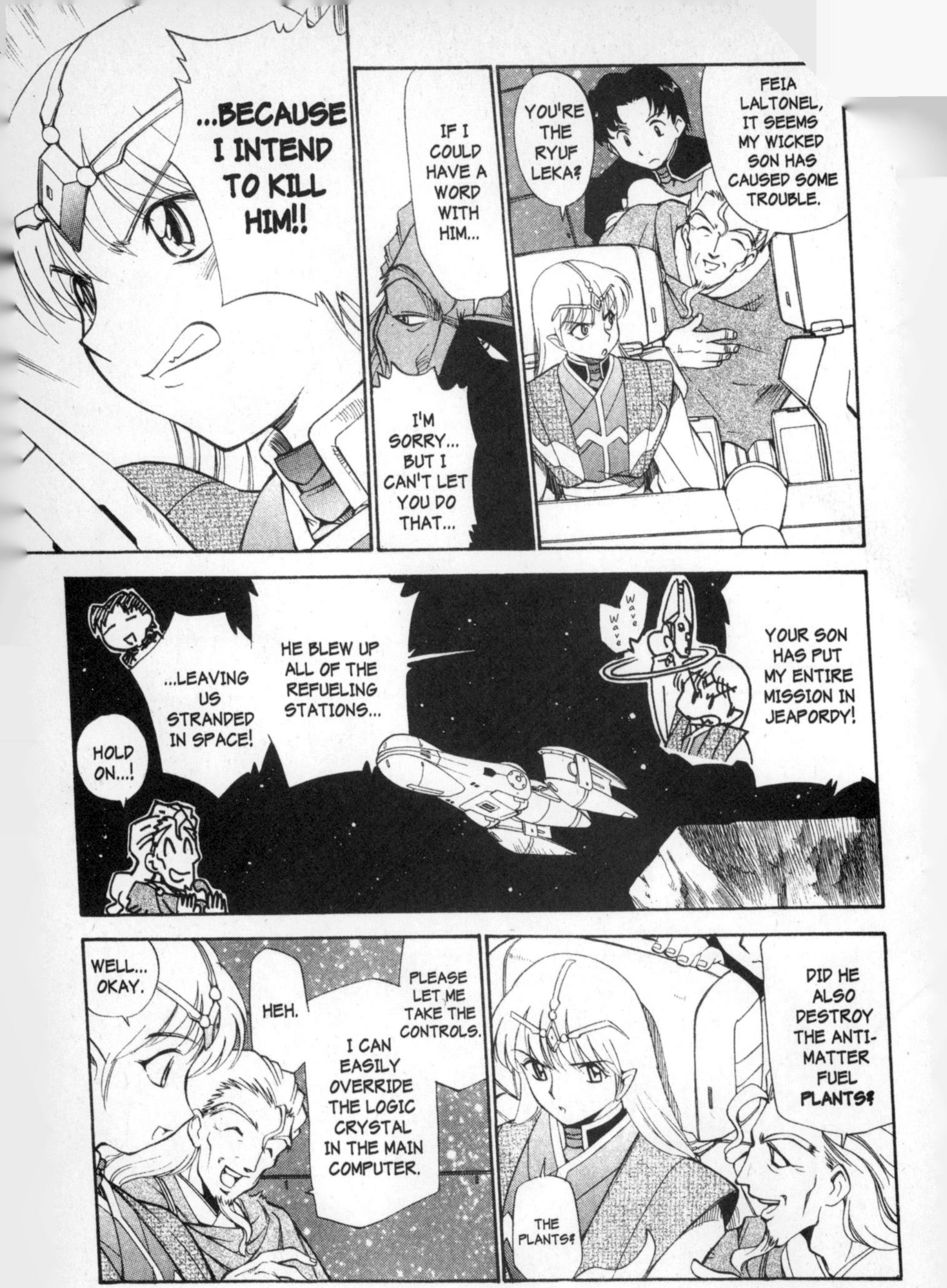
FEIA LALTONEL, IT SEEMS MY WICKED SON HAS CAUSED SOME TROUBLE.
YOU'RE THE RYUF LEKA?
IF I COULD HAVE A WORD WITH HIM...
I'M SORRY... BUT I CAN'T LET YOU DO THAT...
...BECAUSE I INTEND TO KILL HIM!!
YOUR SON HAS PUT MY ENTIRE MISSION IN JEAPORDY!
Wave Wave
HE BLEW UP ALL OF THE REFUELING STATIONS...
...LEAVING US STRANDED IN SPACE!
HOLD ON...!
DID HE ALSO DESTROY THE ANTI-MATTER FUEL PLANTS?
THE PLANTS?
PLEASE LET ME TAKE THE CONTROLS.
HEH.
I CAN EASILY OVERRIDE THE LOGIC CRYSTAL IN THE MAIN COMPUTER.
WELL... OKAY.

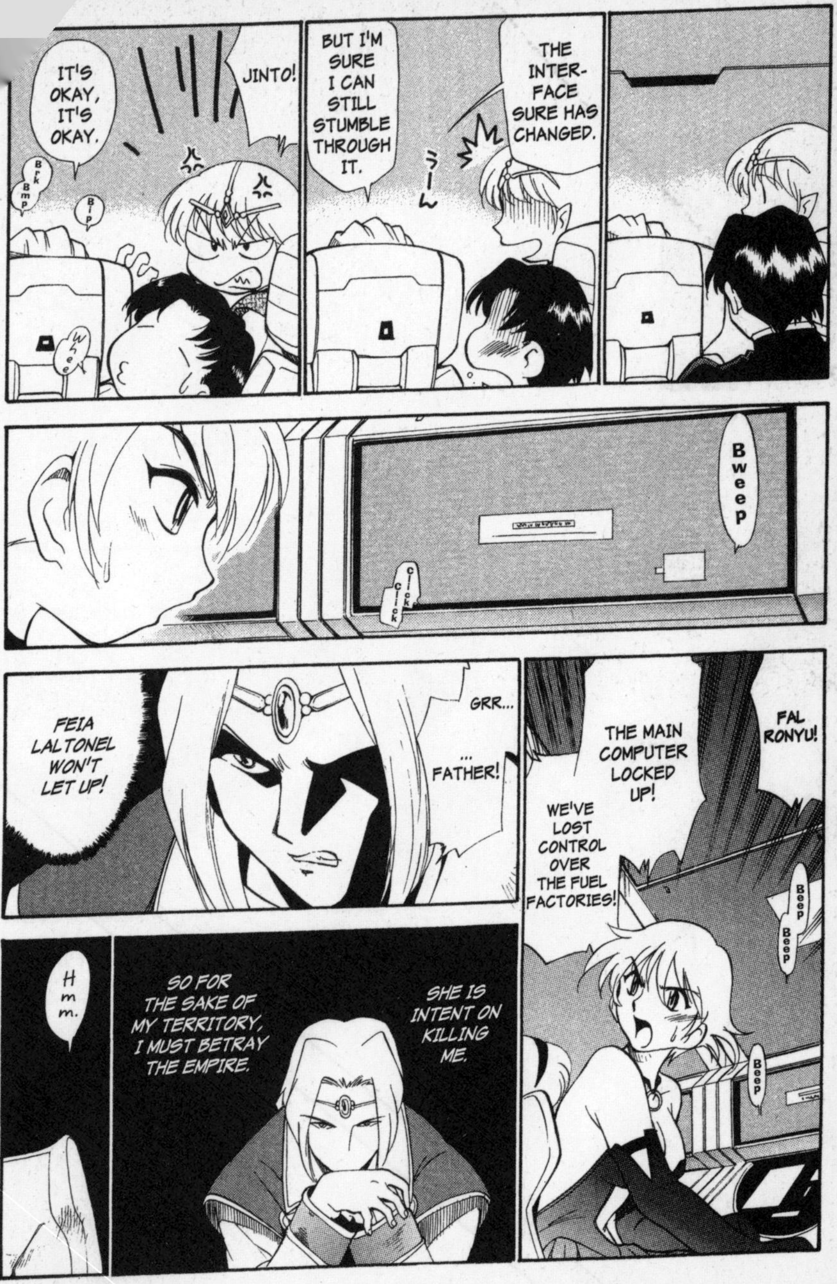
THE INTER-FACE SURE HAS CHANGED.
BUT I'M SURE I CAN STILL STUMBLE THROUGH IT.
ラーん
JINTO!
IT'S OKAY, IT'S OKAY.
Brk Bmp
BiP
Whee
Bweep
Click Click
FAL RONYU!
THE MAIN COMPUTER LOCKED UP!
WE'VE LOST CONTROL OVER THE FUEL FACTORIES!
Beep Beep
Beep
GRR...
... FATHER!
FEIA LALTONEL WON'T LET UP!
SHE IS INTENT ON KILLING ME.
SO FOR THE SAKE OF MY TERRITORY, I MUST BETRAY THE EMPIRE.
Hmm.

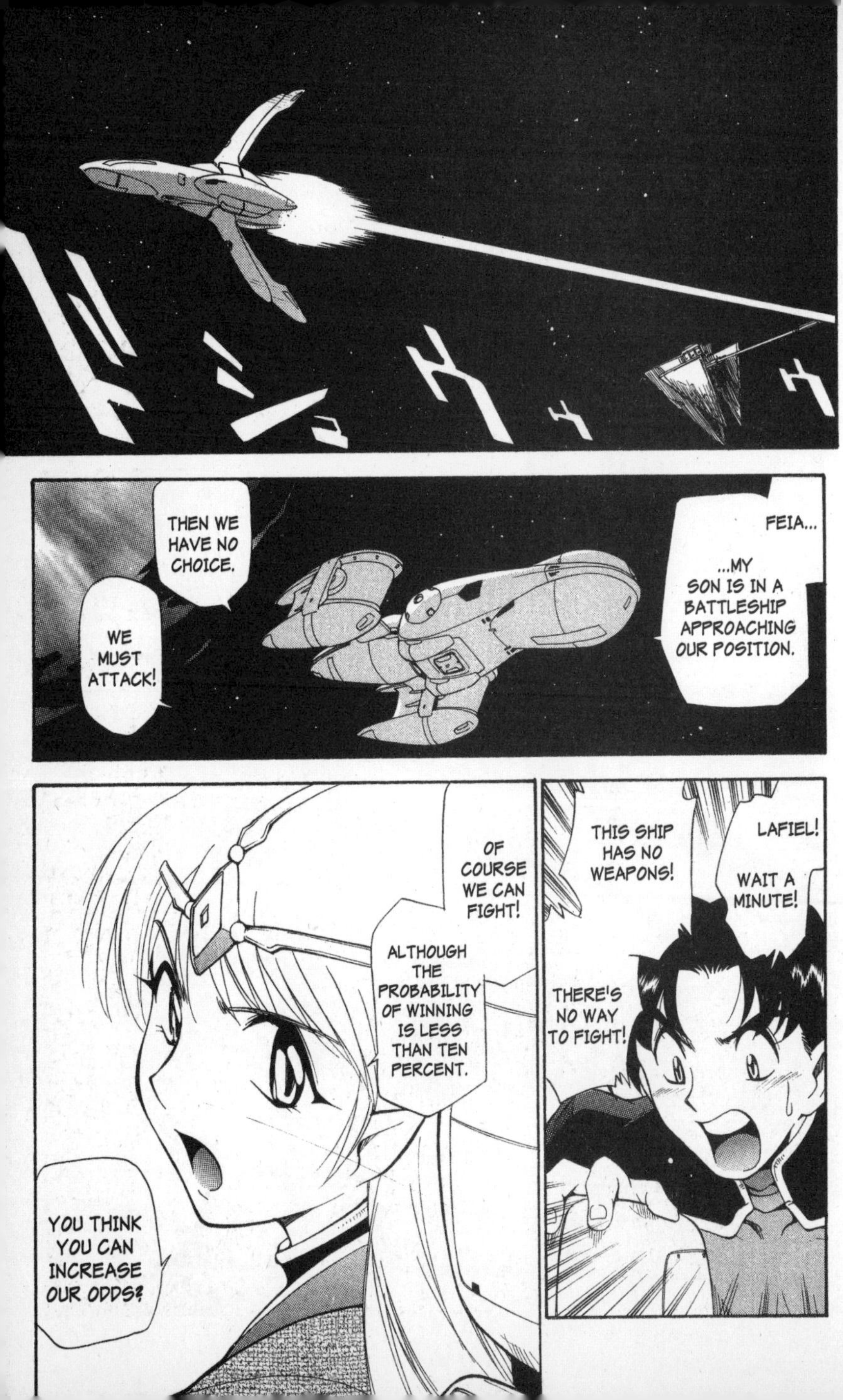
FEIA...
...MY SON IS IN A BATTLESHIP APPROACHING OUR POSITION.
THEN WE HAVE NO CHOICE.
WE MUST ATTACK!
LAFIEL!
WAIT A MINUTE!
THIS SHIP HAS NO WEAPONS!
THERE'S NO WAY TO FIGHT!
OF COURSE WE CAN FIGHT!
ALTHOUGH THE PROBABILITY OF WINNING IS LESS THAN TEN PERCENT.
YOU THINK YOU CAN INCREASE OUR ODDS?

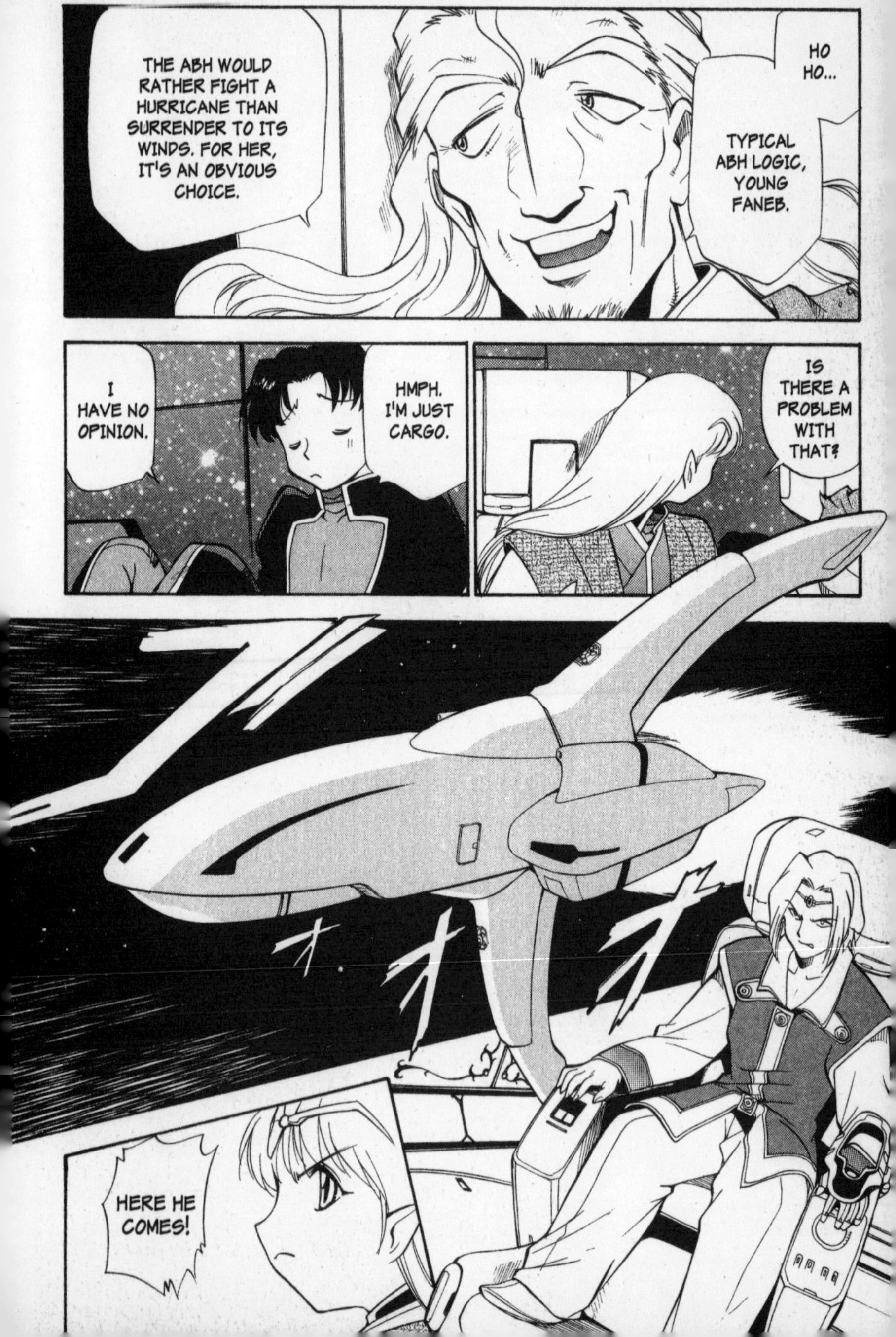
HO HO...
TYPICAL ABH LOGIC, YOUNG FANEB.
THE ABH WOULD RATHER FIGHT A HURRICANE THAN SURRENDER TO ITS WINDS. FOR HER, IT'S AN OBVIOUS CHOICE.
IS THERE A PROBLEM WITH THAT?
HMPH. I'M JUST CARGO.
I HAVE NO OPINION.
HERE HE COMES!

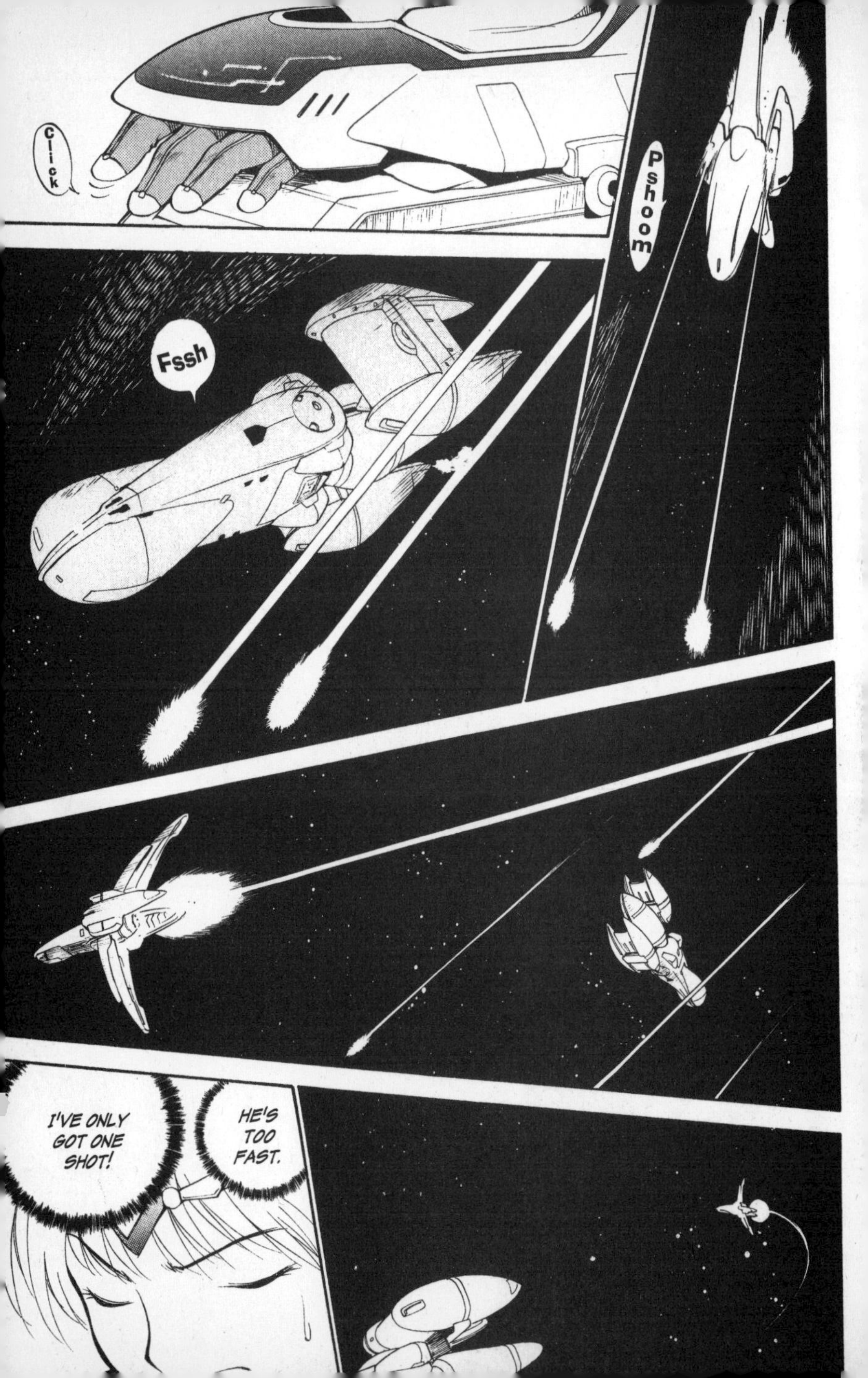
Pshoom
Click
Fssh
HE'S TOO FAST.
I'VE ONLY GOT ONE SHOT!

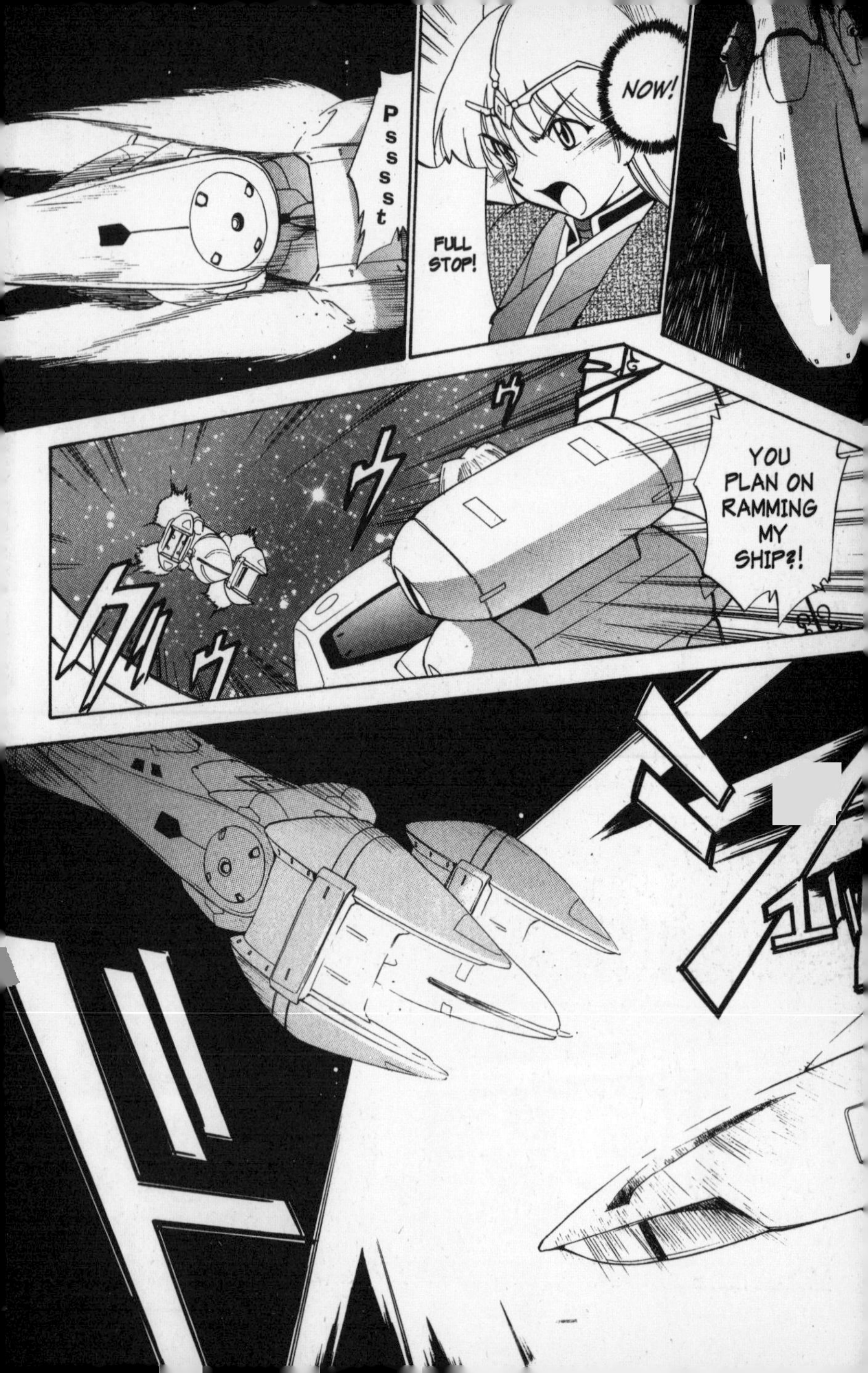
NOW!
FULL STOP!
Psssst
YOU PLAN ON RAMMING MY SHIP?!

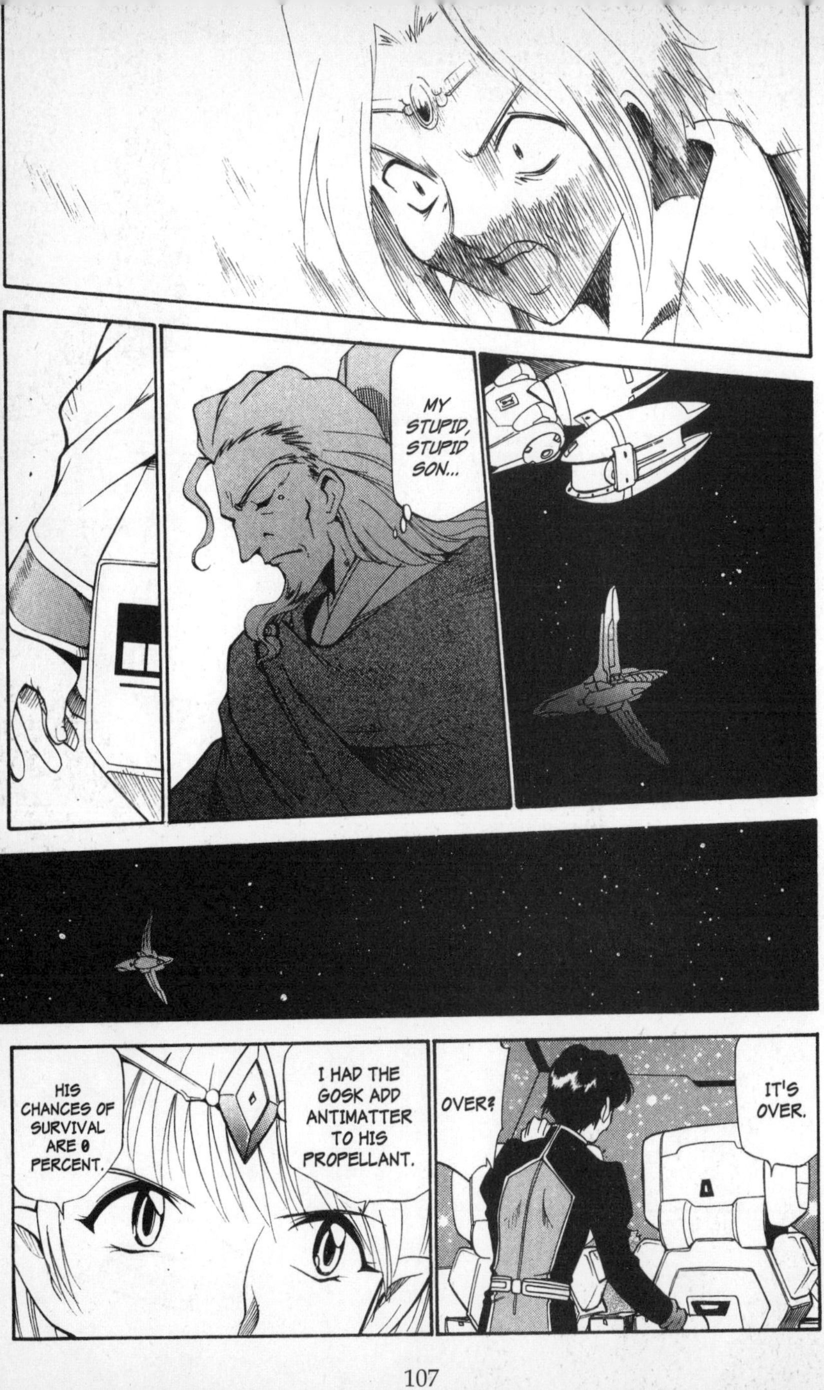
MY STUPID, STUPID SON...
IT'S OVER.
OVER?
I HAD THE GOSK ADD ANTIMATTER TO HIS PROPELLANT.
HIS CHANCES OF SURVIVAL ARE 0 PERCENT.

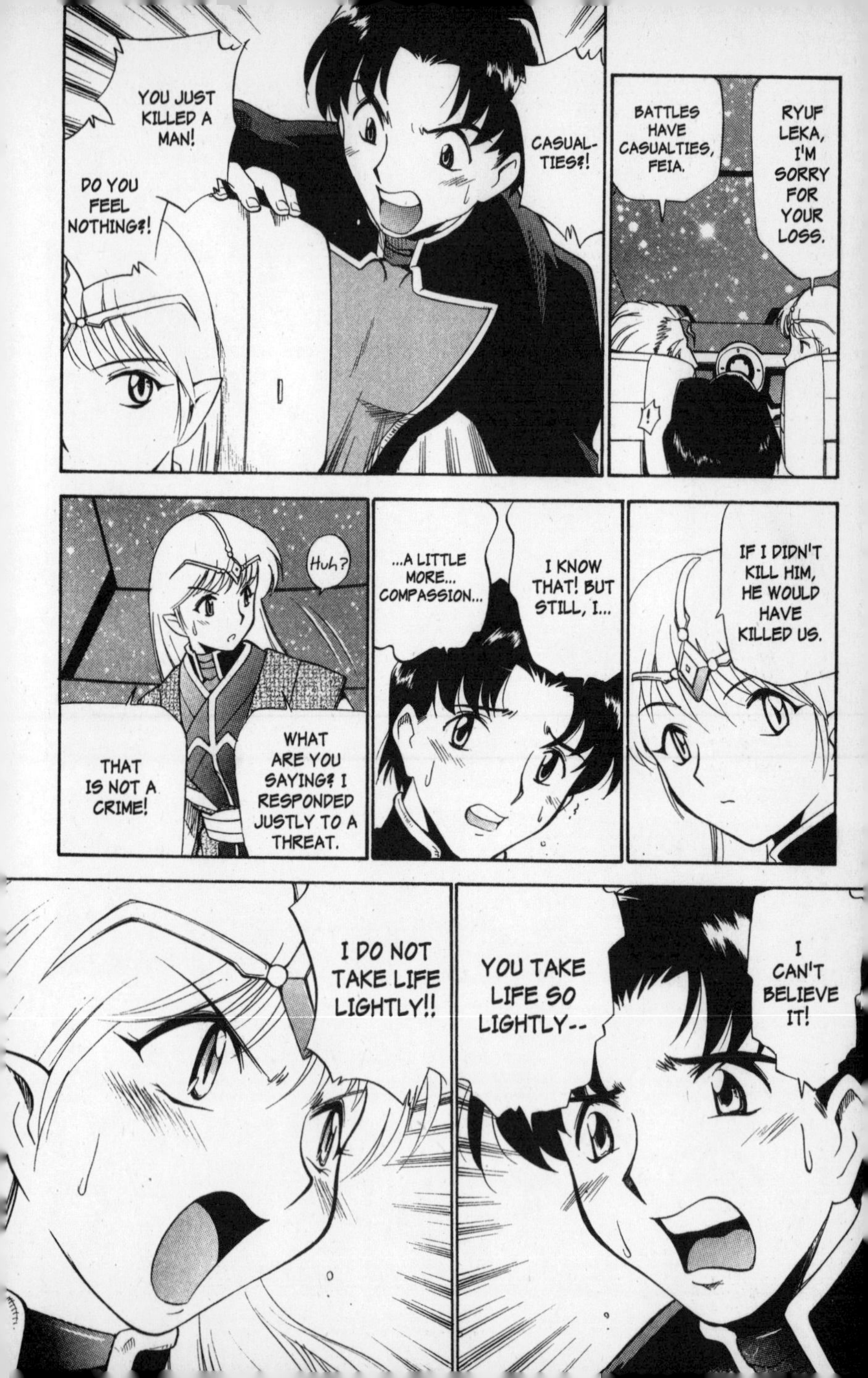
RYUF LEKA, I'M SORRY FOR YOUR LOSS.
BATTLES HAVE CASUALTIES, FEIA.
!
CASUAL-TIES?!
YOU JUST KILLED A MAN!
DO YOU FEEL NOTHING?!
IF I DIDN'T KILL HIM, HE WOULD HAVE KILLED US.
I KNOW THAT! BUT STILL, I...
...A LITTLE MORE... COMPASSION...
Huh?
WHAT ARE YOU SAYING? I RESPONDED JUSTLY TO A THREAT.
THAT IS NOT A CRIME!
I CAN'T BELIEVE IT!
YOU TAKE LIFE SO LIGHTLY--
I DO NOT TAKE LIFE LIGHTLY!!

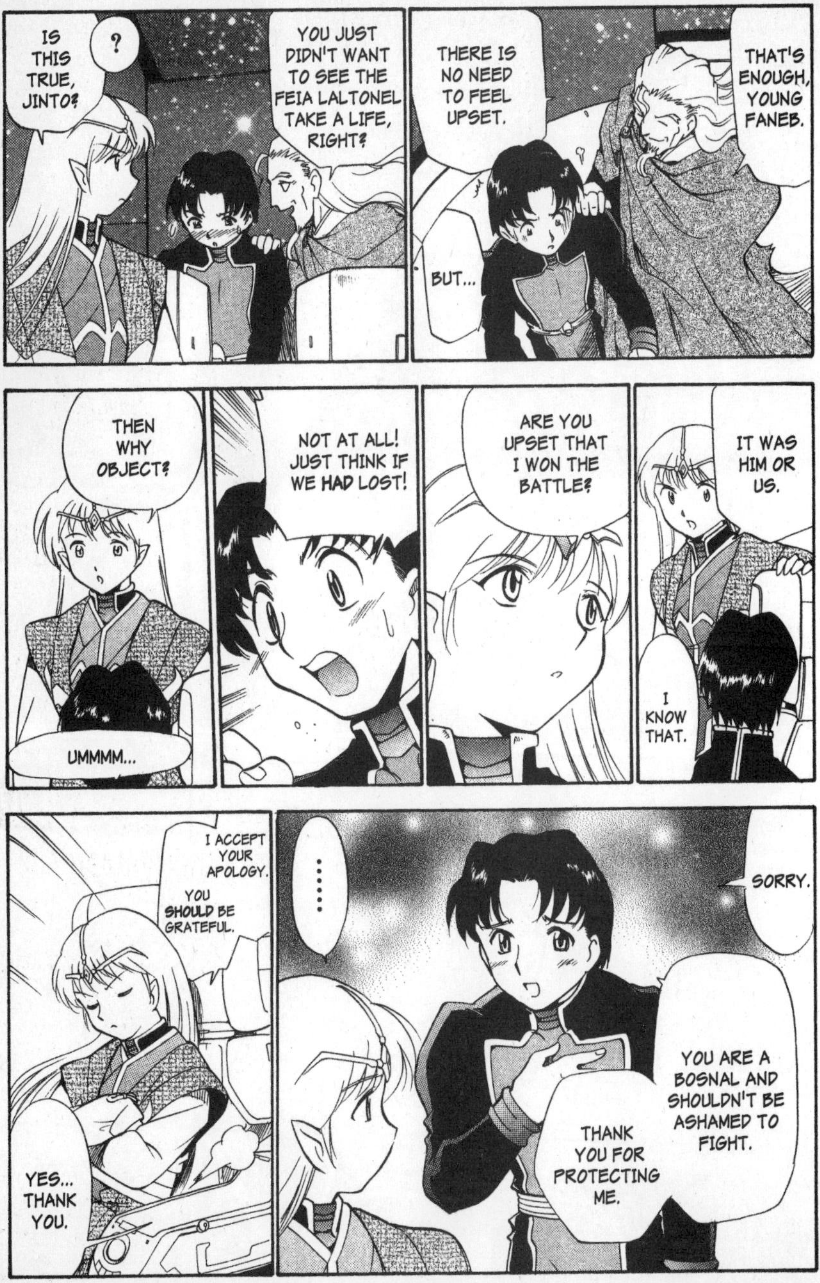
THAT'S ENOUGH, YOUNG FANEB.
THERE IS NO NEED TO FEEL UPSET.
BUT...
YOU JUST DIDN'T WANT TO SEE THE FEIA LALTONEL TAKE A LIFE, RIGHT?
?
IS THIS TRUE, JINTO?
IT WAS HIM OR US.
I KNOW THAT.
ARE YOU UPSET THAT I WON THE BATTLE?
NOT AT ALL! JUST THINK IF WE HAD LOST!
THEN WHY OBJECT?
UMMMM...
SORRY.
......
YOU ARE A BOSNAL AND SHOULDN'T BE ASHAMED TO FIGHT.
THANK YOU FOR PROTECTING ME.
I ACCEPT YOUR APOLOGY.
YOU SHOULD BE GRATEFUL.
YES... THANK YOU.

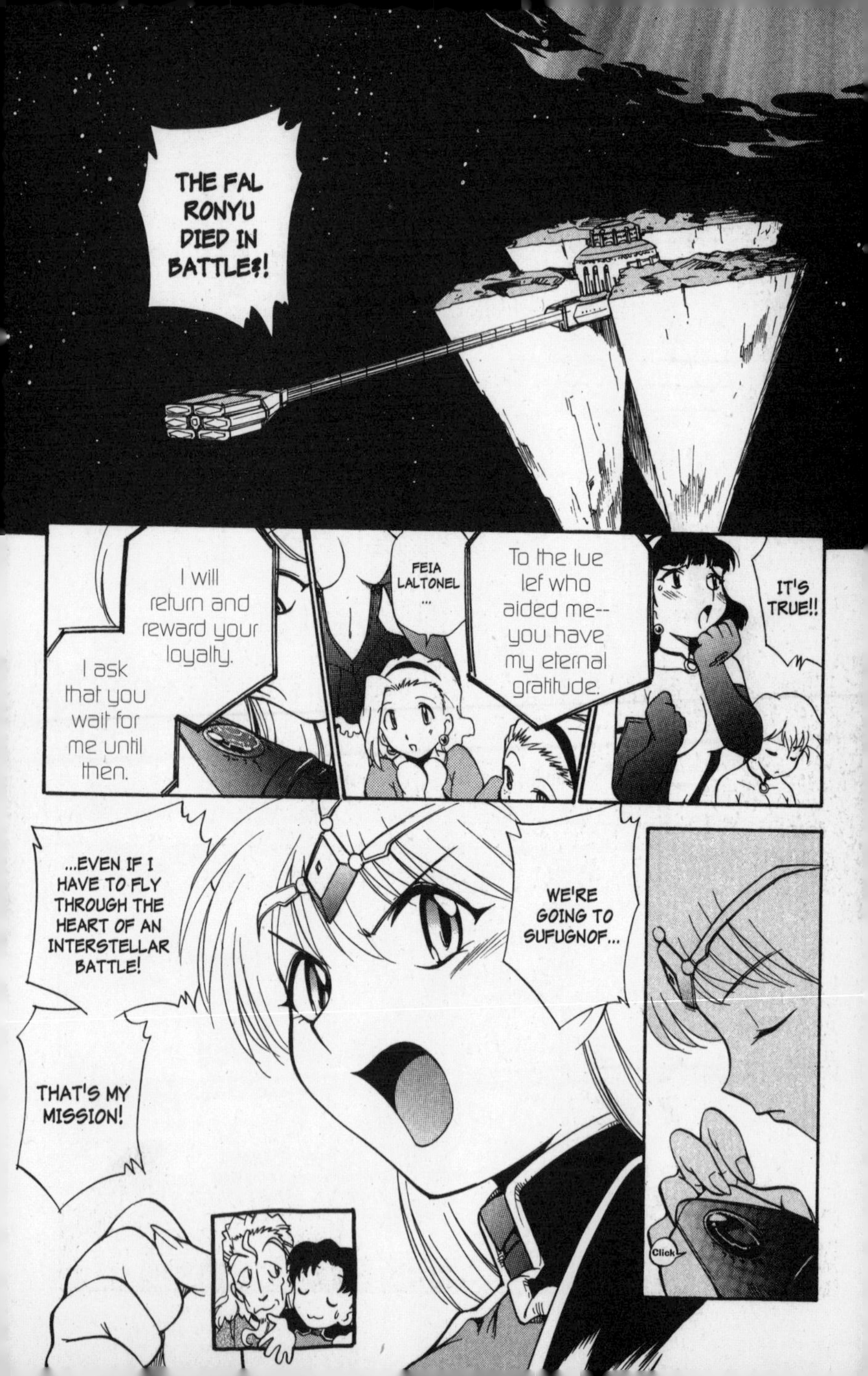
THE FAL RONYU DIED IN BATTLE?!
IT'S TRUE!!
To the lue lef who aided me-- you have my eternal gratitude.
FEIA LALTONEL ...
I will return and reward your loyalty.
I ask that you wait for me until then.
Click
WE'RE GOING TO SUFUGNOF...
...EVEN IF I HAVE TO FLY THROUGH THE HEART OF AN INTERSTELLAR BATTLE!
THAT'S MY MISSION!

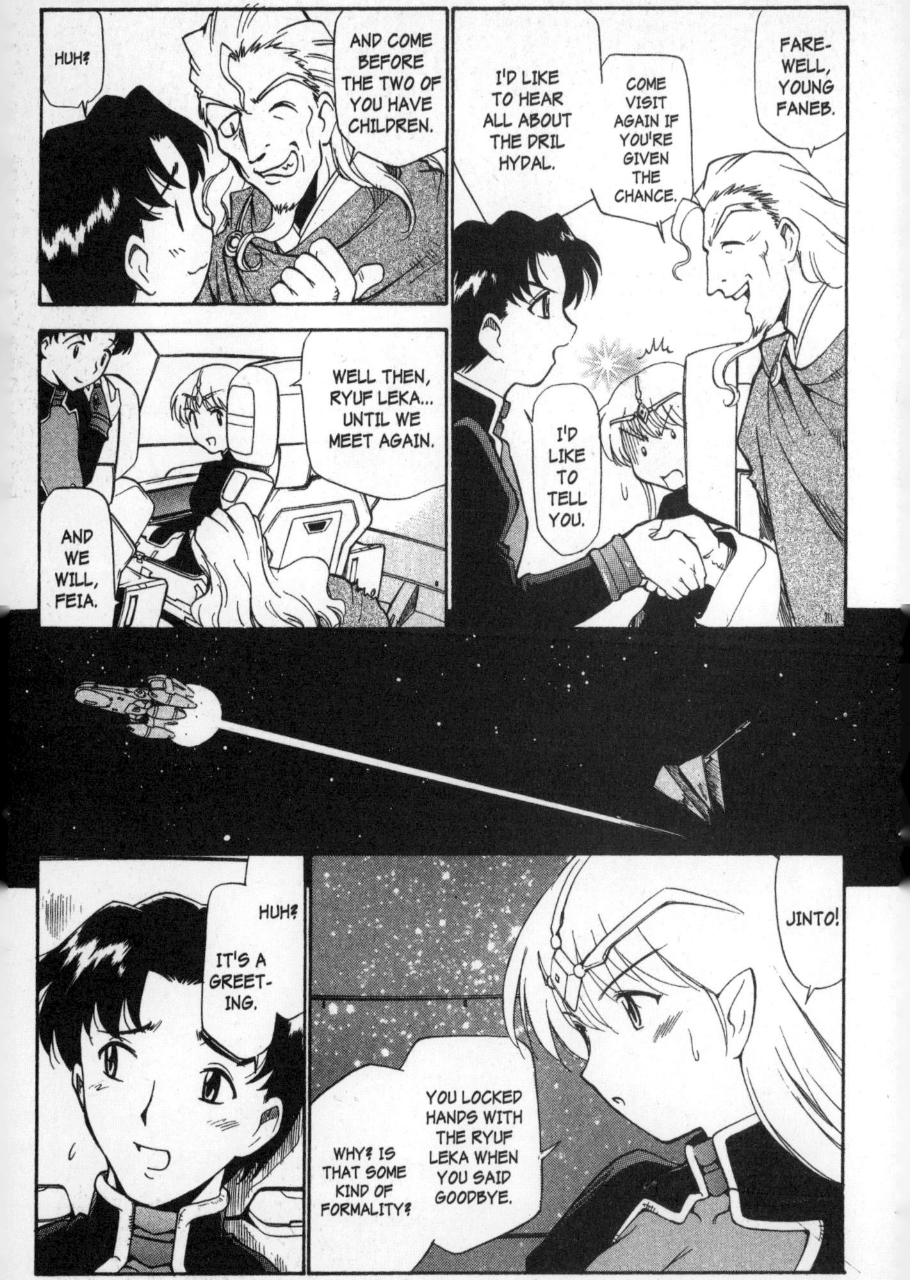
FARE-WELL, YOUNG FANEB.
COME VISIT AGAIN IF YOU'RE GIVEN THE CHANCE.
I'D LIKE TO HEAR ALL ABOUT THE DRIL HYDAL.
I'D LIKE TO TELL YOU.
AND COME BEFORE THE TWO OF YOU HAVE CHILDREN.
HUH?
WELL THEN, RYUF LEKA... UNTIL WE MEET AGAIN.
AND WE WILL, FEIA.
JINTO!
YOU LOCKED HANDS WITH THE RYUF LEKA WHEN YOU SAID GOODBYE.
WHY? IS THAT SOME KIND OF FORMALITY?
HUH?
IT'S A GREETING.

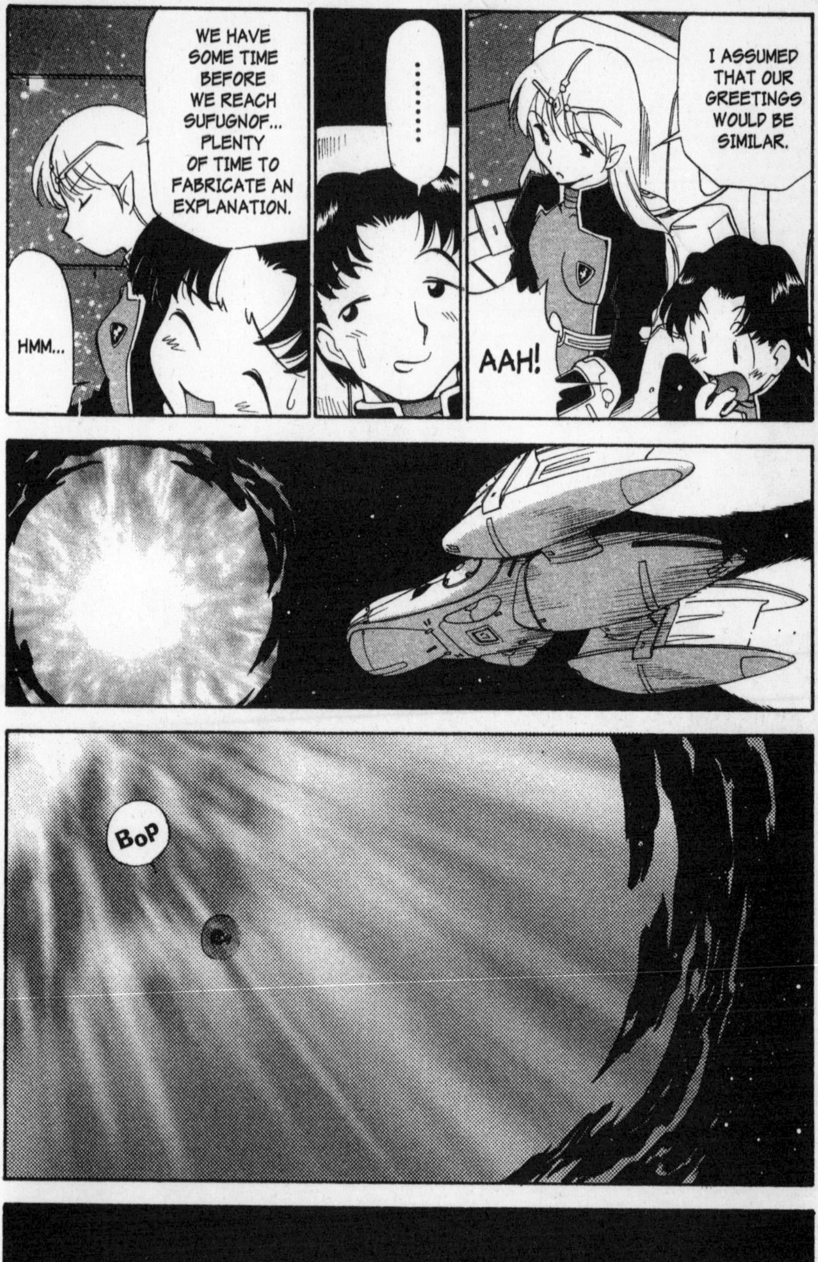
I ASSUMED THAT OUR GREETINGS WOULD BE SIMILAR.
AAH!
......
WE HAVE SOME TIME BEFORE WE REACH SUFUGNOF... PLENTY OF TIME TO FABRICATE AN EXPLANATION.
HMM...
BoP

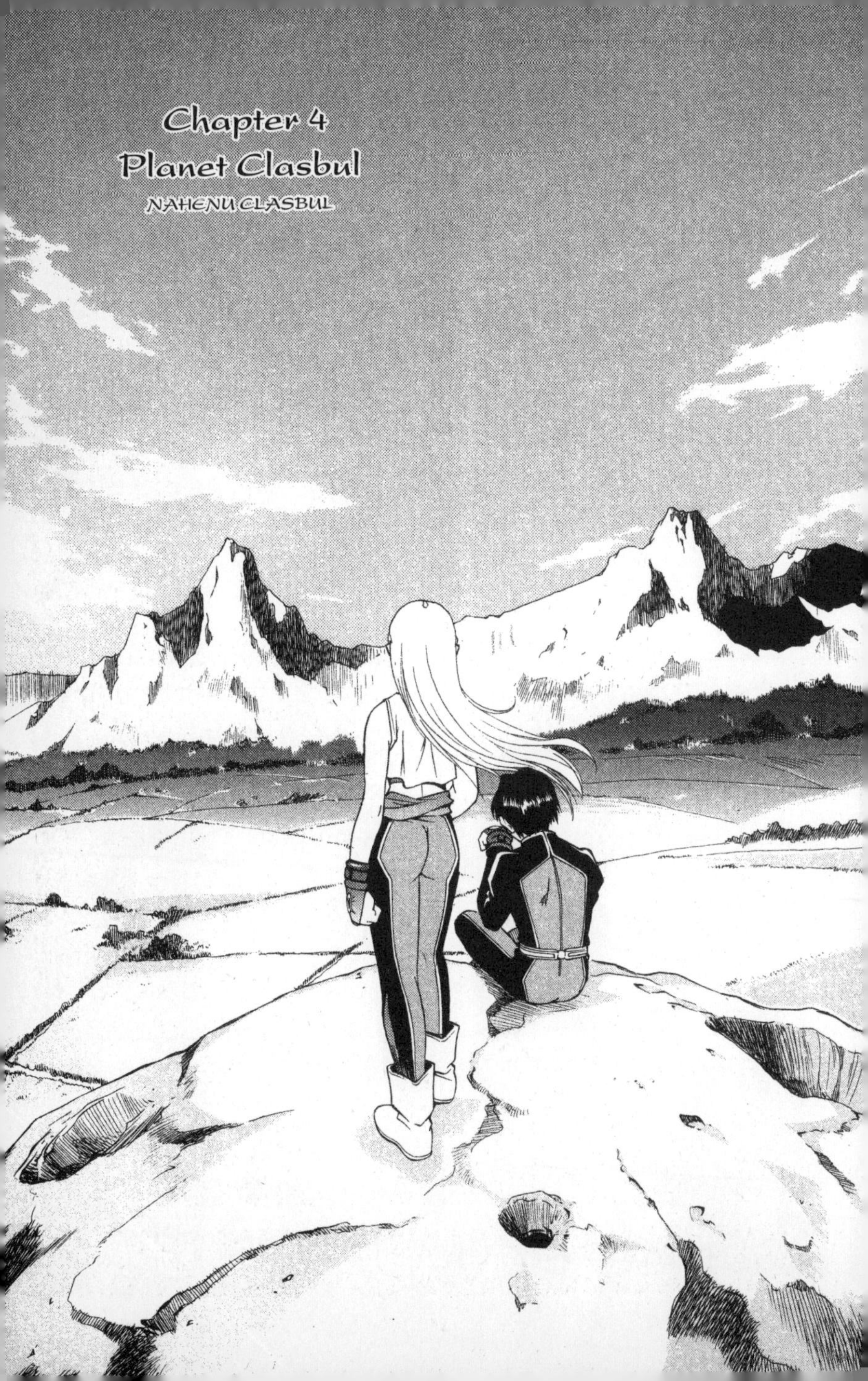
Chapter 4
Planet Clasbul
NAHENU CLASBUL

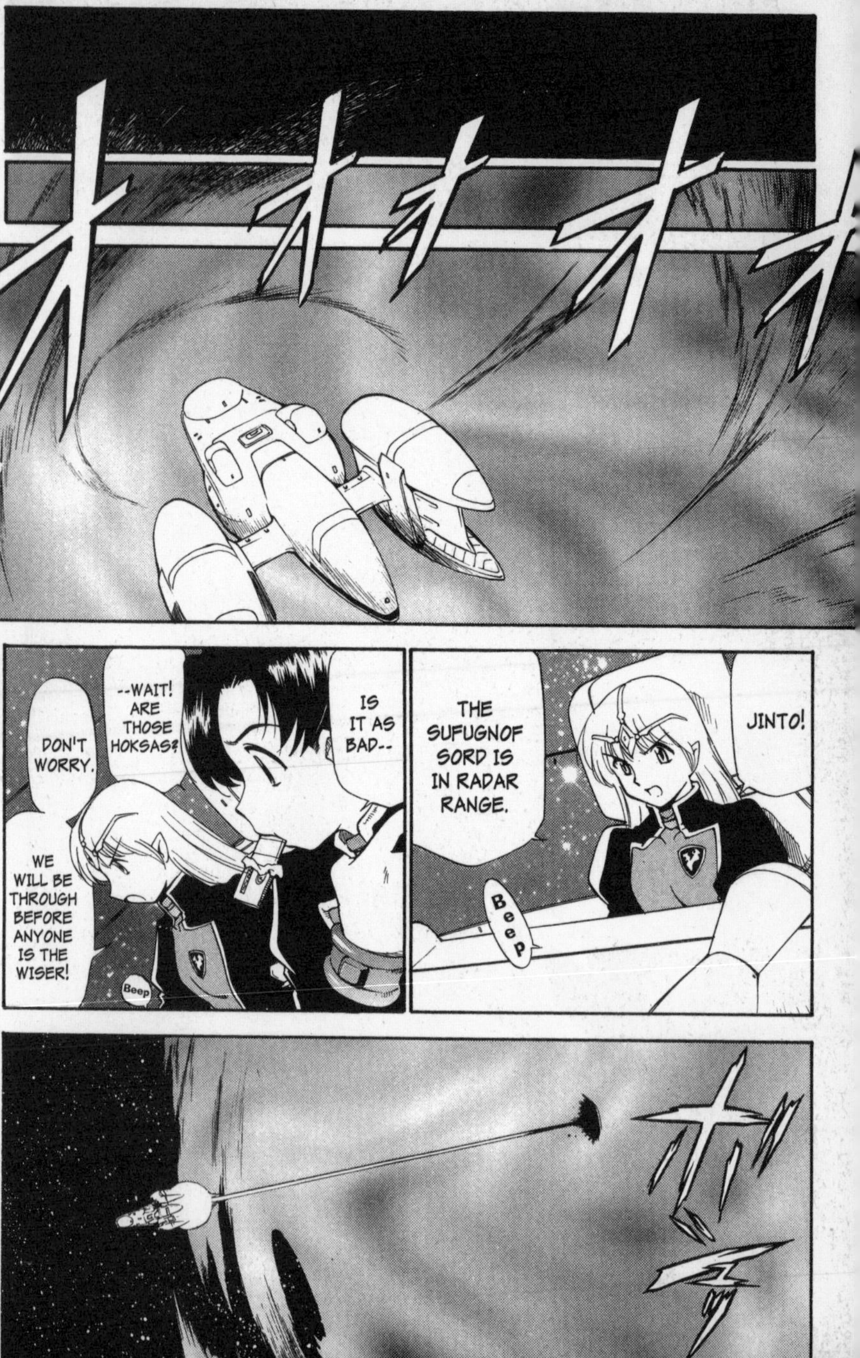
JINTO!
THE SUFUGNOF SORD IS IN RADAR RANGE.
Beep
IS IT AS BAD--
--WAIT! ARE THOSE HOKSAS?
DON'T WORRY.
WE WILL BE THROUGH BEFORE ANYONE IS THE WISER!
Beep

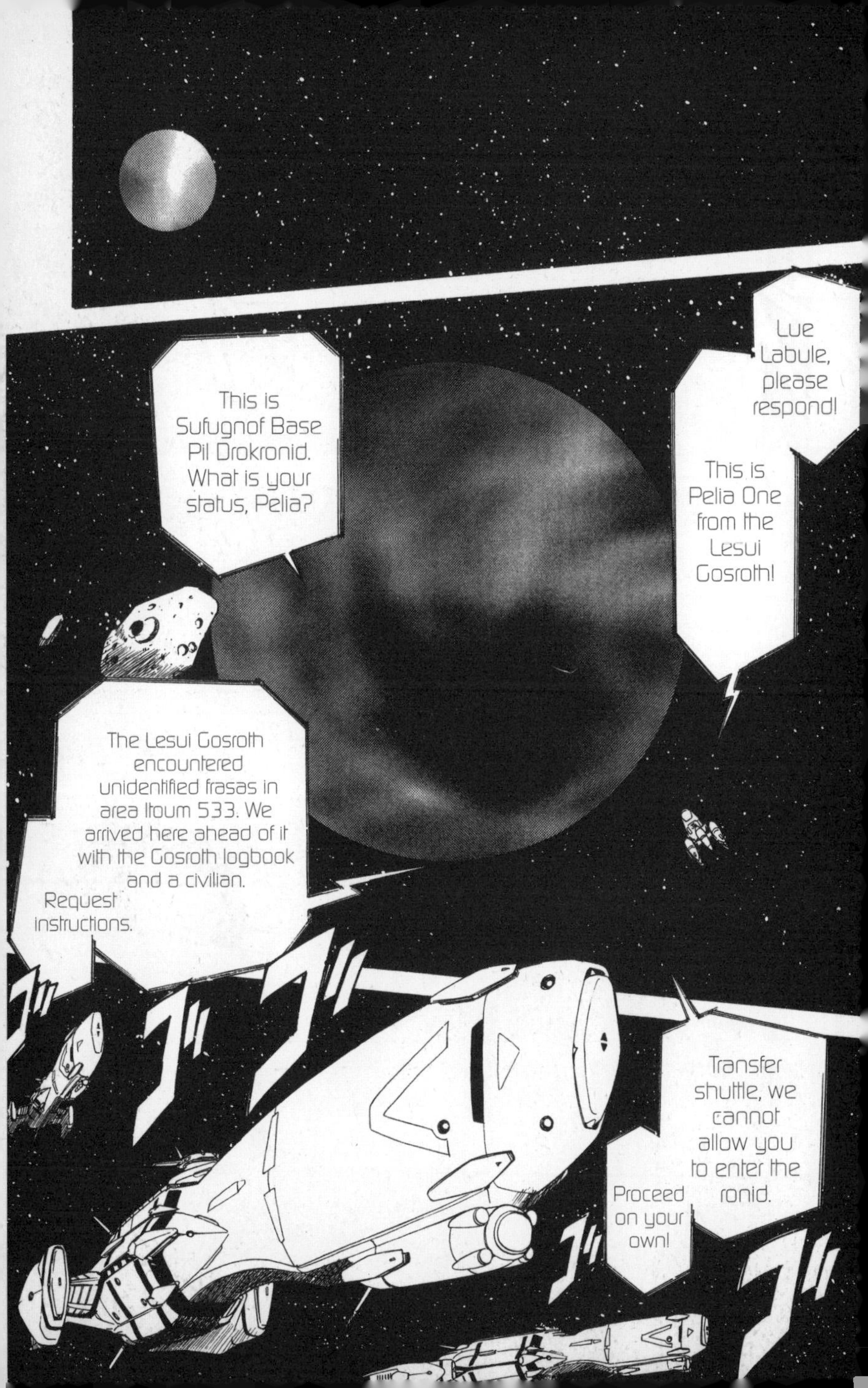
Lue Labule, please respond!
This is Pelia One from the Lesui Gosroth!
This is Sufugnof Base Pil Drokronid. What is your status, Pelia?
The Lesui Gosroth encountered unidentified frasas in area Itoum 533. We arrived here ahead of it with the Gosroth logbook and a civilian.
Request instructions.
Transfer shuttle, we cannot allow you to enter the ronid.
Proceed on your own!
ゴ ゴ ゴ ゴ ゴ ゴ

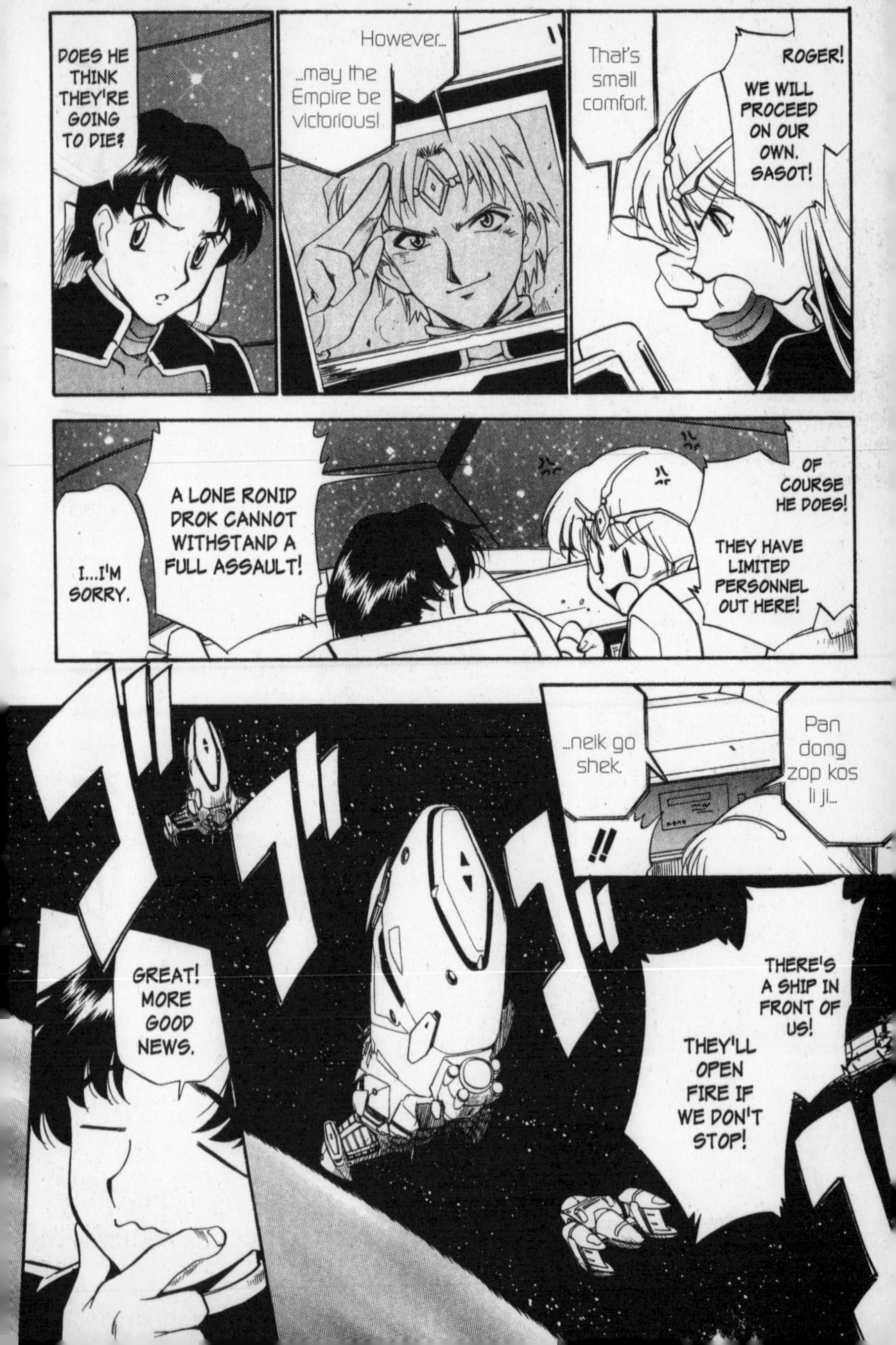
ROGER!
WE WILL PROCEED ON OUR OWN. SASOT!
That's small comfort.
However...
...may the Empire be victorious!
DOES HE THINK THEY'RE GOING TO DIE?
OF COURSE HE DOES!
THEY HAVE LIMITED PERSONNEL OUT HERE!
A LONE RONID DROK CANNOT WITHSTAND A FULL ASSAULT!
I...I'M SORRY.
Pan dong zop kos li ji...
...neik go shek.
!!
THERE'S A SHIP IN FRONT OF US!
THEY'LL OPEN FIRE IF WE DON'T STOP!
GREAT! MORE GOOD NEWS.

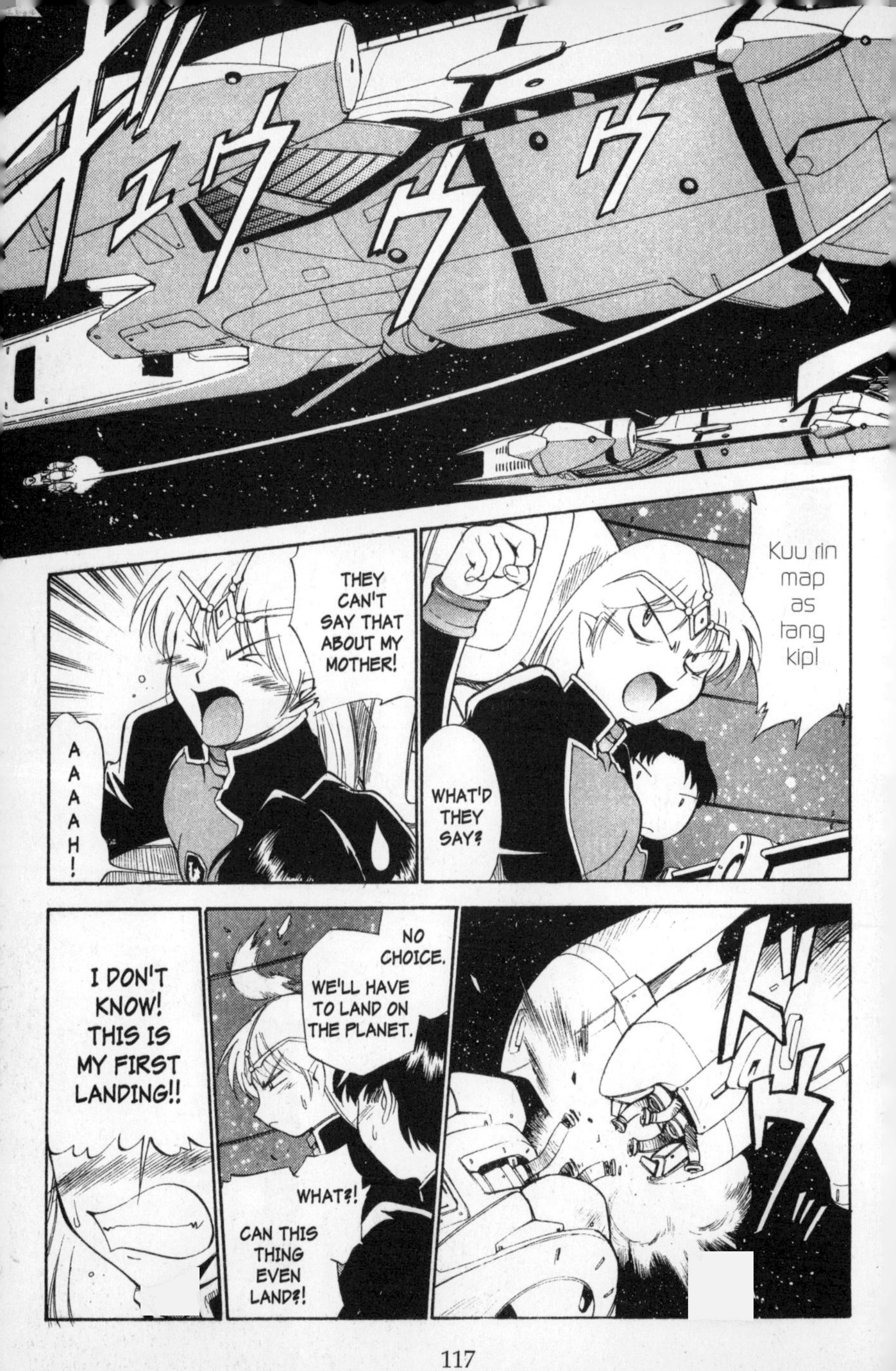
Kuu rin map as tang kip!
WHAT'D THEY SAY?
THEY CAN'T SAY THAT ABOUT MY MOTHER!
AAAAAH!
NO CHOICE.
WE'LL HAVE TO LAND ON THE PLANET.
WHAT?!
CAN THIS THING EVEN LAND?!
I DON'T KNOW! THIS IS MY FIRST LANDING!!

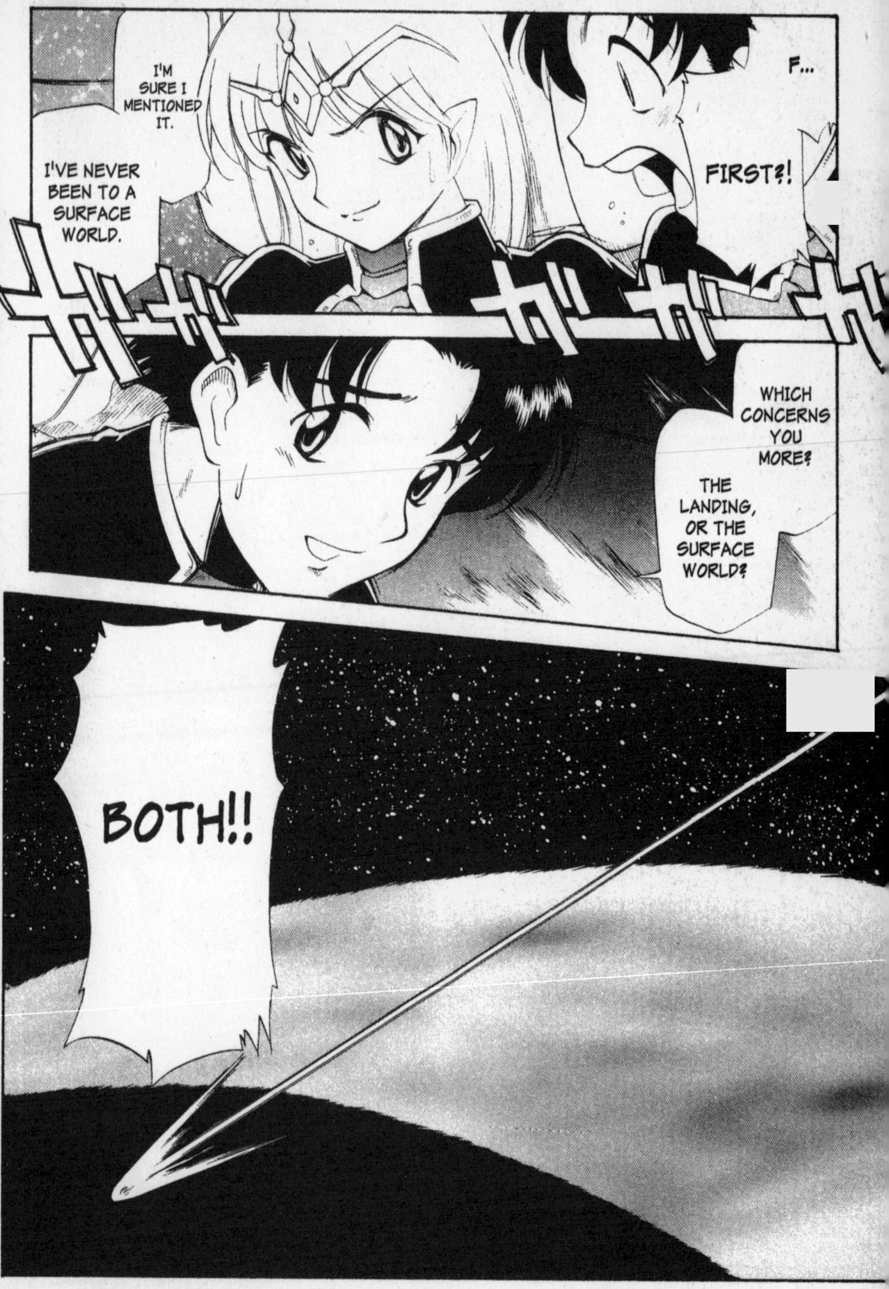
F...
FIRST?!
I'M SURE I MENTIONED IT.
I'VE NEVER BEEN TO A SURFACE WORLD.
ガガガガガ
WHICH CONCERNS YOU MORE?
THE LANDING, OR THE SURFACE WORLD?
BOTH!!

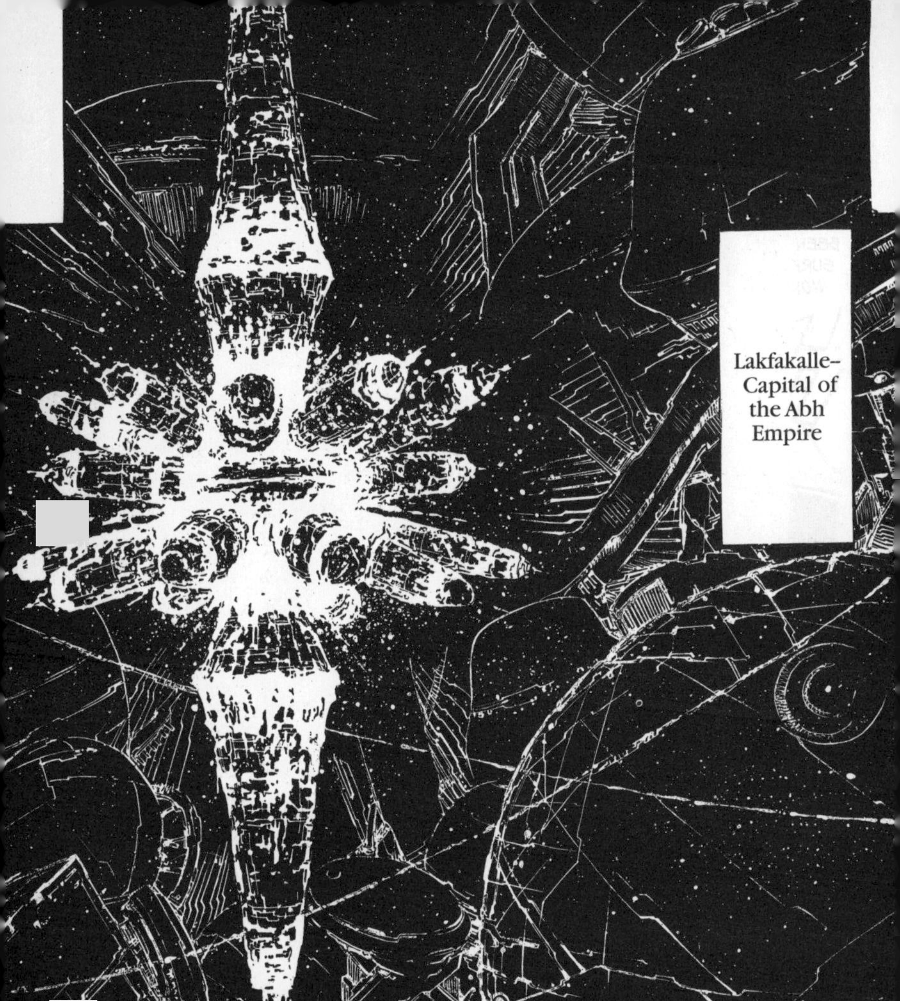
Lakfakalle–
Capital of
the Abh
Empire
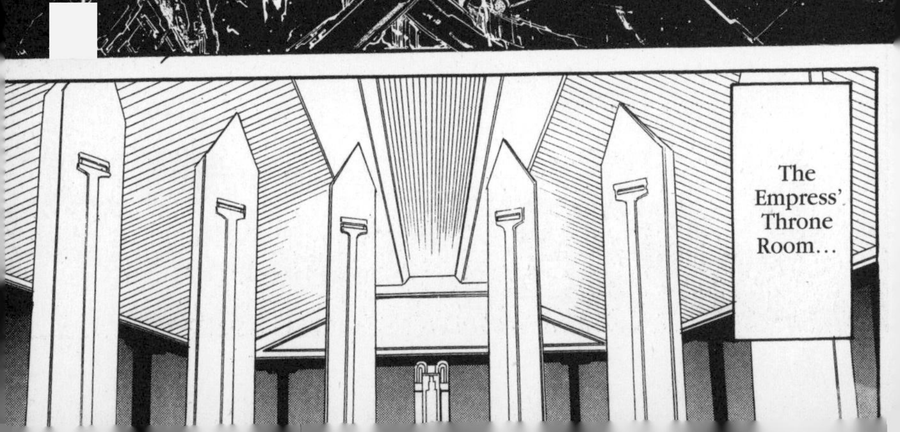
The
Empress'
Throne
Room...

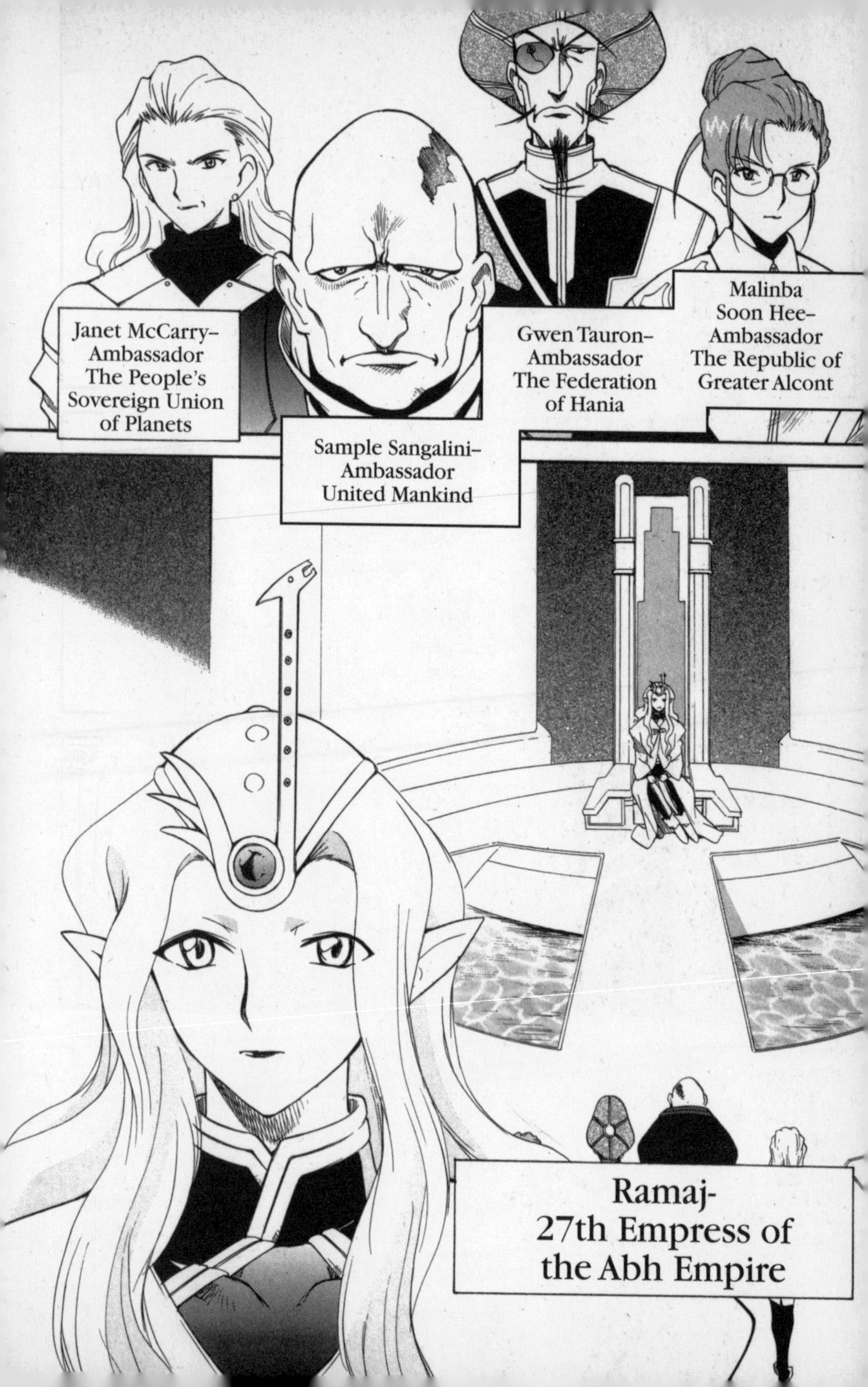
Malinba Soon Hee–Ambassador The Republic of Greater Alcont
Gwen Tauron–Ambassador The Federation of Hania
Sample Sangalini–Ambassador United Mankind
Janet McCarry–Ambassador The People's Sovereign Union of Planets
Ramaj-27th Empress of the Abh Empire

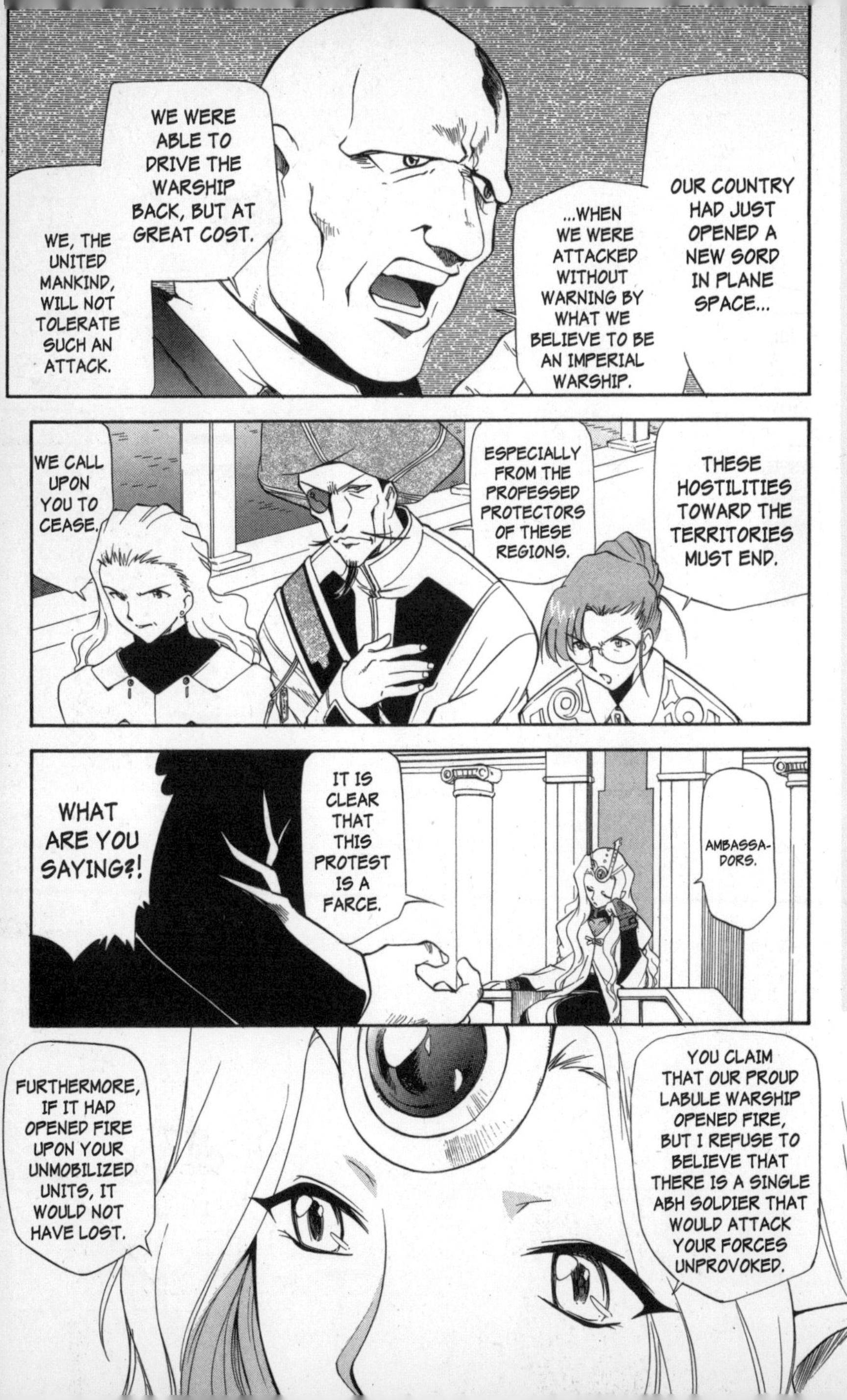
OUR COUNTRY HAD JUST OPENED A NEW SORD IN PLANE SPACE...
...WHEN WE WERE ATTACKED WITHOUT WARNING BY WHAT WE BELIEVE TO BE AN IMPERIAL WARSHIP.
WE WERE ABLE TO DRIVE THE WARSHIP BACK, BUT AT GREAT COST.
WE, THE UNITED MANKIND, WILL NOT TOLERATE SUCH AN ATTACK.
THESE HOSTILITIES TOWARD THE TERRITORIES MUST END.
ESPECIALLY FROM THE PROFESSED PROTECTORS OF THESE REGIONS.
WE CALL UPON YOU TO CEASE.
AMBASSA-DORS.
IT IS CLEAR THAT THIS PROTEST IS A FARCE.
WHAT ARE YOU SAYING?!
YOU CLAIM THAT OUR PROUD LABULE WARSHIP OPENED FIRE, BUT I REFUSE TO BELIEVE THAT THERE IS A SINGLE ABH SOLDIER THAT WOULD ATTACK YOUR FORCES UNPROVOKED.
FURTHERMORE, IF IT HAD OPENED FIRE UPON YOUR UNMOBILIZED UNITS, IT WOULD NOT HAVE LOST.

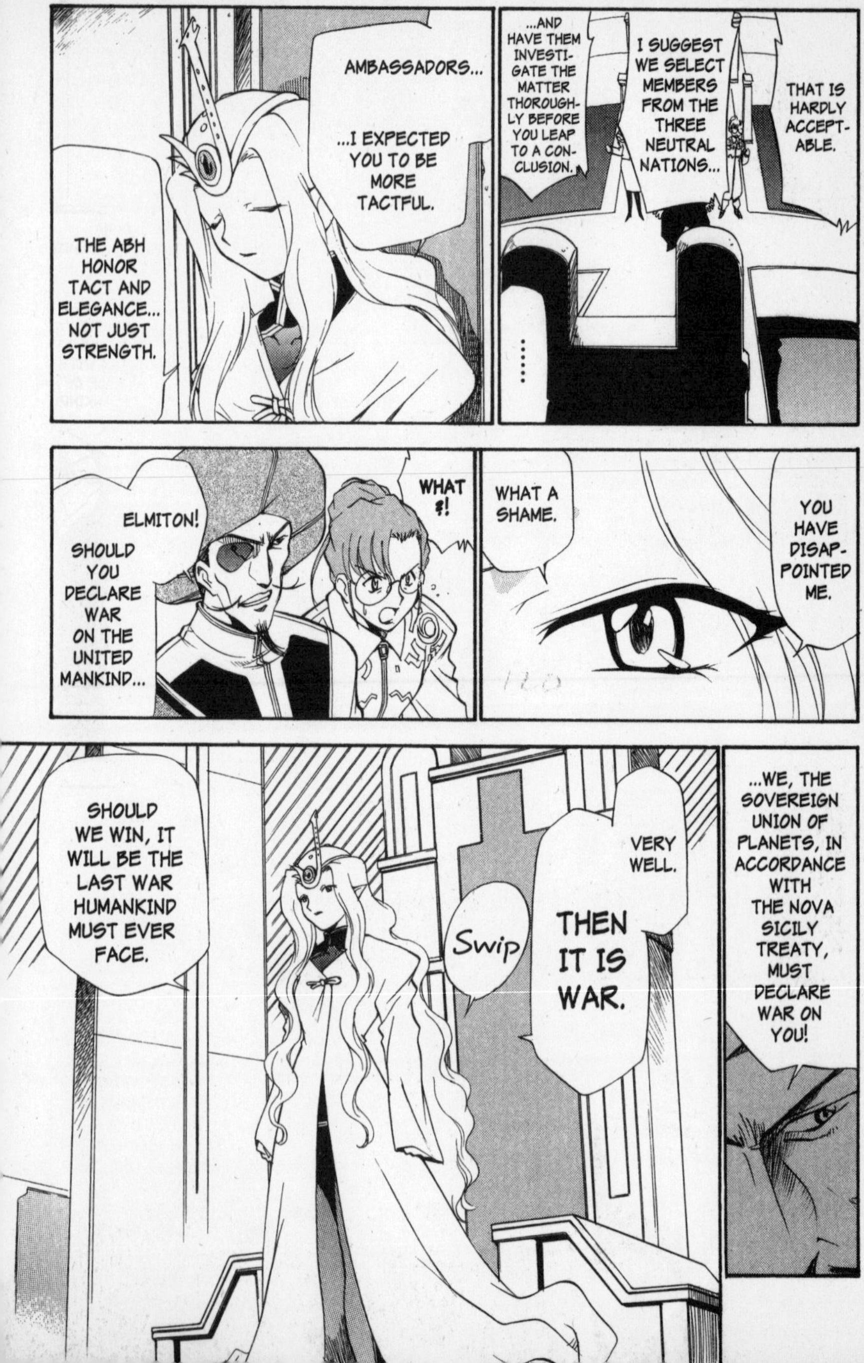
THAT IS HARDLY ACCEPTABLE.
I SUGGEST WE SELECT MEMBERS FROM THE THREE NEUTRAL NATIONS...
...AND HAVE THEM INVESTIGATE THE MATTER THOROUGHLY BEFORE YOU LEAP TO A CONCLUSION.
......
AMBASSADORS...
...I EXPECTED YOU TO BE MORE TACTFUL.
THE ABH HONOR TACT AND ELEGANCE... NOT JUST STRENGTH.
YOU HAVE DISAPPOINTED ME.
WHAT A SHAME.
WHAT?!
ELMITON!
SHOULD YOU DECLARE WAR ON THE UNITED MANKIND...
...WE, THE SOVEREIGN UNION OF PLANETS, IN ACCORDANCE WITH THE NOVA SICILY TREATY, MUST DECLARE WAR ON YOU!
VERY WELL.
THEN IT IS WAR.
Swip
SHOULD WE WIN, IT WILL BE THE LAST WAR HUMANKIND MUST EVER FACE.

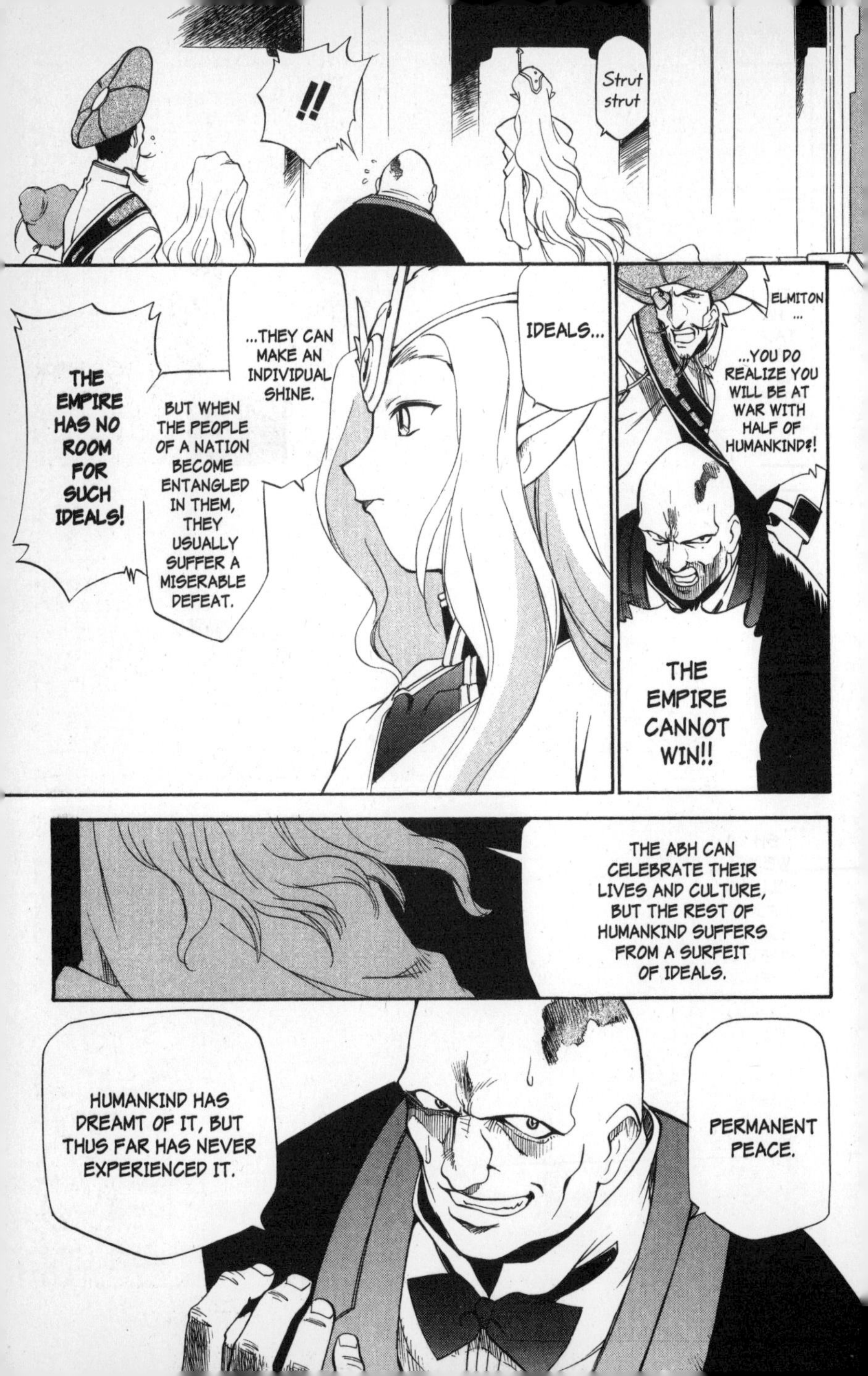
Strut strut
!!
ELMITON ...
...YOU DO REALIZE YOU WILL BE AT WAR WITH HALF OF HUMANKIND?!
THE EMPIRE CANNOT WIN!!
IDEALS...
...THEY CAN MAKE AN INDIVIDUAL SHINE.
BUT WHEN THE PEOPLE OF A NATION BECOME ENTANGLED IN THEM, THEY USUALLY SUFFER A MISERABLE DEFEAT.
THE EMPIRE HAS NO ROOM FOR SUCH IDEALS!
THE ABH CAN CELEBRATE THEIR LIVES AND CULTURE, BUT THE REST OF HUMANKIND SUFFERS FROM A SURFEIT OF IDEALS.
PERMANENT PEACE.
HUMANKIND HAS DREAMT OF IT, BUT THUS FAR HAS NEVER EXPERIENCED IT.

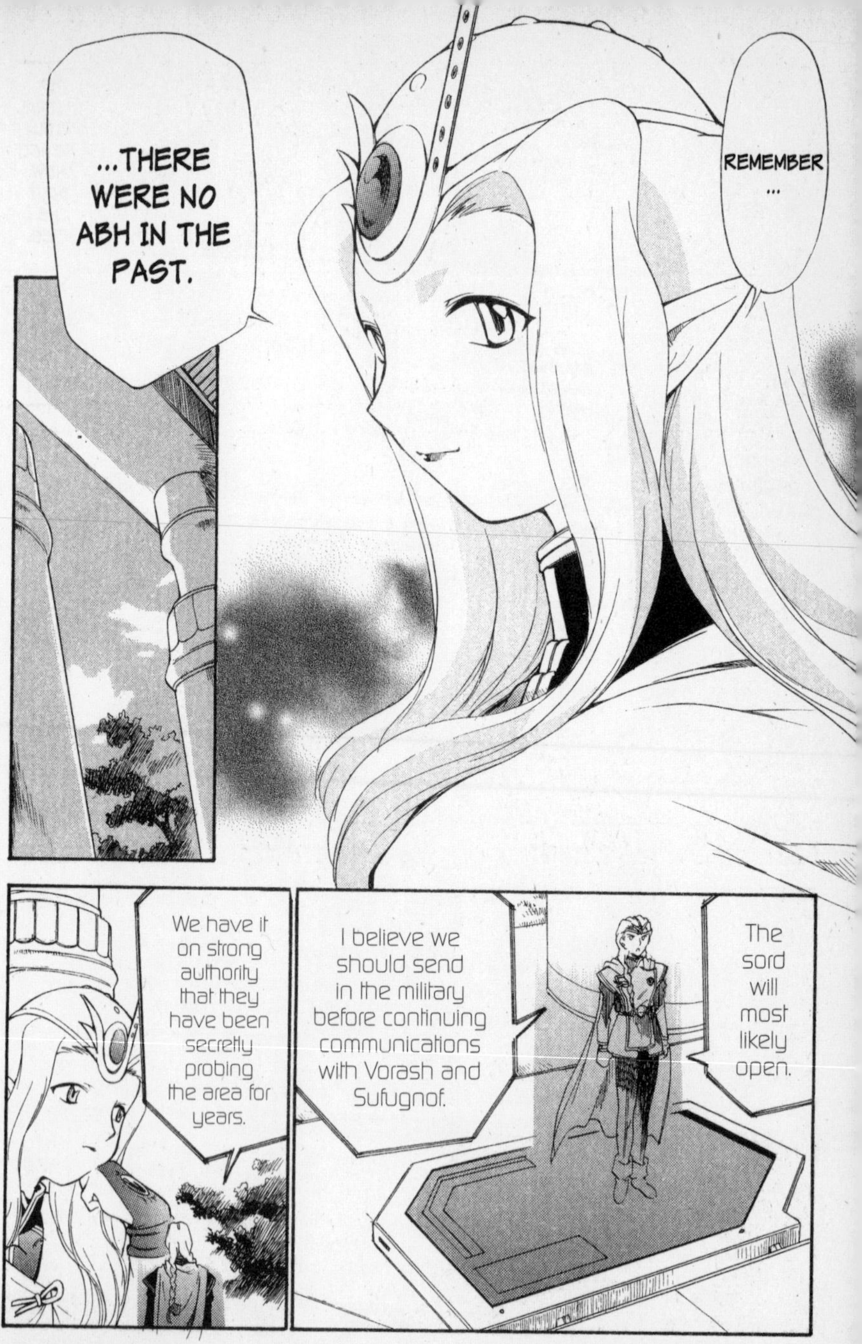
REMEMBER ...
...THERE WERE NO ABH IN THE PAST.
The sord will most likely open.
I believe we should send in the military before continuing communications with Vorash and Sufugnof.
We have it on strong authority that they have been secretly probing the area for years.

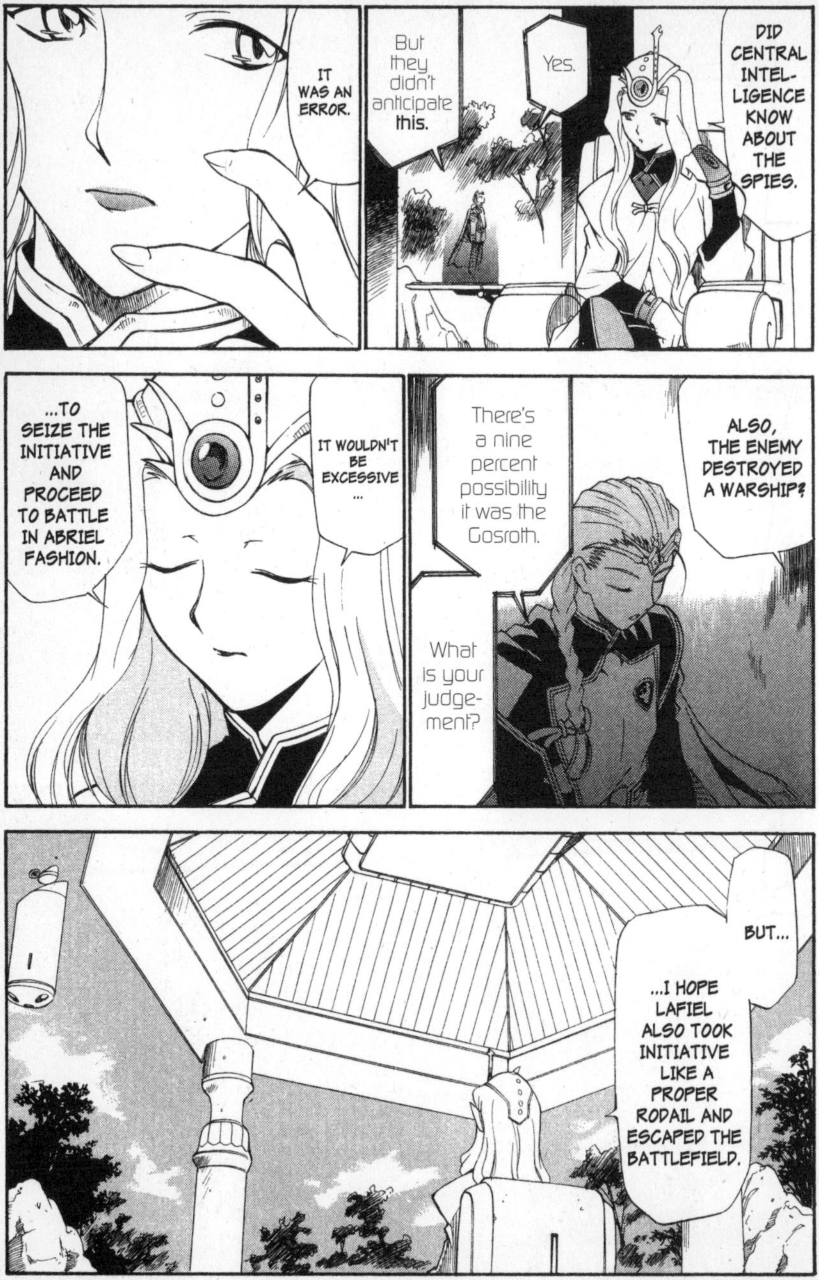
DID CENTRAL INTEL-LIGENCE KNOW ABOUT THE SPIES.
Yes.
But they didn't anticipate this.
IT WAS AN ERROR.
ALSO, THE ENEMY DESTROYED A WARSHIP?
There's a nine percent possibility it was the Gosroth.
What is your judgement?
IT WOULDN'T BE EXCESSIVE ...
...TO SEIZE THE INITIATIVE AND PROCEED TO BATTLE IN ABRIEL FASHION.
BUT...
...I HOPE LAFIEL ALSO TOOK INITIATIVE LIKE A PROPER RODAIL AND ESCAPED THE BATTLEFIELD.

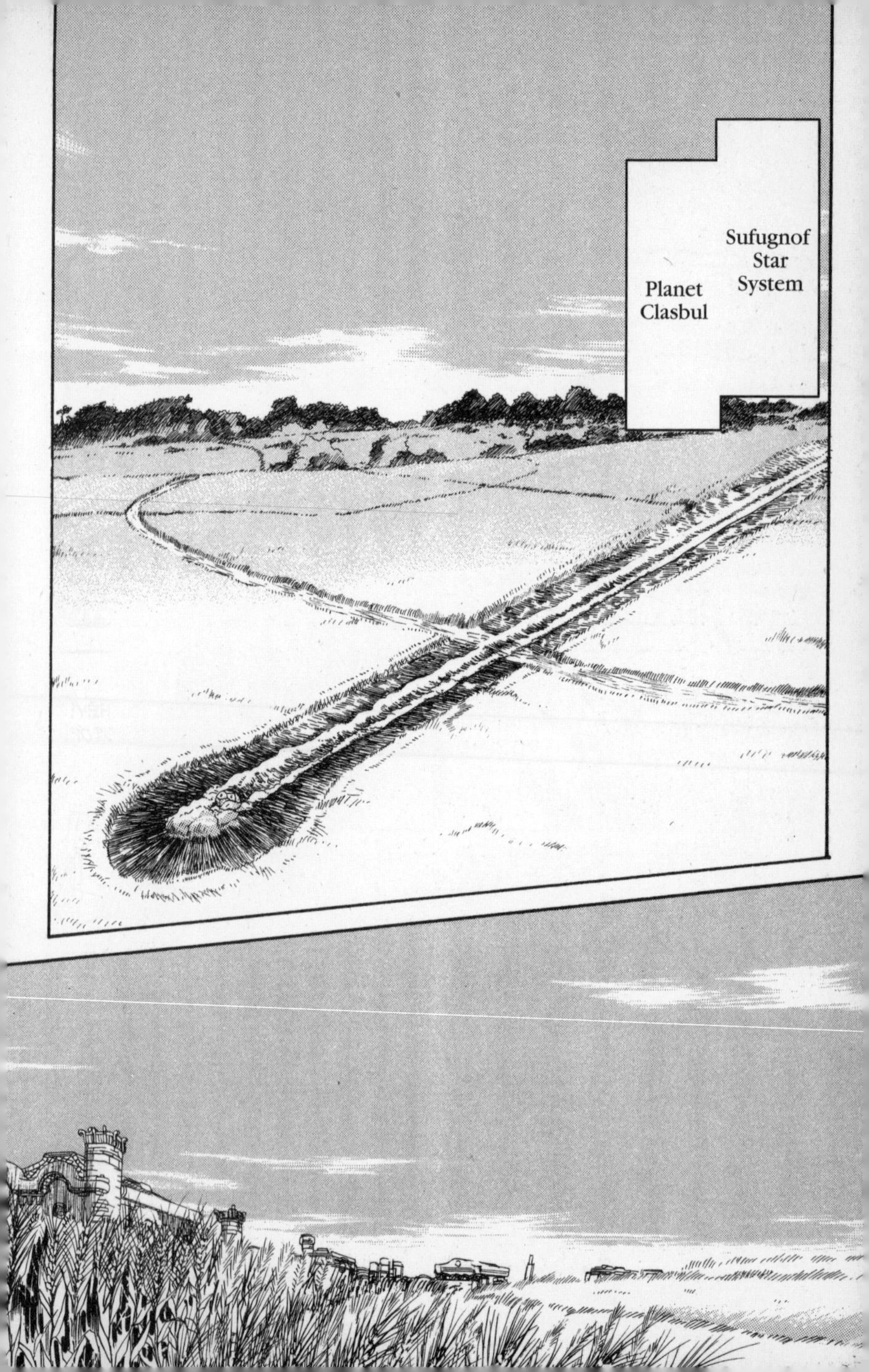
Sufugnof Star System
Planet Clasbul

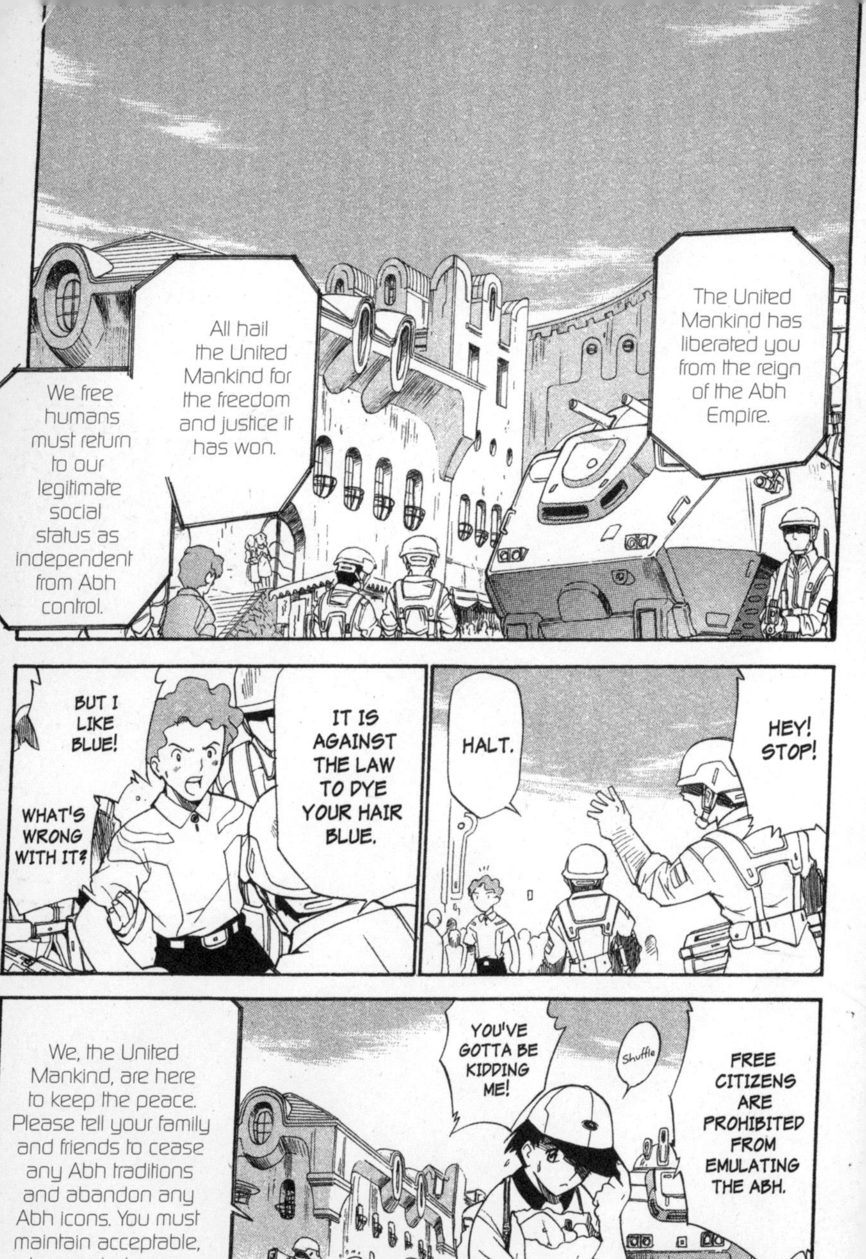
The United Mankind has liberated you from the reign of the Abh Empire.
All hail the United Mankind for the freedom and justice it has won.
We free humans must return to our legitimate social status as independent from Abh control.
HEY! STOP!
HALT.
IT IS AGAINST THE LAW TO DYE YOUR HAIR BLUE.
BUT I LIKE BLUE!
WHAT'S WRONG WITH IT?
FREE CITIZENS ARE PROHIBITED FROM EMULATING THE ABH.
Shuffle
YOU'VE GOTTA BE KIDDING ME!
We, the United Mankind, are here to keep the peace. Please tell your family and friends to cease any Abh traditions and abandon any Abh icons. You must maintain acceptable, human behavior.

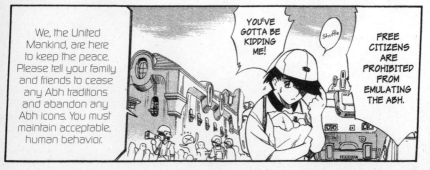

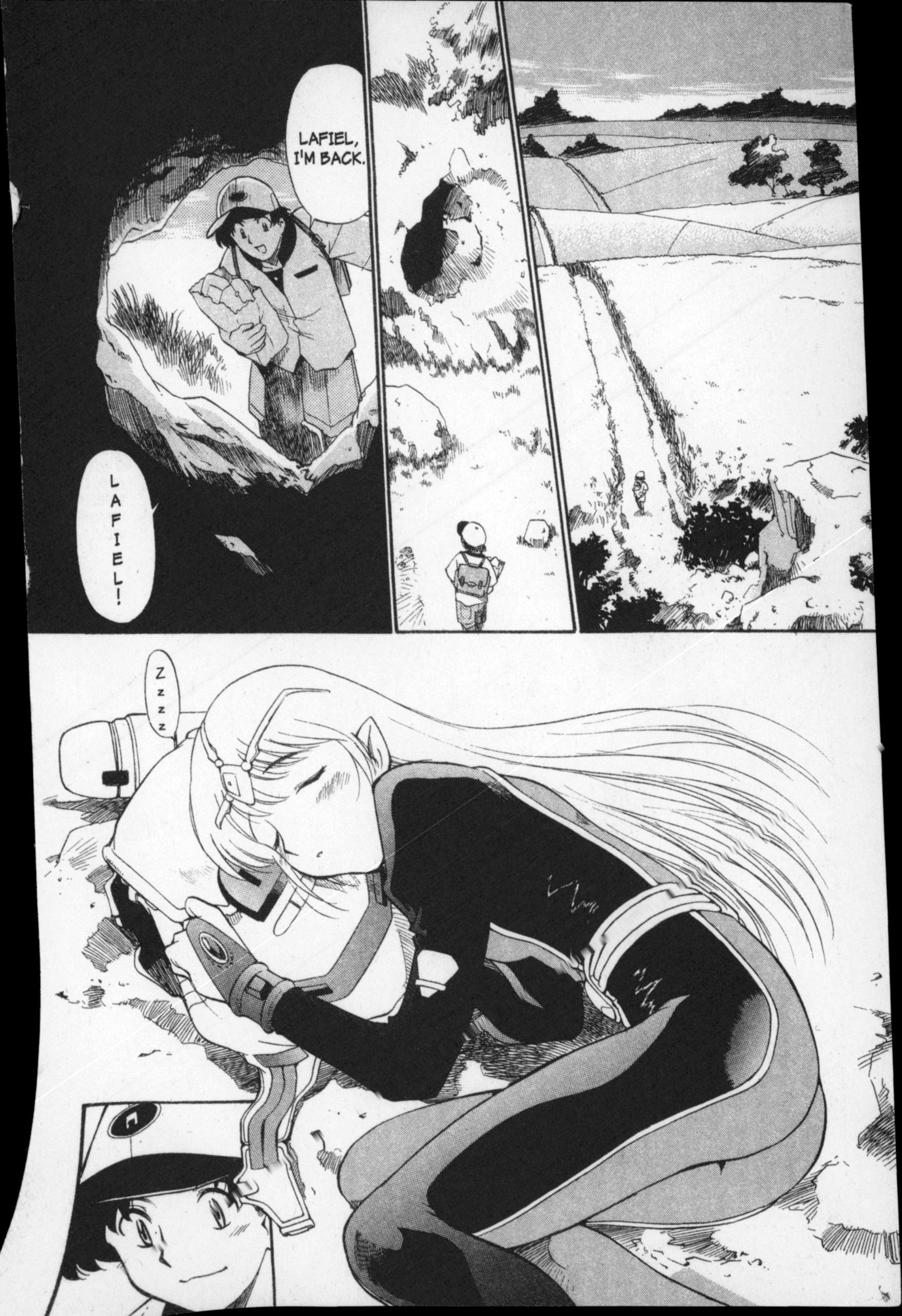
LAFIEL, I'M BACK.
LAFIEL!
Zzzz

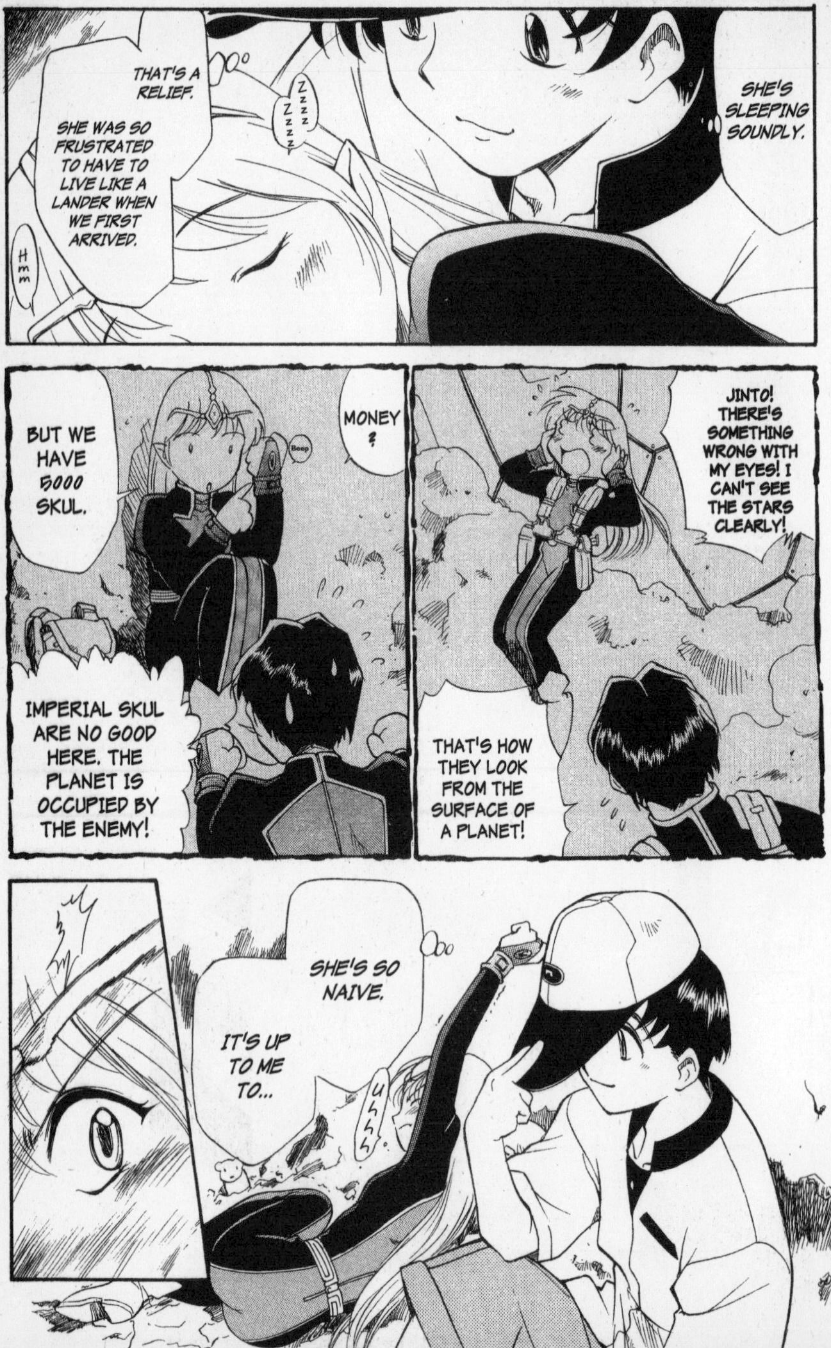
SHE'S SLEEPING SOUNDLY.
Zzzz
THAT'S A RELIEF.
SHE WAS SO FRUSTRATED TO HAVE TO LIVE LIKE A LANDER WHEN WE FIRST ARRIVED.
Hmm
JINTO! THERE'S SOMETHING WRONG WITH MY EYES! I CAN'T SEE THE STARS CLEARLY!
THAT'S HOW THEY LOOK FROM THE SURFACE OF A PLANET!
MONEY?
Beep
BUT WE HAVE 5000 SKUL.
IMPERIAL SKUL ARE NO GOOD HERE. THE PLANET IS OCCUPIED BY THE ENEMY!
SHE'S SO NAIVE.
IT'S UP TO ME TO...

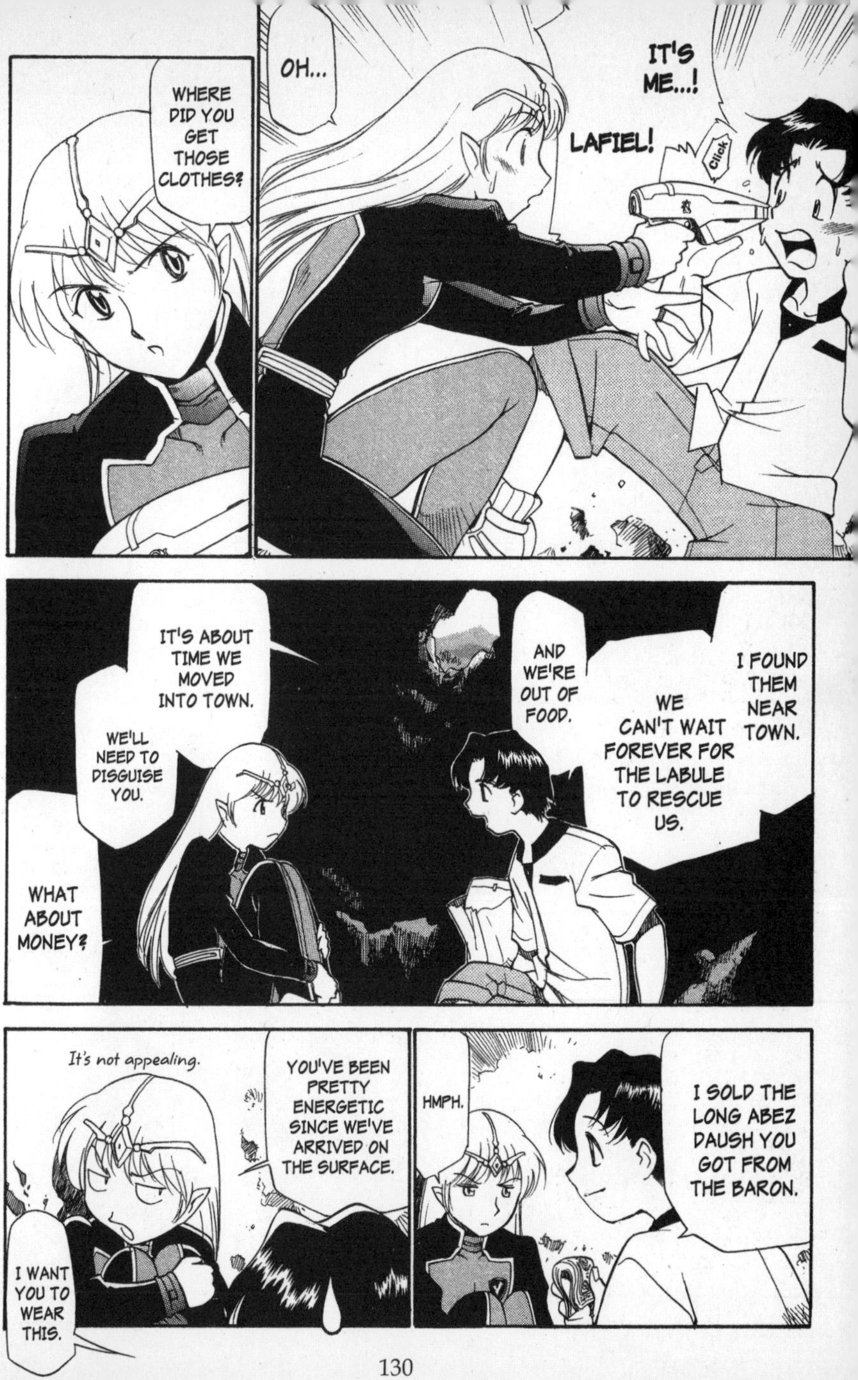
IT'S ME...!
Click
LAFIEL!
OH...
WHERE DID YOU GET THOSE CLOTHES?
I FOUND THEM NEAR TOWN.
WE CAN'T WAIT FOREVER FOR THE LABULE TO RESCUE US.
AND WE'RE OUT OF FOOD.
IT'S ABOUT TIME WE MOVED INTO TOWN.
WE'LL NEED TO DISGUISE YOU.
WHAT ABOUT MONEY?
I SOLD THE LONG ABEZ DAUSH YOU GOT FROM THE BARON.
HMPH.
YOU'VE BEEN PRETTY ENERGETIC SINCE WE'VE ARRIVED ON THE SURFACE.
It's not appealing.
I WANT YOU TO WEAR THIS.

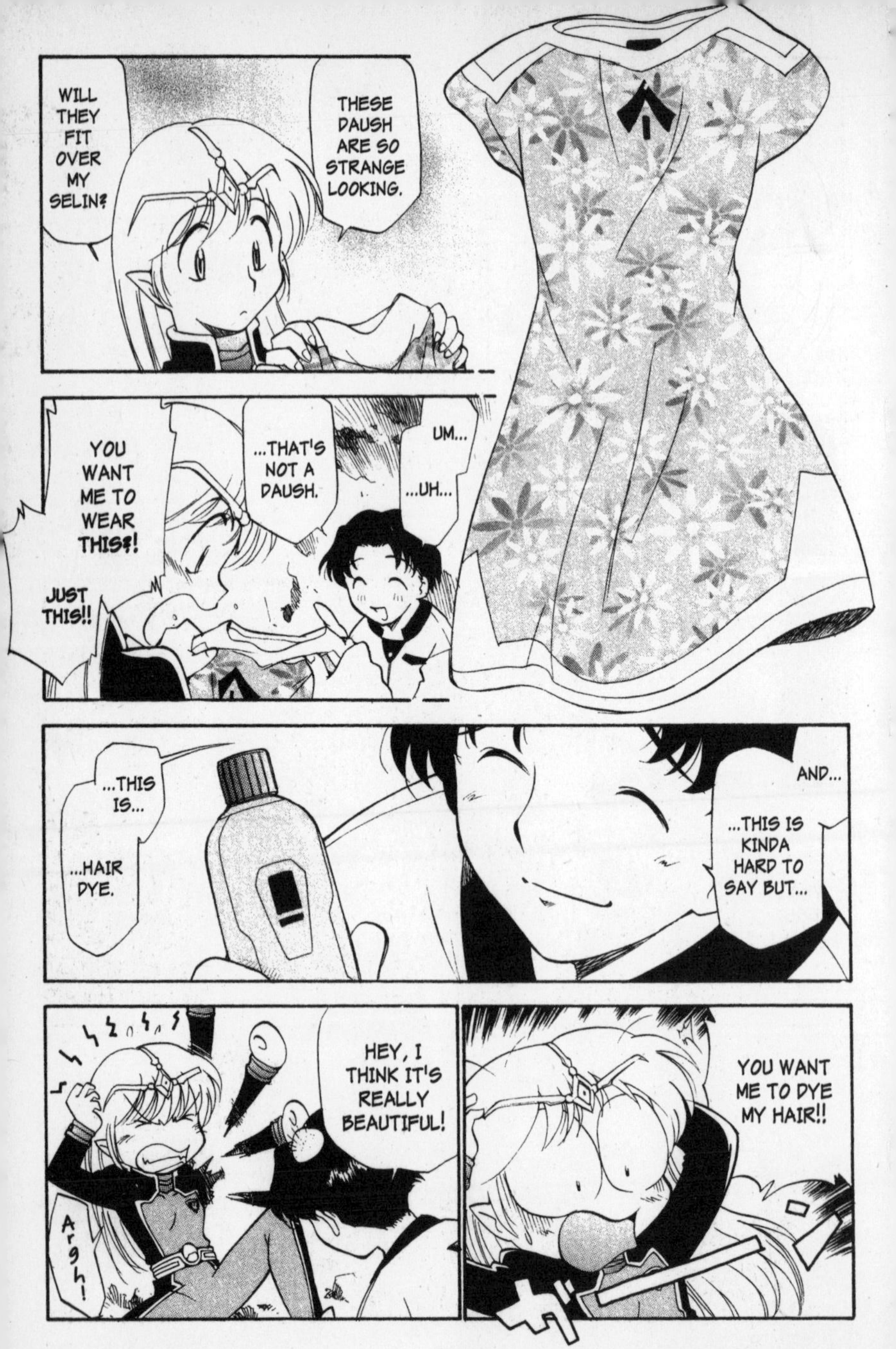
THESE DAUSH ARE SO STRANGE LOOKING.
WILL THEY FIT OVER MY SELIN?
UM... ...UH...
...THAT'S NOT A DAUSH.
YOU WANT ME TO WEAR THIS?!
JUST THIS!!
AND...
...THIS IS KINDA HARD TO SAY BUT...
...THIS IS...
...HAIR DYE.
YOU WANT ME TO DYE MY HAIR!!
HEY, I THINK IT'S REALLY BEAUTIFUL!
Argh!

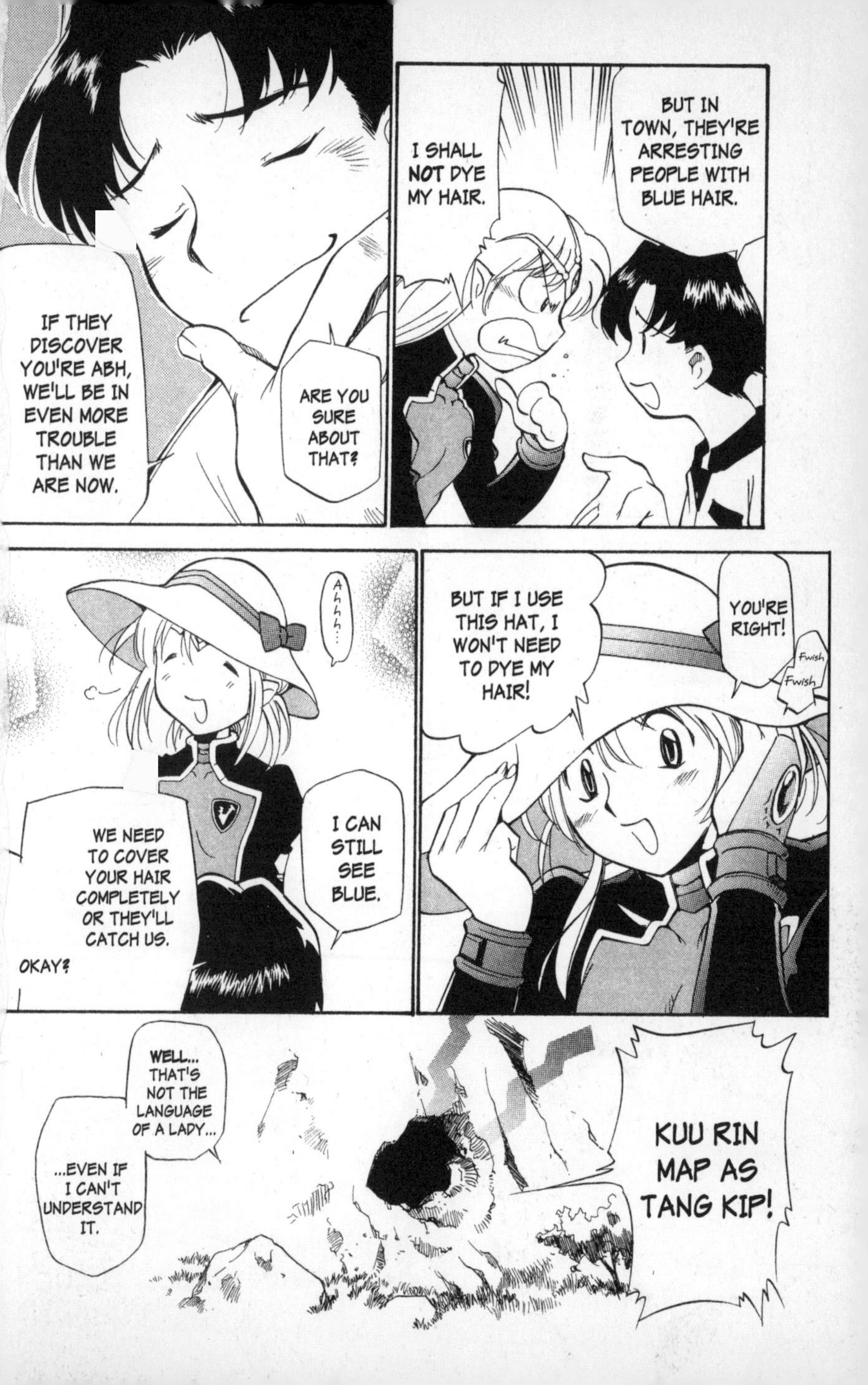
BUT IN TOWN, THEY'RE ARRESTING PEOPLE WITH BLUE HAIR.
I SHALL NOT DYE MY HAIR.
ARE YOU SURE ABOUT THAT?
IF THEY DISCOVER YOU'RE ABH, WE'LL BE IN EVEN MORE TROUBLE THAN WE ARE NOW.
YOU'RE RIGHT!
Fwish
Fwish
BUT IF I USE THIS HAT, I WON'T NEED TO DYE MY HAIR!
Ahhh...
I CAN STILL SEE BLUE.
WE NEED TO COVER YOUR HAIR COMPLETELY OR THEY'LL CATCH US.
OKAY?
KUU RIN MAP AS TANG KIP!
WELL... THAT'S NOT THE LANGUAGE OF A LADY...
...EVEN IF I CAN'T UNDERSTAND IT.

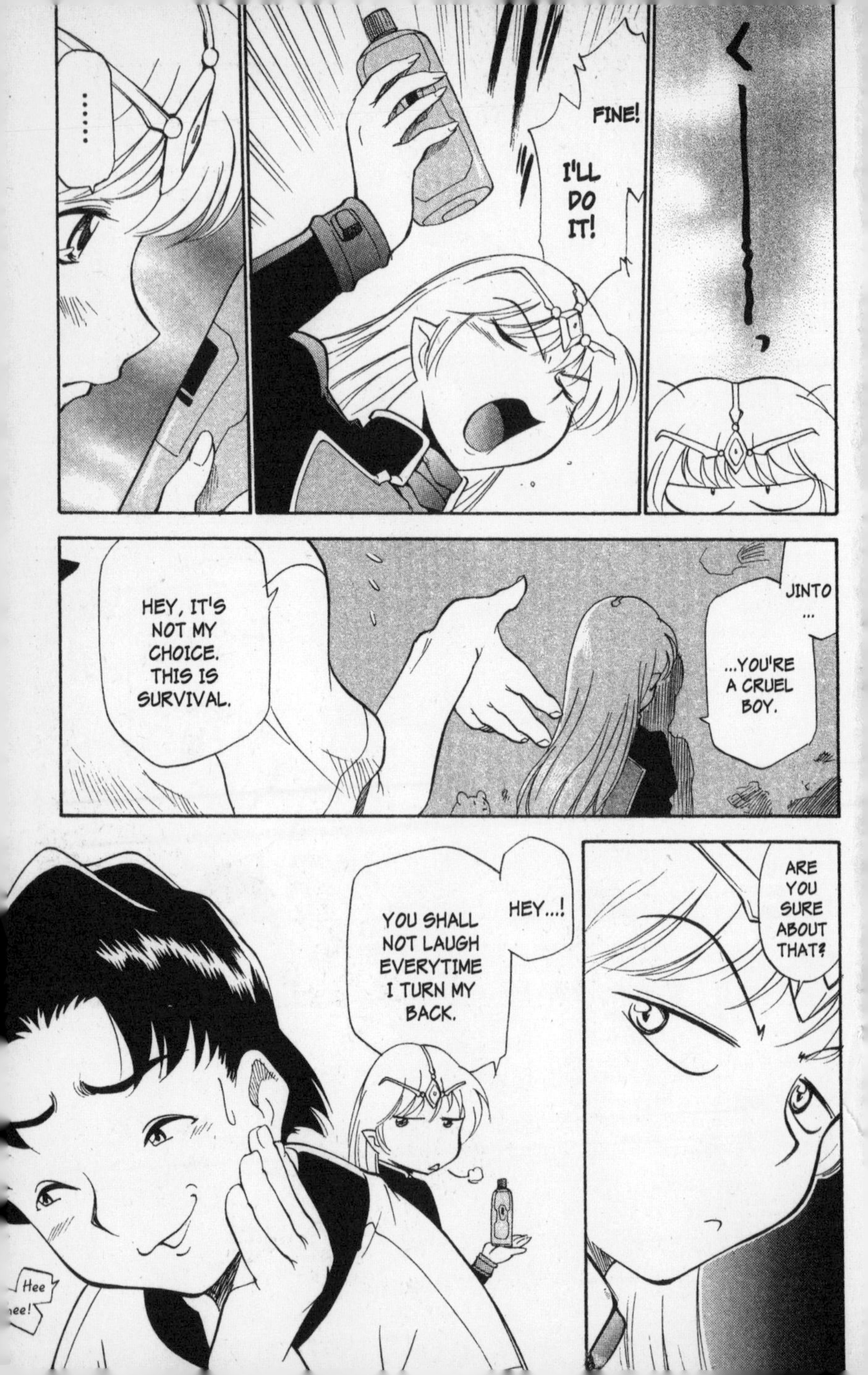
く
FINE!
I'LL DO IT!
......
JINTO ...
...YOU'RE A CRUEL BOY.
HEY, IT'S NOT MY CHOICE. THIS IS SURVIVAL.
ARE YOU SURE ABOUT THAT?
HEY...!
YOU SHALL NOT LAUGH EVERYTIME I TURN MY BACK.
Hee ee!

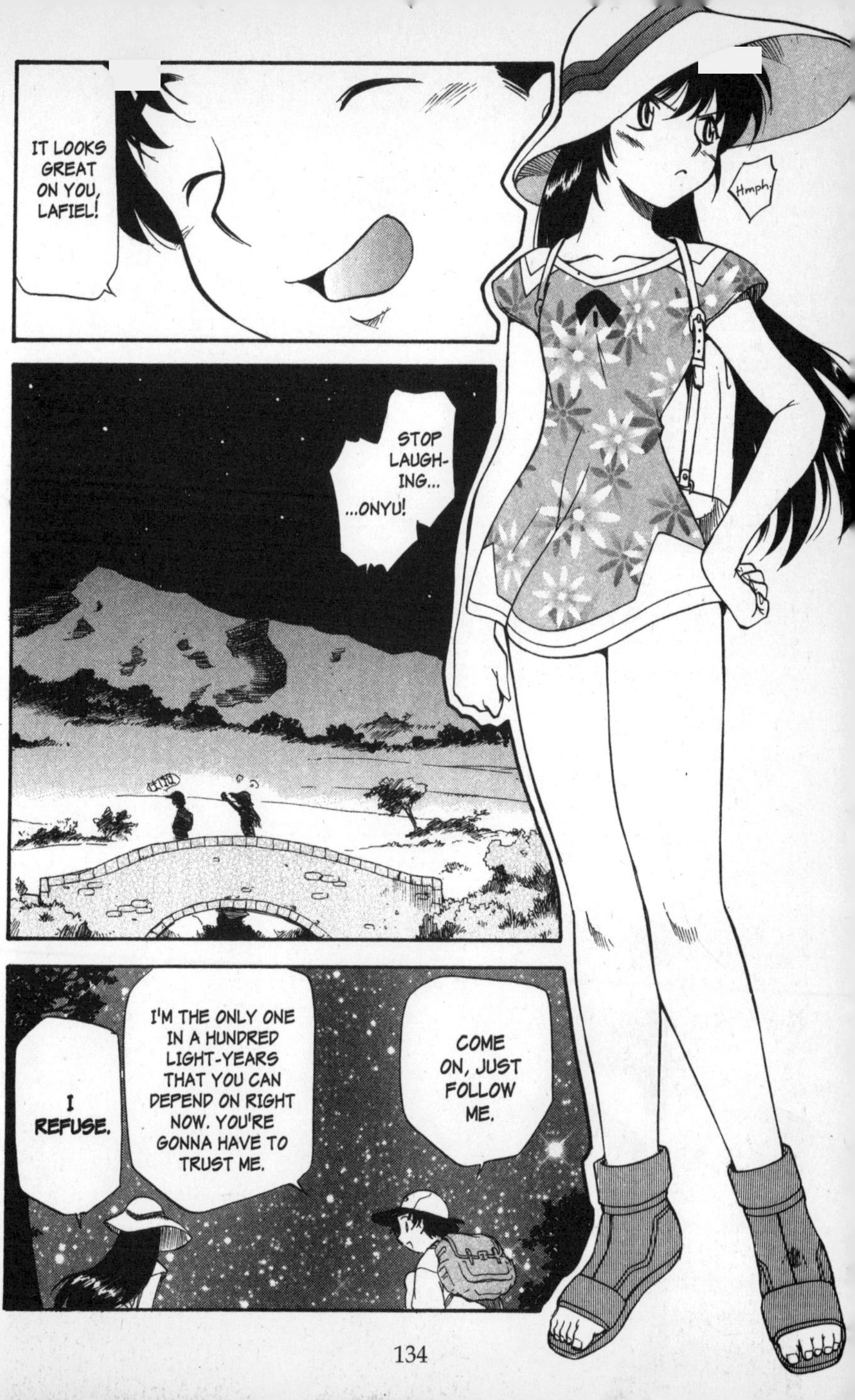
Hmph.
IT LOOKS GREAT ON YOU, LAFIEL!
STOP LAUGHING... ...ONYU!
COME ON, JUST FOLLOW ME.
I'M THE ONLY ONE IN A HUNDRED LIGHT-YEARS THAT YOU CAN DEPEND ON RIGHT NOW. YOU'RE GONNA HAVE TO TRUST ME.
I REFUSE.

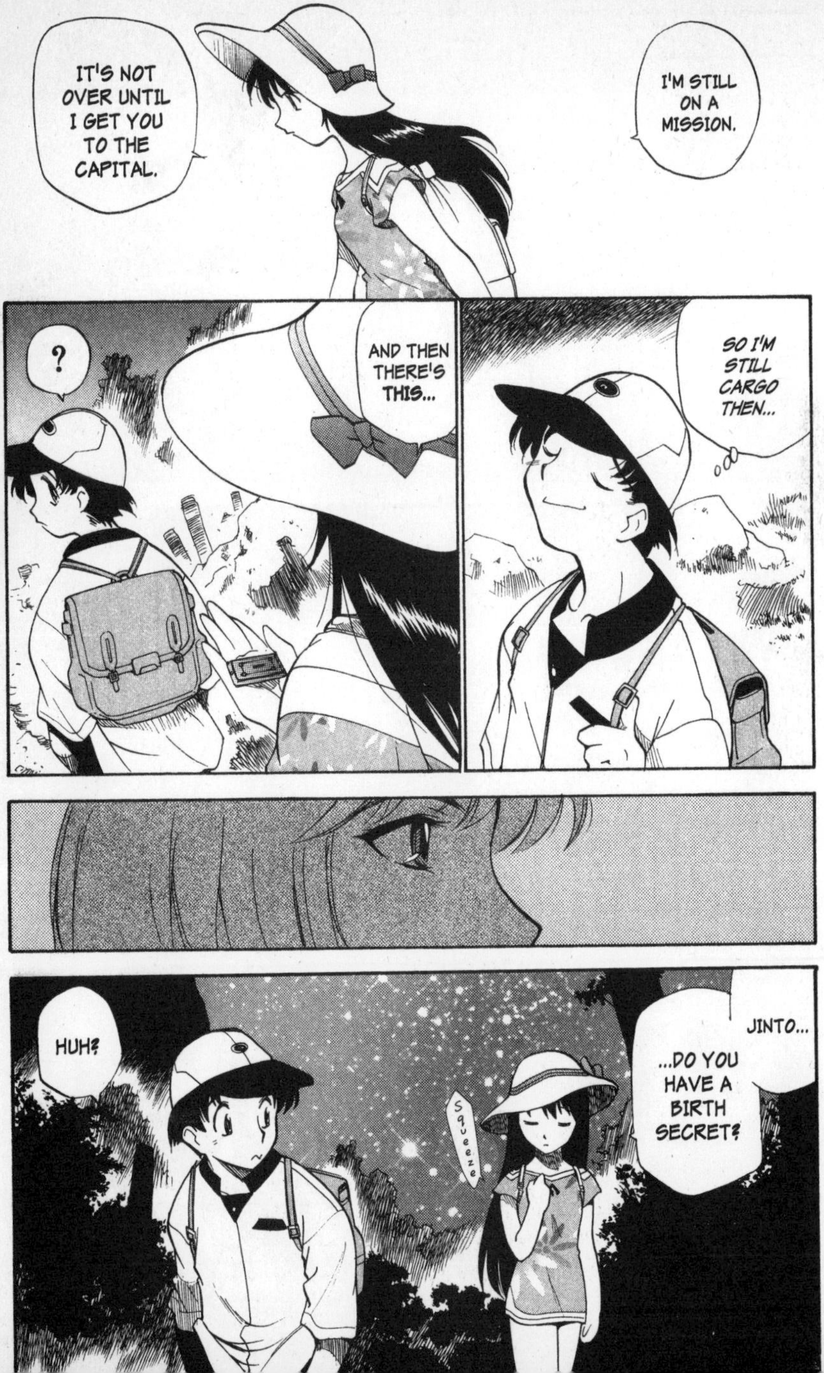
I'M STILL ON A MISSION.
IT'S NOT OVER UNTIL I GET YOU TO THE CAPITAL.
SO I'M STILL CARGO THEN...
AND THEN THERE'S THIS...
?
JINTO...
...DO YOU HAVE A BIRTH SECRET?
Squeeze
HUH?

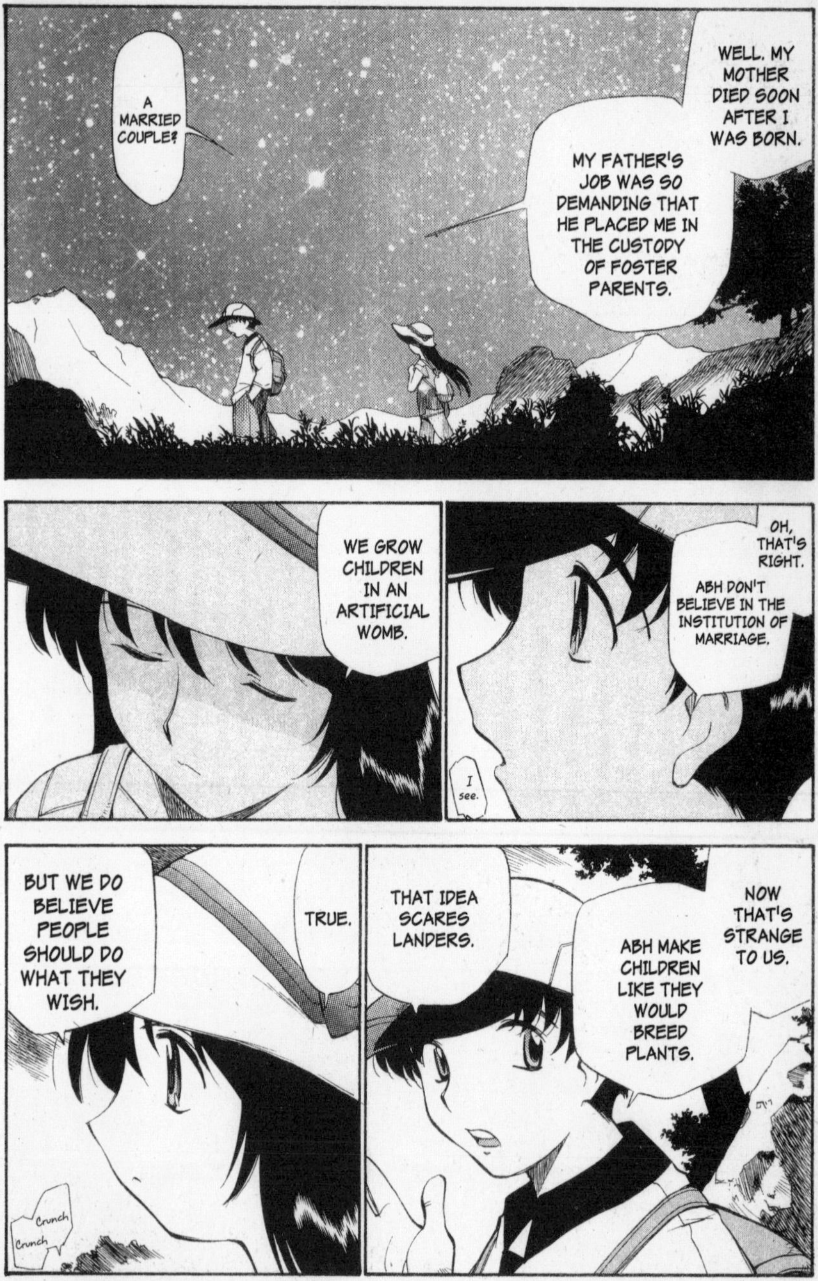
WELL. MY MOTHER DIED SOON AFTER I WAS BORN.
MY FATHER'S JOB WAS SO DEMANDING THAT HE PLACED ME IN THE CUSTODY OF FOSTER PARENTS.
A MARRIED COUPLE?
OH, THAT'S RIGHT.
ABH DON'T BELIEVE IN THE INSTITUTION OF MARRIAGE.
I see.
WE GROW CHILDREN IN AN ARTIFICIAL WOMB.
NOW THAT'S STRANGE TO US.
ABH MAKE CHILDREN LIKE THEY WOULD BREED PLANTS.
THAT IDEA SCARES LANDERS.
TRUE.
BUT WE DO BELIEVE PEOPLE SHOULD DO WHAT THEY WISH.
Crunch
Crunch

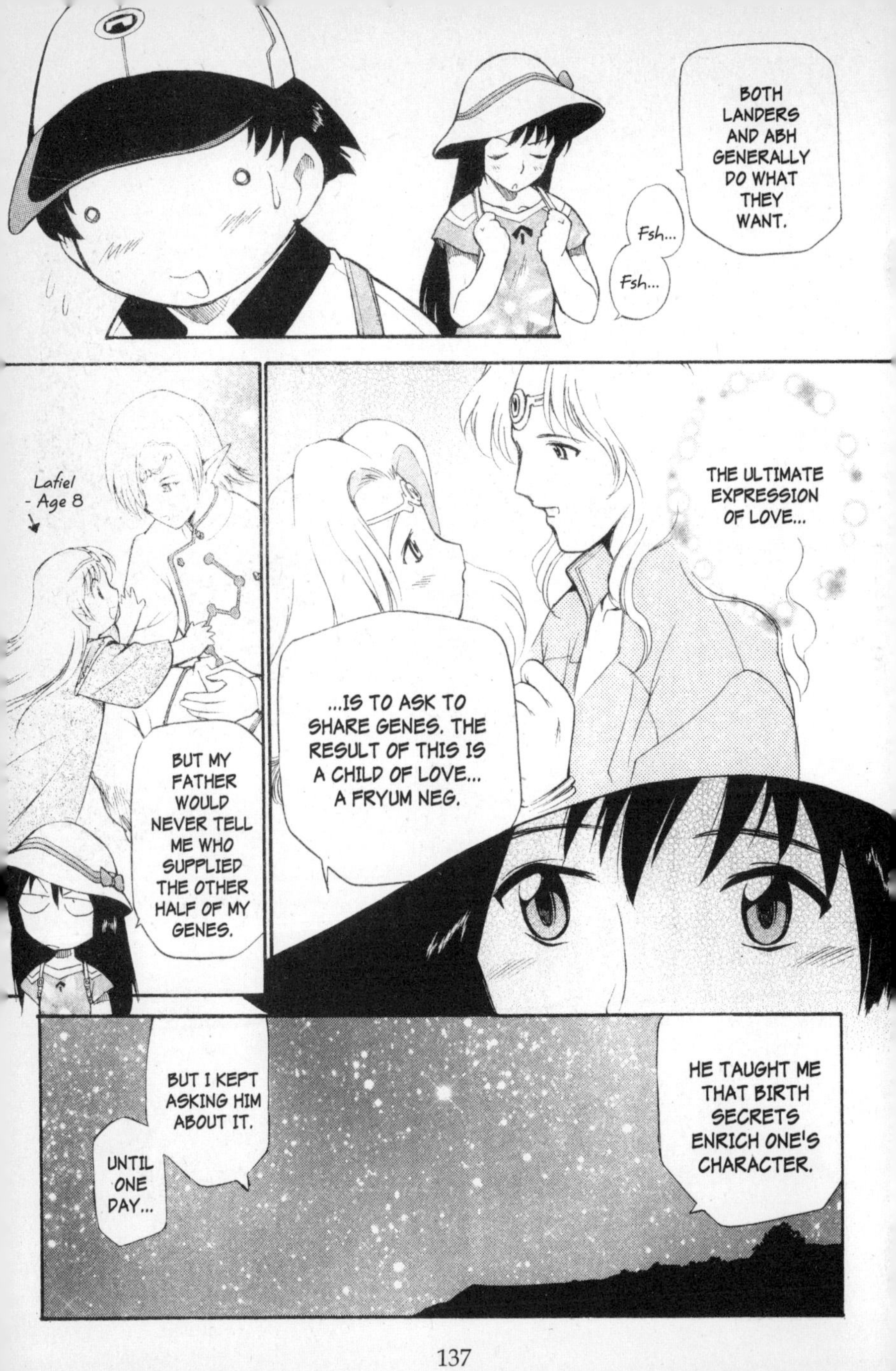
BOTH LANDERS AND ABH GENERALLY DO WHAT THEY WANT.
Fsh...
Fsh...
THE ULTIMATE EXPRESSION OF LOVE...
...IS TO ASK TO SHARE GENES. THE RESULT OF THIS IS A CHILD OF LOVE... A FRYUM NEG.
Lafiel - Age 8
BUT MY FATHER WOULD NEVER TELL ME WHO SUPPLIED THE OTHER HALF OF MY GENES.
HE TAUGHT ME THAT BIRTH SECRETS ENRICH ONE'S CHARACTER.
BUT I KEPT ASKING HIM ABOUT IT.
UNTIL ONE DAY...

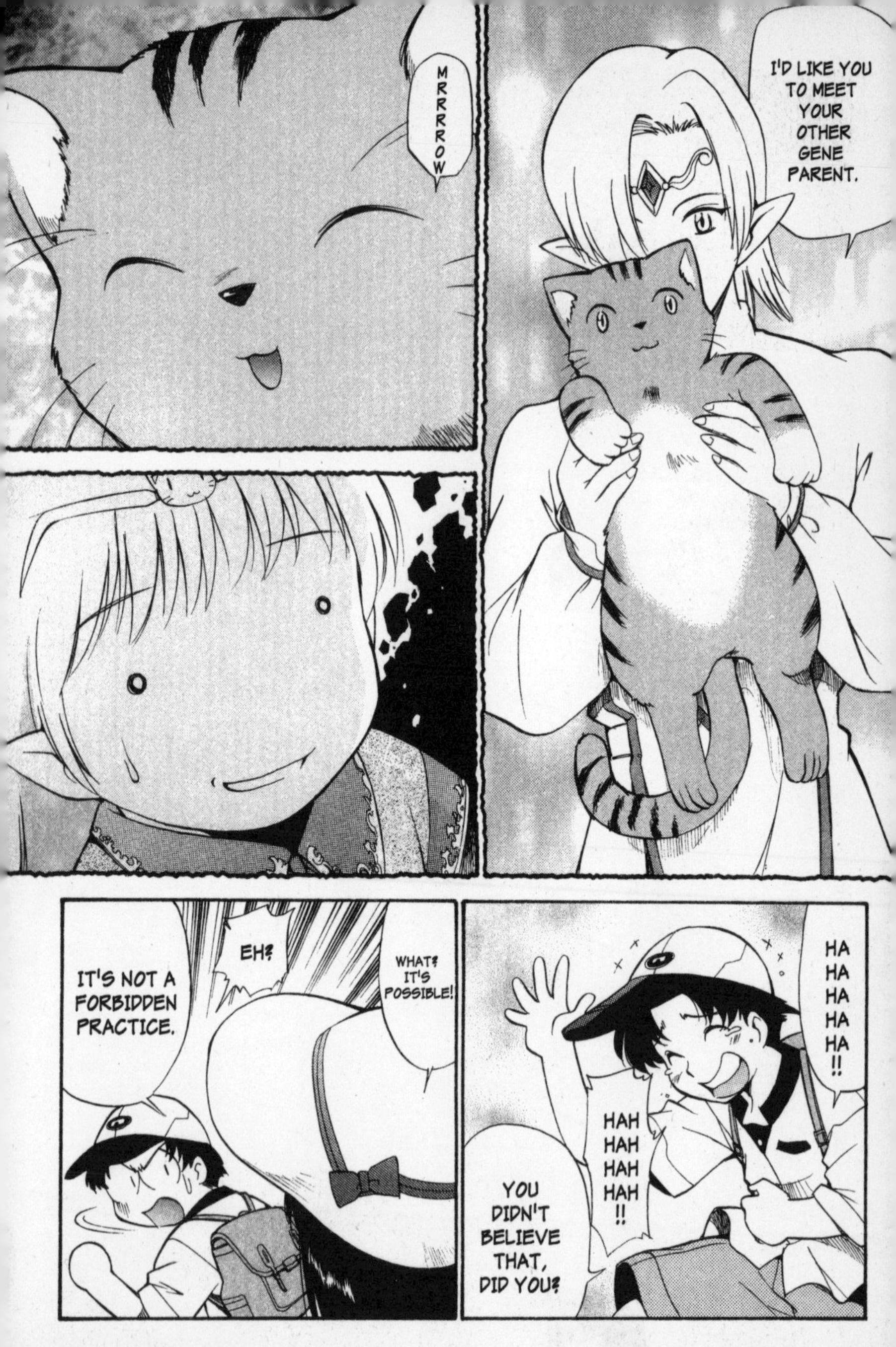
I'D LIKE YOU TO MEET YOUR OTHER GENE PARENT.
MRRRROW
HA HA HA HA HA !!
HAH HAH HAH HAH !!
YOU DIDN'T BELIEVE THAT, DID YOU?
WHAT? IT'S POSSIBLE!
EH?
IT'S NOT A FORBIDDEN PRACTICE.

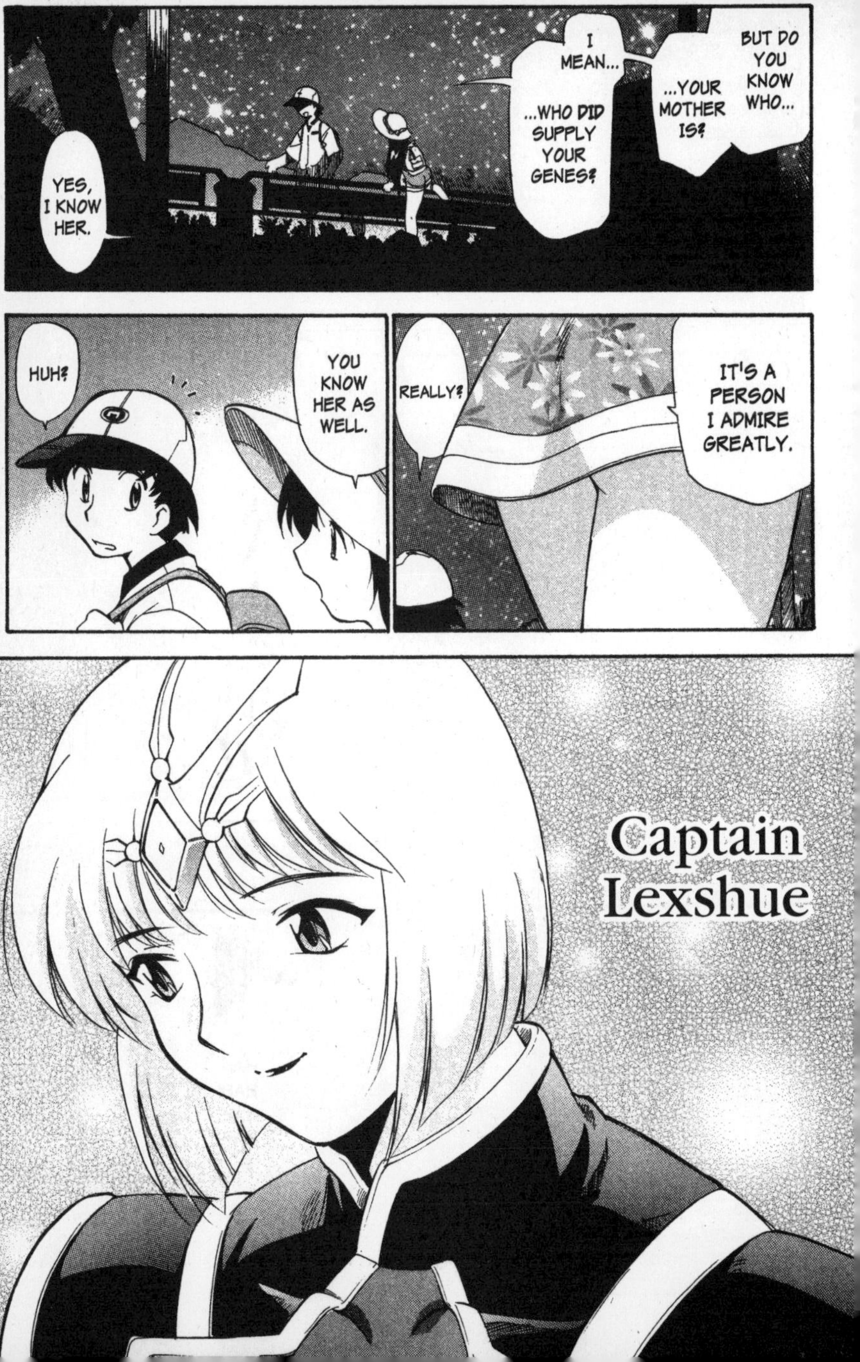
BUT DO YOU KNOW WHO...
...YOUR MOTHER IS?
I MEAN...
...WHO DID SUPPLY YOUR GENES?
YES, I KNOW HER.
IT'S A PERSON I ADMIRE GREATLY.
REALLY?
YOU KNOW HER AS WELL.
HUH?
Captain Lexshue

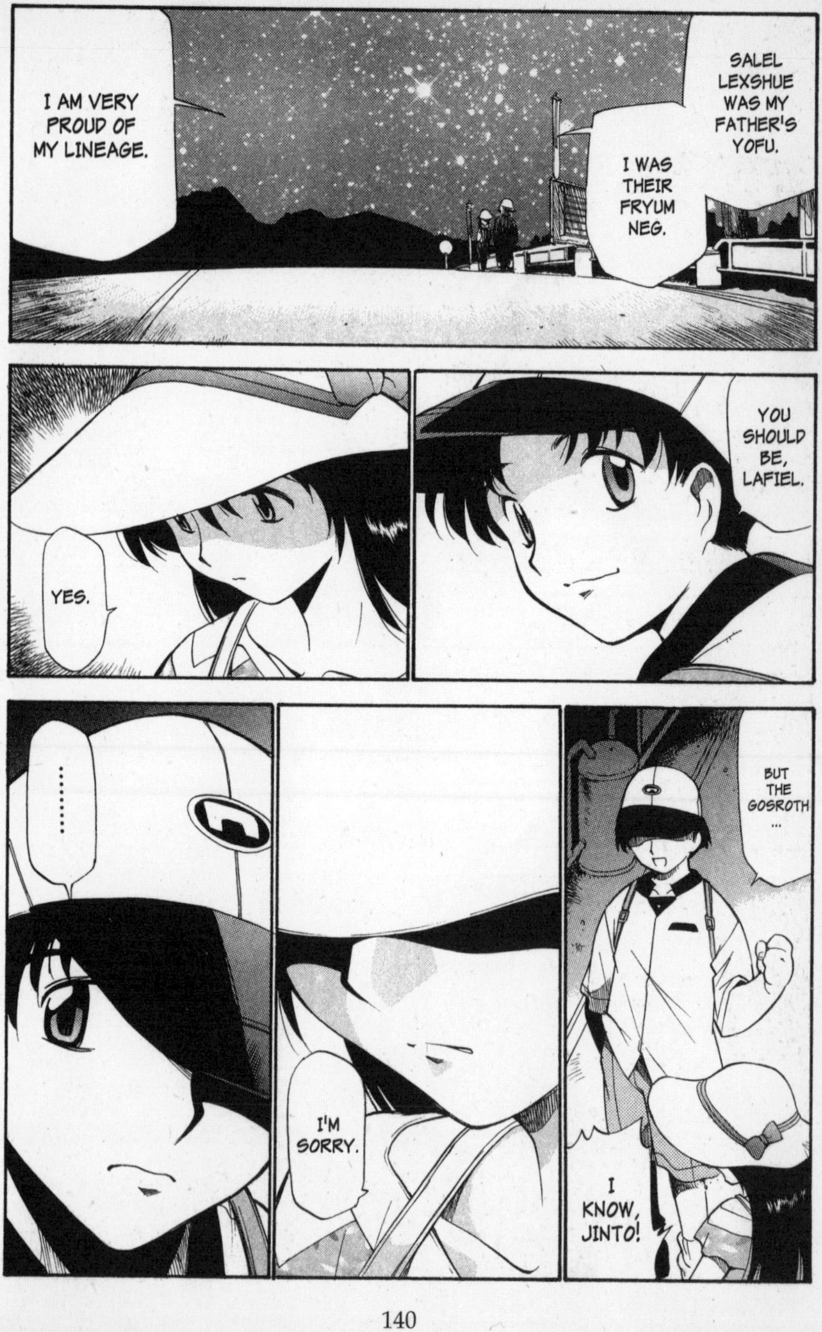
SALEL LEXSHUE WAS MY FATHER'S YOFU.
I WAS THEIR FRYUM NEG.
I AM VERY PROUD OF MY LINEAGE.
YOU SHOULD BE, LAFIEL.
YES.
BUT THE GOSROTH ...
I KNOW, JINTO!
I'M SORRY.
....

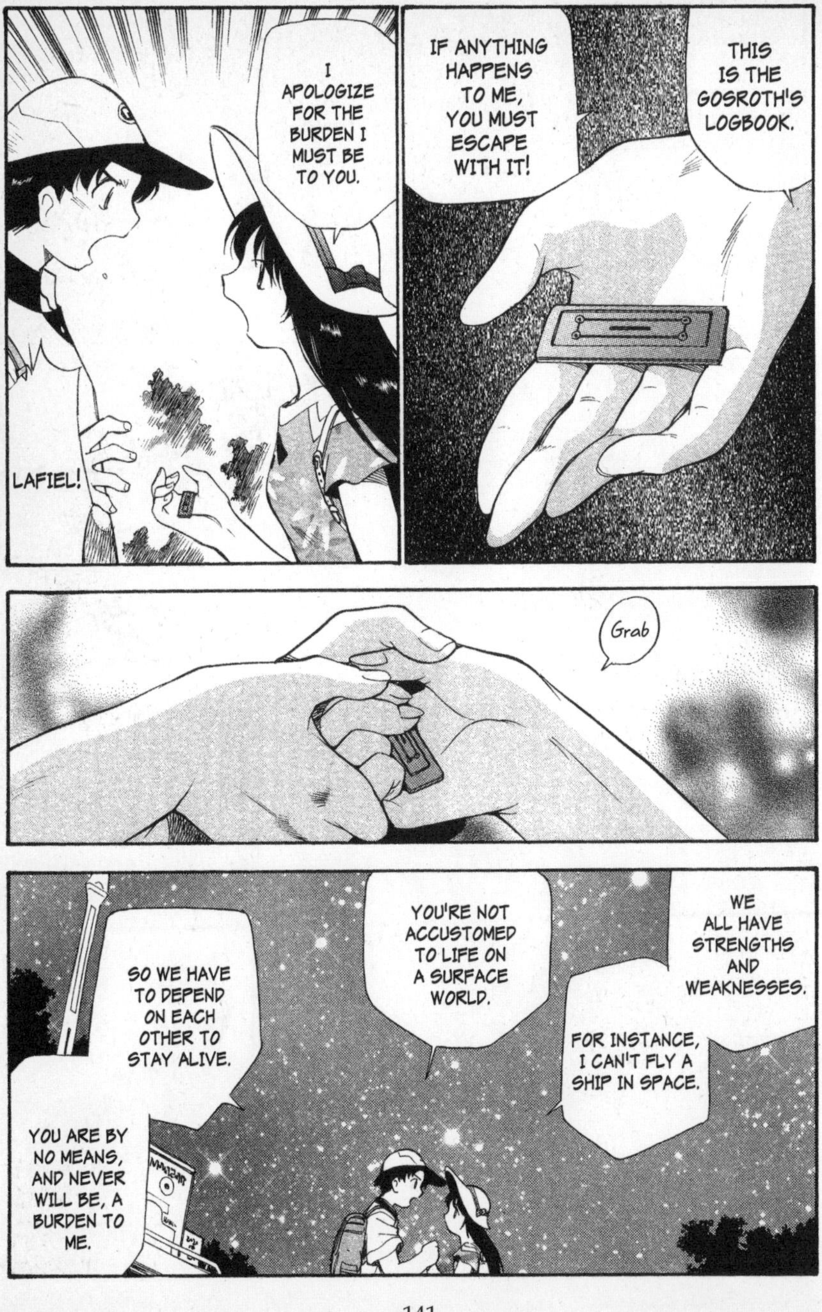
THIS IS THE GOSROTH'S LOGBOOK.
IF ANYTHING HAPPENS TO ME, YOU MUST ESCAPE WITH IT!
I APOLOGIZE FOR THE BURDEN I MUST BE TO YOU.
LAFIEL!
Grab
WE ALL HAVE STRENGTHS AND WEAKNESSES.
FOR INSTANCE, I CAN'T FLY A SHIP IN SPACE.
YOU'RE NOT ACCUSTOMED TO LIFE ON A SURFACE WORLD.
SO WE HAVE TO DEPEND ON EACH OTHER TO STAY ALIVE.
YOU ARE BY NO MEANS, AND NEVER WILL BE, A BURDEN TO ME.

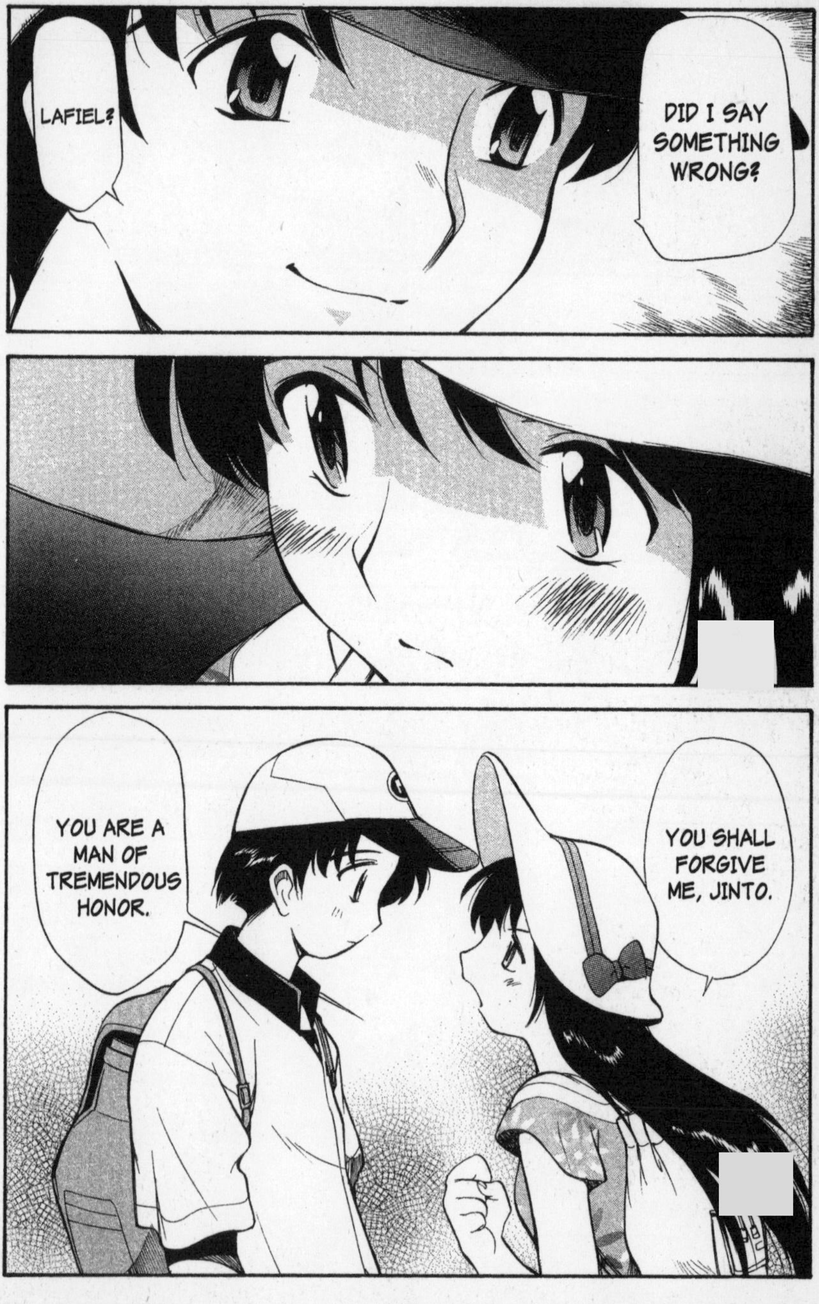
DID I SAY SOMETHING WRONG?
LAFIEL?
YOU SHALL FORGIVE ME, JINTO.
YOU ARE A MAN OF TREMENDOUS HONOR.

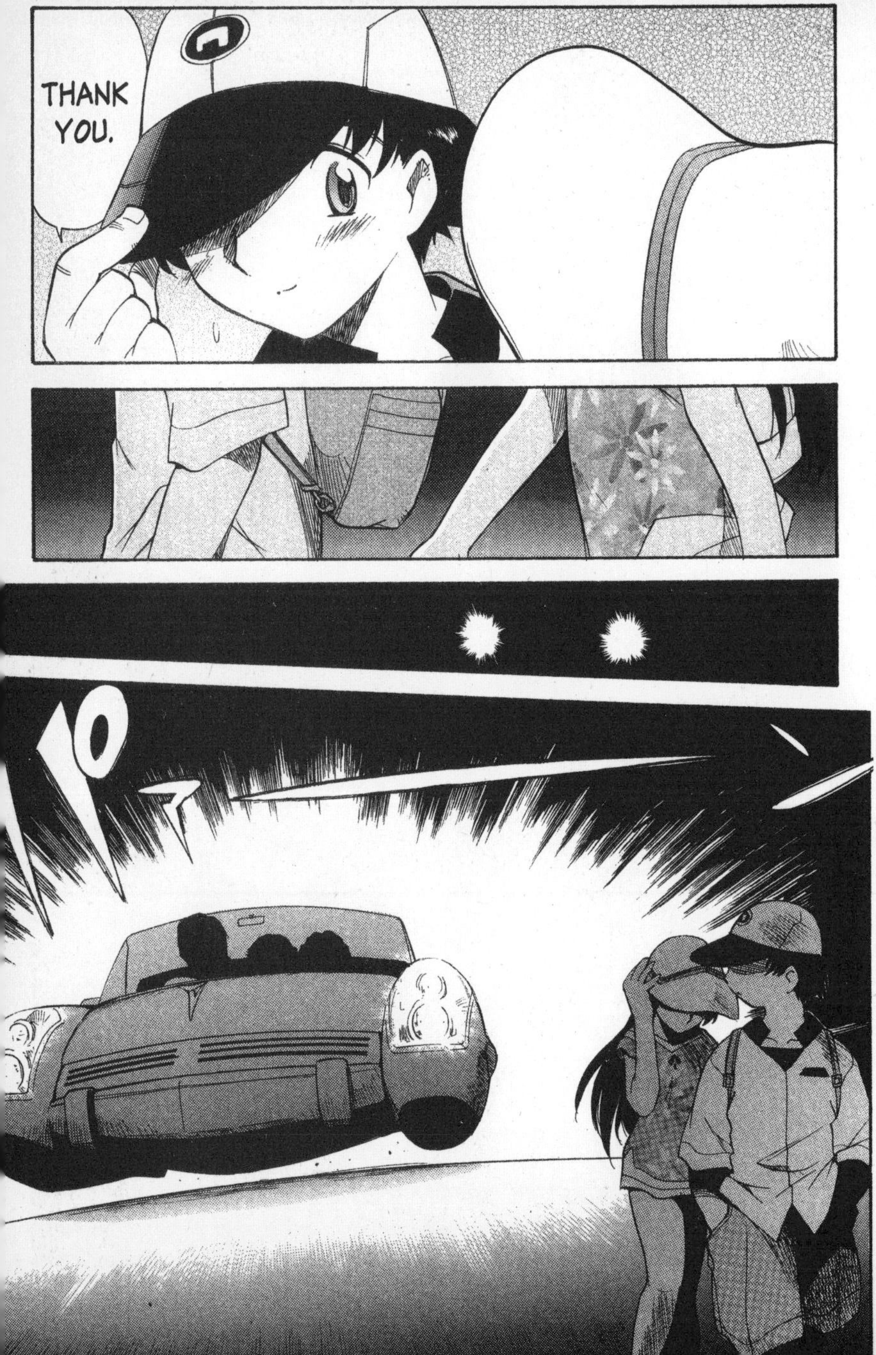
THANK YOU.

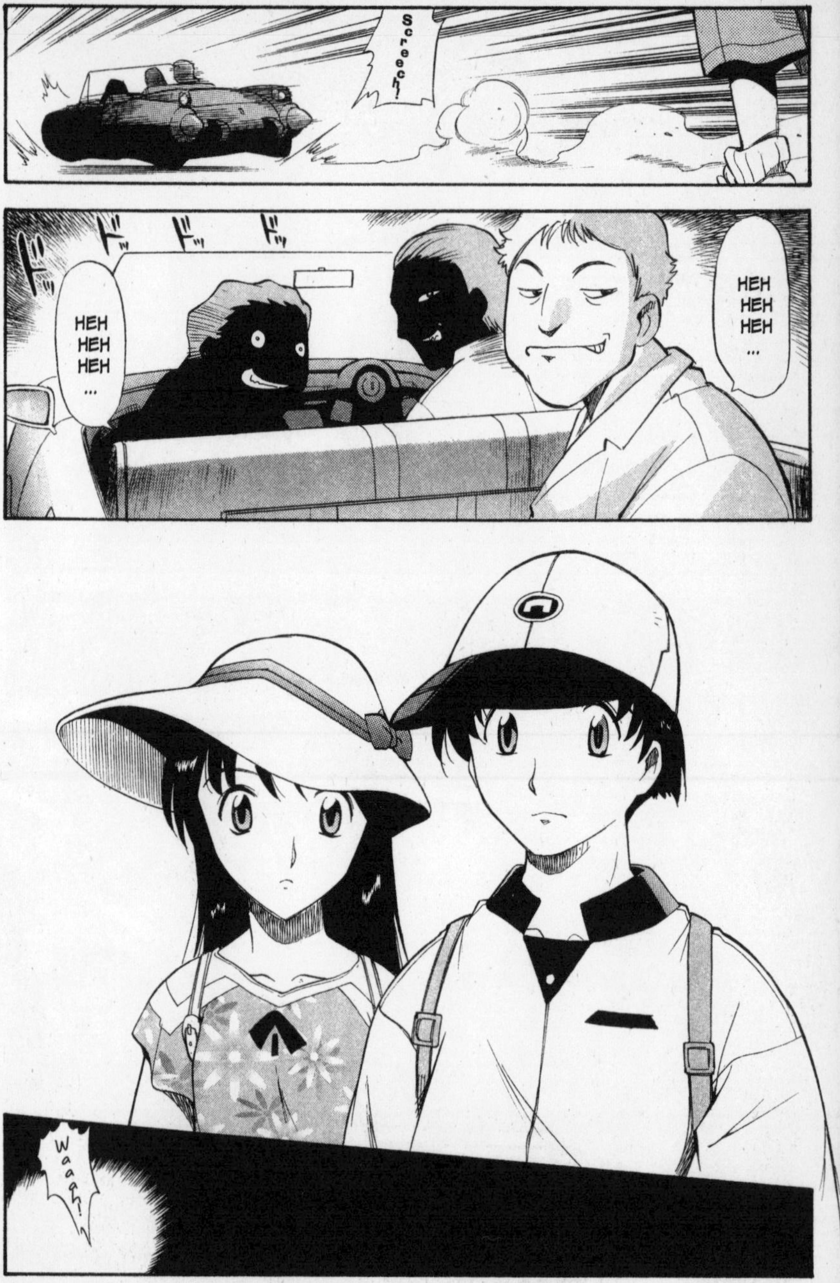
Screech!
HEH HEH HEH ...
ドドッドッドッ
HEH HEH HEH ...
Waaah!

Chapter 5
Collaboration Request

RAD OF OS LOFT

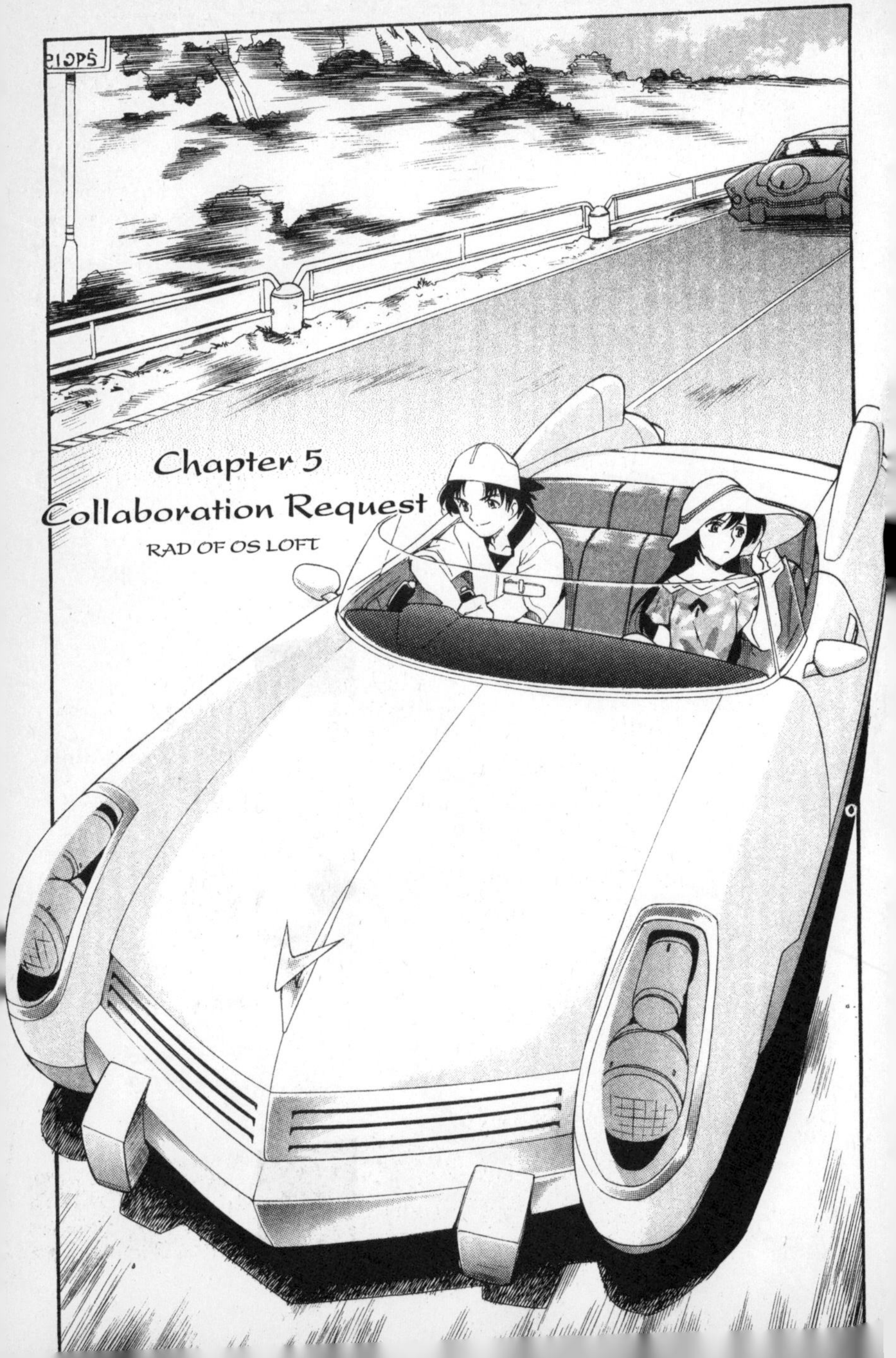

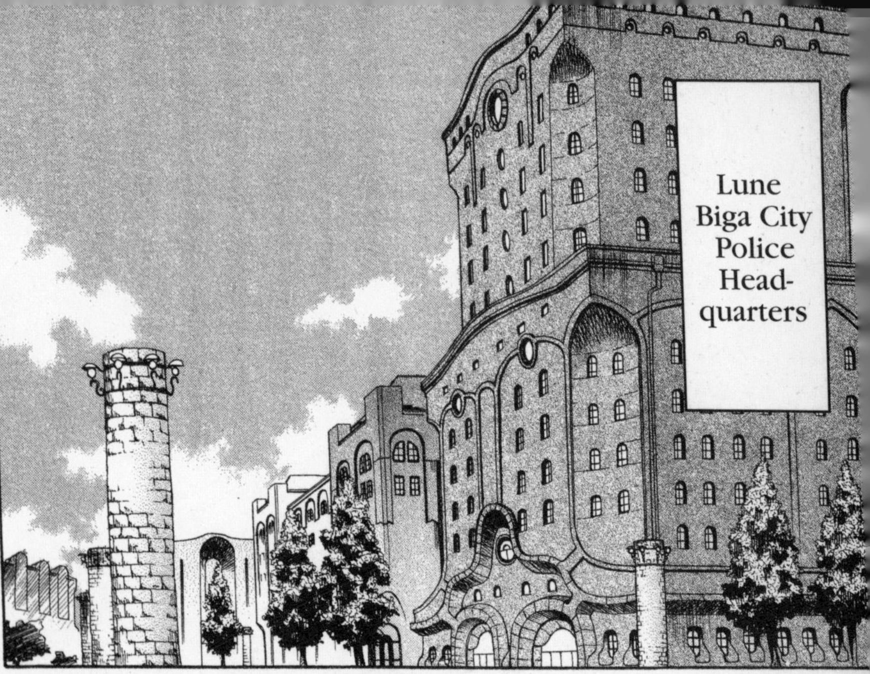
Lune Biga City Police Head-quarters

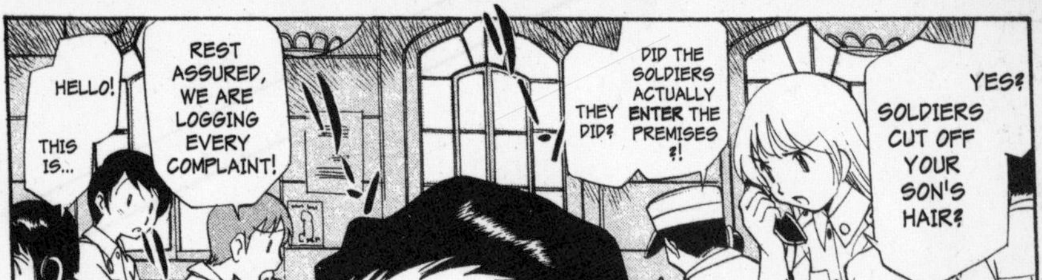
YES? SOLDIERS CUT OFF YOUR SON'S HAIR?
THEY DID? DID THE SOLDIERS ACTUALLY ENTER THE PREMISES?!
REST ASSURED, WE ARE LOGGING EVERY COMPLAINT!
HELLO! THIS IS...

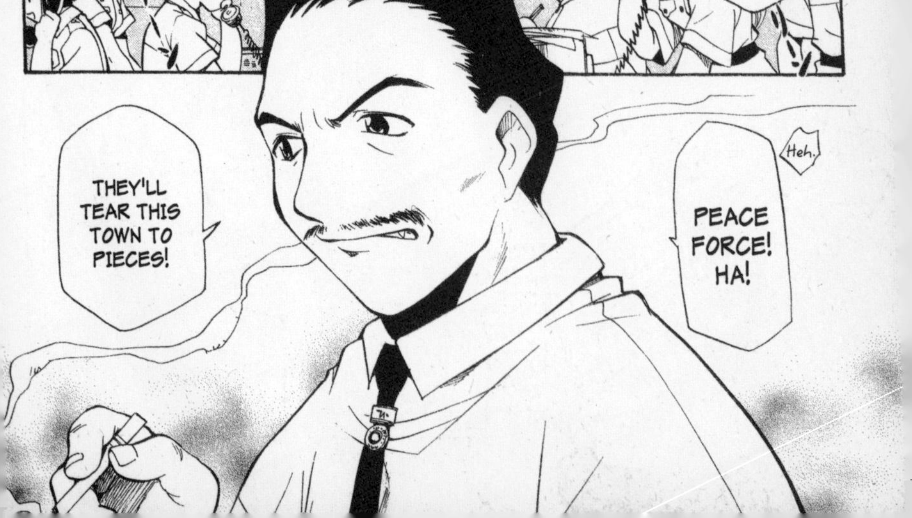
Heh.
PEACE FORCE! HA!
THEY'LL TEAR THIS TOWN TO PIECES!

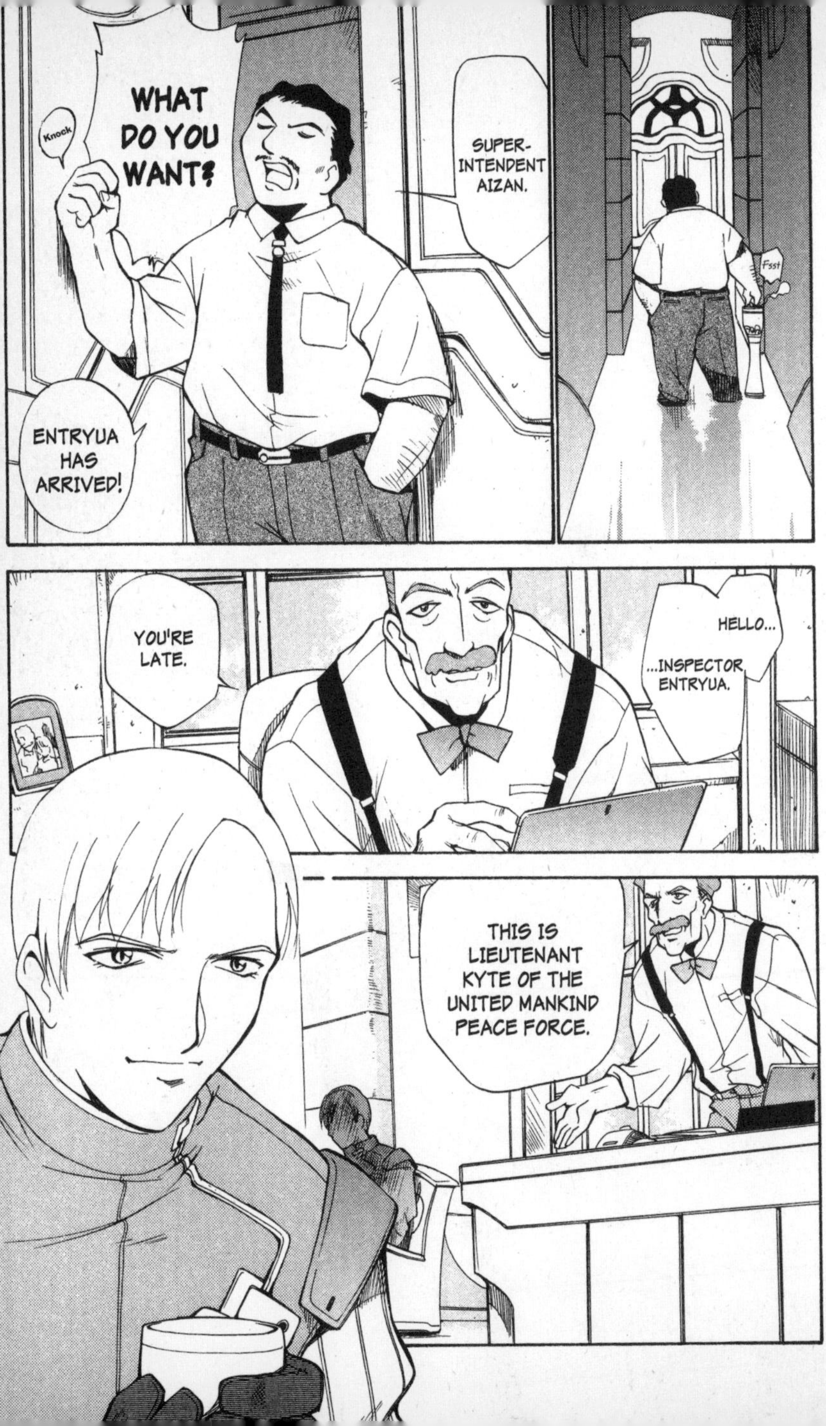
Fsst
Knock
SUPER-INTENDENT AIZAN.
WHAT DO YOU WANT?
ENTRYUA HAS ARRIVED!
HELLO...
...INSPECTOR ENTRYUA.
YOU'RE LATE.
THIS IS LIEUTENANT KYTE OF THE UNITED MANKIND PEACE FORCE.

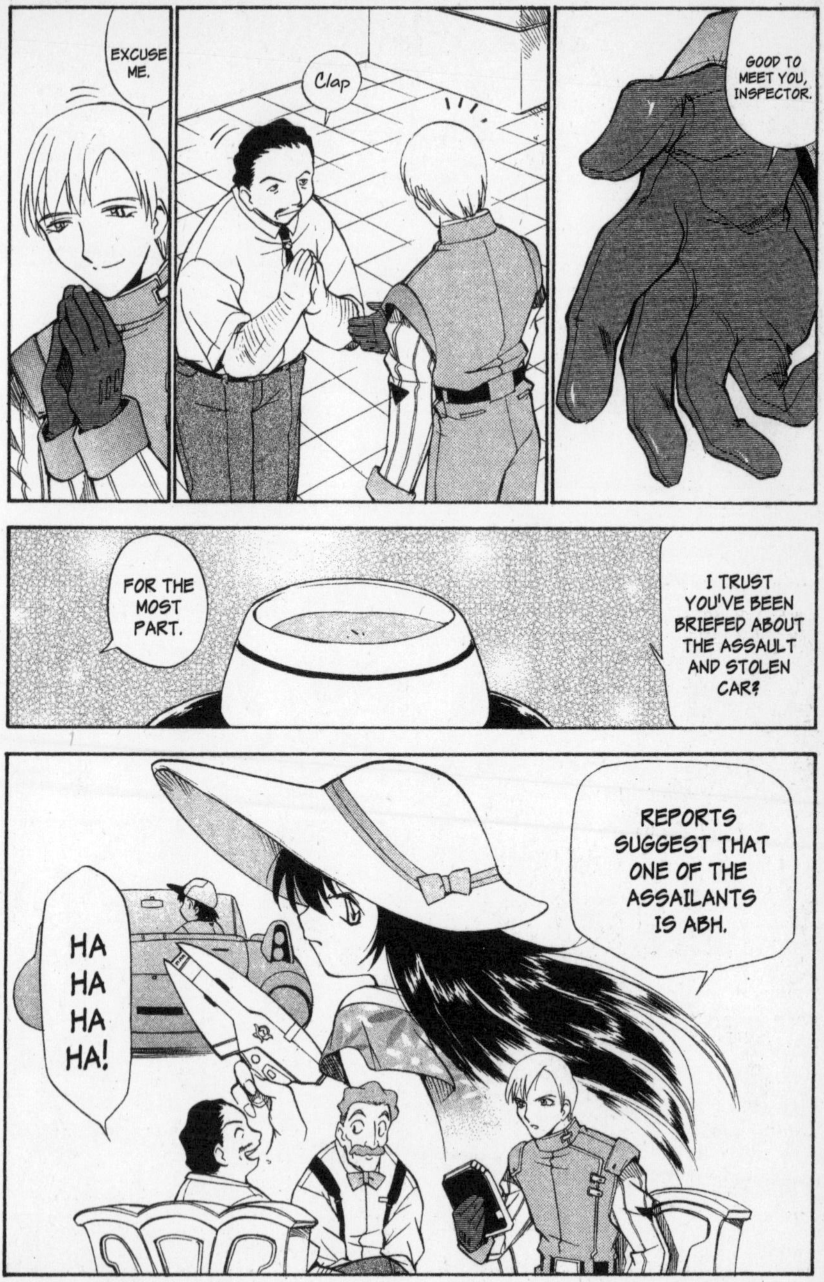
GOOD TO MEET YOU, INSPECTOR.
Clap
EXCUSE ME.
I TRUST YOU'VE BEEN BRIEFED ABOUT THE ASSAULT AND STOLEN CAR?
FOR THE MOST PART.
REPORTS SUGGEST THAT ONE OF THE ASSAILANTS IS ABH.
HA HA HA HA!

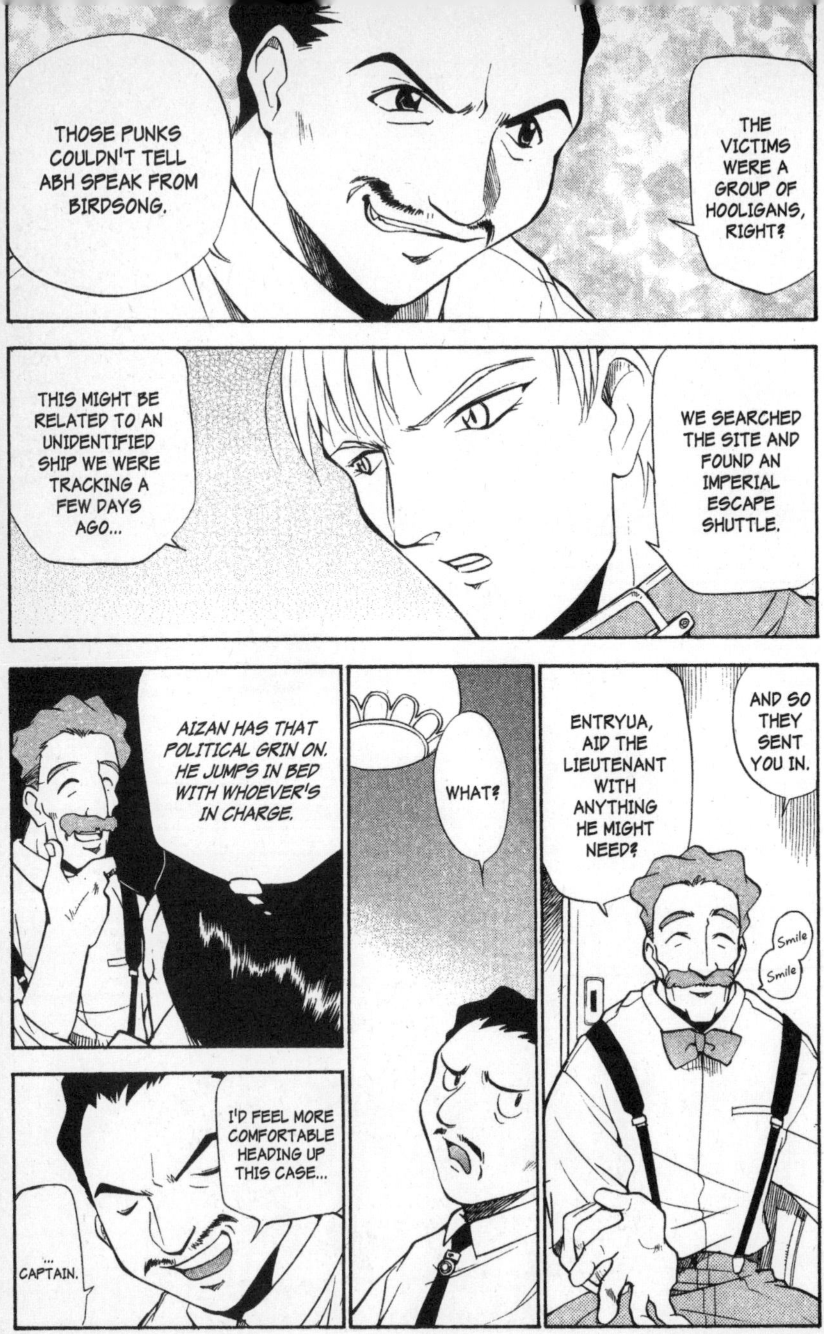
THE VICTIMS WERE A GROUP OF HOOLIGANS, RIGHT?
THOSE PUNKS COULDN'T TELL ABH SPEAK FROM BIRDSONG.
WE SEARCHED THE SITE AND FOUND AN IMPERIAL ESCAPE SHUTTLE.
THIS MIGHT BE RELATED TO AN UNIDENTIFIED SHIP WE WERE TRACKING A FEW DAYS AGO...
AND SO THEY SENT YOU IN.
ENTRYUA, AID THE LIEUTENANT WITH ANYTHING HE MIGHT NEED?
Smile
Smile
WHAT?
AIZAN HAS THAT POLITICAL GRIN ON. HE JUMPS IN BED WITH WHOEVER'S IN CHARGE.
I'D FEEL MORE COMFORTABLE HEADING UP THIS CASE...
... CAPTAIN.

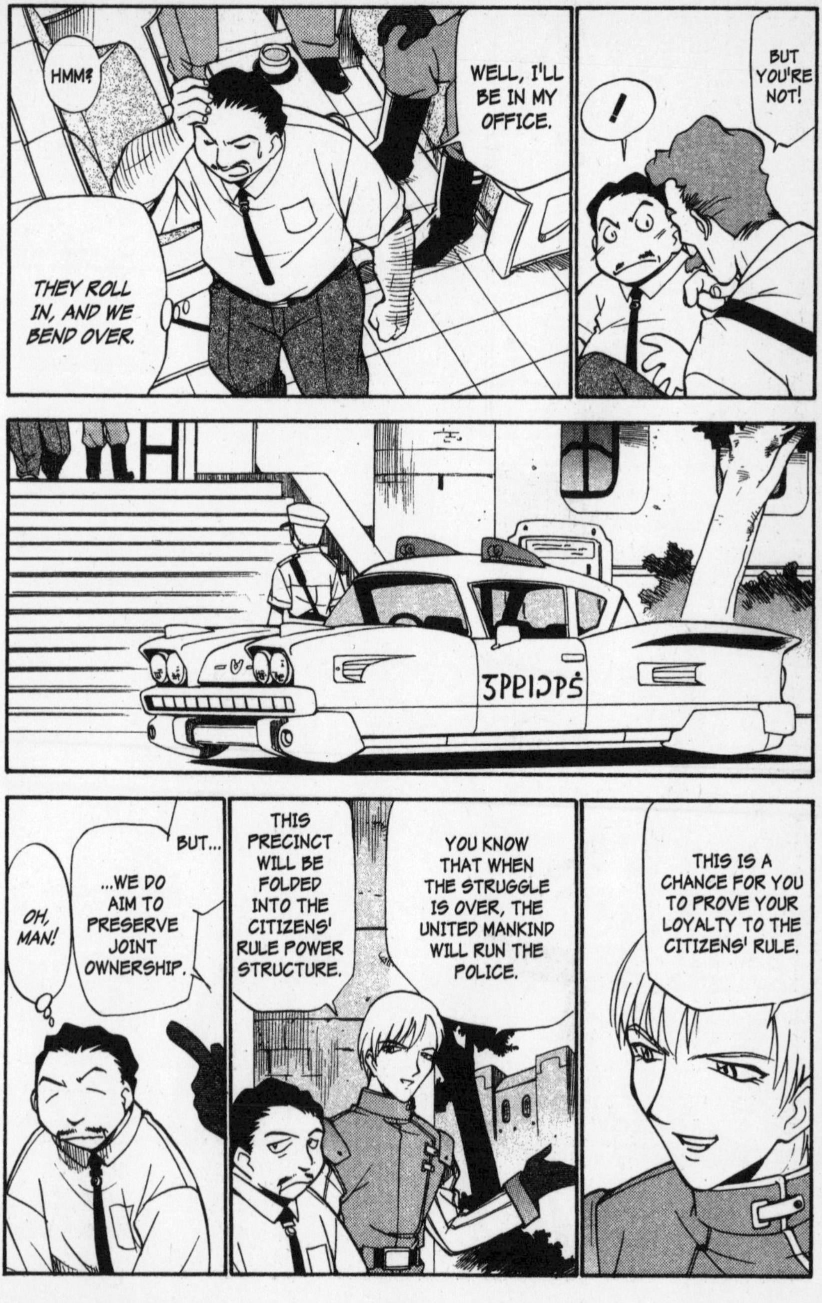
BUT YOU'RE NOT!
!
WELL, I'LL BE IN MY OFFICE.
HMM?
THEY ROLL IN, AND WE BEND OVER.
THIS IS A CHANCE FOR YOU TO PROVE YOUR LOYALTY TO THE CITIZENS' RULE.
YOU KNOW THAT WHEN THE STRUGGLE IS OVER, THE UNITED MANKIND WILL RUN THE POLICE.
THIS PRECINCT WILL BE FOLDED INTO THE CITIZENS' RULE POWER STRUCTURE.
BUT...
...WE DO AIM TO PRESERVE JOINT OWNERSHIP.
OH, MAN!

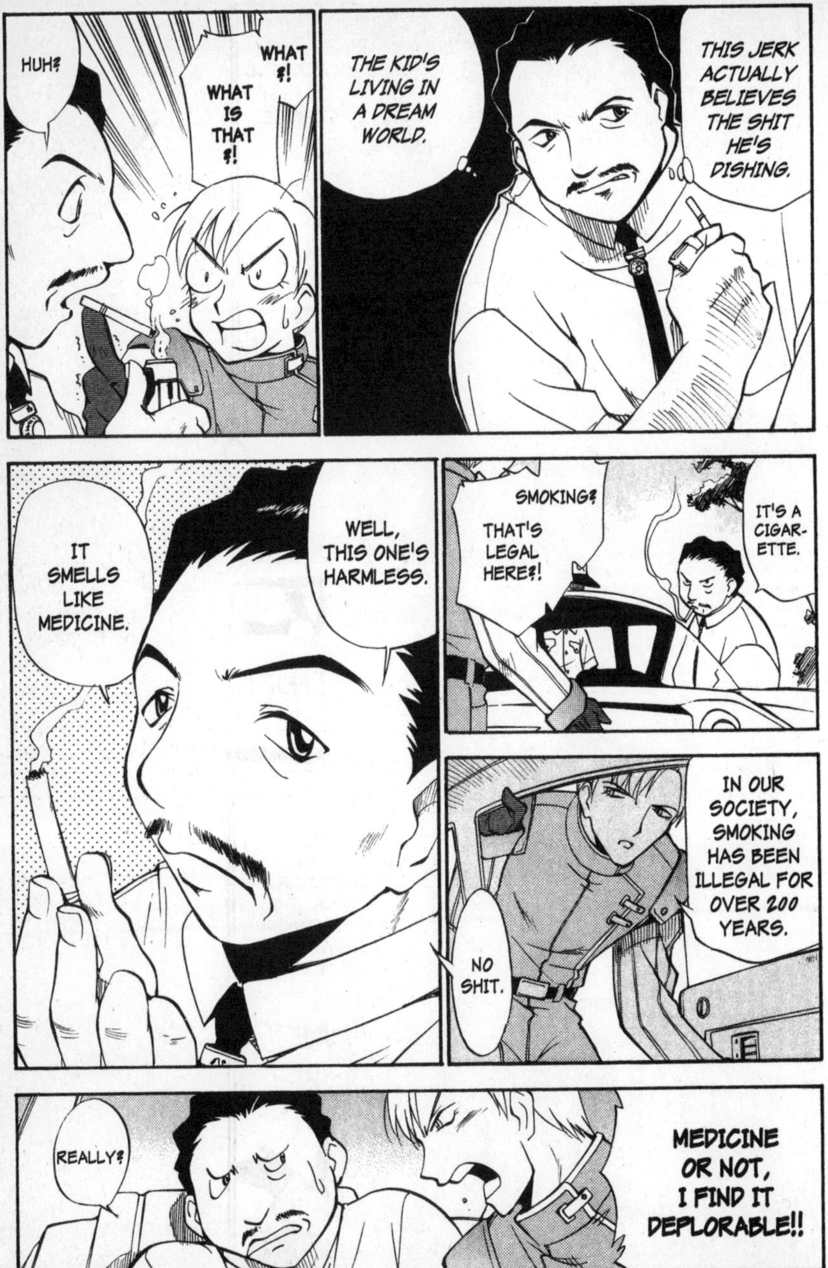
THIS JERK ACTUALLY BELIEVES THE SHIT HE'S DISHING.
THE KID'S LIVING IN A DREAM WORLD.
WHAT ?!
WHAT IS THAT ?!
HUH?
IT'S A CIGARETTE.
SMOKING?
THAT'S LEGAL HERE?!
IN OUR SOCIETY, SMOKING HAS BEEN ILLEGAL FOR OVER 200 YEARS.
NO SHIT.
WELL, THIS ONE'S HARMLESS.
IT SMELLS LIKE MEDICINE.
MEDICINE OR NOT, I FIND IT DEPLORABLE!!
REALLY?

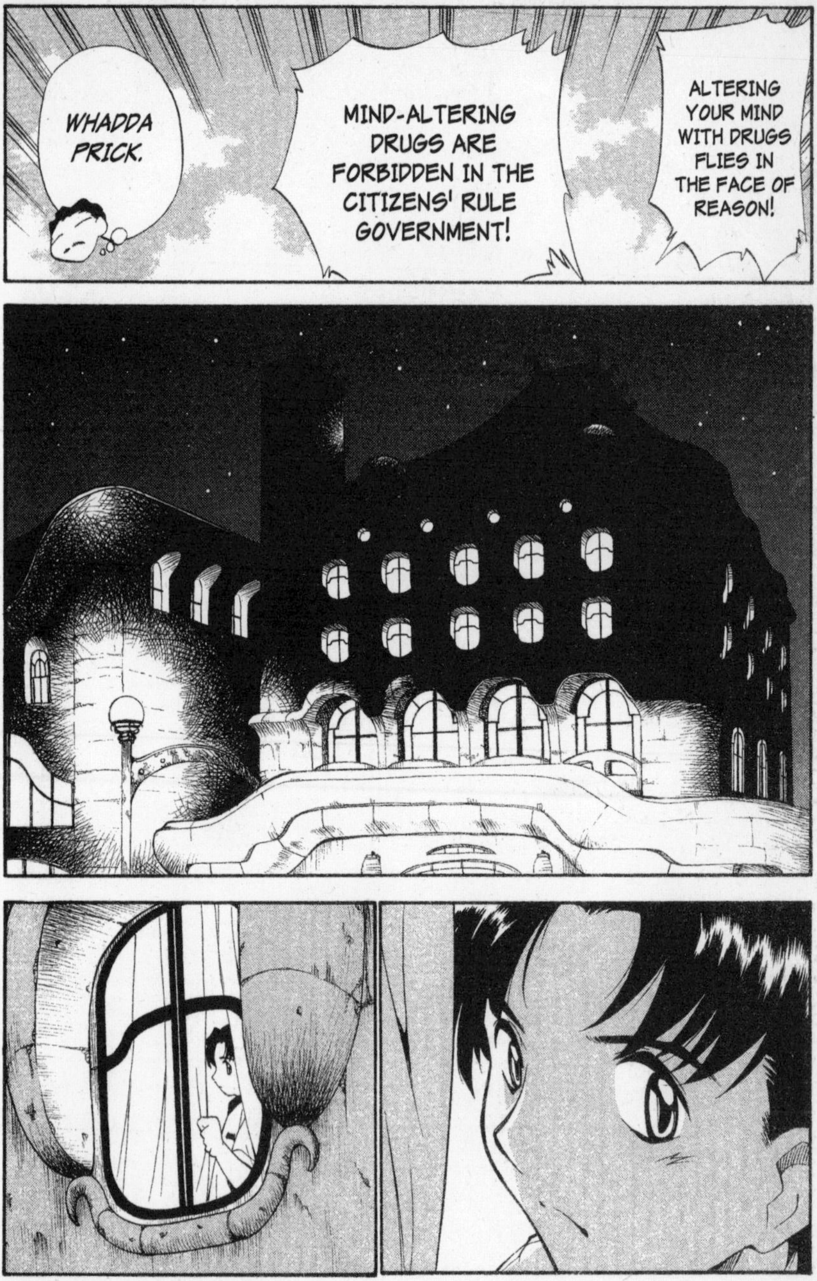
ALTERING YOUR MIND WITH DRUGS FLIES IN THE FACE OF REASON!
MIND-ALTERING DRUGS ARE FORBIDDEN IN THE CITIZENS' RULE GOVERNMENT!
WHADDA PRICK.

[redacted]

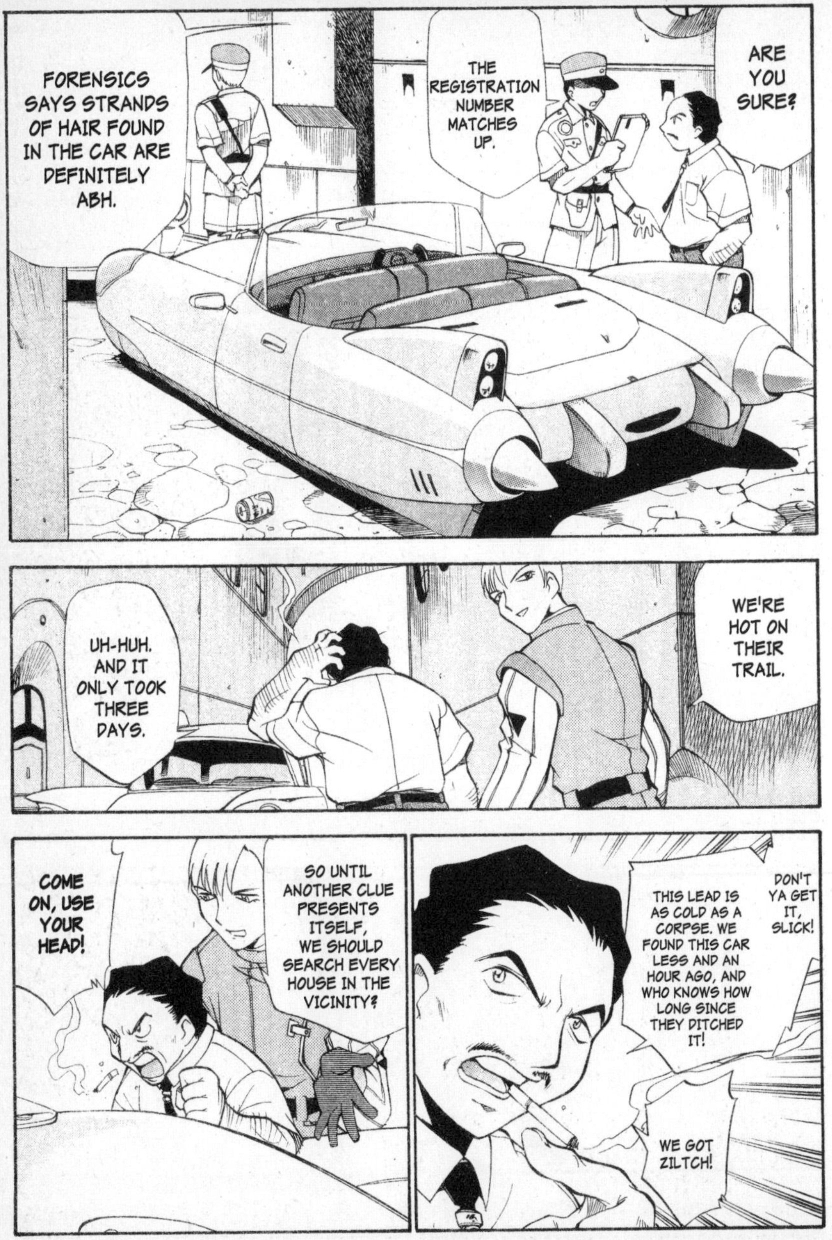

FORENSICS SAYS STRANDS OF HAIR FOUND IN THE CAR ARE DEFINITELY ABH.
THE REGISTRATION NUMBER MATCHES UP.
ARE YOU SURE?
UH-HUH. AND IT ONLY TOOK THREE DAYS.
WE'RE HOT ON THEIR TRAIL.
COME ON, USE YOUR HEAD!
SO UNTIL ANOTHER CLUE PRESENTS ITSELF, WE SHOULD SEARCH EVERY HOUSE IN THE VICINITY?
DON'T YA GET IT, SLICK!
THIS LEAD IS AS COLD AS A CORPSE. WE FOUND THIS CAR LESS AND AN HOUR AGO, AND WHO KNOWS HOW LONG SINCE THEY DITCHED IT!
WE GOT ZILTCH!

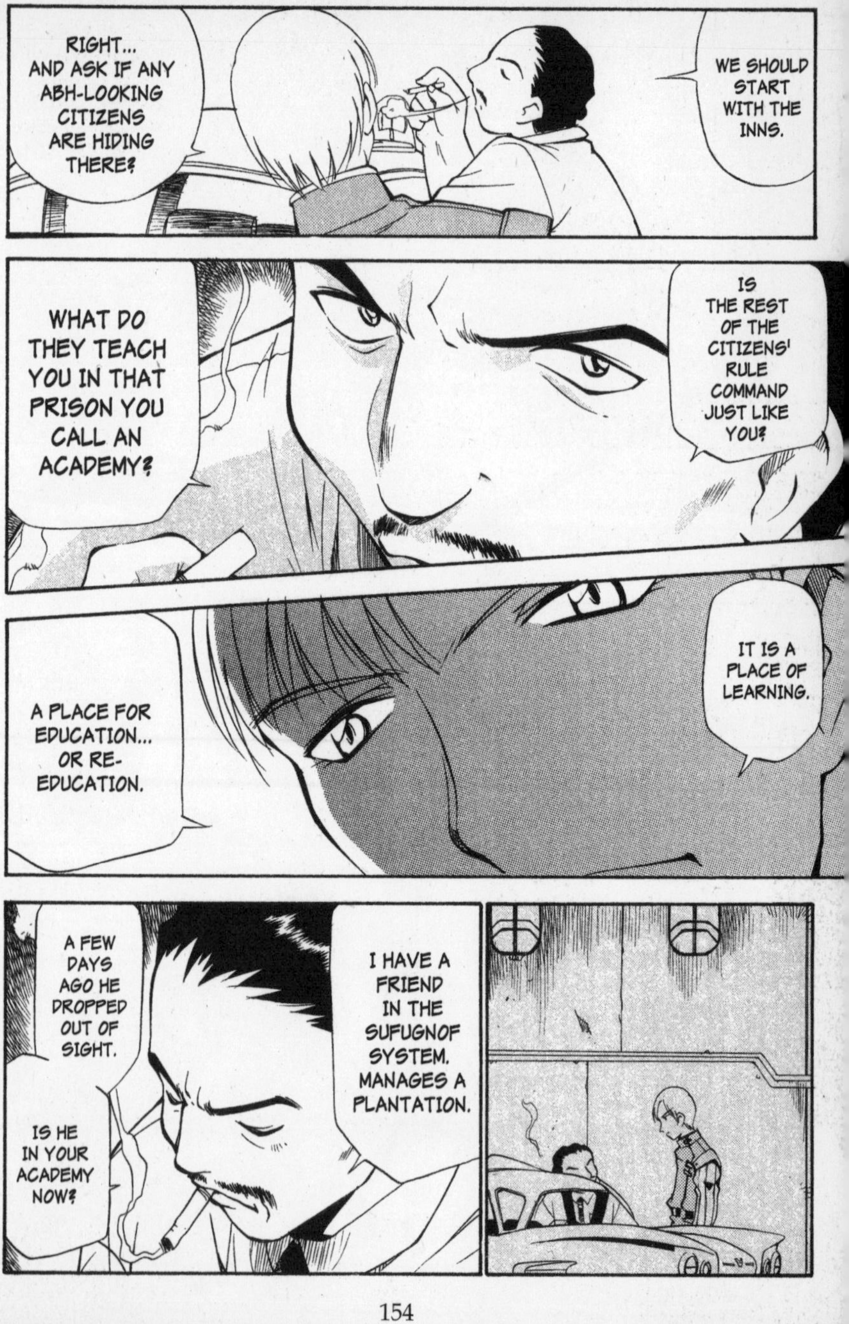
WE SHOULD START WITH THE INNS.
RIGHT... AND ASK IF ANY ABH-LOOKING CITIZENS ARE HIDING THERE?
IS THE REST OF THE CITIZENS' RULE COMMAND JUST LIKE YOU?
WHAT DO THEY TEACH YOU IN THAT PRISON YOU CALL AN ACADEMY?
IT IS A PLACE OF LEARNING.
A PLACE FOR EDUCATION... OR RE-EDUCATION.
I HAVE A FRIEND IN THE SUFUGNOF SYSTEM. MANAGES A PLANTATION.
A FEW DAYS AGO HE DROPPED OUT OF SIGHT.
IS HE IN YOUR ACADEMY NOW?

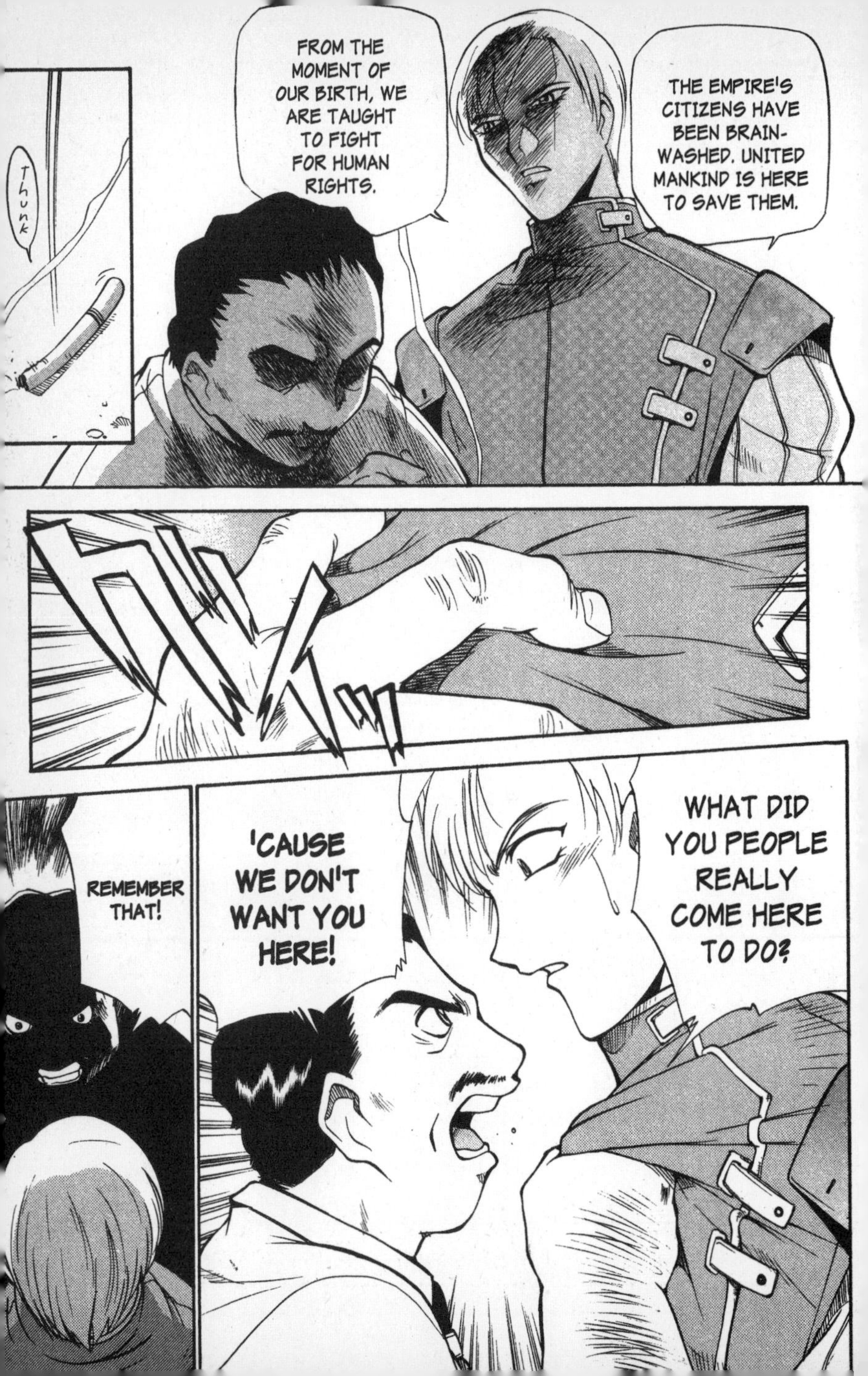
THE EMPIRE'S CITIZENS HAVE BEEN BRAIN-WASHED. UNITED MANKIND IS HERE TO SAVE THEM.
FROM THE MOMENT OF OUR BIRTH, WE ARE TAUGHT TO FIGHT FOR HUMAN RIGHTS.
Thunk
WHAT DID YOU PEOPLE REALLY COME HERE TO DO?
'CAUSE WE DON'T WANT YOU HERE!
REMEMBER THAT!

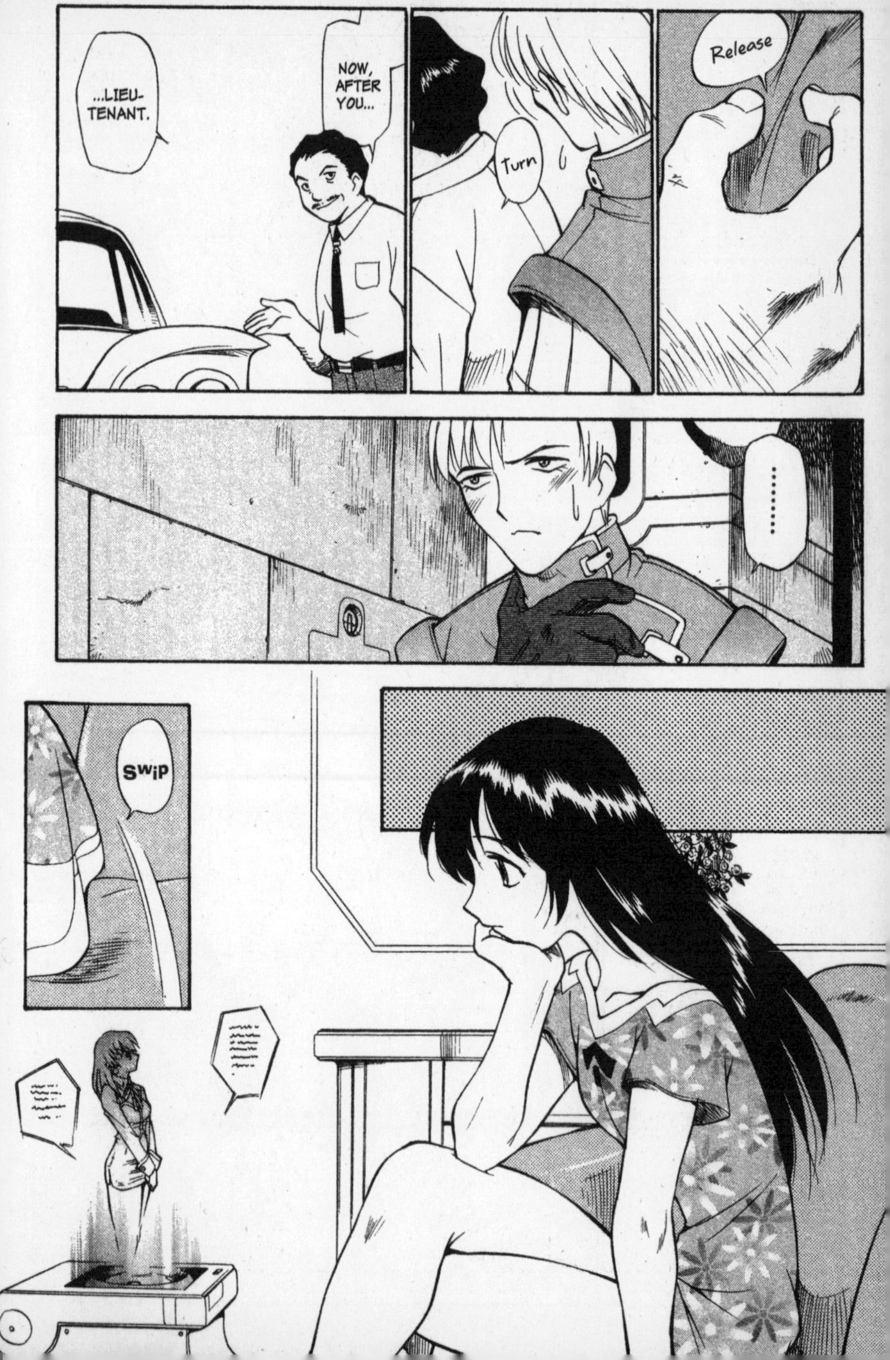
Release
Turn
NOW, AFTER YOU...
...LIEU-TENANT.
....
SWIP

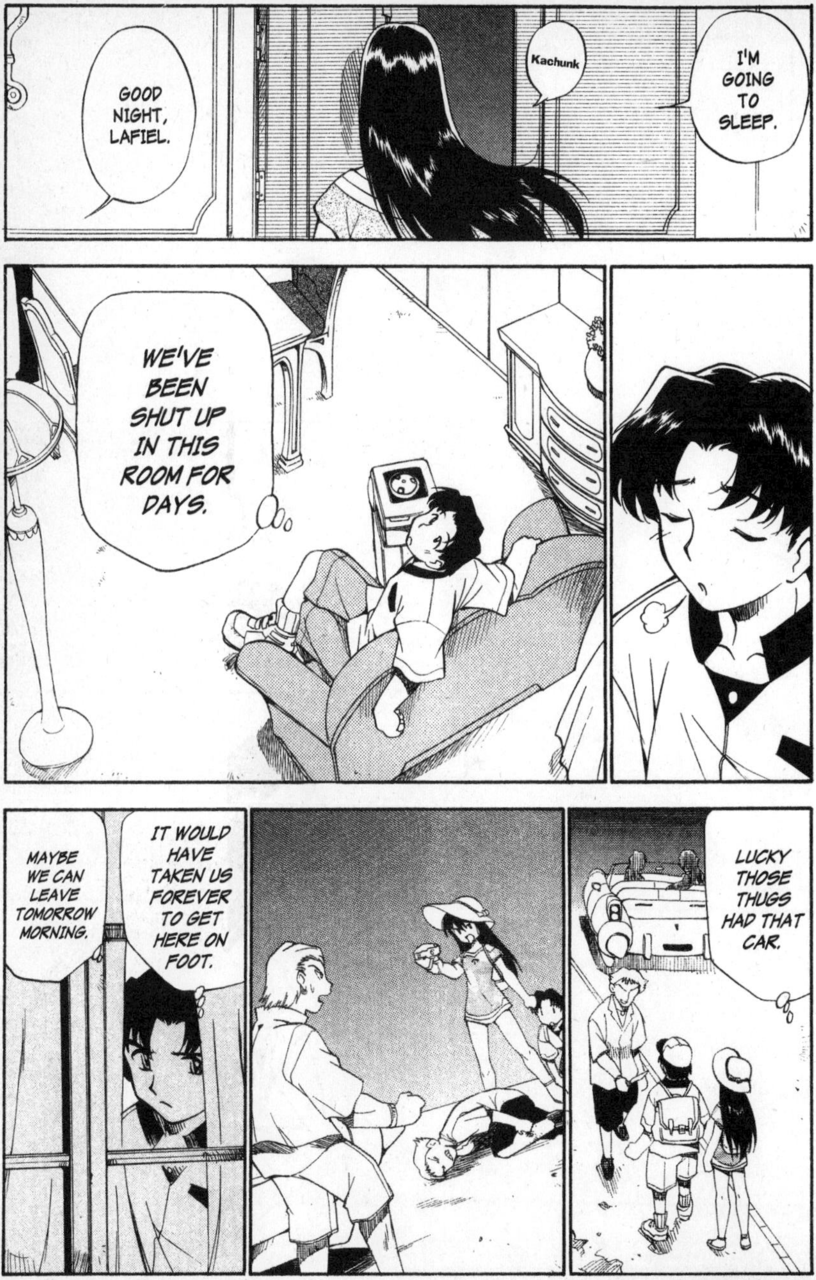
I'M GOING TO SLEEP.
Kachunk
GOOD NIGHT, LAFIEL.
WE'VE BEEN SHUT UP IN THIS ROOM FOR DAYS.
LUCKY THOSE THUGS HAD THAT CAR.
IT WOULD HAVE TAKEN US FOREVER TO GET HERE ON FOOT.
MAYBE WE CAN LEAVE TOMORROW MORNING.

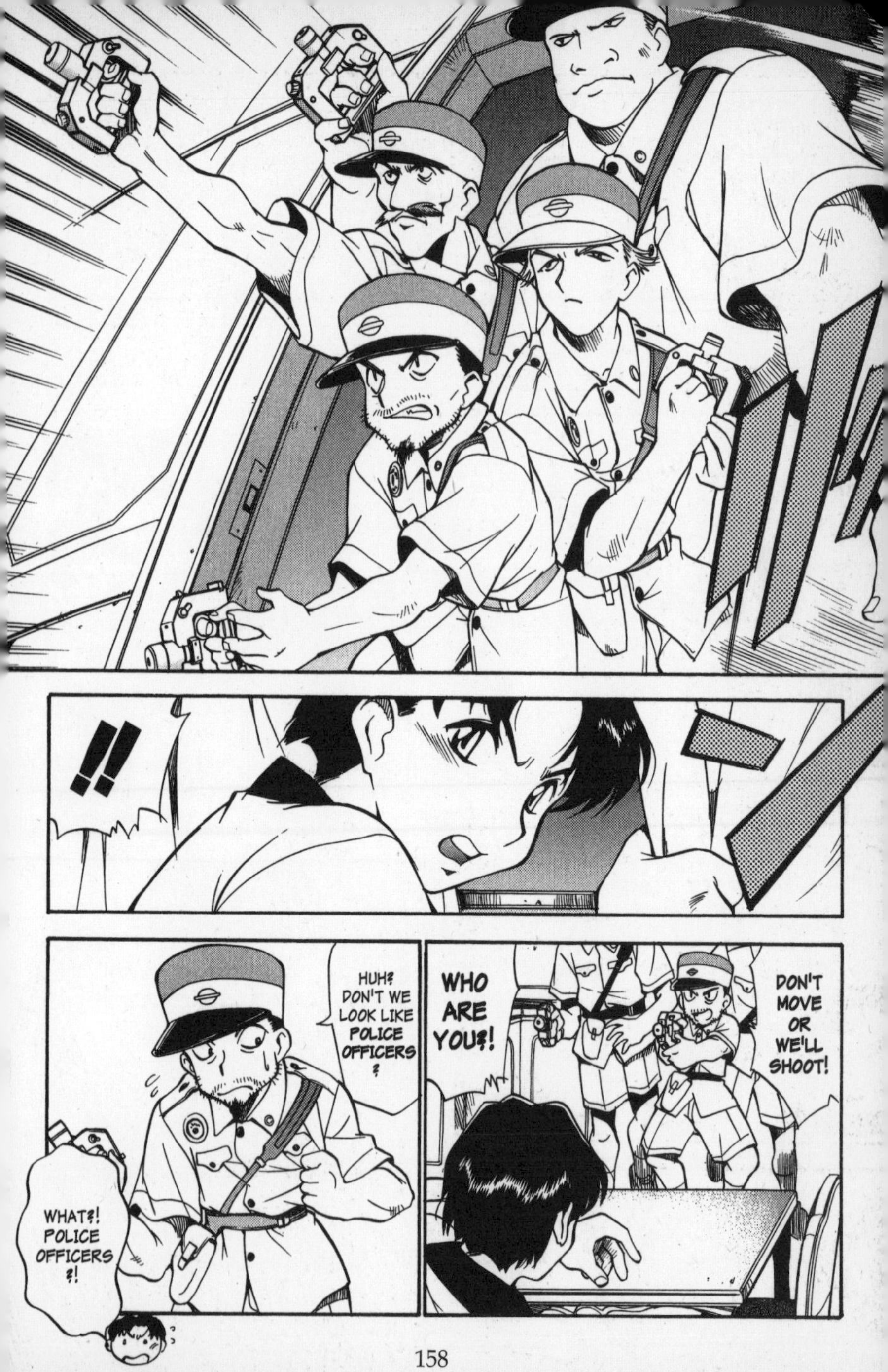
!!
DON'T MOVE OR WE'LL SHOOT!
WHO ARE YOU?!
HUH? DON'T WE LOOK LIKE POLICE OFFICERS?
WHAT?! POLICE OFFICERS?!

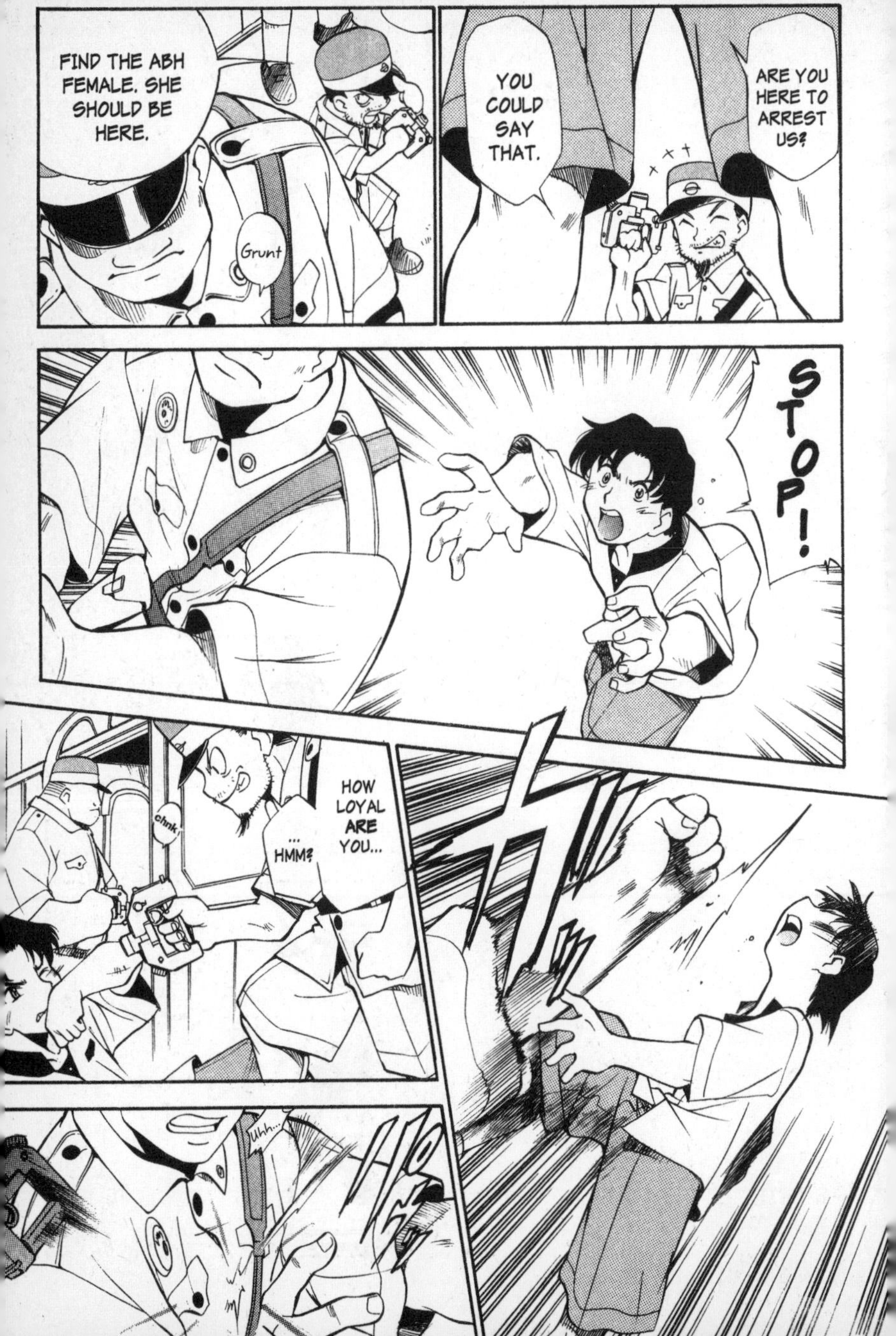
ARE YOU HERE TO ARREST US?
YOU COULD SAY THAT.
FIND THE ABH FEMALE. SHE SHOULD BE HERE.
Grunt
STOP!
HOW LOYAL ARE YOU...
... HMM?
chnk
Uhh...

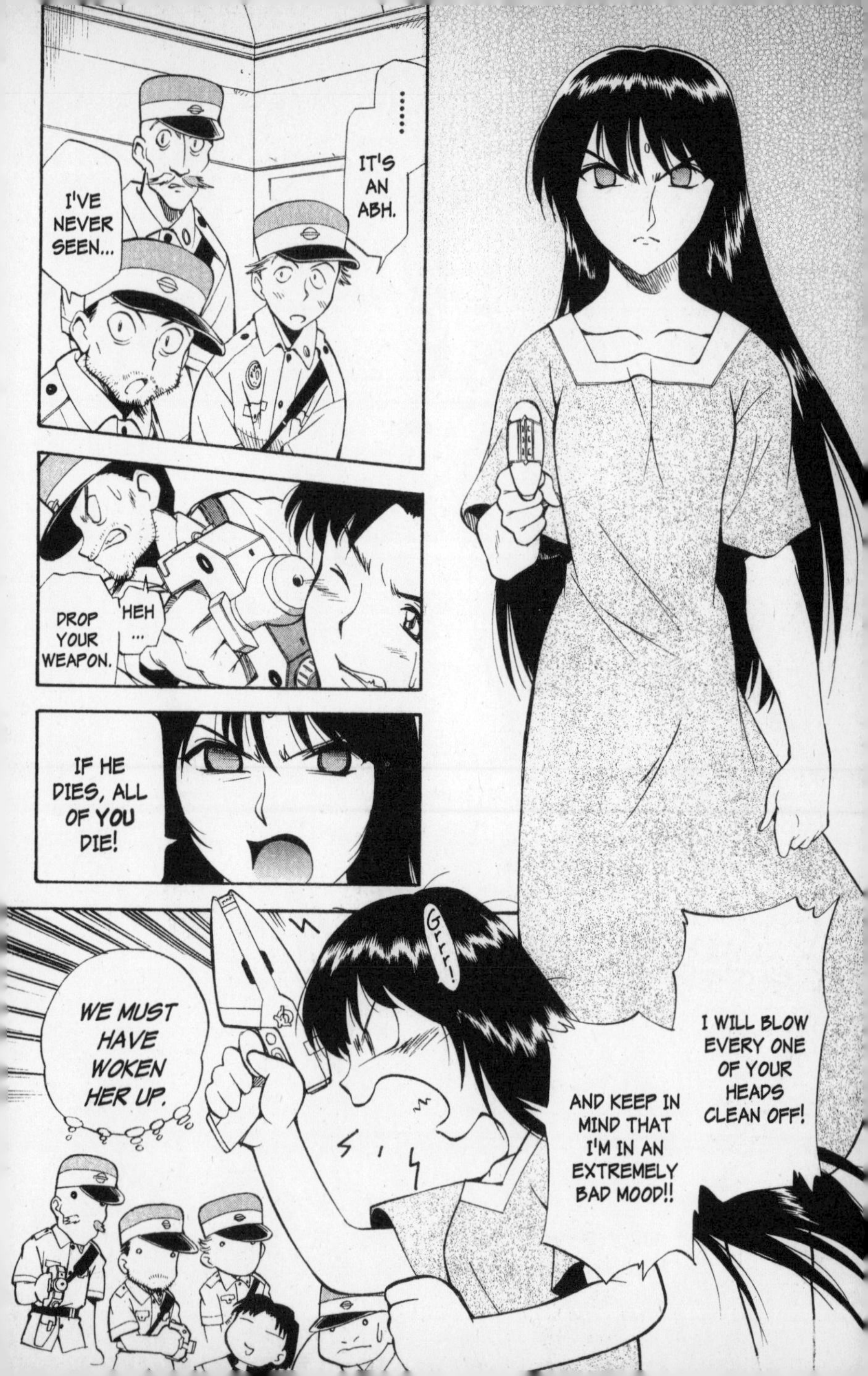
......
IT'S AN ABH.
I'VE NEVER SEEN...
DROP YOUR WEAPON.
HEH...
IF HE DIES, ALL OF YOU DIE!
I WILL BLOW EVERY ONE OF YOUR HEADS CLEAN OFF!
AND KEEP IN MIND THAT I'M IN AN EXTREMELY BAD MOOD!!
Grrr!
WE MUST HAVE WOKEN HER UP.

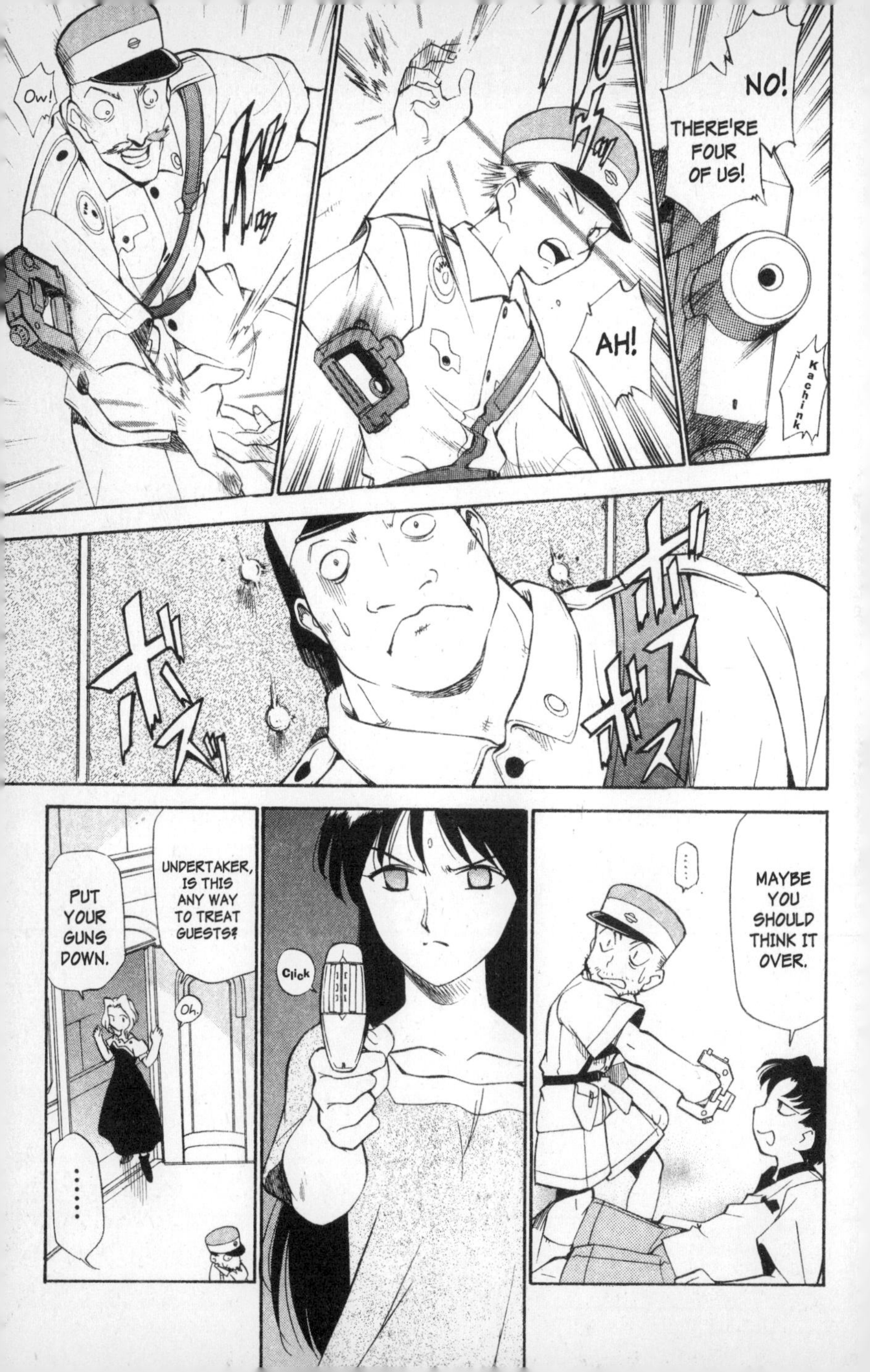
NO!
THERE'RE FOUR OF US!
Kachink
AH!
Ow!
ボス
ボス
ボスッ
......
MAYBE YOU SHOULD THINK IT OVER.
Click
UNDERTAKER, IS THIS ANY WAY TO TREAT GUESTS?
PUT YOUR GUNS DOWN.
Oh.
......

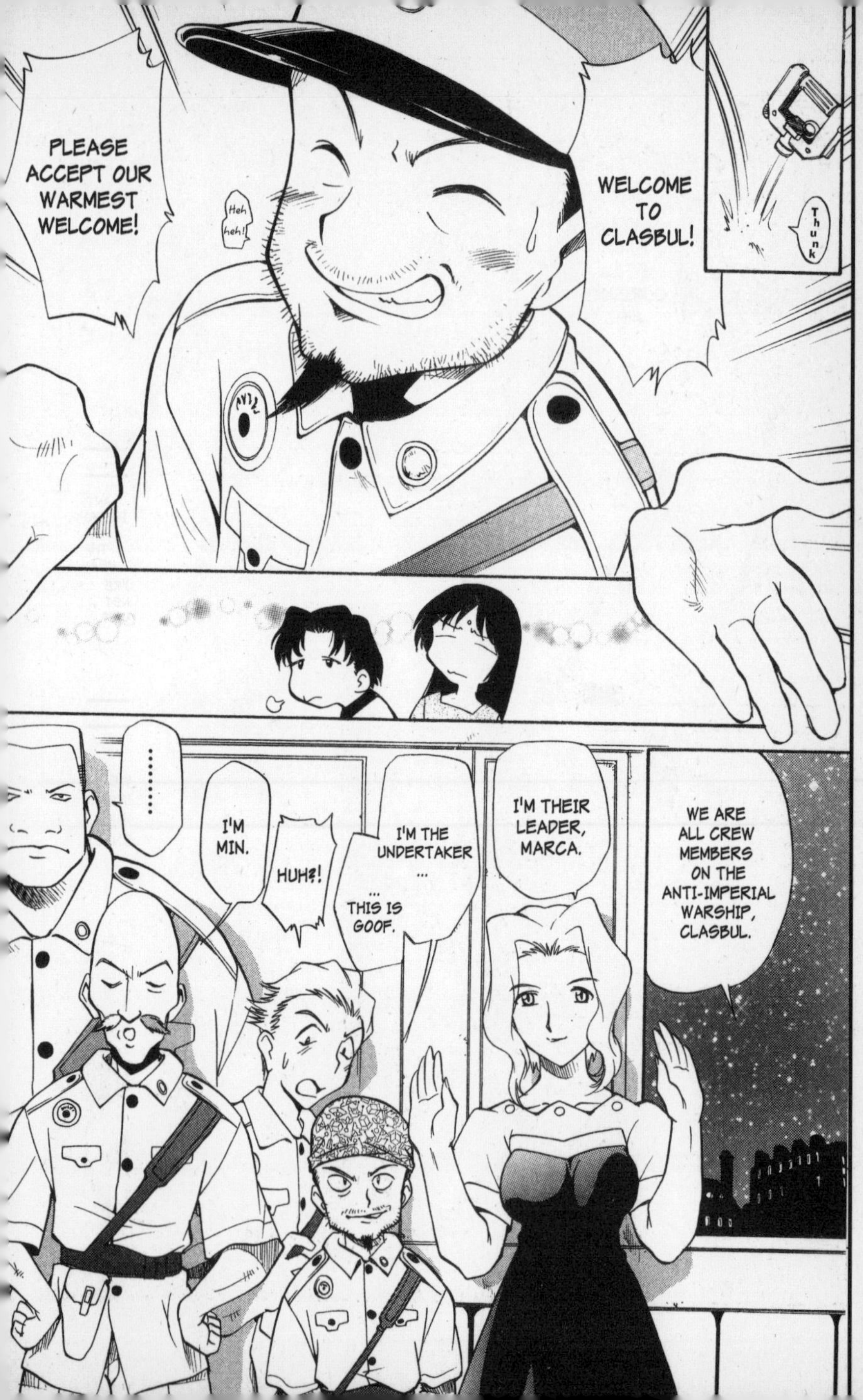
Thunk
WELCOME TO CLASBUL!
Heh heh!
PLEASE ACCEPT OUR WARMEST WELCOME!
WE ARE ALL CREW MEMBERS ON THE ANTI-IMPERIAL WARSHIP, CLASBUL.
I'M THEIR LEADER, MARCA.
I'M THE UNDERTAKER ...
... THIS IS GOOF.
HUH?!
I'M MIN.
....

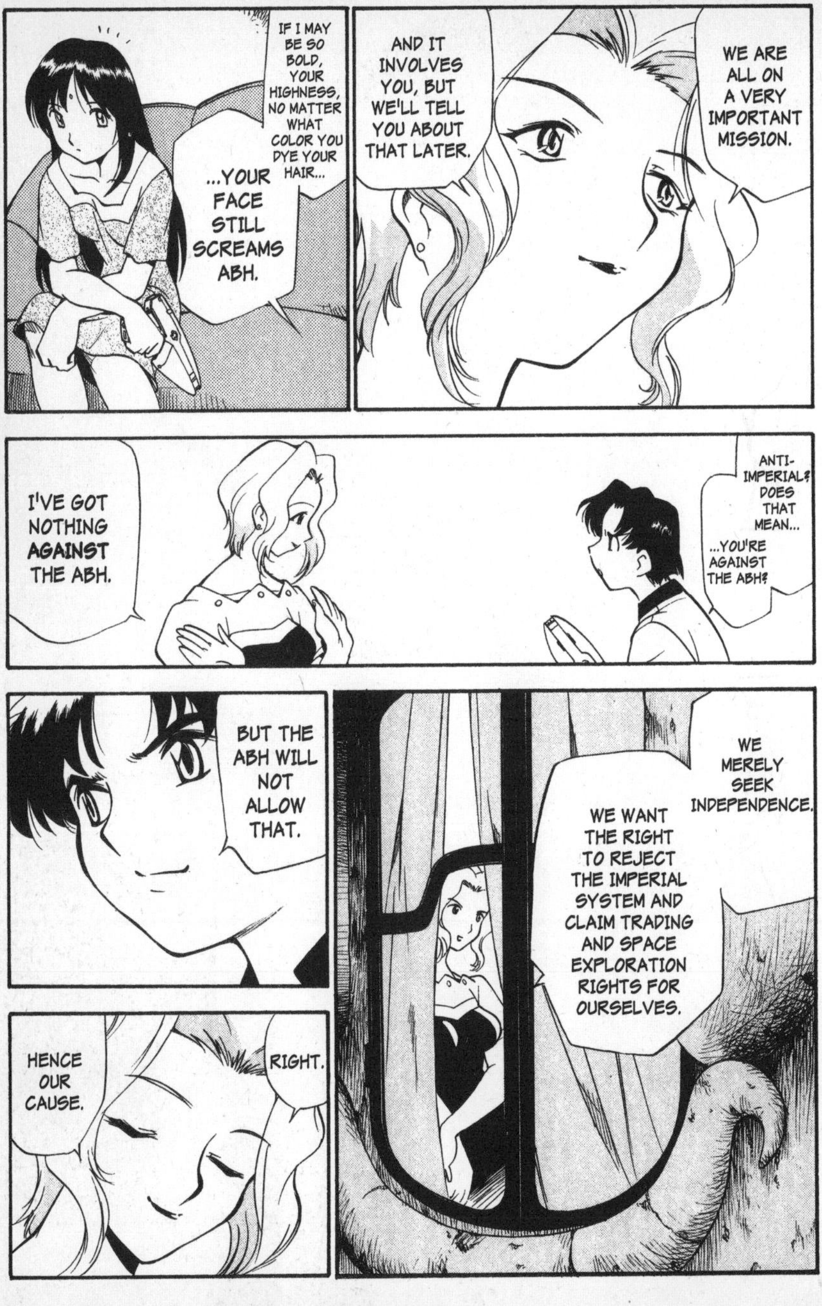
WE ARE ALL ON A VERY IMPORTANT MISSION.
AND IT INVOLVES YOU, BUT WE'LL TELL YOU ABOUT THAT LATER.
IF I MAY BE SO BOLD, YOUR HIGHNESS, NO MATTER WHAT COLOR YOU DYE YOUR HAIR...
...YOUR FACE STILL SCREAMS ABH.
ANTI-IMPERIAL? DOES THAT MEAN...
...YOU'RE AGAINST THE ABH?
I'VE GOT NOTHING AGAINST THE ABH.
WE MERELY SEEK INDEPENDENCE.
WE WANT THE RIGHT TO REJECT THE IMPERIAL SYSTEM AND CLAIM TRADING AND SPACE EXPLORATION RIGHTS FOR OURSELVES.
BUT THE ABH WILL NOT ALLOW THAT.
RIGHT.
HENCE OUR CAUSE.

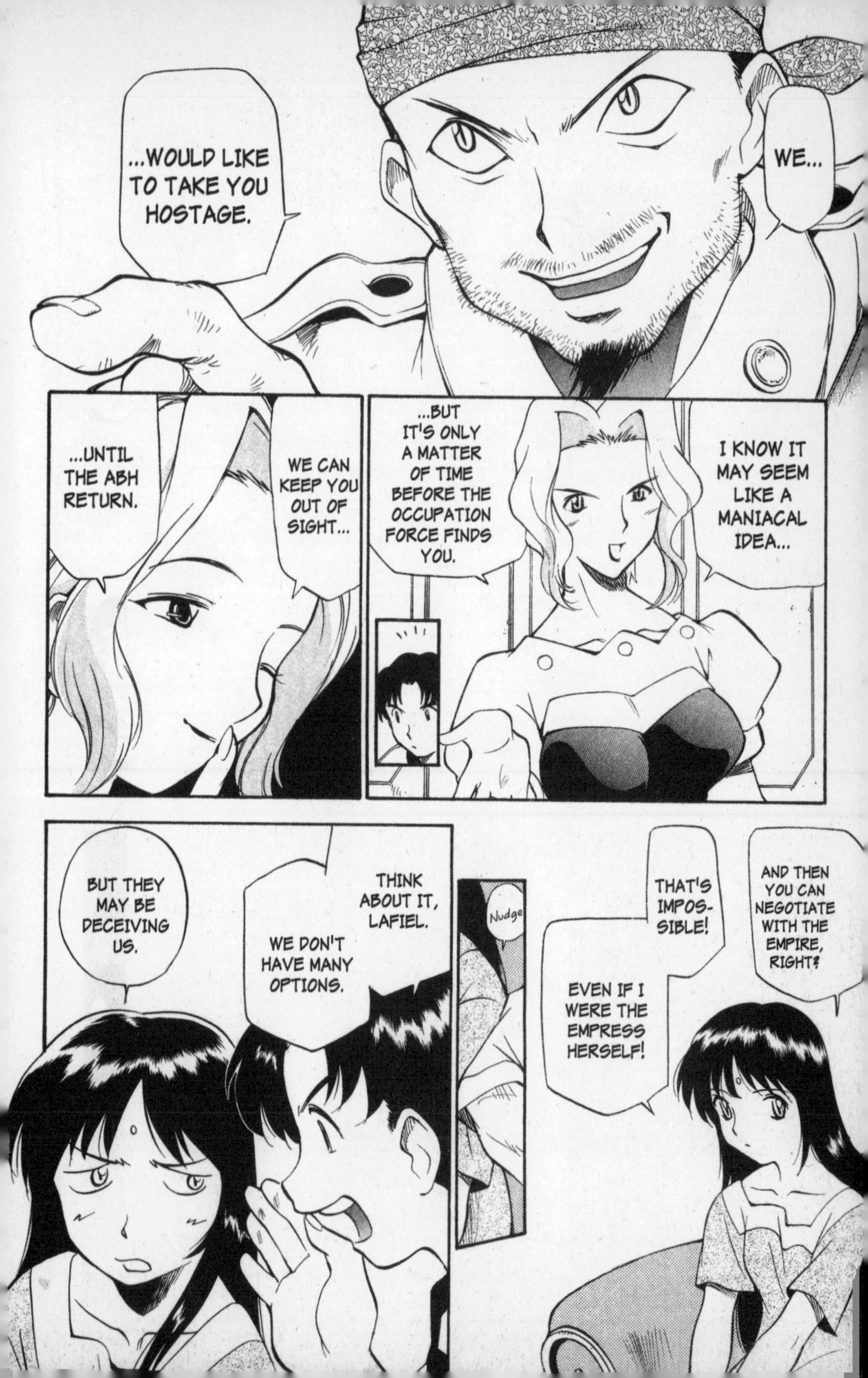
WE...
...WOULD LIKE TO TAKE YOU HOSTAGE.
I KNOW IT MAY SEEM LIKE A MANIACAL IDEA...
...BUT IT'S ONLY A MATTER OF TIME BEFORE THE OCCUPATION FORCE FINDS YOU.
WE CAN KEEP YOU OUT OF SIGHT...
...UNTIL THE ABH RETURN.
AND THEN YOU CAN NEGOTIATE WITH THE EMPIRE, RIGHT?
THAT'S IMPOS-SIBLE!
EVEN IF I WERE THE EMPRESS HERSELF!
Nudge
THINK ABOUT IT, LAFIEL.
WE DON'T HAVE MANY OPTIONS.
BUT THEY MAY BE DECEIVING US.

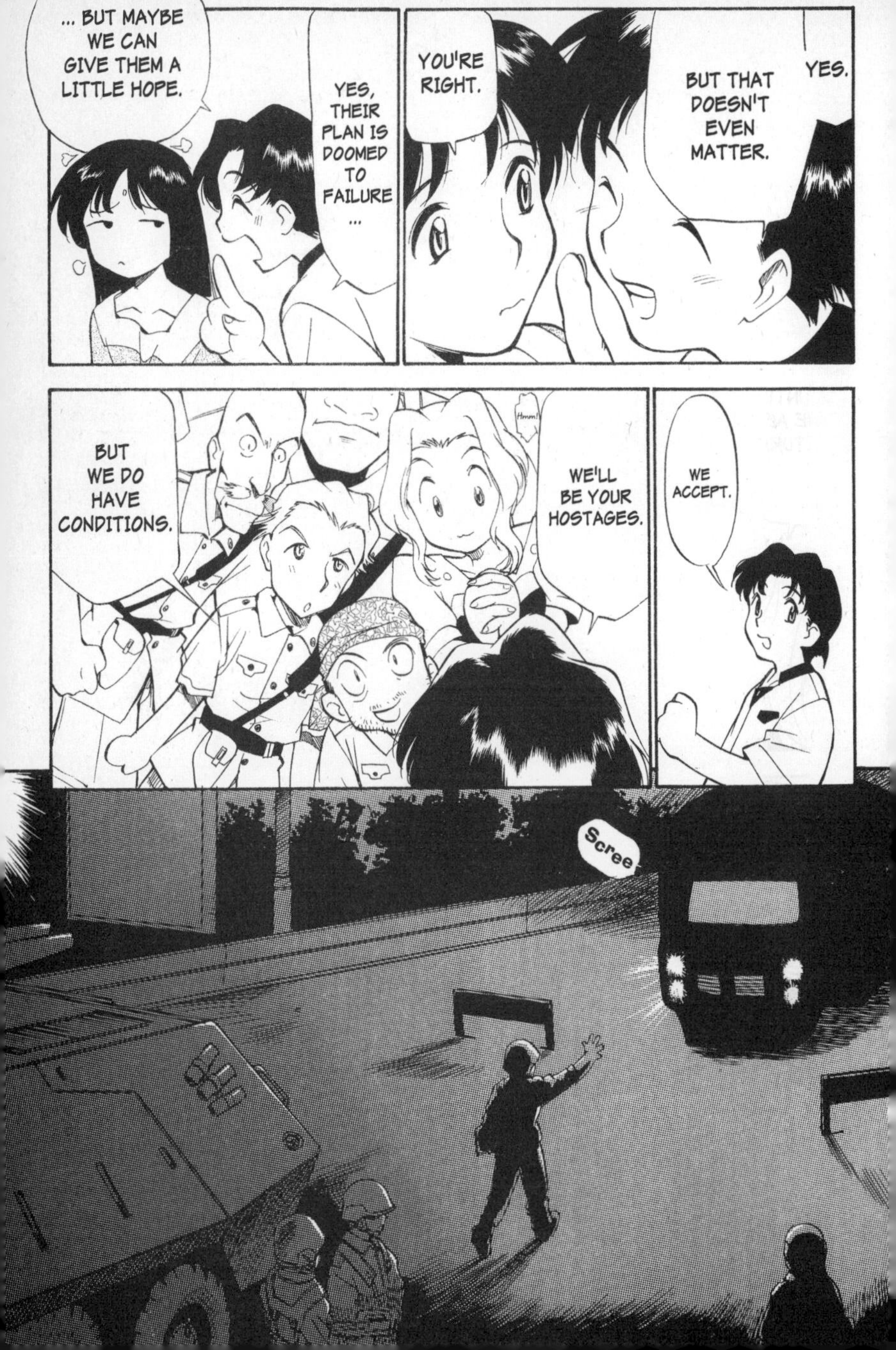
YES.
BUT THAT DOESN'T EVEN MATTER.
YOU'RE RIGHT.
YES, THEIR PLAN IS DOOMED TO FAILURE ...
... BUT MAYBE WE CAN GIVE THEM A LITTLE HOPE.
WE ACCEPT.
Hmm!
WE'LL BE YOUR HOSTAGES.
BUT WE DO HAVE CONDITIONS.
Scree

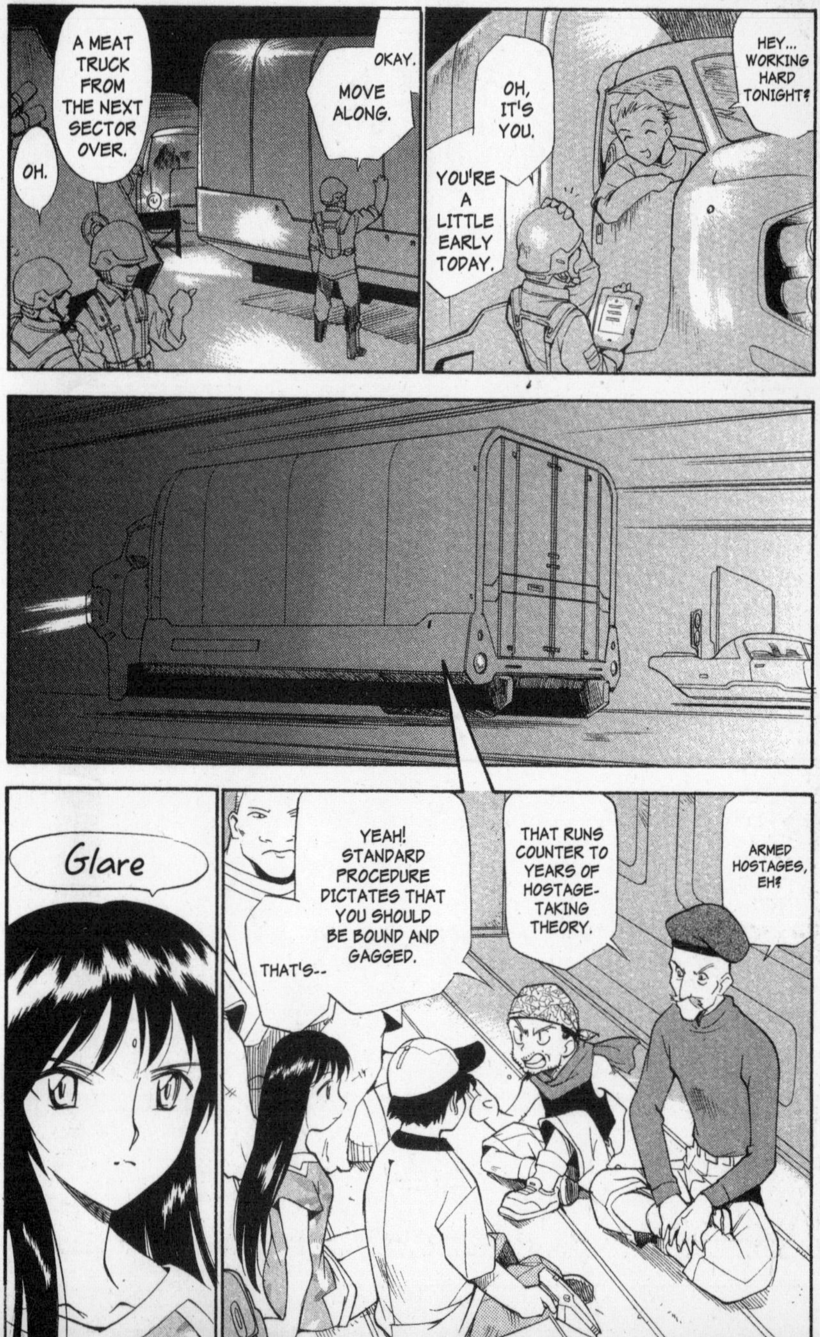
HEY... WORKING HARD TONIGHT?
OH, IT'S YOU.
YOU'RE A LITTLE EARLY TODAY.
OKAY.
MOVE ALONG.
A MEAT TRUCK FROM THE NEXT SECTOR OVER.
OH.
ARMED HOSTAGES, EH?
THAT RUNS COUNTER TO YEARS OF HOSTAGE-TAKING THEORY.
YEAH! STANDARD PROCEDURE DICTATES THAT YOU SHOULD BE BOUND AND GAGGED.
THAT'S--
Glare

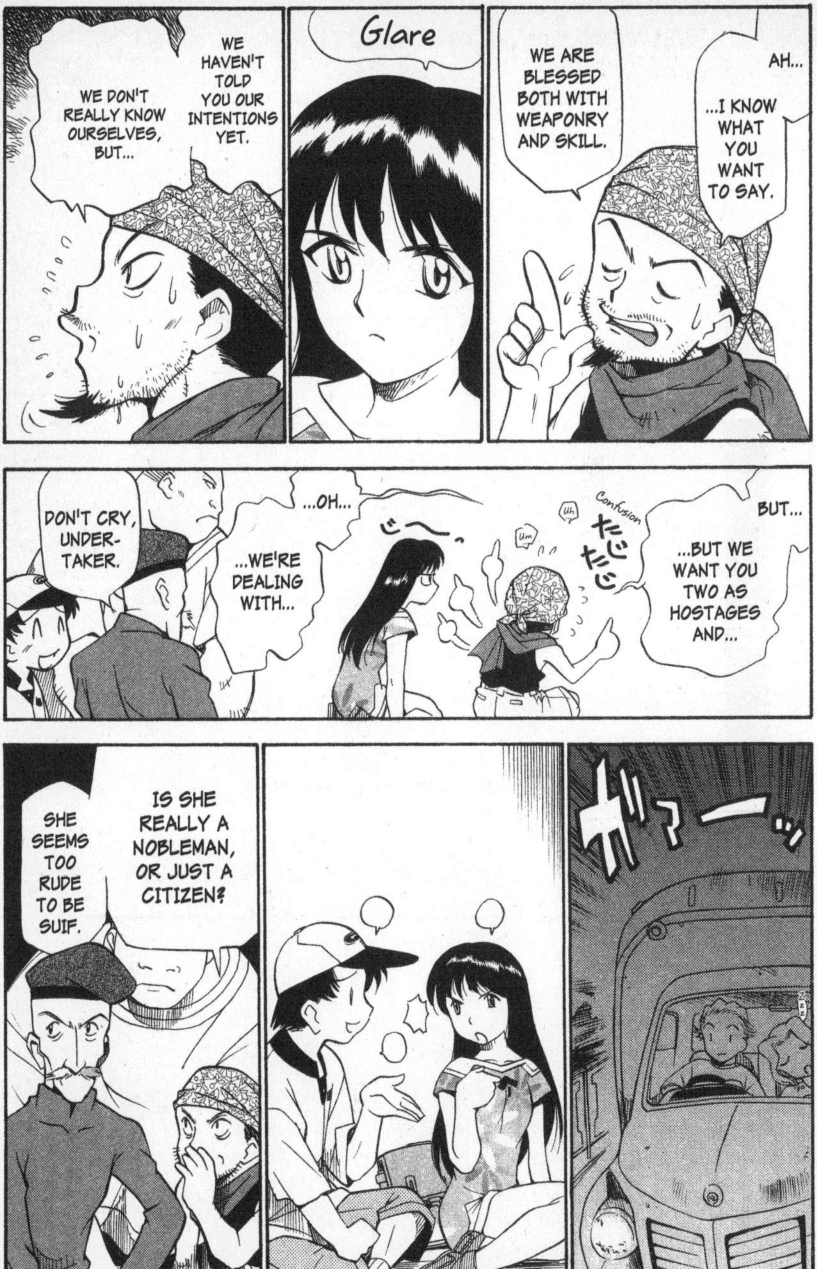
AH...
...I KNOW WHAT YOU WANT TO SAY.
WE ARE BLESSED BOTH WITH WEAPONRY AND SKILL.
Glare
WE HAVEN'T TOLD YOU OUR INTENTIONS YET.
WE DON'T REALLY KNOW OURSELVES, BUT...
BUT...
...BUT WE WANT YOU TWO AS HOSTAGES AND...
Confusion
たじたじ
Uh
Um
じ〜
...OH...
...WE'RE DEALING WITH...
DON'T CRY, UNDER-TAKER.
ギャーッ
IS SHE REALLY A NOBLEMAN, OR JUST A CITIZEN?
SHE SEEMS TOO RUDE TO BE SUIF.

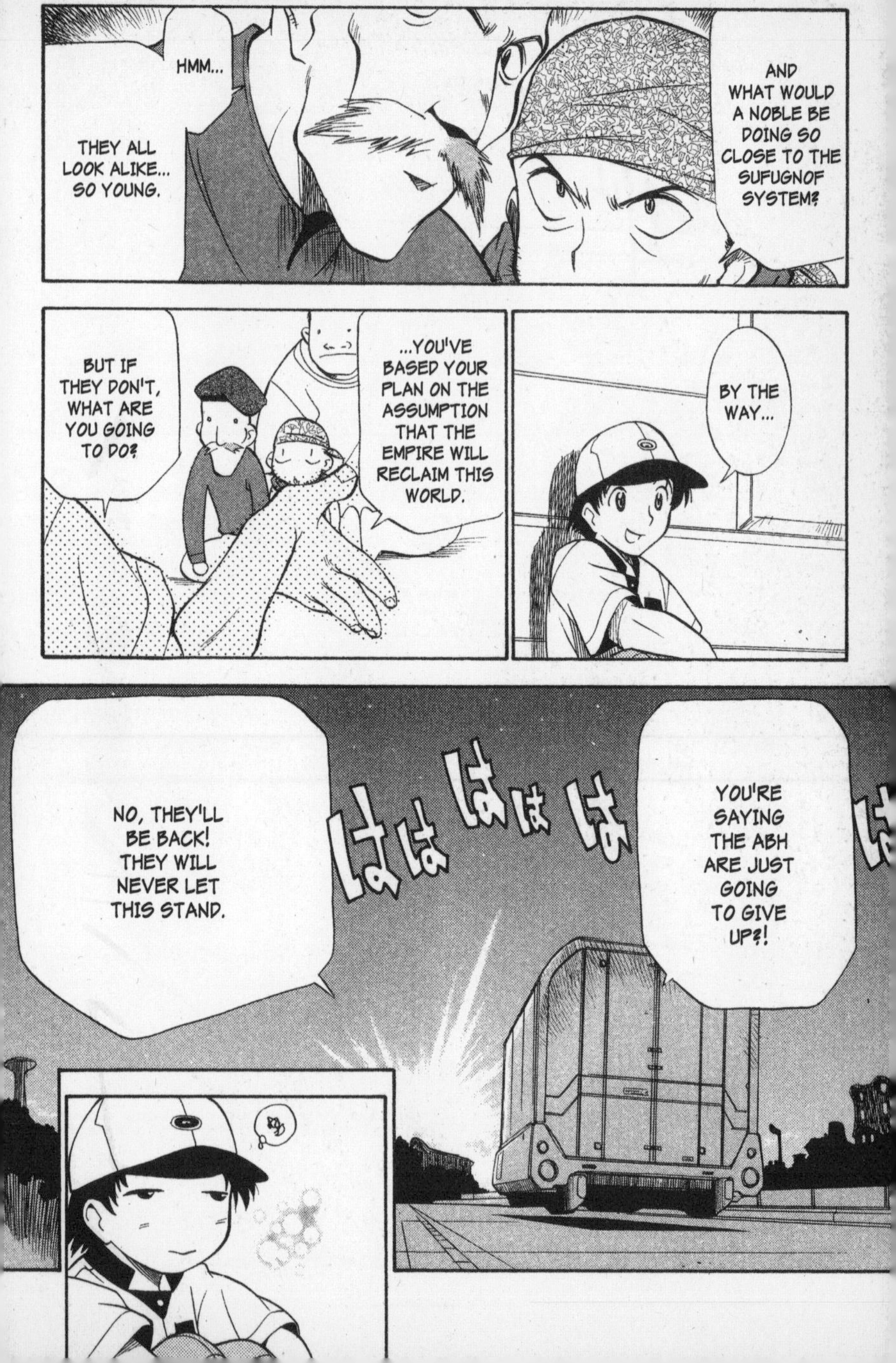
AND WHAT WOULD A NOBLE BE DOING SO CLOSE TO THE SUFUGNOF SYSTEM?
HMM...
THEY ALL LOOK ALIKE... SO YOUNG.
BY THE WAY...
...YOU'VE BASED YOUR PLAN ON THE ASSUMPTION THAT THE EMPIRE WILL RECLAIM THIS WORLD.
BUT IF THEY DON'T, WHAT ARE YOU GOING TO DO?
YOU'RE SAYING THE ABH ARE JUST GOING TO GIVE UP?!
ははははは
NO, THEY'LL BE BACK! THEY WILL NEVER LET THIS STAND.

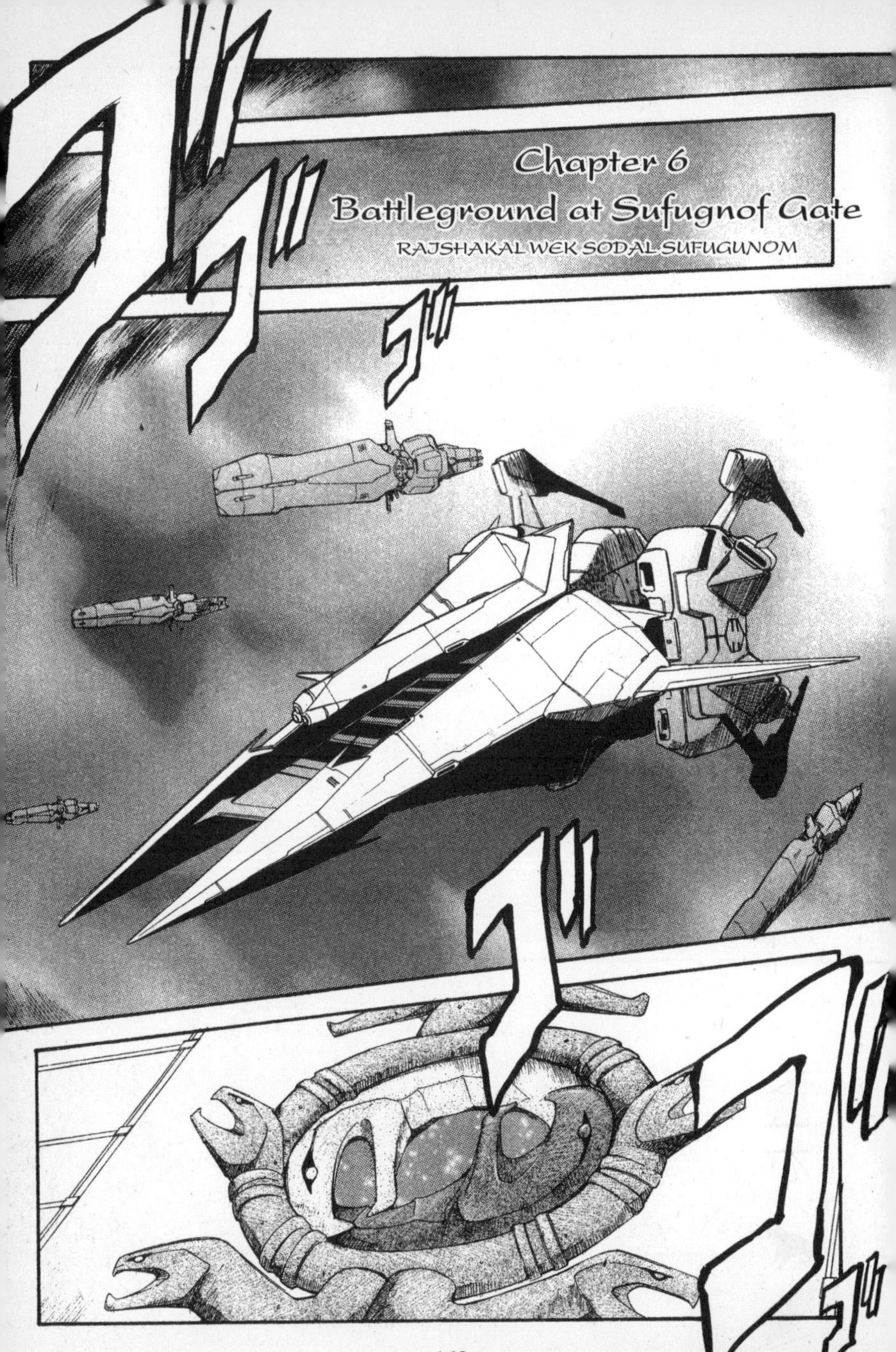
Chapter 6
Battleground at Sufugnof Gate
RAJSHAKAL WEK SODAL SUFUGUNOM

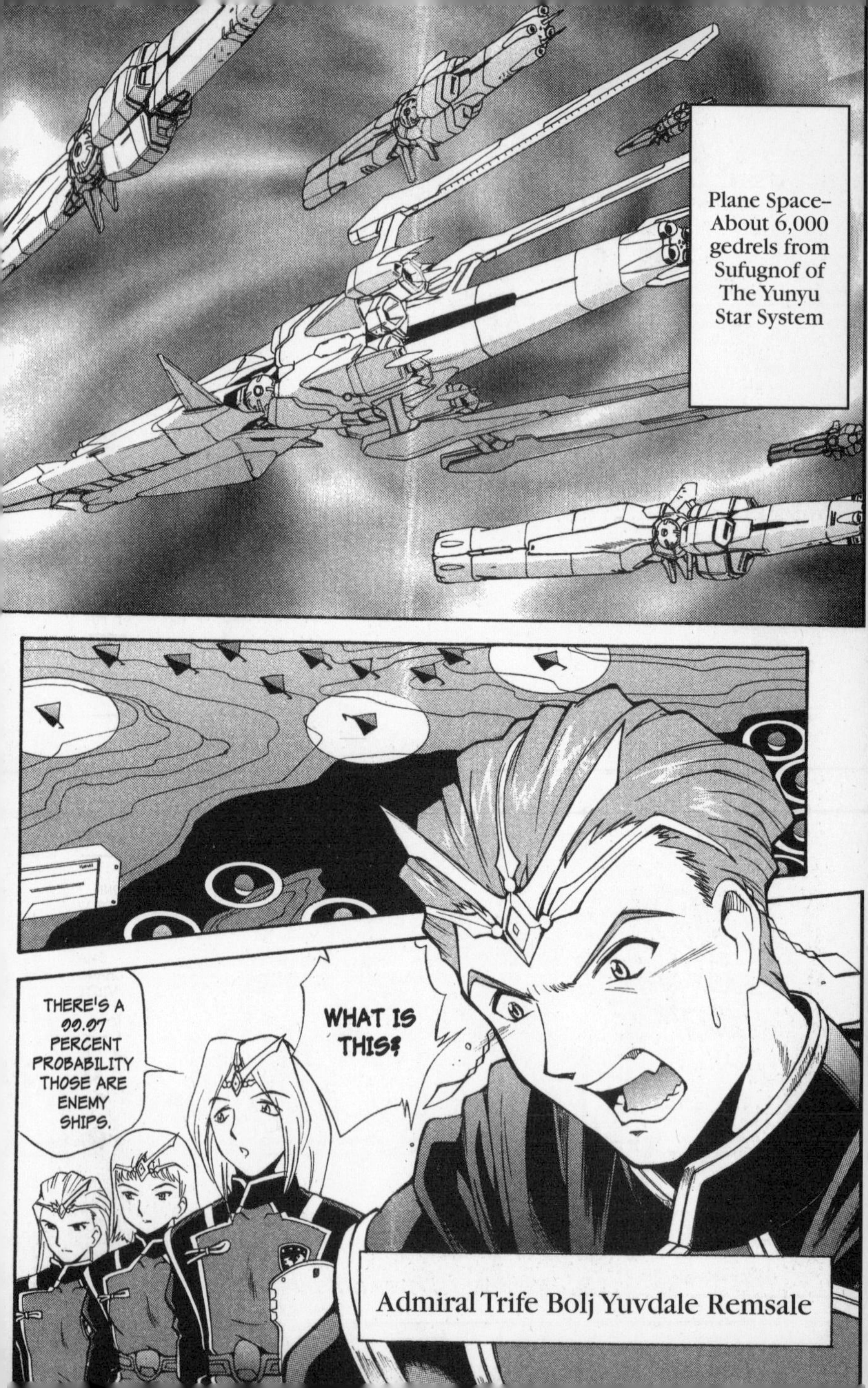
Plane Space–About 6,000 gedrels from Sufugnof of The Yunyu Star System
WHAT IS THIS?
THERE'S A 99.97 PERCENT PROBABILITY THOSE ARE ENEMY SHIPS.
Admiral Trife Bolj Yuvdale Remsale

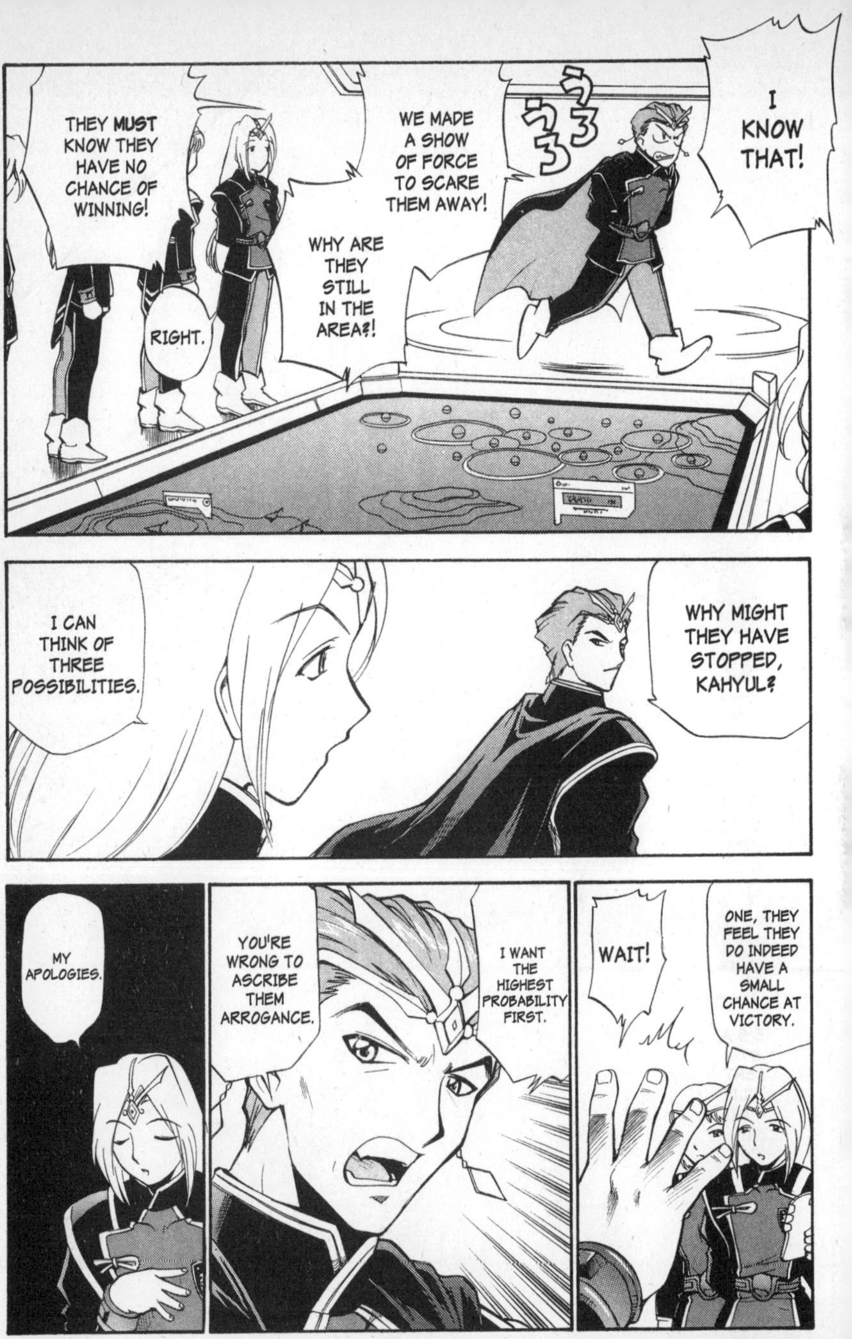
I KNOW THAT!
うろうろ
WE MADE A SHOW OF FORCE TO SCARE THEM AWAY!
WHY ARE THEY STILL IN THE AREA?!
THEY MUST KNOW THEY HAVE NO CHANCE OF WINNING!
RIGHT.
WHY MIGHT THEY HAVE STOPPED, KAHYUL?
I CAN THINK OF THREE POSSIBILITIES.
ONE, THEY FEEL THEY DO INDEED HAVE A SMALL CHANCE AT VICTORY.
WAIT!
I WANT THE HIGHEST PROBABILITY FIRST.
YOU'RE WRONG TO ASCRIBE THEM ARROGANCE.
MY APOLOGIES.

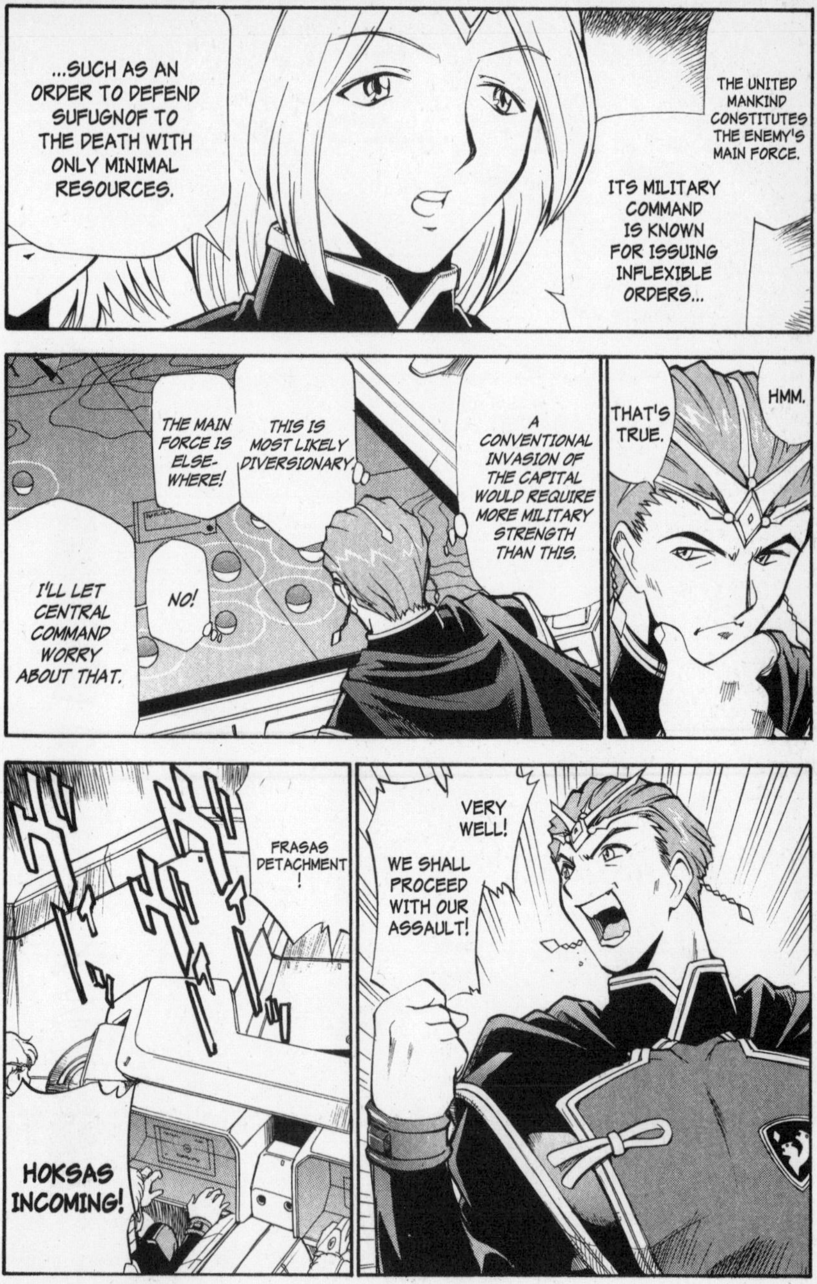
THE UNITED MANKIND CONSTITUTES THE ENEMY'S MAIN FORCE.
ITS MILITARY COMMAND IS KNOWN FOR ISSUING INFLEXIBLE ORDERS...
...SUCH AS AN ORDER TO DEFEND SUFUGNOF TO THE DEATH WITH ONLY MINIMAL RESOURCES.
HMM.
THAT'S TRUE.
A CONVENTIONAL INVASION OF THE CAPITAL WOULD REQUIRE MORE MILITARY STRENGTH THAN THIS.
THIS IS MOST LIKELY DIVERSIONARY.
THE MAIN FORCE IS ELSE-WHERE!
NO!
I'LL LET CENTRAL COMMAND WORRY ABOUT THAT.
VERY WELL!
WE SHALL PROCEED WITH OUR ASSAULT!
FRASAS DETACHMENT!
HOKSAS INCOMING!

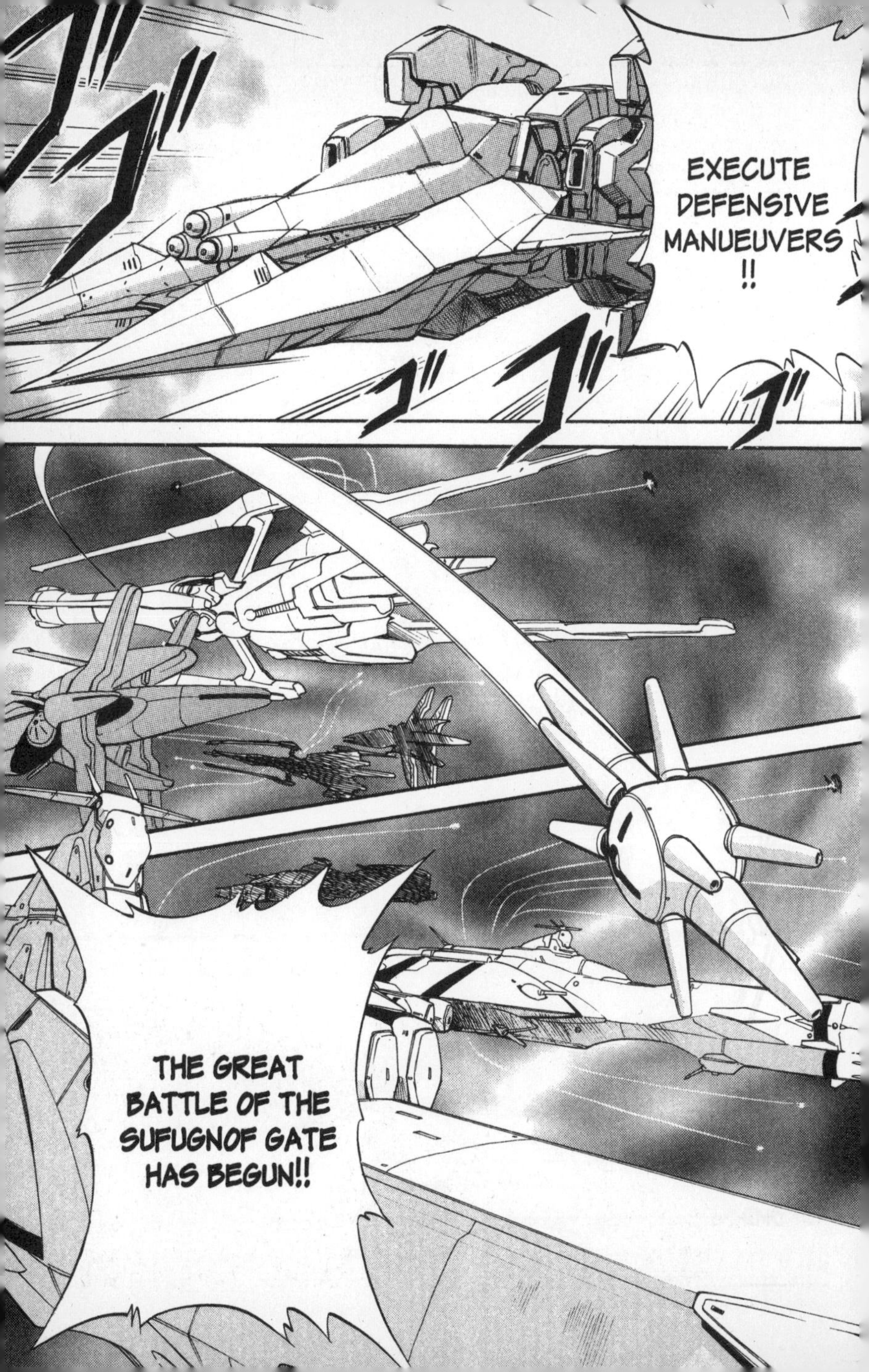
EXECUTE DEFENSIVE MANUEUVERS !!
ゴゴ
ゴゴゴ
THE GREAT BATTLE OF THE SUFUGNOF GATE HAS BEGUN!!

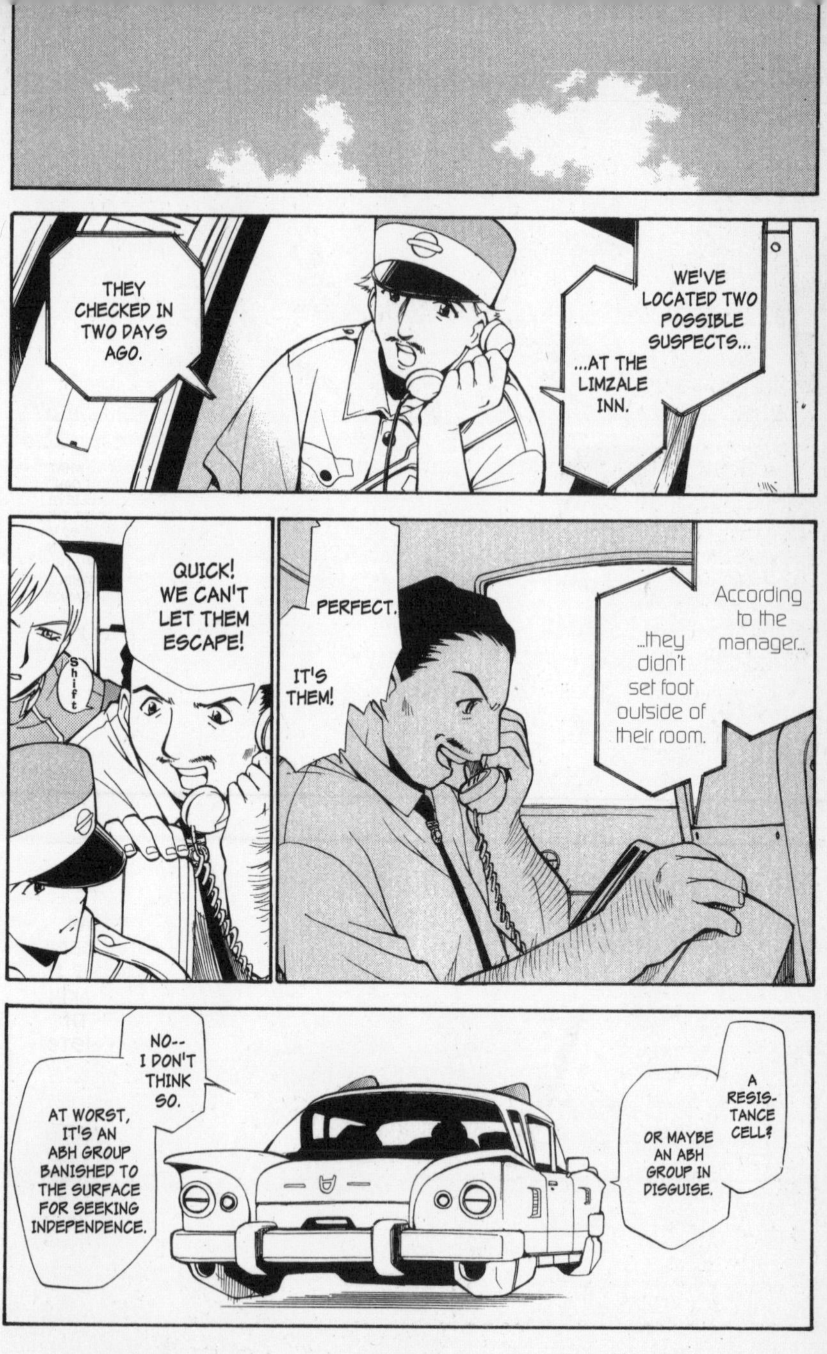
WE'VE LOCATED TWO POSSIBLE SUSPECTS...
...AT THE LIMZALE INN.
THEY CHECKED IN TWO DAYS AGO.
According to the manager...
...they didn't set foot outside of their room.
PERFECT.
IT'S THEM!
QUICK! WE CAN'T LET THEM ESCAPE!
Shift
A RESISTANCE CELL?
OR MAYBE AN ABH GROUP IN DISGUISE.
NO-- I DON'T THINK SO.
AT WORST, IT'S AN ABH GROUP BANISHED TO THE SURFACE FOR SEEKING INDEPENDENCE.

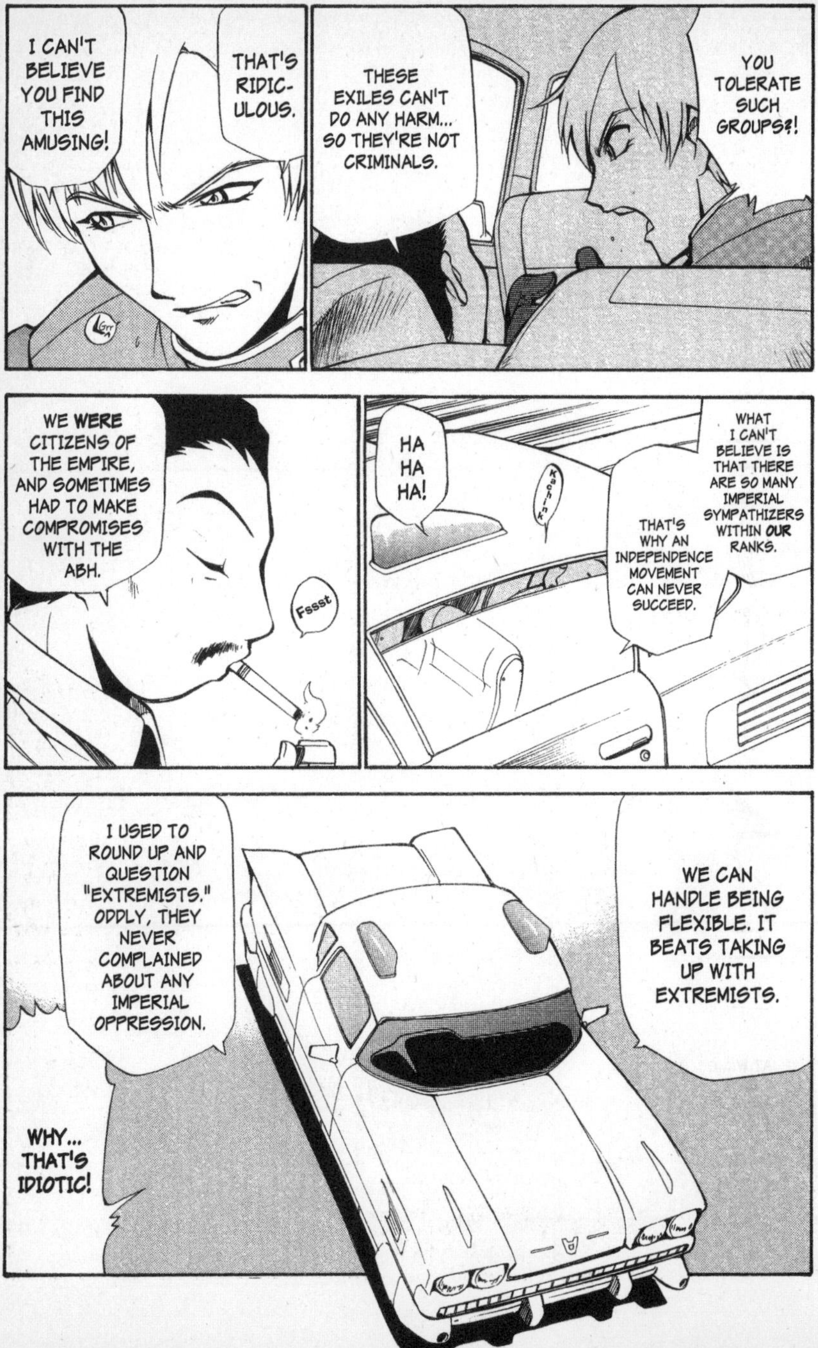
YOU TOLERATE SUCH GROUPS?!
THESE EXILES CAN'T DO ANY HARM... SO THEY'RE NOT CRIMINALS.
THAT'S RIDIC-ULOUS.
I CAN'T BELIEVE YOU FIND THIS AMUSING!
Grr
WHAT I CAN'T BELIEVE IS THAT THERE ARE SO MANY IMPERIAL SYMPATHIZERS WITHIN OUR RANKS.
THAT'S WHY AN INDEPENDENCE MOVEMENT CAN NEVER SUCCEED.
Kachink
HA HA HA!
WE WERE CITIZENS OF THE EMPIRE, AND SOMETIMES HAD TO MAKE COMPROMISES WITH THE ABH.
Fssst
WE CAN HANDLE BEING FLEXIBLE. IT BEATS TAKING UP WITH EXTREMISTS.
I USED TO ROUND UP AND QUESTION "EXTREMISTS." ODDLY, THEY NEVER COMPLAINED ABOUT ANY IMPERIAL OPPRESSION.
WHY... THAT'S IDIOTIC!

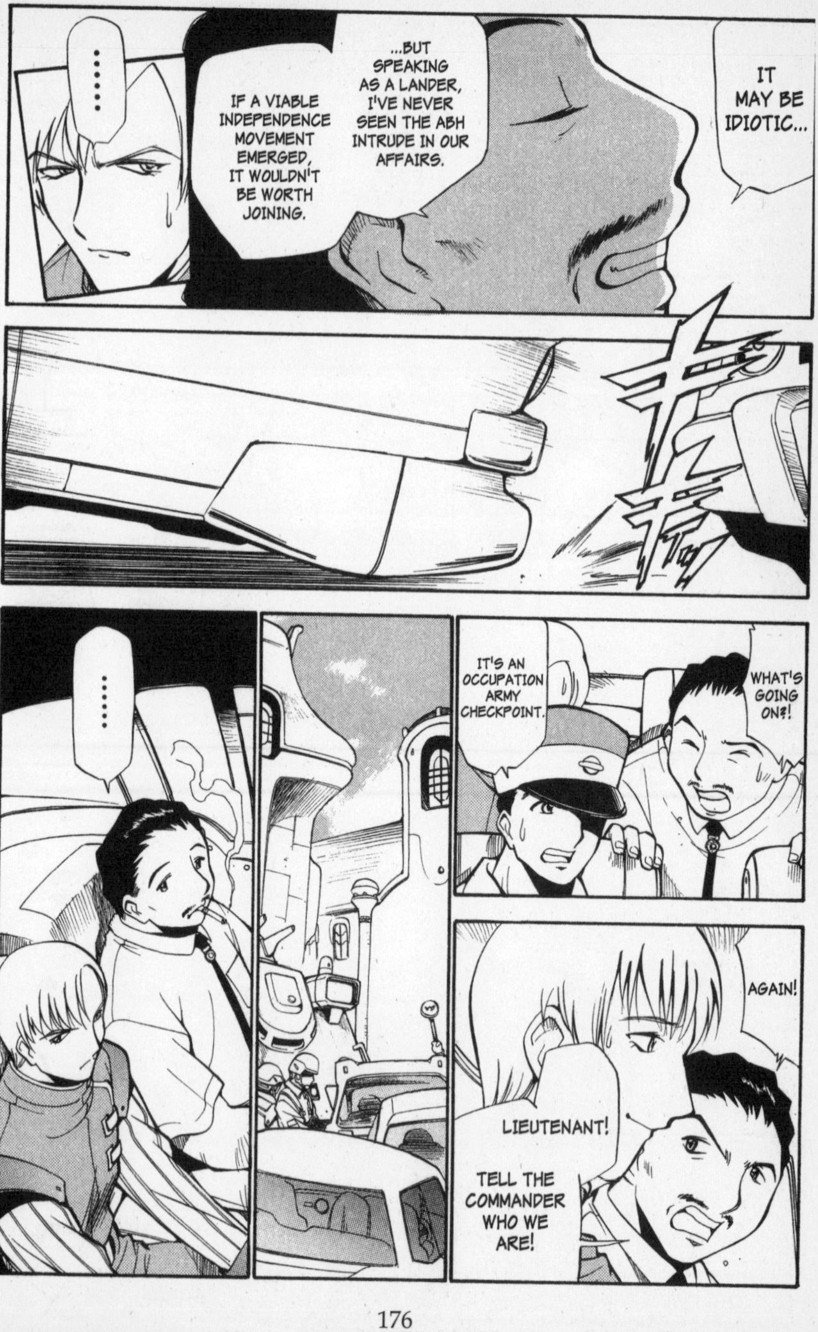
IT MAY BE IDIOTIC...
...BUT SPEAKING AS A LANDER, I'VE NEVER SEEN THE ABH INTRUDE IN OUR AFFAIRS.
IF A VIABLE INDEPENDENCE MOVEMENT EMERGED, IT WOULDN'T BE WORTH JOINING.
......
WHAT'S GOING ON?!
IT'S AN OCCUPATION ARMY CHECKPOINT.
AGAIN!
LIEUTENANT!
TELL THE COMMANDER WHO WE ARE!
......

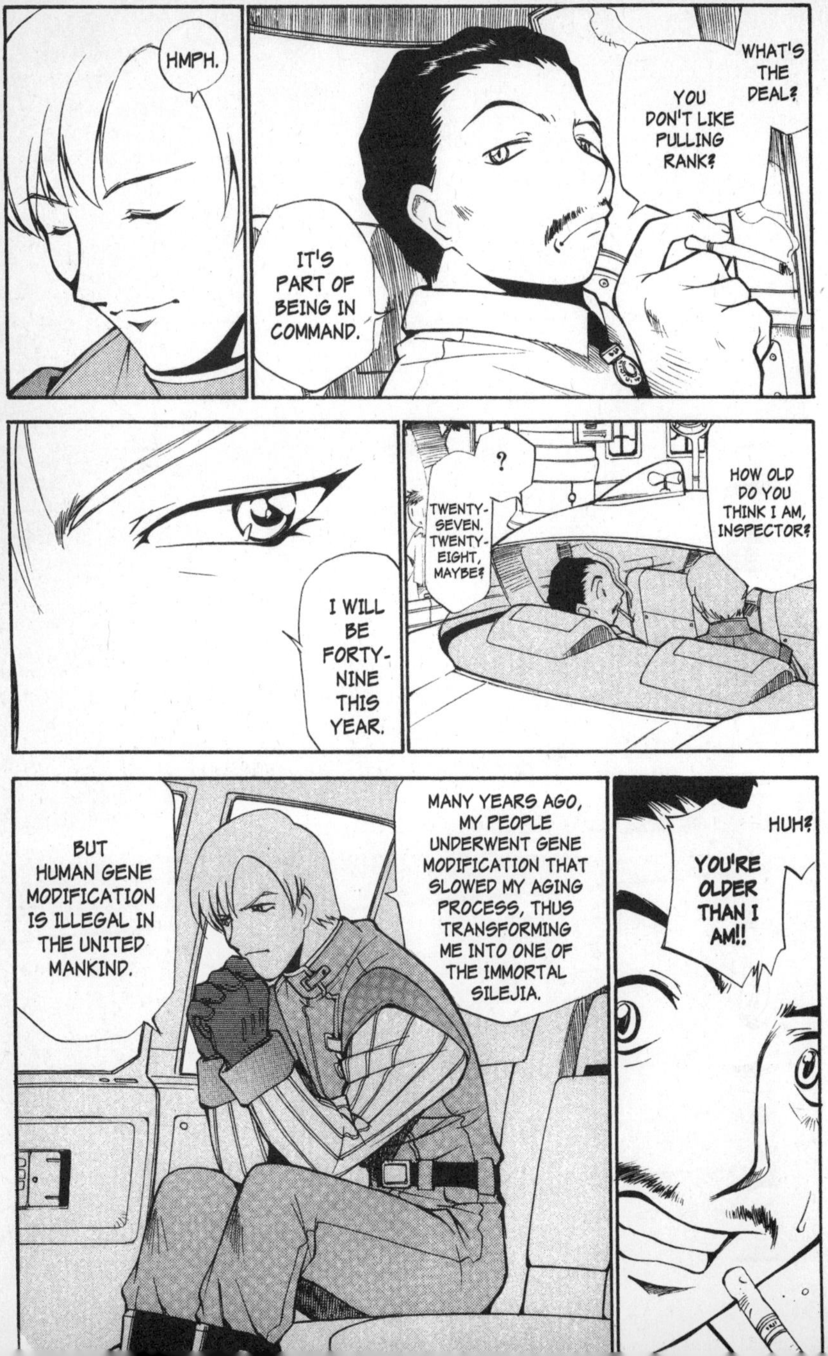
WHAT'S THE DEAL?
YOU DON'T LIKE PULLING RANK?
IT'S PART OF BEING IN COMMAND.
HMPH.
HOW OLD DO YOU THINK I AM, INSPECTOR?
?
TWENTY-SEVEN. TWENTY-EIGHT, MAYBE?
I WILL BE FORTY-NINE THIS YEAR.
HUH?
YOU'RE OLDER THAN I AM!!
MANY YEARS AGO, MY PEOPLE UNDERWENT GENE MODIFICATION THAT SLOWED MY AGING PROCESS, THUS TRANSFORMING ME INTO ONE OF THE IMMORTAL SILEJIA.
BUT HUMAN GENE MODIFICATION IS ILLEGAL IN THE UNITED MANKIND.

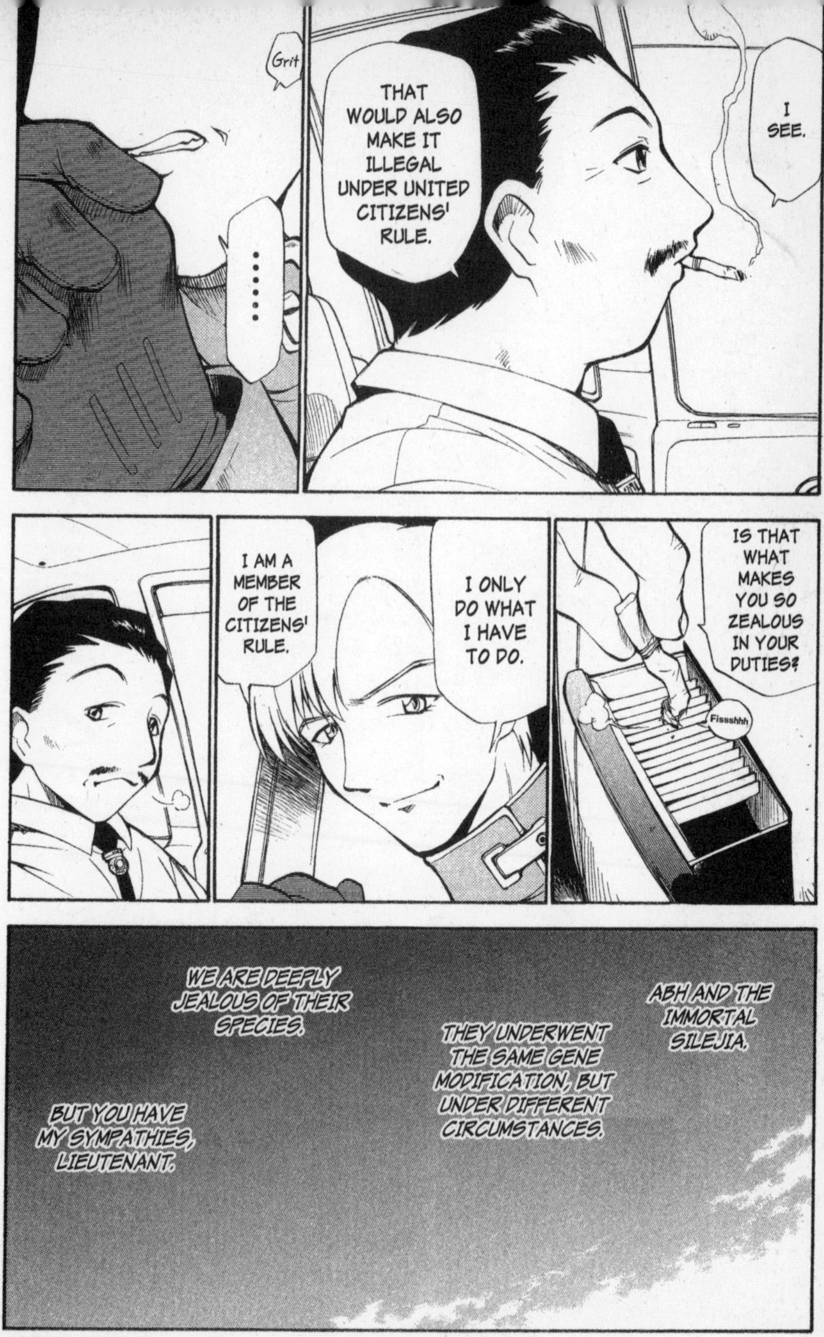
I SEE.
THAT WOULD ALSO MAKE IT ILLEGAL UNDER UNITED CITIZENS' RULE.
Grit
......
IS THAT WHAT MAKES YOU SO ZEALOUS IN YOUR DUTIES?
Fissshhh
I ONLY DO WHAT I HAVE TO DO.
I AM A MEMBER OF THE CITIZENS' RULE.
ABH AND THE IMMORTAL SILEJIA.
THEY UNDERWENT THE SAME GENE MODIFICATION, BUT UNDER DIFFERENT CIRCUMSTANCES.
WE ARE DEEPLY JEALOUS OF THEIR SPECIES.
BUT YOU HAVE MY SYMPATHIES, LIEUTENANT.

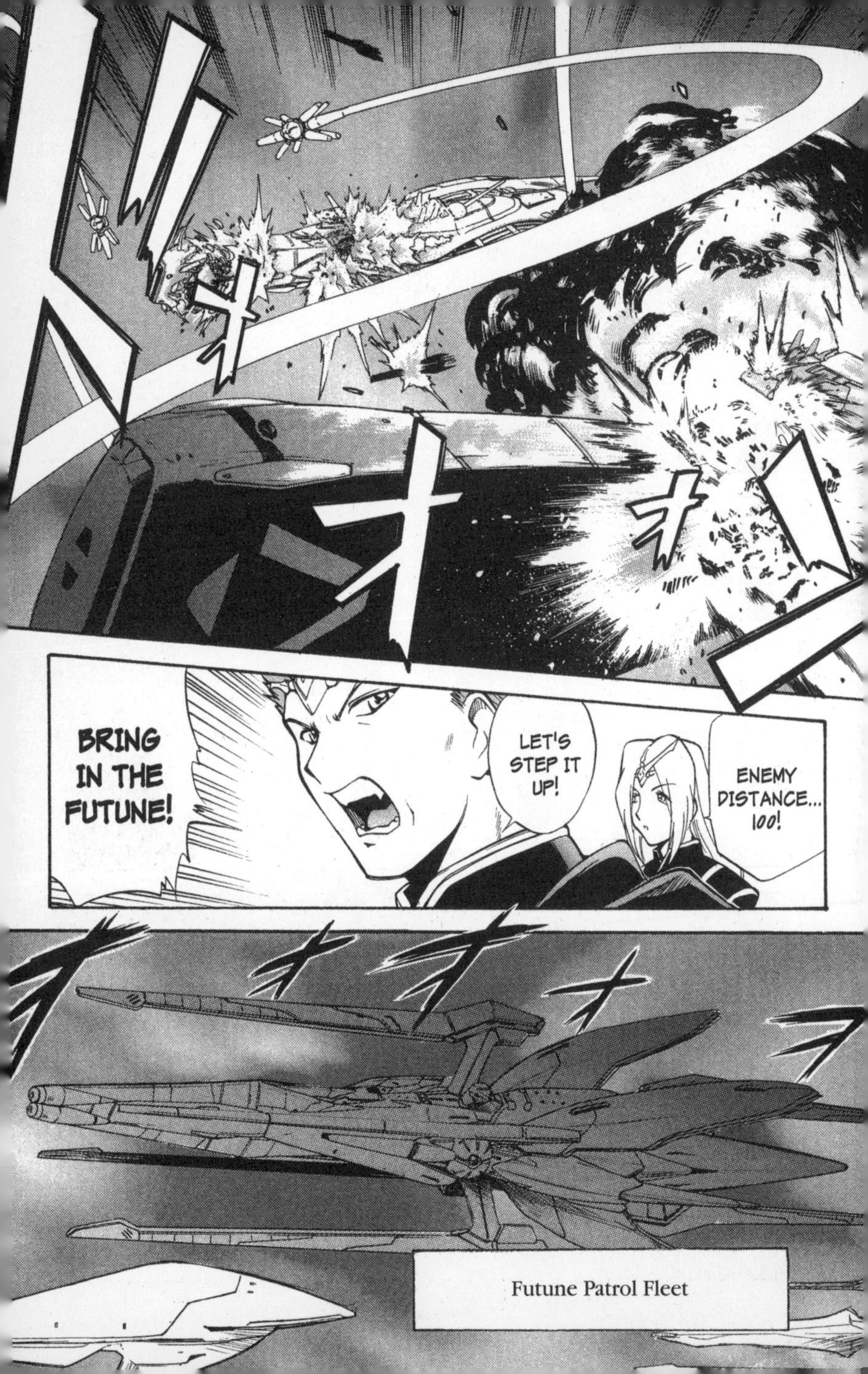
ENEMY DISTANCE... 100!
LET'S STEP IT UP!
BRING IN THE FUTUNE!
Futune Patrol Fleet

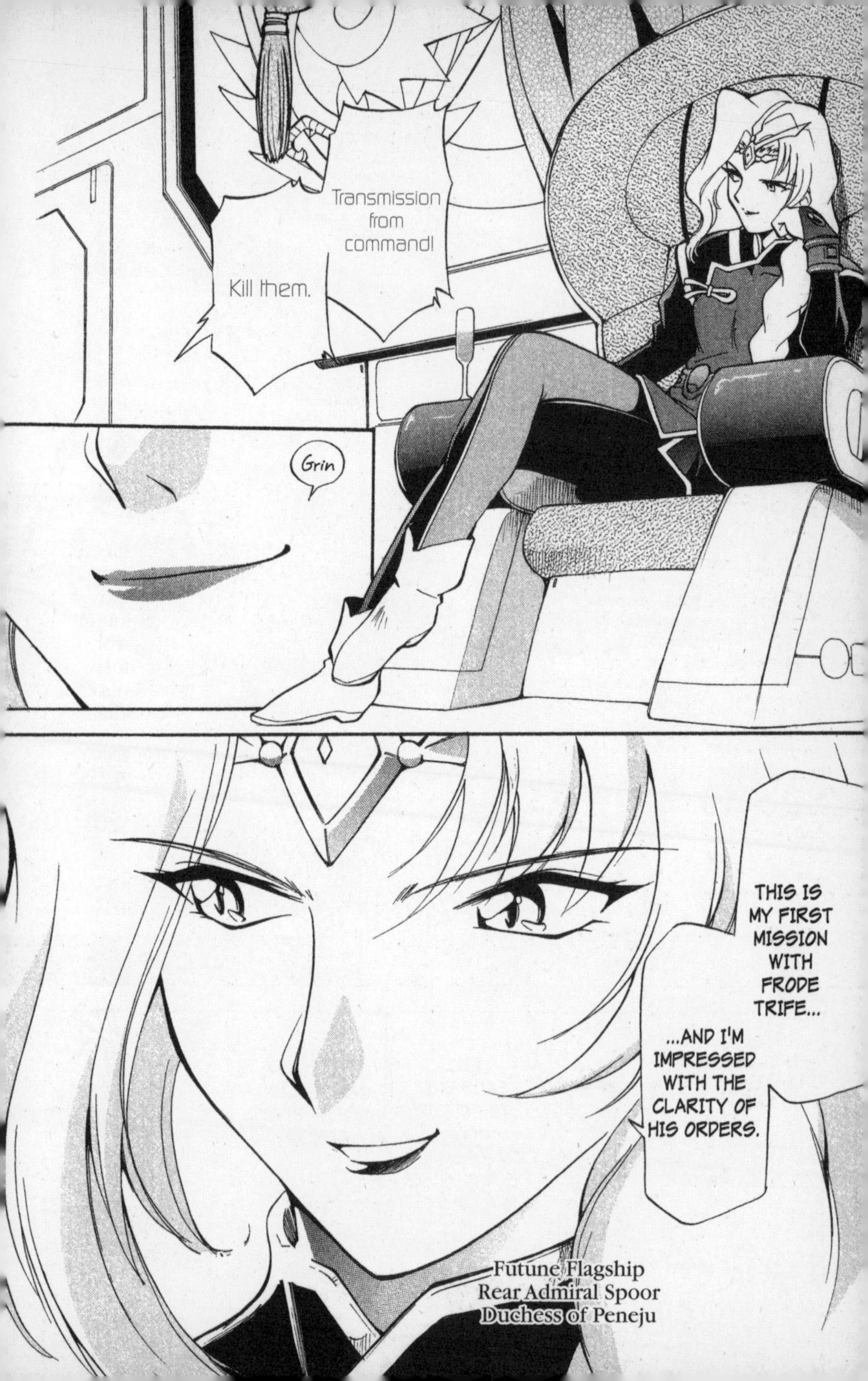
Transmission from command!
Kill them.
Grin
THIS IS MY FIRST MISSION WITH FRODE TRIFE...
...AND I'M IMPRESSED WITH THE CLARITY OF HIS ORDERS.
Futune Flagship
Rear Admiral Spoor
Duchess of Peneju

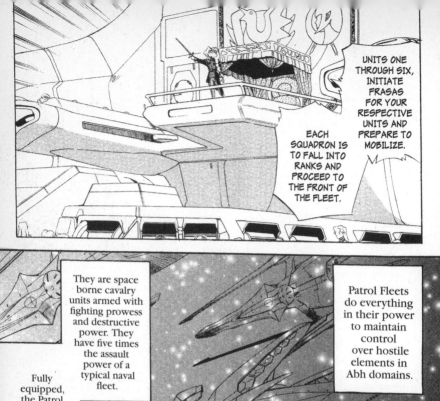

UNITS ONE THROUGH SIX, INITIATE FRASAS FOR YOUR RESPECTIVE UNITS AND PREPARE TO MOBILIZE.
EACH SQUADRON IS TO FALL INTO RANKS AND PROCEED TO THE FRONT OF THE FLEET.
Patrol Fleets do everything in their power to maintain control over hostile elements in Abh domains.
They are space borne cavalry units armed with fighting prowess and destructive power. They have five times the assault power of a typical naval fleet.
Fully equipped, the Patrol Fleet charges through space!
UNIT FOUR HAS FALLEN BEHIND FIVE RANKS!
TELL EACH UNIT TO FOLLOW US ON COURSE 3-1-0. CONTINUOUS MESSAGE!
APPROACHING ENEMY HOKSAS!

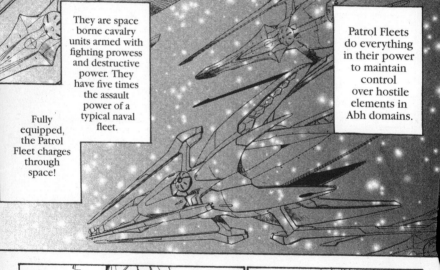

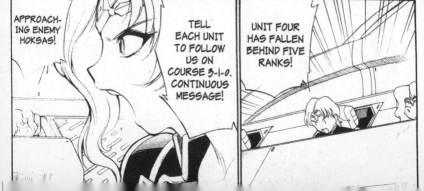

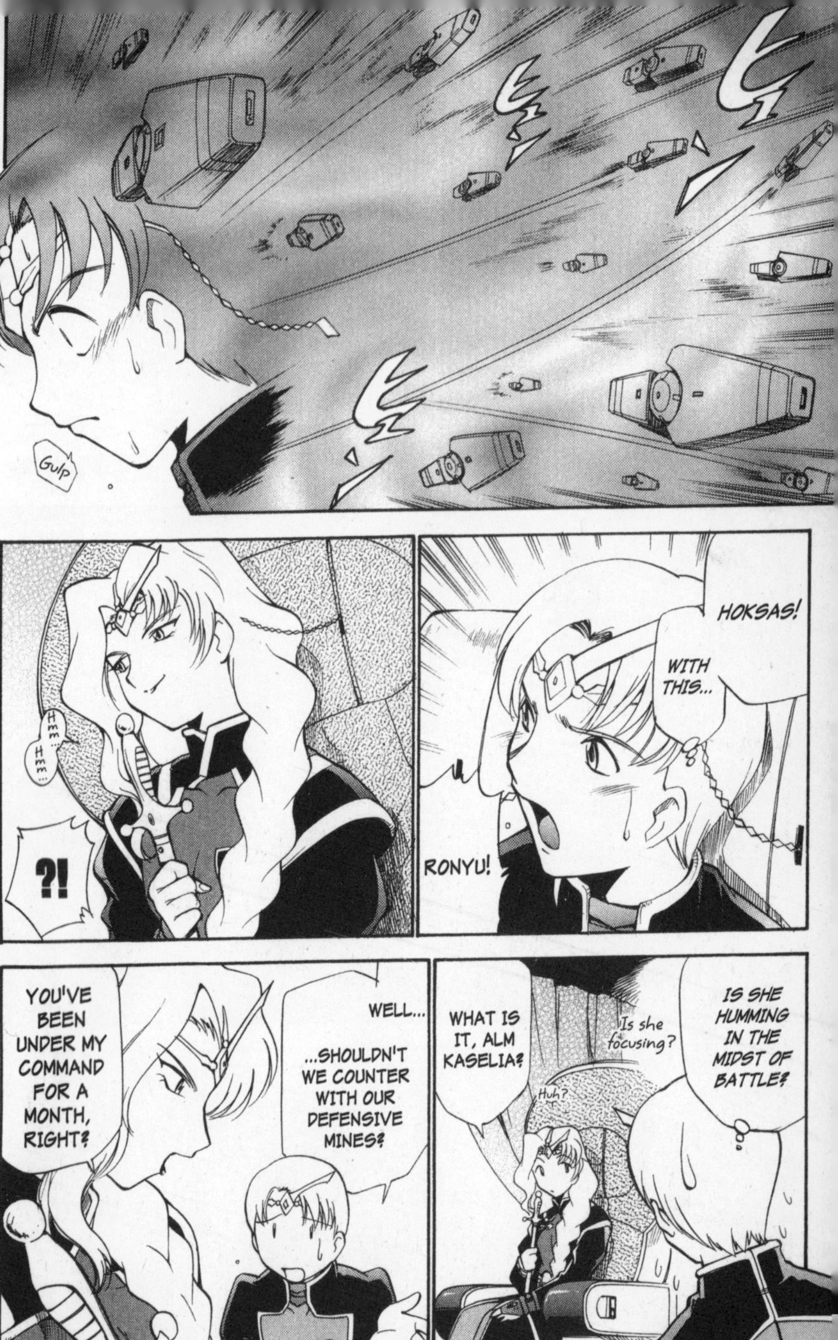
Gulp
HOKSAS!
WITH THIS...
RONYU!
Hmm... Hmm...
?!
IS SHE HUMMING IN THE MIDST OF BATTLE?
Is she focusing?
WHAT IS IT, ALM KASELIA?
Huh?
WELL...
...SHOULDN'T WE COUNTER WITH OUR DEFENSIVE MINES?
YOU'VE BEEN UNDER MY COMMAND FOR A MONTH, RIGHT?

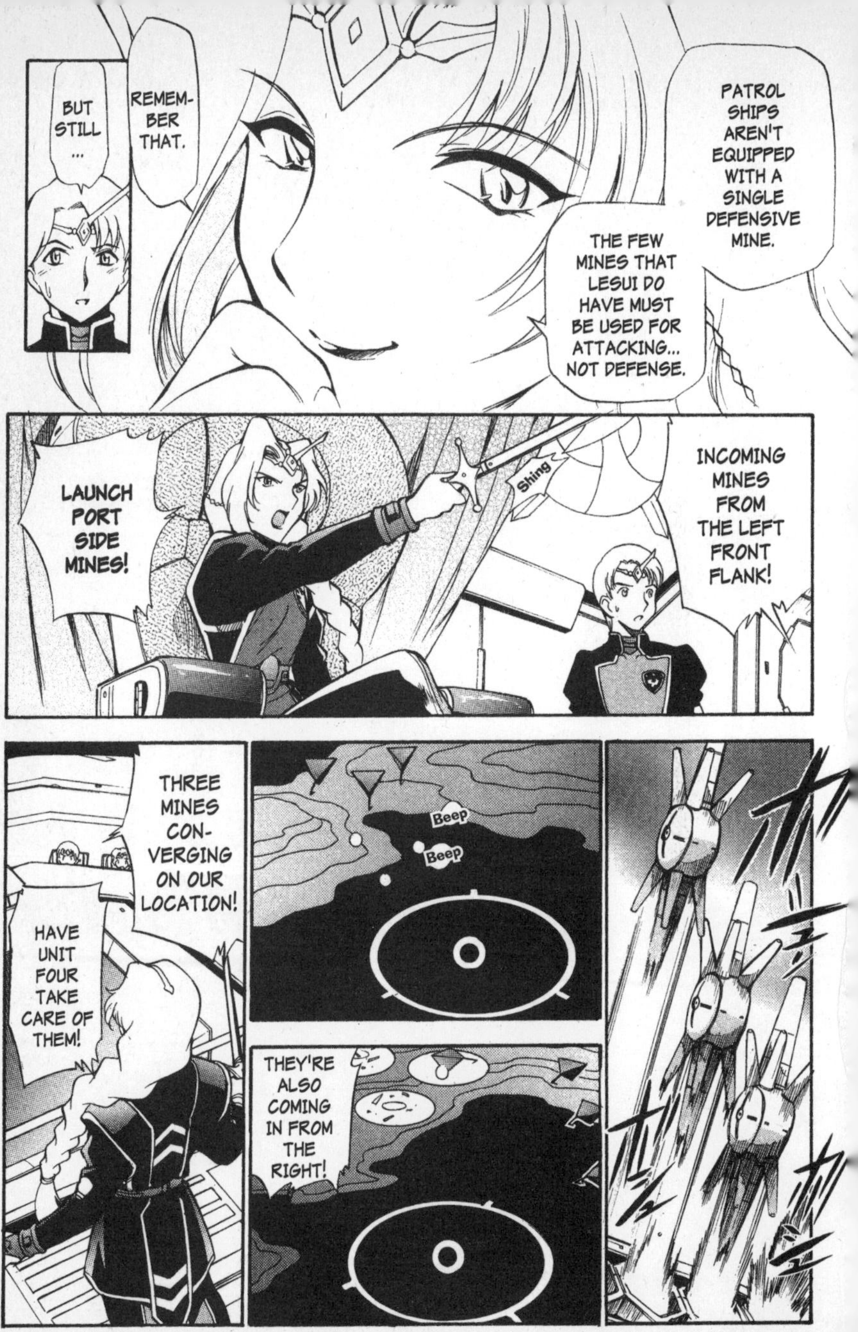
PATROL SHIPS AREN'T EQUIPPED WITH A SINGLE DEFENSIVE MINE.
THE FEW MINES THAT LESUI DO HAVE MUST BE USED FOR ATTACKING... NOT DEFENSE.
REMEM-BER THAT.
BUT STILL ...
INCOMING MINES FROM THE LEFT FRONT FLANK!
Shing
LAUNCH PORT SIDE MINES!
Beep
Beep
THEY'RE ALSO COMING IN FROM THE RIGHT!
THREE MINES CON-VERGING ON OUR LOCATION!
HAVE UNIT FOUR TAKE CARE OF THEM!

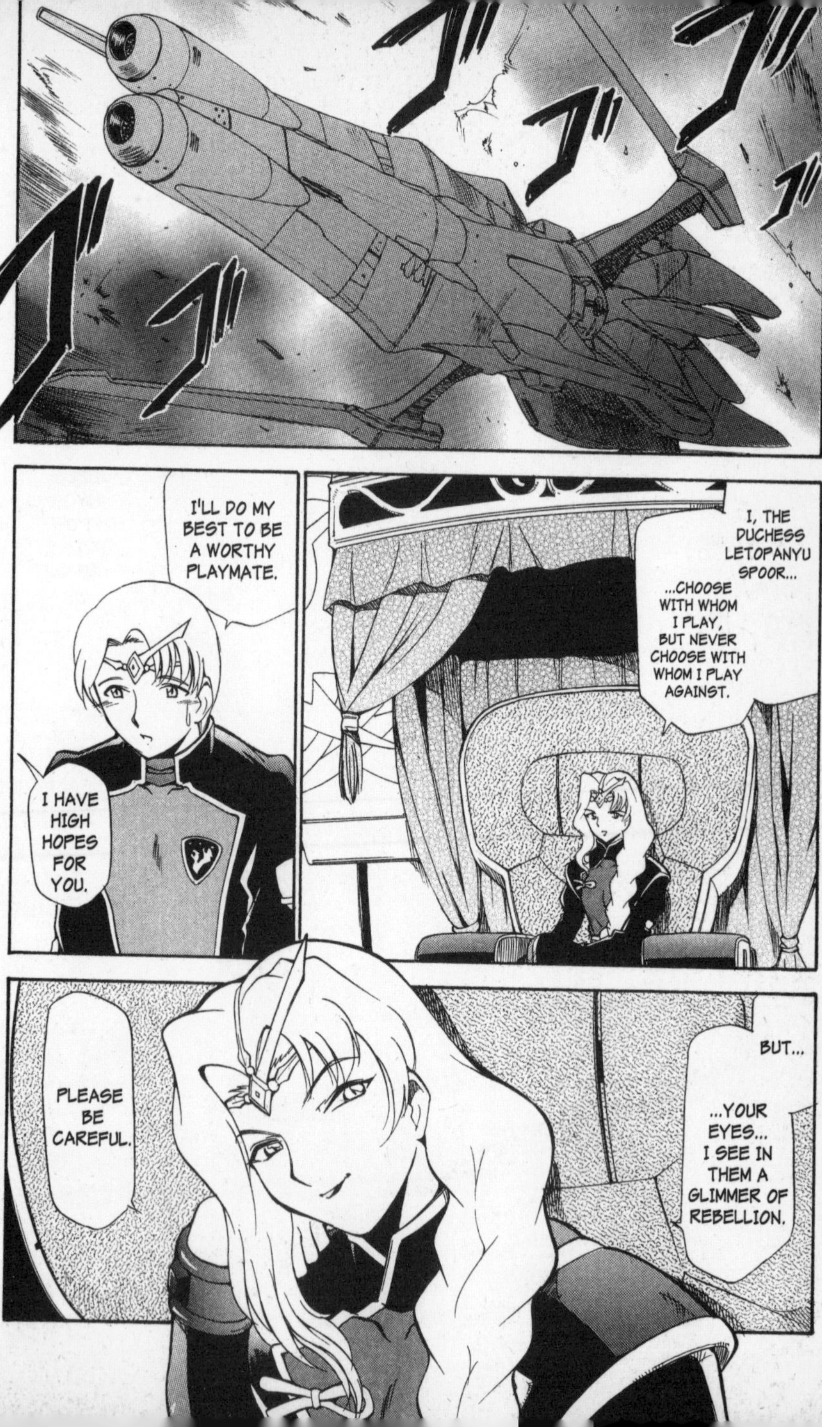
I, THE DUCHESS LETOPANYU SPOOR...
...CHOOSE WITH WHOM I PLAY, BUT NEVER CHOOSE WITH WHOM I PLAY AGAINST.
I'LL DO MY BEST TO BE A WORTHY PLAYMATE.
I HAVE HIGH HOPES FOR YOU.
BUT...
...YOUR EYES... I SEE IN THEM A GLIMMER OF REBELLION.
PLEASE BE CAREFUL.

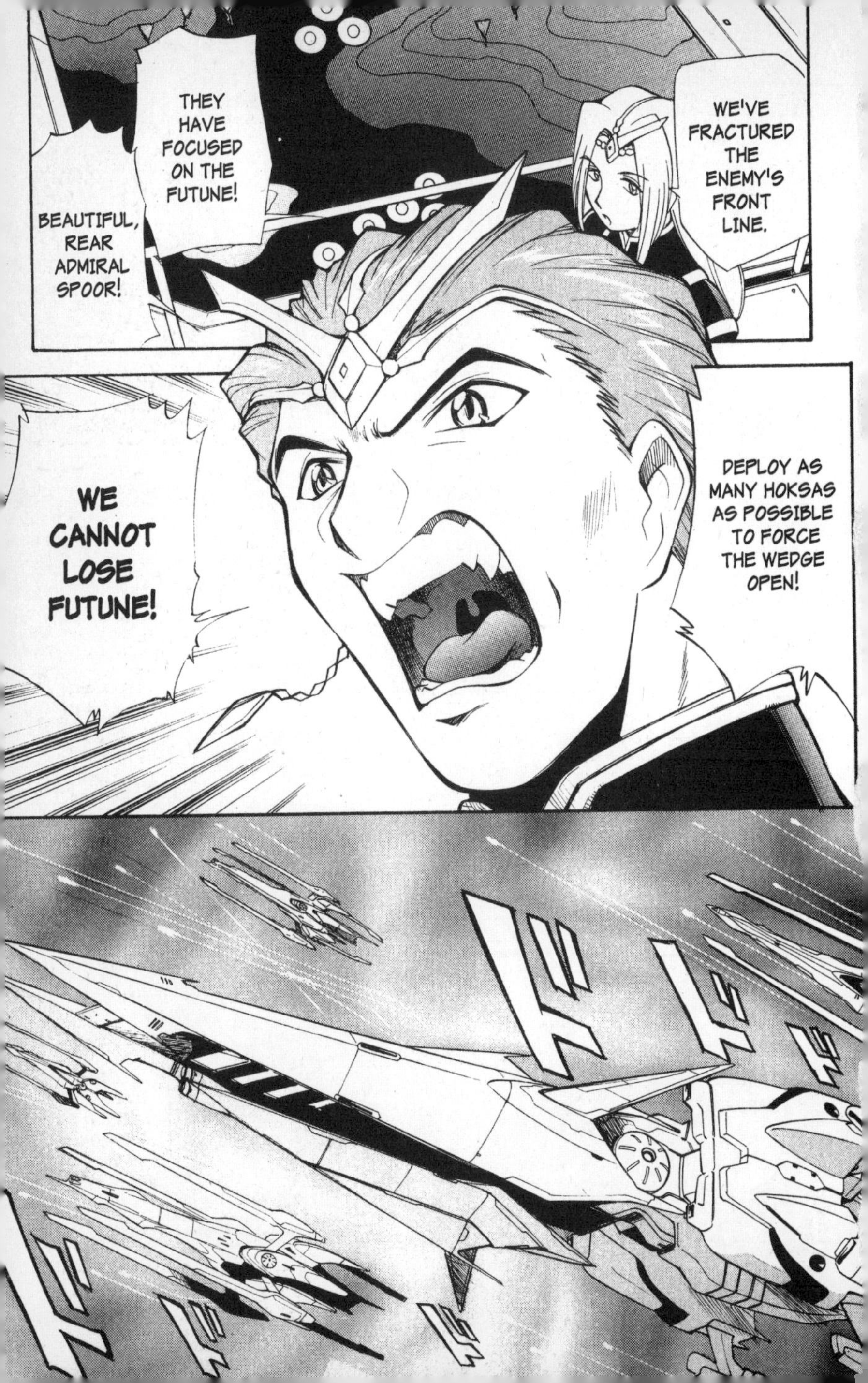
WE'VE FRACTURED THE ENEMY'S FRONT LINE.
THEY HAVE FOCUSED ON THE FUTUNE!
BEAUTIFUL, REAR ADMIRAL SPOOR!
DEPLOY AS MANY HOKSAS AS POSSIBLE TO FORCE THE WEDGE OPEN!
WE CANNOT LOSE FUTUNE!

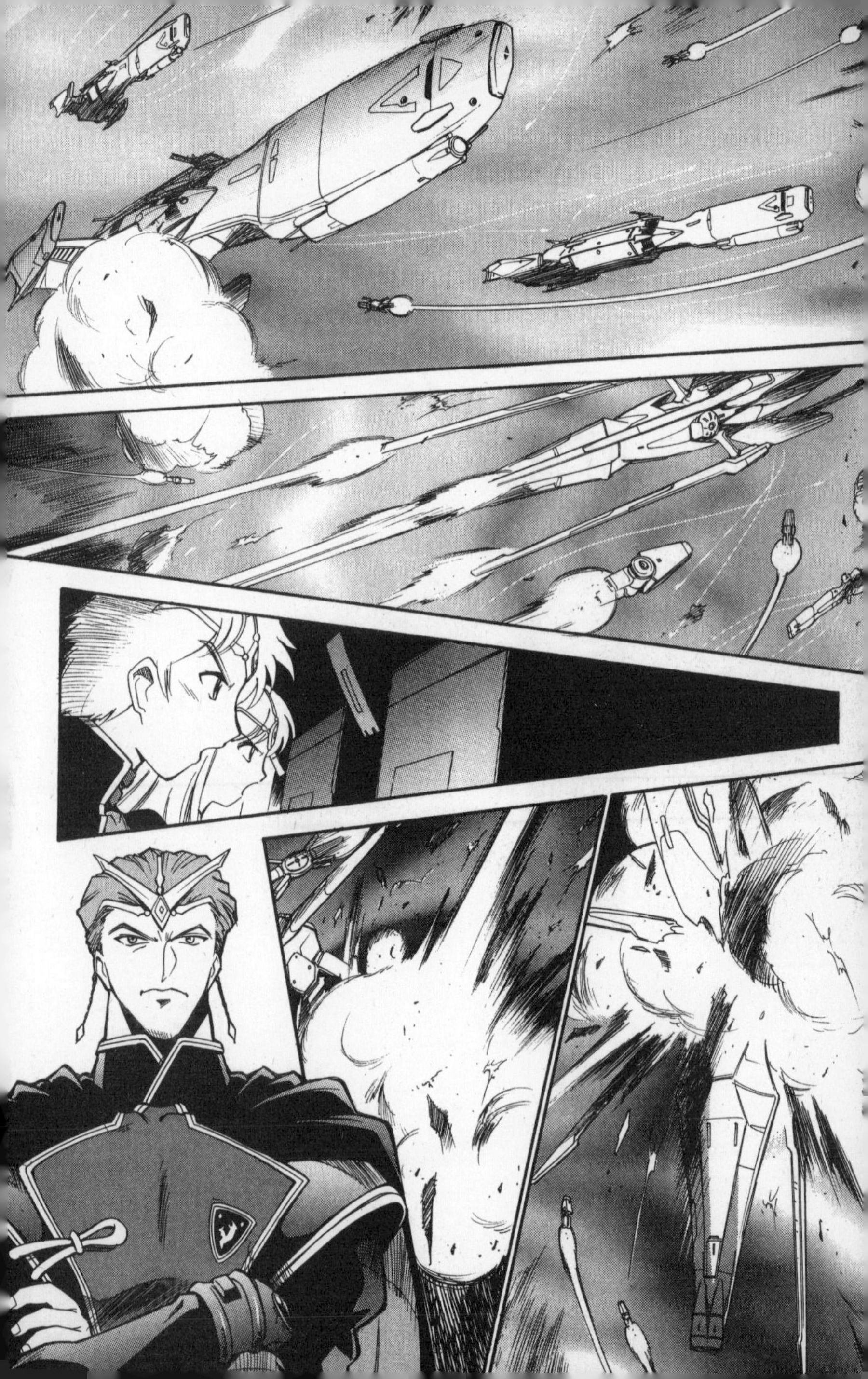

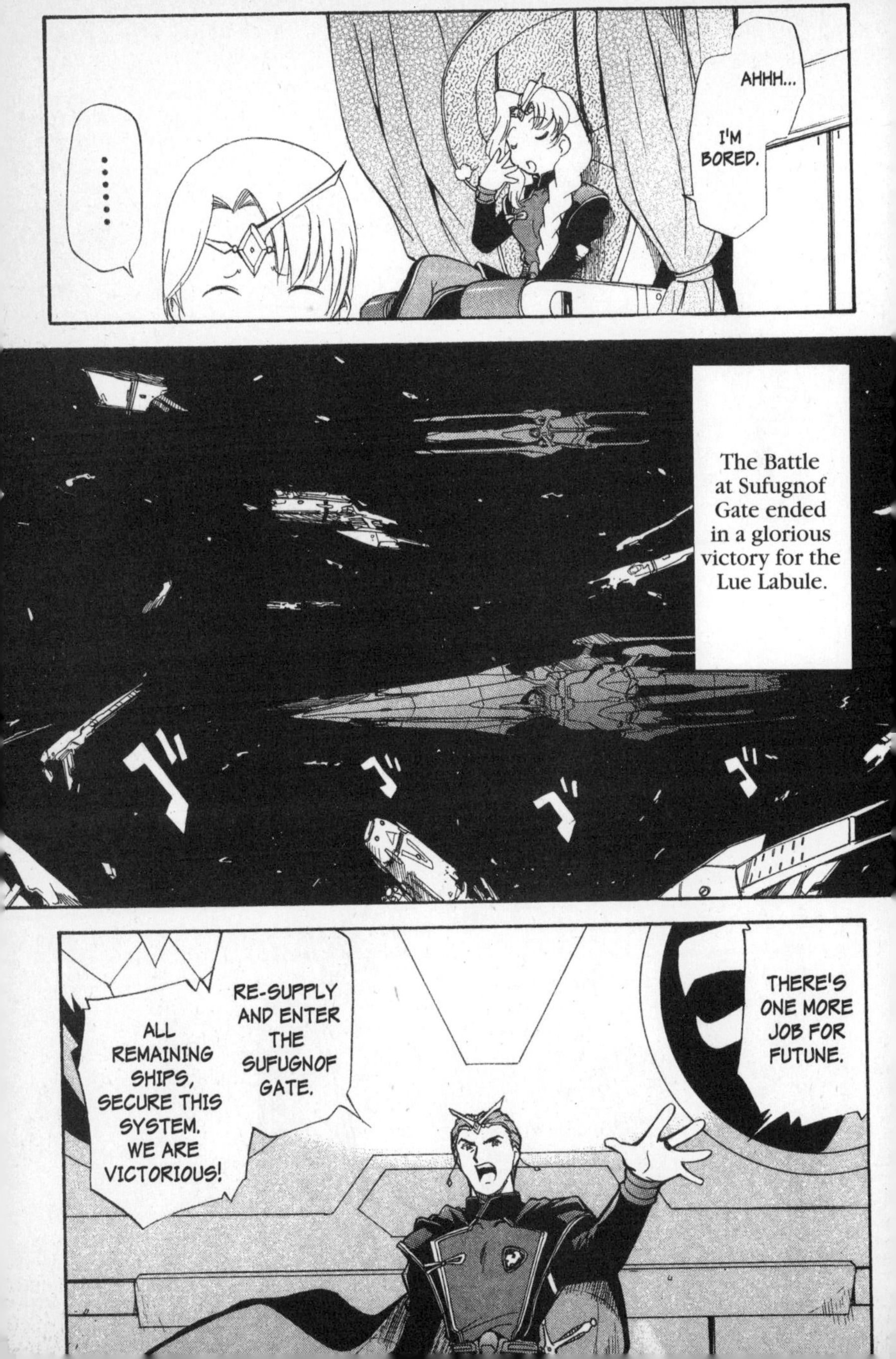
AHHH... I'M BORED.
......
The Battle at Sufugnof Gate ended in a glorious victory for the Lue Labule.
THERE'S ONE MORE JOB FOR FUTUNE.
RE-SUPPLY AND ENTER THE SUFUGNOF GATE.
ALL REMAINING SHIPS, SECURE THIS SYSTEM. WE ARE VICTORIOUS!

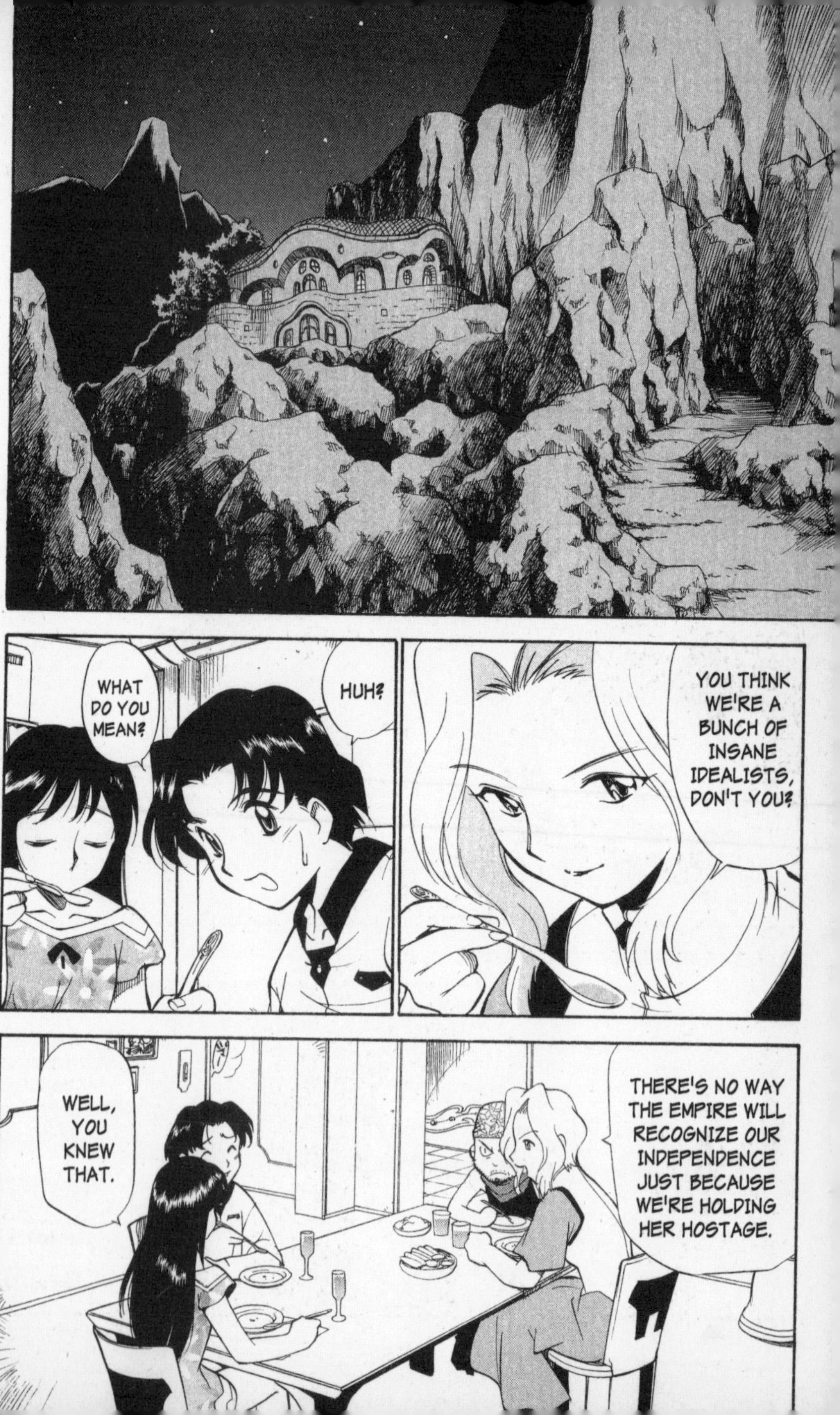
YOU THINK WE'RE A BUNCH OF INSANE IDEALISTS, DON'T YOU?
HUH?
WHAT DO YOU MEAN?
THERE'S NO WAY THE EMPIRE WILL RECOGNIZE OUR INDEPENDENCE JUST BECAUSE WE'RE HOLDING HER HOSTAGE.
WELL, YOU KNEW THAT.

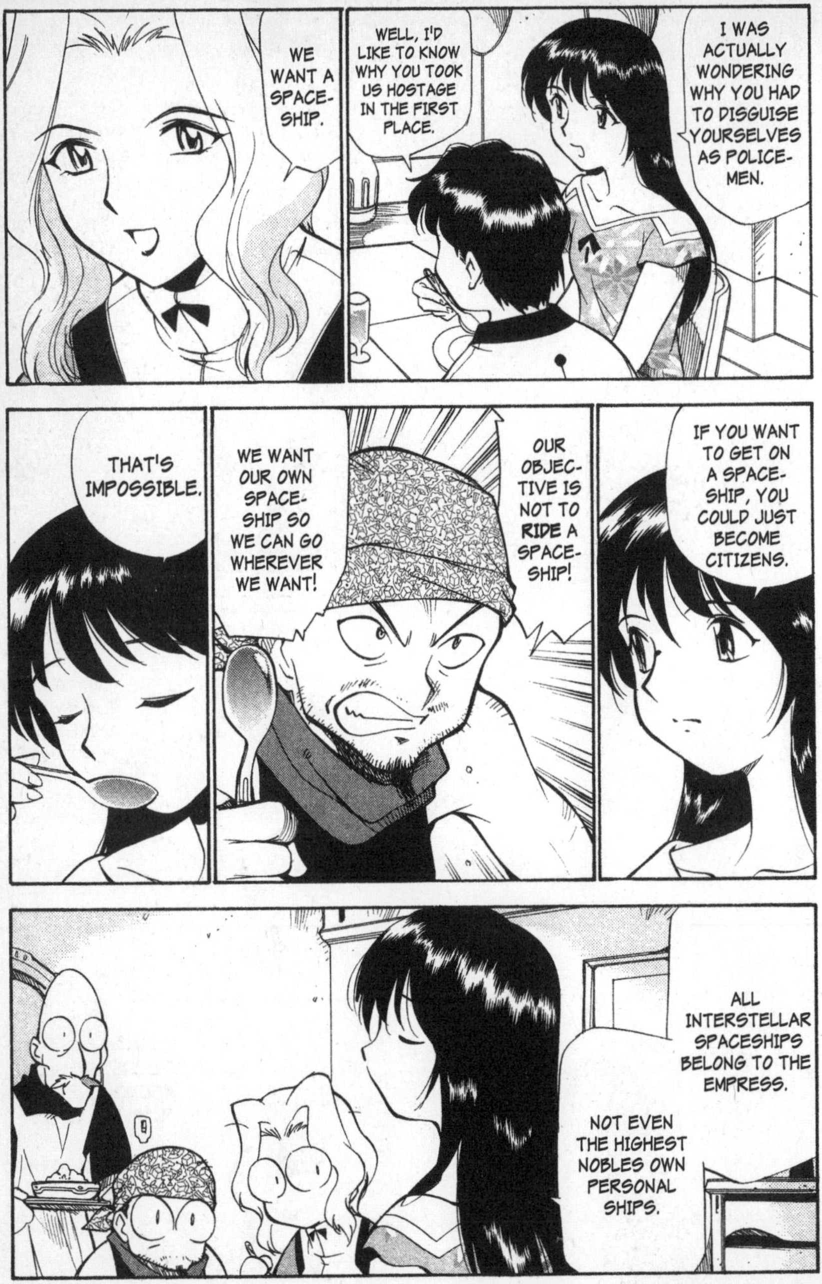

I WAS ACTUALLY WONDERING WHY YOU HAD TO DISGUISE YOURSELVES AS POLICE-MEN.
WELL, I'D LIKE TO KNOW WHY YOU TOOK US HOSTAGE IN THE FIRST PLACE.
WE WANT A SPACE-SHIP.
IF YOU WANT TO GET ON A SPACE-SHIP, YOU COULD JUST BECOME CITIZENS.
OUR OBJEC-TIVE IS NOT TO **RIDE** A SPACE-SHIP!
WE WANT OUR OWN SPACE-SHIP SO WE CAN GO WHEREVER WE WANT!
THAT'S IMPOSSIBLE.
ALL INTERSTELLAR SPACESHIPS BELONG TO THE EMPRESS.
NOT EVEN THE HIGHEST NOBLES OWN PERSONAL SHIPS.

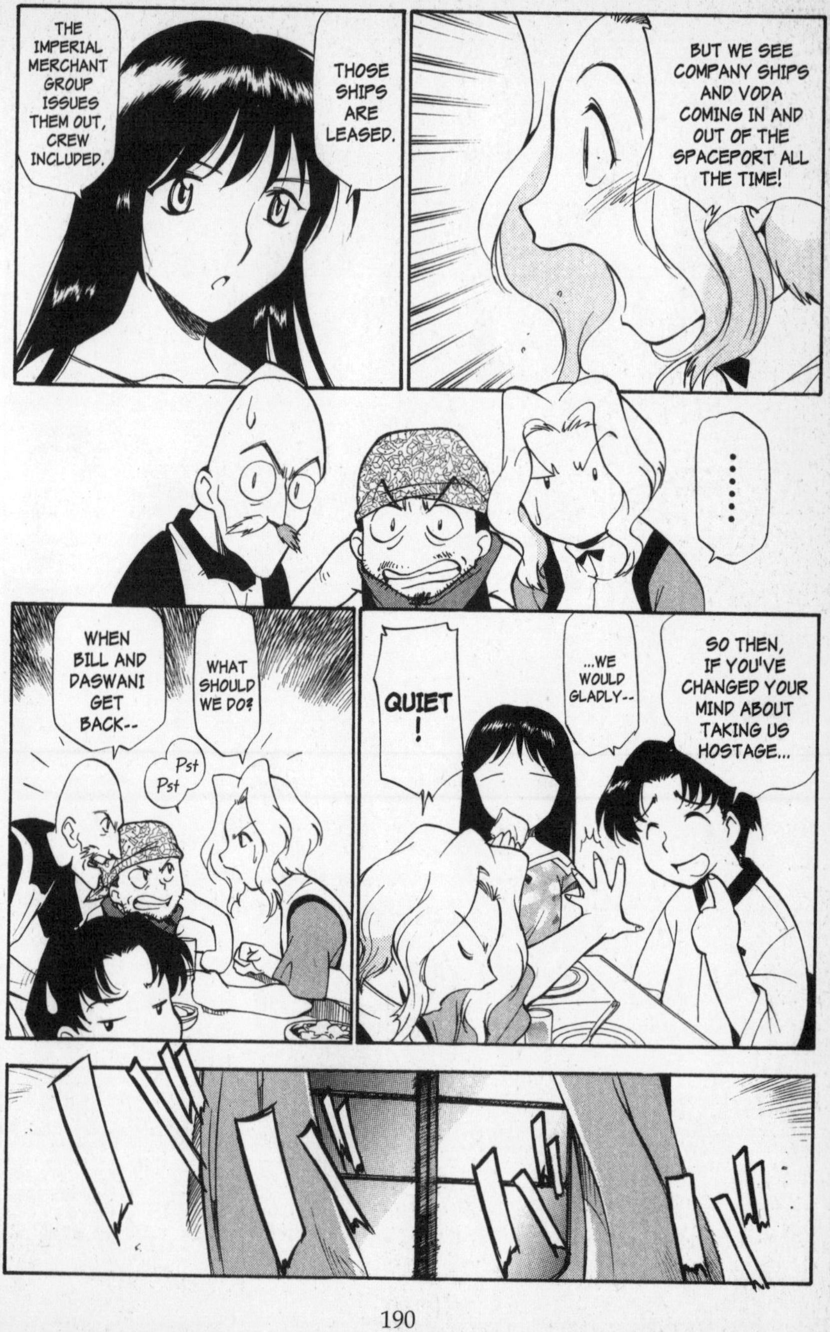
BUT WE SEE COMPANY SHIPS AND VODA COMING IN AND OUT OF THE SPACEPORT ALL THE TIME!
THOSE SHIPS ARE LEASED.
THE IMPERIAL MERCHANT GROUP ISSUES THEM OUT, CREW INCLUDED.
......
SO THEN, IF YOU'VE CHANGED YOUR MIND ABOUT TAKING US HOSTAGE...
...WE WOULD GLADLY--
QUIET!
WHAT SHOULD WE DO?
Pst Pst
WHEN BILL AND DASWANI GET BACK--

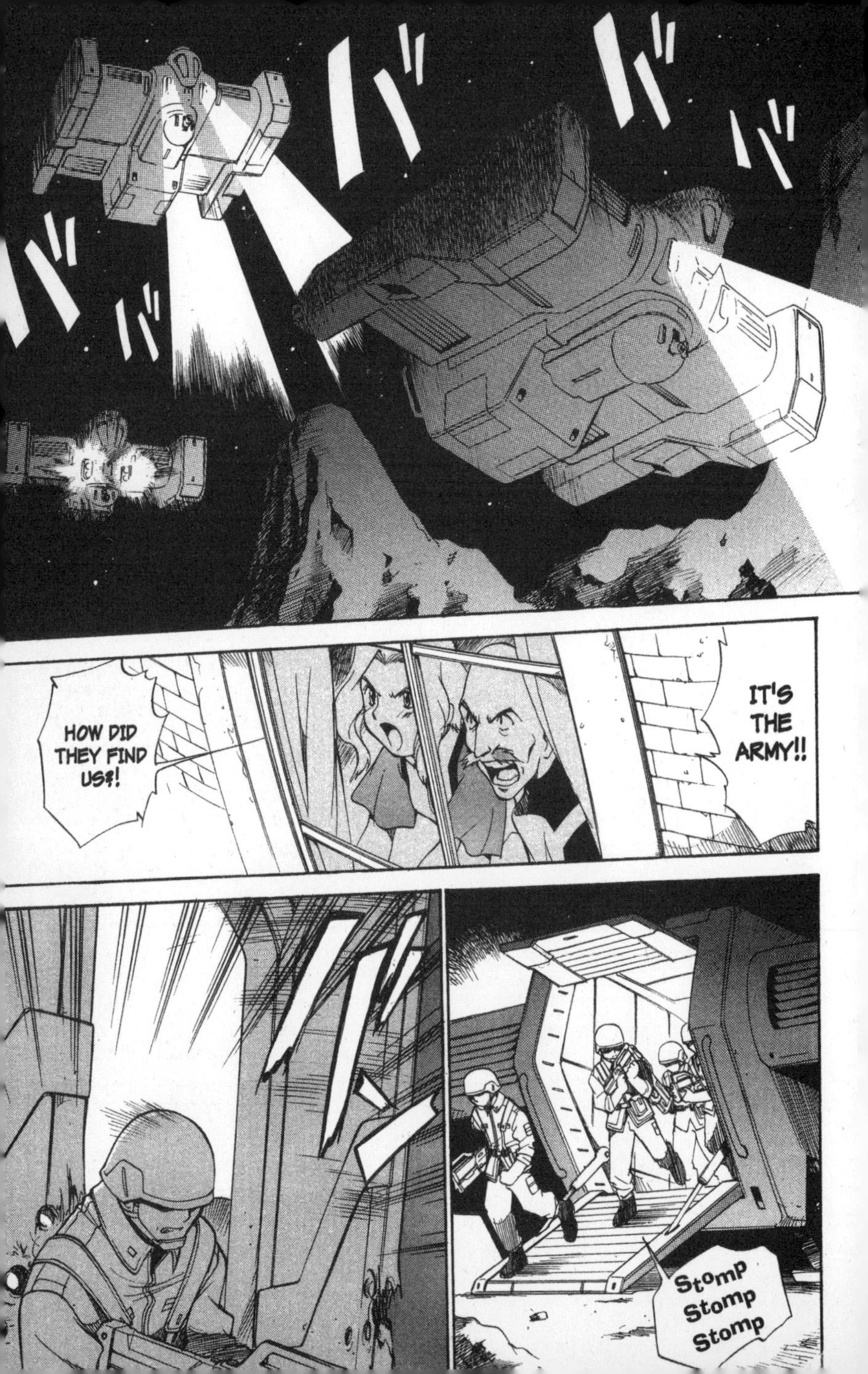
IT'S THE ARMY!!
HOW DID THEY FIND US?!
Stomp Stomp Stomp

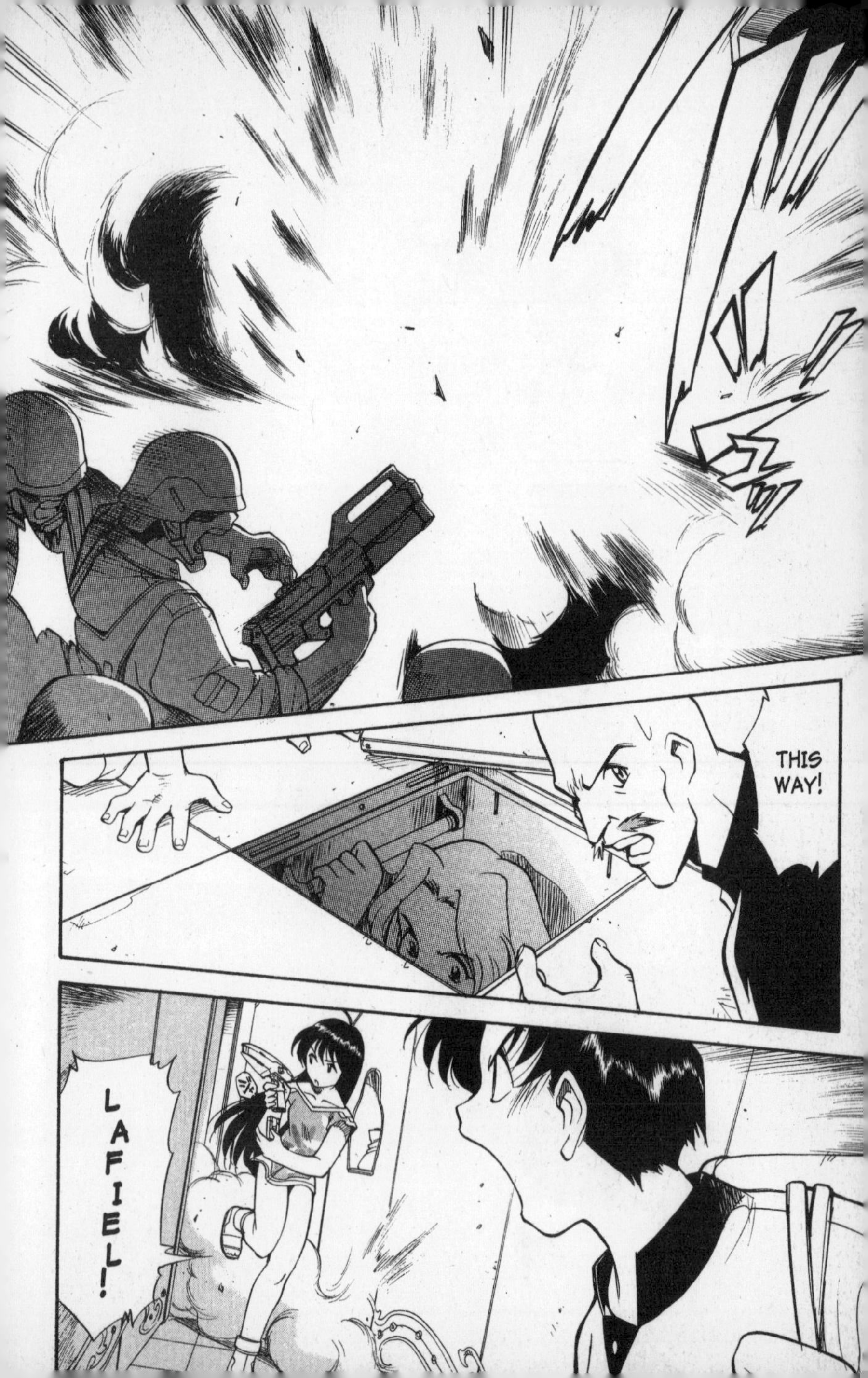
THIS WAY!
LAFIEL!

FwiP

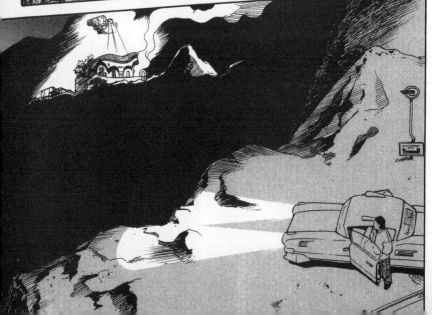

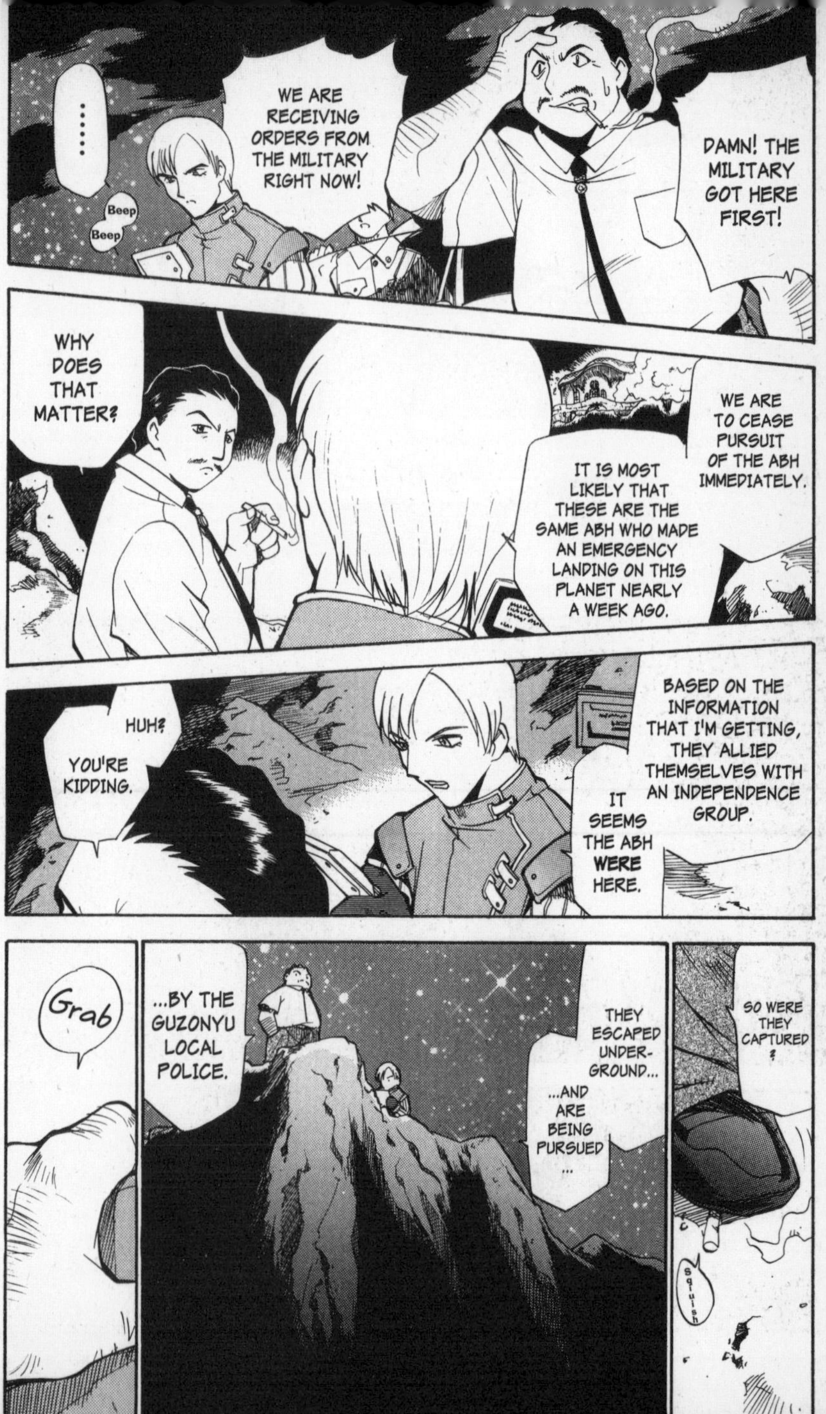
DAMN! THE MILITARY GOT HERE FIRST!
WE ARE RECEIVING ORDERS FROM THE MILITARY RIGHT NOW!
Beep
Beep
......
WE ARE TO CEASE PURSUIT OF THE ABH IMMEDIATELY.
IT IS MOST LIKELY THAT THESE ARE THE SAME ABH WHO MADE AN EMERGENCY LANDING ON THIS PLANET NEARLY A WEEK AGO.
WHY DOES THAT MATTER?
BASED ON THE INFORMATION THAT I'M GETTING, THEY ALLIED THEMSELVES WITH AN INDEPENDENCE GROUP.
IT SEEMS THE ABH **WERE** HERE.
HUH?
YOU'RE KIDDING.
SO WERE THEY CAPTURED?
squish
THEY ESCAPED UNDER-GROUND...
...AND ARE BEING PURSUED ...
...BY THE GUZONYU LOCAL POLICE.
Grab

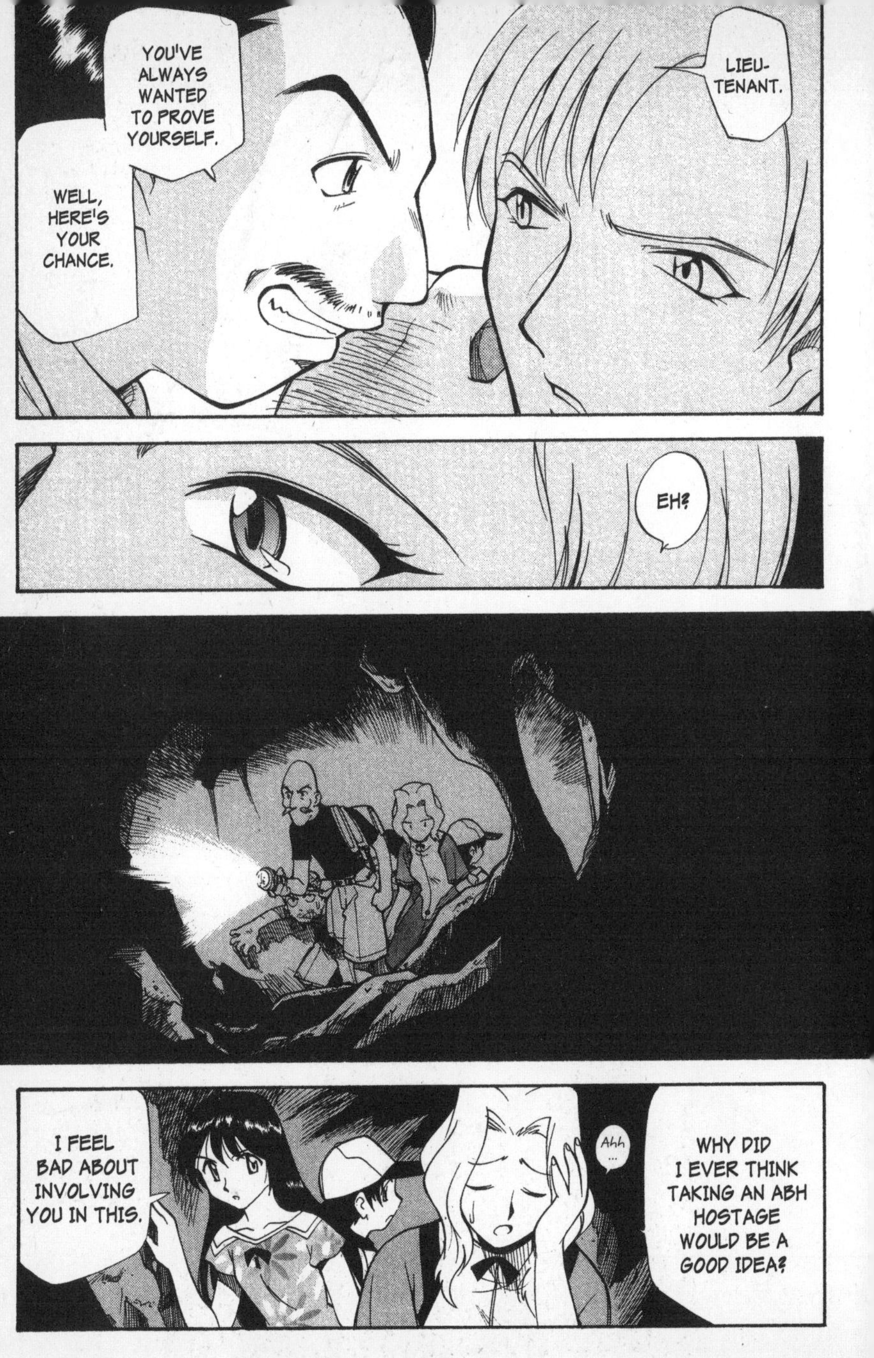
LIEU-TENANT.
YOU'VE ALWAYS WANTED TO PROVE YOURSELF.
WELL, HERE'S YOUR CHANCE.
EH?
WHY DID I EVER THINK TAKING AN ABH HOSTAGE WOULD BE A GOOD IDEA?
Ahh ...
I FEEL BAD ABOUT INVOLVING YOU IN THIS.

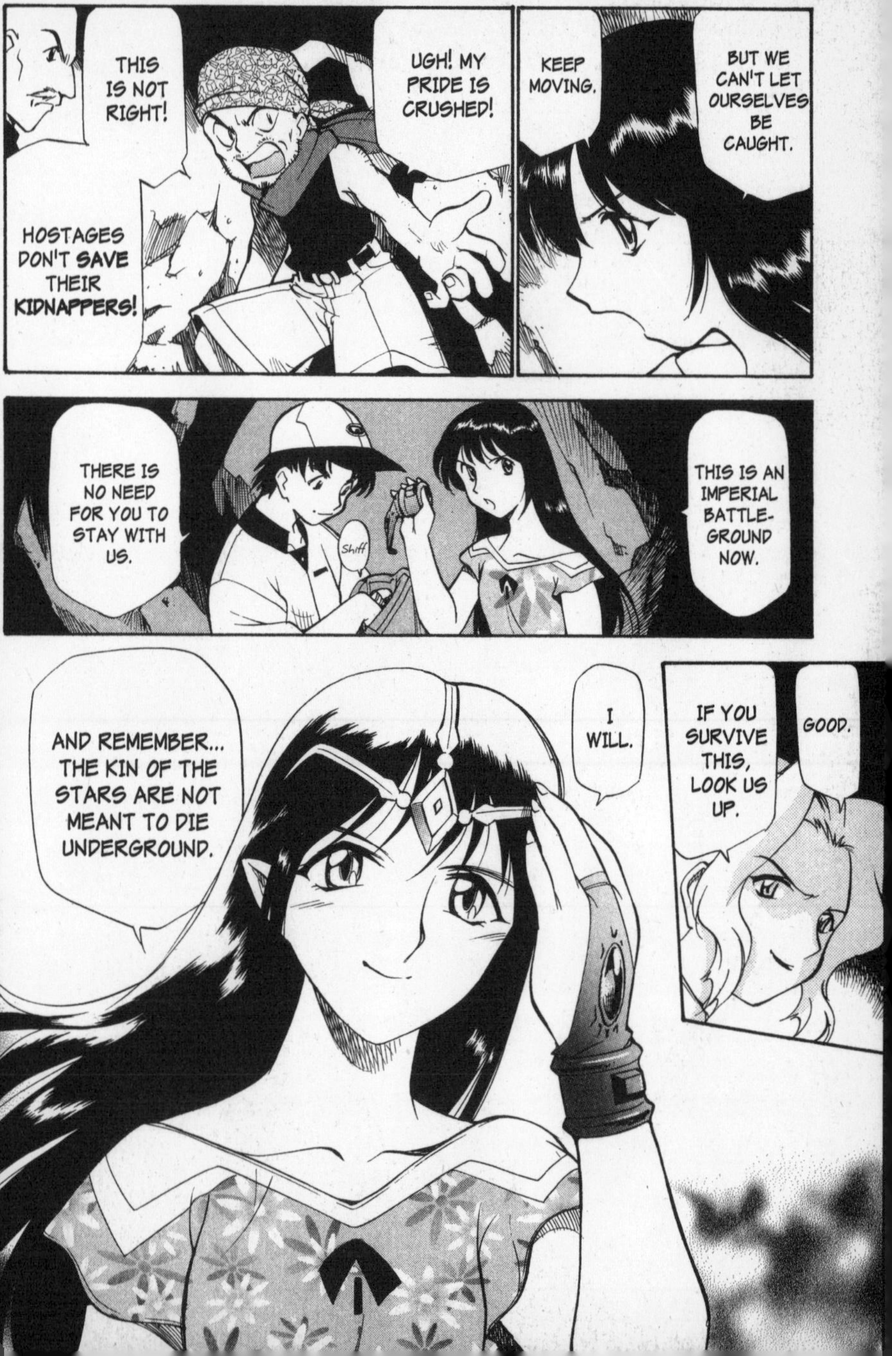
BUT WE CAN'T LET OURSELVES BE CAUGHT.
KEEP MOVING.
UGH! MY PRIDE IS CRUSHED!
THIS IS NOT RIGHT!
HOSTAGES DON'T SAVE THEIR KIDNAPPERS!
THIS IS AN IMPERIAL BATTLE-GROUND NOW.
Shiff
THERE IS NO NEED FOR YOU TO STAY WITH US.
GOOD.
IF YOU SURVIVE THIS, LOOK US UP.
I WILL.
AND REMEMBER... THE KIN OF THE STARS ARE NOT MEANT TO DIE UNDERGROUND.

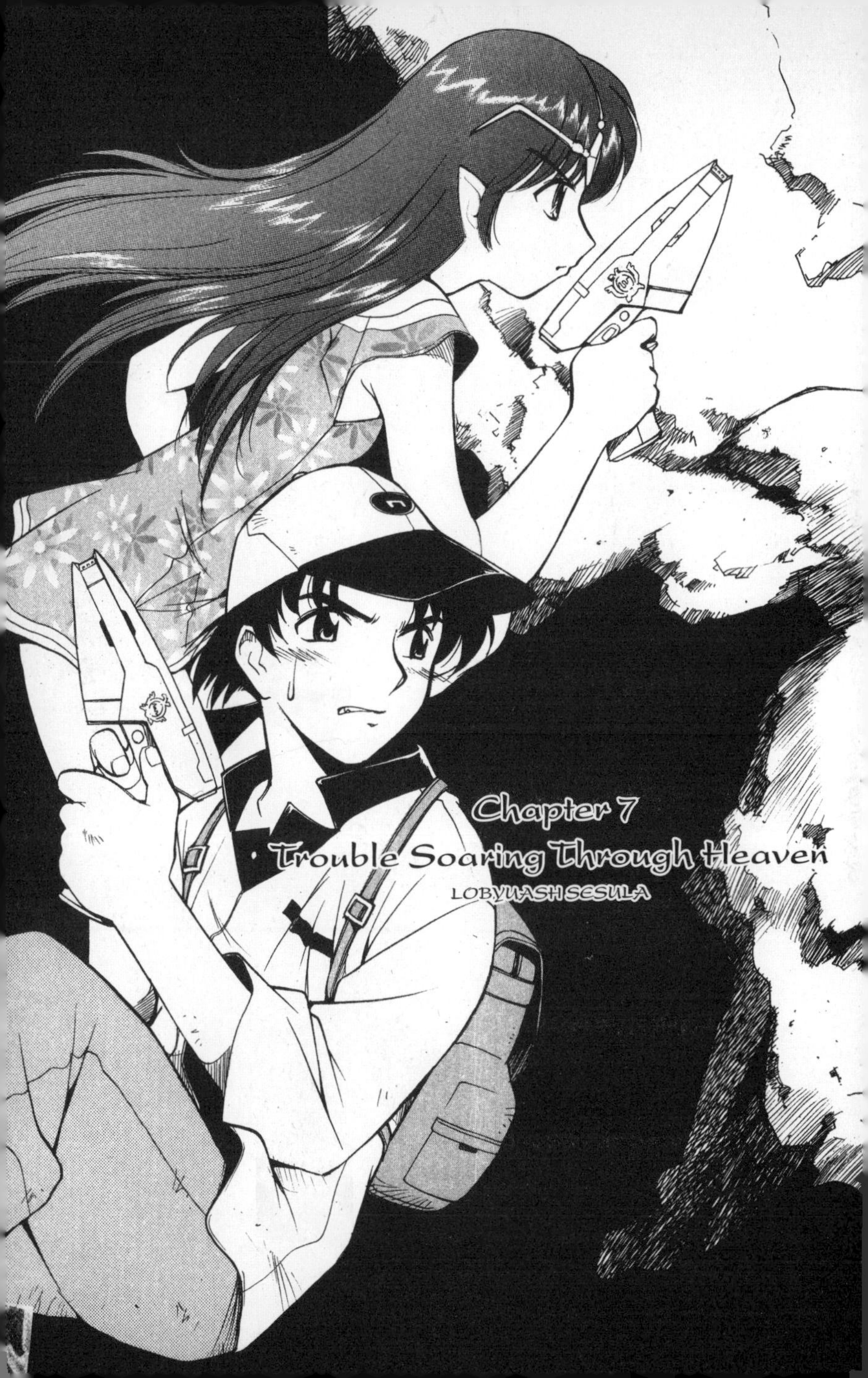
Chapter 7
Trouble Soaring Through Heaven
LOBYUASH SESULA

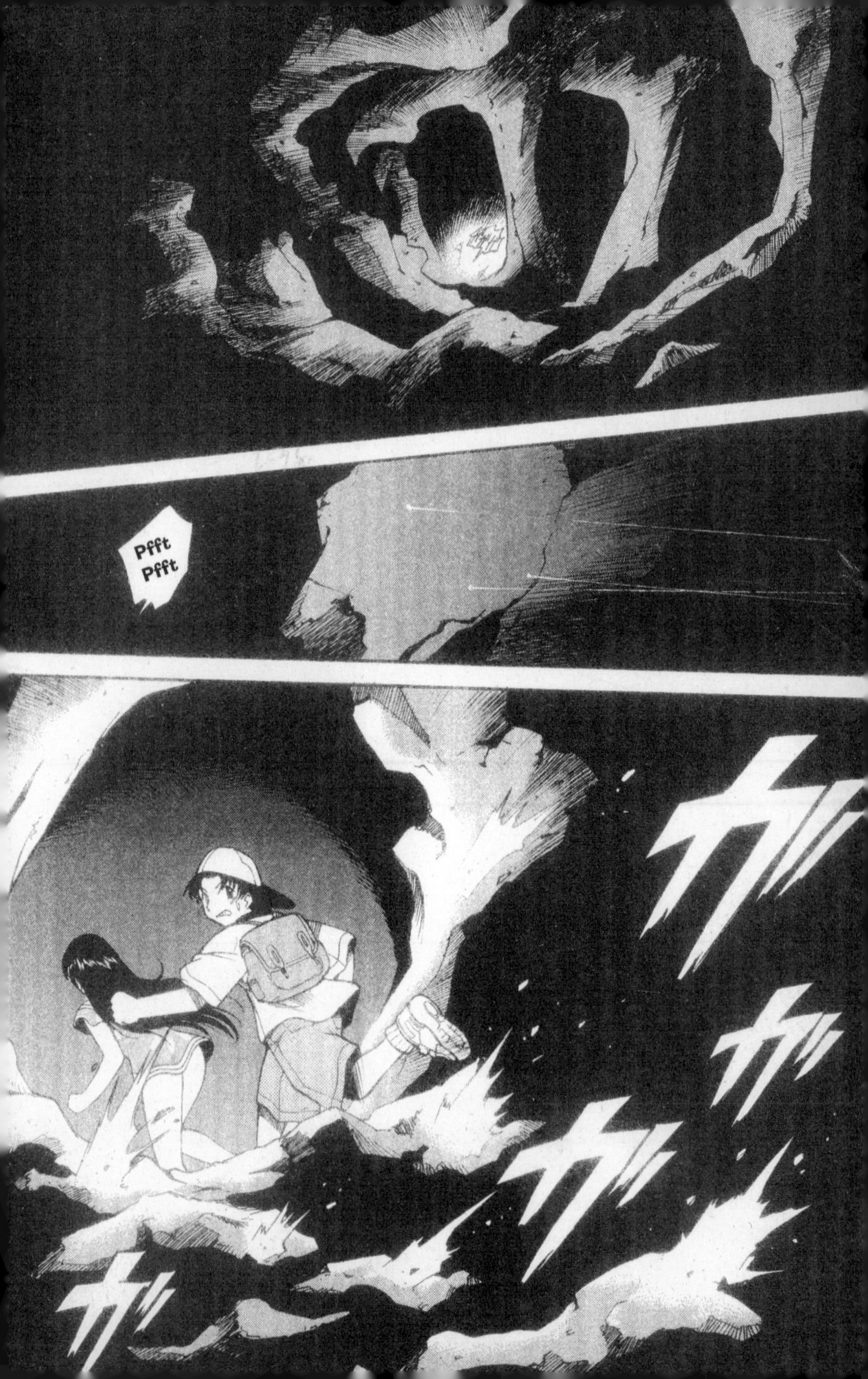
Pfft
Pfft

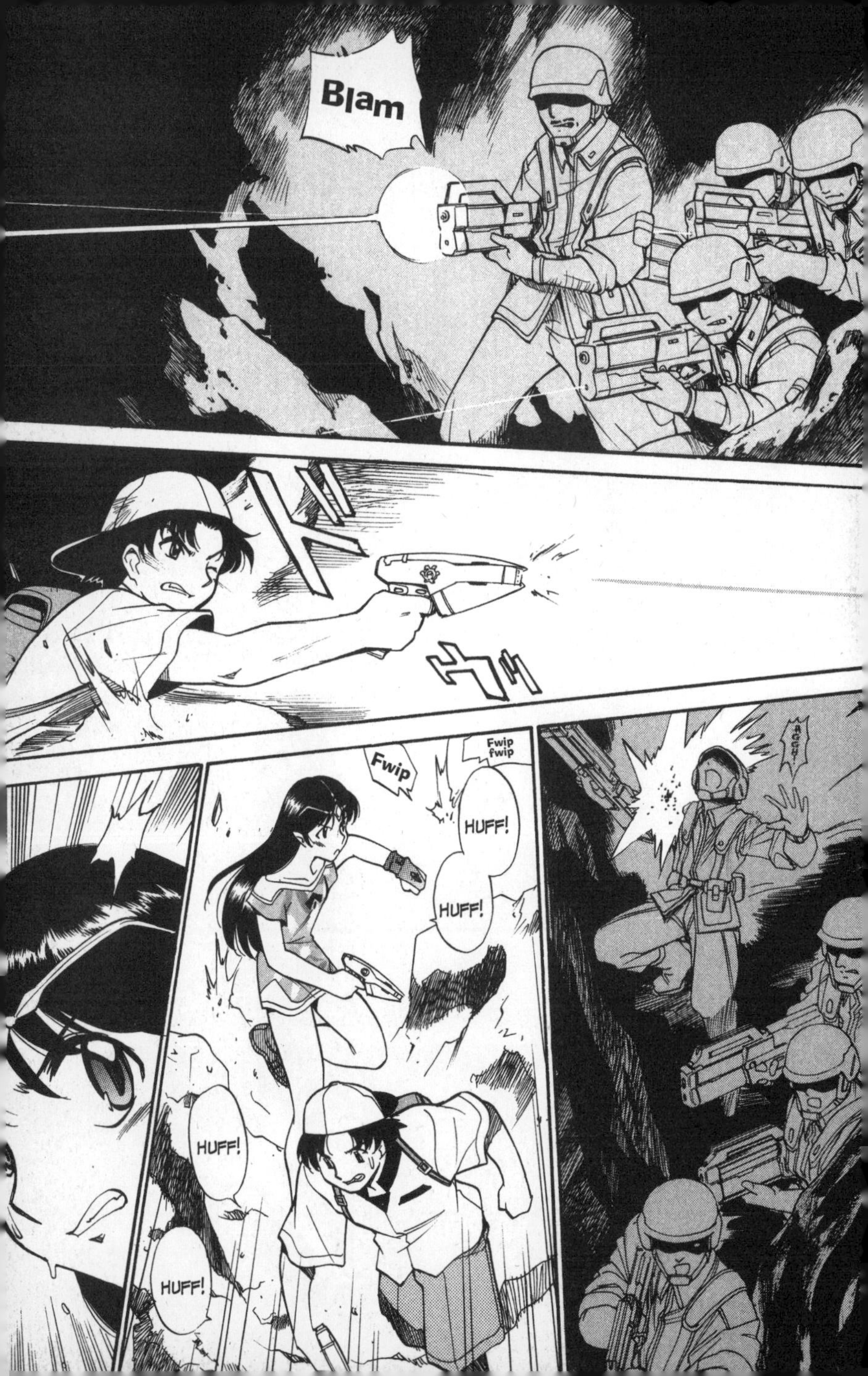

Blam
AGGH!
Fwip fwip
Fwip
HUFF!
HUFF!
HUFF!
HUFF!

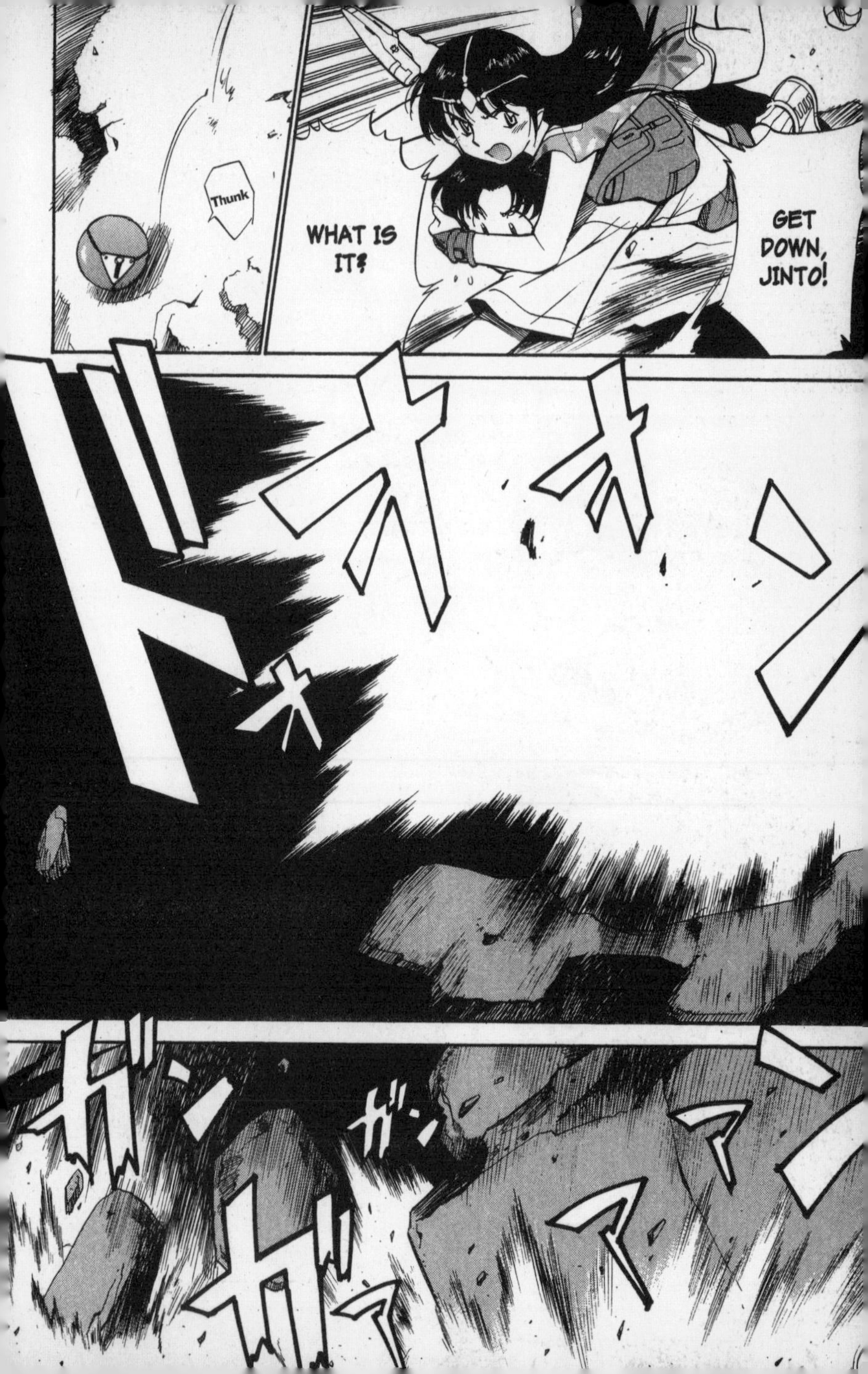
GET DOWN, JINTO!
WHAT IS IT?
Thunk

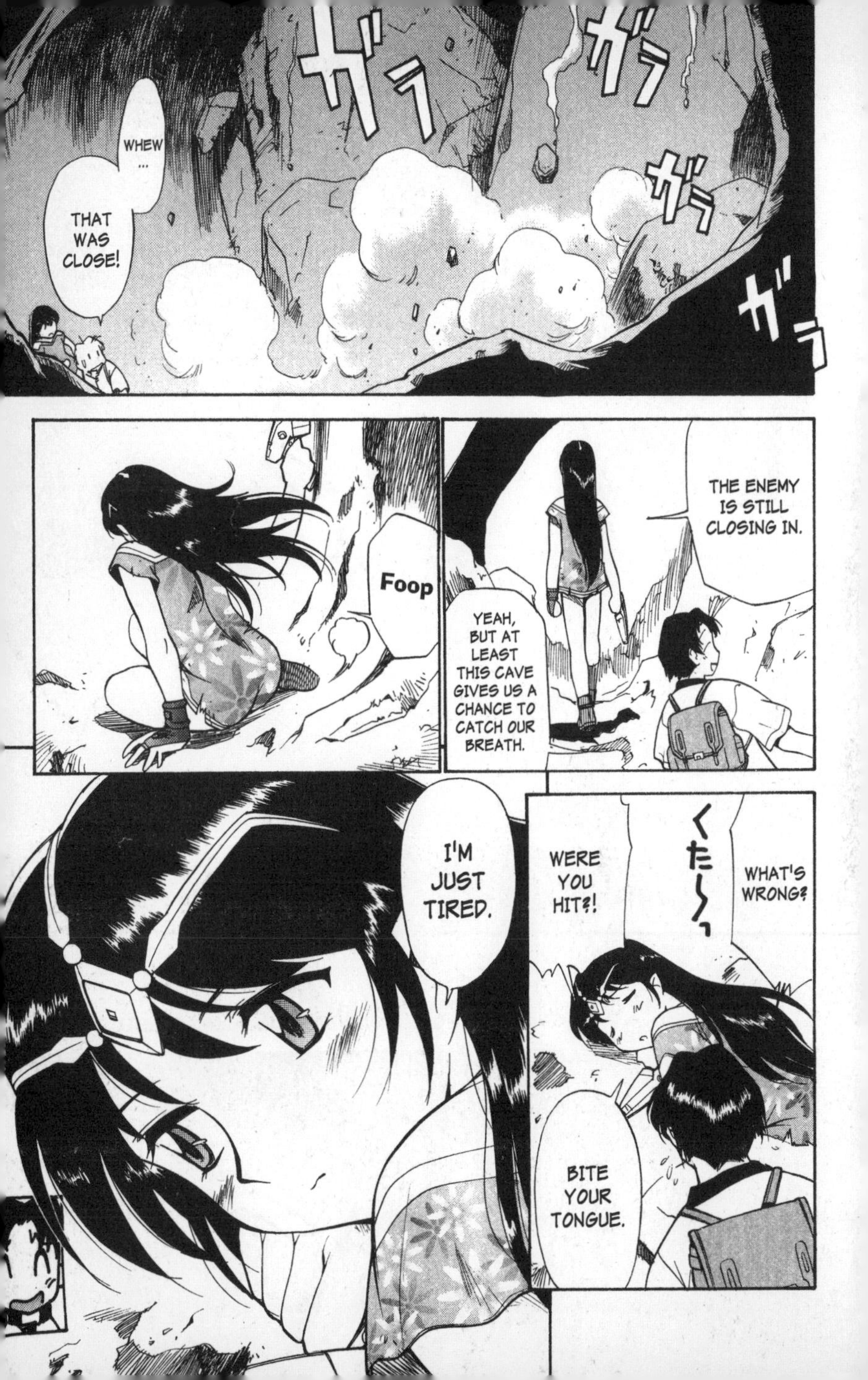
ガラ
ガラ
ガラ
ガラ
WHEW ... THAT WAS CLOSE!
THE ENEMY IS STILL CLOSING IN.
YEAH, BUT AT LEAST THIS CAVE GIVES US A CHANCE TO CATCH OUR BREATH.
Foop
WHAT'S WRONG?
くた～っ
WERE YOU HIT?!
BITE YOUR TONGUE.
I'M JUST TIRED.

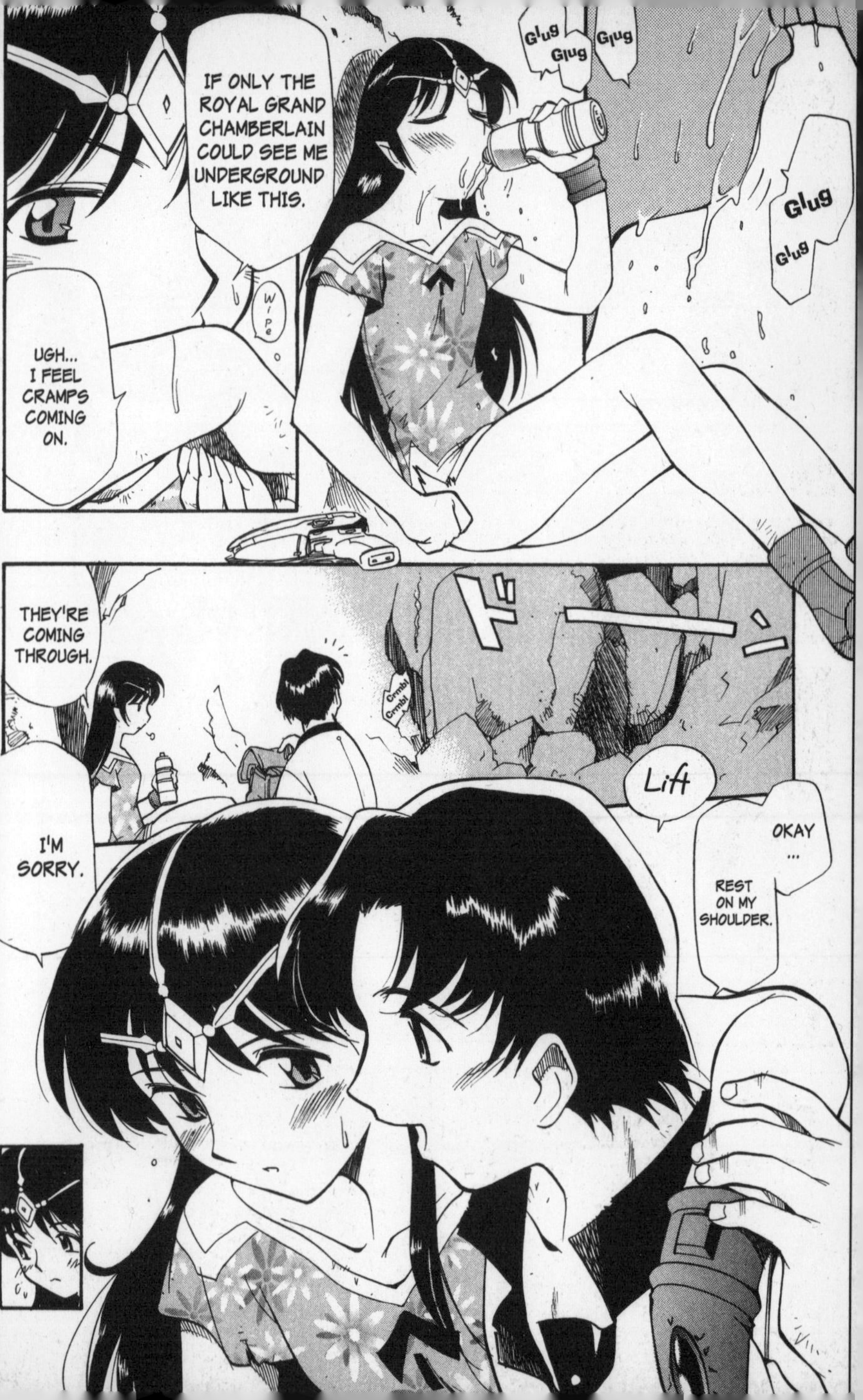
Glug Glug Glug
Glug Glug
IF ONLY THE ROYAL GRAND CHAMBERLAIN COULD SEE ME UNDERGROUND LIKE THIS.
Wipe
UGH... I FEEL CRAMPS COMING ON.
ドー
Crmbl Crmbl
THEY'RE COMING THROUGH.
Lift
OKAY ... REST ON MY SHOULDER.
I'M SORRY.

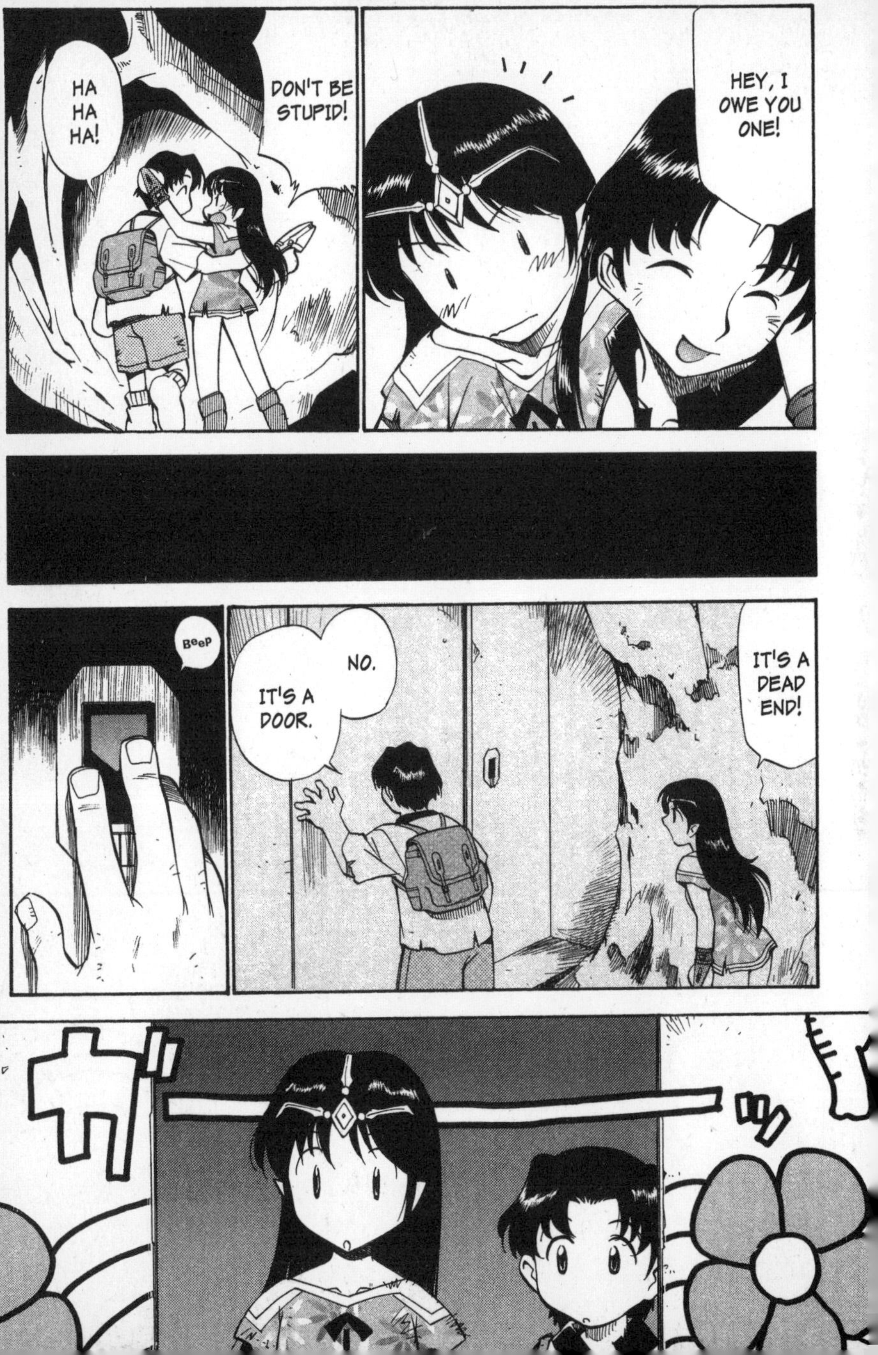
HEY, I OWE YOU ONE!
DON'T BE STUPID!
HA HA HA!
IT'S A DEAD END!
NO.
IT'S A DOOR.
Beep

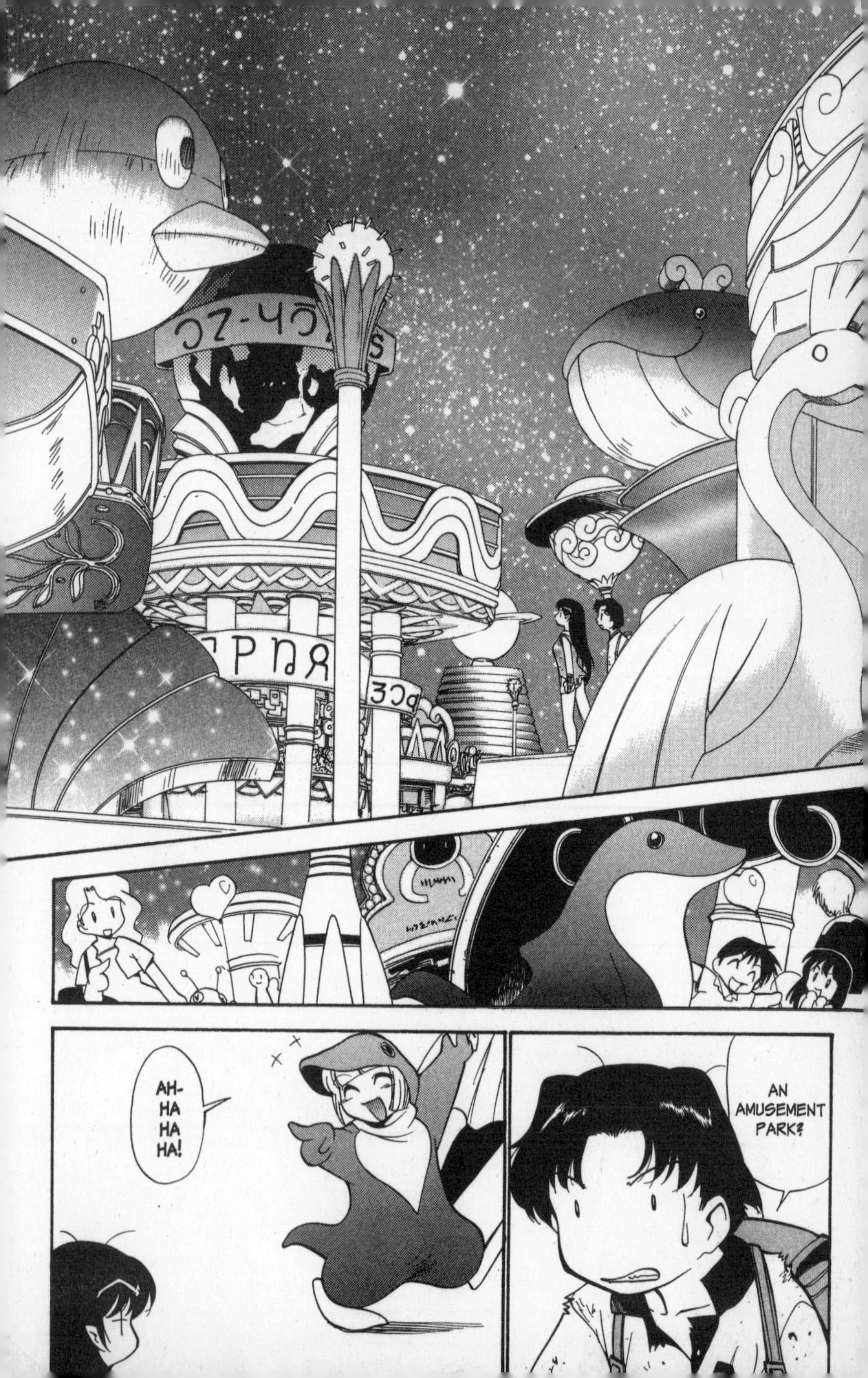
AN AMUSEMENT PARK?
AH-HA HA HA!

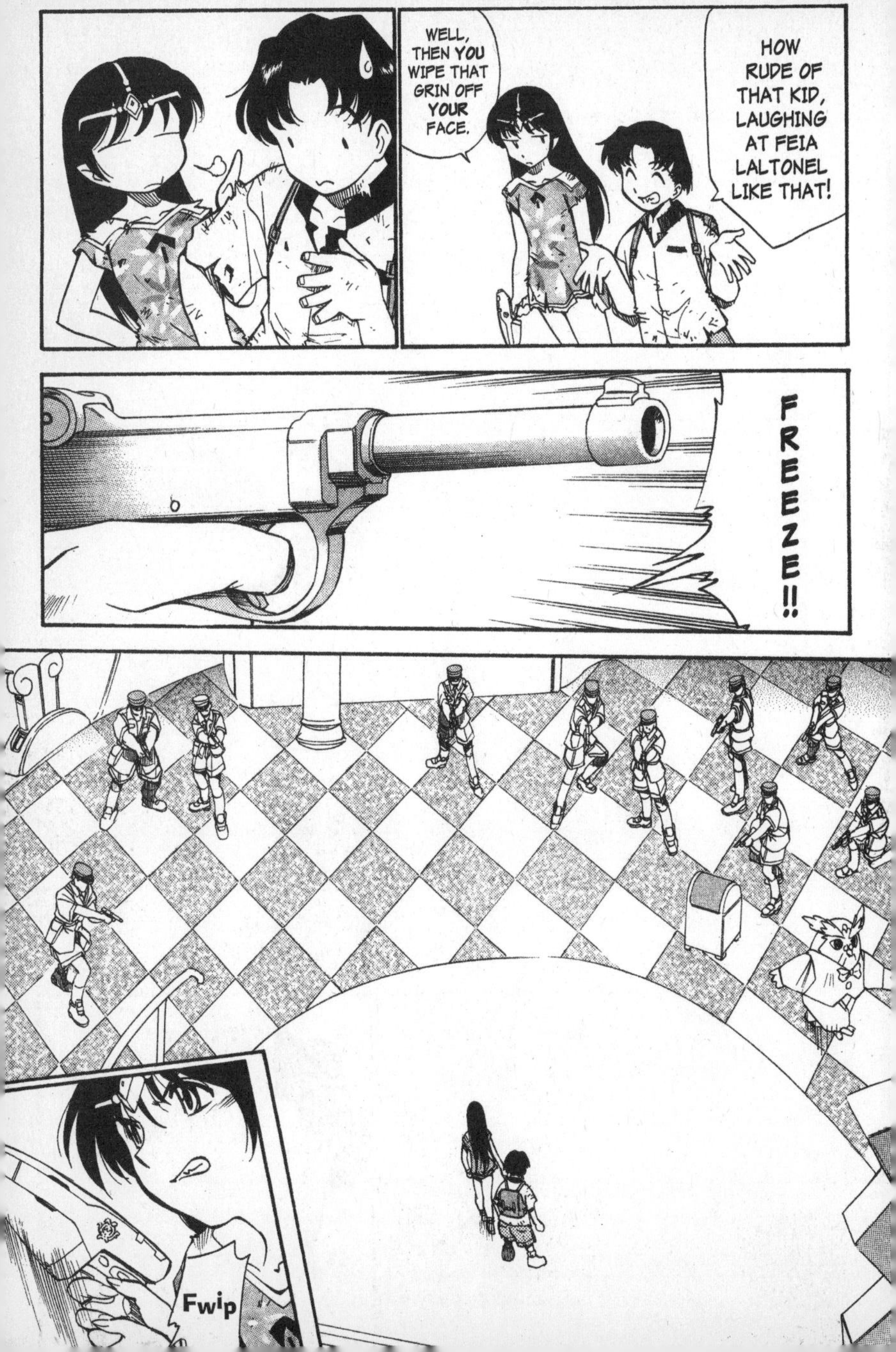
HOW RUDE OF THAT KID, LAUGHING AT FEIA LALTONEL LIKE THAT!
WELL, THEN YOU WIPE THAT GRIN OFF YOUR FACE.
FREEZE!!
Fwip

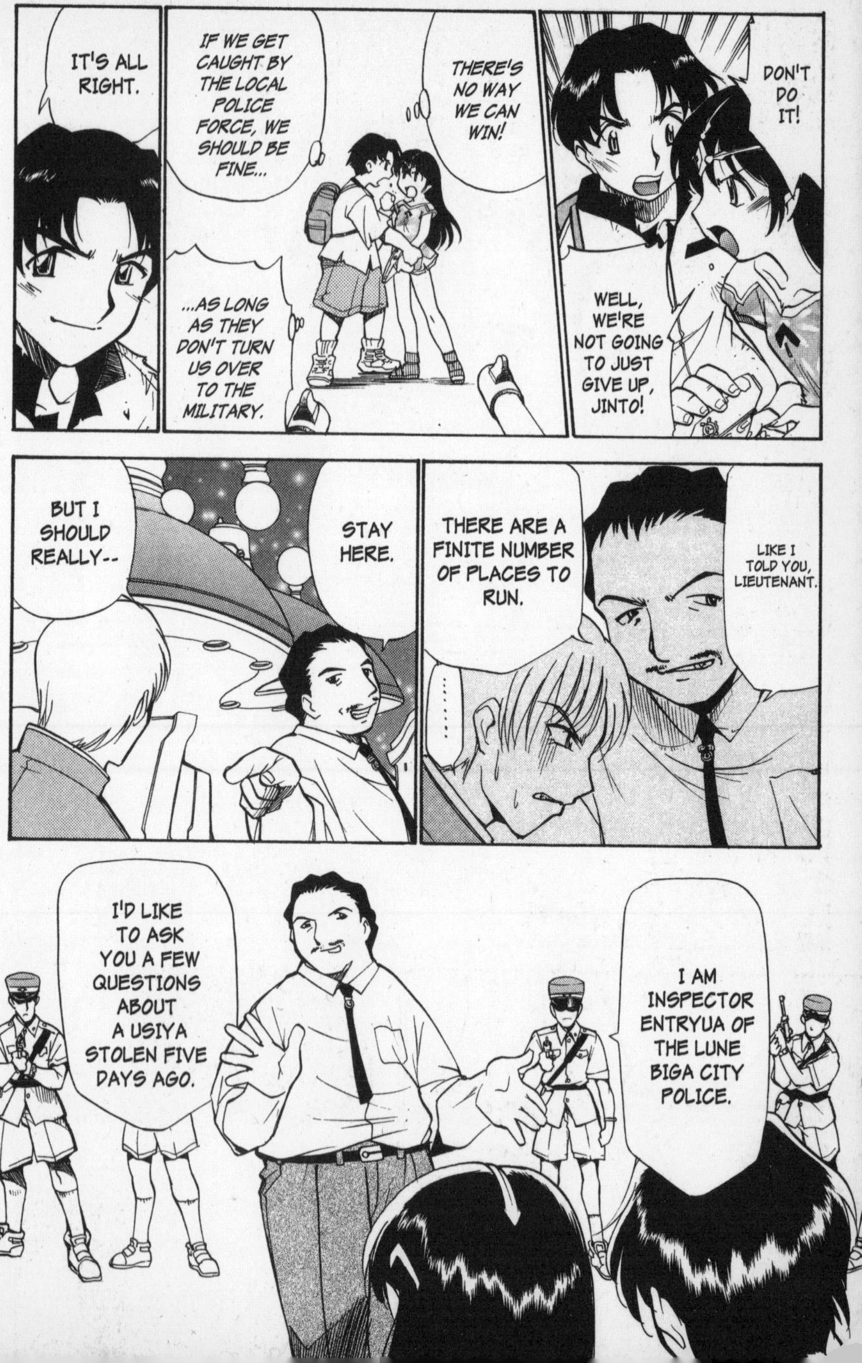
DON'T DO IT!
WELL, WE'RE NOT GOING TO JUST GIVE UP, JINTO!
THERE'S NO WAY WE CAN WIN!
IF WE GET CAUGHT BY THE LOCAL POLICE FORCE, WE SHOULD BE FINE...
...AS LONG AS THEY DON'T TURN US OVER TO THE MILITARY.
IT'S ALL RIGHT.
LIKE I TOLD YOU, LIEUTENANT.
THERE ARE A FINITE NUMBER OF PLACES TO RUN.
......
STAY HERE.
BUT I SHOULD REALLY--
I AM INSPECTOR ENTRYUA OF THE LUNE BIGA CITY POLICE.
I'D LIKE TO ASK YOU A FEW QUESTIONS ABOUT A USIYA STOLEN FIVE DAYS AGO.

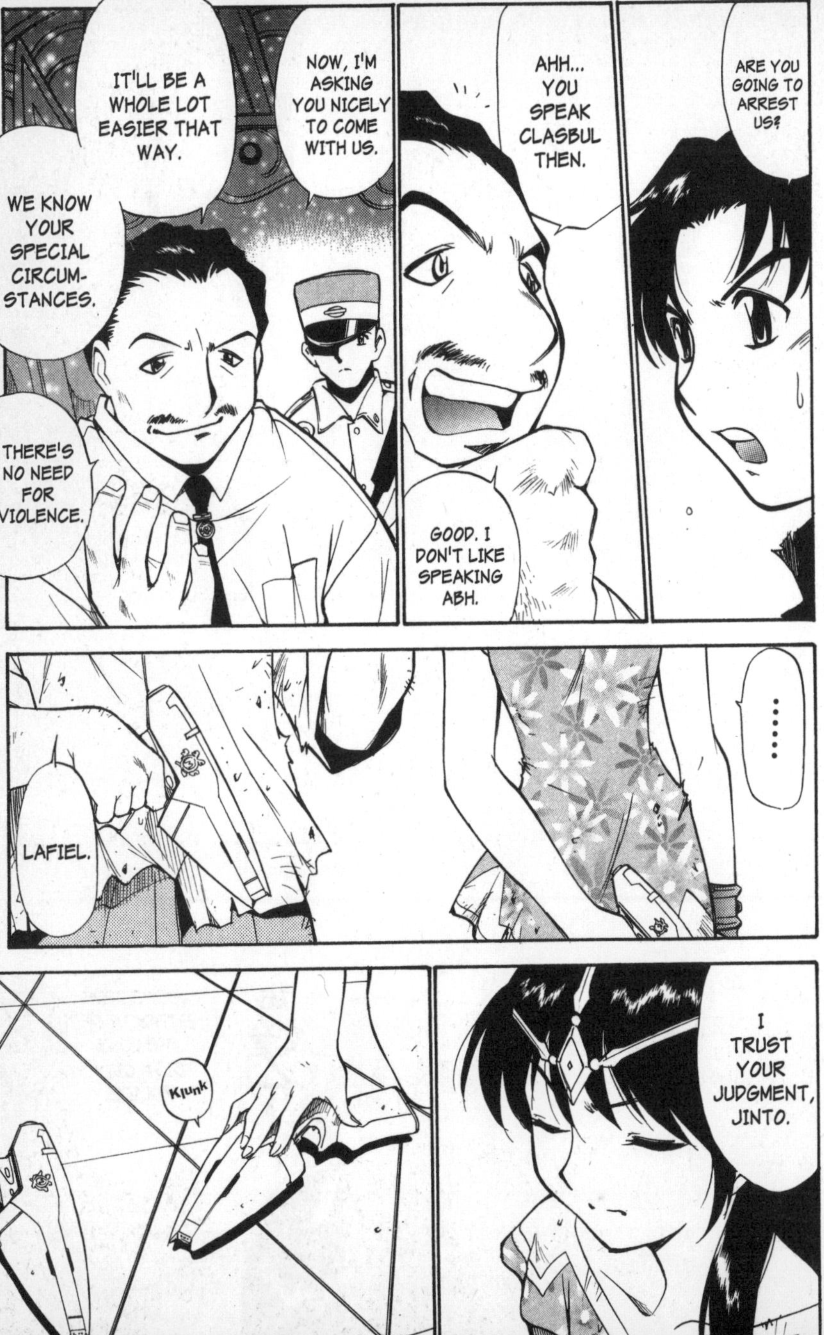
ARE YOU GOING TO ARREST US?
AHH... YOU SPEAK CLASBUL THEN.
GOOD. I DON'T LIKE SPEAKING ABH.
NOW, I'M ASKING YOU NICELY TO COME WITH US.
IT'LL BE A WHOLE LOT EASIER THAT WAY.
WE KNOW YOUR SPECIAL CIRCUM-STANCES.
THERE'S NO NEED FOR VIOLENCE.
......
LAFIEL.
I TRUST YOUR JUDGMENT, JINTO.
Klunk

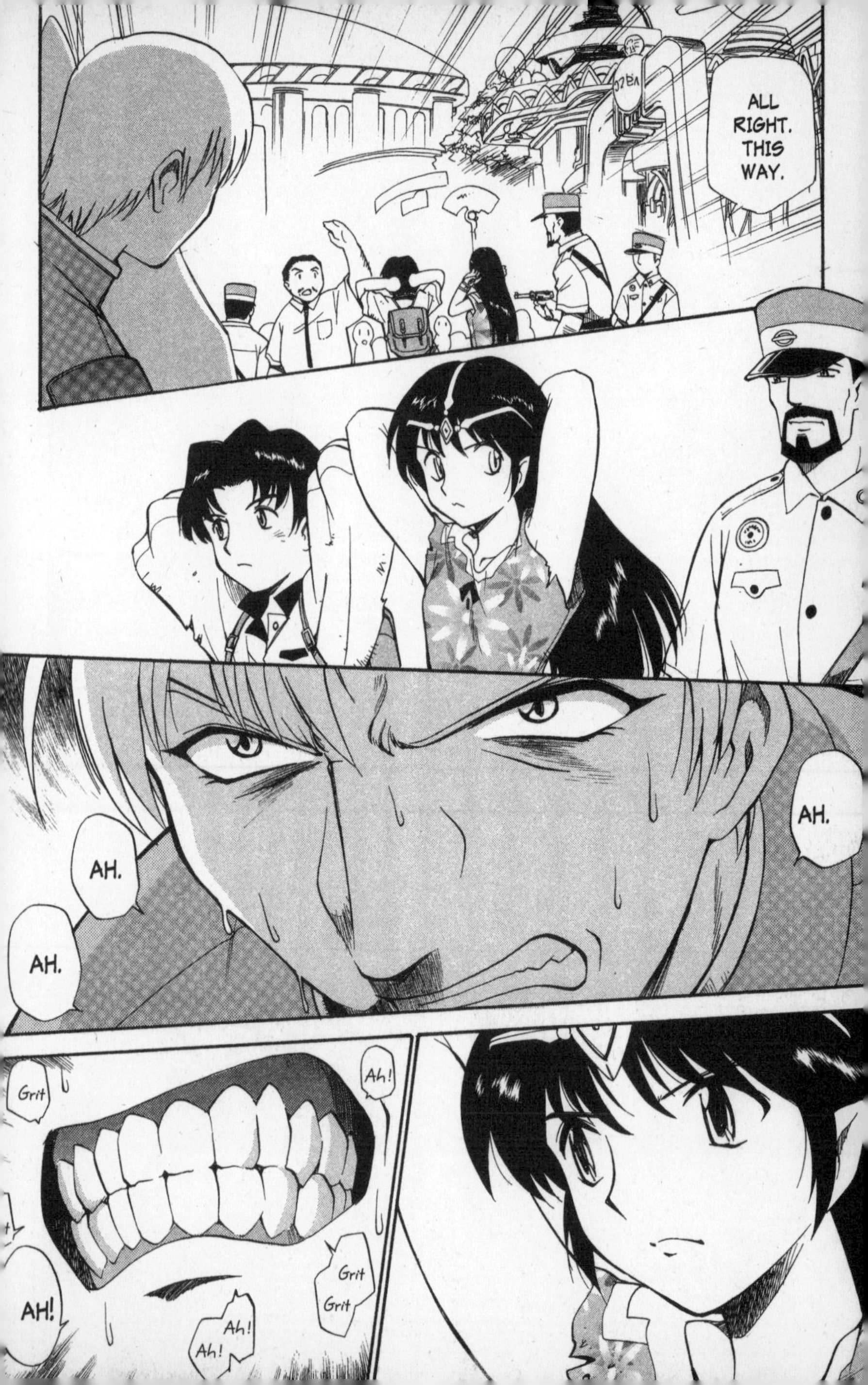
ALL RIGHT. THIS WAY.
AH.
AH.
AH.
Ah!
Grit
Grit
Grit
Ah!
Ah!
AH!

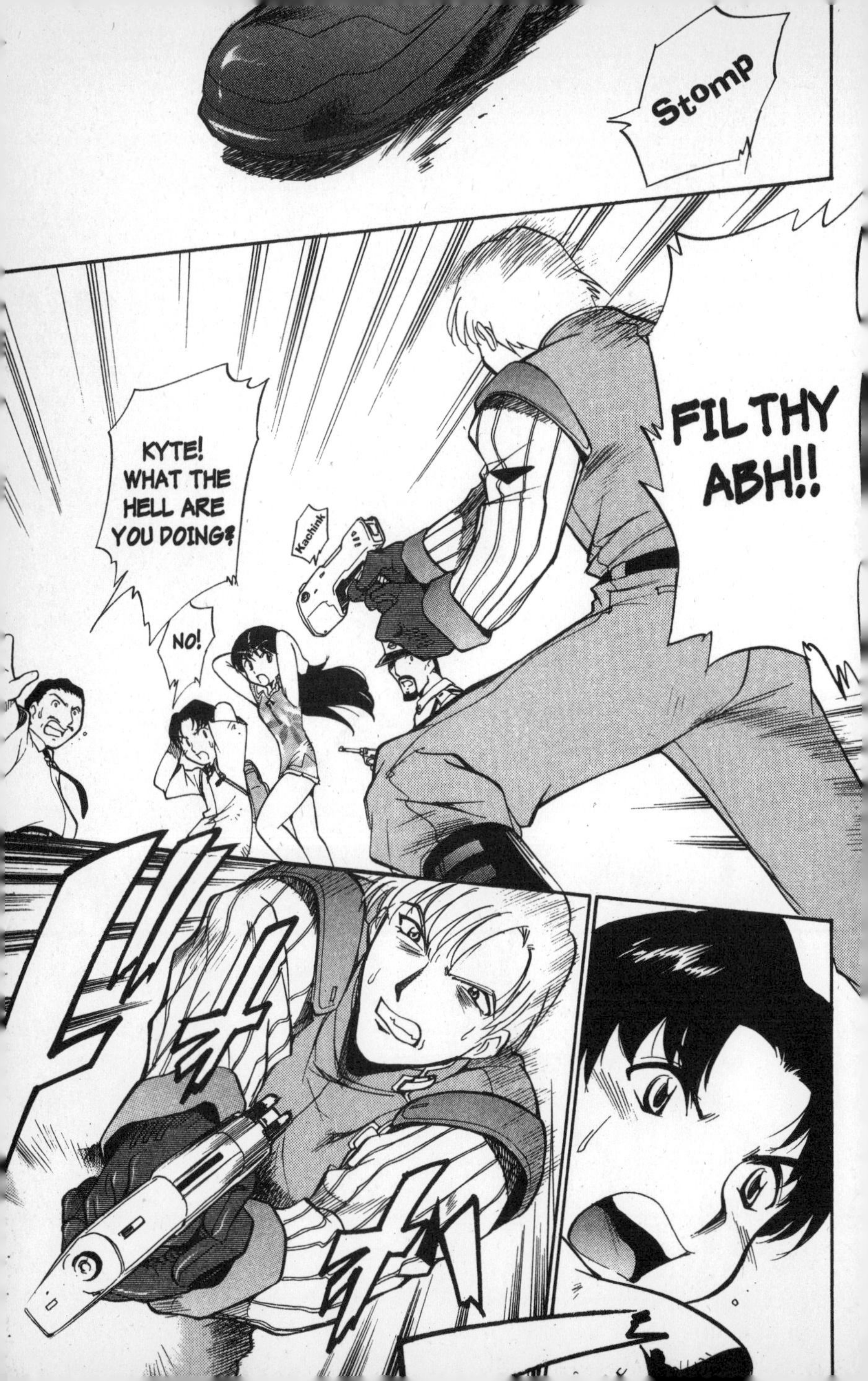
Stomp
FILTHY ABH!!
KYTE! WHAT THE HELL ARE YOU DOING?
Kachink
NO!

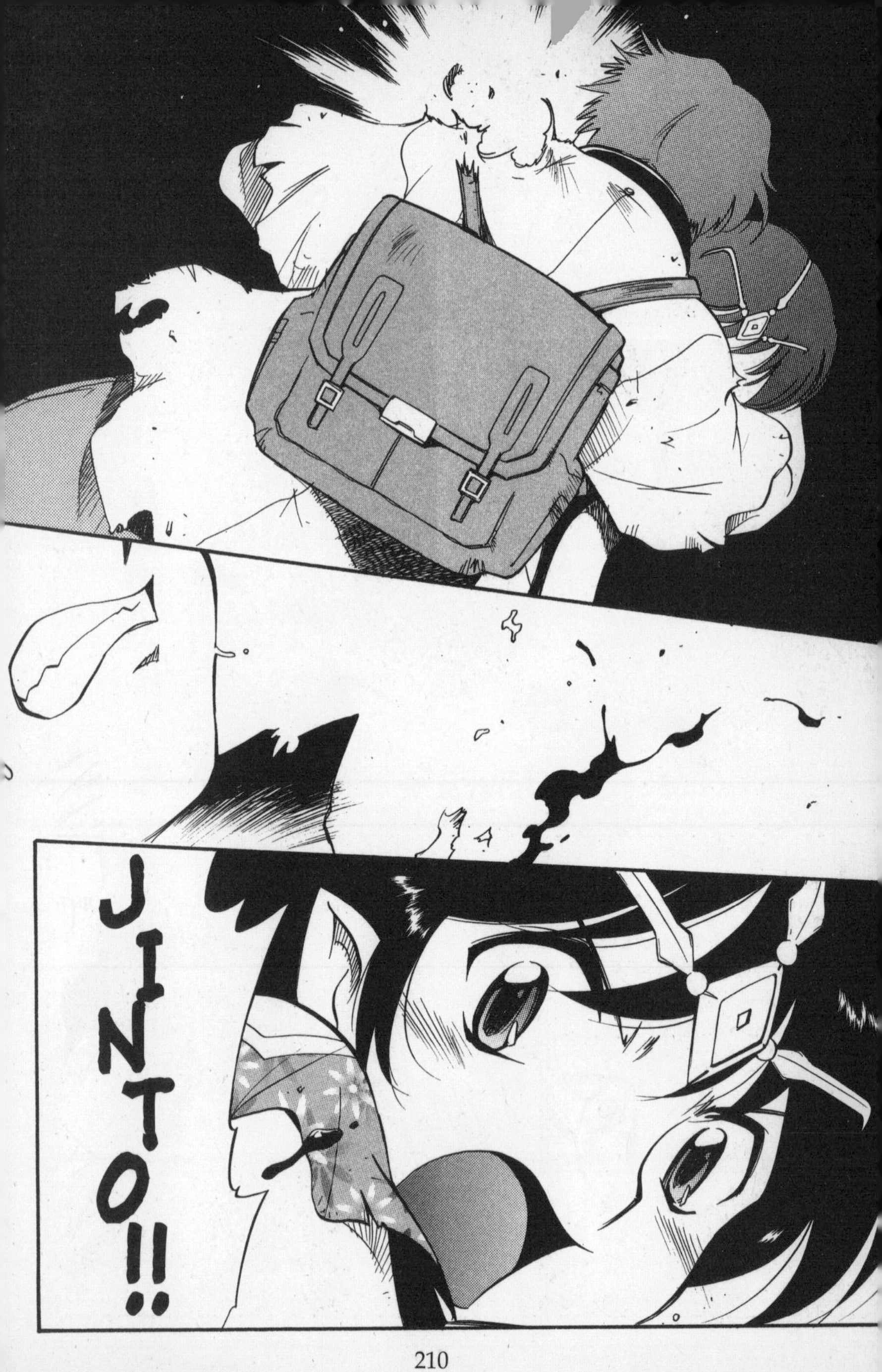
JINTO!!

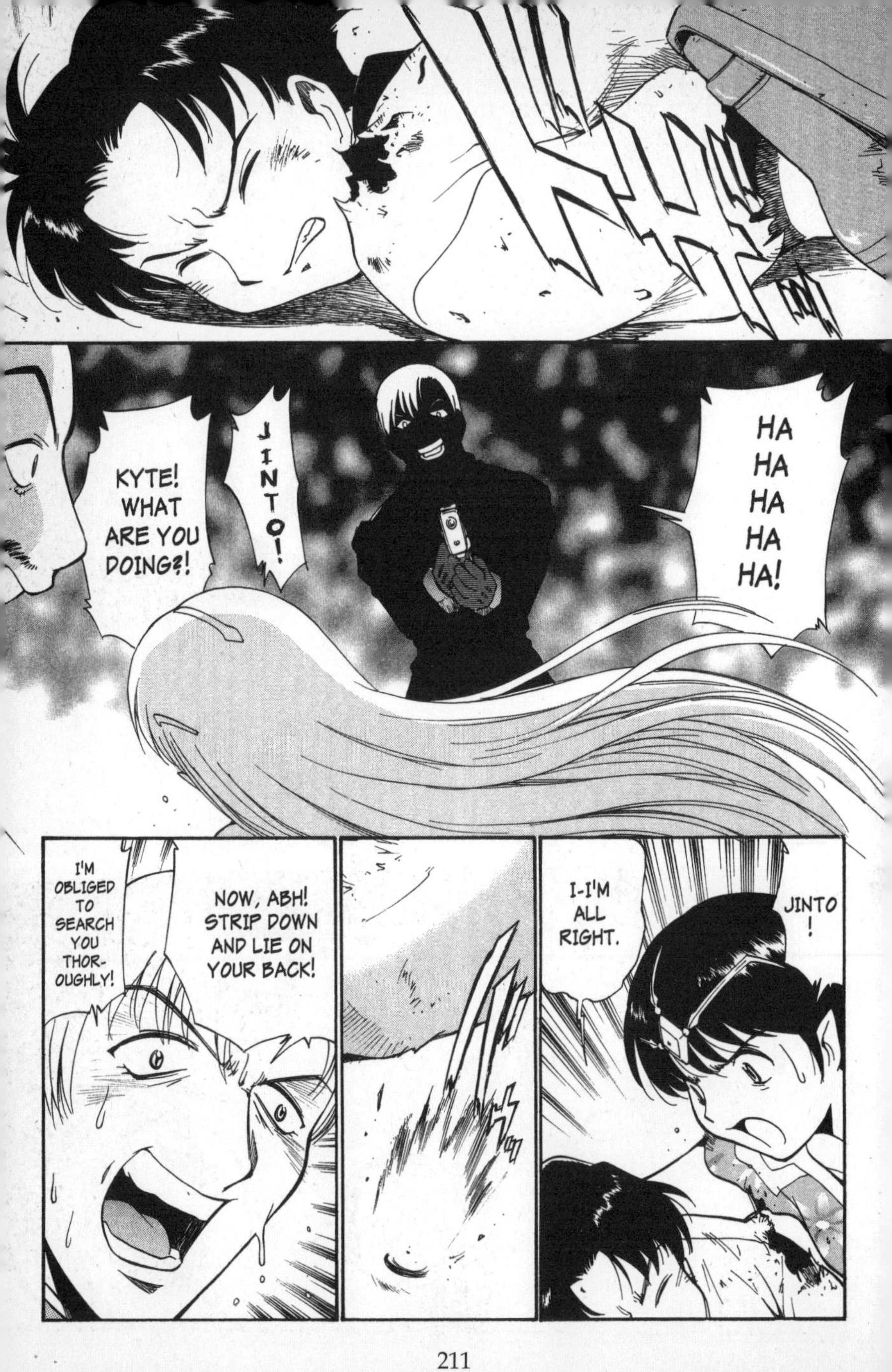
HA HA HA HA HA!
JINTO!
KYTE! WHAT ARE YOU DOING?!
JINTO!
I-I'M ALL RIGHT.
NOW, ABH! STRIP DOWN AND LIE ON YOUR BACK!
I'M OBLIGED TO SEARCH YOU THOROUGHLY!

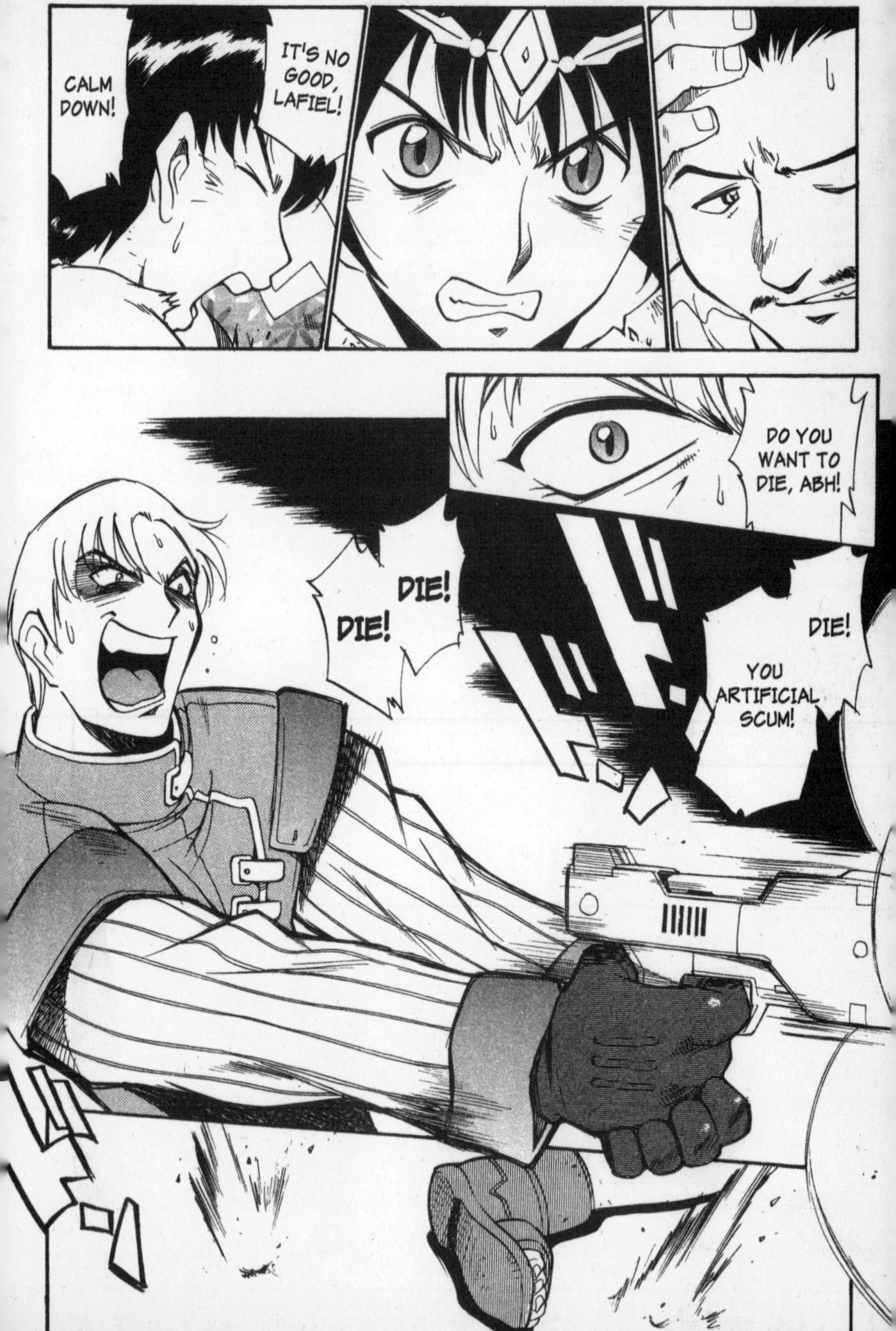
IT'S NO GOOD, LAFIEL!
CALM DOWN!
DO YOU WANT TO DIE, ABH!
DIE!
YOU ARTIFICIAL SCUM!
DIE!
DIE!

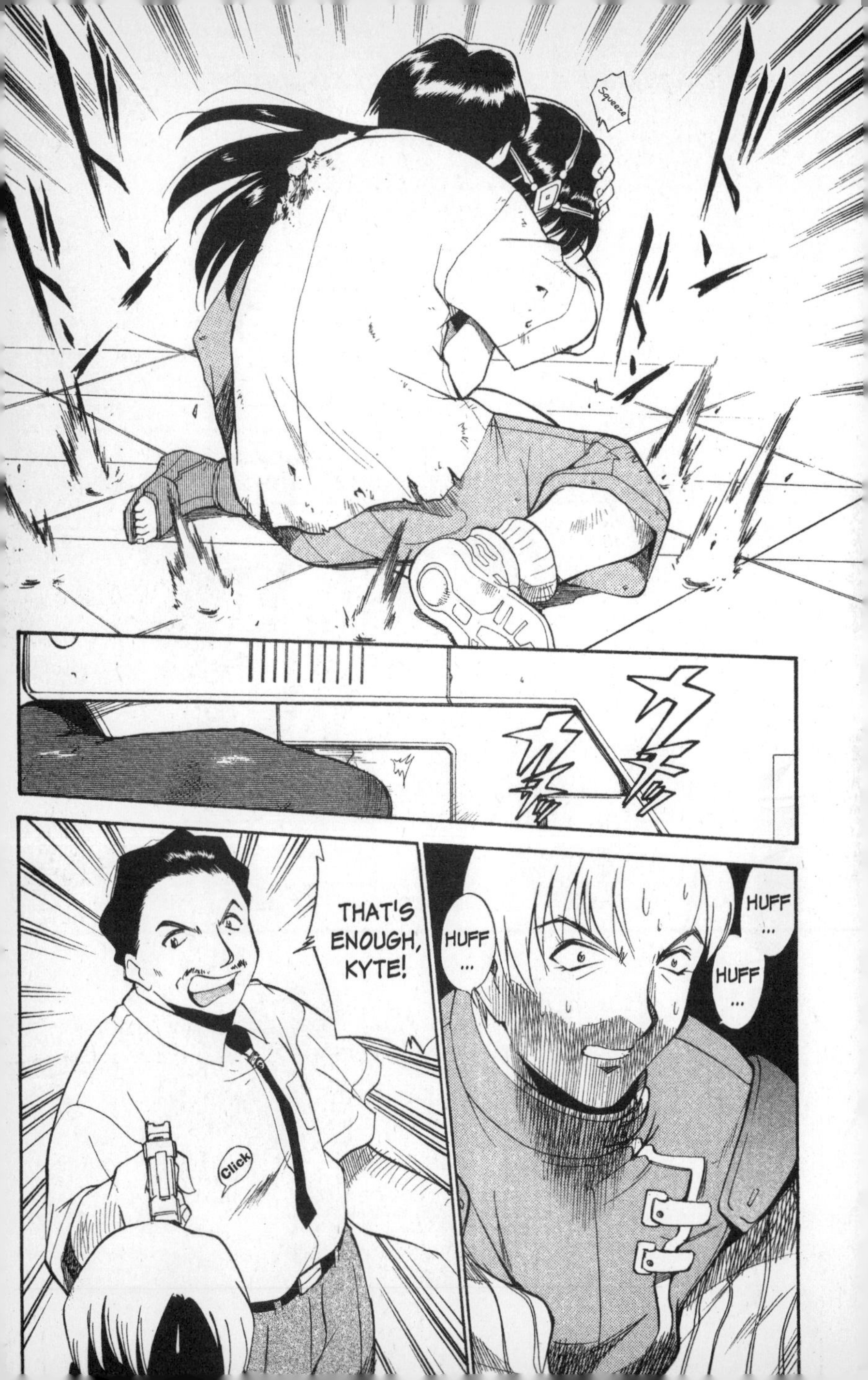
Squeeze
HUFF ...
HUFF ...
HUFF ...
THAT'S ENOUGH, KYTE!
Click

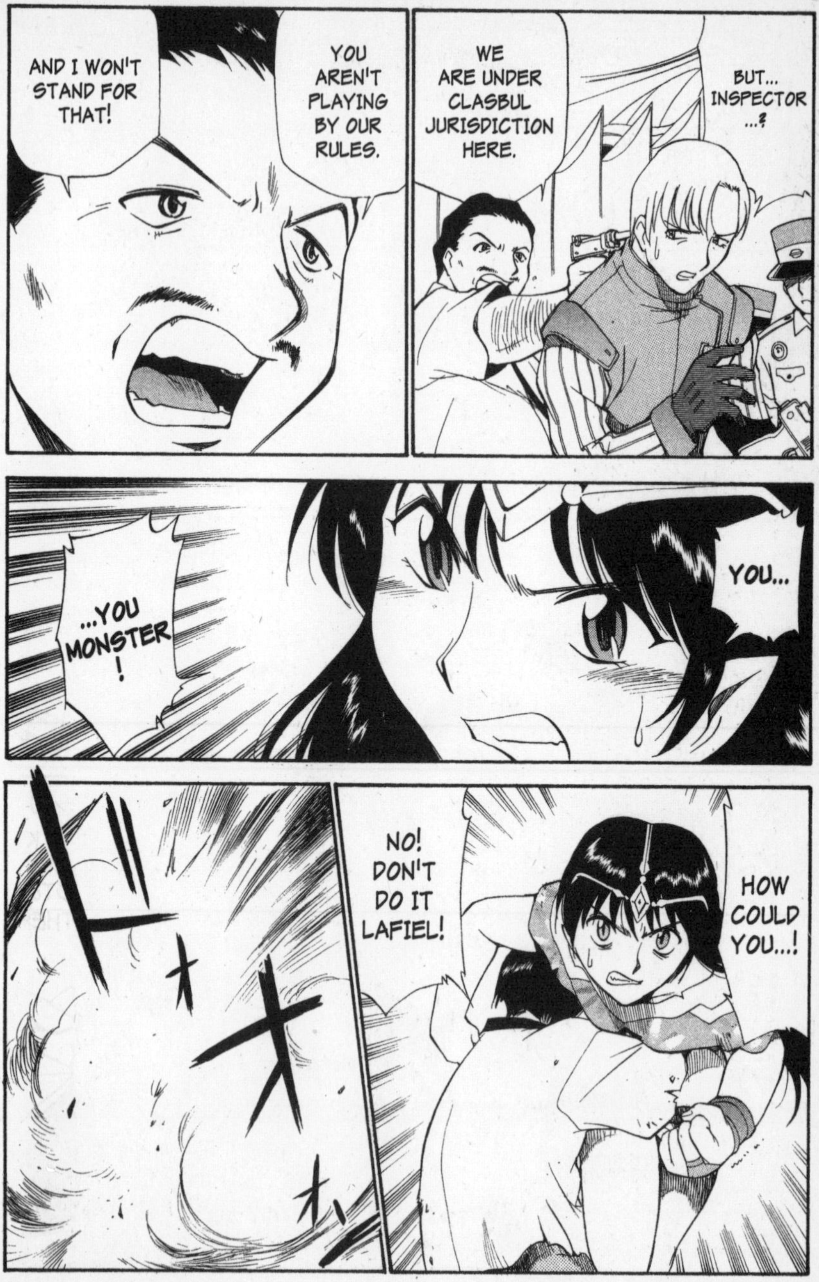
BUT... INSPECTOR ...?
WE ARE UNDER CLASBUL JURISDICTION HERE.
YOU AREN'T PLAYING BY OUR RULES.
AND I WON'T STAND FOR THAT!
YOU...
...YOU MONSTER!
HOW COULD YOU...!
NO! DON'T DO IT LAFIEL!

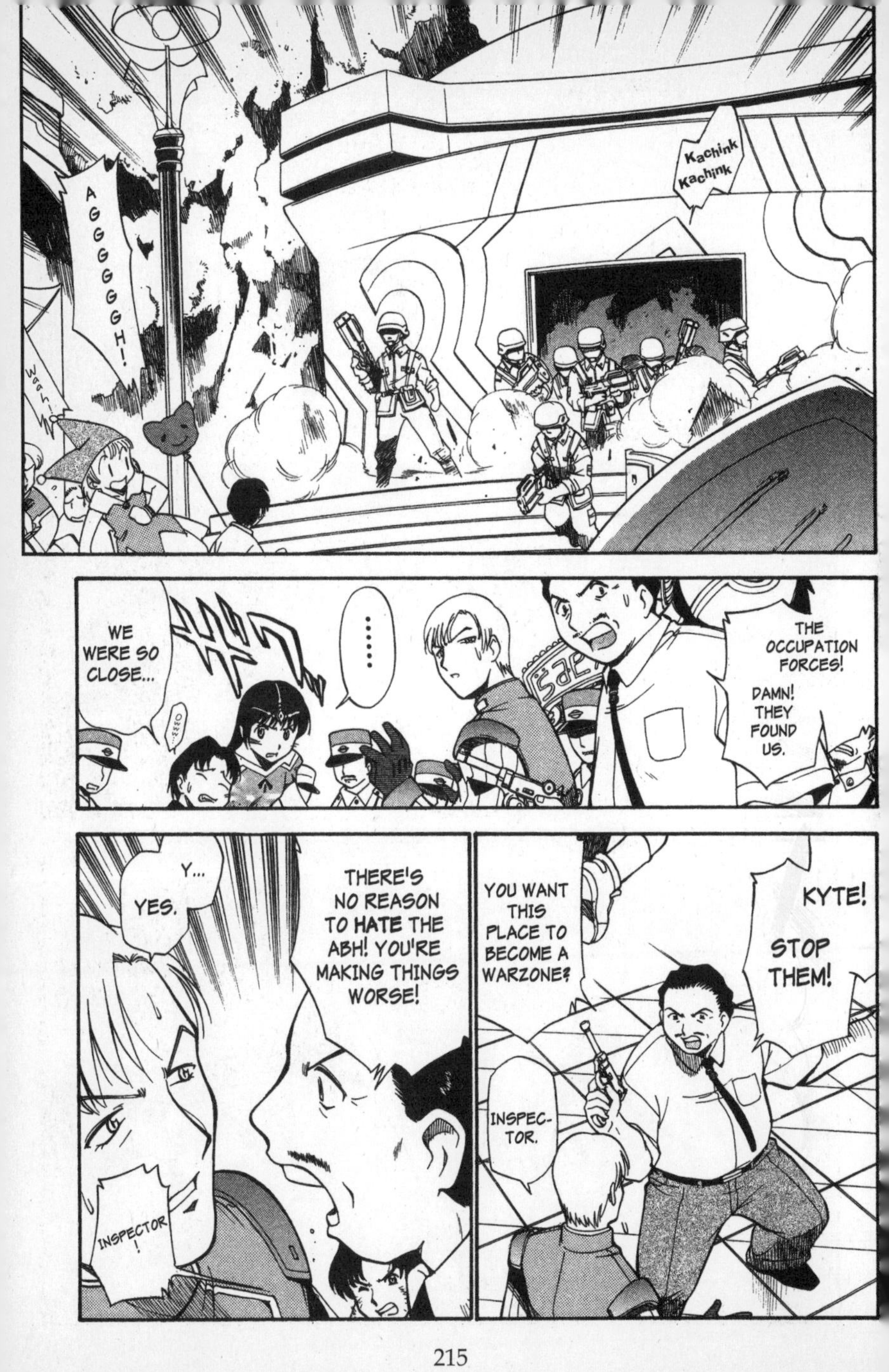
Kachink Kachink
AGGGGGGH!
Waah!
THE OCCUPATION FORCES!
DAMN! THEY FOUND US.
......
WE WERE SO CLOSE...
KYTE!
STOP THEM!
YOU WANT THIS PLACE TO BECOME A WARZONE?
INSPECTOR.
THERE'S NO REASON TO HATE THE ABH! YOU'RE MAKING THINGS WORSE!
Y... YES.
INSPECTOR!

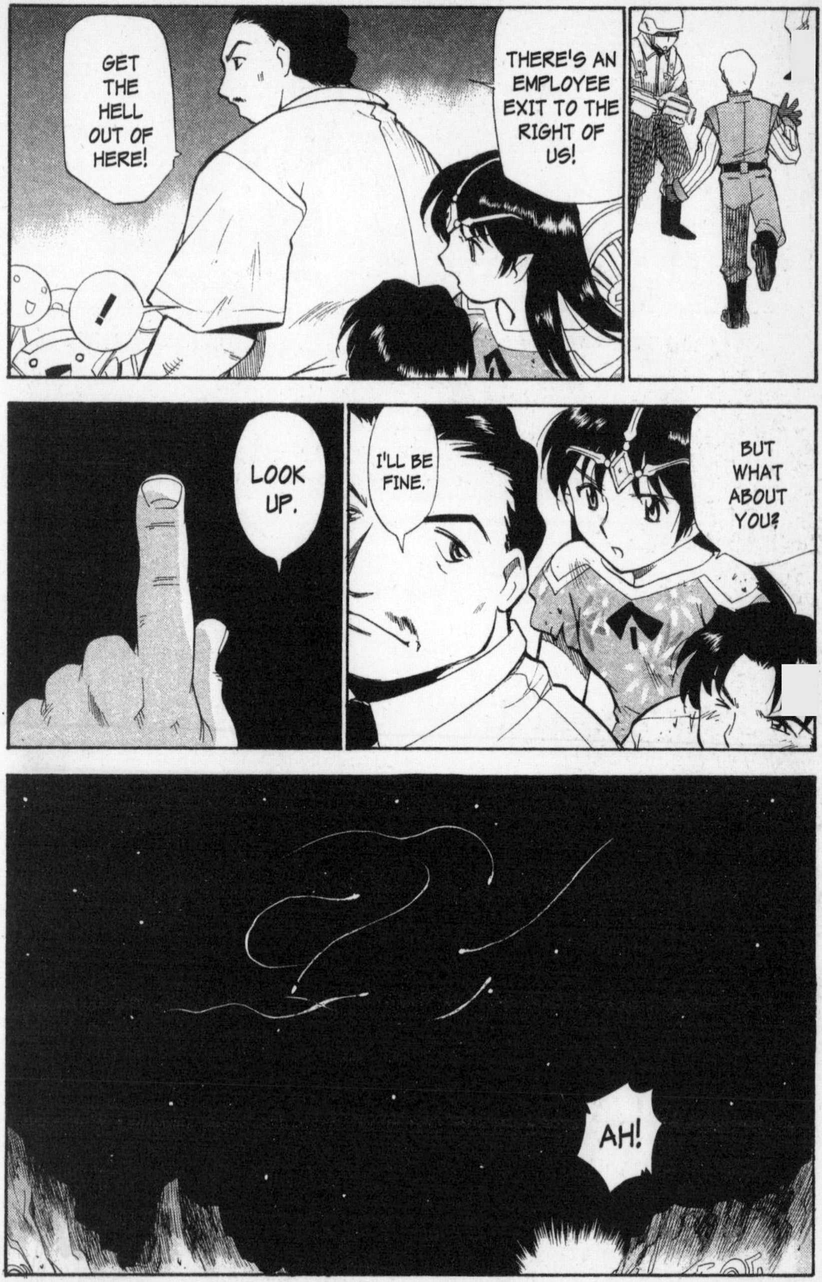
THERE'S AN EMPLOYEE EXIT TO THE RIGHT OF US!
GET THE HELL OUT OF HERE!
!
BUT WHAT ABOUT YOU?
I'LL BE FINE.
LOOK UP.
AH!

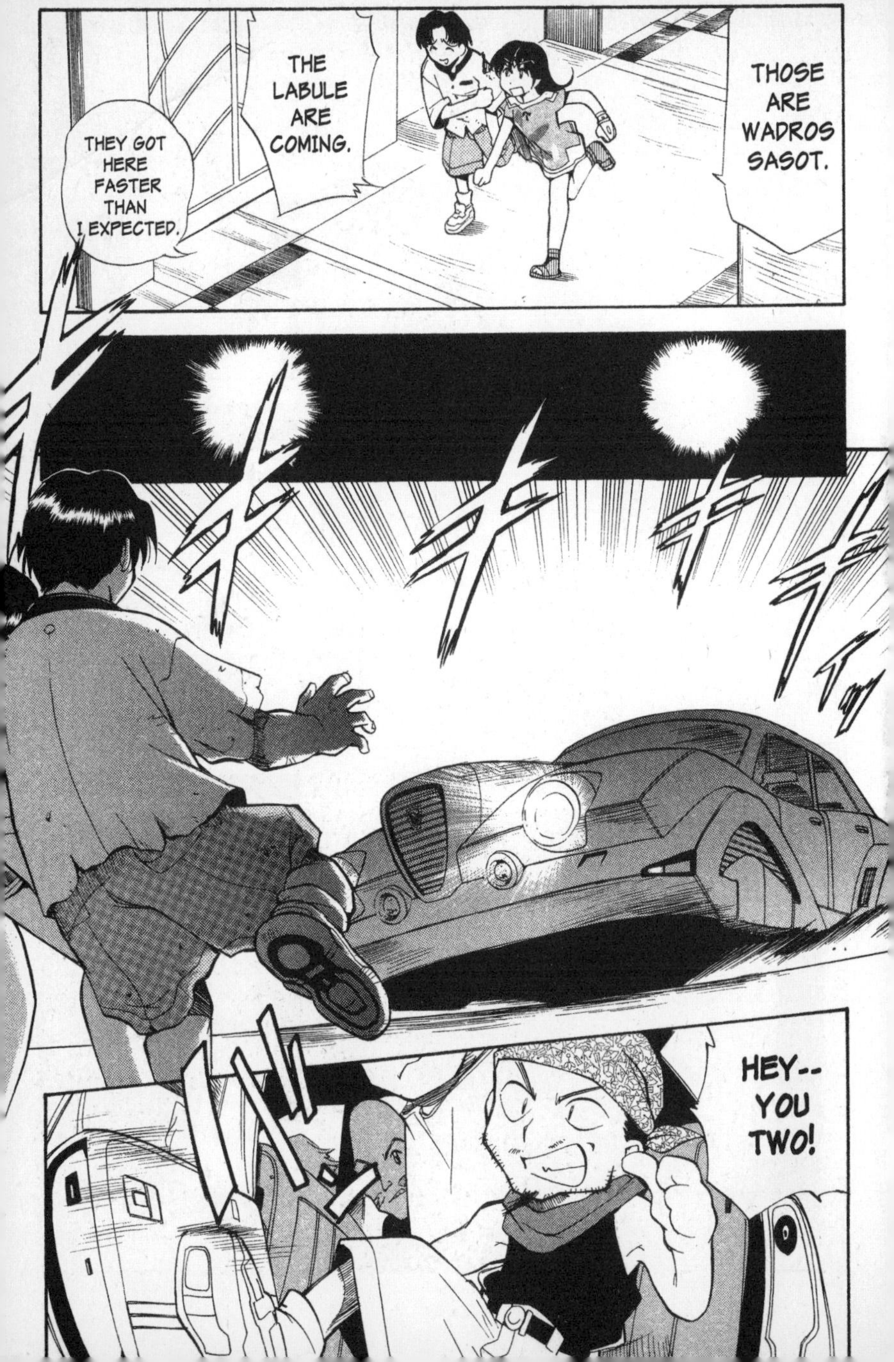
THOSE ARE WADROS SASOT.
THE LABULE ARE COMING.
THEY GOT HERE FASTER THAN I EXPECTED.
HEY-- YOU TWO!

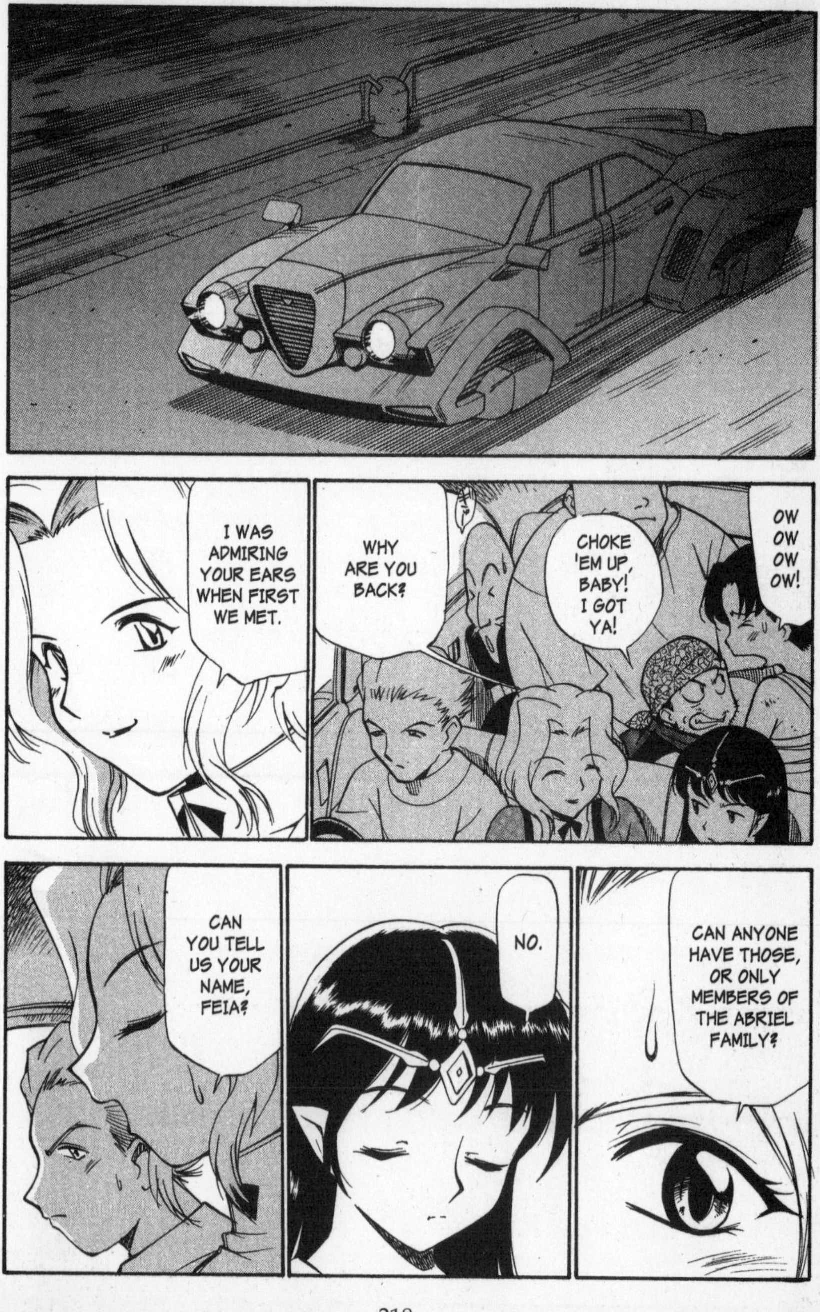
OW OW OW OW!
CHOKE 'EM UP, BABY! I GOT YA!
WHY ARE YOU BACK?
I WAS ADMIRING YOUR EARS WHEN FIRST WE MET.
CAN ANYONE HAVE THOSE, OR ONLY MEMBERS OF THE ABRIEL FAMILY?
NO.
CAN YOU TELL US YOUR NAME, FEIA?

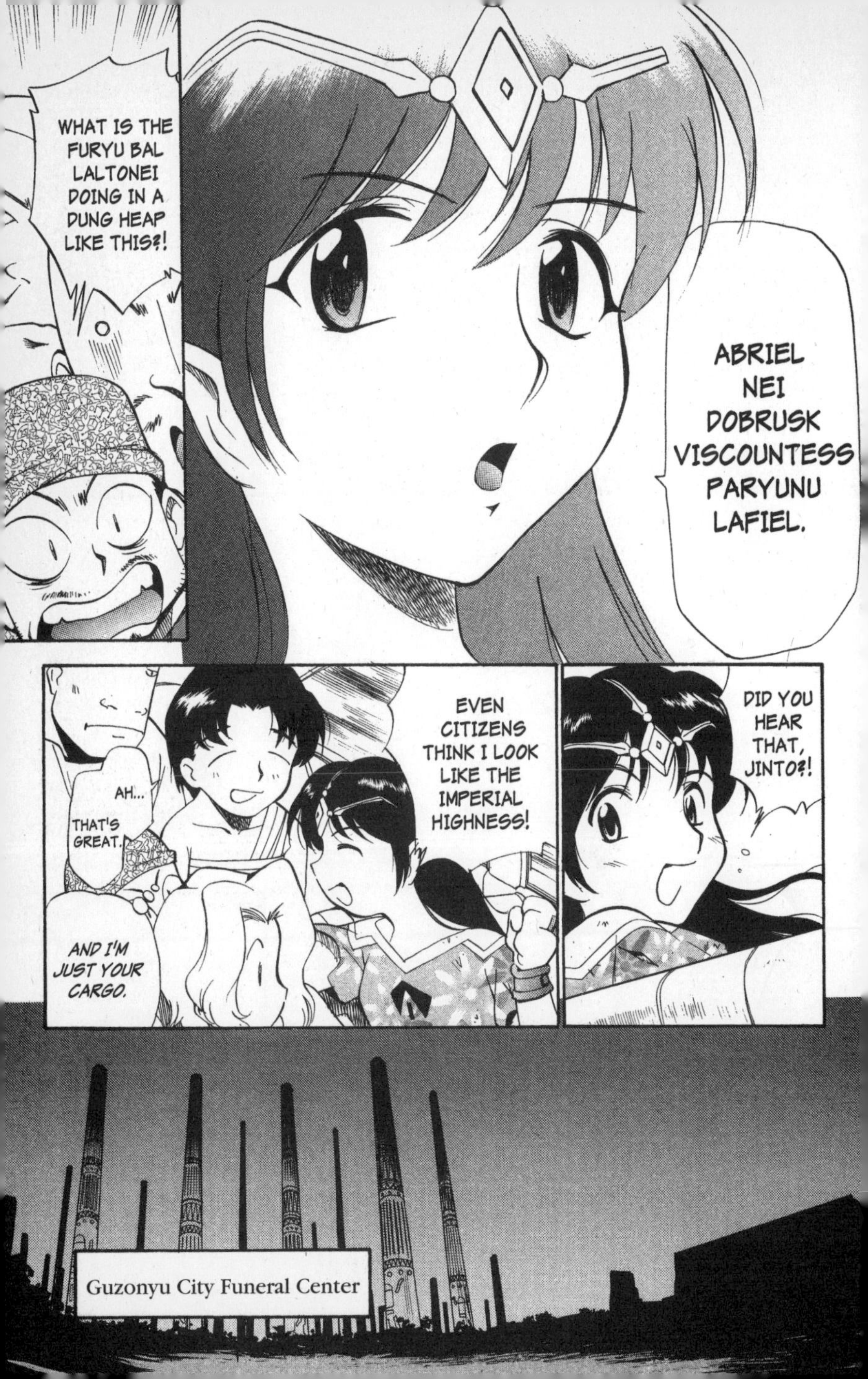
ABRIEL NEI DOBRUSK VISCOUNTESS PARYUNU LAFIEL.
WHAT IS THE FURYU BAL LALTONEI DOING IN A DUNG HEAP LIKE THIS?!
DID YOU HEAR THAT, JINTO?!
EVEN CITIZENS THINK I LOOK LIKE THE IMPERIAL HIGHNESS!
AH... THAT'S GREAT.
AND I'M JUST YOUR CARGO.
Guzonyu City Funeral Center

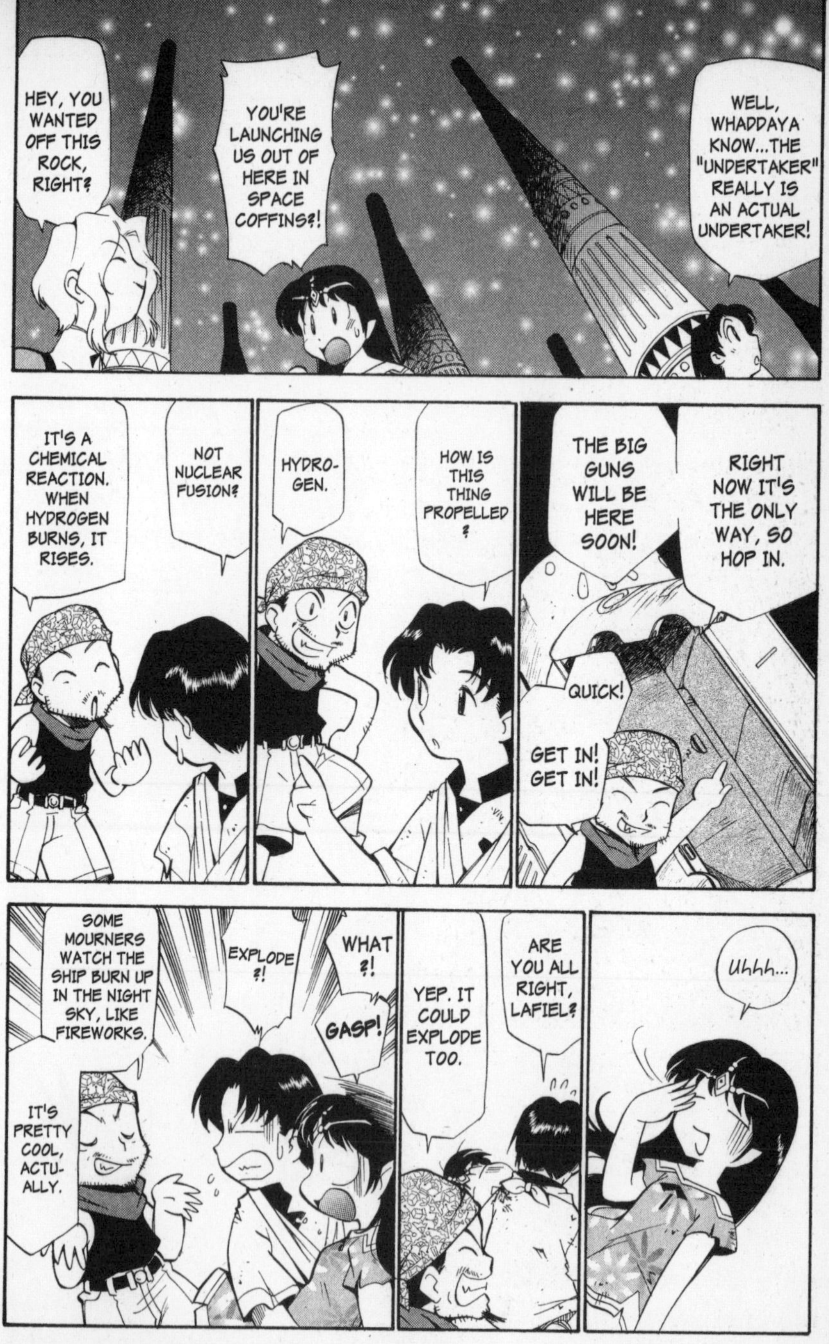
WELL, WHADDAYA KNOW...THE "UNDERTAKER" REALLY IS AN ACTUAL UNDERTAKER!
YOU'RE LAUNCHING US OUT OF HERE IN SPACE COFFINS?!
HEY, YOU WANTED OFF THIS ROCK, RIGHT?
RIGHT NOW IT'S THE ONLY WAY, SO HOP IN.
THE BIG GUNS WILL BE HERE SOON!
QUICK!
GET IN! GET IN!
HOW IS THIS THING PROPELLED?
HYDRO-GEN.
NOT NUCLEAR FUSION?
IT'S A CHEMICAL REACTION. WHEN HYDROGEN BURNS, IT RISES.
Uhhh...
ARE YOU ALL RIGHT, LAFIEL?
YEP. IT COULD EXPLODE TOO.
WHAT?!
EXPLODE?!
GASP!
SOME MOURNERS WATCH THE SHIP BURN UP IN THE NIGHT SKY, LIKE FIREWORKS.
IT'S PRETTY COOL, ACTU-ALLY.

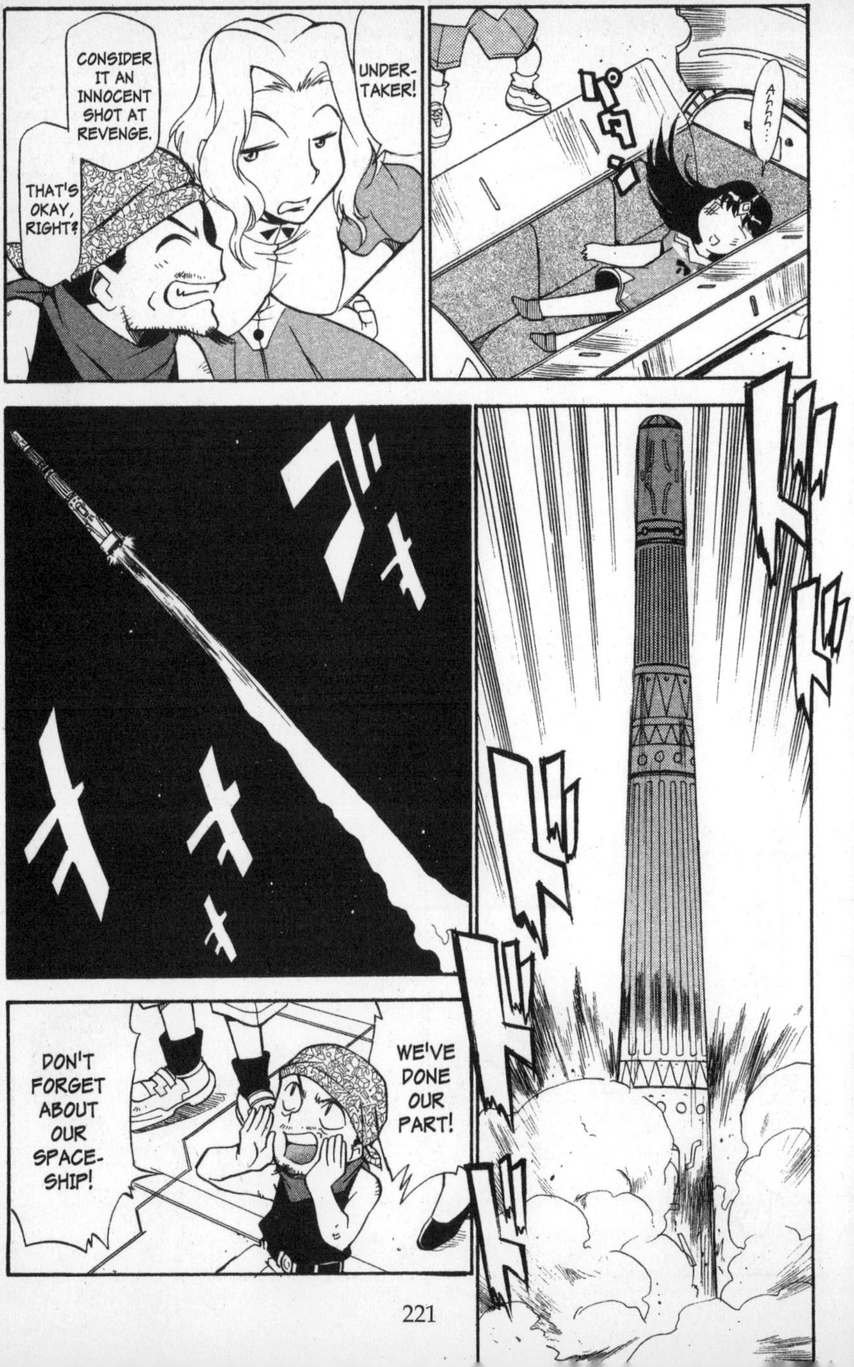
Ahhh...
UNDER-TAKER!
CONSIDER IT AN INNOCENT SHOT AT REVENGE.
THAT'S OKAY, RIGHT?
WE'VE DONE OUR PART!
DON'T FORGET ABOUT OUR SPACE-SHIP!

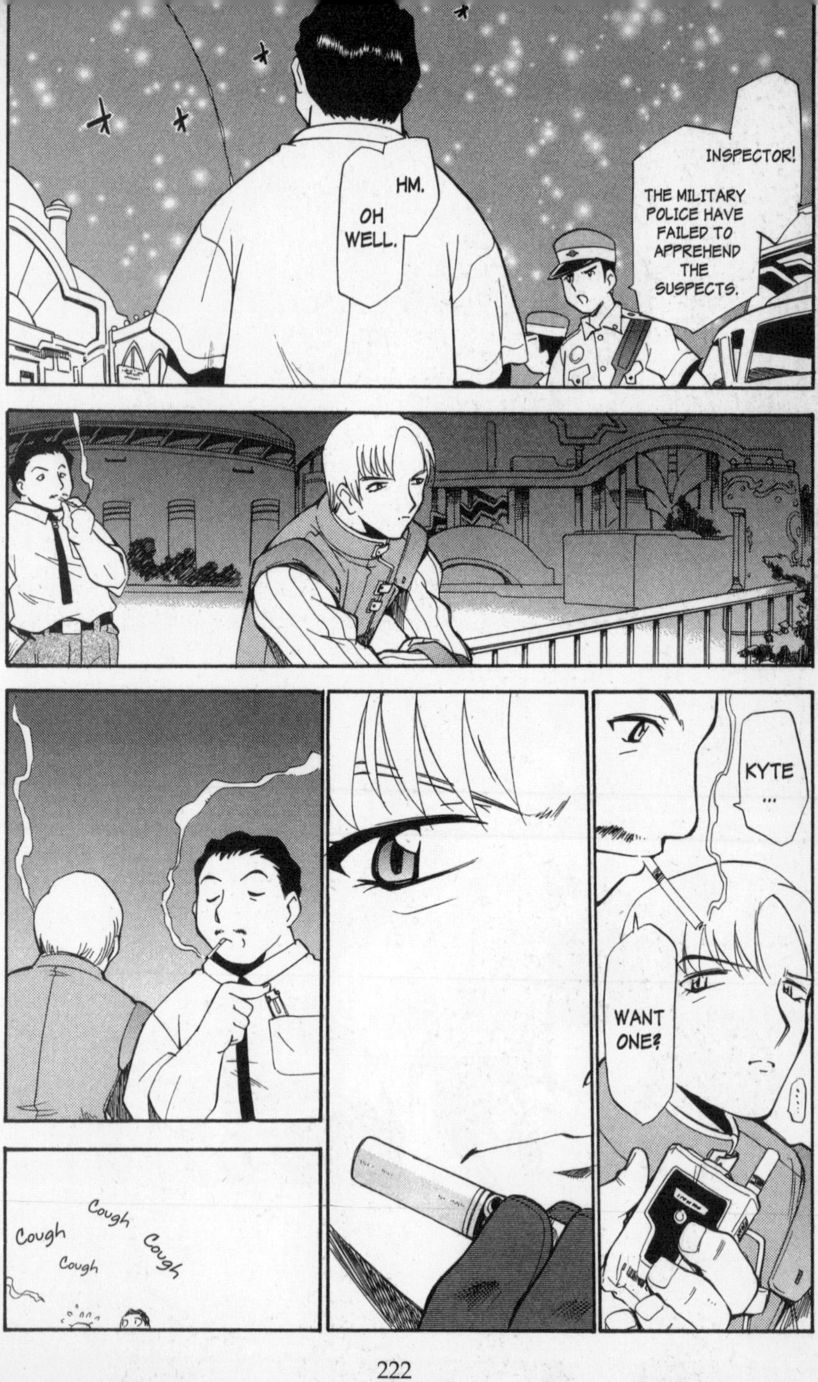
INSPECTOR!
THE MILITARY POLICE HAVE FAILED TO APPREHEND THE SUSPECTS.
HM.
OH WELL.
KYTE ...
WANT ONE?
.....
Cough
Cough
Cough
Cough

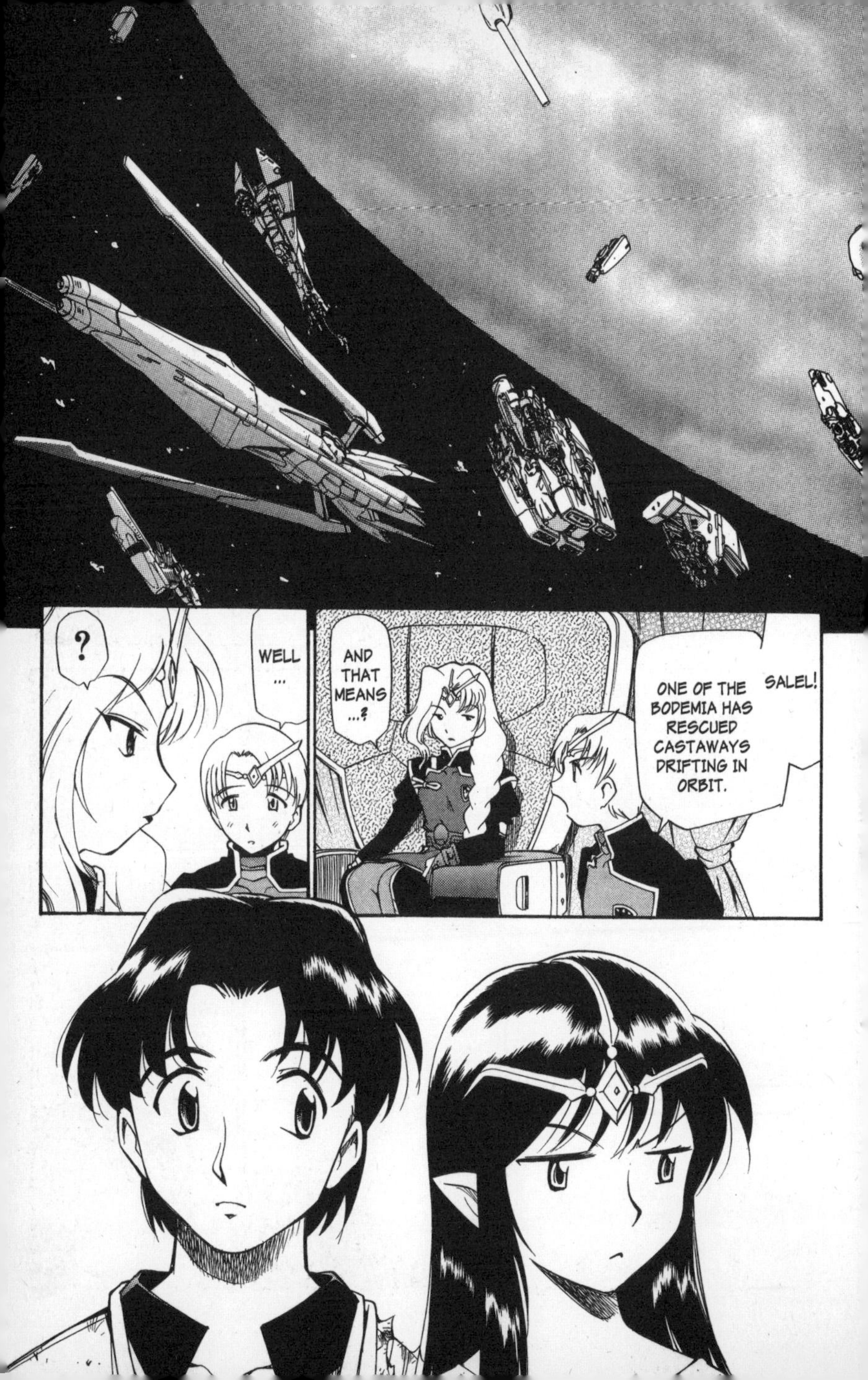
SALEL!
ONE OF THE BODEMIA HAS RESCUED CASTAWAYS DRIFTING IN ORBIT.
AND THAT MEANS ...?
WELL ...
?

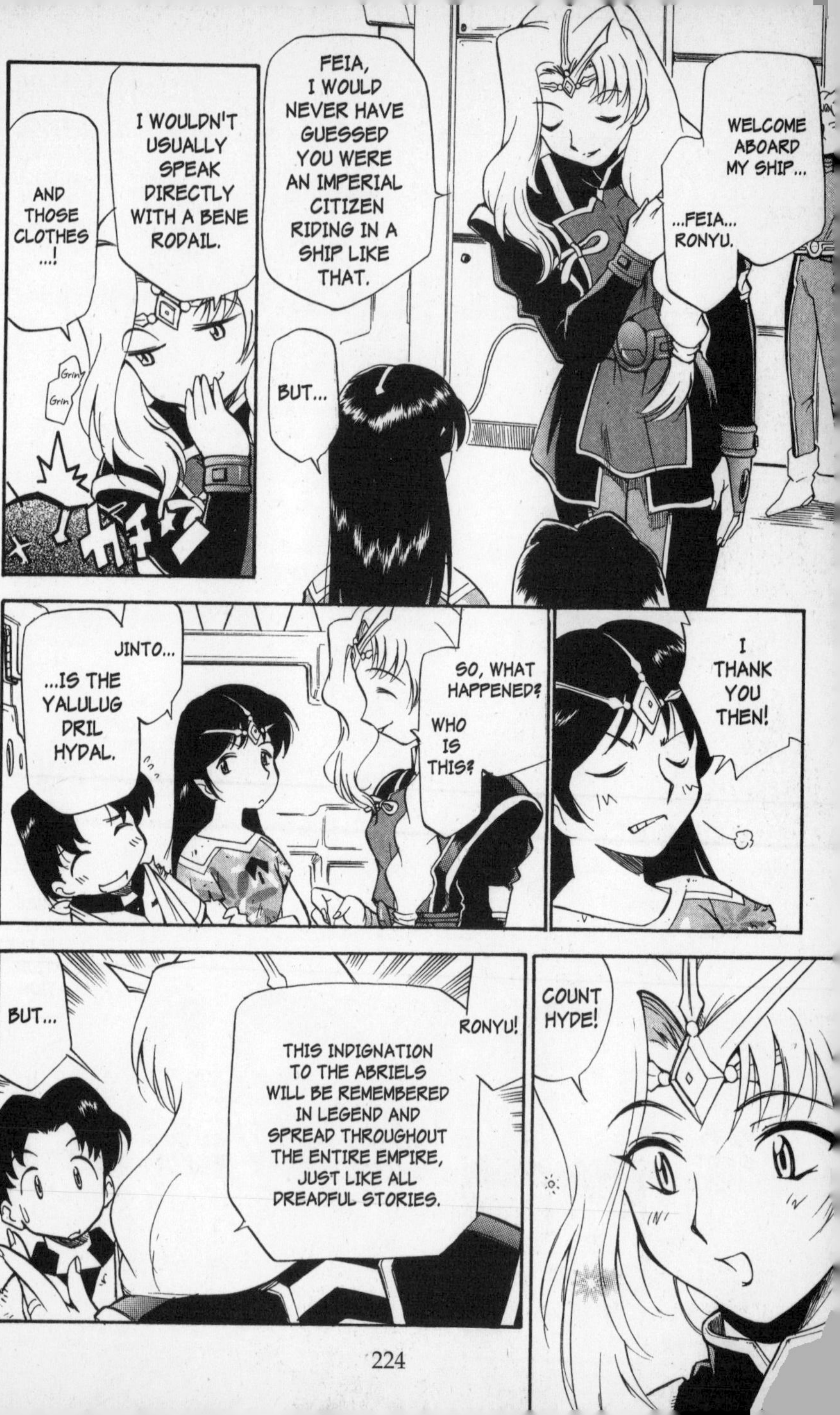
WELCOME ABOARD MY SHIP...
...FEIA... RONYU.
FEIA, I WOULD NEVER HAVE GUESSED YOU WERE AN IMPERIAL CITIZEN RIDING IN A SHIP LIKE THAT.
BUT...
I WOULDN'T USUALLY SPEAK DIRECTLY WITH A BENE RODAIL.
AND THOSE CLOTHES ...!
Grin
Grin
I THANK YOU THEN!
SO, WHAT HAPPENED?
WHO IS THIS?
JINTO...
...IS THE YALULUG DRIL HYDAL.
COUNT HYDE!
RONYU!
THIS INDIGNATION TO THE ABRIELS WILL BE REMEMBERED IN LEGEND AND SPREAD THROUGHOUT THE ENTIRE EMPIRE, JUST LIKE ALL DREADFUL STORIES.
BUT...

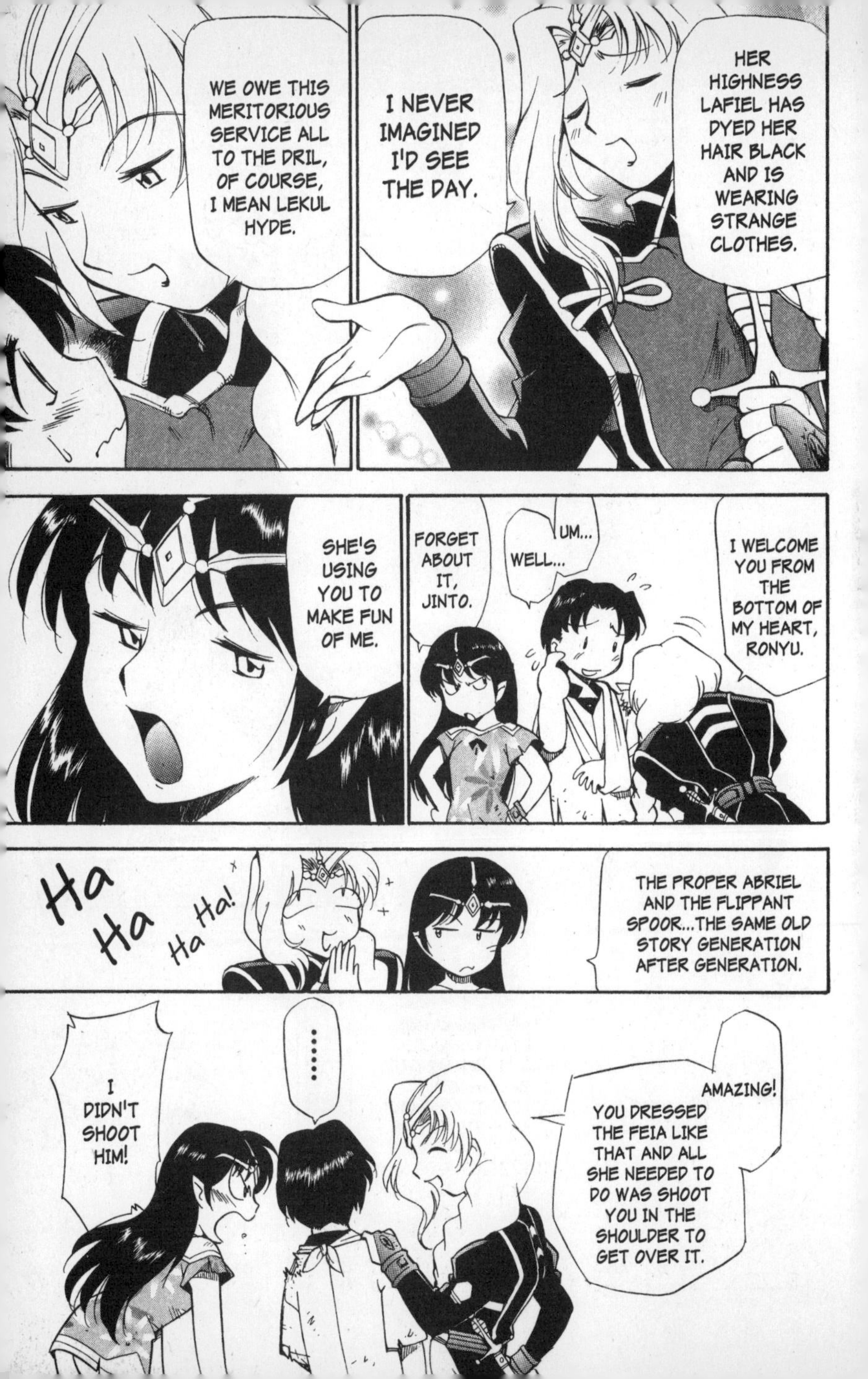
HER HIGHNESS LAFIEL HAS DYED HER HAIR BLACK AND IS WEARING STRANGE CLOTHES.
I NEVER IMAGINED I'D SEE THE DAY.
WE OWE THIS MERITORIOUS SERVICE ALL TO THE DRIL, OF COURSE, I MEAN LEKUL HYDE.
I WELCOME YOU FROM THE BOTTOM OF MY HEART, RONYU.
UM... WELL...
FORGET ABOUT IT, JINTO.
SHE'S USING YOU TO MAKE FUN OF ME.
THE PROPER ABRIEL AND THE FLIPPANT SPOOR...THE SAME OLD STORY GENERATION AFTER GENERATION.
Ha Ha Ha Ha!
AMAZING! YOU DRESSED THE FEIA LIKE THAT AND ALL SHE NEEDED TO DO WAS SHOOT YOU IN THE SHOULDER TO GET OVER IT.
......
I DIDN'T SHOOT HIM!

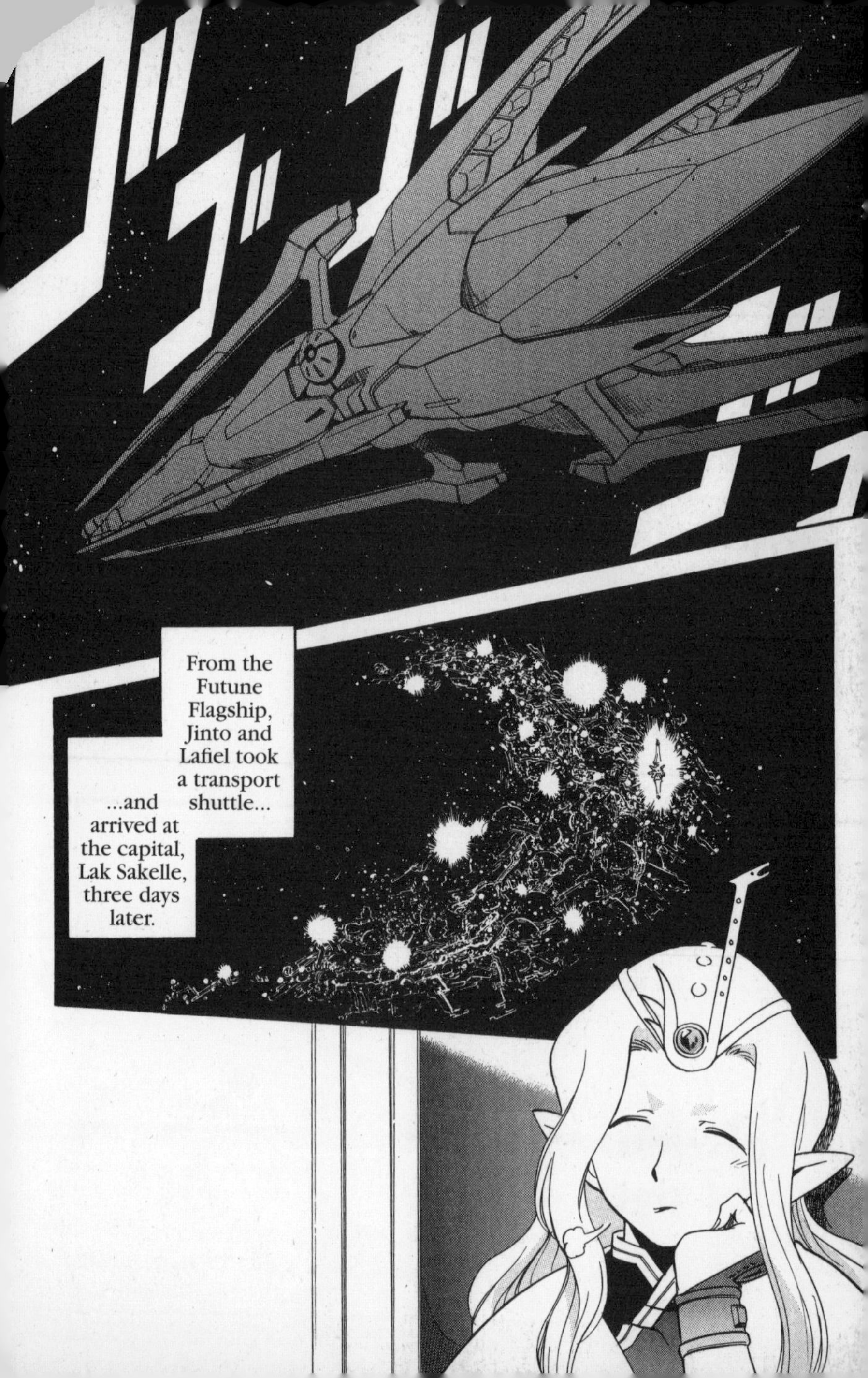
From the Futune Flagship, Jinto and Lafiel took a transport shuttle...
...and arrived at the capital, Lak Sakelle, three days later.

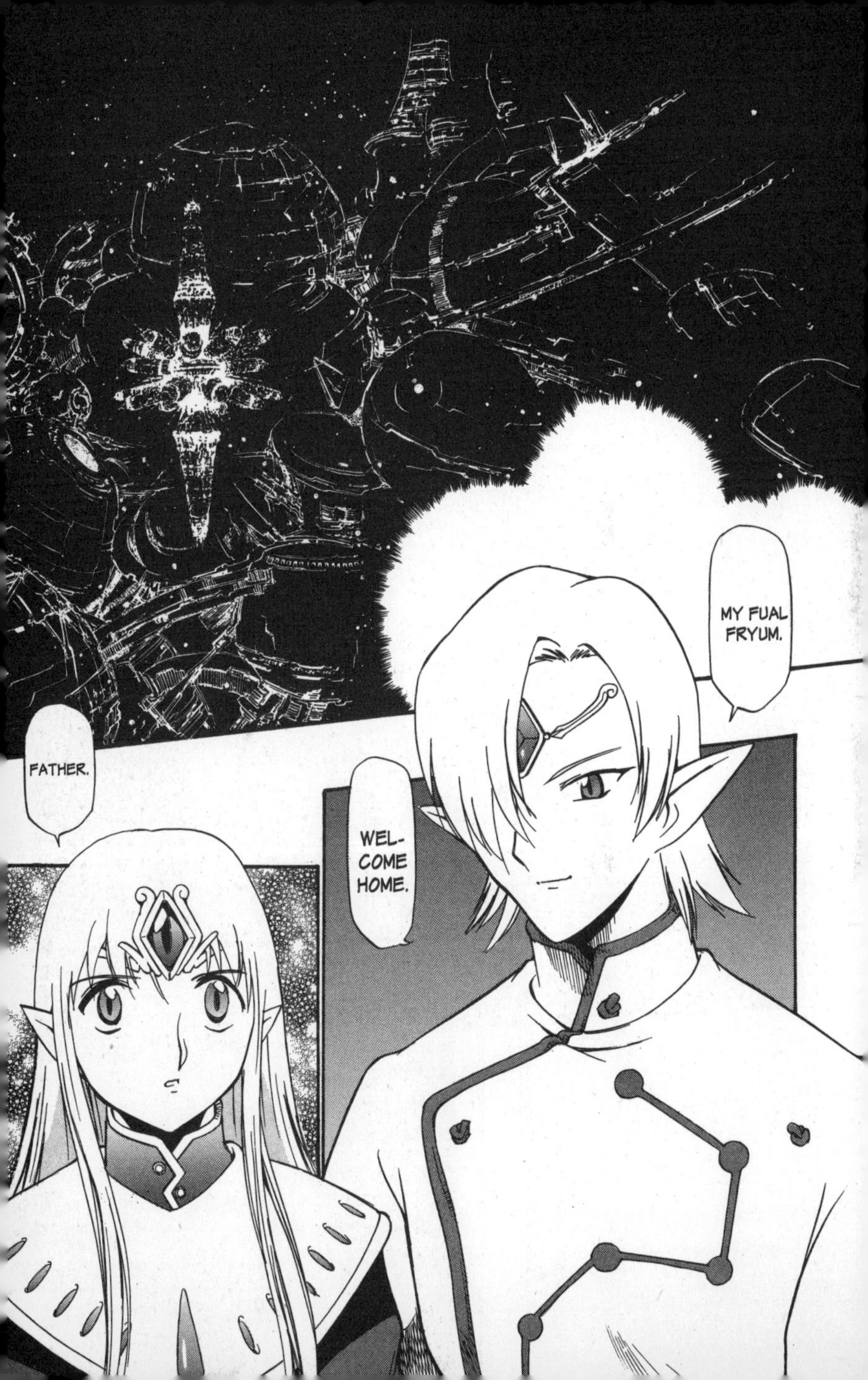
MY FUAL FRYUM.
WEL-COME HOME.
FATHER.

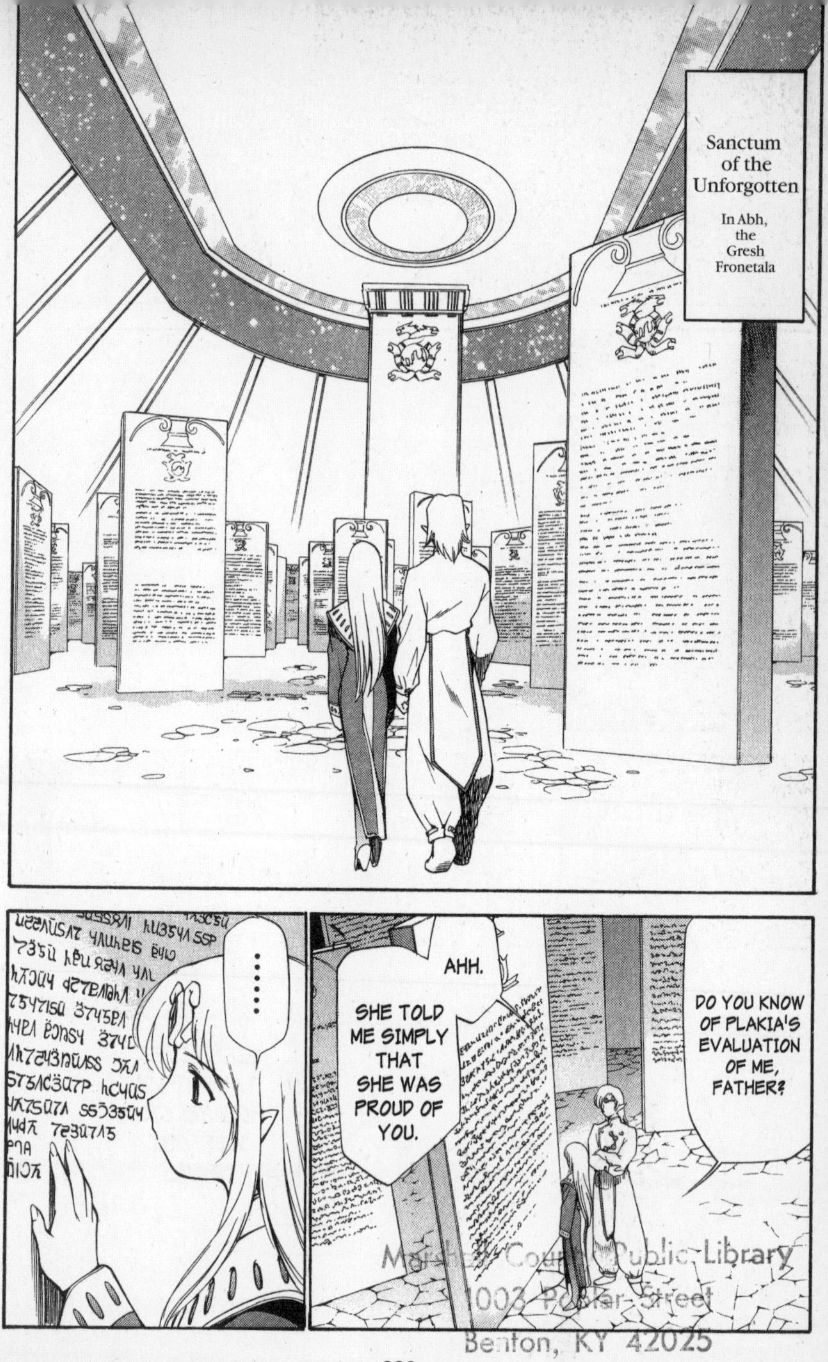
Sanctum of the Unforgotten
In Abh, the Gresh Fronetala
DO YOU KNOW OF PLAKIA'S EVALUATION OF ME, FATHER?
AHH.
SHE TOLD ME SIMPLY THAT SHE WAS PROUD OF YOU.
......

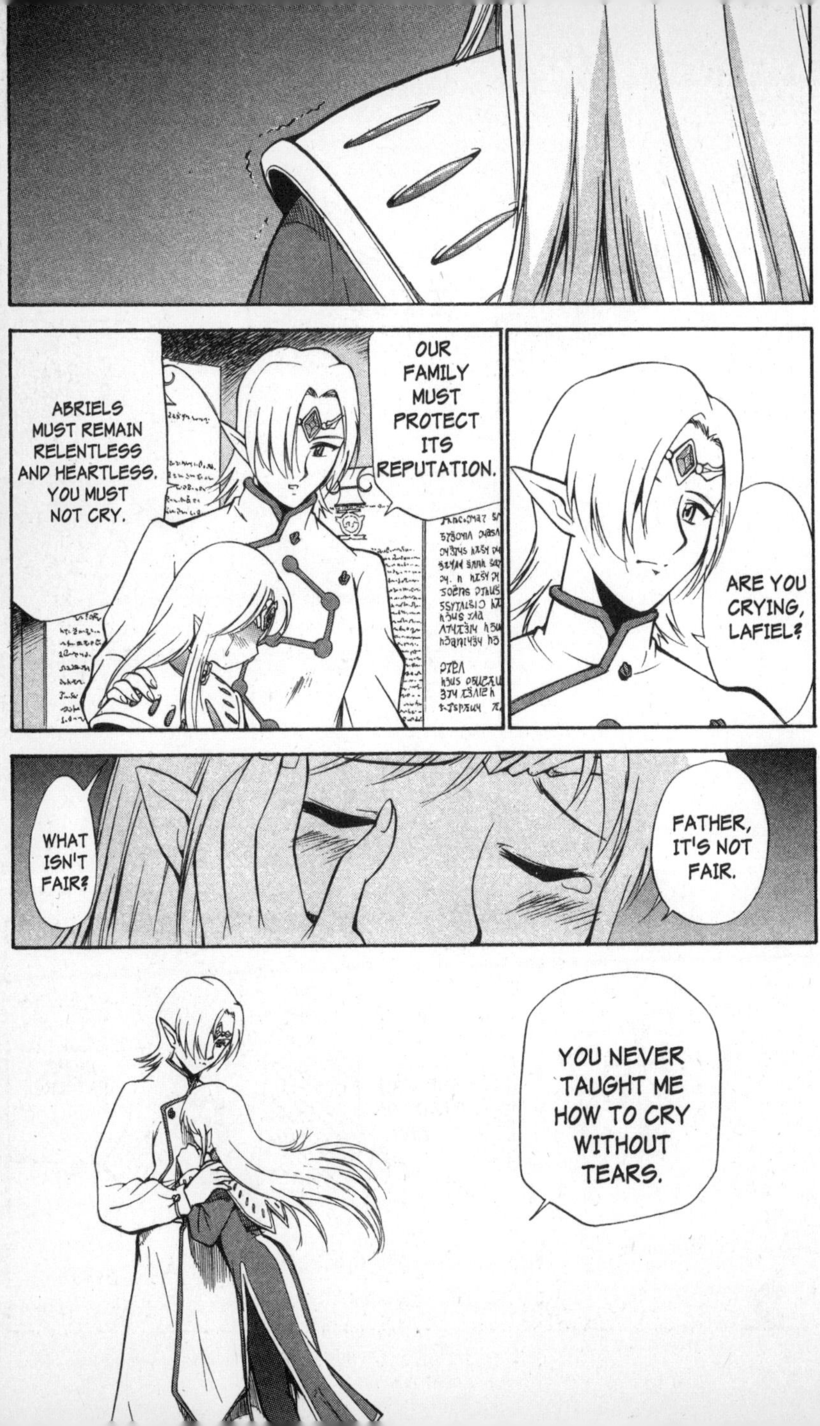

ARE YOU CRYING, LAFIEL?
OUR FAMILY MUST PROTECT ITS REPUTATION.
ABRIELS MUST REMAIN RELENTLESS AND HEARTLESS. YOU MUST NOT CRY.
FATHER, IT'S NOT FAIR.
WHAT ISN'T FAIR?
YOU NEVER TAUGHT ME HOW TO CRY WITHOUT TEARS.

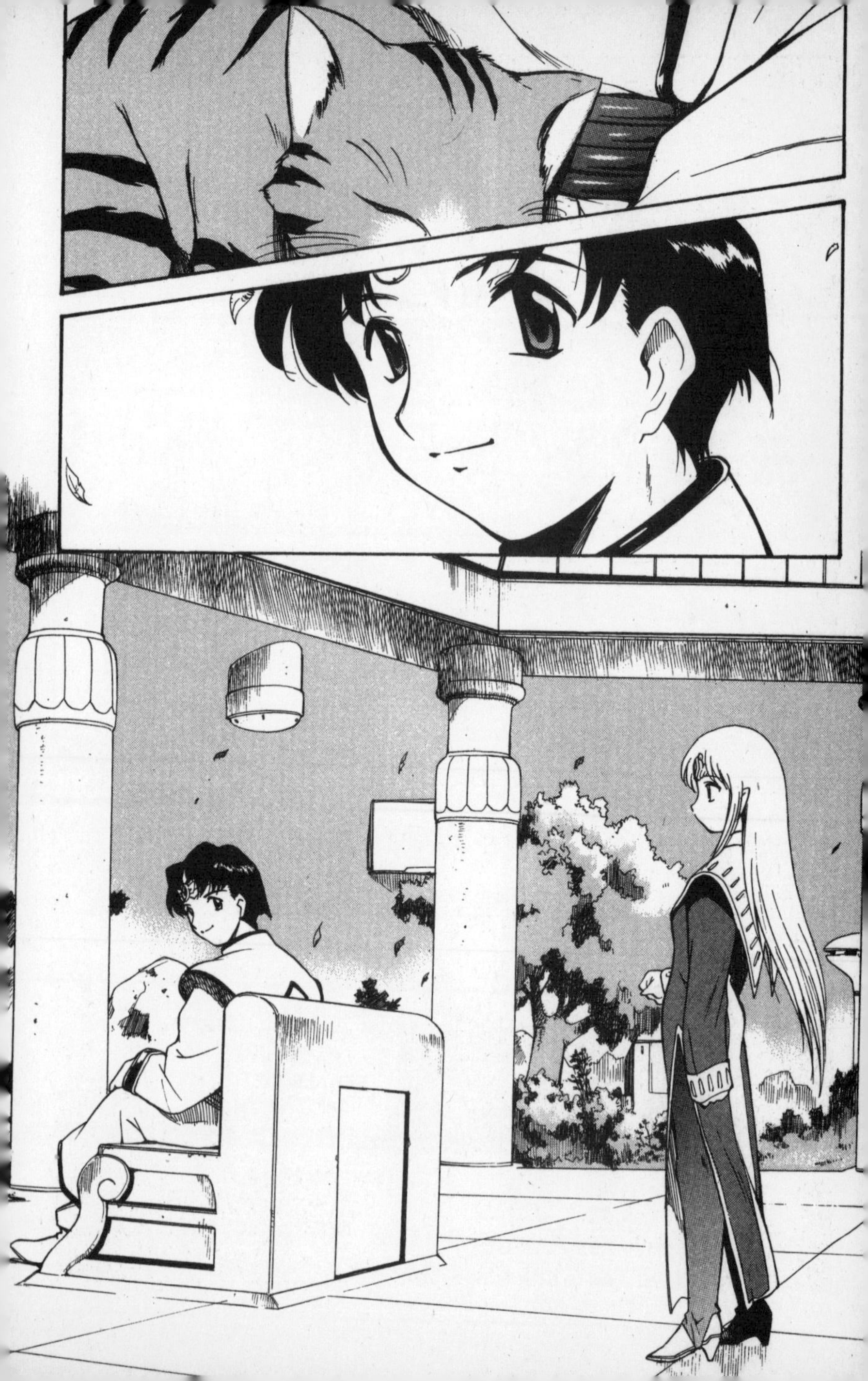

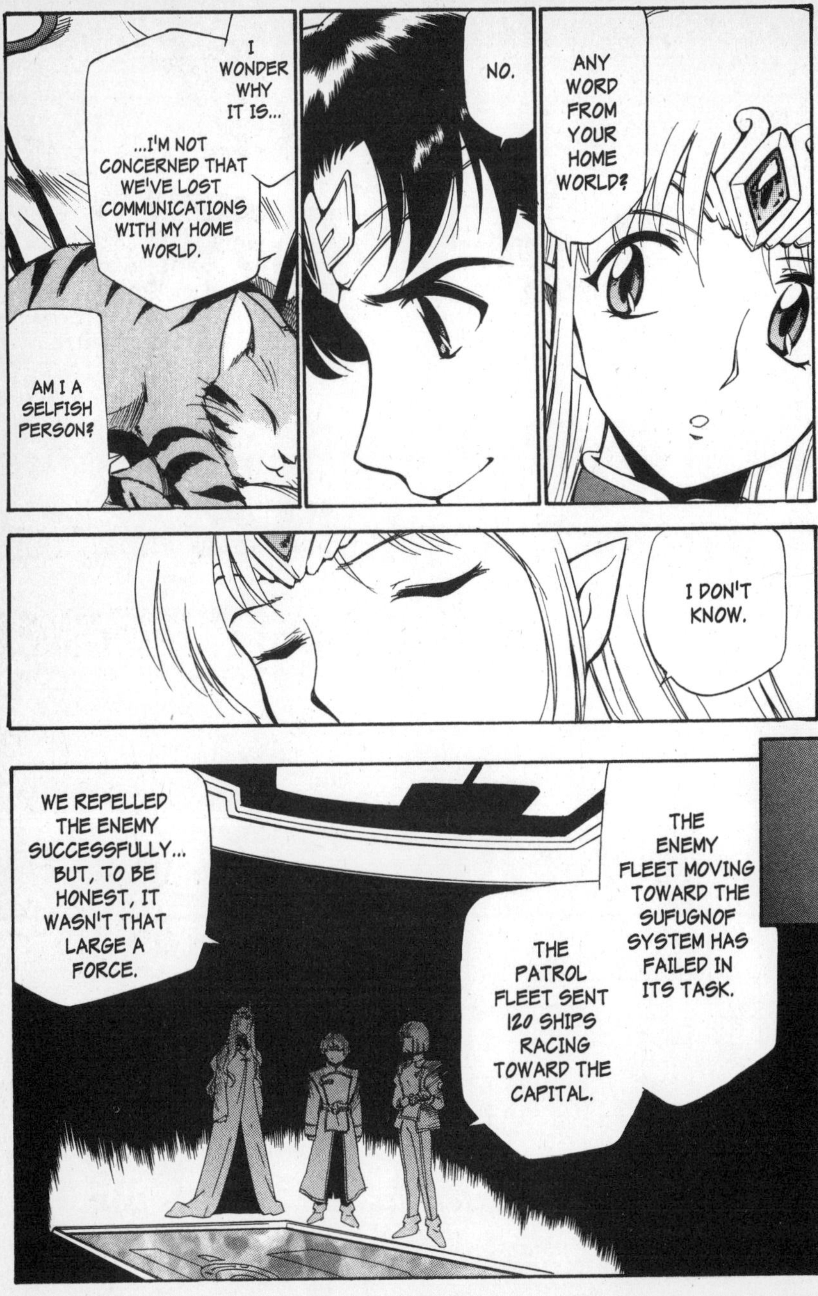
ANY WORD FROM YOUR HOME WORLD?
NO.
I WONDER WHY IT IS...
...I'M NOT CONCERNED THAT WE'VE LOST COMMUNICATIONS WITH MY HOME WORLD.
AM I A SELFISH PERSON?
I DON'T KNOW.
THE ENEMY FLEET MOVING TOWARD THE SUFUGNOF SYSTEM HAS FAILED IN ITS TASK.
THE PATROL FLEET SENT 120 SHIPS RACING TOWARD THE CAPITAL.
WE REPELLED THE ENEMY SUCCESSFULLY... BUT, TO BE HONEST, IT WASN'T THAT LARGE A FORCE.

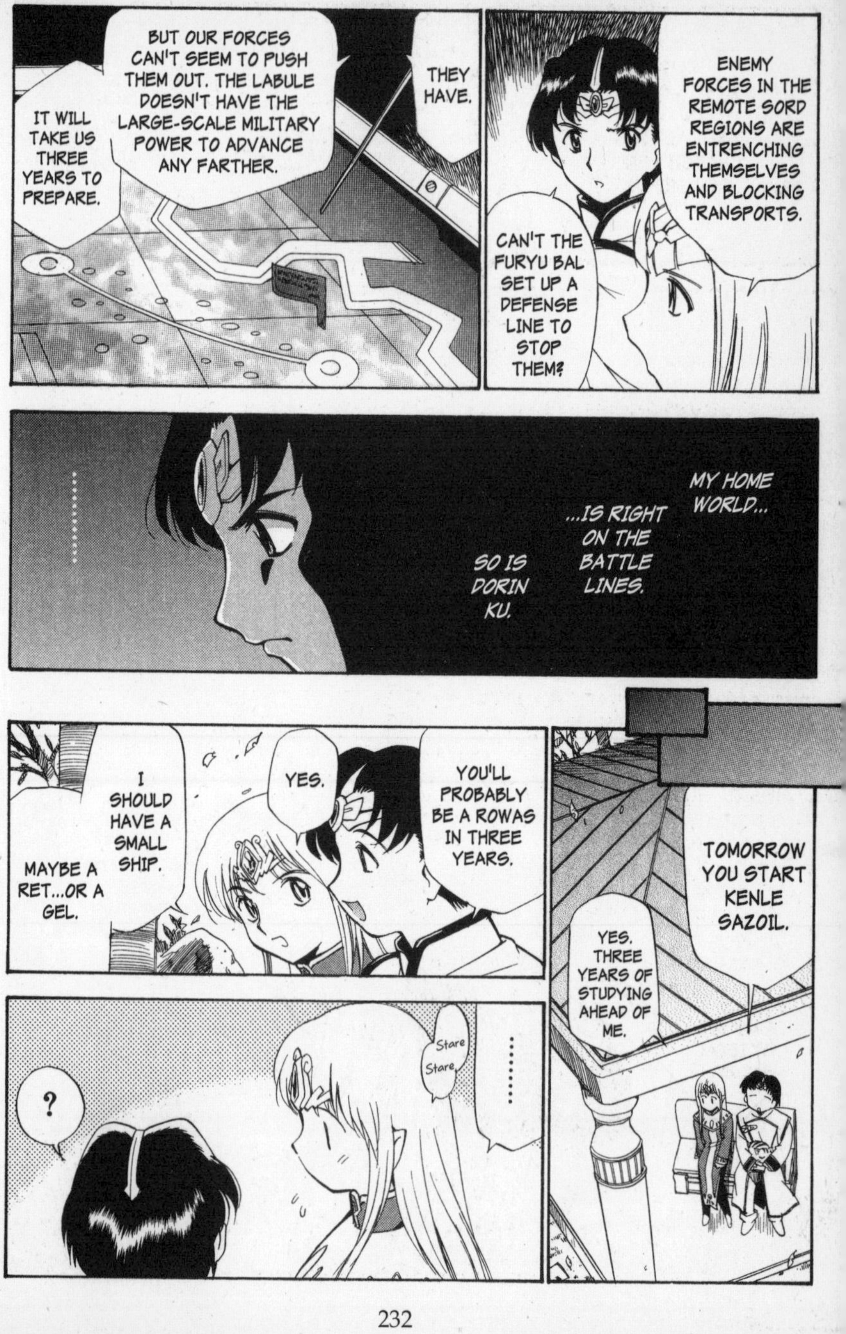

ENEMY FORCES IN THE REMOTE SORD REGIONS ARE ENTRENCHING THEMSELVES AND BLOCKING TRANSPORTS.
CAN'T THE FURYU BAL SET UP A DEFENSE LINE TO STOP THEM?
THEY HAVE.
BUT OUR FORCES CAN'T SEEM TO PUSH THEM OUT. THE LABULE DOESN'T HAVE THE LARGE-SCALE MILITARY POWER TO ADVANCE ANY FARTHER.
IT WILL TAKE US THREE YEARS TO PREPARE.
MY HOME WORLD...
...IS RIGHT ON THE BATTLE LINES.
SO IS DORIN KU.
....
TOMORROW YOU START KENLE SAZOIL.
YES. THREE YEARS OF STUDYING AHEAD OF ME.
YOU'LL PROBABLY BE A ROWAS IN THREE YEARS.
YES.
I SHOULD HAVE A SMALL SHIP.
MAYBE A RET...OR A GEL.
......
Stare
Stare
?

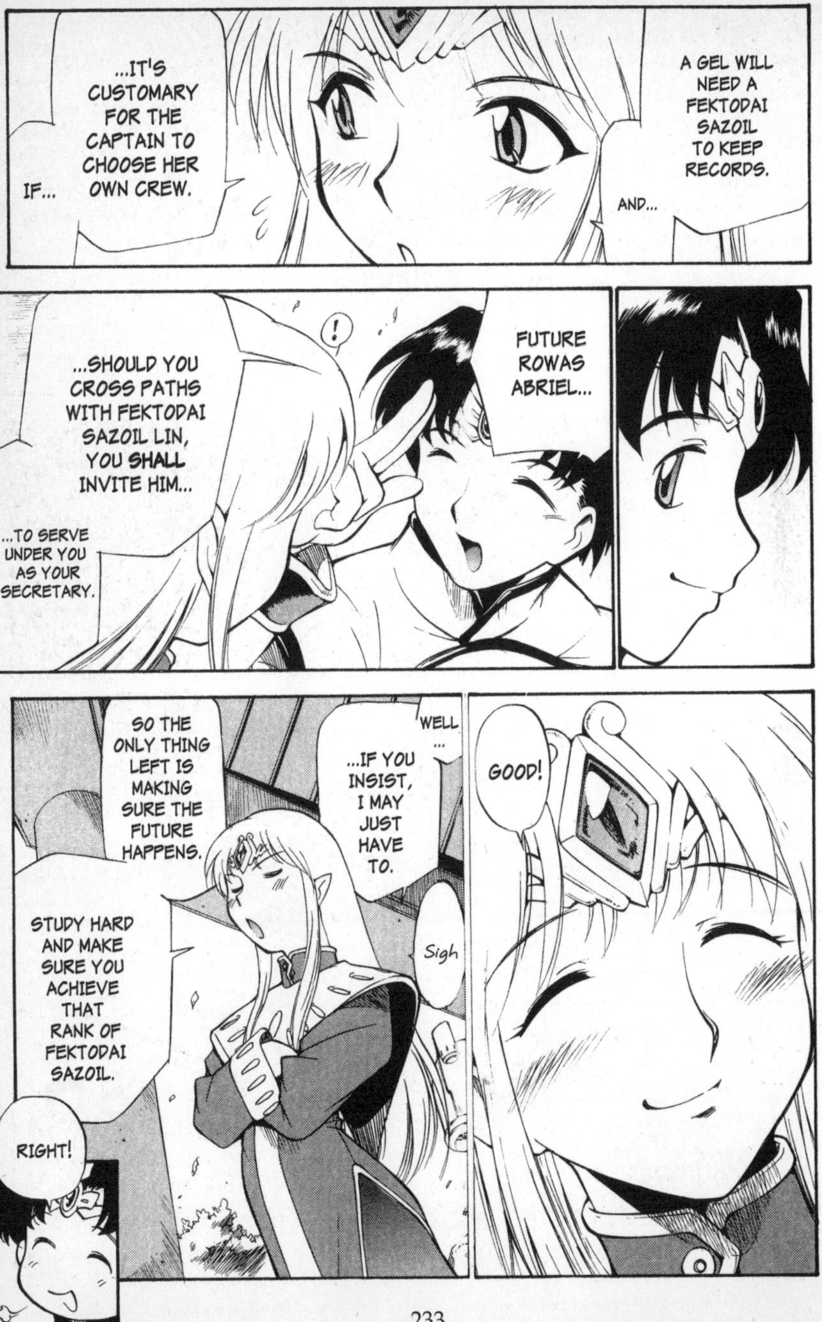

A GEL WILL NEED A FEKTODAI SAZOIL TO KEEP RECORDS.
AND...
...IT'S CUSTOMARY FOR THE CAPTAIN TO CHOOSE HER OWN CREW.
IF...
FUTURE ROWAS ABRIEL...
!
...SHOULD YOU CROSS PATHS WITH FEKTODAI SAZOIL LIN, YOU SHALL INVITE HIM...
...TO SERVE UNDER YOU AS YOUR SECRETARY.
GOOD!
WELL ...
...IF YOU INSIST, I MAY JUST HAVE TO.
SO THE ONLY THING LEFT IS MAKING SURE THE FUTURE HAPPENS.
Sigh
STUDY HARD AND MAKE SURE YOU ACHIEVE THAT RANK OF FEKTODAI SAZOIL.
RIGHT!

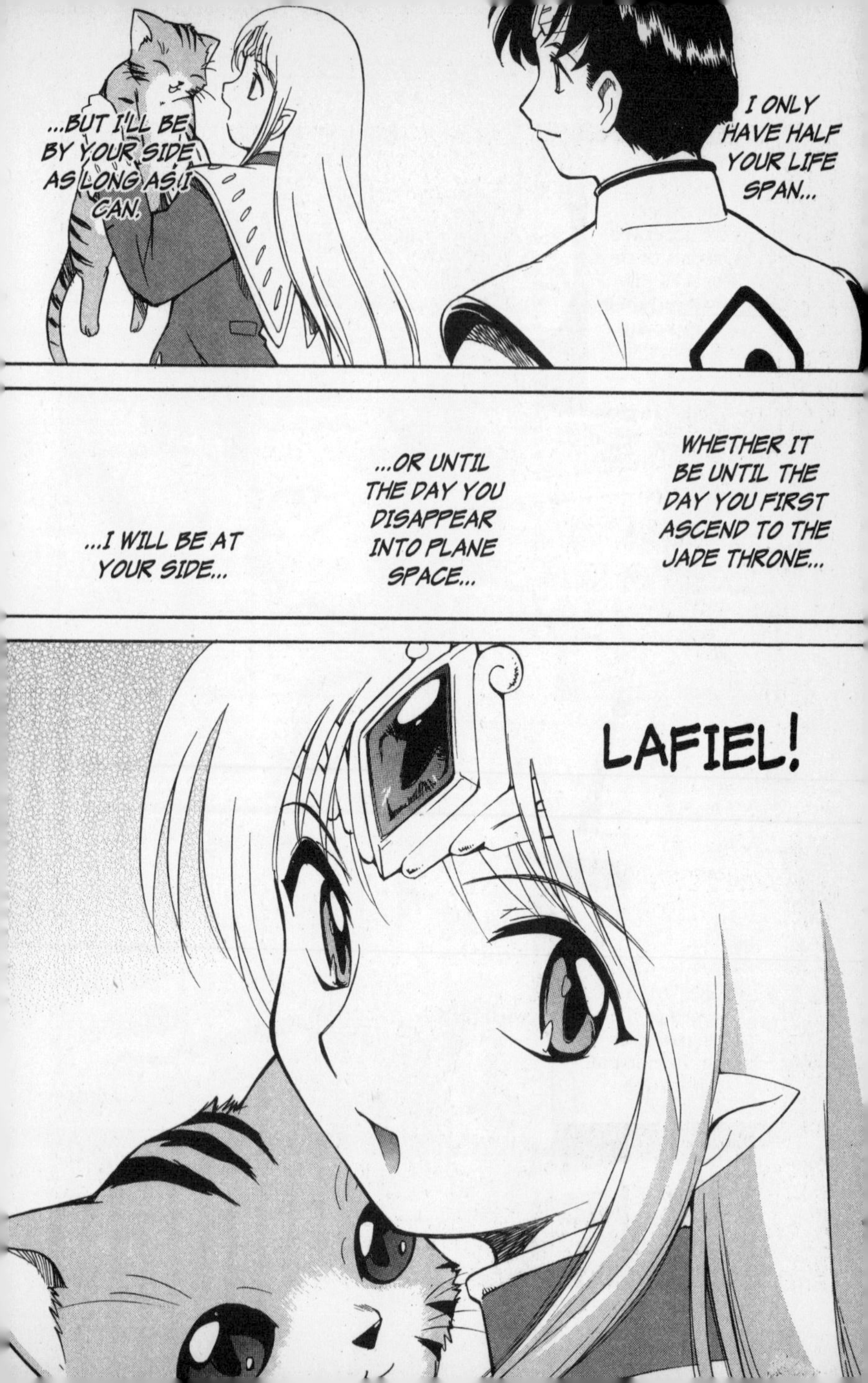
I ONLY HAVE HALF YOUR LIFE SPAN...
...BUT I'LL BE BY YOUR SIDE AS LONG AS I CAN.
WHETHER IT BE UNTIL THE DAY YOU FIRST ASCEND TO THE JADE THRONE...
...OR UNTIL THE DAY YOU DISAPPEAR INTO PLANE SPACE...
...I WILL BE AT YOUR SIDE...
LAFIEL!

Three years later...

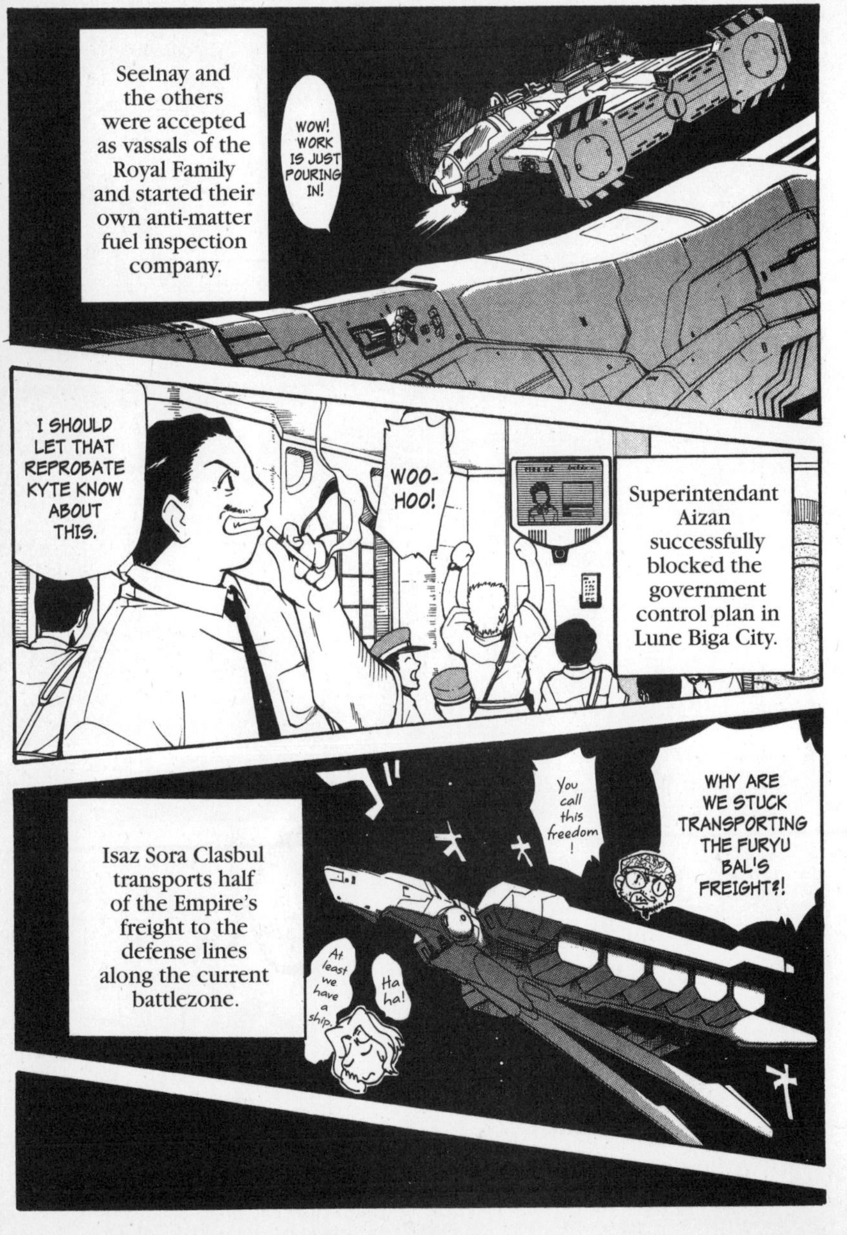

WOW! WORK IS JUST POURING IN!
Seelnay and the others were accepted as vassals of the Royal Family and started their own anti-matter fuel inspection company.
Superintendant Aizan successfully blocked the government control plan in Lune Biga City.
WOO-HOO!
I SHOULD LET THAT REPROBATE KYTE KNOW ABOUT THIS.
WHY ARE WE STUCK TRANSPORTING THE FURYU BAL'S FREIGHT?!
You call this freedom!
Ha ha!
At least we have a ship.
Isaz Sora Clasbul transports half of the Empire's freight to the defense lines along the current battlezone.

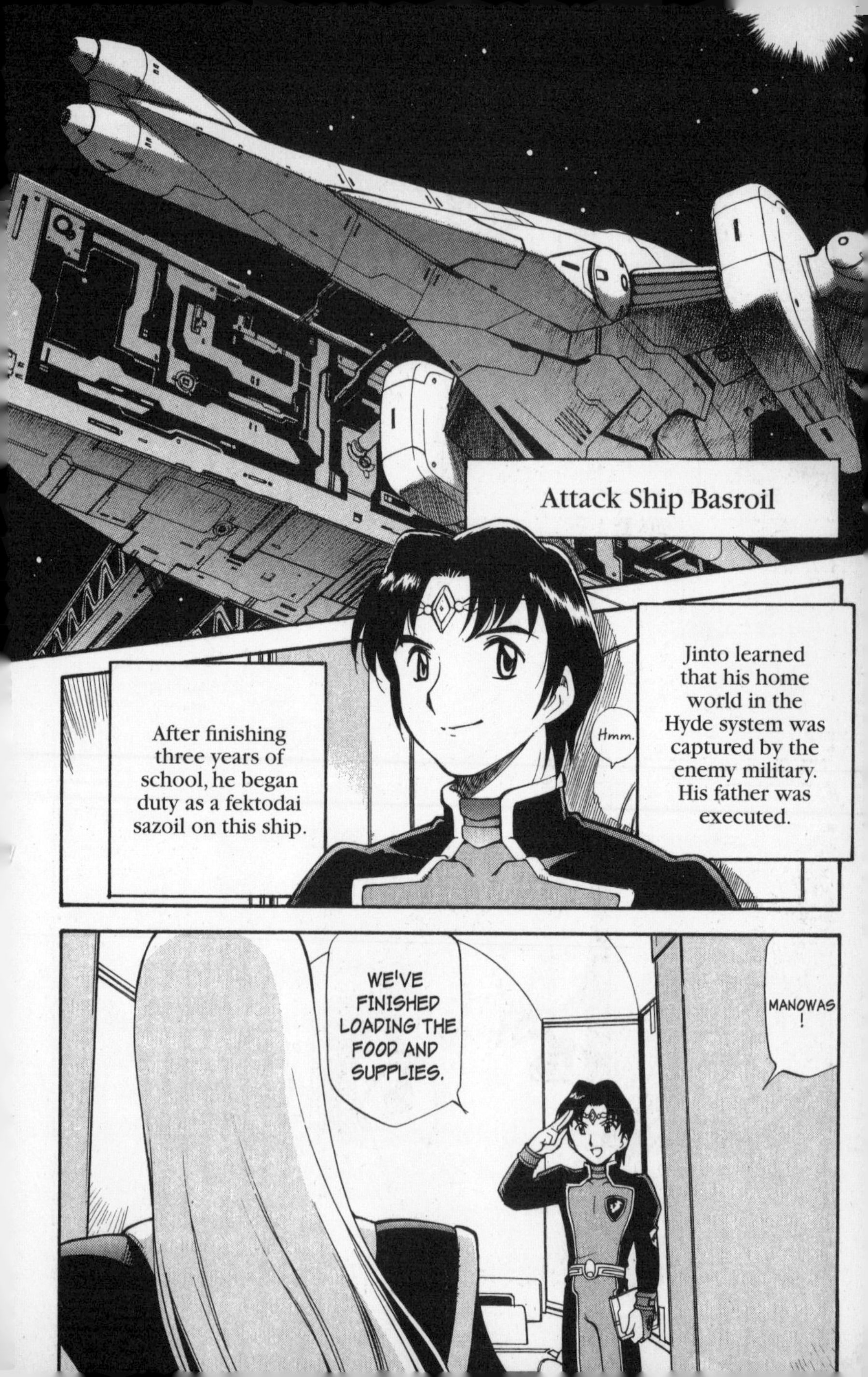
Attack Ship Basroil
Jinto learned that his home world in the Hyde system was captured by the enemy military. His father was executed.
Hmm.
After finishing three years of school, he began duty as a fektodai sazoil on this ship.
MANOWAS!
WE'VE FINISHED LOADING THE FOOD AND SUPPLIES.

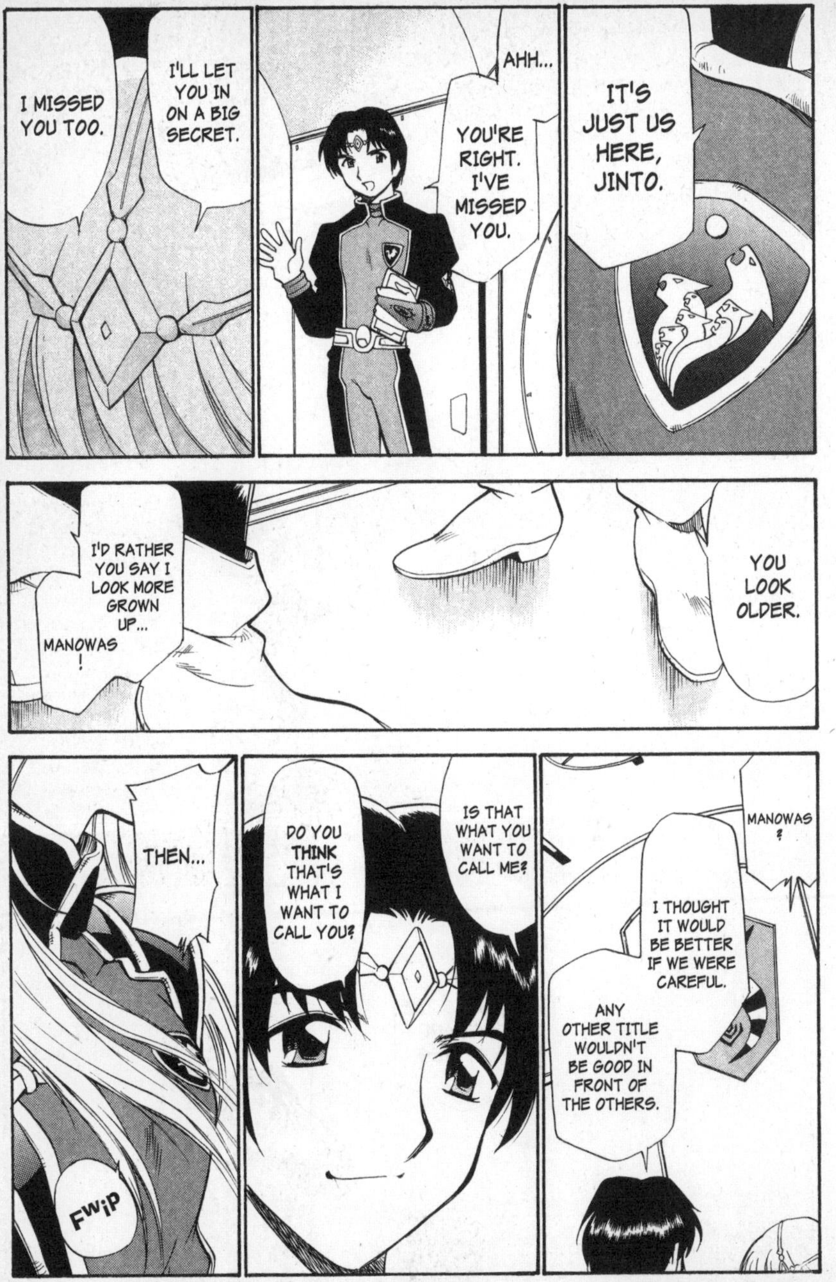
IT'S JUST US HERE, JINTO.
AHH...
YOU'RE RIGHT. I'VE MISSED YOU.
I'LL LET YOU IN ON A BIG SECRET.
I MISSED YOU TOO.
YOU LOOK OLDER.
I'D RATHER YOU SAY I LOOK MORE GROWN UP...
MANOWAS !
MANOWAS ?
I THOUGHT IT WOULD BE BETTER IF WE WERE CAREFUL.
ANY OTHER TITLE WOULDN'T BE GOOD IN FRONT OF THE OTHERS.
IS THAT WHAT YOU WANT TO CALL ME?
DO YOU THINK THAT'S WHAT I WANT TO CALL YOU?
THEN...
FWIP

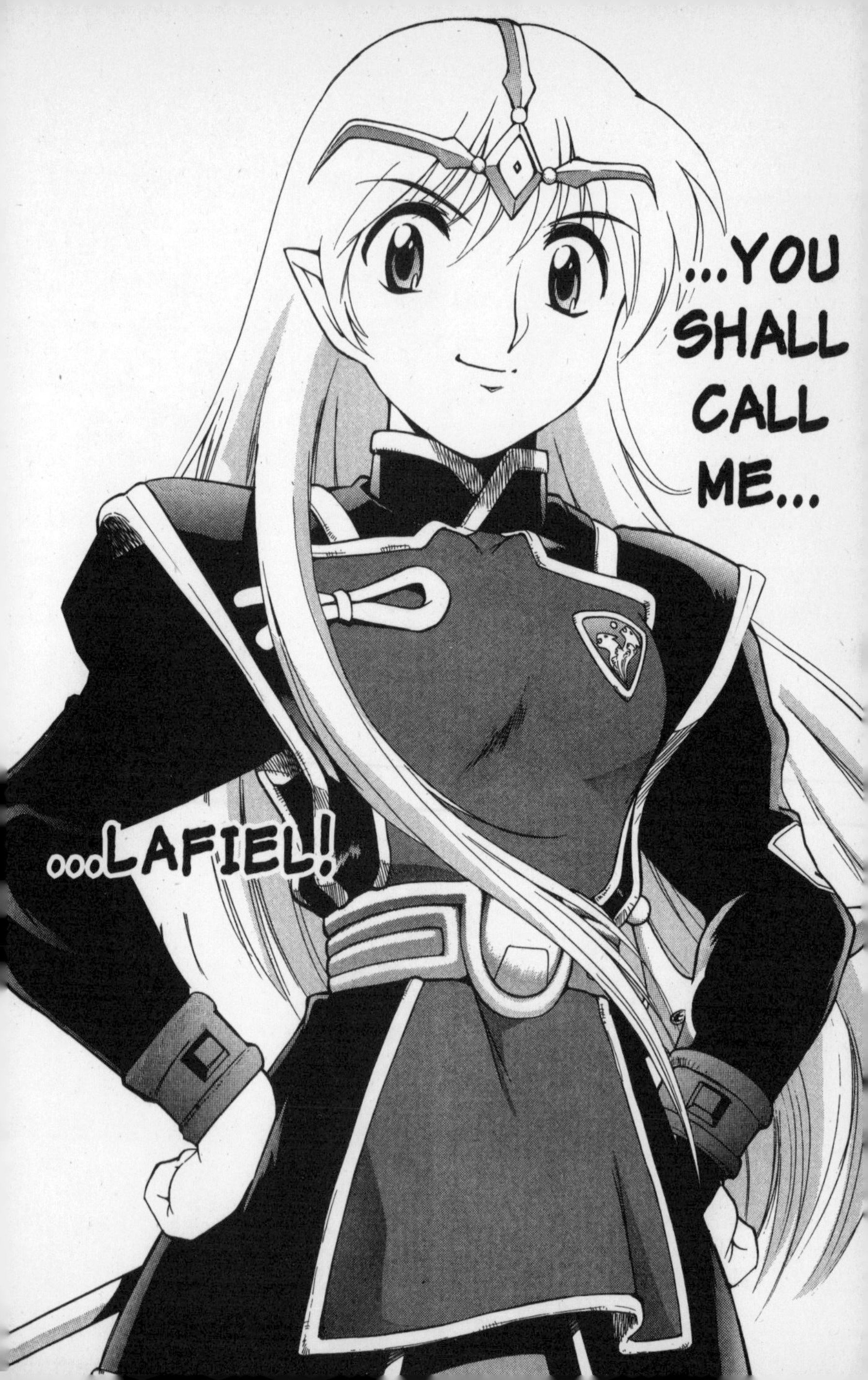
...YOU SHALL CALL ME...
...LAFIEL!

Crest of the Stars
The End

//PREVIEW://
NEXT VOLUME

SEIKAI TRILOGY
BANNER OF THE STARS

Three years have passed since Lafiel and Jinto's escape from Planet Clasbul. Lafiel is now captain of her own Assault Ship, the Basroil, and has requested the services of Jinto Lin as her supply officer. But their struggle has only begun. Lafiel must deal with the pressures of command; Jinto works to make himself worthy of his Empire and of Lafiel's friendship. In the meantime, both are haunted by a phantom from the past and menaced by a numerically superior enemy fleet.

The conflict between the Abh Empire and the United Mankind has entered one of its hottest phases as the Abh initiate Operation Phantom Flame to capture a huge swath of enemy territory.

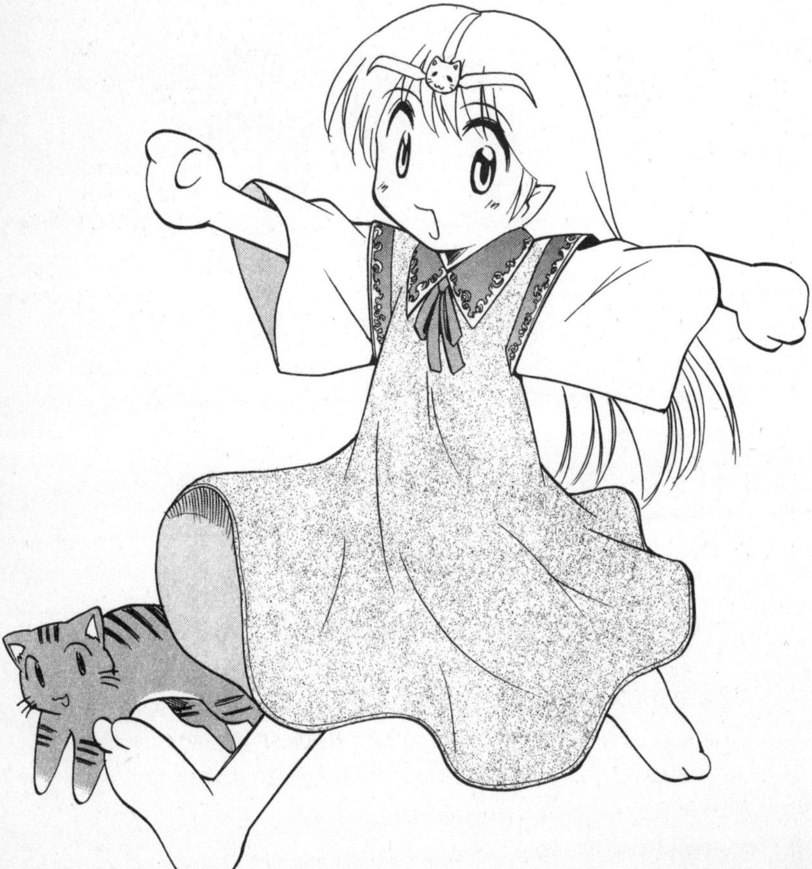

cally engineered humans designed to live in the vacuum of space.

kasna *n.* two

kenle sazoil *n.* school of accounting

Labule. Star Forces, the Abh interstellar military

Lakfakalle. the capital of the Abh Empire

lals *n.* king

lef *n.* citizens

leklun *n.* state

Lengarf Glorf. the name of an Abh transport vessel

lepahunyu *n.* star system

lesui *n.* patrol ship

libyun *n.* territory, usually ruled by a voda

lue *adj.* imperial

lue suif *n.* imperial uniform worn by the nobility

lue bogne *n.* imperial granddaughter

lue lazem *n.* imperial domain

lue lef *n.* citizens of the empire

luk *n.* family

manowas *n.* captain

mata *n.* one

nahenu *n.* planet

onyu *n.* idiot

opsei *n.* main engines

pelia *n.* transfer shuttle

ponew *n.* armed ship

ret *n.* escort ship

ronid *n.* base

ronyu loom leka *n.* the baron's father

ronyu *n.* excellency, term of respect used to members of the nobility and royalty

rumusko *n.* baronial domain

ryuf *n.* baron

sabo luga *exp.* commence battle

sakas lazasot *n.* imperial high court

salel *n.* fleet commander

sasot *exp.* Abh expression for good luck

selin *n.* uniform

skul *n.* unit of currency for the Abh Empire

sord *n.* space-time gate that links distant points in space

spot lelag *n.* information bureau

Sufagnom. Abh word for the star system Sufugnof

Sufugnof. an Abh planet on the front lines of the war with the United Mankind

suif luk *n.* noble family

suif *n.* nobility; used to describe individual (a suif) or the whole of nobility as a separate class (the suif)

sune *n.* court rank or title

usiya *n.* car

vesh *n.* anti-matter

voda *n.* a landholding noble in the Abh empire; lord

Vorash. an Abh planet on the front lines of the war with the United Mankind

wadros sasot *n.* victory lights

yadbiru *n.* fleet

yofu *n.* gene partner

yogodozvos *n.* combat status

Yunyu. one of the star systems in the Abh Empire

Abh *n.* a race of humans genetically engineered to live in the vacuum of space. Abh have twice the lifespan of unmodified humans, blue hair, pale skin and heightened brain functions. *adj.* having the quality of Abh.

aga izofot *exp.* a challenge to battle

alm kaselia *n.* executive officer

alm trakia *n.* gunnery officer

alpha *n.* control tiara worn by most Abh

arosh *n.* imperial capital. To the Abh, it is the city of Lakfalle.

Pal Lepenew *exp.* an Abh idiom that means Pride of the Abh

bara *n.* roses

bene rodial *n.* pilot trainee

bodemia *n.* scout ship

bogne *n.* granddaughter

bosnal *n.* military officer or soldier

Clasbul. the name of a planet near the Sufugnof border

clyuno *n.* proper name for the Abh's primary communication device

daisele *n.* an order to launch in Labule terminology

daush *n.* long, imperial robes

Delbisks. an Abh artist who specialized in landscapes

dril *n.* a count; a member of the nobility

drok *n.* communications

elmita *n.* her majesty

elmiton *n.* your majesty

Estote. a state in the Abh Empire; the location of the Star Forces officer training school

fabeut *n.* high lord

fal suif *n.* master

faneb *n.* young man

fasenzal *n.* princess; designation of royalty

feia *n.* highness

feia kufena *n.* little royal princess

feia laltonel *n.* your royal highness

feia luel *n.* your highness

fektodai sazoil *n.* supply officer

frasas *n.* space-time clusters that allow Abh to travel through hyper-space

frasatei *adj.* having the quality of frasas

frode *n.* admiral

fryum neg *n.* a child born of Abh parents who decide to share genes

fual fryum *n.* precious daughter

furyu bal *n.* empire

Futune *n.* name of the main Abh patrol fleet as well as its flagship

Gaff Laka. an Abh artist who specialized in landscapes; painted Bal Reprenew

gedrels *n.* units of space travel

gel *n.* an assault ship

gooheik *n.* control stick for Abh space vessels. It works in concert with an Alpha so that Abh pilots can use their brain waves to maneuver space craft.

gosk lan *n.* vassal

gosk *n.* vassals

hoksas *n.* mines

hydal. *adj.* the Abh adjective for the Hyde star system as in the phrase drill hydal (the Count of Hyde)

karsal gululak *exp.* kin of the stars, an idiom used to refer to the Abh, geneti-

Illustration Gallery

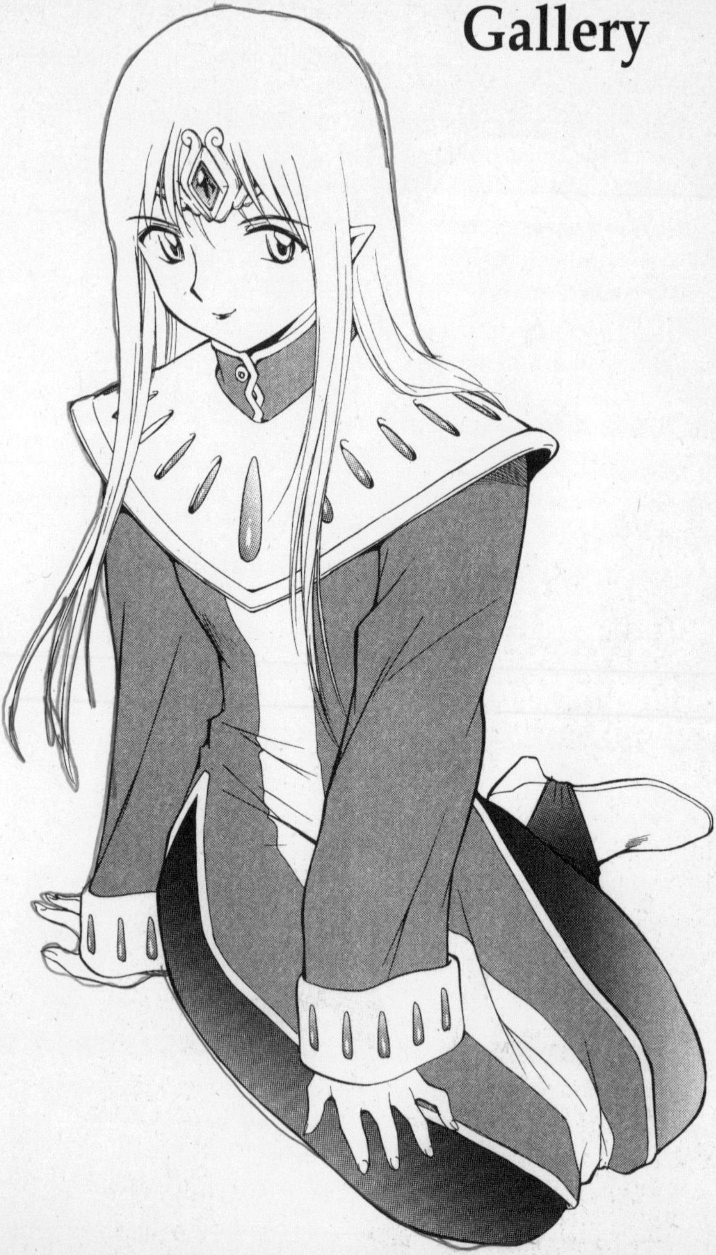

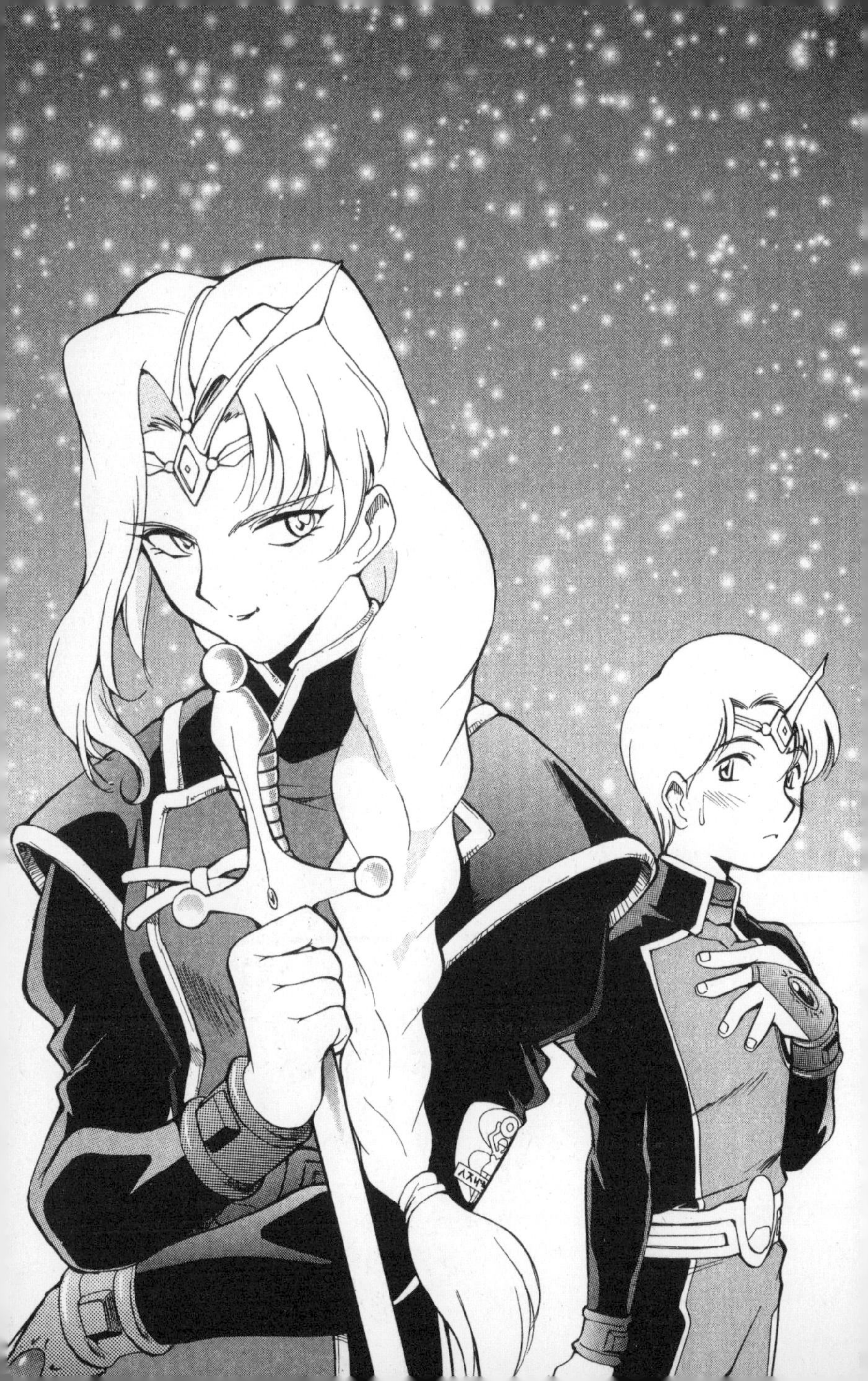

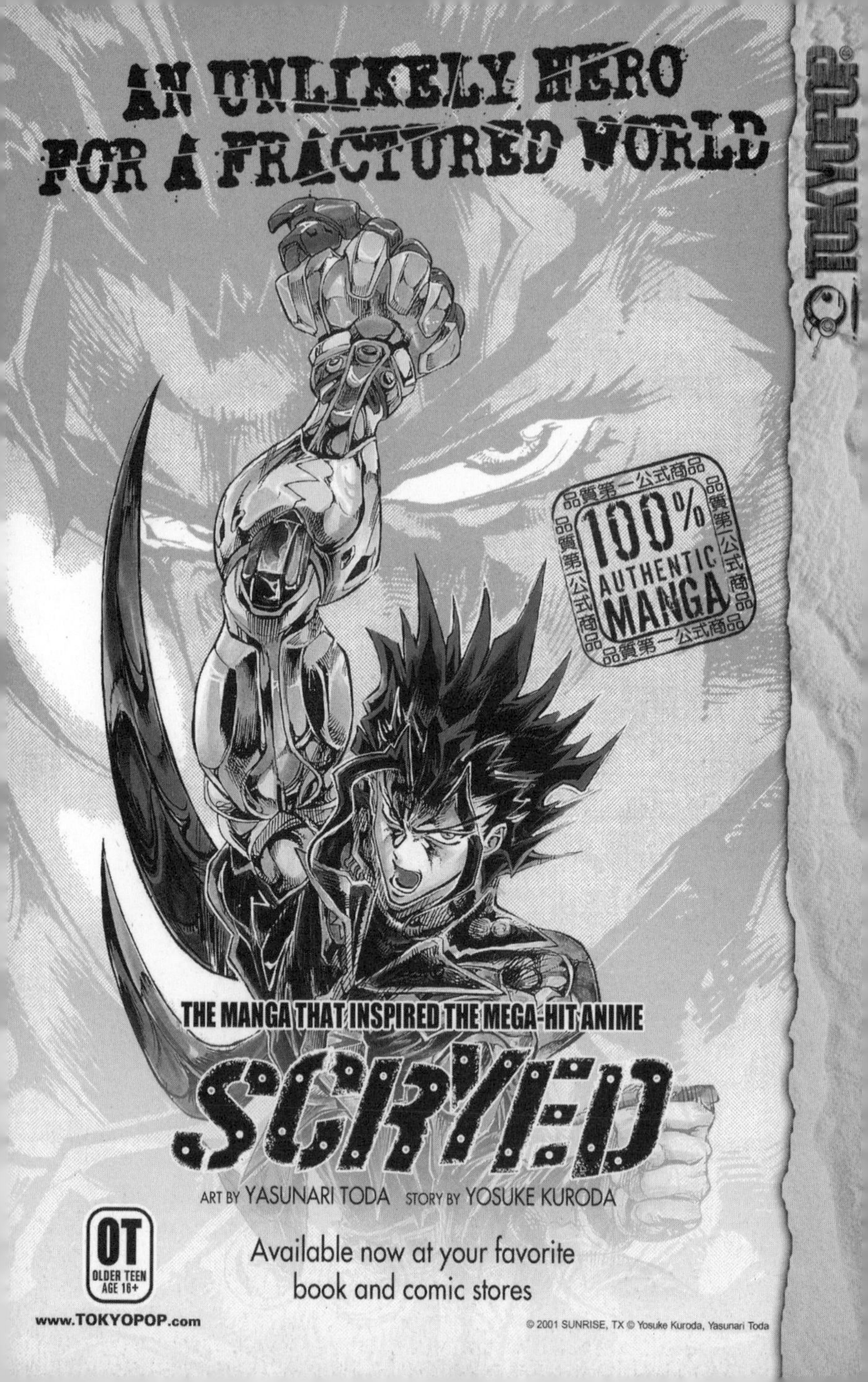
AN UNLIKELY HERO FOR A FRACTURED WORLD
TOKYOPOP
100% AUTHENTIC MANGA
品質第一公式商品
THE MANGA THAT INSPIRED THE MEGA-HIT ANIME
SCRYED
ART BY YASUNARI TODA STORY BY YOSUKE KURODA
OT OLDER TEEN AGE 16+
Available now at your favorite book and comic stores
www.TOKYOPOP.com
© 2001 SUNRISE, TX © Yosuke Kuroda, Yasunari Toda

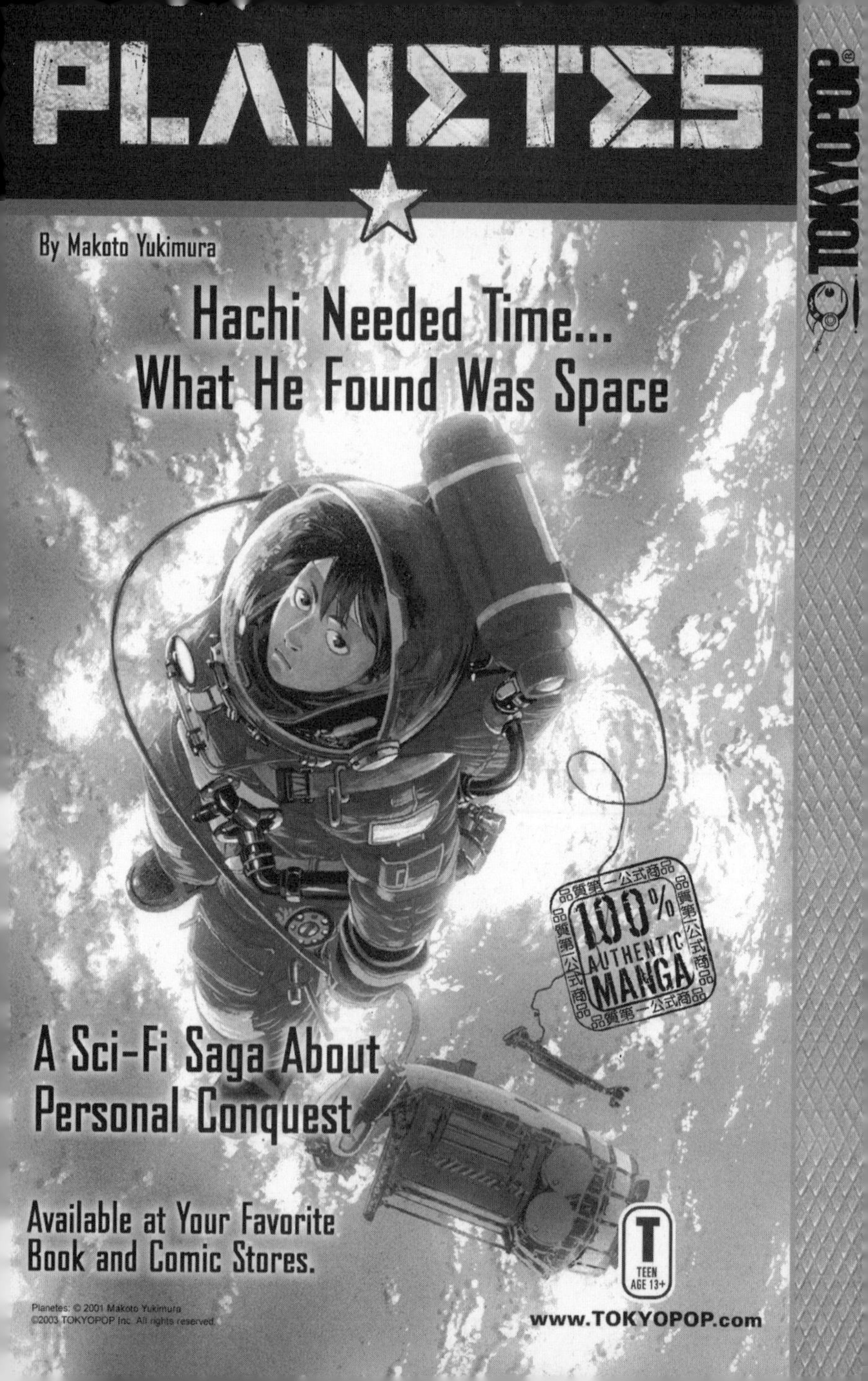
PLANETES
TOKYOPOP®
By Makoto Yukimura
Hachi Needed Time...
What He Found Was Space
100% AUTHENTIC MANGA
品質第一公式商品
A Sci-Fi Saga About
Personal Conquest
Available at Your Favorite
Book and Comic Stores.
T
TEEN
AGE 13+
Planetes: © 2001 Makoto Yukimura
©2003 TOKYOPOP Inc. All rights reserved.
www.TOKYOPOP.com

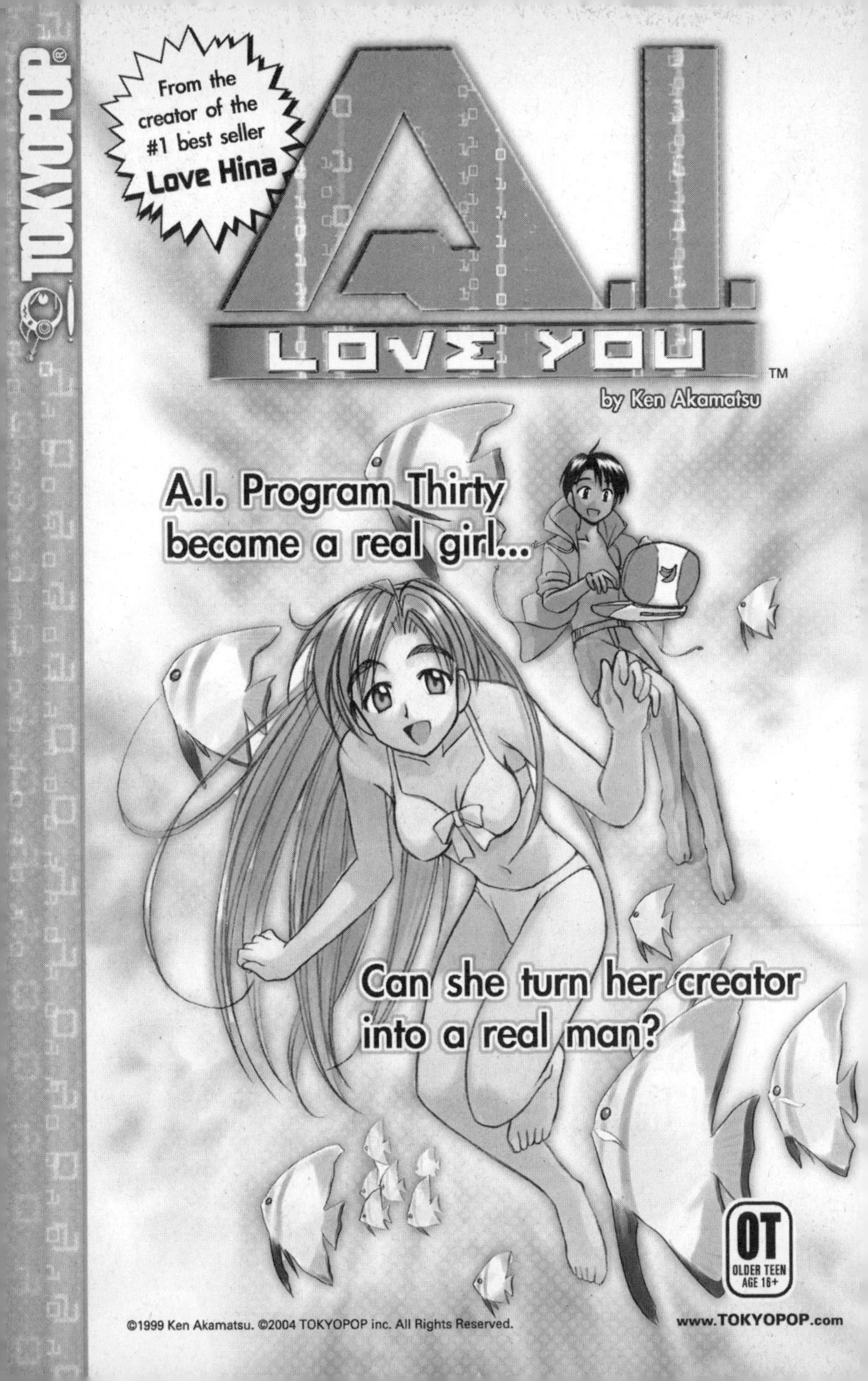
TOKYOPOP
From the creator of the #1 best seller Love Hina
A.I. LOVE YOU™
by Ken Akamatsu
A.I. Program Thirty became a real girl...
Can she turn her creator into a real man?
OT OLDER TEEN AGE 16+
©1999 Ken Akamatsu. ©2004 TOKYOPOP inc. All Rights Reserved.
www.TOKYOPOP.com

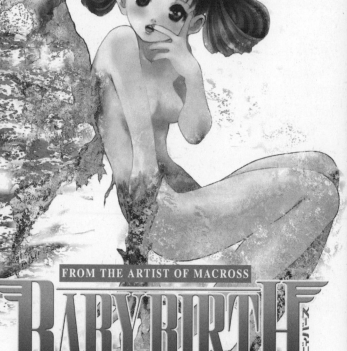

PSYCHIC ACADEMY™

You don't have
to be a great psychic to
be a great hero
...but it helps.

ALSO AVAILABLE FROM TOKYOPOP®

PITA-TEN
PL T LADDER
PL TES
PR
PR ESS AI
PS IC ACADEMY
QU 'S KNIGHT, THE
RA AROK
RA MASTER
RE Y CHECK
RE TH
RE UND
RE TE
RI STARS OF MANGA
SA R MARIONETTE J
SA R MOON
SA TAIL
SA KI
SA JRAI DEEPER KYO
S JRAI GIRL REAL BOUT HIGH SCHOOL
S ED
S N TRILOGY, THE
S FROG
S OLIN SISTERS
S AHIME-SYO: SNOW GODDESS TALES
S TTERBOX
S L MAN, THE
S W DROP
S CERER HUNTERS
S NE
S ODEN III
S
EADS OF TIME
YO BABYLON
YO MEW MEW
YO TRIBES
MPS LIKE US
DER THE GLASS MOON
MPIRE GAME
ON OF ESCAFLOWNE, THE
RRIORS OF TAO
D ACT
SH
RLD OF HARTZ
DAY
DIAC P.I.

OVELS

AMP SCHOOL PARANORMAL INVESTIGATORS
RMA CLUB
ILOR MOON
AYERS

RT BOOKS

RT OF CARDCAPTOR SAKURA
RT OF MAGIC KNIGHT RAYEARTH, THE
EACH: MIWA UEDA ILLUSTRATIONS

ANIME GUIDES

COWBOY BEBOP
GUNDAM TECHNICAL MANUALS
SAILOR MOON SCOUT GUIDES

TOKYOPOP KIDS

STRAY SHEEP

CINE-MANGA™

ALADDIN
CARDCAPTORS
DUEL MASTERS
FAIRLY ODDPARENTS, THE
FAMILY GUY
FINDING NEMO
G.I. JOE SPY TROOPS
GREATEST STARS OF THE NBA
JACKIE CHAN ADVENTURES
JIMMY NEUTRON: BOY GENIUS, THE ADVENTURES OF
KIM POSSIBLE
LILO & STITCH: THE SERIES
LIZZIE MCGUIRE
LIZZIE MCGUIRE MOVIE, THE
MALCOLM IN THE MIDDLE
POWER RANGERS: DINO THUNDER
POWER RANGERS: NINJA STORM
PRINCESS DIARIES 2
RAVE MASTER
SHREK 2
SIMPLE LIFE, THE
SPONGEBOB SQUAREPANTS
SPY KIDS 2
SPY KIDS 3-D: GAME OVER
THAT'S SO RAVEN
TOTALLY SPIES
TRANSFORMERS: ARMADA
TRANSFORMERS: ENERGON
VAN HELSING

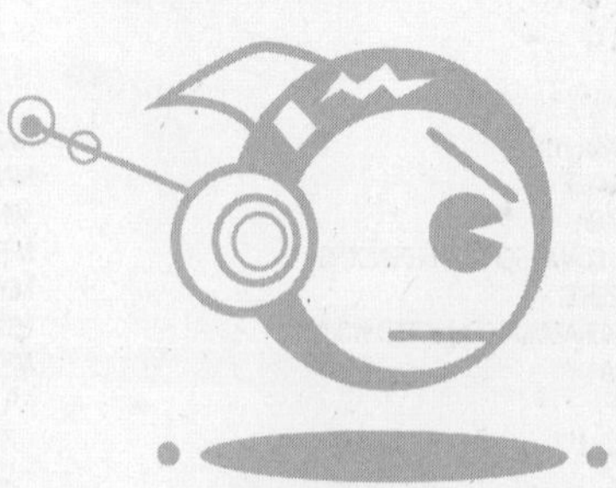

For more information visit www.TOKYOPOP.com

03.30.04T

STOP!

This is the back of the book.
You wouldn't want to spoil a great ending!

This book is printed "manga-style," in the authentic Japanese right-to-left format. Since none of the artwork has been flipped or altered, readers get to experience the story just as the creator intended. You've been so TOKYOPOP® delivered: authentic, hot-off-the-press, fun!

DIRECTIONS

If this is your first time reading manga-style, here's a quick guide to help you understand how it works.

It's easy... just start in the top right panel and follow the numbers. Have fun, and look for more 100% authentic manga from TOKYOPOP®!

MANGA